macmillanhighered.com
/mediaessentials3e

Streaming Music Videos
On the Media Essentials LaunchPad, watch clips of recent music videos from Katy Perry.
Discussion: Music videos get less TV exposure than they did in their heyday, but they can still be a crucial part of major artists' careers. How do these videos help sell Perry's music?

and the paid version of Spotify. Spotify, Rdio, YouTube, and Ve iHeartRadio), ringtones, and sy various media, such as film, TV two-thirds of the U.S. market a cent of all music recordings pu iTunes is the leading retailer o

Subscription and streaming United States and now accou revenues. The difference betw streaming radio (e.g., Pandora to stream specific songs, whe a genre or style of music.

The international recording i vices because they are a new re online file-sharing—still exists, t services has satisfied consume illegal file-swapping. There are r wide.[11] Spotify, one of the leadin songs to stream globally, with d carries so many songs that 20 p

LaunchPad for *Media Essentials* goes beyond the printed textbook

Media Essentials emphasizes convergence and practices it, too. Callouts in the boxes and margins throughout the book direct students to the wealth of video clips available on LaunchPad for *Media Essentials*.

We've added clips from movies, TV shows, and other media texts to the site's array of interviews, diversifying the book's extensive video program.

Videos are accompanied by critical thinking questions that invite students to offer their own analysis and reactions—perfect for media response papers and class discussions. For a complete list of available clips, see the last book page.

LearningCurve

LaunchPad for *Media Essentials* also includes LearningCurve, a game-like adaptive quizzing system designed to help students review. Each chapter's LearningCurve uses a wealth of review questions and adaptive technology that analyzes student answers, helping them to figure out what they already know and master the concepts they still need to learn.

LaunchPad for *Media Essentials* can be packaged with the book or purchased on its own. To learn more, see the inside back cover or visit **launchpadworks.com**.

For more information about *Media Essentials*, please visit **macmillanhighered.com/mediaessentials3e**.

148 Mass Media Industries

macmillanhighered.com
/mediaessentials3e
Use **LearningCurve** to review concepts from this chapter.

The Early Histor

Early inventors' work and a product that en uct's format changed moving from records loads and digital mus product's quality; for ity of CDs over "scrato technology—online d tically reduced sales o dustry players to look

From Cylinders to Di Becomes a Mass Med

In the development stage

MEDIA ESSENTIALS

MEDIA ESSENTIALS

A Brief Introduction

Third Edition

Richard Campbell

MIAMI UNIVERSITY

Christopher R. Martin

UNIVERSITY OF NORTHERN IOWA

Bettina Fabos

UNIVERSITY OF NORTHERN IOWA

with

Shawn Harmsen

UNIVERSITY OF IOWA

Bedford/St. Martin's

A Macmillan Education Imprint

Boston • New York

For Bedford/St. Martin's

Vice President, Editorial, Macmillan Higher Education Humanities: Edwin Hill
Publisher for Communication: Erika Gutierrez
Senior Developmental Editor: Jesse Hassenger
Senior Production Editor: Jessica Gould
Media Producer: Rand Thomas
Senior Production Supervisor: Jennifer Wetzel
Marketing Manager: Kayti Corfield
Copy Editor: Jamie Thaman
Indexer: Kirsten Kite
Photo Researcher: Sue McDermott Barlow
Director of Rights and Permissions: Hilary Newman
Senior Art Director: Anna Palchik
Text Design: TODA (The Office of Design and Architecture)
Cover Design: Billy Boardman
Cover Photo: © Ronald Reyna/EyeEm/Getty Images
Composition: Cenveo Publisher Services
Printing and Binding: RR Donnelley and Sons

Manufactured in the United States of America.

0 9 8 7 6 5
f e d c b a

For information, write: Bedford/St. Martin's, 75 Arlington Street, Boston, MA 02116
    (617-399-4000)

ISBN 978-1-4576-9376-2
ISBN 978-1-319-05238-6 (Loose-leaf Edition)

About the Authors

Richard Campbell, director of the journalism program at Miami University, is the author of *"60 Minutes" and the News: A Mythology for Middle America* (1991) and coauthor of *Cracked Coverage: Television News, the Anti-Cocaine Crusade, and the Reagan Legacy* (1994). Campbell has written for numerous publications, including *Columbia Journalism Review, Journal of Communication,* and *Media Studies Journal,* and he has served on the editorial boards of *Critical Studies in Mass Communication and Television Quarterly.* He holds a PhD from Northwestern University.

Christopher R. Martin is a professor of journalism at the University of Northern Iowa and author of *Framed! Labor and the Corporate Media* (2003). He has written articles and reviews on journalism, televised sports, the Internet, and labor for several publications, including *Communication Research, Journal of Communication, Journal of Communication Inquiry, Labor Studies Journal,* and *Culture, Sport, and Society.* He is also on the editorial board of the *Journal of Communication Inquiry.* Martin holds a PhD from the University of Michigan and has also taught at Miami University.

Bettina Fabos, an award-winning video maker and former print reporter, is an associate professor of visual communication and interactive media studies at the University of Northern Iowa. She is the author of *Wrong Turn on the Information Superhighway: Education and the Commercialized Internet* (2003). Her areas of expertise include critical media literacy, Internet commercialization and education, and media representations of popular culture. Her work has been published in *Library Trends, Review of Educational Research,* and *Harvard Educational Review.* Fabos has a PhD from the University of Iowa.

Shawn Harmsen straddles the line between the professional and academic worlds. His journalism career has, since 1995, spanned radio, television, and newsroom jobs, including reporter, anchor, photojournalist, and news director. After getting his MA in communication education from the University of Northern Iowa in 2005, he continued to work in television news as a freelancer while also serving as an adjunct faculty member at the University of Wisconsin–Superior. He is set to receive his PhD from the University of Iowa's School of Journalism and Mass Communication in 2016. While at Iowa, Shawn edited the *Journal of Communication Inquiry* and coauthored work published in *Journalism Practice* and *Journalism and Mass Communication Quarterly.* His research interests involve the intersection of journalism, politics, and social justice issues.

Brief Contents

Preface

THE DIGITAL FUTURE OF MASS MEDIA HAS ARRIVED, and we're experiencing it firsthand. Not only has there been a fundamental change in the ways we use and consume media, but also in the many ways that media messages saturate our lives. As media industries continue to evolve and converge, we want students to have the critical tools they need to understand the media-saturated world around them. These tools, and an understanding of the fundamentals of media studies, are exactly what we had in mind when we wrote *Media Essentials*.

Media Essentials distills media industries and major concepts like digital convergence and legal controls down to their essence. Each chapter offers incisive historical context, frames key concepts up front, and uses pivotal examples to tell the broader story of how different forms of media have developed, how they work, and how they connect to us today. For example, Chapter 10, "Digital Gaming and the Media Playground," explores the roots of electronic gaming in early twentieth-century penny arcades, then goes on to explain how new technologies facilitated the medium's evolution into computer and console games played in arcades and at home and its eventual development into a socially driven mass medium. It then follows the money through an in-depth section on the economics of the video game industry, moves into discussions of regulation and its implications for democracy, and, in a new Converging Media Case Study box, discusses the ways game criticism has affected harassment on social media.

In addition to a wealth of content offered in every chapter, *Media Essentials* continues to be 30 percent briefer than competing books. In the third edition we've combined the chapters on newspapers and journalism into a single, streamlined chapter that better reflects the way journalism has changed and converged over the years. Throughout the book, our coverage is succinct, accessible, and peppered with memorable examples, and the book's unique approach—distilling media information to its core—gives instructors the space to add in personal research or social perspectives.

We've also further emphasized the importance of convergence by expanding our Converging Media boxes and our Media Literacy boxes, going in depth on timely issues like self-publishing, binge-watching, net neutrality, race in Hollywood, social media marketing, online activism, and more. Because the book also practices convergence, *Media Essentials* has an expanded online video program in LaunchPad, with clips that offer students firsthand experience with important (and attention-grabbing) media texts, covering everything from modern television drama to music videos, from groundbreaking films like *12 Years a Slave* to vintage Saturday-morning cartoons like *Transformers*. LaunchPad also includes access to LearningCurve, an adaptive quizzing system that helps students figure out what they know—and what material they need to review. LaunchPad for *Media Essentials* can be packaged with the book at a deep discount.

Hallmark Features of *Media Essentials*, Third Edition

Clear, streamlined, and accessible. Thirty percent briefer than competing texts, *Media Essentials* addresses all the topics typically covered in introductory mass communication books. From the media industries to legal controls, it offers just the right amount of detail, ensuring that students have enough information to make connections and develop media literacy.

An organization that supports learning. *Media Essentials* offers a chronological table of contents and consistent organization. Each chapter includes a brief history of the topic, a discussion of the evolution of the medium, a look at media economics, and coverage of the medium's relationship to democracy, media literacy, and convergence. This consistent organization and focus helps students make their way through the material while they grasp themes both big and small. Under each major heading, a preview paragraph highlights key ideas and contextualizes them, guiding students through the material.

Learning tools help students master the material. Each chapter opens with a bulleted list of objectives highlighting what students should expect to learn, while timelines preview important historical events necessary for understanding the chapter's theme. Converging Media and Media Literacy Case Study boxes address relevant topics in greater detail and help students think critically about them. Finally, each chapter concludes with Chapter Essentials, a useful study guide that helps students review material and prepares them for quizzes and exams.

New to This Edition

Expanded video clips. Call-outs in the boxes and margins throughout the book direct students to the wealth of video clips available on LaunchPad for *Media Essentials*. We've added clips from movies, TV shows, and other media texts like *Breaking Bad*, *Gravity*, *2 Broke Girls*, *Frozen*, *30 Rock*, *Real Housewives*, and more to the site's array of interviews, diversifying the book's impressive video program by providing extensive examples of the book's core concepts. Videos are accompanied by thoughtful questions that invite students to offer their own analysis and reactions—perfect for media response papers and class discussions. For a complete list of available clips, see the inside back cover. LaunchPad for *Media Essentials* can be purchased on its own or packaged with the text.

Expanded media literacy and convergence coverage. The Converging Media Case Study and Media Literacy Case Study boxes have been expanded and updated to accommodate more examples, visuals, and video. These boxes now go even more in depth on topics like race in Hollywood, investigative reporting, binge-viewing habits, magazines on social media, net neutrality, harassment among gaming fans, and stereotypes in advertising.

A newly revised journalism chapter. The newly revised Chapter 3, "Newspapers to Digital Frontiers: Journalism's Journey," merges chapters on newspapers and journalism into one comprehensive, streamlined, and forward-looking profile of journalism's future and past.

The most current and engaging examples. More than a dozen new chapter openers bring students into the stories of the media with current and attention-grabbing coverage of recent events, like the rise of GoPro cameras, threats over the Sony e-mail hacks and *The Interview*, the popularity of cord-cutting, surprise album releases, success in self-publishing, and more.

Updated industry coverage. *Media Essentials* keeps pace with all of the latest developments in the world of mass media, like Amazon's price wars, the boom in satirical fake news, the shifting economics of streaming music and video content, public relations failures on social media, the rise of the digital conglomerates, and more.

LaunchPad: Where Students Learn

Digital tools for *Media Essentials*, Third Edition, are available on LaunchPad, a dynamic new platform that combines a curated collection of videos, home-work assignments, e-book content, and the LearningCurve adaptive quizzing program, organized for easy assignability, in a simple user interface. LaunchPad for *Media Essentials* features:

- **An easy-to-use interface.** Ready-made interactive LaunchPad units give you the building blocks to assign instantly as is, or customize to fit your course. A unit's worth of work can be assigned in seconds, significantly decreasing the amount of time it takes for you to get your course up and running.
- **Intuitive and useful analytics.** The Gradebook allows you to quickly review progress at the class and individual level, providing useful information to help you make the most of the teaching and learning experience.
- **Fully interactive e-book.** Every LaunchPad e-book comes with powerful study tools, multimedia content, and easy customization for instructors.

- **LearningCurve offers adaptive quizzing and a personalized learning program.** In every chapter, call-outs prompt students to tackle the game-like LearningCurve quizzes to test their knowledge and reinforce learning of the material. Based on research as to how students learn, LearningCurve motivates students to engage with course materials, while the reporting tools let you see what content students have mastered, allowing you to adapt your teaching plan to their needs.
- **Integrated video clips that extend and complement the book.** A rich library of videos offers easy access to clips from movies, TV shows, music videos, interviews, and more, along with thought-provoking discussion questions that can be assigned in or out of class.
- **Video tools let you create video assignments for the class, individuals, and groups.** Instructors and students can upload their own videos, embed from sites like YouTube, and use publisher-provided videos in assignments and then analyze and assess them using time-based commenting features and rubrics.
- **The newest edition of our *Media Career Guide*.** LaunchPad includes a digital version of this practical, student-friendly guide to media jobs, featuring tips and career guidance for students considering a major in the media industries.

Find out more at **www.launchpadworks.com.** LaunchPad is available to purchase on its own, or at a discount when packaged with the print book. Contact your Bedford/St. Martin's sales representative for more details.

Digital and Print Formats

For more information on these formats and packaging information, please visit the online catalog at **macmillanhighered.com/catalog/mediaessentials3e**.

LaunchPad for *Media Essentials* at macmillanhighered.com/mediaessentials3e

Packaged at a discount with *Media Essentials* or available for purchase separately, LaunchPad features an array of video clips, homework assignments, e-book content, and the LearningCurve adaptive quizzing program, organized for easy assignability in a simple user interface. To order LaunchPad packaged with the print book, use ISBN 978-1-319-05550-9. To order LaunchPad on its own, use ISBN 978-1-319-02789-6.

Your e-book. Your way.

A variety of e-book formats are available for use on computers, tablets, and e-readers, featuring portability, customization options, and affordable prices. For more information, visit **macmillanhighered.com/ebooks**.

Student and Instructor Resources

For more information or to order or download the instructor resources, please visit the online catalog at **macmillanhighered.com/catalog/mediaessentials3e**.

Media Career Guide: Preparing for Jobs in the 21st Century, Tenth Edition
Sherri Hope Culver; ISBN 978-1-319-01953-2

Practical, student-friendly, and revised to include recent statistics on the job market, this guide includes a comprehensive directory of media jobs, practical tips, and career guidance for students considering a major in the media industries. The *Media Career Guide* can also be packaged for free with the print text. An electronic version comes integrated in LaunchPad for *Media Essentials*.

Instructor's Resource Manual
James E. Mueller, Christopher R. Martin, Bettina Fabos, and Richard Campbell; ISBN 978-1-319-02792-6

This downloadable manual provides instructors with a comprehensive teaching tool for the introduction to mass communication course. Every chapter offers teaching tips and activities culled from dozens of instructors who teach thousands of students. In addition, this extensive resource provides a range of teaching approaches, tips for facilitating in-class discussions, suggestions for using LaunchPad in and out of class, sample answers for LaunchPad's video discussion questions, writing assignments, outlines, lecture topics, lecture spin-offs, critical-process exercises, classroom media resources, and an annotated list of more than two hundred video resources.

Lecture Slides
Lecture slide presentations to help guide each chapter's lecture are available for download at **macmillanhighered.com/catalog/mediaessentials3e** on the instructor side and exist within LaunchPad.

Test Bank
James E. Mueller, Christopher R. Martin, Bettina Fabos, and Richard Campbell; ISBN 978-1-319-02793-3

Available as software formatted for Windows and Mac, the Test Bank includes multiple choice, true/false, fill-in-the-blank, and short and long essay questions for every chapter in *Media Essentials*. The Test Bank is also available within LaunchPad.

Acknowledgments

We wish every textbook author could have the kind of experience we've had while working on *Media Essentials* and would like to thank everyone at Bedford/ St. Martin's who supported this project through its editions and stages, including

Vice President Edwin Hill, Publisher Erika Gutierrez, Development Manager Susan McLaughlin, Marketing Manager Kayti Corfield, and Senior Editor Jesse Hassenger, who helped us develop this book over the past two editions. We also appreciate the tireless work of Senior Project Editor Jessica Gould, who kept the book on schedule while making sure all details were in place; Senior Production Supervisors Dennis J. Conroy and Jennifer Wetzel; and Associate Editor Catherine Burgess. We are also grateful to our research assistant, Susan Coffin. We extend particular and heartfelt thanks to our collaborator and contributor Shawn Harmsen, for all of his invaluable ideas, expertise, and excellent writing, as well as past contributor Jimmie Reeves, particularly for his knowledge in the world of digital gaming.

We also want to thank the many fine and thoughtful reviewers who contributed ideas to earlier editions of *Media Essentials*: Ajje-Ori Agbese, *University of Texas Pan American*; Julie Andsager, *University of Iowa*; Jerome D. DeNuccio, *Graceland University*; Jennifer Fleming, *California State University–Long Beach*; Peter Galarneau Jr., *West Virginia Wesleyan College*; Mary-Lou Galician, *Arizona State University*; Neil Goldstein, *Montgomery Country Community College*; August Grant, *University of South Carolina*; Jennifer Greer, *University of Alabama*; Jodie Hallsten, *Illinois State University*; Allison Hartcock, *Butler University*; Kirk Hazlett, *Curry College*; Amani E. Ismail, *California State University, Northridge*; Sharon Mazzarella, *James Madison University*; Daniel G. McDonald, *Ohio State University*; Gary Metzker, *California State University–Long Beach;* James E. Mueller, *University of North Texas;* Robert M. Ogles, *Purdue University;* Daniel A. Panici, *University of Southern Maine;* Kenneth Payne, *Western Kentucky University;* Zengjun Peng, *St. Cloud State University;* Samantha Phillips, *University of Miami;* Selene Phillips, *University of Louisville;* David Pierson, *University of Southern Maine;* Jennifer Proffitt, *Florida State University;* Arthur A. Raney, *Florida State University;* Steve H. Sohn, *University of Louisville;* Mark Steensland, *Pennsylvania State–Erie;* Carl Sessions Stepp, *University of Maryland;* Melvin Sunin, *Pennsylvania State–Erie;* Mike Trice, *Florida Southern College;* Richard West, *University of Texas at San Antonio;* Mark J. P. Wolf, *Concordia University Wisconsin;* and Yanjun Zhao, *Morrisville State College.*

We'd also like to thank the excellent reviewers who gave us feedback as we prepared the third edition: Vince Benigni, *College of Charleston;* Michael Bowman, *Arkansas State University;* Scott Brown, *California State University, Northridge;* Ted Carlin, *Shippensburg University of Pennsylvania;* Cheryl Casey, *Champlain College;* Doug Ferguson, *College of Charleston;* Barbara Eisenstock, *California State University, Northridge*; David Flex, *College of DuPage*; Katie Foss, *Middle Tennessee State University*; Nathaniel Frederick, *Winthrop University;*

Kate Joeckel, *Bellevue University*; Ileana Oroza, *University of Miami*; Lawrence Overlan, *Wentworth Institute of Technology*; D. Matthew Ramsey, *Salve Regina University*; Chadwick Lee Roberts, *University of North Carolina, Wilmington*; Martin David Sommerness, *Northern Arizona University*; and Matthew Turner, *Radford University*.

Special thanks from Richard Campbell: I am grateful to all my former students at the University of Wisconsin–Milwaukee, Mount Mary College, the University of Michigan, and Middle Tennessee State University, as well as to my current students at Miami University. Some of my students have contributed directly to this text, and thousands have endured my courses over the years—and made them better. My all-time favorite former students, Chris Martin and Bettina Fabos, are coauthors, as well as the creators of our book's Instructor's Manual and Test Bank. I am grateful for all their work, ideas, and energy.

Special thanks from Christopher Martin and Bettina Fabos: We would like to thank Richard Campbell, with whom it is a delight working on this project. We also appreciate the great devotion, creativity, and talent that everyone at Bedford/St. Martin's brings to the book. We would like to thank reviewers and our own journalism and media students for their input and for creating a community of sorts around the theme of critical perspectives on the media. Most of all, we'd like to thank our daughters, Olivia and Sabine, who bring us joy and laughter every day, and a sense of mission to better understand the world of media in which they live.

Please feel free to e-mail us at **mediaessentials@bedfordstmartins.com** with any comments, concerns, or suggestions!

Contents

MASS MEDIA INDUSTRIES

© JGI/Tom Grill/Blend Images/Corbis

LaunchPad For videos, review quizzing, and more, visit **macmillanhighered.com/mediaessentials3e.**

Jerod Harris/WireImage/Getty Images

2   Books and the Power of Print   36

3 Newspapers to Digital Frontiers: Journalism's Journey   69

The Granger Collection

4   Magazines in the Age of Specialization   113

Chester Higgins Jr./The New York
Times/Redux Pictures

Dave Benett/Getty Images

Kevin Mazur/WireImage/Getty Images

© Warner Bros. Pictures/Everett
Collection

Matt Dinnerstein/© Fox/Everett
Collection

8 **Television, Cable, and Specialization
in Visual Culture** 253

Columbia Pictures/Everett Collection

© incamerastock/Alamy

MEDIA FRAMING INDUSTRIES

11 Advertising and Commercial Culture   363

Emmanuel Foudrot/Reuters/Landov

12 Public Relations and Framing the Message   401

Ray Tamarra/Newscom

MEDIA EXPRESSIONS

13 Legal Controls and Freedom of Expression   433

Drew Angerer/Getty Images

Gabriel Bouys/AFP/Getty Images

Warner Bros./Everett Collection

MEDIA ESSENTIALS

1

Mass Communication: A Critical Approach

Prior to the 1980s, the vast majority of people watched video content (television programs) on their television sets from three or four broadcasters over the local airwaves. Then cable television exploded; currently, an estimated 85 percent of homes with a television pay for some kind of cable or satellite television.[1] The still-increasing numbers of channels include networks and local affiliates as well as cable-only channels and premium offerings, such as HBO. At the same time, a growing number of consumers are finding ways to watch their favorite programs without signing up for traditional cable service.

The process is called *cord cutting*, a term created to describe people who cancel their cable or satellite-television subscriptions in favor of watching similar content streamed online. Industry researchers estimate that by the end of 2013, about 7.6 million homes had "cut" their cable cords, up from about 5 million homes in 2010. Although that represents only about 6.5 percent of all U.S. households, a closer look at the numbers reveals some interesting details about this trend. Customers under the age of thirty-five are twice as likely to cut the cord as older users, and customers who have a Hulu or Netflix account or own a smartphone or digital tablet are also much more likely to ditch their cable subscriptions.[2] The ability to watch streaming video using mobile devices is a major driving force in changing viewing and cable-purchasing habits. Researchers have also found that not only are younger users more likely to cut the cord, but more and more of them go straight to online streaming and never bother getting hooked up to cable in the first place.

Though this is a significant change, it doesn't exactly liberate consumers from the major cable companies. Consider, for example, the cable company Comcast. Its recent purchase of entertainment conglomerate NBC Universal means that it still produces content, for which it still gets paid through services like Hulu and Netflix, which license TV shows and stream them for their users. Comcast and other cable providers often provide the same broadband Internet services being used by cord cutters. That means cable companies can structure prices and bundle services like cable, Internet, and even telephone landlines in such a way as to encourage users to keep all three. They have also been pushing for regulators at the FCC to allow them to charge companies such as Netflix more money to get faster Internet service, although the FCC has so far decided against the tiered pricing schemes favored by large Internet providers. Such a tiered service would mean that only large, well-established companies would be able to pay for this faster Internet, stifling the innovation of small Internet start-ups. These regulatory, legislative, and judicial battles over net neutrality, technological innovation, and multiplatform corporations will continue to shape our digital media world for years to come. The tensions between innovation, control, consumer interests, and commercial profits will be a recurring theme throughout this book.

THINKING ABOUT OUR RELATIONSHIP—with all the small, medium, and large screens in our world generates many compelling questions. For example, what does research tell us about how media both reflect and shape our world? What roles and responsibilities do mass media have? What is our role in media processes, such as the development and distribution of content? And how (if at all) should these processes be changed? In this book, we take up such questions by examining the history and business of mass media as well as scholarly research into how media and people interact. We take stock of the media's positive and negative aspects, seeking ideas for ways to use media to improve the quality of our lives.

At their best, media, in all their forms, try to help us understand the events and trends affecting us. At their worst, they can erode the quality of our lives in numerous ways. For one thing, media's appetite for telling and selling stories can lead them to misrepresent those events or exploit them (and the people they most affect) for profit. Many critics disapprove of how media—particularly TV, cable, and tabloid magazines—seem to hurtle from one event to another, often dwelling on trivial, celebrity-driven content rather than meaningful analysis of more important events. Critics also fault media for failing to fulfill their responsibility as a watchdog for democracy—which sometimes calls for challenging our leaders and questioning their actions. Finally, the formation and growth of media industries, commercial culture, and new converging technologies—smartphones, laptop computers, digital television—have some critics worrying that we are now spending more time consuming media than interacting with one another.

Like anything else, mass media have their good sides and bad, their useful effects and destructive ones. And that's why it is so important for us to acquire media literacy—an understanding of the media that are powerfully shaping our world (and being shaped by it). Only by being media literate can we have a say in the roles that media play around us.

In this chapter, we will take steps to strengthen that literacy by:

- tracing the evolution of mass communication—from oral and written forms to print and electronic incarnations

- examining mass media and the process of communication, including the steps a new medium travels on its journey to mass medium status, and the role that mass media play in our everyday lives

- considering two main models of media literacy—cultural and social scientific—which reflect different approaches to understanding how mass communication works and how media affect us

- taking a closer look at cultural approaches to media literacy

- taking a closer look at social scientific approaches to media literacy

- exploring ways of critiquing the mass media, and reflecting on the importance of doing so

LaunchPad
**macmillanhighered.com
/mediaessentials3e**
Use **LearningCurve** to review
concepts from this chapter.

The Evolution of Mass Communication

The mass media surrounding us have their roots in mass communication. **Mass media** are the industries that create and distribute songs, novels, newspapers, movies, Internet services, TV shows, magazines, and other products to large numbers of people. The word *media* is a Latin plural form of the singular noun *medium*, meaning an intervening material or substance through which something else is conveyed or distributed.

We can trace the historical development of media through several eras, all of which still operate to varying degrees. These eras are oral, written, print, electronic, and digital. In the first two eras (oral and written), media existed only in tribal or feudal communities and agricultural economies. In the last three eras (print, electronic, and digital), media became vehicles for **mass communication**: the creation and use of symbols (e.g., languages, Morse code, motion pictures, and binary computer codes) that convey information and meaning to large and diverse audiences through all manner of channels.

Although the telegraph meant that by the middle of the 1800s reporters could almost instantly send a report to their newspaper across the country, getting that news out to a mass audience still had to wait on printing and delivery of a physical object. But with the start of the electronic age in the early twentieth century, radio and then television made mass communication even more widely, and instantly, accessible. If a person were in range of a transmitter, news and entertainment now came at the flick of a switch. By the end of the twentieth century, the Internet revolutionized the entire field of mass communication, and continues to change it today. Consider, for example, that a smartphone that fits into the palm of a person's hand offers every earlier form of communication anywhere there is a Wi-Fi or cellular signal. One could use the phone to make a call or video chat (oral communication), send a text or an e-mail (written communication), read a book (print communication), listen to an online radio station or watch a television program on a service like Hulu (electronic communication), and then send a tweet about the movie they watched on Netflix (digital communication). As shown throughout this book, older forms of communication don't go away but are adapted and converged with newer forms and technologies.

The Oral and Written Eras

In most early societies, information and knowledge first circulated slowly through oral (spoken) traditions passed on by poets, teachers, and tribal storytellers. However, as alphabets and the written word emerged, a manuscript (written) culture developed and eventually overshadowed oral communication. Painstakingly documented and transcribed by philosophers, monks, and stenographers, manuscripts were commissioned by members of the ruling classes, who used them to record religious works and prayers, literature, and personal chronicles. Working people, most of whom were illiterate, rarely saw manuscripts. The shift from oral to written communication created a wide gap between rulers and the ruled in terms of the two groups' education levels and economic welfare.

These trends in oral and written communication unfolded slowly over many centuries. Although exact time frames are disputed, historians generally date the oral and written eras as ranging from 1000 BCE to the mid-fifteenth century. Moreover, the transition from oral to written communication wasn't necessarily smooth. For example, some philosophers saw oral traditions (including exploration of questions and answers through dialogue between teachers and students) as superior. They feared that the written word would hamper conversation between people.

AP Photo/U.S. Army Signal Corps

These army cadets from the 1940s train in sending and receiving Morse code, one of the earliest mass communication technologies.

The Print Era

What we recognize as modern printing—the wide dissemination of many copies of particular manuscripts—became practical in Europe around the middle of the fifteenth century. At this time, Johannes Gutenberg's invention of movable metallic type and the printing press in Germany ushered in the modern print era. Printing presses—and the publications they enabled—spread rapidly across Europe in the late 1400s and early 1500s. But early on, many books were large, elaborate, and expensive. It took months to illustrate and publish these volumes, which were typically purchased by wealthy aristocrats, royal families, church leaders, prominent merchants, and powerful politicians.

In the following centuries, printers reduced the size and cost of books, making them available and affordable to more people. Books were then being mass-produced, making them the first mass-marketed products in history. This development spurred four significant changes: an increasing resistance to authority, the rise of new socioeconomic classes, the spread of literacy, and a focus on individualism.

Resistance to Authority

Since mass-produced printed materials could spread information and ideas faster and farther than ever before, writers could use print to disseminate views that challenged traditional civic doctrine and religious authority. This paved the way for major social and cultural changes, such as the Protestant Reformation and the rise of modern nationalism. People who read contradictory views began resisting traditional clerical authority. With easier access to information about events in nearby places, people also started seeing themselves not merely as members of families, isolated communities, or tribes, but as participants in larger social units—nation-states—whose interests were broader than local or regional concerns.

Bibliotheque Nationale, Paris/Scala-Art Resource

Before the invention of the printing press, books were copied by hand in a labor-intensive process. This beautifully illuminated page is from an Italian Bible from the early 1300s.

New Socioeconomic Classes

Eventually, mass production of books inspired mass production of other goods. This development led to the Industrial Revolution and modern capitalism in the mid-nineteenth century. The nineteenth and twentieth centuries saw the rise of a consumer culture, which encouraged mass consumption to match the output of mass production. The revolution in industry also sparked the emergence of a middle class. This class was composed of people who were neither poor laborers nor wealthy political or religious leaders, but who made modest livings as merchants, artisans, and service professionals, such as lawyers and doctors.

In addition to a middle class, the Industrial Revolution also gave rise to an elite class of business owners and managers who acquired the kind of influence once held only by the nobility or the clergy. These groups soon discovered that they could use print media to distribute information and maintain social order.

Spreading Literacy

Although print media secured authority figures' power, the mass publication of pamphlets, magazines, and books also began democratizing knowledge—making it available to more and more people. Literacy rates rose among the working and middle classes, and some rulers fought back. In England, for instance, the monarchy controlled printing press licenses until the early nineteenth century to constrain literacy and therefore sustain the Crown's power over the populace. Even today, governments in many countries worldwide control presses, access to paper, and advertising and distribution channels for the same reason. In most industrialized countries, such efforts at control have met with only limited success. After all, building an industrialized economy requires a more educated workforce, and printed literature and textbooks support that education.

Focus on Individualism

The print revolution also nourished the idea of individualism. People came to rely less on their local community and their commercial, religious, and political leaders for guidance on how to live their lives. Instead, they read various ideas and arguments, and came up with their own answers to life's great questions. By the mid-nineteenth century, individualism had spread into the realm of commerce. There, it took the form of increased resistance to government interference in the affairs of self-reliant entrepreneurs. Over the next century, individualism became a fundamental value in American society.

The Electronic and Digital Eras

In Europe and America, the rise of industry completely transformed everyday life, with factories replacing farms as the main centers of work and production. During the 1880s, roughly 80 percent of Americans lived on farms and in small towns; by the 1920s and 1930s, most had moved to urban areas, where new industries and economic opportunities beckoned. This shift set the stage for the final two eras in mass communication: the electronic era (whose key innovations included the telegraph, radio, and television) and the digital era (whose flagship invention is the Internet).

The Electronic Era

In America, the gradual transformation from an industrial, print-based society to one fueled by electronic innovation began with the development of the telegraph in the 1840s. Featuring dot-dash electronic signals, the telegraph made media messages instantaneous, no longer reliant on stagecoaches, ships, or the pony express. It also enabled military, business, and political leaders to coordinate commercial and military operations more easily than ever. And it laid the

Culver Pictures/The Art Archive at Art Resource, NY

In the 1930s and 1940s, radio or television sets—encased in decorative wood and sold as stylish furniture—occupied a central place in some American homes.

groundwork for future technological developments, such as wireless telegraphy, the fax machine, and the cell phone (all of which ultimately led to the telegraph's demise).

The development of film at the start of the twentieth century and radio in the 1920s were important milestones, but the electronic era really took off in the 1950s and 1960s with the arrival of television—a medium that powerfully reshaped American life.

The Digital Era

With the arrival of cutting-edge communication gadgetry—ever-smaller personal computers, cable TV, e-mail, DVDs, DVRs, direct broadcast satellites, cell phones, PDAs—the electronic era gave way to the digital era. In **digital communication**, images, texts, and sounds are converted (encoded) into electronic signals (represented as combinations of ones and zeros) that are then reassembled (decoded) as a precise reproduction of, say, a TV picture, a magazine article, a song, or a voice on the telephone. On the Internet, various images, text, and sounds are digitally reproduced and transmitted globally.

New technologies, particularly cable television and the Internet, have developed so quickly that those who had long controlled the dispersal of information—for example, newspaper editors and network television news producers—have lost some of that power. Moreover, e-mail and text messages—digital versions of both oral and written culture—now perform some of the functions of the postal service and are outpacing some governments' attempts to control communications beyond national borders.

Media Convergence

The electronic and digital eras have ushered in the phenomenon of **media convergence**, a term that has two very different meanings. According to one meaning, media convergence is the technological merging of content in different mass media. For example, magazine articles and radio programs are also accessible on the Internet; and songs, TV shows, and movies are now available on computers, iPods, and cell phones.

Such technological convergence is not entirely new. For instance, in the late 1920s, the Radio Corporation of America (RCA) purchased the Victor Talking Machine Company and introduced machines that could play both radio and recorded music. However, contemporary media convergence is much broader because it involves digital content across a wider array of media.

The term *media convergence* can also be used to describe a particular business model by which a company consolidates various media holdings—such as cable connections, phone services, television transmissions, and Internet access—under one corporate umbrella. The goal of such consolidation is not necessarily to offer consumers more choices in their media but to better manage resources, lower costs, and maximize profits. For example, a company that owns TV stations, radio outlets, and newspapers in multiple markets—as well as in the same cities—can deploy one reporter or producer to create three or four versions of the same story for various media outlets. Thus, the company can employ fewer people than if it owned only one media outlet.

Tony Cenicola/The New York Times/Redux Pictures

The convergence of online media into one simple device is still a new media concept for many people—an enormous shift from the multiple single-purpose devices most Americans grew up with.

Mass Media and the Process of Communication

To understand how mass media shape the communication process, let's look at the stages a medium goes through on its journey to becoming a mass medium. Then let's examine the ways in which the media have affected everyday life.

The Evolution of a New Mass Medium

A new medium emerges not just from the work of inventors, such as Thomas Edison, but also from social, cultural, political, and economic changes. For instance, the Internet arose to meet people's desire to transport messages and share information more rapidly in an increasingly mobile and interconnected global population.

Typically, each media industry goes through three stages in its evolution. First is the *development stage* (sometimes referred to as the novelty stage). During this stage, inventors and technicians try to solve a particular problem, such as making pictures move, transmitting messages between ships and shore, or sending mail electronically.

Comcast Extends Its Reach

Convergence and accompanying concerns about possible monopolies are not new to the mass media landscape. But some corporate behemoths push the envelope of what is possible in the current digital media world. One such company is Comcast. Started in the 1960s as a small cable company serving just over a thousand subscribers, Comcast has grown those numbers to almost twenty-two million. But Comcast is hardly just a cable company anymore. As the government has relaxed its rules about competition and ownership, Comcast has become the largest video, Internet, and phone provider in the United States—and its reach exceeds even those services. Comcast's biggest recent purchase was NBC Universal, meaning that a single company not only owns the wires that bring programming into over twenty million homes but also owns NBC and its affiliated networks, a substantial number of cable stations (Bravo, E!, Golf Channel, MSNBC, Oxygen, USA, the Weather Channel), Telemundo, the online TV service Hulu, almost a dozen broadcast TV stations in the nation's largest cities, Universal Pictures, and Universal Studios theme parks. In 2014, Comcast expressed interest in merging with fellow media giant Time Warner Cable, although opponents have asked the Federal Communications Commission to block the move.

What does this mean for the average consumer? Considering all of the ways a megamedia corporation like Comcast interacts with consumers could take an entire book of its own; instead, we will briefly consider the hypothetical merger with Time Warner Cable. A Comcast press release claims the merger would create "a company that delivers maximum value for our shareholders, enormous opportunities for our employees and a superior experience for our customers."[1] On the other hand, media watchdogs argue that despite those friendly words, corporations exist to maximize profits, and this means a push toward monopolization and away from consumer choice and satisfaction. A 2014 survey by the American Customer Satisfaction Index seems to support the critics, ranking Comcast and Time Warner as the worst in terms of customer satisfaction among major Internet providers.[2]

The picture is about much more than customer service. Not only is Comcast Corporation the largest cable operator and largest home Internet service provider (ISP) in the United States, but it is also listed by political watchdog Web site OpenSecrets.org as a "heavy hitter."[3] That means it is among the top 140 overall donors to federal elections since 1990, spending over $20 million

▶ **Visit LaunchPad** to watch a scene from *30 Rock* that parodies the reach of cable companies. How might *30 Rock*'s parent company have affected the writers' satire?

in contributions to political campaigns and over $120 million in lobbying. In addition to the proposed merger, Comcast is also mobilized to oppose strong net neutrality protections, including those called for by President Obama in late 2014. With Comcast's deep pockets and powerful control of several media outlets, including one of the Big Three news networks, advocates for greater ownership diversity and net neutrality have their work cut out for them.

Throughout this book, we consider how the digital turn and media convergence have changed the way we consume media—and also the way we connect with others. A more converged business model offers more profits to those companies that downsize their workforce while increasing their media holdings in many markets. But although it's easy to see the benefits for media owners, this model presents serious disadvantages for society. For one thing, it limits the range of perspectives from which messages are delivered, as media content becomes concentrated in fewer and fewer hands. For instance, as conglomerates buy up more and more newspapers and employ fewer reporters, citizens are exposed to a narrower range of interpretations of news events. Simultaneously, media owners' personal biases and interests (in culture, politics, and economics) gain more influence, because the content they control gets disseminated more widely than content controlled by smaller companies or media outlets.

Convergence also affects which companies have the greatest economic power. Whereas much media content is still produced by traditional media industries (the music industry, the film industry, the publishing industry, and so forth), distribution channels have expanded to include a great variety of services and devices. This in turn has caused an ongoing economic shift, in which cable and Internet providers, cell phone companies, and digital retailers like Amazon and iTunes receive a greater share of the money spent on media consumption, while traditional outlets like movie theaters, book stores, and record labels may struggle. Media consumption still absorbs a massive amount of time and money, but convergence ensures that this time and money will be flowing in new and different directions.

Second is the *entrepreneurial stage*, in which inventors and investors determine a practical and marketable use for the new device. For example, the Internet has some roots in scientists' desire for a communication system that could enable their colleagues across the country to share time on a few rare supercomputers.

Third is the *mass medium stage*. At this point, businesses figure out how to market the new device as a *consumer product*. To illustrate, Pentagon and government researchers developed the prototype for the Internet, but commercial interests extended the medium's usefulness to individuals and businesses.

Debating Media's Role in Everyday Life

Even as far back as ancient times, human beings have discussed and debated the media's merits and dangers. The earliest recorded debates in Western society about the impact of the written word on daily life date back to the ancient Greeks—in particular, to Socrates, Euripides, and Plato. These men argued over whether theatrical plays would corrupt young people by exposing them to messages that conflicted with those promulgated by their teachers.

Today, we still debate these sorts of questions. At the turn of the twentieth century, for example, newly arrived immigrants to the United States who spoke little English gravitated toward vaudeville shows and silent films, which they could enjoy without having to understand English. These popular events occasionally became a flash point for some groups. For example, the Daughters of the American Revolution, local politicians, religious leaders, and police vice squads feared that these "low" cultural forms would undermine what they saw as traditional American values.

Since then, print, electronic, and digital communications have extended their reach, and people have begun spending more time consuming them (see Table 1.1). Mass media now play an even more controversial role in society. For instance, some people are frustrated by the overwhelming amount of information available. Others decry what they view as mass media's overly commercial and sensationalistic quality. In their view, too many talk shows exploit personal problems for commercial gain, and too many TV shows and video games feature graphic violence.

People also keep grappling with the question, To what extent do mass media shape our values and behaviors, and to what extent do our values and behaviors shape the media? Researchers have continued searching for answers to this question. For example, some have designed studies to determine whether watching violent TV shows makes viewers more likely to commit violent acts. Other scholars argue that violent TV shows don't cause violent behavior in viewers;

TABLE 1.1 // HOURS PER PERSON PER YEAR USING CONSUMER MEDIA

Year	Total TV	Broadcast & Satellite Radio	Newspaper	Consumer Internet	Video Games	Total*
1999	1,427	939	205	65	58	3,280
2002	1,519	991	194	147	70	3,430
2006	1,555	975	179	190	82	3,499
2009	1,562	984	165	203	96	3,555
2012	1,597	729	150	197	142	3,515
Seven- and Six-Year Changes						
1999–2006	+128	+36	–26	+125	+24	+219
2006–2012	+42	–246	–29	+7	+60	+16

*Total hours includes time spent with recorded music, consumer magazines, consumer books, home video/DVD, box office, interactive TV, and wireless content, and time spent media multitasking—using media simultaneously.

Data from: Veronis Suhler Stevenson Communications Industry Forecast

rather, people who already have violent tendencies are drawn to violent TV shows. Still others suggest that certain variables—such as age, upbringing, or genetic predisposition—might be the root cause of violence. Research into such questions of media and violence hasn't yielded conclusive answers, but it does encourage us to keep asking questions and to examine the approaches we use to analyze the media's role in our lives.

Finally, people have expressed concern about the financial power of mass media industries. In the United States, these industries earn more than $200 billion annually, then reinvest those revenues to research how we choose our media content, what we do with that content, and how they can better serve our needs and influence our behaviors (from shopping to voting) so that they can make more money.

Like the air we breathe, the mass media surrounds us, and we often take its impact, like that of the air, for granted. And if we don't take it for granted, we frequently can't agree on its quality. To monitor the media's "air quality" more proactively and productively, we must become media literate. We can start by examining several models for understanding media's nature and impact.

Mass media play a significant role in capturing important historical and controversial events. This Pulitzer Prize–winning photo by Stanley Forman, "The Soiling of Old Glory," shows a white teenager attacking an African American lawyer with a flagpole bearing the American flag at a protest over court-ordered busing to desegregate schools in Boston on April 5, 1976.

© Stanley Forman Photo, Pulitzer Prize 1976

Media Literacy: Ways of Understanding

Experts have used a variety of approaches to understand how the various media work and what influence they have on our lives in order to strengthen our **media literacy**. These approaches to mass communication include the linear model (which focuses on the communication process), the cultural model (which views mass communication as a cultural characteristic and uses anecdotal evidence to interpret media), and the social scientific model (which uses numerical data-gathering and statistical analysis).

The Linear Model

The linear model represents a traditional approach to interpreting media content. The model attempts to explain how a mass medium actually communicates messages and how people understand those messages. According to this model, mass communication is a *linear process* by which media producers deliver messages to large audiences. **Senders** (authors, producers, organizations) transmit **messages** (programs, texts, images, sounds, ads) through a **mass media channel** (newspapers, books, magazines, radio, television, the Internet) to large groups of **receivers** (readers, viewers, consumers). In the process, **gatekeepers** (news editors, executive producers of TV shows and movies) filter those messages by making decisions about which messages get produced for which audiences. This linear process allows **feedback**, in which citizens and consumers, if they choose, return messages to senders or gatekeepers through letters, phone calls, e-mail, Web postings, tweets, or talk shows.

The problem with the linear model is that it doesn't capture certain complexities of the mass communication process. In reality, media messages do not always get to their intended receivers, nor do receivers always interpret these messages in the way media producers want. For example, people might ignore an advertisement or a new movie, or draw an entirely different message from a magazine article or TV show than what the content creator intended to communicate. The cultural and social scientific models have since developed more sophisticated approaches to media study that improve on the limitations of the linear model.

The Cultural Model

The cultural model of media literacy views media content as a part of culture. Culture consists of the ways in which people live and represent themselves at

Photofest (top); © 20th Century Fox/Photofest (bottom)

Often, popular stories and characters evolve in our culture over time, acquiring new meaning. Consider the classic 1931 film *Frankenstein* (*top*) and the 1974 parody *Young Frankenstein* (*bottom*). How does each story reflect changes in cultural attitudes?

© Greg Whitesell/Reuters/Corbis

By analyzing the news media's coverage of the recent wars in Afghanistan and Iraq, the cultural model shows how media content shapes attitudes and beliefs. Graphic portrayals of the human casualties caused many people to oppose the wars.

particular historical times, as manifested in things like fashion, sports, architecture, education, religion, science, and media.

As cultural forms, the media help us make sense of daily life and articulate our values. When we listen to music, read a book, watch television, or scan the Internet, we assign meaning to that song, book, TV program, or Web site. And different people often assign different meanings to the same media content. Take the Harry Potter book series. Some readers see the series as an innocent coming-of-age children's story. Others interpret it as more adult literature, containing pointed metaphors about good and evil that parallel current political events. Still others construe the series as a tool for luring children into a life of witchcraft. And others use the books merely for entertainment, inventing Harry Potter parodies in almost every imaginable media form.

We describe this model for understanding media content as cultural because it recognizes that individuals assign diverse meanings to messages depending on personal characteristics, such as gender, age, educational level, ethnicity, occupation, and religious beliefs. According to this model, audiences actively affirm, interpret, refashion, select, or reject the messages flowing through various media channels. One manifestation of this active audience in the digital age is the Internet meme. Coined by British evolutionary biologist Richard Dawkins, the term *meme* has come to mean a digital experience—a video, a sound recording, even just a catchphrase—that is passed electronically from one consumer to another—sometimes with new variations (remakes, remixes, mash-ups, and so forth)—often very quickly. This widespread, rapid transmission is frequently referred to as *viral*, and includes brief cultural touchstones, like Rebecca Black's "Friday" video, Charlie Sheen's use of "winning," or Three Wolf Moon T-shirts. Unlike network celebrities and corporate brands, the meme is a product of an interactive culture in dialogue with itself.

But even as we shape media content, it shapes us, too. For instance, during the recent wars in Afghanistan and Iraq, journalists' work increased people's awareness of the wars and in some cases altered attitudes toward them. Graphic depictions of the wars' human toll prompted many people to vocally oppose the wars. This opposition in turn influenced political leaders to reconsider their military strategies.

Thus, the cultural approach to studying the media critically analyzes media content, the ways in which audiences interpret the content, and the circumstances of how the media produce such content.

The Social Scientific Model

The social scientific model also asks important questions about the media, but it is informed by an approach that tests hypotheses with measurable data. The model has its roots in the natural sciences' pursuit of objective research. However, as social scientific researchers know, applying rigorous social scientific methods to the study of human behavior is much less reliable than applying such methods to a highly controlled chemistry or physics laboratory environment.

Nevertheless, social scientific research has provided valuable insight into questions about how the media affect us and has become more sophisticated with the rise of electronic and digital media in the twentieth century. Early research looked at the effects of movies, using electric mechanisms attached to viewers' skin to detect heightened responses to frightening or romantic scenes. More recent research has continued to test hypotheses about media effects, using controlled laboratory experiments. For example, researchers might set out to chart the relationship among stereotypical magazine representations of women of color and readers' occupational expectations for women of color in general.

Politics and public opinion also have long attracted the interest of media researchers, beginning with the rise of **survey research** in the twentieth century. Today, media researchers—working for universities, news organizations, the government, and political parties—conduct regular national and regional surveys to take snapshots of the public's opinions on all manner of issues. They also use that information as a basis for action. For example, public opinion researchers (usually working as consultants for political parties or campaigns) test words, ideas, and images on small focus groups to see how different ways of framing a topic—such as "global warming" versus "climate change"—affect voters' decisions.

Just as media research can help political candidates formulate their campaign strategies, it can also help businesses develop and market their products. For instance, consumer product companies use quantitative methods to track the effectiveness of their advertisements; Hollywood studios regularly screen-test movies to figure out which ending works best for viewers; and ratings services track audience numbers for radio, television, and Web sites, compiling immense stores of data that companies use to gauge the effectiveness of their ad spending.

The goal of social scientific media research, then, is to develop testable hypotheses (or predictions) about the media, gather relevant data, and determine whether the data verifies the hypotheses.

A Closer Look at the Cultural Model: Surveying the Cultural Landscape

In the pages that follow, we examine the cultural model of media literacy, which provides many ways to study media content through the lens of culture. We discuss two metaphors researchers use to describe the way people judge media content, and present ways to trace changes in our cultural values as media adapt and change.

© Comedy Central/Everett Collection

Animated comedy series like *South Park* reflect a mix of high and low culture, with their often raunchy parodies and attacks on what the creators perceive as hypocrisies within society.

The "Culture as Skyscraper" Metaphor

Throughout the twentieth century, many Americans envisioned our nation's culture as consisting of ascending levels of superiority—like floors in a skyscraper. They identified **high culture** (the top floors of the building) with good taste, higher education, and fine art supported by wealthy patrons and corporate donors. And they associated **low** or **popular culture** (the bottom floors) with the questionable tastes of the masses, who lapped up the commercial junk circulated by the mass media, such as reality TV shows, celebrity gossip Web sites, and action films.

Some cultural researchers have pointed out that this high–low hierarchy has become so entrenched that it powerfully influences how we view and discuss culture today.[3] For example, people who subscribe to the hierarchy metaphor believe that low culture prevents people (students in particular) from appreciating fine art, exploits high culture by transforming classic works into simplistic forms, and promotes a throwaway ethic. These same critics accuse low culture of driving out higher forms of culture. They also argue that it inhibits political discourse and social change by making people so addicted to mass-produced media that they lose their ability to see and challenge social inequities (also referred to as the Big Mac Theory).[4]

The "Culture as Map" Metaphor

Other researchers think of culture as a map. In this metaphor, culture—rather than being a vertically organized structure—is an ongoing process that accommodates diverse tastes. Cultural phenomena, including media—printed materials we read, movies and TV programs we watch, songs and radio shows we listen to—can take us to places that are conventional, recognizable, stable, and comforting. However, they can also take us to places that are innovative, unfamiliar, unstable, and challenging.

Human beings are attracted to both consistency and change, and cultural media researchers have pointed out that most media can satisfy both of those desires. For example, a movie can contain elements that are familiar to us (such as particular plots) as well as elements that are completely new and strange (such as a cinematic technique we've never seen before).

Tracing Changes in Values

In addition to examining metaphors of culture that we use to understand media's role in our lives, cultural researchers examine the ways in which our values have changed along with changes in mass media. Researchers have been particularly interested in how values have shifted during the modern era and the postmodern period.

The Modern Era

From the Industrial Revolution to the mid-twentieth century—which historians call the **modern era**—four values came into sharp focus across the American cultural landscape. These values were influenced by developments that unfolded during the era and the media's responses to those developments:

- **Working efficiently.** As businesses used new technology to create efficient manufacturing centers and produce inexpensive products more cheaply and profitably, advertisers (who operate in all mass media) spread the word about new gadgets that could save Americans time and labor, reinforcing the benefits of efficiency.
- **Celebrating the individual.** Media described and interpreted new scientific discoveries, enabling ordinary citizens to gain access to new ideas beyond what their religious leaders and local politicians communicated to them. With access to novel ideas, people began celebrating the individual's power to pick and choose from ideas instead of merely following what leaders told them.
- **Believing in a rational order.** Being modern also meant valuing logic and reason and viewing the world as a rational place. In this orderly place, the printed mass media—particularly newspapers—served to educate the citizenry, helping to build and maintain an organized society.[5]
- **Rejecting tradition and embracing progress.** Within the modern era was a shorter phenomenon: the **Progressive Era**. This period of political and social reform lasted roughly from the 1890s to the 1920s and inspired many Americans—and mass media—to break with tradition and embrace change. For example, journalists began focusing their reporting on immediate events. They ignored the foundational developments that led up to those events, further reinforcing the notion that the past matters far less than the present and the future.

The Postmodern Period

In the **postmodern period**—from roughly the mid-twentieth century to today—cultural values changed shape once more, influenced again by developments in our society and the media's responses to those developments. Cultural researchers have identified the following dominant values in today's postmodern period:

- **Celebrating populism.** As a political idea, **populism** tries to appeal to ordinary people by setting up a conflict between "the people" and "the elite." For example, populist politicians often run ads criticizing big corporations and political favoritism.

© Warner Bros./Photofest

Directed by the Wachowski siblings and released in 1999, *The Matrix* is both a reflection and a critique of the postmodern period's value of embracing technology. The film's innovative special effects would come to define the look of many action films that followed.

And many famous film actors champion oppressed groups, even though their work makes them wealthy global icons of consumerist culture.

- **Reviving older cultural styles.** Mass media now borrow and then transform cultural styles from the modern era. For example, in music, hip-hop deejays and performers sample old R&B, soul, and rock classics to reinvent songs. And in the noir genre of moviemaking, directors use moody photography and retro costuming to create the same look and feel of movies crafted in the earlier era.

- **Embracing technology.** Even as we and our media can't seem to get enough of retro cultural styles, we passionately embrace new technologies. The huge popularity of movies that feature technology at their core—like *Guardians of the Galaxy* and *Interstellar*—testifies to this paradox.

- **Interest in the supernatural.** Some people have begun challenging the argument that scientific reasoning is the only way to interpret the world, and have gravitated toward traditional religion or the supernatural. Mass media reflect this shift. For example, since the late 1980s, a host of popular TV programs emerged that featured mystical themes—including *Twin Peaks*, *The X-Files*, *Buffy the Vampire Slayer*, *Supernatural*, *American Horror Story*, and *The Vampire Diaries*.

A Closer Look at the Social Scientific Model: Gathering Data

The social scientific model of media literacy differs in key ways from the cultural model. In this section, we compare analyses of two studies to examine the differences between the two models, and we look more closely at how social scientific researchers gather data to analyze the content of media messages and consumers' responses to those messages.

Comparing Analyses of Cancer News Coverage

Cultural and social scientific media researchers often study the same topics, but they ask different types of questions about those topics. For example, two studies recently analyzed news coverage of cancer. The study informed by the cultural approach, titled "Constructing Breast Cancer in the News: Betty Ford and the Evolution of the Breast Cancer Patient," explored a historical turning point in how the media and consumers interpret breast cancer. The study centered on how the news media covered First Lady Betty Ford's mastectomy operation in 1974. The author of the study concluded that coverage of Ford's mastectomy still influences contemporary news coverage of breast cancer today. Specifically, many stories on this topic emphasize "the need for breast cancer patients to maintain their femininity."[6]

Research by social scientists asked a question about cancer news coverage that was perhaps less expansive but more measurable. In an article titled "A Comprehensive Analysis of Breast Cancer News Coverage in Leading Media Outlets Focusing on Environmental Risks and Prevention," researchers analyzed the contents of newspaper, television, and magazine accounts of the topic over a two-year span. The researchers didn't interpret the meanings of the news stories (as cultural researchers might have). Instead, they focused on the data they gathered, describing their analysis in more objective terms. For example, the authors noted that "about one-third of the stories included prevention content, primarily focusing narrowly on the use of pharmaceutical products. Little information described risk reduction via other individual preventive behaviors (e.g., diet, exercise, and smoking), parental protective measures, or collective actions to combat contamination sites."[7]

Gathering and Analyzing Data

The social scientists analyzing cancer news coverage used a technique called **content analysis** to gather data. Through content analysis, researchers code and count the content of various types of media. For instance, they total up the number of news stories that contain specific types of information regarding the topic in question (such as how to prevent cancer), count song lyrics containing references to a topic (e.g., sex), or total up the number of occurrences of certain behaviors (e.g., violent acts) shown in a set of movies.

But content analysis is only one way to gather data using the social science approach. Researchers also conduct **experiments** using randomly assigned subjects (college students are popular test subjects) to test people's self-reported recall of or reactions to media content. To illustrate, experimenters might use devices such as eye trackers to record what part of a page or screen each viewer is watching.[8] Researchers can also gather data through surveys they've designed or use data from the many surveys the federal government funds and makes available.

Critiquing Media

To acquire media literacy, we can read the findings of cultural and social science researchers who have studied various aspects of the media. However, both models have their limits; thus, it's important to view their conclusions with a critical eye. We can also learn to critique media content ourselves in a methodical, disciplined way. Whatever approach we use to develop media literacy, it's helpful to always keep in mind the benefits of a critical perspective.

Evaluating Cultural and Social Scientific Research

Examining the findings of both cultural and social scientific research on media can help us follow a **critical process** that consists of describing, analyzing, interpreting, evaluating, and engaging with mass media. But the two models have strengths and weaknesses that are important to keep in mind. The cultural model is best at recognizing the complexity of media culture and providing analyses that draw on descriptive, critical, historical, ethnographic, political, and economic traditions. Yet this model has a downside: Although cultural studies can help us see media from new perspectives, the conclusions laid out in a particular study may simply be the author's interpretation. Thus, they may not necessarily explain cause-and-effect connections in situations other than what the author examined.

The social scientific model seeks to develop and test theories about how the media affect individuals and society in measurable ways. This approach produces conclusions based on hard numbers, which policy makers often find comforting. It may suggest a clear chain of cause and effect, or at least a statistical relationship between the media and an effect.

But like the cultural model, the social scientific model has limits, too. For example, the options provided in a multiple-choice survey question might not cover all the possible responses that participants could give. As a result, researchers obtain an incomplete picture of how people respond to particular media. Also, definitions of what is being measured may confuse things. To illustrate, researchers might count a bonk on the head shown in a movie as an act of violence, even though the event could be purposeful, accidental, deserved, or part of a character's fantasy. Researchers can thus neglect to ask more nuanced questions, such as whether accidental incidents of violence have a different effect on movie viewers than do purposeful acts of violence. Finally, many social scientific studies are limited to questions that their funding sources—the government, media industry associations, or granting agencies—ask them to study. This situation further constrains the scope of their research.

Ultimately, though, the quality of any media research—cultural or social scientific—depends on the nature of the questions asked and the rigor of the method used. Often, "triangulating" with two or more approaches to test a question makes for much stronger conclusions. For those of us seeking to strengthen our media literacy by consulting research, the best approach may be to balance findings on a particular question from both the cultural and the social scientific models.

Conducting Our Own Critiques

If we want to conduct our own critiques of specific media, we'll need a working knowledge of the particular medium being addressed—whether it's a book, a TV show, a song, a movie, a video game, a magazine, a radio show, or some other form. For example, suppose our goal is to develop a meaningful critique of the TV show *Dexter* (in which the main character is a serial killer), Rush Limbaugh's conservative radio program, or weekly magazines' obsession with Kate Middleton. In each case, we will need to thoroughly familiarize ourselves with the show, program, or magazines in question and start thinking about what messages they seem to be conveying. As we begin this process, we will also need to transcend our own preferences and biases. For instance, we may like or dislike hip-hop, R&B, pop music, or country, but if we want to criticize the messages in one or more of these musical genres intelligently, we need to understand what they have to say and consider why their messages appeal to particular audiences.

Familiarization and a certain amount of self-conscious detachment, then, are the preliminaries of a rigorous process that moves beyond matters of taste or, worse, a cynical, wholesale dismissal of culturally significant experiences. Becoming truly media literate requires mastering this critical process and applying it to everyday encounters with the communication media. The process encompasses five steps: Description, Analysis, Interpretation, Evaluation, and Engagement (see "The Critical Process behind Media Literacy" on page 28).

One way to critique the media is to analyze the highly stylized advertisements and information that appear before us. In trailers and advertisements for the 2014 film *Dawn of the Planet of the Apes*, what is being sold, and what does it reveal about American audiences?

Powerful celebrities like Oprah Winfrey have a profound influence on popular opinion and belief. Developing an informed critical perspective on the media allows individuals to engage in discussions about their impact on the world.

Case Study

Football, *Fútbol*, and Soccer

Since World War II disrupted film production in Europe and gave American filmmakers a chance to solidify their spot at the top of the international entertainment market, the United States has been a leading exporter of cultural mass media products. In addition to (or perhaps because of) U.S. economic and political power following World War II, American-made entertainment and advertising campaigns have been popular or at least widely recognized around the globe. Some see this as positive, citing the influence of American popular culture (and the values it espouses) as inspiring uprisings against oppressive regimes, and crediting American communication platforms such as Facebook and Twitter with the Arab Spring revolts that began in 2011. On the other hand, critics say this globalization of American popular culture

Jim Rogash/Getty Images (top); Victor Carretero/Real Madrid via Getty Images (bottom)

macmillanhighered.com/mediaessentials3e

▶ **Visit LaunchPad** to watch a clip from *The Simpsons* about American reactions to soccer. How have cultures changed since this aired in the late 1990s?

disadvantages local and long-established cultures of people around the globe, which may not be as slick or flashy as what comes from Hollywood or Madison Avenue, by distracting the youth of these cultures from traditional values and practices. Often, this discussion involves a smaller, less-developed country worrying about the influence of a larger or more powerful country. From the position of the more powerful country, it might be too easy to dismiss these concerns, at least for some. But what happens when the roles are reversed?

The 2014 World Cup became the catalyst for just such a role reversal. For most of the world, "football" (*fútbol*) is the game Americans call soccer; in America, "football" is a very different sport. Outside of the United States, soccer is king, whereas sports like basketball, baseball, and American football dominate in the United States. But soccer and soccer culture have been growing rapidly in the last several decades. The phrase "soccer mom" has been used to describe a segment of the American public since at least the 1990s, and President Obama has been quoted as describing himself as a "soccer dad." FIFA (Fédération Internationale de Football Association) estimates that there are twenty million young Americans participating in youth soccer programs.[1] But this growth in soccer and the popularity of the World Cup competition also draws sharp criticism from social and political conservatives who see it as a kind of threat to American values. Some even go so far as to describe the popularity of soccer as part of a socialist plot, a sign of moral decay, and strike a xenophobic note criticizing the sport as being bad because it is "foreign" and associated with undocumented immigrants.

This blurring of physical and political boundaries, the exchange of ideas and cultural products (from films to *fútbol*), and the lack of consensus on what it all means and if it should be seen as good or bad is part of what it is to be living in a postmodern world. Trying to determine that meaning and what it says about who is and who isn't privileged in a global society are key questions for critical cultural scholars who study questions of globalization.

APPLYING THE CRITICAL PROCESS

Investigate the influence of American popular culture on other parts of the world. Look at stories on the home page of at least four international news sources from four different countries. If you are fluent in other languages, good; if you read only English, try the *Guardian*, the *Independent*, the *Telegraph* (all United Kingdom), the *Mail & Guardian* (South Africa), the *Sydney Morning Herald* (Australia), the *Globe and Mail* (Canada), *NHK* (Japan), the *Straits Times* (Singapore), AlJazeera.net (Qatar), and the *Times of India*.

DESCRIPTION Describe the content of the four newspapers, paying particular attention to any U.S.-related content.

ANALYSIS What patterns emerge in the U.S.-related content? Does the content have to do with international politics, sports, entertainment, or some other topic? What percentage of the stories on the home page of each newspaper is about the United States or American culture? Are there any other countries that dominate the news in each newspaper?

INTERPRETATION Does your analysis support the idea that U.S. culture is influential throughout the world? Does the United States have any rivals to the global strength of its culture?

EVALUATION Discuss the advantages and disadvantages of American culture becoming so popular worldwide. Is there evidence that other cultures are influencing American culture? Is that a good or a bad trend?

ENGAGEMENT Continue to read international newspapers, and consider the influence of other countries' culture on the United States. Contact an editor at your local newspaper and ask why an important story you saw in an international paper isn't news here.

THE CRITICAL PROCESS BEHIND MEDIA LITERACY

Becoming literate about communication media involves striking a balance between taking a critical stand (developing knowledgeable interpretations and judgments) and being tolerant of diverse forms of expression (appreciating the distinctive variety of cultural products and processes). Finding this balance in a media-literate critical perspective involves completing five overlapping stages that build on one another.

Stage One: Description

Develop descriptive skills associated with breaking down a story into character types and plot structure. Focus on how music, dialogue, camerawork, and editing come together in a way that encourages audience engagement. Master the terms and understand the techniques of telling stories in a particular medium.

Examples

- Describe how the conventions of the documentary are used in sitcoms like *Modern Family* and *Parks and Recreation*.
- Describe the use of gritty or graphic content in a network show like *NCIS* and a cable series like *The Walking Dead*.

Stage Two: Analysis

Focus on and discuss the significant patterns that emerge during the Description stage. Make connections. How does this song or story connect with other items of popular culture?

Examples

- How does the satirical approach of *Last Week Tonight* compare to that of *The Daily Show*?
- What are the similarities and differences between *Fox & Friends* and NBC's *Today*?

Stage Three: Interpretation

Interpret findings. Ask yourself, What does it mean? If there is a distinct pattern, what is the cause or reason? Consider whether comedy, irony, and satire complicate this stage of the critical process.

Examples

- What does the presence of criminal protagonists mean for shows like *Orange Is the New Black*, *Better Call Saul*, and *Breaking Bad*?
- What does it mean when Jeff Dunham fashions a comedy act around Achmed, the Dead Terrorist? Why do Dunham's fans find the "I keel you" line so funny?

Stage Four: Evaluation

Arrive at a critical judgment that goes beyond your personal tastes. Does the media product under analysis cause harm? Does it inspire thought? Does it perpetuate a dehumanizing view of a group? Does it promote active citizenship or passive consumerism?

Examples

- The movie adaptation of *Gone Girl* depicts contentious relationships between men and women. Should the movie be condemned for misogyny?
- The villain in *The Muppets* (2011) is a greedy oil tycoon. Is this film anticapitalist propaganda?

Stage Five: Engagement

Make your voice heard. Take action that connects your critical perspective to your role as a citizen. Become involved in doing your part to challenge media institutions and make them accountable.

Examples

- Write letters to media editors about blind spots in news coverage.
- Contact companies that perpetuate harmful images of women in their advertising and recommend more socially responsible ways of selling their products.

Benefits of a Critical Perspective

Developing an informed critical perspective on the media enables us to participate in a debate about media's impacts on our democracy and culture. For instance, on the one hand, the media can be a force for strengthening our democracy and making the world a better place. Consider the role of television in documenting racism and injustice in the 1960s—coverage that encouraged the Civil Rights movement. Or consider how the cultural traditions surrounding sports and games can build bridges between peoples even as it generates a backlash (see "Media Literacy Case Study: Football, *Fútbol*, and Soccer" on pages 26–27).

On the other hand, the media have helped create a powerful commercial culture in our nation—a culture in which fewer and fewer multinational corporations dominate our economy and generate more and more of the media messages we consume. A society in which only a few voices are telling us stories about what's important, what our values should be, and how we should behave is hardly a healthy democracy.

Because the media constitute forces for both good and ill, it's that much more important for each of us to think carefully about which media we consume; what messages we draw from those media; and how those messages affect our actions, the quality of our lives, and the health of our democracy. We also need to ask questions, such as the following:

- Why might some people continue clinging to either/or thinking about media (such as high-brow versus low-brow books or movies) when so many boundaries in our society have blurred? Does this either/or thinking reflect a desire to keep people in their "proper" socioeconomic class?
- What does it mean that public debate and news about everyday life now seem just as likely to come from Oprah, *The Daily Show*, or bloggers as from the *New York Times* or the *NBC Nightly News*?[9] Can we no longer distinguish real news from entertainment? If so, does this affect how well informed we are?
- How can we hone our awareness of the economic interests fueling the messages delivered through the media we consume? For example, do you listen to a talk show on a radio station that survives on advertising revenue? If so, ask yourself how the host might distort information (e.g., deliberately inciting conflict between guests) to attract more listeners and therefore bring in more advertising revenue. (Advertisers only want to spend money on ads that will reach as many people as possible.) If such distortion is taking place, how reliable is the information you're consuming by listening to the show?

Unfortunately, we can't rely only on professional media critics or watchdog organizations to do all the work of critiquing the media for us and analyzing their effects on our lives. Each of us is responsible for doing some of that work ourselves. As you read through the chapters in this book, you'll learn more about each type of media—and you'll hone your ability to examine each with a critical eye.

CHAPTER ESSENTIALS

Now that you have finished reading this chapter, you can use the following tools:

REVIEW

Understand the Evolution of Mass Communication

- **Mass media** are the industries that create and distribute songs, novels, newspapers, movies, Internet services, TV shows, magazines, and other products to large numbers of people. **Mass communication** is the creation and use of symbols (such as languages, motion pictures, and computer codes) that convey information and meaning to large and diverse audiences through all manner of channels (pp. 6–7).

- In the oral and written eras (1000 BCE to the mid-fifteenth century), information and knowledge circulated first through spoken traditions (oral) and then through manuscripts (written) commissioned by elites (p. 7).

- In the print era (beginning in the mid-fifteenth century), wide dissemination of manuscripts became possible, thanks to the emergence of movable type and the printing press. Mass production of books spurred four significant changes: an increasing resistance to authority, the rise of new socioeconomic classes, the spread of literacy, and a focus on individualism (pp. 7–9).

- In the electronic and digital eras (the late nineteenth century to today), the telegraph, radio, and television (electronic media) made messages instantaneous and reshaped American life. **Digital communication**, whereby images, texts, and sounds are converted into electronic signals and reassembled as a precise reproduction of an image, a piece of text, or a sound, has changed the rules about who controls the dispersal of information (p. 9).

- The electronic and digital eras also ushered in **media convergence**, which can refer to the technological merging of media content (such as the availability of a magazine article in print and online form) or to a business model used by media companies that consolidate media holdings to reduce costs and maximize profits (pp. 10–11).

Explain How Mass Media Relate to the Process of Communication

- A new medium goes through three stages on its journey toward mass medium status: the development (or novelty) stage (inventors and technicians try to solve a particular problem), the entrepreneurial stage (inventors and investors find a marketable use for the new device), and the mass medium stage (businesses figure out how to market the new device as a consumer product) (pp. 11, 14).

- Human beings have long debated the media's merits and dangers. Some people today are worried that the media are overly commercial and sensationalistic, that they cause violent behavior, and that they have too much financial power (pp. 14–15).

Describe How Media Literacy Represents Ways of Understanding Media

- One approach to **media literacy**—the attempt to understand how the media work and what impact they have on our lives—is the linear model. According to this model, **senders** (authors, producers, organizations) transmit **messages** (programs, texts, images, sounds, ads) through a **mass media channel** (newspapers, books, magazines, radio, television, the Internet) to large groups of **receivers** (readers, viewers, consumers). **Gatekeepers** (news editors, TV and movie producers) filter those messages. Citizens and consumers return **feedback**, or messages, to senders or gatekeepers through letters, phone calls, e-mail, Web postings, tweets, or talk shows. The linear model doesn't capture certain complexities of the mass communication process (p. 16).

- The cultural model of media literacy views media content as part of culture and recognizes that different people assign different meanings to media content. Adherents believe that even as we shape media content, it shapes us (pp. 16–18).

- The social scientific model seeks to test hypotheses about media's effects by gathering and analyzing measurable data. Politicians and businesses often use **survey research** to formulate strategies (pp. 18–19).

Describe the Cultural Model of Media Literacy in Greater Detail

- Cultural researchers of media have offered several metaphors to describe how people judge different media content. The "culture as skyscraper" metaphor holds that some people associate **high culture** with "good taste," higher education, and fine art, and **low** or **popular culture** with the "masses" and commercial "junk" (pp. 19–20).

- The "culture as map" metaphor holds that culture is an ongoing process that accommodates diverse tastes, and that various media can satisfy human desires for both familiarity and newness (p. 20).

- Cultural researchers trace changes in values that accompany changes in mass media. The **modern era** saw the rise of four values: efficient work, celebration of the individual, belief in a rational order, and rejection of tradition and an embracing of progress (in particular, during the **Progressive Era**). The **postmodern period** witnessed the emergence of its own values: celebration of **populism**, a revival of older cultural styles, an embracing of technology, and an interest in the supernatural (pp. 20–22).

Describe the Social Scientific Model of Media Literacy in Greater Detail

- Social scientific media researchers ask different types of questions about media than cultural researchers ask. In a comparison of studies analyzing news coverage of cancer, a study informed by the cultural model explored how coverage of Betty Ford's mastectomy informs news coverage of cancer today, including an emphasis on women's need to maintain their femininity. A study informed by the social scientific model reported findings based on data, such as the percentage of news stories that included content about how to prevent cancer (pp. 22–23).

- Social scientists use **content analysis** to gather data—they code and count the content of various types of media. They also conduct **experiments** to generate data, and gather data through surveys (p. 23).

Explain Why Critiquing Media Is Important and How to Approach This Activity

- Citizens can examine the findings of cultural and social scientific research on media to follow a **critical process** consisting of describing, analyzing, interpreting, evaluating, and engaging with mass media. Both models have strengths and limitations (pp. 24–25).

- To conduct our own critiques of specific media, we must acquire a working knowledge of each medium we want to study, as well as transcend our own preferences or biases regarding the media we're studying (pp. 25, 28).

- A critical perspective on the mass media is valuable because it enables us to take part in debates about the media's impact on our democracy and culture (p. 29).

STUDY QUESTIONS

1. Explain the interrelationship between *mass communication* and *mass media*.
2. What are the stages a medium goes through before becoming a mass medium?
3. Describe the skyscraper model of culture and the map model of culture. What are their strengths and limitations?
4. What are the major differences in how the linear, cultural, and social scientific models approach the study of media?
5. Why is the critical process important?

MEDIA LITERACY PRACTICE

With the use of smartphones and tablets increasing every year and the areas covered by some kind of wireless Internet signal always expanding, people are arguably more connected to mass media now than ever before. For this exercise, we ask you to try and disconnect yourself for one day.

DESCRIBE the experience of giving up all media for one day—including television, radio, movies, books, magazines, newspapers, and the Internet (even connections on a mobile phone).

ANALYZE the patterns you discover. Which media were the most difficult to avoid using? Which were the easiest?

INTERPRET what these patterns mean. For example, what missing elements (news, social contact, entertainment) affected your daily life the most? Did the deprivation experience open up new possibilities for you?

EVALUATE the role of the media in your life and in your social circle. What is good and bad about it? Is it too easy to demonize all media as "bad"? Is it too easy to overindulge in media content?

ENGAGE with the community by sharing your story with local news outlets, on a social networking page, or on a relevant Web site. Or ask your instructor to collect your entire class's media deprivation outcomes for public presentation.

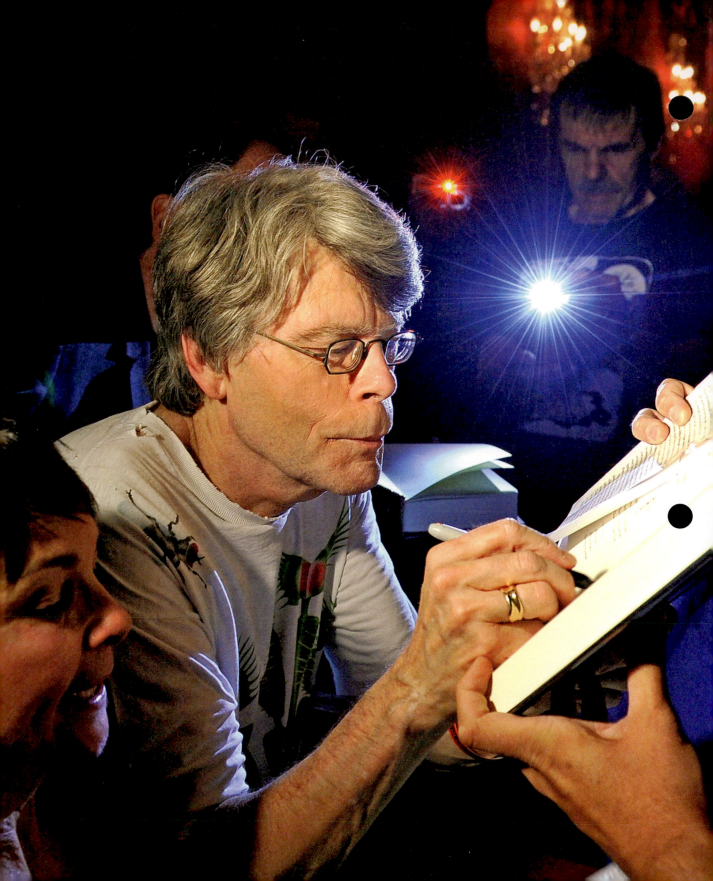

2

Books and the Power of Print

Since its 1994 founding, Amazon has grown from a scrappy upstart to the leading Internet bookseller to a vast online retailer selling not just media but clothing, household items, and hardware—including its Kindle, the first e-reader to achieve real commercial success and a nod to its origins as a bookstore. Today, Amazon is the largest seller of e-books and printed books, easily accounting for over 40 percent of sales in the United States.[1] The Web site's easy-to-use 1-Click and Pre-order buttons, along with quick shipping options, make buying convenient for consumers and help books sell—that is, as long as Amazon is not fighting with the book's publisher.

In 2014, the 1-Click and Pre-order buttons disappeared from the pages advertising certain books, and delivery times for shipping some books mysteriously jumped from a few days to a few weeks. Far from accidental, these changes affected only those books published by Hachette—one of the world's largest publishing companies—because of a contract dispute with Amazon.[2] The dispute generated national headlines, with high-profile authors like David Baldacci, Nora Roberts, and Stephen King (shown signing books for fans in the photo to the left) calling for a quick resolution that would be fair to authors who were suffering as a result of Amazon's making book purchases from Hachette less convenient (a big deal for an Internet business model built around customer convenience). Although not all details were made public, key issues seemed to involve pricing and how much Hachette would have to pay for promotion on Amazon's Web site. One high-profile author caught in the crossfire was J.K. Rowling of Harry Potter fame, whose new book under the pseudonym Robert Galbraith couldn't be pre-ordered on the Amazon site.[3] Not all authors have sided with Hachette; although some critics worry that Amazon's rapid growth has hurt writers as well as independent bookstores, some low-profile authors have praised Amazon for allowing independent writers greater opportunities to publish digitally, sidestepping traditional publishing houses.

The two sides reached an agreement in mid-November 2014, returning Hachette titles to "normal availability" just in time for the annual holiday shopping season. Few details of the agreement have been made public, but part of the deal appears to allow Hachette to set e-book prices on Amazon, with incentives to offer discounts. And although there is a degree of relief among authors, one group of authors is still concerned about Amazon's position in the bookselling marketplace and says it intends to ask the U.S. Department of Justice to review Amazon's business practices.[4]

Although important for authors and publishers, the deal with Hachette (and an earlier deal with Simon & Schuster)

might not be as noticeable to consumers as another recent Amazon announcement. Amazon says its new Kindle Unlimited service offers more than 700,000 books and audio books for reading and listening for a set monthly fee (about ten dollars), similar to the model used by Netflix for video content.[5] This announcement raises questions about how the smaller companies, like Oyster and Scribd, that already offer all-you-can-read subscriptions for a monthly fee will be able to compete with the powerful retail behemoth.

Whether discussing a handful of big publishing houses or a single giant retailer, many familiar with the publishing industry worry about how too few powerful interests might abuse their ability to decide which books will get published and promoted. Will there be too much temptation for these powerful interests along political or ideological lines? Will the emerging publishing business model mean the quiet death of important but commercially risky books? As the next few pages will explain, the history of books is also the history of mankind's most important ideas. As such, the battles in book publishing about costs, prices, and contracts are also about the free flow of ideas—and our access to them.

FOR HUNDREDS OF YEARS—before newspapers, radio, and film, let alone television and the Internet—books were the only mass medium. Books have fueled major developments throughout human history, from revolutions and the rise of democracies to new forms of art (including poetry and fiction) and the spread of religions. When cheaper printing technologies laid the groundwork for books to become more widely available and more quickly disseminated, people gained access to knowledge and ideas that were previously reserved for only the privileged few.

With the emergence of new types of mass media, some critics claimed that books would cease to exist. So far, however, that's not happening. In 1950, U.S. publishers introduced more than 11,000 new book titles; by 2007, that number had reached more than 190,000 (see Table 2.1 on page 39). Though books have adapted to technology and cultural change (witness the advent of e-books), our oldest mass medium still plays a large role in our lives. Books remain the primary repository of history and everyday experience, passing along stories, knowledge, and wisdom from generation to generation.

In this chapter, we will trace the history of this enduring medium and examine its impact on our lives today by:

- assessing books' early roots—including the inventions of papyrus (the first writing surface) and the printing press, as well as the birth of the publishing industry in colonial America

- exploring the unique characteristics of modern publishing, such as how publishing houses are structured

- taking stock of the many types of books that are available today, from the variety of print books to both electronic and digital books

- examining the economics of the book industry, including how players in the industry make money, and what they spend it on to fulfill their mission

- considering the role of books in our democracy today, as this mass medium confronts several challenges

LaunchPad

macmillanhighered.com
/mediaessentials3e
Use **LearningCurve** to review
concepts from this chapter.

The Early History of Books: From Papyrus to Paperbacks

Books have traveled a unique path in their journey to mass medium status. They developed out of early innovations, including papyrus (scrolls made from plant reeds), parchment (treated animal skin), and codex (sheets of parchment sewn together along the edge and then bound and covered). They then entered an entrepreneurial stage, during which people explored new ways of clarifying or illustrating text and experimented with printing techniques, such as block printing, movable type, and the printing press. The invention of the printing press set the stage for books to become a mass medium, complete with the rise of a new industry: publishing.

Papyrus, Parchment, and Codex: The Development Stage of Books

The ancient Egyptians, Greeks, Chinese, and Romans all produced innovations that led up to what looked roughly like what we today think of as a book. It all began some five thousand years ago, in ancient Sumeria (Mesopotamia) and Egypt, where people first experimented with pictorial symbols called *hieroglyphics* or early alphabets. Initially, this writing was placed on wood strips or stones, or pressed into clay tablets. Eventually, these objects were tied or stacked together to form the first "books." Around 1000 BCE, the Chinese were using strips of wood and bamboo with writing on them, tied together to make a booklike object.

Then, in 2400 BCE, the Egyptians began turning plants found along the Nile River into a material they could write on called **papyrus** (from which the word *paper* is derived). Between 650 and 300 BCE, the Greeks and Romans adopted the use of papyrus scrolls. Gradually, **parchment**—treated animal skin—replaced papyrus in Europe. Parchment was stronger, smoother, more durable, and less expensive than papyrus. Around 105 CE, the Chinese began making paper from cotton and linen, though paper did not replace parchment in Europe until the thirteenth century.

The first protomodern book was most likely produced in the fourth century by the Romans, who created the **codex**—sheets of parchment sewn together along one edge, then bound with thin pieces of wood and covered with leather. Whereas scrolls had to be rolled and unrolled for use, a codex could be opened to any page, and people could write on both sides of a page.

TABLE 2.1 // ANNUAL NUMBERS OF NEW BOOK TITLES PUBLISHED, SELECTED YEARS

Year	Number of Titles
1778	461
1798	1,808
1880	2,076
1890	4,559
1900	6,356
1910	13,470 (peak until after World War II)
1915	8,202
1919	5,714 (low point as a result of World War I)
1925	8,173
1930	10,027
1935	8,766 (Great Depression)
1940	11,328
1945	6,548 (World War II)
1950	11,022
1960	15,012
1970	36,071
1980	42,377
1990	46,473
1996	68,175*
2001	114,487
2004	164,020
2007	190,502*
2011	177,126

Changes in the Almanac's methodology in 1997 and for the years 2004–2007 resulted in additional publications being assigned ISBNs and included in the count.

Data from: Figures through 1945 from John Tebbel, A History of Book Publishing in the United States, 4 vols. (New York: R. R. Bowker, 1972–81); figures after 1945 from various editions of the Library and Book Trade Almanac formerly The Bowker Annual (Information Today, Inc.) and Bowker press releases

Writing and Printing Innovations: Books Enter the Entrepreneurial Stage

Books entered the entrepreneurial stage with the emergence of **manuscript culture**. In this stage, new rules about written language and book design were

Erich Lessing/Art Resource, NY

Illuminated manuscripts were handwritten by scribes and illustrated with colorful and decorative images and designs.

codified—books were elaborately lettered, decorated, and bound by hand. Inventors also began experimenting with printing as an alternative to hand lettering and a way to speed up the production and binding of manuscript copies.

Manuscript Culture

During Europe's Middle Ages (400 to 1500 CE), Christian priests and monks transcribed the philosophical tracts and religious texts of the period, especially versions of the Bible. These **illuminated manuscripts** featured decorative, colorful illustrations on each page and were often made for churches or wealthy clients. These early publishers developed certain standards for their works, creating rules of punctuation, making distinctions between small and capital letters, and leaving space between words to make reading easier. Some elements of this manuscript culture remain alive today in the form of design flourishes, such as the drop capitals occasionally used for the first letter in a book chapter.

Block Printing

If manuscript culture involved advances in written language and book design, it also involved hard work: Every manuscript was painstakingly copied one book at a time. From as early as the third century, Chinese printers came up with an innovation that made mass production possible.

These Chinese innovators developed **block printing**. Using this technique, printers applied sheets of paper to large blocks of inked wood into which they had hand-carved a page's worth of characters and illustrations. The oldest dated block-printed book still in existence is China's *Diamond Sutra*, a collection of Buddhist scriptures printed by Wang Chieh in 868 CE.

CHAPTER 2 // TIMELINE

2400 BCE Papyrus
Made from plant reeds, papyrus is first used as paper and rolled into scrolls.

1000 BCE The Earliest Books
The Chinese make booklike objects from strips of wood and bamboo.

Fourth Century CE Codex
The first protomodern book is produced by the Romans.

600 Illuminated Manuscripts
These books are created by priests and monks throughout Europe.

1000 Movable Type
The Chinese invent movable type, significantly speeding up printing time.

Movable Type

The next significant step in printing came with the invention of movable type in China around the year 1000. This was a major improvement (in terms of speed) over block printing because, rather than carving each new page on one block, printers carved commonly used combinations of characters from the Chinese language into smaller, reusable wood (and later ceramic) blocks. They then put together the pieces needed to represent a desired page of text, inked the small blocks, and applied the sheets of paper. This method enabled them to create pages of text much more quickly than before.

The Printing Press and the Publishing Industry: Books Become a Mass Medium

Books moved from the entrepreneurial stage to mass medium status with the invention of the printing press (which made books widely available for the first time) and the rise of the publishing industry (which arose to satisfy people's growing hunger for books).

The Printing Press

The **printing press** was invented by Johannes Gutenberg in Germany between 1453 and 1456. Drawing on the principles of movable type, and adding to them a device adapted from the design of a wine press, Gutenberg's staff of printers produced the first so-called modern books, including two hundred copies of a Latin Bible—twenty-one of which still exist. The Gutenberg Bible (as it's now known) was printed on a fine calfskin-based parchment called **vellum**.

Printing presses spread rapidly across Europe in the late 1400s and early 1500s. Many of these early books were large, elaborate, and expensive. But printers gradually reduced the size of books and developed less-expensive grades of paper. These changes made books cheaper to produce, so printers could sell them for less, making the books affordable to many more people.

1453 Printing Press
Gutenberg invents the printing press, forming the prototype for mass production.

1640 The First Colonial Book
Stephen Daye prints a collection of biblical psalms.

1751 Encyclopedias
French scholars begin compiling articles in alphabetical order.

1800s Publishing Houses
The book industry forms prestigious companies that produce and market works of respected writers.

1836 Textbooks
William H. McGuffey publishes the first in his series of Eclectic Readers, helping American students learn how to read.

The New York Public Library/Art Resource, NY

The weekly paperback series *Tip Top Weekly*, which was published between 1896 and 1912, featured the most popular dime novel hero of the day, Yale football star and heroic adventurer Frank Merriwell.

The spread of printing presses and books sparked a major change in the way people learned. Previously, people followed the traditions and ideas framed by local authorities—the ruling class, clergy, and community leaders. But as books became more broadly available, people gained access to knowledge and viewpoints far beyond their immediate surroundings and familiar authorities, leading some of them to begin challenging the traditional wisdom and customs of their tribes and leaders.[6] This interest in debating ideas would ultimately encourage the rise of democratic societies in which all citizens had a voice.

The Publishing Industry

In the two centuries following the invention of the printing press, publishing—the establishment of printing shops to serve the public's growing demand for books—took off in Europe, eventually spreading to England and finally to the American colonies. In the late 1630s, English locksmith Stephen Daye set up the first colonial print shop in Cambridge, Massachusetts. By the mid-1760s, all thirteen colonies had printing shops. Some publishers, such as Benjamin Franklin, grew quite wealthy in this profession.

However, in the early 1800s, U.S. publishers had to find ways to lower the cost of producing books to meet the exploding demand. By the 1830s, machine-made paper replaced the more expensive handmade varieties, cloth covers supplanted costlier leather ones, and **paperback books** were made with cheaper paper covers (introduced in Europe), all of which helped to make books even more accessible to the masses. Further reducing the cost of books, publishers introduced paperback **dime novels** (so called because they sold for five or ten cents) in 1860. By 1885, one-third of all books published in the United States consisted of popular paperbacks and **pulp fiction** (a reference to the cheap, machine-made pulp paper dime novels were printed on).

CHAPTER 2 // TIMELINE continued

1870s Mass Market Paperbacks
Pulp-fiction paperbacks become popular among middle- and working-class readers.

Mid-1880s Linotype and Offset Lithography
New printing techniques lower the cost of books in the United States.

1926 Book Clubs
The Book-of-the-Month Club and the Literary Guild are formed.

1960s Professional Books
The book industry targets various occupational groups.

1971 Borders Is Established
The chain formation of superstores begins.

Meanwhile, the printing process itself also advanced. In the 1880s, the introduction of **linotype** machines enabled printers to save time by setting type mechanically using a typewriter-style keyboard. The introduction of steam-powered and high-speed rotary presses also permitted the production of even more books at lower costs. With the development of **offset lithography** in the early 1900s, publishers could print books from photographic plates rather than from metal casts. This greatly reduced the cost of color illustrations and accelerated the production process, enabling publishers to satisfy Americans' steadily increasing demand for books.

The Evolution of Modern Publishing

As demand for books skyrocketed, the publishing industry morphed to satisfy it. Companies that participated in this industry, often called publishing houses, were initially small and focused on offering the works of quality authors. Over time, major corporations with ties to international media conglomerates snapped up these companies. However, regardless of what subject matter they focus on or who owns them, publishing houses are structured in similar ways to carry out the process of attracting authors, developing manuscripts, and marketing published books.

Early Publishing Houses

The modern book industry in the United States developed gradually in the 1800s with the formation of "prestigious" publishing houses: companies that identified and produced the works of respected writers.[7] The oldest American houses

1995 Amazon.com
The first online book distributor is established.

2007 Harry Potter
Harry Potter and the Deathly Hallows has record-breaking sales of 13.1 million copies.

2007 Kindle
Amazon.com introduces the Kindle, the most successful e-book reader to date.

2011 Borders Closes
The chain files bankruptcy and the same year closes all of its stores, as brick-and-mortar stores lose business to digital sales.

2014 Hachette Dispute
Amazon fights publicly with Hachette over prices.

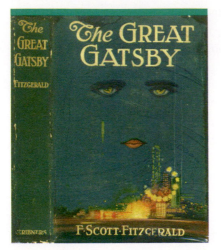

Photo by Princeton University Library. Rare Books Division. Department of Rare Books and Special Collections. Princeton University Library.

Scribner's—known more for its magazine in the late 1800s than for its books—became the most prestigious literary house of the 1920s and 1930s, publishing F. Scott Fitzgerald (The Great Gatsby, 1925) and Ernest Hemingway (The Sun Also Rises, 1926).

include J. B. Lippincott (1792); Harper & Bros. (1817), which became Harper & Row in 1962 and HarperCollins in 1990; Houghton Mifflin (1832); Little, Brown (1837); G. P. Putnam (1838); Scribner's (1842); E. P. Dutton (1852); Rand McNally (1856); and Macmillan (1869).

Between 1880 and 1920, as more people moved from rural areas to cities and learned to read, Americans became interested in reading all kinds of books—novels, historical accounts, reference materials, instructional resources. This caught the attention of entrepreneurs eager to profit by satisfying this demand. A savvy breed of publishing house—those focused on marketing—was born. These firms included Doubleday & McClure Company (1897), McGraw-Hill Book Company (1909), Prentice Hall (1913), Alfred A. Knopf (1915), Simon & Schuster (1924), and Random House (1925).

The Conglomerates

Book publishing sputtered from the 1910s into the 1940s, as the two world wars and the Great Depression turned Americans' attention away from books. But as the U.S. economy recovered during the 1950s and 1960s, the industry bounced back. Major corporations and international media conglomerates began acquiring the smaller houses to expand their markets and take advantage of the **synergy** (the promotion and sale of different versions of a media product across the various subsidiaries of a conglomerate) between books and other media types.

Nowadays book publishing is dominated by a handful of these giants. Penguin Random House (jointly owned since 2013 by Bertelsmann and Pearson), Simon & Schuster (owned by CBS), Hachette (owned by Lagardère, based in France), HarperCollins (owned by News Corp.), and Macmillan (owned by German-based Holtzbrinck) are the five largest publishers of trade books (popular general-audience books) in the United States.

Looking globally and at all kinds of publishing (see Table 2.2), the top five book publishers in terms of revenue are Pearson (textbooks, educational materials), Reed Elsevier (professional books), Thomson Reuters (professional books), Wolters Kluwer (professional books), and Random House (Bertelsmann) (trade books).

The consolidation of the book industry has raised concerns among observers who mourn the loss of the older houses' distinctive styles and their associations with renowned literary figures, like Mark Twain and Nathaniel Hawthorne. Moreover, the large corporations that now define the industry's direction have huge marketing budgets and can buy needed resources (such as paper, printing, and binding services) at a discount and thus charge less for their product. Few independent publishers have been able to compete against them.

TABLE 2.2 // TEN LARGEST BOOK PUBLISHERS, 2014 (GLOBAL REVENUE IN MILLIONS OF U.S. DOLLARS)

Rank/Publishing Company (Group or Division)	Home Country	Revenue in $ Millions
1 Pearson	U.K.	$9,330
2 Reed Elsevier	U.K./NL/U.S.	$7,288
3 Thomson Reuters	U.S.	$5,576
4 Wolters Kluwer	NL	$4,920
5 Random House (Bertelsmann)	Germany	$3,664
6 Hachette Livre (Lagardère)	France	$2,851
7 Holtzbrinck	Germany	$2,222
8 Grupo Planeta	Spain	$2,161
9 Cengage (Apax Partners)	U.S./Canada	$1,993
10 McGraw-Hill Education	U.S.	$1,992

Data from: "The World's 56 Largest Book Publishers, 2014," June 27, 2014, http://www.publishersweekly.com/pw/by-topic/industry-news/financial-reporting/article/63004-the-world-s-56-largest-book-publishers-2014.html

Note: Cengage emerged from bankruptcy in 2014. Its ranking is based on 2012 revenue.

The Structure of Publishing Houses

Regardless of their size or the types of books they publish, publishing houses are structured similarly. For example, they have teams or divisions responsible for acquisitions and manuscript development; copyediting, design, and production; marketing and sales; and administration. And unlike daily newspapers but similar to magazines, most publishing houses pay independent printers to produce their books.

The majority of publishers employ **acquisitions editors** to seek out authors and offer them contracts to publish specific titles. For fiction, this might mean discovering talented writers through book agents or reading unsolicited manuscripts. For nonfiction, editors might examine unsolicited manuscripts and letters of inquiry or match a known writer to a project (such as a celebrity biography). Acquisitions editors also handle **subsidiary rights** for an author—that is, selling the rights to a book for use in other media, such as a mass market paperback, or as the basis for a screenplay.

After a contract is signed, the acquisitions editor may turn the book over to a **developmental editor**, who helps the author draft and revise the manuscript by providing his or her own feedback and soliciting advice from reviewers. If a book is to contain illustrations, editors work with photo researchers to select photographs or find artists to produce the needed drawings or other graphics. At this point, the production staff enters the picture. While **copy editors** fix any spelling, punctuation, grammar, or style problems in the manuscript, **design managers** determine the look and feel of the book, making decisions about type styles, paper, cover design, and layout of page spreads.

Simultaneously, the publishing house determines a marketing strategy for the book, including identifying which readers will be most interested in the title, deciding how many copies to print and what price to charge, and selecting advertising channels for reaching the target customers. Marketing budgets usually make up a large part of a publishing company's expenses, and marketing managers are often fairly high up in the organization.

Types of Books: Tradition Meets Technology

Until fairly recently, books of all kinds took printed form: pages bound together through various devices (such as glue or spiral wire) and enclosed by a cover (cardboard, leather, paper). But with the rise of electronic and digital publishing, book formats have expanded beyond print to include audio books ("books on tape," now available as CDs or MP3 downloads) and e-books (which are accessed on the Internet and read on a computer or a handheld device). Regardless of the format, however, books are still highly diverse in terms of their subject matter.

Print Books

Today, the publishing industry produces titles that fall into a wide variety of categories—everything from trade books and textbooks to mass market paperbacks and reference books. These categories have been formally defined by various trade organizations, such as the Association of American Publishers (AAP), the Book Industry Study Group (BISG), and the American Booksellers Association (ABA).

Trade

One of the most lucrative markets in the industry, **trade books** include hardbound and paperback books aimed at general readers and sold at commercial retail outlets. The industry distinguishes among adult trade, juvenile trade, and comics and graphic novels (which contain pictures rather than type). Adult trade books include hardbound and paperback fiction; current nonfiction and biographies; literary classics; books on hobbies, art, and travel; popular science, technology, and computer publications; self-help books; and cookbooks. Juvenile trade categories range from preschool picture books to young-adult or young-reader books, such as the Dr. Seuss books, the Lemony Snicket series, and the Harry Potter series.

Professional

Professional books target various occupational groups, not the general consumer market. This area of publishing capitalizes on the growth of professional specialization that has characterized the U.S. job market, particularly since the 1960s. Traditionally, the industry has subdivided professional books into the areas of law, business, medicine, and technology-science. These books are sold mostly through mail order, the Internet, or sales representatives knowledgeable about the various subject areas.

Textbooks

Textbooks such as McGuffey's Eclectic Readers have served a nation intent on improving literacy rates and public education and are divided into elementary through high school (el-hi) texts, college texts, and vocational texts. In about half the states in the country, local school districts determine which el-hi textbooks are appropriate for their students. The remaining states, including Texas and California, have statewide adoption policies governing which texts can be used. Unlike el-hi texts, which are subsidized by various states and school districts, college texts are paid for by students (or their parents) and are sold primarily through college bookstores. The increasing cost of textbooks has led some students to trade, resell, or rent textbooks or to download them more cheaply from sites like Amazon.com or BarnesandNoble.com. For the 2007–08 school year, the average college student spent between $921 and $988 on textbooks and other required course materials.[8] (See Figure 2.1 on page 48.)

First published in 1836, McGuffey Readers helped enable the nineteenth-century U.S. literacy movement and the wave of western expansion. After the Civil War, they were the standard textbooks in thirty-seven states. With 130 million copies published since the first edition, the readers are still in print and in use, with the latest revised version published in the late 1990s.

Mass Market Paperbacks

Unlike the larger-sized trade paperbacks, which are sold mostly in bookstores, **mass market paperbacks** are sold on racks in drugstores, supermarkets, and airports, as well as in bookstores. Contemporary mass market paperbacks—often the work of blockbuster authors such as Stephen King, Danielle Steel, and John Grisham—represent the largest segment of the industry in terms of units sold. But because the books are priced low (under $10), they generate less revenue than trade books. Paperbacks first became popular back in the 1870s, when middle- and working-class

FIGURE 2.1 // WHERE THE NEW TEXTBOOK DOLLAR GOES*

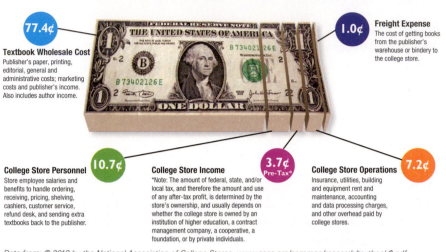

77.4¢

Textbook Wholesale Cost
Publisher's paper, printing, editorial, general and administrative costs; marketing costs and publisher's income. Also includes author income.

1.0¢

Freight Expense
The cost of getting books from the publisher's warehouse or bindery to the college store.

10.7¢

College Store Personnel
Store employee salaries and benefits to handle ordering, receiving, pricing, shelving, cashiers, customer service, refund desk, and sending extra textbooks back to the publisher.

3.7¢
Pre-Tax*

College Store Income
*Note: The amount of federal, state, and/or local tax, and therefore the amount and use of any after-tax profit, is determined by the store's ownership, and usually depends on whether the college store is owned by an institution of higher education, a contract management company, a cooperative, a foundation, or by private individuals.

7.2¢

College Store Operations
Insurance, utilities, building and equipment rent and maintenance, accounting and data processing charges, and other overhead paid by college stores.

Data from: © 2013 by the National Association of College Stores, www.nacs.org/common/research/textbook$.pdf

*College store numbers are averages and reflect the most current data gathered by the National Association of College Stores.

readers popularized dime novels. In 1939, when publisher Pocket Books lowered the price of these books from fifty or seventy-five cents to just twenty-five cents by slashing costs, such as author royalties, readers devoured even more of them.

A major innovation in mass market paperback publishing came with the **instant book**, a marketing strategy that involves publishing a topical book right after a major event occurs. Pocket Books produced the first instant book, *Franklin Delano Roosevelt: A Memorial*, six days after FDR's death in 1945. However, these books suffer from the same problems that their TV counterparts do: Because these accounts are cranked out so quickly, they have been accused of containing shoddy writing, lacking in-depth analysis and historical perspective, and simply exploiting tragedies.

Religious

The best-selling book of all time is the Bible, in all its diverse versions. Over the years, the success of Bible sales has created a large industry for religious books, and many religious-book publishers have extended their offerings to include serious secular titles on such topics as war and peace, race, poverty, gender, and civic responsibility. After a record year in 2004 (twenty-one thousand new titles), this category has seen a slight decline. Yet it continues to play an important role in the book industry, especially during turbulent social times.

Reference

Reference books include dictionaries, encyclopedias, atlases, almanacs, and volumes related to particular professions or trades, such as legal casebooks and medical manuals. Encyclopedias and dictionaries have traditionally accounted for the largest portion of reference sales. But these reference works have moved mostly to online formats since the 1990s in response to competition from companies offering different formats. These rival formats include free online or built-in word-processing software dictionaries, search engines such as Google, and online resources like Wikipedia.

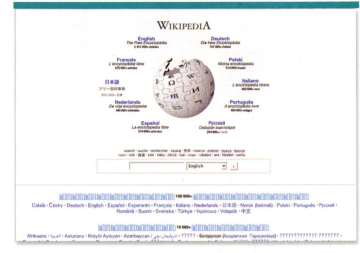

Wikipedia

Since its launch in 2001, Wikipedia has grown to include more than nineteen million entries in 270 languages. Despite the controversies about bias, inconsistency, and incorrect information, the site is one of the most popular on the Web for general information.

University Press

The smallest market in the printed-book industry is the nonprofit **university press**, which publishes scholarly works for small groups of readers interested in specialized areas, such as literary theory and criticism, art movements, and contemporary philosophy. Whereas large commercial trade houses are often criticized for publishing only high-selling, mainstream books, university presses often suffer the opposite criticism—that they produce mostly obscure books that only a handful of scholars read.

Electronic and Digital Publishing

Within the formal categories previously discussed, publishers are continually experimenting with alternatives to the printed-book format to remain competitive and to leverage the advantages of new technologies now available in the digital age. Examples of these alternatives include audio books and e-books.

Audio Books

Audio books (once known as "books on tape," though they are now available primarily on CD or as MP3 downloads) became popular in the 1990s and early 2000s and generally feature actors or authors reading versions of popular fiction and nonfiction trade books. Indispensable to many sightless readers and older readers with diminishing vision, audio books are also popular among readers who have long commutes by car or train, or who want to listen to a book while doing something else, like exercising. By the early 2000s, audio books were readily available on the Internet for downloading to iPods and other portable devices.

E-Books

The first electronic digital copies of books (or **e-books**) that could be shared and read using a computer can be traced back to the early 1970s. But it would be decades before the idea of digitizing copyrighted books, like current best-sellers, in the form of *commercial e-books* would gather steam.

There were some attempts by RCA and Sony in the early 1990s to create portable reading devices for e-books, but those early e-readers were criticized for being too heavy, too expensive, and too difficult to read, as well as for offering too few choices. It wasn't until 2007 when Amazon, already the largest online bookseller, introduced its Kindle e-reader that the long-predicted digital book market started gaining traction. Bookselling giant Barnes and Noble soon followed with a competing product called the Nook. Apple, already experiencing success with its iTunes online store, opened the iBookstore. Since then, Amazon and Barnes and Noble have introduced more sophisticated e-readers (like the Kindle Fire) that resemble tablet computers, while certain apps allow smartphones and tablets to act as e-readers, even allowing a user to link multiple devices to a single online account. For example, a reader might download (in about a minute) a new book in the morning and start reading it on her Kindle, then resume reading it on the bus to work on her smartphone (on the exact same page she left off that morning), and then do the same thing over lunch on her iPad.

The allure of this convenience as well as numerous discounts for some e-book titles has turned electronic publishing into a juggernaut. In 2013, little more than a half decade since the Kindle was introduced, e-books accounted for 38 percent of adult fiction sales in the United States (in terms of revenue). Projections indicate that e-books will surpass the print book market by 2017.[9]

In 2011, in recognition of the boom in sales, the *New York Times* started publishing e-book best-seller lists in fiction and nonfiction. The giant Borders bookstore chain, in contrast, missed the e-book boom, which many believe contributed to its bankruptcy and closing in 2011.

The Economics of the Book Industry

To serve customers profitably, the book business (like other mass media industries) must bring in money while also investing in needed resources. Publishers make money by selling books through specific channels (such as brick-and-mortar stores and online stores) and by selling television and movie rights; publishers spend money on essential activities such as book production, distribution, and marketing.

Money In

Compared with other mass media industries, book publishing has seen only a relatively modest increase in revenues over the decades. From the mid-1980s to 2013, total revenues went from $9 billion to about $27 billion (see Figure 2.2), but the industry continues to seek new and bigger sources of growth. Publishers bring in money through a variety of channels.

Book Sales

The most obvious source of revenue for publishers is sales of the books themselves—whether they're in print, audio, or e-book form. There are several main outlets for selling books:

1. **Brick-and-mortar stores.** These include traditional bookstores, department stores, drugstores, used-book stores, and toy stores. Since the 2011 bankruptcy of Borders, the single largest chain—Barnes & Noble—now dominates book sales. Barnes & Noble operates 661 superstores and 700 college bookstores, though it closed its last remaining B. Dalton bookstores in 2010. The rise of book superstores—along with competition from online stores—severely cut into independent bookstores' business, dropping their number from 5,100 in 1991 to only about 1,900 today. Many independents have formed regional or statewide groups to develop survival tactics.

David Paul Morris/Bloomberg via Getty Images

Amazon's warehouses go far beyond the stockrooms of typical brick-and-mortar stores, housing more than one hundred employees in each location, of which there are dozens across the United States and throughout the world.

2. **Online stores.** Since the late 1990s, online booksellers have created an entirely new book-distribution system on the Internet. The trailblazer is Amazon.com, established in 1995 by then thirty-year-old Jeff Bezos. In 1997, Barnes & Noble, the leading retail store bookseller, launched its own heavily invested and carefully researched bn.com site. In 1999, the ABA launched BookSense.com to help more than a thousand independent bookstores

establish an online presence. Despite this competition, Amazon remains the top online retailer, controlling 41 percent of U.S. book sales by 2014 (print and e-books combined).[10] The strength of online sellers lies in their convenience and low prices, especially their ability to offer backlist titles and the works of less-famous authors that even superstores don't carry on their shelves. Many online customers also appreciate the ability to post their own book reviews at online stores, read those of fellow customers, and receive book recommendations based on their searches and past purchases. As book readers turn to e-books, online stores are better situated for this transition. By 2011, customers were buying more e-books than print books from Amazon.

3. **Book clubs.** Similar to music clubs, book clubs entice new members with introductory offers, such as five books for a dollar, then require regular purchases from their list of recommended titles. The Book-of-the-Month Club and the Literary Guild are two examples, both launched in 1926. Originally, this business model helped generate revenues when bookstores were not as numerous as they are today. But since the 1980s, book clubs' sales have declined. Today, twenty remaining book clubs—including the Book-of-the-Month Club, the Literary Guild, and Doubleday—are consolidated under a single company, Pride Tree Holdings, which also owns DVD and music clubs.

4. **Mail order.** Mail-order bookselling was another tactic introduced before bookstores became a major channel for selling, now used primarily by trade, professional, and university press publishers. Like a book club, a mail-order company immediately notifies readers about new book titles. This channel appeals to customers who want to avoid the hassle of shopping in stores or who want their purchases (for example, of sexually explicit materials) to remain private.

Regardless of what channel a publisher sells its books through, trade publishers are constantly on the hunt for the next *best-seller*—dating back to the huge success of Harriet Beecher Stowe's abolitionist novel *Uncle Tom's Cabin*, which sold 15,000 copies in just fifteen days in 1852. (A total of three million copies flew off the shelves before the Civil War.) A best-seller can come from anywhere—a celebrity who pens his or her autobiography, a respected scientist who offers a provocative new perspective on artificial intelligence, a first-time novelist whose work is chosen for Oprah's Book Club.

Indeed, publishers have learned that TV can help sell books. Through TV exposure, books by or about talk-show hosts, actors, and politicians sell millions of copies—enormous sales in a business in which 100,000 units sold constitutes remarkable success. In national polls conducted from the 1980s through today, nearly 30 percent of respondents said they had read a book after seeing a story about it or a promotion on television. A major force in promoting books on TV was Oprah's Book Club. Each selection by the club—before it made its transition online to Oprah's Book Club 2.0 in 2012—became an immediate best-seller.

© Neville Elder/Corbis

The Strand is an independent bookstore in New York City. Open since 1927, it is famous for its "18 miles of books," which include more than 2.5 million new, used, and rare books.

FIGURE 2.2 // 2013 TRADE BOOK SALES BY BOOK TYPE

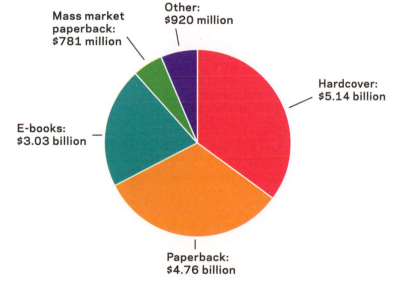

Mass market paperback: $781 million

Other: $920 million

Hardcover: $5.14 billion

E-books: $3.03 billion

Paperback: $4.76 billion

Data from: Jim Milliot, "Industry Sales Flat in 2013; Trade Dropped 2.3%," Publishers Weekly, June 26, 2014, http://www.publishersweekly.com/pw/by-topic/industry-news/financial-reporting/article/63052-industry-sales-flat-in-2013-trade-dropped-2-3.html

Although still a multibillion-dollar industry, 2013 saw a slight drop in total book sales from 2012 (from $27.12 billion to $27.01 billion). Experts attribute some of this to a tapering off of the big boost the trade book segment of the industry got in 2012 from the Fifty Shades and Hunger Games trilogies. This graph shows the breakdown of the trade segment (still the publishing industry's largest segment, with $14.63 billion in sales) by type of book.

CONVERGING MEDIA

Case Study

Self-Publishing Redefined

Media convergence—in the form of e-book readers and e-ink apps for tablets and laptops—is clearly changing the way people read books. But there is another dimension to the e-book revolution that is even more threatening to the traditional print publishing powers: Media convergence is also transforming the way people publish books. Amazon's Kindle Direct Publishing has made self-publishing so cheap and easy that, as one Amazon executive put it, "The only really necessary people in the publishing process now are the writer and reader."[1]

Of course, self-publishing has long been stigmatized as a vain enterprise (hence the term *vanity press*). Being self-published has been equated with amateurism and work that is not worthy of the considerable expenses and promotional resources associated with one of the big publishing houses. In the new media landscape, however, those notions are becoming increasingly inaccurate. Erika Leonard took the pen name E. L. James and self-published her e-book *Fifty Shades of Grey* (which she began writing as *Twilight* fan fiction). When it vaulted to the top of the best-seller list in the e-book format, she signed with publisher Vintage Books, who issued the print version as well as published the following two books in the Fifty Shades trilogy. All three became best-sellers in both formats, and the first book has already been made into a top-grossing movie, with sequels on the way. A self-published expansion of fan fiction became a multimedia empire of sorts. James published an additional spin-off novel in summer 2015, retelling the story from a different point of view.

A number of established authors have also started testing the waters of self-publishing e-books. But the publishing industry response to these flirtations can be harsh. For instance, when Kiana Davenport e-published a compilation of short stories, her publishing house at the time declared that she was "sleeping with the enemy," canceled the publication of a forthcoming novel, and demanded the return of a $20,000 advance. Davenport then came full circle, signing a new publishing deal with Amazon imprint Thomas & Mercer.[2] The established publishers have reason to

macmillanhighered.com/mediaessentials3e

▶ **Visit LaunchPad** to watch a clip from the *Fifty Shades of Grey* trailer. How does the advertising frame the movie?

Chuck Zlotnick/© Focus Features/Everett Collection

guard their turf: Self-published authors need not pay 10 percent to a literary agency, and they receive a significantly larger piece of the overall pie. Whereas the authors of paper-based books claim royalties of between 5 and 15 percent, authors with Amazon receive between 35 and 70 percent of the purchase price.[3] A 2014 study of author earnings showed self-published books now represent 31 percent of e-book sales on Amazon's Kindle Store.[4]

But Amazon's entry into the publishing world is not limited to simply giving self-published authors a platform. As in the case with Davenport, Amazon is also signing authors to its own publishing arm to produce both print and electronic versions of books.[5] Publishers may soon face the kind of competition that booksellers have seen from Amazon over the past decade—and self-publishing authors may still struggle against authors with greater promotional muscle behind them.

Murray Close/© Lionsgate/Everett Collection

Over the years, many movies have been based on books; *The Hunger Games* is a recent example. Movie rights bring in substantial revenue for the book industry.

macmillanhighered.com
/mediaessentials3e

Based On: Making Books into Movies
Writers and producers discuss the process that brings a book to the big screen.
Discussion: How is the creative process of writing a novel different from that of making a movie? Which would you rather do, and why?

TV and Movie Rights

One of the most dramatic (literally and figuratively) examples of media convergence happens in the relationship between book publishing and the big (and little) screens. Many TV shows and films get their story ideas from books, a process that generates enormous movie-rights revenues for the book industry and its authors. The most profitable movie-rights deals for the book industry in recent years have included the Hunger Games and Harry Potter series as well as Peter Jackson's movie adaptations of J. R. R. Tolkien's *Lord of the Rings* (first published in the 1950s).

The subgenre of comic books and graphic novels has led to countless films on its own, including several top box-office hits, like the *Dark Knight* trilogy and Marvel's interconnected series of superhero films. And just as a popular book can help generate interest for a movie, a movie or TV show can boost book sales. HBO's adaptation of *A Game of Thrones*, the first book in George R. R. Martin's A Song of Ice and Fire series, pushed Martin's work to the top of best-seller lists and promoted the publication of the fifth book in the series, *A Dance with Dragons*. TV or movie promotion can also boost sales in new media: In September 2011, Martin joined Amazon's Kindle Million Club, meaning that e-book sales of his work have exceeded one million downloads. Even classic and *public domain* books (those no longer subject to copyright law) can create profits for the book industry. For example, in 2011, a screen version of Charlotte Brontë's 1847 novel *Jane Eyre* boosted sales of the reissued novel.

Money Out

To generate sales, publishers must spend money on producing books, distributing their products, and promoting or marketing newly launched titles.

Production

To produce books, publishing houses have expenditures such as overhead (including salaries for the employees who edit and design books) as well as paper, printing, and binding. Also, as part of their contracts, authors sometimes require that publishers pay them *advance money*, an up-front payment that's subtracted from royalties later earned from book sales (see Figure 2.3). Typically, an author's royalty

FIGURE 2.3 // HOW A PAPERBACK'S REVENUE IS DIVIDED

Despite their low profit margins, mass market paperbacks remain an important segment of the book industry. For example, two-thirds of Random House's income comes from paperbacks. A Random House paperback, retail priced at $10, breaks down this way:

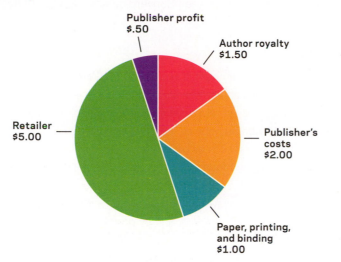

Publisher profit
$.50

Author royalty
$1.50

Publisher's costs
$2.00

Retailer
$5.00

Paper, printing, and binding
$1.00

Data from: Arianne Cohen, "A Publishing Company: Random House," New York, *http://nymag.com/news/features/2007/profit/32906/*

is 5 to 15 percent of the net price of the book. New authors may receive little or no advance from a publisher, but commercially successful authors can receive millions. For example, *Interview with a Vampire* author Anne Rice hauled in a $17 million advance from Knopf in a contract for writing three more vampire novels. Celebrities such as actors, musicians, or politicians can also get million-dollar advances. In 2012, *Girls* writer, director, and star Lena Dunham got a $3.5 million advance for her book. J.K. Rowling got a reported $8 million advance for her 2012 book, *The Casual Vacancy.*

Distribution

Distribution costs include maintaining inventory of books to be sold and fulfilling orders (shipping books to commercial outlets or college bookstores). Publishers monitor their warehouse inventories to ensure that enough copies of a book will be available to meet demand. Anticipating demand, though, is a tricky business. No publisher wants to be caught short if a book proves more popular than originally predicted. Nor does it want to get stuck with books it can't sell, as the company must then absorb the cost of returned books. As one way to avoid both of these costly scenarios, distributors, publishers, and bookstores have begun taking advantage of digital technology to print books on demand rather than stockpiling them in warehouses. Through this technology, they can revive books that would otherwise have gone out of print because of limited demand—and avoid the expense of carrying unsold books (see "Converging Media Case Study: Self-Publishing Redefined" on pages 54–55).

Marketing

Publishers spend a significant amount of money on marketing, which includes advertising and generating favorable reviews. For trade books and some scholarly books, publishing houses may send advance copies of a book to appropriate magazines and newspapers with the hope of receiving positive reviews that can be used in promotional materials, such as brochures. A house may also send well-known authors on book-signing tours and arrange radio and TV talk-show interviews to promote their books. College textbook firms "seed adoptions" by paying instructors an honorarium to review a book that's in development, by sending free examination copies to potential adopters, and by promoting new titles through direct-mail brochures.

To help create a best-seller, trade publishing houses often give large illustrated cardboard bins, called *dumps*, to bookstores to display a particular book in bulk quantities. Large trade houses buy shelf space from major chains to ensure prominent locations in bookstores. Publishers also buy ad space in newspapers and magazines and on buses, billboards, television, radio, and the Web—all to pump up interest in a new book.

Books in a Democratic Society

Books have played a vital role in our democracy—not only by spreading the notion of democracy itself but also by disseminating ideas that inspire people to drive change. For example, Harriet Beecher Stowe's *Uncle Tom's Cabin* sparked outrage over slavery, helping to end the institution in the 1860s. Rachel Carson's *Silent Spring* exposed the perils of the pesticide industry in the 1960s, prompting the American public to demand reform. And Michael Pollan's *The Omnivore's Dilemma* has people thinking about the ethical and nutritional issues connected with factory farming and buying more locally raised meats and vegetables. Books have enabled people to share ideas freely, discuss those ideas' merits and flaws, and make informed choices—all key elements in any democracy.

Indeed, the ability to write whatever one wants has its very roots in our founding documents: Amendment I of the U.S. Constitution's Bill of Rights guarantees freedom of the press.

Though books have long played this crucial role and will continue to do so, they face several challenges that threaten to dilute their impact. These challenges include the persistence of censorship, the decline of bookstores and libraries, and the loss of old books to physical deterioration.

Censorship

Throughout human history, rulers intent on maintaining their power have censored or banned books to prevent people from learning about alternative ideas and ways of living. For example, in various parts of the world, some versions of the Bible, Karl Marx's *Das Kapital* (1867), *The Autobiography of Malcolm X* (1965), and Salman Rushdie's *The Satanic Verses* (1989) have all been banned at one time or another. (For more on banned books, see "Media Literacy Case Study: Banned Books and 'Family Values'" on pages 60–61.)

In the United States, censorship and book banning are illegal. But citizens can sometimes force the removal of a particular book from public or school libraries if enough people file a formal complaint—a **book challenge**—about subject matter they find objectionable. The American Library Association (ALA) compiles a list of the most challenged books in the United States. Common reasons for challenges include sexually explicit passages, offensive language, occult themes, violence, homosexual themes, promotion of a religious viewpoint, nudity, and racism. The ALA defends the right of libraries to offer

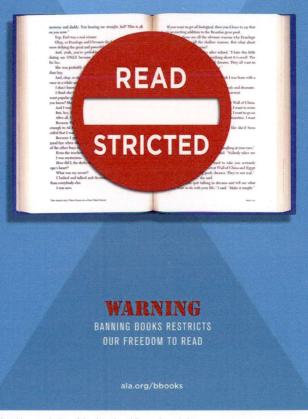

Reprinted by permission of the American Library Association

Banned Books Week is an event sponsored by the American Library Association to raise awareness of challenges to reader freedoms and attempts to ban books.

MEDIA LITERACY

Case Study

Banned Books and "Family Values"

Ulysses by James Joyce, *The Scarlet Letter* by Nathaniel Hawthorne, *Leaves of Grass* by Walt Whitman, *The Diary of a Young Girl* by Anne Frank, *Lolita* by Vladimir Nabokov, and *To Kill a Mockingbird* by Harper Lee have all been banned by a U.S. community, school, or library at one time or another.

In fact, the most censored book in U.S. history is Mark Twain's *The Adventures of Huckleberry Finn*, the 1884 classic that still sells tens of thousands of copies each year. Often, the impulse behind calling for a book's banishment is to protect children in the name of a community's "family values."

LaunchPad

macmillanhighered.com/mediaessentials3e

▶ **Visit LaunchPad** to watch a clip from a film adaptation of *Huckleberry Finn*. What audience does it seem to be aimed at?

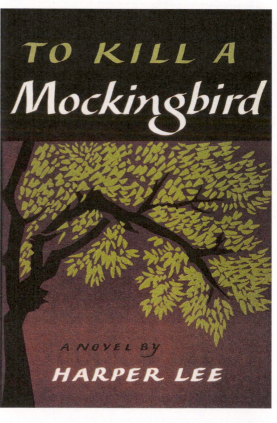

The Granger Collection

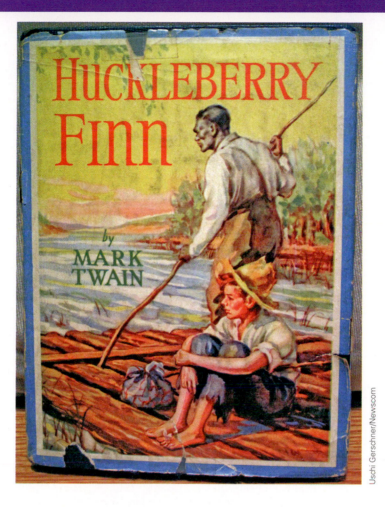

Uschi Gerschner/Newscom

APPLYING THE CRITICAL PROCESS

DESCRIPTION Identify two contemporary books that have been challenged or banned in two separate communities. (Check the American Library Association Web site—www.ala.org—for information on the most frequently challenged and banned books, or use the LexisNexis database.) Describe the two communities involved and what sparked the challenges or bans.

ANALYSIS Look at the patterns that emerge: the main arguments for censoring these books and for defending these books, and any middle-ground positions or unusual viewpoints brought up in the book controversies.

INTERPRETATION Why did these issues arise, and what do you think are the actual reasons why people would challenge or ban a book? For example, does it seem as though people are genuinely concerned about protecting young readers, or do they just seem personally offended by particular books?

EVALUATION Who do you think is right and wrong in these controversies? How are First Amendment protections of printed materials significant here?

ENGAGEMENT Contact your local library and ask what policies are in place to respond to book challenges, and whether it observes the ALA's annual Banned Books Week each September.

material with a wide range of views and does not support removing books on the basis of partisan or doctrinal disapproval.

This tension between citizens' desire to suppress printed materials they find objectionable and the desire to uphold freedoms guaranteed by the Constitution has long characterized our democracy—and will likely continue to do so.

Decline of Bookstores and Libraries

As we enter the digital age, many bookstores are closing, from the small, independent stores to even the megachains that once threatened smaller stores. Bookstores of all shapes and sizes can offer more than sales: book clubs, author readings, and other live events, as well as a general sense of community. Though their aim is more commercial, many bookstores have taken on a role once assigned to public libraries: as social gathering spaces for readers. But just as libraries now face slashed budgets, many bookstores find it difficult to compete with the discounts of online retailers or the convenience of e-books. In many cases, a customer choosing a local bookstore over online options will essentially mean agreeing to pay a higher price to support the face-to-face social interaction of brick-and-mortar bookstores.

Physical Deterioration

Many older books, especially those from the nineteenth century printed on acid-based paper, gradually deteriorate. To prevent loss of the knowledge in these books, research libraries have built climate-controlled depositories for older books that have permanent research value. Also, recent projects by Xerox and Cornell University have produced electronic copies of old books through computer scanning.

The Google Books Library Project represents a similar effort. Begun in 2004, the project features partnerships with the New York Public Library and several major university research libraries to scan millions of books and make them available online and searchable through Google. The Authors Guild and the Association of American Publishers initially resisted having Google digitize books without permission. Google responded that displaying only a limited portion of the books was legal under "fair use" rules. After years of legal battles, a U.S. Court of Appeals sided with Google's fair-use argument in 2013 and dismissed the lawsuit. The Authors Guild vowed to appeal the decision. An alternative group, the Open Content Alliance, was dissatisfied with the Google Books Library Project's intent to restrict scanned book content to Google's search service. In 2007, the alliance started a competing nonprofit service that partners with the Boston Public Library, several New England university libraries, and Yahoo! to digitize millions of books with expired copyrights and make them freely available through the Internet Archive.

Censorship, the decline of bookstores and libraries, and the physical deterioration of books all present daunting challenges to books as a mass medium essential to our democracy. But like other mass media, books—and the people who love them—have adapted as needed to keep this medium alive and vital. Witness the proliferation of book groups, the greater array of formats through which books are now available, and the power of a writer like J.K. Rowling to resurrect a passion for reading in children and adults alike. The ultimate value of books is their ability to encourage the exchange and exploration of ideas. Clearly, they are still serving this purpose—despite the challenges and changes that have reshaped this oldest of media.

CHAPTER ESSENTIALS

Now that you have finished reading this chapter, you can use the following tools:

LaunchPad for *Media Essentials*

Go to **macmillanhighered.com/mediaessentials3e** for videos, review quizzes, and more.

LaunchPad for *Media Essentials* includes:

- **REVIEW WITH LEARNINGCURVE**
  LearningCurve uses gamelike quizzing to help you master the concepts you need to learn from this chapter.

- **VIDEO: TURNING THE PAGE: BOOKS GO DIGITAL**
  Authors discuss how e-books are changing both how books are consumed and how they are written.

REVIEW

Evaluate the Early History of Books

- Books first developed due to innovations made by the Egyptians, Greeks, Chinese, and Romans. Egyptians created **papyrus** (scrolls made from plant reeds) in 2400 BCE. Gradually, people began writing on **parchment** (treated animal skin) because of its durability and cheaper cost; by the fourth century CE, Romans created the first proto-modern book with the **codex** (sheets of parchment sewn together along one edge, then bound with thin pieces of wood and covered with leather) (p. 38).

- Books entered the entrepreneurial stage in the Middle Ages, at which time people explored new ways of writing. This led to the emergence of **manuscript culture**, whereby priests and monks advanced the art of book-making with **illuminated manuscripts**, which featured decorative, colorful illustrations on each page. At the same time, inventors experimented with printing techniques that sped up the hand-lettering process, such as **block printing**—in which printers applied sheets of paper to large blocks of inked wood into which they had hand-carved a page's worth of characters and illustrations—and movable type (pp. 39–41).

- The invention of the **printing press** by Gutenberg between 1453 and 1456 allowed for the mass production of books, such as the Bible. (The first Gutenberg Bible was printed on a fine calfskin-based parchment called **vellum**.) This advancement marked books' move to the mass medium stage, complete with the rise of the publishing industry two centuries later. By the 1830s, **paperback books** were introduced in the United States, and by the 1870s, **dime novels** (coined as **pulp fiction**—a reference to the cheap, machine-made pulp paper they were printed on) were made accessible to the masses. Meanwhile, in the 1880s, the introduction of **linotype** machines enabled printers to save time by setting type mechanically using a typewriter-style keyboard, and the introduction of **offset lithography** in the 1900s allowed publishers to print books from photographic plates rather than from metal casts—cutting costs and saving more time (pp. 41–43).

Outline the Evolution of Modern Publishing

- Initially, publishing houses were small and focused on offering the works of prestigious authors, but over time—by the 1950s and 1960s—they were snapped up by major corporations with ties to international media conglomerates that took advantage of **synergy**, or the promotion and sale of different versions of a media product across the various subsidiaries of the conglomerate (pp. 43–45).

- Regardless of their size or the types of books they publish, all publishing houses are structured similarly: **Acquisitions editors** seek out authors, offer them contracts, and handle **subsidiary rights** (the selling of the rights to a book for use in other media); **developmental editors** help the author draft and revise a manuscript by providing feedback and soliciting reviewer advice; **copy editors** fix spelling, punctuation, and other grammar issues; **design managers** determine the look and feel of a book; and marketing departments identify consumer patterns and help determine business plans accordingly (pp. 45–46).

Explain the Types of Books That Exist

- Until recently, books of all kinds took only printed form. Some of the categories include **trade books** (hardbound and paperback books aimed at general readers and sold at commercial retail outlets); **professional books** (targeted at various occupational groups, not the general consumer market); **textbooks** (educational books divided into elementary through high school, college, and vocational categories); **mass market paperbacks** (sold on racks in drugstores, supermarkets, and airports, in addition to bookstores) and **instant books** (an innovation in mass market paperback publishing that involves putting out a topical book right after a major event occurs); religious books; **reference books** (including dictionaries, encyclopedias, atlases, almanacs, and volumes related to particular professions or trades); and **university press books** (nonprofit scholarly works for small groups of readers) (pp. 46–49).

- With the rise of electronic and digital publishing, book formats have expanded beyond print to include audio books—known originally as "books on tape" (now available on CDs and as MP3 downloads), which became popular in the 1990s and early 2000s—and **e-books**—digital books read on a computer or electronic reading device. Publishers in the e-book market are continually looking for ways to improve on printed books (pp. 49–50).

Understand the Economics of the Book Industry

- The book business makes money by selling books through brick-and-mortar stores, online stores, book clubs, and mail order, and also by selling TV and movie rights (pp. 50–53, 56).

- The book business spends money on essential activities, such as book production, distribution, and marketing (pp. 56–58).

Consider the Role of Books in a Democratic Society

- Books have played a vital role in democracy by spreading its very notion and disseminating ideas that have inspired people to drive change (pp. 58–59).

- Despite the crucial role of books, they face many challenges. For example, censorship prevents people from learning about alternative ideas or ways of living. Although censorship is illegal in the United States, citizens can sometimes force the removal of books from public or school libraries by filing a complaint—a **book challenge**—about subject matter they find objectionable. In addition, the decline of bookstores and libraries and the physical deterioration of books pose problems (pp. 59, 62–63).

STUDY QUESTIONS

1. Why was the printing press such an important and revolutionary invention?
2. Why did publishing houses develop?
3. What are the main ways in which digital technologies have changed the publishing industry?
4. What are the main sources of revenue in book publishing?
5. How do books play a vital role in our society?

MEDIA LITERACY PRACTICE

Although there are more than a quarter million new books published every year, it's sometimes too easy to forget about the oldest mass medium when we talk about "the media." To reconsider the impact of books, investigate the influence of books on another medium: the movies.

DESCRIBE the current state of movies by developing a list of the top twenty movies from the past year.

ANALYZE your list by noting patterns: Which movies were based on books, and which movies inspired later books?

INTERPRET what these patterns mean. For example, are only popular books made into movies? Do movies increase the sales of related books? Do popular movies launch new books?

EVALUATE the synergy of books with movies. Do movies bring attention to books that might otherwise go unnoticed, or do movies completely overshadow books?

ENGAGE with the community by contacting your local library or a bookstore. Since reading for pleasure strongly correlates with academic achievement, you could work with the library or bookstore to develop a promotion or reading series built around the influence of books on movies.

3

Newspapers to Digital Frontiers: Journalism's Journey

The Granger Collection

In 1887, a young reporter left her job at the *Pittsburgh Dispatch* to seek her fortune in New York City. Only twenty-three years old, Elizabeth "Pink" Cochrane had grown tired of writing for the society pages and answering letters to the editor; she wanted to be on the front page. At that time, it was considered "unladylike" for women journalists to use their real names, so the *Dispatch* editors, borrowing from a Stephen Foster song, had dubbed her "Nellie Bly."

After four months of persistent job hunting and freelance writing, Nellie Bly earned a tryout at Joseph Pulitzer's *New York World*, the nation's largest paper. Her assignment: to investigate conditions at the Women's Lunatic Asylum on Blackwell's Island. Her method: to get herself committed to the asylum. After practicing the look of a disheveled lunatic in front of mirrors, she wandered city streets unwashed and seemingly dazed, and acted strangely around her fellow boarders in a New York rooming house.[1] Her tactics worked: Doctors declared her mentally deranged and had her committed.

Ten days later, an attorney from the *World* went in to get her out. Her two-part story appeared in October 1887 and caused a sensation. Nellie Bly's dramatic first-person account documented harsh, cold baths; attendants who abused and taunted patients; and newly arrived immigrant women, completely sane, who had been dragged to the asylum simply because no one could understand them. Bly became famous. Pulitzer gave her a permanent job, and New York City committed $1 million toward improving its asylums. Through her courageous work, Bly pioneered what was then called *detective* or *stunt* journalism—a model that would pave the way toward the twentieth-century practice of investigative journalism.

JOURNALISM IS THE ONLY MEDIA ENTERPRISE THAT democracy absolutely requires—and is the only media practice and business specifically protected by the U.S. Constitution. However, with the decline in traditional news audiences, mounting criticism of "celebrity" journalists, the growth of partisanship in politics, and the rise of highly opinionated twenty-four-hour cable news and Internet news blogs, mainstream journalists have begun losing their credibility with the public. To understand where journalism and all of its current print and electronic forms are today, it's useful to explore the often partisan and sensationalistic history of newspapers. In this chapter, we look at how the profession of journalism, the technology of gathering and sharing the news, and the economics of the news business shaped each other over the last three hundred years by:

- exploring journalism's early history, including the rise of the political-commercial press, penny papers, and yellow journalism

- assessing the modern era of print journalism, including the tensions between objective and interpretive journalism

- considering how the transition from tradecraft to profession in the twentieth century created values, ethics, practices, and cultures recognizable in most newsrooms

- looking at journalism in the Information Age, including changing definitions of "news" and the evolution of journalism's values

- considering the diverse array of newspaper types in existence today, such as local and ethnic papers as well as the underground press

- examining the economics behind print journalism

- taking stock of the challenges facing journalism today, such as industry consolidation and the digitization of content

- considering how journalism's current struggles may affect the strength of our democracy

The Early History of American Journalism

Human beings have always valued **news**—the process by which people gather information and create narrative reports to help one another make sense of events happening around them. The earliest news was passed along *orally*—from family to family and from tribe to tribe—by community leaders and oral historians. Soon after moving from oral to written form, the news shifted from an information source accessible only to elites and local leaders to a mass medium that satisfied a growing audience's hunger for information. In the earliest days of American newspapers (the late 1600s through the 1800s), written news took on a number of formats—political analyses printed on expensive, handmade paper; cheaper accounts printed on machine-made paper; and sensationalist and investigative reports. Each of these formats fulfilled Americans' "need to know"—whether they wanted coverage of the political scene, exposés of corruption in business, or even humorous or entertaining perspectives on current events.

Colonial Newspapers and the Partisan Press

Inspired by the introduction of the printing press in Europe, American colonists began producing their first newspapers in the late seventeenth century. Two main types of early papers developed: the **partisan press** and commercial shipping news. The partisan press got its name because unlike the business models we are familiar with today, these papers were increasingly being sponsored by political parties, politicians, and other partisan groups. They served a vital function

© British Library Board Publick Occurrences, 1690, p. 1

The first colonial newspaper, *Publick Occurrences, Both Forreign and Domestick*, was published in 1690 and banned after one issue for its negative portrayal of British rule.

before, during, and after the Revolutionary period, critiquing government and disseminating the views of political parties. Other papers were more focused on markets and news about ships that were coming in and out of colonial ports, or they reprinted news (several weeks or months old) from European magazines and newspapers brought on board those ships. In the partisan press, one can see a forerunner to today's editorial pages as well as partisan cable news channels and Web sites. In the commercial papers, one can see the ancestor of today's business sections, as well as numerous papers, cable news programs, and Web sites focused on business news.

The first newspaper, *Publick Occurrences, Both Forreign and Domestick*, was published on September 25, 1690, by Boston printer Benjamin Harris, but it was banned after just one issue for its negative view of British rule. In the early 1700s, other papers cropped up, including Benjamin Franklin's *Pennsylvania Gazette*—which many historians regard as the best of the colonial papers. The *Gazette* was also one of the first papers to make money by printing advertisements alongside news.

One significant colonial paper, the *New-York Weekly Journal*, was founded in 1733 by the Popular Party, a political group that opposed British rule. *Journal* articles included attacks on the royal governor of New York. The party had installed John Peter Zenger as printer of the paper, and in 1734 he was arrested for *seditious libel* when one of his writers defamed a public official's character in print. Championed by famed Philadelphia lawyer Andrew Hamilton, Zenger won his case the following year. The

---

CHAPTER 3 // TIMELINE

1690 First Colonial Newspaper
Boston printer Benjamin Harris publishes *Publick Occurrences, Both Forreign and Domestick*.

1734 Press Freedom
John Peter Zenger is arrested for seditious libel; jury rules in his favor in 1735, establishing freedom of the press and newspapers' right to criticize the government.

1827 First African American Newspaper
Freedom's Journal is founded.

1828 First Native American Newspaper
The *Cherokee Phoenix* is founded.

Zenger decision helped lay a foundation—the right of a democratic press to criticize public officials—for the First Amendment to the Constitution, adopted as part of the Bill of Rights in 1791.

By 1765, the American colonies boasted about thirty newspapers, all of them published weekly or monthly. In 1784, the first daily paper began operations. But even the largest of these papers rarely reached a circulation of fifteen hundred. Readership was largely confined to educated or wealthy men who controlled local politics and commerce (and who could afford newspaper subscriptions).

The Penny Press: Becoming a Mass Medium

During the 1830s, a number of forces transformed newspapers into an information source available to, valued by, and affordable for all—a true mass medium. For example, thanks to the Industrial Revolution, factories could make cheap, machine-made paper to replace the expensive handmade kind previously in use. At the same time, the rise of the middle class, enabled by the growth of literacy, set the stage for a more popular and inclusive press. And with steam-powered presses replacing mechanical presses, publishers could crank out as many as four thousand copies of their newspapers every hour, which dramatically lowered their cost. Popular **penny papers** soon began outselling the six-cent elite publications previously available. The success of penny papers would

North Wind Picture Archives

Andrew Hamilton defends John Peter Zenger, a New York printer arrested for seditious libel in 1734. Zenger eventually won his case, which established the precedent that today allows U.S. journalists and citizens to criticize public officials.

1833 Penny Press
Printer Benjamin Day founds the *New York Sun* and helps usher in the penny press era.

1848 Associated Press
Six New York newspapers form the Associated Press (AP), relaying news stories around the country via telegraph.

1883 Yellow Journalism
Pulitzer buys the *New York World*; the battle with Hearst's *New York Journal* heats up in 1895 during the heyday of yellow journalism.

1887 Nellie Bly
Nellie Bly's first article on the conditions in women's insane asylums is printed in the *New York World*, an early effort in investigative journalism.

North Wind Picture Archives

Founded by Benjamin Day in 1833, the *New York Sun* helped usher in the penny press era, bringing news to the working and emerging middle class.

change not only who was reading newspapers but also how those papers were written.

The First Penny Papers

In 1833, printer Benjamin Day founded the *New York Sun*, lowered the price of his newspaper to one penny, and eliminated subscriptions. The *Sun* (whose slogan was "It shines for all") highlighted local events, scandals, and police reports. It also ran fabricated and serialized stories, making legends of frontiersmen Davy Crockett and Daniel Boone and blazing the trail for Americans' enthusiasm for celebrity news. Within six months, the *Sun* had a circulation of eight thousand—twice that of its nearest competitor. The *Sun*'s success unleashed a barrage of penny papers that favored **human-interest stories**: news accounts that focused on the daily trials and triumphs of the human condition, often featuring ordinary individuals who had faced down extraordinary challenges.

In 1835, James Gordon Bennett founded another daily penny paper, the *New York Morning Herald*. Considered the first U.S. press baron, Bennett—not any one political party—completely controlled his paper's content. He established an independent publication that served middle- and working-class readers. The *Herald* carried political essays and reports of scandals, business stories, a letters section, fashion notes, moral reflections, religious news, society gossip, colloquial tales and jokes, sports stories, and, later, reports from the Civil War fronts. By 1860, the *Herald* had nearly eighty thousand readers, making it the world's largest daily paper.

CHAPTER 3 // TIMELINE continued

1896 Modern Journalism
Adolph Ochs buys the *New York Times*, jump-starting modern objective journalism.

1920 First Radio Newscast
The *Detroit News*, a Scripps-owned newspaper, airs the first radio newscast on August 31 on what would later become WWJ 950 AM.

1948 First Regular Anchored Television Newscasts
CBS Television News starts a regular fifteen-minute nightly newscast with a news anchor (earlier televised news was simulcast from CBS Radio). Newscasts would be extended to a half hour in 1963.

1951 First Television-Newsmagazine-Style Program
Veteran reporter Edward R. Murrow and producer Fred W. Friendly bring their radio-magazine-style show *Hear It Now* to television, giving it the new name *See It Now*.

Changing Business Models, Changing Journalism

As ad revenues and circulation skyrocketed, the newspaper industry expanded overall. In 1830, about 650 weekly and 65 daily papers operated in the United States, reaching a circulation of 80,000. Just ten years later, the nation had a total of 1,140 weeklies and 140 dailies, attracting more than 300,000 readers.

As they proliferated and gained new readers, penny papers shifted not just their business models but also the way the news was presented and, as a result, the practice of journalism. Papers had previously been funded primarily by the political parties that sponsored them, and their content emphasized overt political views. But as they expanded, they realized they could derive even more revenues from the market—by selling space for advertisements and by hawking newspapers on the streets and through newsstands. Editors began putting their daily reporting on the front page, moving overt political viewpoints to the editorial page. In other words, as the business model relied more on selling to a mass audience, there was a financial incentive to appeal to customers with a wider range of political beliefs. This trend toward an "objective" style as a result of commercial pressures would also be supported by services that provided content for several different newspapers.

The First News Wire Service

In 1848, the enormous expansion of the newspaper industry led six New York newspapers to form a cooperative arrangement and found the Associated Press (AP), the first major news wire service. **Wire services** began as commercial and cooperative organizations that relayed news stories and information around the country and the world using telegraph lines (and, later, radio waves and digital transmissions). In the case of the AP, which functioned as a kind of news co-op, the founding New York papers provided access to their own stories and those from other newspapers.

1980 First 24-Hour Cable News
The Cable News Network (CNN) becomes the first television station to provide 24-hour news and information programming.

1980 First Online Paper
Ohio's *Columbus Dispatch* becomes the first newspaper to go online.

1982 Postmodern News
Gannett chain launches *USA Today*, ushering in the postmodern era, in which news is modeled after television.

2009 Some Major Dailies Go Online Only
In the wake of the 2008 recession, some newspapers fail and others, like the *Seattle Post-Intelligencer*, stop printing paper copies and become online only.

Such companies enabled news to travel rapidly from coast to coast, setting the stage for modern journalism in the United States. And because the papers still cost only a penny, more people than ever now had access to a widening array of news. Clearly, newspapers had moved from the entrepreneurial stage to the status of mass media.

As individual newspapers, which certainly still retained elements of political ideology, became aware of the financial rewards of not alienating those with differing political viewpoints, wire services also saw the need to offer material that as many newspapers as possible would buy. Based on both this economic need and the chance that unreliable telegraph lines might cut off the last part of a report, a journalistic style of writing called the **inverted pyramid** was developed.

Developed by Civil War correspondents working for individual papers or wire services,[2] inverted-pyramid reports were often stripped of adverbs and adjectives, and began—as they do today—with the most dramatic or newsworthy information. They answered the questions who, what, where, when—and, less frequently, why and how—at the top of the story and then narrowed the account down to its less significant details. This approach offered an important advantage: If wars or natural disasters disrupted the telegraph transmissions of these dispatches, at least readers would get the crucial information. Still a staple of introductory news writing courses, this form tends to emphasize immediate events and facts over deeper discussions of context or partisan debate.

But a move away from overt political partisanship on the front page wasn't the only way the economic desire for larger and larger audiences changed the way journalism was practiced.

Yellow Journalism

Following the tradition established by the *New York Sun* and the *New York Morning Herald*, a new brand of papers arose in the late 1800s. These publications ushered in the era of **yellow journalism**, which emphasized exciting human-interest stories, crime news, large headlines, and easy-to-digest copy. Generally regarded as the direct forerunner of today's tabloid papers, reality TV, and celebrity-obsessed Web sites like TMZ, yellow journalism featured two major characteristics:

1. Overly dramatic—or sensational—stories about crime, celebrities, disasters, scandals, and intrigue
2. News reports exposing corruption, particularly in business and government— the foundation for *investigative journalism*

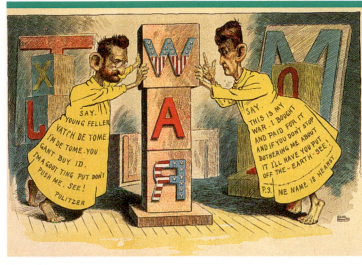

Library of Congress

AP Photo

Generally considered America's first comic-strip character, the Yellow Kid was created in the mid-1890s by cartoonist R. F. Outcault. The cartoon was so popular that newspaper barons Joseph Pulitzer and William Randolph Hearst fought over Outcault's services, giving yellow journalism its name.

The term *yellow journalism* has its roots in the press war that pitted Joseph Pulitzer's *New York World* against William Randolph Hearst's *New York Journal*. During their furious fight to win readers, the two papers ultimately took turns hosting the first popular cartoon strip, *The Yellow Kid*, created in 1895 by artist R. F. Outcault. Pulitzer, a Jewish-Hungarian immigrant, had bought the *New York World* in 1883 for $346,000. Aimed at immigrant and working-class readers, the *World* crusaded for improved urban housing, better treatment of women, and equitable labor laws, while railing against big business. It also manufactured news events and printed sensational-ized stories on crime and sex. By 1887, its Sunday circulation had soared to more than 250,000—the largest anywhere.

The *World* faced its fiercest competition when William Randolph Hearst in 1895 bought the *New York Journal* (a penny paper founded by Pulitzer's brother Albert) and then raided Joseph Pulitzer's paper for editors, writers, and cartoon-ists. Hearst focused on lurid, sensational stories and appealed to immigrant readers by using large headlines and bold layout designs. To boost circulation, the *Journal* invented interviews, faked pictures, and provoked conflicts that might result in eye-catching stories. In 1896, its daily circulation reached 450,000. A year later, the circulation of the paper's Sunday edition rivaled the *World's* 600,000.

Yellow journalism has been vilified for its sensationalism and aggressive tactics to snatch readers from competitors by appealing to their low-brow inter-ests, but this unique era gave birth to several newspaper elements still valued by many readers today, including advice columns and feature stories. It even laid the foundation for the prestigious Pulitzer Prizes, which today recognize quality writing, reporting, and research in such categories as poetry, history, international reporting, editorial cartooning, public service, and explanatory reporting.

The Evolution of Newspaper Journalism: Competing Models and the Rise of Professionalism

In the late 1800s, as newspapers pushed to expand circulation even further, two distinct types of journalism emerged: the story-driven model, which dramatized important events and characterized the penny papers and the yellow press; and "the facts" model, an approach that seemed more impartial and was favored by the six-cent papers.[3] Provocative questions arose: Could news accounts be entirely objective? Should reporters actively interpret the meaning of particular events for readers? And later, as the profession and culture of journalism moved from print into broadcasting and online reporting, these new media, with their different sets of abilities and limitations, required different approaches to the news.

"Objectivity" and Professionalization in Modern Journalism

Throughout the mid-1800s, the more a newspaper appeared not to take sides on its front pages, the more readers it could attract. Also at this time, wire service organizations were serving a variety of newspaper clients in different regions of the country. To satisfy all their clients, newspapers strived for the appearance of impartiality—presenting "the facts" and leaving it up to readers to interpret the implications for their own lives. At the same time, the more sensational aspects of yellow journalism created an image problem for newspapers and their style of journalism, with journalists seen at best as low-status tradesmen and at worst as disreputable. But with the approach of the twentieth century, newspapers and journalism were about to start changing.

Adolph Ochs and the *New York Times*

The ideal of an impartial, or purely informational, news model was reinvented by Adolph Ochs, who bought the *New York Times* in 1896. Through wise hiring, Ochs and his editors rebuilt the paper around substantial news coverage and provocative editorial pages. To distance the *Times* from the yellow press, the editors also downplayed sensational stories, favoring the documentation of major events or issues and developing a powerful marketing message touting the *Times* as the higher-brow choice.

With the Hearst and Pulitzer papers capturing the bulk of working- and middle-class readers, managers at the *Times* initially tried to use their straightforward, "no frills" reporting to appeal to more affluent and educated readers. In 1898, Ochs also lowered the paper's price to a penny. Soon middle-class readers gravitated to the paper as a status marker for the educated and well informed. Between 1898 and 1899, circulation soared from 25,000 to 75,000. By 1921, the *Times* had a daily circulation of 330,000 and a Sunday circulation of 500,000.

Andrew Harrer/Bloomberg via Getty Images

Known for getting information and presenting news in a straightforward way—without the opinion of the reporter—the *New York Times* was the first truly modern newspaper. It established itself as the official paper of record by the 1920s and maintains a venerable reputation today.

"Just the Facts, Please": Journalism Gets Professional

Early in the twentieth century, with reporters adopting a more "scientific" attitude to news- and fact-gathering, the ideal of objectivity took a firmer hold in journalism. In **objective journalism**, which distinguishes factual reports from opinion columns, reporters strive to maintain a neutral attitude toward the issue or event they cover. They also search out competing points of view among the sources for a story in an effort to provide balanced coverage.

The early twentieth century was also a time when even the most notorious yellow journalists wanted to boost the respectability of the news business. That, combined with a broader cultural trend that favored a more "scientific" approach to the world, pushed the training of new journalists away from apprenticeships and toward universities. Early in the century, Joseph Pulitzer approached Columbia University in New York about setting up the first journalism school. He wanted to see the status of journalists rise to that of other professionals, such as lawyers and doctors. But the reputation of journalism was such that it took several years for the directors of the school to accept the millions Pulitzer offered, finally founding the school in 1912. (In addition to offering graduate degrees, the school began awarding the coveted Pulitzer Prizes in journalism in 1917 and continues to do so to this day.) But the distinction of being the first journalism school in the United States goes to a different Columbia: the School of Journalism at the University of Missouri in Columbia, Missouri, founded in 1908.[4]

Interpretive Journalism

By the 1920s, people began wondering whether the impartial approach to news reporting was sufficient for helping readers understand complex national and global developments. As one news scholar contended, it was partly as a result of "drab, factual, objective reporting" that "the American people were utterly amazed when [World War I] broke out in August 1914, as they had no understanding of the foreign scene to prepare them for it."[5] Such concerns triggered the rise of **interpretive journalism**, which aims to explain the ramifications of key issues or events and place them in a broader historical or social context.

Editor and columnist Walter Lippmann insisted that although objectivity should serve as journalism's foundation, the press should do more. He ranked three press responsibilities: (1) "to make a current record"; (2) "to make a running analysis of it"; and (3) "on the basis of both, to suggest plans."[6]

The rise of radio in the 1930s intensified tensions between the objective and interpretive models of print journalism. As radio gained in popularity, broadcasters increasingly took their news directly from papers and wire services. Seeking to maintain their dominion over "the facts," some newspaper editors and lobbyists argued that radio should provide only interpretive commentary. Other print journalists argued that it was interpretive stories, not objective reports, which could best help newspapers compete against radio. However, most U.S. dailies continued relegating interpretive content to a few editorial and opinion pages.

It wasn't until the 1950s—with the outbreak of the Korean War, the development of atomic power, the deepening of the Cold War, and the U.S. anticommunist movement—that newspapers began providing more interpretive journalism. They did so in part to compete with the latest news medium: television. And their interpretive material often took the form of an "op-ed" page—which appeared opposite the traditional editorial page. The op-ed page offered a wider variety of columns, news analyses, and letters to the editor.

Journalism Evolves across Media

The rise of radio and the coming of television would give way to new forms of journalism. Nearly every new mass medium has eventually found a home for journalism of some kind, from radio and television in the first half of the twentieth century, to the addition of cable television in the 1980s, to the emergence and convergence of the Internet in the 1990s through the present day. Many mass media have coexisted with traditional print journalism, but the converged media offered by the Internet has been the catalyst for some of the biggest changes in the journalism world since its early days.

Journalism on the Airwaves

By the time America plunged into the Great Depression, the unique abilities of broadcasting were becoming apparent. For example, President Franklin Delano Roosevelt tapped this potential during his now-famous "fireside chats." Later, news icon Edward R. Murrow made a name for himself and CBS News during World War II with his broadcasts from rooftops during the bombing of London and his taking a recorder with him as he flew on B-17 bombing missions over Germany, taping commentary for later broadcast. By the 1950s, the rules and rituals surrounding journalism would shift with the popularity of the newest medium, television, to which many radio news icons, such as Murrow, would switch. In 1951, his radio program *Hear It Now* was retitled *See It Now*, and it went on to challenge Senator Joseph McCarthy (for his reckless abuse of power and disregard for evidence in the name of labeling others as communists in the United States) and was among the first to warn of the dangers of smoking tobacco. However, as much as Murrow and his work on radio and television are lauded and held in high esteem to this day by broadcast journalists (one of the industry's highest awards is named after him), it's worth noting that his coverage of controversial subjects and the accompanying offense taken by advertisers often brought Murrow into conflict with CBS owner William S. Paley and ultimately doomed the program.

AP Photo

The rules and rituals governing American journalism began shifting in the 1950s. In the early days, the most influential and respected news program was CBS's *See It Now*, coproduced by Edward R. Morrow. The show practiced a kind of TV journalism lodged between the neutral and the narrative traditions.

The Power of Visual Language

The shift from a print-dominated culture to an electronic-digital culture brings up the question of how the power of visual imagery compares with the power of the printed word. For the second half of the twentieth century, TV news dramatized America's key events visually. Civil Rights activists, for instance, acknowledge that the movement benefited enormously from televised news that documented the plight of southern blacks in the 1960s in evocative moving images. Many people

MEDIA LITERACY

Case Study

From Uncovering Scandals to Being the Scandal

The 1960s and 1970s are sometimes referred to as a "golden age" of American journalism. Although in retrospect there were serious problems during this period (including the lack of women and minorities in mainstream newsrooms), this was a time when journalists could document and influence great social changes of the time, from the Civil Rights struggle to the Vietnam War.

It was also a time of investigative reporting that would influence generations of journalists, especially because of a story known by a single word: Watergate. *Washington Post* reporters Bob Woodward and Carl Bernstein started researching after five men were arrested for breaking into and entering the Democratic National Committee headquarters at the Watergate office complex in

AP Photo

Washington, D.C., on June 17, 1972. By the time they were done, they had uncovered information that this break-in was just one of many illegal activities that President Richard Nixon had authorized and was carried out by Nixon's staff. Ultimately, the House of Representatives started investigating, and on August 8, 1974, Nixon resigned before the House could decide on impeachment.

Fast-forward a few decades, and one of the great scandals of recent years was about a news operation that was largely being exposed by another newspaper (not to say there weren't other scandals involving journalists and news organizations in between, of course). But this time the stories delved into both corruption (of the corporate variety) and a shameful breakdown of journalistic ethics, at least on the part of some of the players. Media mogul Rupert Murdoch was forced to withdraw his $12 billion takeover bid for British Sky Broadcasting after a phone hacking scandal involving key figures in his publishing empire brought down Murdoch's *News of the World*, one of Britain's oldest newspapers. In the continuing fallout of the phone hacking scandal, Murdoch's News Corp. announced in 2012 that it would divide its publishing companies (newspapers and books) from its entertainment holdings (television and movie studios).

A rival paper, the *Guardian*, played a prominent role in publicizing the lurid details of the case. Reporter Nick Davies continued to investigate the *News of the World* after the police, the government, and the rest of the press accepted the News Corp. story that the hacking of British royal family members, including Prince Charles, was an isolated event. When Davies discovered that James Murdoch (son of Rupert) paid more than $1 million in hush money to cover up another instance of phone hacking, the scandal took on new life, reaching a tipping point when Davies reported that the *News of the World* had hacked into the phone calls of Milly Dowler, a missing teenager. Davies revealed that the hackers had deleted Dowler's voice messages so they could listen to new ones—a transgression that gave her parents false hope that she was still alive. This revelation damaged News Corp. from top to bottom; intrepid reporting from Nick Davies and the *Guardian* curtailed Murdoch's stranglehold on British politics and media.[1]

Davies, then, demonstrates that courageous reporting can make a real difference on a grand scale, even or especially if it involves standing up to a media conglomerate in the news business. Imagine, for example, what might have been avoided if such investigative journalism had addressed the abuses of Wall Street and the too-big-to-fail banks in the lead-up to the financial collapse of 2008. The story of journalism taking the practices that took down corrupt political leaders and applying them to a corrupt conglomerate should inspire business reporters to do more to be better watchdogs over corporate interests.

© Lucy Nicholson/Reuters/Corbis

APPLYING THE CRITICAL PROCESS

DESCRIPTION Choose two major newspapers, and investigate how each covered the phone hacking scandal and other media business stories. How does the coverage differ in terms of the number of articles devoted to the scandal in May, June, and July of 2011? How many editorial and opinion pieces are devoted to the scandal during this three-month period?

ANALYSIS How do the two newspapers characterize the scandal? Are there differences in the editorial treatment of Rupert Murdoch and his son James?

INTERPRETATION Write a two- to three-paragraph critical interpretation of the "meanings" of the scandal proposed by the two newspapers. Are there differences in the coverage of Murdoch being forced to withdraw his bid for British Sky Broadcasting?

EVALUATION Determine which papers and stories you would judge as good and which ones you would judge as weaker models for how business and media stories should be covered. Are some elements that should be included missing from the coverage? If so, make suggestions.

ENGAGEMENT Contact a business editor from a newspaper and ask how he or she makes content decisions. What kind of business and economic reporting catches the editorial department's eye? What considerations are made when business editors decide what to cover?

find visual images far more compelling and memorable than written descriptions of events or individuals. If listening to President Roosevelt on the radio was part of creating a national shared experience, the effect was amplified as a nation watched and celebrated together shared milestones, from the first man to walk on the moon to the inauguration of the first African American U.S. president.

But just as sound and moving pictures provide powerful communication tools, the technical requirements and styles that have developed also bring along some shortcomings. As previously discussed, TV news reporters share many values and conventions with their print counterparts, yet they also differ from them in significant ways. First, whereas print editors fit stories around ads on the printed page, TV news directors have to time stories to fit between commercials, which can make the ads seem more intrusive to viewers. Second, newspapers can increase or decrease the number of pages, but time is a finite commodity. This has led commercial news operations to often place strict limits on the length of individual news stories (from twenty to ninety seconds in many cases) in the twenty or so minutes of time left in a half-hour newscast after time is taken for commercials. Of that remaining twenty minutes, around half is typically used for local weather and sports. Third, whereas modern print journalists derive their credibility from their apparent neutrality, TV news reporters gain credibility from providing live, on-the-spot reporting; believable imagery; and an earnest, personable demeanor that makes them seem more approachable, even more trustworthy, than the detached, faceless print reporters. As TV news reporting evolved, it developed a style of its own—one defined by attractive, congenial newscasters skilled at perky banter (sometimes called "happy talk"), and short, seven- to eight-second quotes (or "sound bites") from interview subjects. Print and TV reporters must also compete with Internet-only outlets, which combine elements of both television and print journalism.

Cable News Enters the Field

The transformation of TV news by cable—with the arrival of CNN in 1980—led to dramatic changes in TV news delivery at the national level. Prior to cable news (and the Internet), most people tuned to their local and national news late in the afternoon or evening on a typical weekday, with each program lasting just thirty minutes. But today, the 24/7 news cycle means that we can get TV news anytime, day or night, and the constant need for new content (sometimes called "feeding the beast" by insiders) has led to major changes in what is considered news. Because it is expensive to dispatch reporters to document stories or to maintain foreign news bureaus to cover international issues, the much less expensive "talking head" pundit has become a standard for cable news channels.

Such a programming strategy requires few resources beyond the studio and a few guests.

Today's main cable channels have built their evening programs along partisan lines and follow the model of journalism as opinion and assertion: Fox News goes right with pundit stars like Bill O'Reilly (the ratings king of cable news) and Sean Hannity; MSNBC leans left with Rachel Maddow and Lawrence O'Donnell; and CNN stakes out the middle with hosts who try to strike a more neutral pose, like Anderson Cooper. CNN, the originator of cable news, does much more original reporting than Fox News and MSNBC and does better in nonpresidential election years, as well as during natural disasters and crime tragedies.

Broadcast and cable news organizations play an important role in society with their (somewhat) traditional approach to television programming. But it's nearly impossible to define or describe the current state of journalism, from whatever source, without discussing its convergence with the Internet.

Paul Zimmerman/WireImage/Getty Images

Internet Convergence Accelerates Changes to Journalism

For mainstream print and TV reporters and editors, online news has added new dimensions to journalism. Both print and TV news can continually update breaking stories online, and many reporters now post their online stories first and then work on traditional versions. This means that readers and viewers no longer have to wait until the next day for the morning paper or for the local evening newscast for important stories. To enhance the online reports, which do not have the time or space constraints of television or print, newspaper reporters are increasingly required to provide video or audio for their stories. This allows readers and viewers to see full interviews rather than just selected print quotes in the paper or short sound bites on the TV report. Journalists might augment stories with interactive tools (like maps plotting reports of crimes in a city over time) or a song recording added to the end of an interview with a musician.

However, online news comes with a special set of problems. Print reporters, for example, can do e-mail interviews rather than leave the office to question a subject in person. Many editors discourage this practice because they think relying on e-mail gives interviewees too much control over shaping their answers. Although some might argue that this provides more thoughtful answers,

The popularity of 24/7 cable news has led to increased screen time for news anchors, which can mean both more exposure and more room for errors. CNN's Don Lemon is featured heavily on the news channel, but has also been cited for a series of embarrassing on-air gaffes.

KM1/ZOB/WENN/Newscom

When actor Idris Elba (The Wire, Luther, Thor, Mandela: Long Walk to Freedom) was interviewed by the Guardian in late 2014, the topic wasn't his acting but his crossover into making music. The online version of this article (circulated on the paper's Facebook page) included not just the typical written account of the interview but photographs, an embedded video clip from Mandela, and the album itself, which could be listened to for free.

journalists say it takes the elements of surprise and spontaneity out of the traditional news interview, during which a subject might accidentally reveal important information—something less likely to occur in an online setting.

Another problem for journalists is, ironically, the wide-ranging resources of the Internet, including access to versions of stories from other papers and broadcast stations. The mountain of information available on the Internet has made it all too easy for journalists to—unwittingly or intentionally—copy other journalists' work. In addition, access to databases and other informational sites can keep reporters at their computers rather than out tracking down new kinds of information, cultivating sources, and staying in touch with their communities.

Most notable, however, for journalists in the digital age are the demands that convergence has made on their reporting and writing. Print journalists at newspapers (and magazines) are expected to carry digital cameras so that they can post video along with the print versions of their stories. TV reporters are expected to write print-style news reports for their station's Web site to supplement the streaming video of their original TV stories. And both print and TV reporters are often expected to post the Internet versions of their stories first, before the versions they do for the morning paper or the six o'clock news. In addition, journalists today are increasingly expected to tweet and blog.

The Culture of News and Rituals of Reporting

Throughout the twentieth century, sets of beliefs and practices came to define what was accepted as news and what it meant to be a journalist reporting that news. Despite the technical and inherent stylistic differences among print, radio, and television, mainstream journalists in all media shared a similar mission, encountered similar ethical issues, and developed methods designed to get and share information. These concepts have proven invaluable for news operations trying to do the never-ending job of providing the information the public needs to make informed and intelligent decisions. They also provide a framework within which journalists say they are adhering to principles of unbiased truth-seeking and from which they derive a great portion of their authority. Critics suggest that these practices are just as likely to create biases, derail honest discussions about those biases, and paint a picture that distorts reality. But before one can discuss what is a useful tool and what is a potential pitfall, it's helpful to understand more about news culture and the common customs of gathering the news, starting with the most basic question of journalism: What is news?

What Is News?

News is the process of gathering information and making reports that use a narrative framework; in other words, news reports tell stories. News reports (whether in print, on TV, or on the Internet) help the public make sense of prominent people, important events, and unusual happenings in everyday life. Over time, journalists have developed a set of criteria for determining whether information is **newsworthy**—that is, whether it merits transformation into news stories. These criteria include timeliness, proximity, conflict, prominence, human interest, consequence, usefulness, novelty, and deviance:[7]

- Most issues and events that journalists cover are *timely* or *new*. Reporters, for instance, cover speeches, meetings, crimes, and court cases that have just happened.
- The bulk of these events usually occur close by, or in *proximity* to, the readers and viewers who will consume the news stories.
- In developing news narratives, reporters often seek contentious quotes from those with opposing or *conflicting* views. In theory, this helps create balance. In practice, it can lead to seeking the most extreme positions, rather than a range of positions, to create drama.
- Surveys indicate that most people identify more closely with an individual than with an abstract issue. Therefore, the news media tend to report stories that feature *prominent*, powerful, or influential people.
- However, reporters also look for the *human-interest* story: extraordinary incidents that happen to "ordinary" people. In fact, reporters often relate a story

about a complicated issue (such as unemployment, health care, or homelessness) by illustrating its impact on an "average" person or a "typical" family.

- Many editors and reporters believe that some news must also be of *consequence* to a majority of their readers or viewers. For example, they might include stories about new business regulations that affect credit cards or home mortgages.
- Likewise, many people look for *useful* stories: for instance, those offering hints on how to buy a used car or choose a college.
- When events happen that are outside the routine of daily life—that is, they are *novel*—they will likely generate news coverage. Examples might include a seven-year-old girl who tries to pilot a plane across the country or a fading celebrity who gets arrested for drunk driving.
- Reporters also cover events that appear to *deviate* from social norms, including murders, rapes, fatal car or plane crashes, fires, political scandals, and wars.

In producing news stories that meet many of these criteria, journalists influence our interpretations of what is going on around us and thus the decisions we make. For example, if we read a story in the newspaper emphasizing the consequences of failing to save for retirement, we may conclude that such saving is important—and that we'd better do more of it. If we see a lot of stories about crime and violence, even as fewer and fewer violent crimes are actually being committed, we might conclude that the world is a more dangerous place than the facts actually suggest.

Values in American Journalism

In addition to telling us how journalists define news, newsworthiness criteria begin to paint a picture of the values that came to define American journalism in the 1970s and 1980s. This was a time some refer to as the "golden age" of journalism, when newspapers enjoyed consistent profitability and the Big Three TV networks (NBC, CBS, and ABC) hadn't yet encountered the competition from cable and online news. It was also a time when the journalism profession was enjoying a boost in prestige and popularity in the wake of big stories about the Watergate scandal and the Pentagon Papers (see "Media Literacy Case Study: From Uncovering Scandals to Being the Scandal" on pages 82–83). It was from this time that researchers started identifying and critiquing the values—not always recognized by the journalists themselves at the time—that influenced how stories were covered (or not).

Putting It in Neutral

Perhaps the most prominent and obvious of these values is neutrality, or the apparent lack of bias—a quality that remains prized even in a more polarized environment that has given rise to more opinion-ated forms of news. Many professional journalists believe strongly that their job is to gather and then present facts without judging them. Conventions such as the inverted-pyramid news lead (starting reports with the most important information), the careful attribution of sources (favoring quoted interview subjects rather than the reporter's analysis), the minimal use of adverbs and adjectives (getting rid of ornate, flowery language in order to look "factual"), and the detached third-person point of view (using the omniscient, or all-knowing, authorial point of view favored by many novelists) all help reporters present their findings in a supposedly neutral way.

Erik S. Lesser/The New York Times/Redux Pictures

CNN's world headquarters is located in Atlanta, but the cable channel maintains bureaus in many other U.S. cities, including New York, Chicago, Boston, New Orleans, and San Francisco.

Journalists argue that this dedication to neutrality (and related concepts of fairness, balance, independence, objectivity, and so on) boosts their credibility and is an important part of what separates news from propaganda. Generations of journalists have spent careers trying to live up to these ideals as part of what they see as their mission to serve their audiences and communities. At its best, a commitment by individual journalists to these traditional news values have helped them get the news, hold the powerful to account, and resist manipulation by those who would deceive the public.

However, critics in and out of the profession say this approach also brings a set of problems. In practice, neutrality is itself an unrealistic goal. In deciding which stories to cover with limited resources, news operations make judgments about what is worthy of attention (or not) by the public. Merely by deciding which information and experience to include in a news story, journalists cannot help but present a point of view on the story's topic. And although the pursuit of personal detachment might have become part of a well-intentioned set of ethics, it is still true that the origins of the shift from partisan to objective journalism in the 1800s had at least as much to do with economics as with ethics.

Another problem with the concept of "neutrality" for journalism might be the way in which believing one's judgment to be neutral can create dangerous blind spots, which ultimately undermine the ethical intentions of journalists.

Assumptions about what is normal or "natural" are often involved when trying to find the neutral position, especially when dealing with social issues. Take, for example, the experience of the *New York Times* during the 1970s and 1980s and the way it covered—or, rather, often ignored—gay rights and the AIDS epidemic. The antigay positions of the paper's management and owners at the time (including Ochs's daughter Iphigene Ochs Sulzberger) became the target for critics who said the silence of this "objective" newspaper slowed public attention and public support for the fight against AIDS, contributing to the ultimate death toll from the disease, before the *Times* changed its policies in the late 1980s.[8]

Diversity in the Newsroom

An important part of the critique of the ability of newsrooms to achieve neutrality or objectivity involves the ways in which the demographics of a newsroom reflect the demographics of the community it covers. For much of the twentieth century, mainstream news operations were dominated by white men and, as such, lacked the perspective that comes with the different lived experiences of other groups in society. This hurts the ability of a newsroom to question what it considers "normal" or "neutral," which is really based on a very non-neutral worldview.

Beginning in the 1970s, there was a push to make newsrooms more diverse. The good news is that from 1977 to 1994, the number of minority reporters in newspaper newsrooms nearly tripled, from 4 percent to 11 percent. The bad news is that the number hasn't improved much in the last twenty years. As of 2012, minority journalists made up only 12 percent of the total newspaper newsroom workforce, whereas in the rest of America, nonwhites make up about 39 percent of the population. Women (half of the population) still make up less than half of newsroom employees, and only about a third of newsroom managers.[9]

Getting a Good Story

According to Don Hewitt, the creator and longtime executive producer of *60 Minutes*, "There's a very simple formula if you're in Hollywood, Broadway, opera, publishing, broadcasting, newspapering. It's four very simple words—tell me a story."[10] For most journalists, the bottom line is "Get the story"—an edict that overrides most other concerns. This is the standard against which many reporters measure themselves and their profession. At its best, it can provide inspiration to keep digging to uncover important information or perspectives that might be difficult to get or that someone is trying to hide from public view. At its worst, it can lead to a variety of unethical and even criminal behaviors (see "Media Literacy Case Study: From Uncovering Scandals to Being the Scandal" on pages 82–83). It has also occasionally led journalists to make up stories, such as in the early 1980s, when former *Washington Post* reporter Janet Cooke won a Pulitzer Prize for a story she made up about a mother who contributed to the heroin addiction of her eight-year-old son (the prize was later revoked). Or in the early 2000s, when it came to light that *New York Times* reporter Jayson Blair had frequently plagiarized and fabricated stories. These more extreme cases are typically career ending and generate condemnation from the journalistic community.

Getting a Story First

In addition to getting a good story, one of the most valued achievements for a reporter is getting the story first. It is a badge of honor to be a reporter who can *scoop* the competition—that is, uncover and report a story before anyone else. Again, this creates a double-edged sword: It provides motivation for carrying out the necessary and sometimes difficult news-gathering tasks of reporting, but also applies pressure that too often results in poorly researched stories, rampant misinformation, little or no fact-checking, and all-around sloppy reporting.

What's not always clear is how the public is better served by a journalist's claim to have gotten a story first. What *is* clear is that the problems that have always existed because of the pressure to get the story first have intensified with 24/7 cable news channels, the Internet, and competition from bloggers. We discuss this again later in the chapter when we look more closely at how the entire journalism profession is changing and being challenged in the digital era.

Getting a Story "Right"

Although journalists certainly value being the first ones to uncover an interesting story and tell it in a compelling way, it would be a mistake to ignore the importance to professional journalists of getting the facts correct. Traditionally, serious journalists pride themselves on the results of careful news-gathering, ideally using multiple sources to confirm controversial information and allegations made in news stories. From the lessons learned in journalism schools to the awarding of top prizes for reporting, getting accurate information is the gold standard. More than just a professional standard, getting the truth also carries legal responsibilities. Journalists are taught that the best defense against a libel lawsuit is that the report can be shown to be factually true. However, critics are quick to point out that in practice, the gold standard isn't always met. Reasons for this can range from an honest mistake (journalists are human, after all) or deadline and workload pressures preventing adequate fact-checking, to outright lying or omission of important information due to a desire for self-promotion by sources and sometimes journalists themselves. In addition, journalists often face the task of sifting through information provided by public relations practitioners who are paid to make their clients look good to the public. As of 2013, U.S. labor statistics indicated that there were almost five public relations practitioners for every journalist.[11]

Other Values in Journalism

Some sociologists—including Herbert Gans, who studied the newsroom cultures of CBS, NBC, *Newsweek*, and *Time* in the 1970s—generalize that several basic "enduring values" have been shared by most American reporters and editors. These values include ethnocentrism (viewing other cultures through an American "lens"), responsible or benign capitalism (the assumption that the main goal of business is to enhance prosperity for everyone), small-town pastoralism (favoring small, rural communities over big cities), and a major emphasis on individualism and personal stories over the operations of large institutions or organizations.[12] Many of these beliefs are still prevalent in today's more fragmented news culture, though they are undergoing shifts along with the rest of the industry.

- **Ethnocentrism.** By ethnocentrism, Gans means that reporters judge other countries and cultures on the basis of how "they live up to or imitate American practices and values."[13] This remains true of many news outlets, although the ubiquity of the Internet has greatly increased the diversity of news sources available in some countries, making other perspectives more accessible to many Americans.

- **Responsible capitalism.** Another value Gans described as being held by American journalists—responsible capitalism—assumes that the purpose of business is not to maximize profits but "to create increased prosperity for all." Gans points out that although most reporters and editors condemn monopolies, they provide "little implicit or explicit criticism of the oligopolistic nature of much of today's economy."[14] This continues today, complicated by the fact that many news outlets are owned by large, multinational corporations. In the wake of the 2008–09 financial crisis, more news outlets began to report on wrongdoing in the business world, but conflicts of ownership remain.

- **Small-town pastoralism.** Another value that Gans identified was small-town pastoralism, whereby journalists tend to favor the small over the large and the rural over the urban in stories that feature the "goodness" of small-town America. Many journalists continue to frame stories about rustic communities with crime or drug problems—for example, illegal meth labs springing up in isolated rural areas—as country life being contaminated by corrupt big-city values.

- **Individualism.** According to Gans, many reporters have been attracted to the journalism profession because it has tended toward or praised an individualistic, rugged tenacity for confronting and exposing corruption. This value is further revealed in the many news stories that focus on individuals who have overcome personal adversity. Yet such stories neglect to acknowledge or analyze the role of large social organizations and institutions in individual and personal achievements.

When Values Collide: Ethics and the News Media

Up to this point, we have been talking about some of the common practices, values, and goals by which professional journalists tend to define who they are and what they do. As you might already have noticed, these values can sometimes conflict with one another and with the realities of gathering the news (deadlines, shrinking newsroom staffs, bigger demands on limited resources).

Journalists regularly face many such conflicts and ethical dilemmas. For example, they must decide when to protect government secrets and when to reveal those secrets to the public. They must consider whether it is ethically acceptable to use deception or to invade someone's privacy to get information the public deserves to know, and they must guard against accepting gifts or favors in return for producing a news story or presenting a story's subject in a favorable light.

Mark Sagliocco/Getty Images

David Carr covered media and culture for the *New York Times,* among other publications. When writing his addiction memoir, *The Night of the Gun,* Carr treated his own life as he would a news story. He remained at the *Times* until his death from lung cancer in 2015.

Professional Codes of Ethics

So how do journalists decide what to do in these cases? One way is to refer to sets of ethical guidelines produced by professional journalistic groups, like the Society of Professional Journalists (SPJ), the Radio Television Digital News Association (RTDNA, formerly the Radio-Television News Directors Association), and the National Press Photographers Association (NPPA). Although each has a slightly different focus, all three instruct journalists to seek the truth, hold the powerful accountable, maintain integrity, and consider the consequences of each news report, especially on people who appear in the news. Journalism education programs typically contain stand-alone ethics courses or attempt to integrate ethics into other classes—or both. Each newsroom might have its own printed code of ethical guidelines or, more likely, might rely on veteran reporters and editors to pass along to newer journalists what's considered acceptable in that particular news department. It's also worth noting that these printed codes of ethical conduct are not etched in stone. All of these groups review and update their ethics—now more than ever, with the new ethical dilemmas that have come with the Internet and social media.

Applying Ethics and Values Inside the Job

Codes of ethics can be helpful, but they would be impossibly long if they were to cover every possible situation a reporter might find. There are times when parts of a given code will come in conflict with one another. What's more, these dilemmas mostly happen when reporters are facing the crush of deadlines and daily duties. Many times the necessity for making a quick decision means answering these questions in a way that has become established professional practice—that is, the way it has always been done. Although relying on the experience of the individual or the organization can be helpful and save time, it can also undermine careful critical examination of a given situation.

In addition to guidelines designed specifically for the profession, a journalist might also borrow from other philosophical approaches to ethics when confronted with an ethical quandary. Although this isn't intended to be a complete list of those approaches, the next few paragraphs attempt to offer a few useful examples.

The Greek philosopher Aristotle offered an early ethical concept, the "golden mean," as a guideline for seeking balance between competing positions. For Aristotle, the golden mean referred to the desirable middle ground between extreme positions. For example, Aristotle saw ambition as the golden mean between sloth and greed.

Another ethical principle entails the "categorical imperative," developed by German philosopher Immanuel Kant (1724–1804). This idea suggests that a society must adhere to moral codes that are universal and unconditional, applicable in all situations at all times. For example, the ideal to always tell the truth might lead a Kantian to argue that it's never okay to use deception to get a news story.

British philosophers Jeremy Bentham (1748–1832) and John Stuart Mill (1806–1873) promoted a general ethics principle derived from "the greatest good for the greatest number." This principle directs us "to distribute a good consequence to more people rather than to fewer, whenever we have a choice."[15]

Applying Ethics and Values Outside the Job

Although the Internet, bloggers, social media, and partisan cable stations and Web sites have blurred the lines between journalist and nonjournalist, most mainstream news organizations have ethical expectations of their journalists that extend beyond the hours spent on the job. Journalism's code of ethics also warns reporters and editors not to place themselves in positions that create a **conflict of interest**—that is, situations in which journalists may stand to benefit personally from producing a story or from presenting the subject in a certain light. "Journalists should refuse gifts, favors, fees, free travel and special treatment," the code states, "and avoid political and other activities that may compromise integrity or impartiality, or may damage credibility."[16]

Many news outlets attempt to protect journalists from getting into compromising positions. For instance, in most cities, journalists do not actively participate in politics or support social causes. Some journalists will not reveal their political affiliations, and some have even declined to vote. If a journalist has a tie to any organization, and that organization is later suspected of involvement in shady or criminal activity, the reporter's ability to report fairly on the organization will be compromised—along with the credibility of the news outlet for which he or she works. Conversely, other journalists believe that not participating in politics or social causes means abandoning one's civic obligations.

The Economics of Journalism in the Twenty-First Century

Ask almost any veteran reporter to list the challenges facing the profession of journalism, and either at or near the top will be a concern about rapidly shrinking numbers of reporters, editors, and photographers in the newsroom. Although the business models for broadcasters (see Chapters 6 and 8 for more specifics on the radio and TV broadcasting industries) are not quite the same as that for print newsrooms, they do share this common concern: Budget cuts, for whatever reason, mean cuts to newsroom staff. A 2011 Federal Communications Commission report expressed concern that layoffs, cutbacks, and ownership consolidation were leaving too few broadcast reporters to adequately serve as watchdogs over the government and businesses in their local communities. For newspapers, the situation is even more troubling, with full-time U.S. professional newsroom employment down from a peak of 56,900 in 1990 to less than 37,000 in 2014. Almost all of this drop (well over one-third of total newspaper reporters) happened in the seven-year period since the economy began its recession in 2007.[17] Because newspapers are the legacy format for journalism and still represent the lion's share of reporting in most communities, it's important to spend some time in this chapter examining the business side of newspapers and consider what recent developments are doing to the ability of newspapers to fulfill their journalistic missions.

Money In

For most newspapers, the majority of their revenues derive from selling advertising space. For some papers, ads provide the *only* source of revenue. Indeed, the majority of large daily papers devote as much as one-half to two-thirds of their pages to advertisements. What remains after the advertising department places the ads in the paper is called the **newshole**, the space not taken up by ads and devoted to front-page news reports, special regional or topical sections, horoscopes, advice columns, crossword puzzles, and letters to the editor. Newspaper advertising—in print and online—can take forms ranging from expensive full-page spreads for department stores to classifieds, which individual consumers can purchase for a few dollars to sell everything from used cars to furniture to exercise equipment. Of course, one of the biggest problems for print newspapers is that consumers can now place most of these classified ads online free of charge.

The other way newspapers make money is by selling the paper to readers. Readers can buy papers from vending machines, newsstands, or other sources on an individual basis, or subscribe and have every edition of the paper delivered, usually at a somewhat discounted rate.

More and more newspapers are trying to boost income by placing content behind a subscriber-only **paywall**. The *Wall Street Journal* was one of the first major papers to put up a paywall in 1997. Other newspapers and newspaper chains have been experimenting with paywalls, which can be controversial and unpopular with potential readers who are used to getting free content online. To balance this, the *New York Times* and other newspaper operations (like major chain Gannett) have gone to a hybrid model. A person might

The *New York Times* is one of the papers trying to balance the need to generate income with not angering readers who are now accustomed to free content on the Internet. It has a hybrid paywall model in which a user can read up to ten articles a month for free online, after which he or she has to buy a subscription. By the middle of 2014, the *Times* had about 830,000 online subscribers.

Andrew Harrer/Bloomberg via Getty Images

access a limited number of articles for free each month (typically ten to twenty), but access to any more than that or to other premium products (like online newspaper archives) requires a paid subscription.

In addition, news companies are finding ways to cater to readers' increasingly digital lifestyles, developing material for new digital platforms like the touchscreen tablet or smartphone. In some cases, the digital subscription rates are also tailored, depending on the device (and particular app) the reader is going to use.

Money Out

Like any other enterprise, a newspaper has to spend money to fulfill its mission. Its costs include overhead (such as rent and utilities), salaries and wages, marketing and sales, and any investments in wire services or feature syndication required to offer content for readers.

Salaries and Wages

A major expense for most newspapers comes in the form of salaries and wages paid to the various editors and reporters working for the paper, though in the last five to ten years newspapers have shrunk not only their newshole but the size of their reporting staffs. Traditionally, most large papers have a publisher and an owner, an editor in chief and a managing editor in charge of the daily news-gathering and writing processes, and assistant editors and news managers running different news divisions. These key divisions include features, sports, photos, local news, state news, and a wire service containing much of the day's national and international news reports.

Reporters work for editors. *General assignment reporters* handle all sorts of stories that might emerge—or break—in a given day. *Specialty reporters* are assigned to particular beats (police, courts, schools, local and national government) or topics (education, religion, health, environment, technology). On large dailies, *bureau reporters* also file reports from other major cities. In addition, large daily papers feature columnists and critics who cover various aspects of culture, such as books, television, movies, and food. Since 2000, some newspapers have added staff solely responsible for online operations, although newsroom cuts have increasingly led to the shifting of these duties to the remaining reporters and editors.

Wire Services and Feature Syndication

To provide adequate coverage of important events from other places, many newspapers rely on wire services and syndicated feature services to supplement local coverage by their own reporters and writers. A few major dailies, such as the *New York Times*, run their own wire services, selling their stories to other papers to reprint. Other agencies, such as the Associated Press (AP), United Press International (UPI), and Reuters (based in London), have hundreds of staffers stationed throughout major U.S. cities and world capitals. These agencies submit stories, photos, and videos each day for distribution to newspapers, newscasts, and online sites across the country and sometimes internationally.

Daily papers generally pay monthly fees for access to all wire stories. Although they use only a fraction of what's available over the wires, editors carefully monitor wire services each day for important stories and ideas for local angles.

In addition, newspapers may contract with **feature syndicates**, such as Universal uClick (formerly United Features) and Tribune Media Services, to provide work from the nation's best political writers, editorial cartoonists, comic-strip artists, and self-help columnists. These companies serve as brokers, distributing horoscopes and crossword puzzles as well as the columns and comic strips that appeal to a wide audience; however, with the downsizing of newspapers in terms of space, most papers today offer less syndicated content than they did in the 1990s.

Consolidation and a Crash

Although the fundamental elements of the business side of newspapers remain the same, the way the money flows into and out of the paper's coffers and what that has meant for the news has changed dramatically since the early 2000s. Some of these changes are certainly due to convergence with the Internet, but arguably it is the combination of the entry into the digital age with widespread ownership consolidation and the 2007 economic crash that upset the newspaper apple cart.

Newspaper chains—newspapers in different cities owned by the same person or company—have been around since the late 1800s. By the 1980s, more than 130 chains owned an average of nine papers each, with the 12 largest chains accounting for 40 percent of the total circulation in the United States. This trend continued to pick up steam through the end of the twentieth century, and by the early 2000s, the top ten chains controlled over half the nation's total newspaper circulation. Gannett, the nation's largest chain, owns over eighty daily papers and hundreds of nondailies worldwide.

As large media corporations were adding up the numbers of newspapers (and often radio and television stations) they owned, they were also adding up the amount of money they were borrowing to make those purchases. Through the 1990s and the first few years of the 2000s, newspapers typically made enough money to make payments on these *leveraged* purchases. And then the economy started to tank in 2007.

By 2008, the economy was in full recession, and a lot of the major advertisers for high-priced goods like cars cut back their ad spending. By this time newspapers had already lost the revenue from classified ads to free Internet sites like Craigslist. To make matters worse, the decades-long slide in newspaper circulation gathered speed in the 2000s as more and more people canceled subscriptions, in many cases switching to free news sources on the Internet. When newspaper revenues from ads and subscriptions dropped dramatically, large chains went from *leveraged* to *overleveraged*, no longer able to keep up with loan payments. In some cases, this meant filing bankruptcy; in other cases, it meant being forced to sell off newspapers; and in still other cases, it meant shutting down altogether. Although some smaller newspaper owners avoided being overleveraged, they still had to deal with the reality of shrinking revenues. Thus, the industry-wide reaction has been to cut costs by laying off huge numbers of editors, reporters, and photographers, and closing bureaus at state and national capitals.

More than just bad news for the workers who lost their jobs, this trend raises concerns for the communities they are meant to serve. The newspaper industry as a whole lacks competition nationwide, as almost all the cities that once had multiple competing dailies have lost all but one of those daily papers. Critics and journalists worry about the ability of the remaining journalists to meet the information needs of local communities. Additionally, the coverage of national and state politics has dropped precipitously, as bureaus at the national and state capitols were among the first victims of budget cuts.

Changes and Challenges for Journalism in the Information Age

In modern America, journalism's highest role has been to provide information that enables citizens to make intelligent decisions. Today, this guiding principle has been partially derailed. Why? First, the media may be producing too much information through too many communication channels, making it harder to confirm facts and engage in thoughtful discussion about them. Second, the information the media now provide has apparently not improved the quality of public and political life—a core mission of journalism. For example, many people feel disconnected from the stories about the major institutions and political processes that serve as the foundation of democratic society.

Earlier in this chapter (see pages 85–86), we discussed some of the ways in which the Internet has changed how professional journalists do their jobs—many of which are internal in nature. But there are also external changes, happening outside of professional newsrooms, affecting the ways in which audiences consume and understand news—and sometimes even the manner in which journalists are expected to report.

News Aggregation

"Frankly, the *New York Times* is a bore. As are actually most news organizations which continue to write for an older world. I mean, the *New York Times* writes as though one is only reading the *New York Times*."[1]

These fighting words were spoken by Michael Wolff, editorial director of *Adweek* and founder of *Newser*. Like the *Drudge Report* and the *Huffington Post*, *Newser* thrives on a new type of content convergence called *news aggregation*, in which a site packages news summaries, usually providing links to the sources from which it draws (such as online versions of a newspaper, magazine, or wire service). The *Drudge Report* is the oldest and most famous of these sites. With a Web 1.0 look, the *Drudge Report* presents links to news reports, opinion pieces, and blogs with a general conservative

bent. The *Huffington Post* (bought by AOL in 2011), though claiming to be independent, often reverses *Drudge*'s partisanship with a liberal slant. *Newser* steers clear of partisanship, branding itself as "a news curator with a kick."[2] The site reduces the long, "boring" stories from, say, the *New York Times* to summaries with links to the original reports, intended to be readable in a variety of formats: desktop, laptop, or mobile device.

In recent years, news aggregators have come under public attack for promoting a form of journalism that only takes and gives nothing back. In September 2009, media entrepreneur Mark Cuban took aim at *Newser*, declaring that major media companies should use software that blocks links, thus preventing hyperlink access to the offending sites.[3] Wolff's response, "Mark Cuban Is a Big Fat Idiot—News Will Stay Free," claimed *Newser* should be thanked, not condemned, because some readers click through to the original stories.[4]

A year later, it was Arianna Huffington's turn to deflect the barbs of an "old news" representative. In a lecture, former executive editor of the *Washington Post* Len Downie named the *Huffington Post* as an example of a news media "parasite," condemning news aggregation as thievery.[5] Huffington dismissed his concerns: "Once again, some in the old media have decided that the best way to save, if not journalism, at least themselves, is by pointing fingers and calling names."[6]

As the name-calling feuds suggest, media convergence often arouses passion and arrogance on both sides of the new/old media divide. But we don't have to pick sides to recognize the paradox of Wolff's declaration that the "news will stay free."

LaunchPad

macmillanhighered.com/mediaessentials3e

▶ **Visit LaunchPad** to watch a clip of Arianna Huffington. How does she represent a different personality in media ownership?

Despite his argument that he provides a service to his hosts, Wolff doesn't pay any newsroom salaries. As such, it's possible that news aggregation could help hasten the demise of businesses that do actually pay reporters—after all, if there's no one to report and write up the news, there will be nothing for the aggregators to aggregate. Clearly, audiences are seeking new forms of journalism, and many media companies are working to find a model that makes financial sense. What's not yet clear is where this process will leave organizations like *Newser*—or their audiences.

Social Media

One of the fastest-growing areas of research among those who study journalism has been trying to determine what the rise of social media sites (Facebook, Twitter, Instagram) means to journalism and journalists. Although it's simply too soon to know what all of the changes will mean long term, it is possible to make a few observations.

First of all, the vast majority of news operations use social media to promote their work, hoping readers will share articles and stories. Often, journalists, reporters, anchors, and editors are required to have social media accounts for use as part of their reporting duties (some have separate accounts for just friends and family), from sharing work to finding sources for stories. Some media organizations have also created social media policies to act as ethical guidelines in the digital context.

Social media is also changing the way some people consume the news. For example, a person on Facebook might get a combination of news from dozens of sources based on what friends share or post as well as on what is posted by the news outlets they follow. And those sources aren't limited to whatever lineup might appear on the local airwaves or cable.

Another way consuming news on social media is different is the immediacy and variety of sources in a breaking-news event. For example, a person on Twitter the night of the first demonstrations in Ferguson, Missouri, in August 2014 might have been able to watch the events unfold in 140-character tweets, pictures, and video several hours before even the 24-hour cable news channels started covering the events. In addition, by tweeting and retweeting from their feeds, news consumers became conduits for—and often commentators on—information on those same events. At the same time, that immediacy also removes the chance for fact-checking and other benefits that come from thorough reporting.

Blogs

What began in the late 1990s and early 2000s as amateur, sideline journalism has become a major source of news—one that has begun calling papers' authority into question. Widely read blogs like *Daily Kos*, the *Huffington Post*, Andrew Sullivan's the *Dish*, the *Drudge Report*, *Talking Points Memo*, and *Politico* have moved this Internet feature into the realm of traditional journalism. In fact, many reporters now write a blog in addition to their regular newspaper, television, or radio work. And some big-name newspapers, such as the *Washington Post* and the *New York Times*, even hire journalists to blog exclusively for their Web sites.

As discussed earlier, getting the story first is an important news value that can pressure journalists to cut corners on their ethical judgment. But in many cases the race used to be only against other journalists who might be expected to adhere to similar standards of reporting. Now it's also against bloggers who aren't required to check their sources rigorously. A blogger merely has to post his or her opinion about an issue or an event, yet many readers swallow this content whether or not it has been backed by rigorous reporting practices. On the other hand, some blogs have won respect as viable information sources. In 2008, the *Talking Points Memo* blog, headed by Joshua Micah Marshall, won a George Polk Award for legal reporting. Today, some blog sites stand alongside printed papers as trusted, authoritative sources of news (see "Converging Media Case Study: News Aggregation" on pages 100–101).

Koni Takahashi/Bloomberg via Getty Images

The *Huffington Post*, a news blog founded in 2005, offers original content as well as aggregated headlines.

One way technology has allowed citizens to become involved in the reporting of news is through cell phone photos and videos. Witnesses can now pass on what they have captured to mainstream news sources.

Citizen Journalism

Another development influencing the field is **citizen journalism**, also known as *public journalism* or *community journalism*. Through citizen journalism, people who are not professional journalists—such as activists concerned about a specific issue—use the Internet and blog sites to disseminate information and opinions about their favorite issues. With steep declines in newsroom staffs, numerous news media organizations—like CNN (iReport) and many regional newspapers—are increasingly drawing on citizen journalists' work to make up for the loss of professional journalists through newsroom downsizing. Some community journalism efforts also attempt to bring members of the public and journalists together in meetings and panel discussions.

But the citizen journalism efforts have generated criticism. Editors and reporters argue that public journalism was co-opted by the marketing department, blurring the

Ahmad Gharabli/AFP/Getty Images

lines between the editorial and business functions of a news organization. Some journalists fear this turns them from community watchdogs into community boosters. There is also a fear that over-utilization of members of the public who lack the education, training, and experience of professional journalists results in a news product that ultimately undermines the news organization's credibility.

The Echo Chamber

The "echo chamber" refers to the idea that as cable news channels, Web sites, and other media consciously cater to the ideological and political viewpoints of a portion of society, those people will seek out only those sources with which they agree and avoid any news that might challenge their worldview. For example, a very conservative person might only watch Fox News on TV, listen to Rush Limbaugh on the radio, and visit Breitbart.com and the *Drudge Report* online. A more left-leaning person might only watch MSNBC on TV and read online news from a source like *Daily Kos*.

One problem with this approach is that the information from these sources might not just be biased toward a particular worldview; in fact, researchers are increasingly discovering that information from these sources is inaccurate and wrong at a much higher rate than that from other sources, like CNN, National Public Radio, or the *New York Times*. Several attempts have been made to determine which of these networks are the most—and least—accurate. One such study in 2012 found that viewers of Fox News are the least informed (in some studies, even less informed than people who don't watch any news).[18] The same study found that listeners to NPR scored the best on questions of national and international news. A more recent effort by fact-checking site PolitiFact.com attempted to rate the truthfulness of fact claims made by pundits and on-air personalities for TV networks. On the scorecard released in 2014, only 18 percent of claims made on CNN got rated mostly false, false, or "pants on fire"; for Fox and FoxNews Channel, that number jumps to 60 percent.[19]

The full implications of these findings become clearer when one realizes that according to television ratings agency Nielsen, Fox News has been the most watched cable news network for over a decade. Not only does that call into question the core reason for journalism in a democracy—to inform the public, who will then make public policy decisions based on that information—but it also creates pressure on other networks eager to capture higher ratings (and more ad dollars) to copy the approach of the Rupert Murdoch–owned Fox News.[20]

"Fake" News and Satiric Journalism

It comes as little surprise to most long-term observers of American journalism that a source like National Public Radio would be at the top of a list of reliable news sources. But one of the more surprising results of the 2012 study—and a

2007 study by the Pew Research Center's Project for Excellence in Journalism—is that one of the other best-informed audiences was the group that got its news from *The Daily Show with Jon Stewart*.

Following in the tradition of *Saturday Night Live*, which began satirizing television news as a regular part of its program in 1975, shows like *The Daily Show* and spin-off *The Colbert Report* found success using humor to criticize news conventions and the political system.

The Daily Show uses a combination of monologue, reports from comedians acting as correspondents, and interviews (occasionally even with past and present U.S. presidents). As news court jester, Stewart displays more amazement, irony, outrage, laughter, and skepticism than would be acceptable for a real news anchor. Stewart has repeatedly rejected the label of journalist, often reminding people that he is a comedian. But he does often provide audiences with informative and insightful looks at current events, issues, and figures in the news. He regularly exposes hypocrisy by juxtaposing what a politician or pundit said recently in the news with the opposite position articulated by the same politician months or years earlier. In late 2014, Colbert ended his show after eleven seasons, and Comedy Central replaced *The Colbert Report* with *The Nightly Show* hosted by comedian Larry Wilmore. In early 2015, Stewart announced he would be stepping down after sixteen years at the anchor desk, and the network named South African comic Trevor Noah to take his place.

Another *Daily Show* alum, John Oliver, has also branched off and created a show on HBO called *Last Week Tonight*. Clearly related to the satirical and humorous take on the news that is the hallmark of *The Daily Show*, Oliver's program changes the formula a bit to allow for longer, more detailed, and well-researched reports on institutions and issues, often relying on the inherent and unadorned ridiculousness of those involved to deliver the punch line. This approach is already making waves. For example, after one episode on which Oliver called for people to comment on the Federal Communications Commission's Web site in favor of net neutrality, the response was so overwhelming it crashed the FCC Web site. If *The Daily Show* is the satirical version of the nightly news, then Oliver's program might be thought of as the *60 Minutes* of the genre.

Eric Liebowitz/© HBO/Everett Collection

Satirical news has become something of a cottage industry in recent years, stemming from *Saturday Night Live*'s Weekend Update segment and dominated by *The Daily Show*. *Last Week Tonight*—a fake-news program on HBO hosted by former *Daily Show* "correspondent" John Oliver—isn't especially "fake": It mixes satirical commentary with real reporting and advocacy.

Journalism in a Democratic Society

Journalism is central to democracy: Both citizens and the media must have access to the information needed to make important decisions. Conventional journalists will fight ferociously for the principles that underpin journalism's basic tenets—questioning the government, freedom of the press, the public's right to know, and two sides to every story. These are mostly worthy ideals, but they do have limitations. For example, they do not generally acknowledge any moral or ethical duty for journalists to improve the quality of daily life. Rather, conventional journalism values its news-gathering capabilities and the well-constructed news narrative, leaving the improvement of civic life to political groups, nonprofit organizations, business philanthropists, individual citizens, and practitioners of Internet activism.

Social Responsibility

Although reporters have traditionally thought of themselves first and foremost as observers and recorders, some journalists have acknowledged a social responsibility. Among them was James Agee in the 1930s. In his book *Let Us Now Praise Famous Men*, which was accompanied by the Depression-era photography of Walker Evans, Agee regarded conventional journalism as dishonest, partly because the act of observing intruded on people and turned them into story characters that newspapers and magazines exploited for profit.

Agee also worried that readers would retreat into the comfort of his writing—his narrative—instead of confronting what for many families was the horror of the Great Depression. For Agee, the question of responsibility extended not only to journalism and to himself but to the readers of his stories as well.

Deliberative Democracy

According to advocates of public journalism, when reporters are chiefly concerned with maintaining their antagonistic relationship to politics and are less willing to improve political discourse, news and democracy suffer. *Washington Post* columnist David Broder thinks that national journalists like him—through rising salaries, prestige, and formal education—have distanced themselves "from the people that we are writing for and have become much, much closer to people we are writing about."[21] Broder believes that journalists need to become activists, not for a particular party but for the political process and in the interest of reenergizing public life. For those who advocate for public journalism, this might also involve mainstream media spearheading voter registration drives or setting up pressrooms or news bureaus in public libraries or shopping malls, where people converge in large numbers.

Public journalism offers people models for how to deliberate in forums, and then covers those deliberations. This kind of community journalism aims to re-invigorate a *deliberative democracy,* in which citizen groups, local government, and the news media work together more actively to shape social, economic, and political agendas. In a more deliberative democracy, a large segment of the community discusses public life and social policy before advising or electing officials who represent the community's interests.

The Troubled Future of Journalism and Journalism's First Home

While pondering the future of the newspaper—and of our democracy—we must recognize that a free press isn't free, nor is its survival certain.

As newsroom cutbacks accelerate; as state, national, and foreign bureaus close down; and as industry consolidation continues apace, we must ask ourselves where we will get the thorough reporting we need to make informed choices and present well-considered viewpoints—two hallmarks of a vibrant democracy. A host of current developments in print journalism undermine the newspaper's role as a bulwark of democracy. Many cities now have just one newspaper, which tends to cover only issues and events of interest to middle- and upper-middle-class read-ers. The experiences and events affecting poorer and working-class citizens get short shrift, and with the rise of newspaper chains, the chances that mainstream daily papers will publish a diversity of opinions, ideas, and information will likely decrease. Moreover, chain ownership—often concerned first about the bottom line and saving money—has tended to discourage watchdog journalism, the most expensive type of reporting. This means that we, as citizens, must remain ever mindful of our news sources and consider the motivations and interests concealed behind the news we're receiving and ask ourselves why we're receiving it.

As news increasingly reaches us through a wide range of digital distribution channels, print journalism is losing readers and advertisers and may eventually cease to exist. Editor John Carroll described the situation in no uncertain terms. Having presided over thirteen Pulitzer Prize–winning reports at the *Los Angeles Times* as editor from 2000 to 2005, Carroll left the paper to protest deep cor-porate cuts to the newsroom. He lamented the apparently imminent demise of newspapers, proclaiming: "Newspapers are doing the reporting in this country. Google and Yahoo! and those people aren't putting reporters on the street in any numbers at all. Blogs can't afford it. Network television is taking reporters off the street. . . . Newspapers are the last ones standing, and newspapers are threatened. . . . Reporting is absolutely an essential thing for democratic self-government. Who's going to do it? Who's going to pay for the news? If news-papers fall by the wayside, what will we know?"[22]

CHAPTER ESSENTIALS

Now that you have finished reading this chapter, you can use the following tools:

LaunchPad for *Media Essentials*

Go to **macmillanhighered.com/mediaessentials3e** for videos, review quizzes, and more.

LaunchPad for *Media Essentials* includes:

- **REVIEW WITH LEARNINGCURVE**
  LearningCurve uses gamelike quizzing to help you master the concepts you need to learn from this chapter.

- **VIDEO: THE OBJECTIVITY MYTH**
  Pulitzer Prize–winning journalist Clarence Page and *Onion* editor Joe Randazzo explore how objectivity began in journalism and how reporter biases may nonetheless influence news stories.

REVIEW

Explain Major Developments in Newspapers' Early History

- The social impact of **news**—the process by which people gather information and create narrative reports to make sense of events surrounding them—accelerated with the invention of the printing press, leading to the creation of the first colonial newspapers. Known as the **partisan press**, these papers critiqued government, spread the views of different political parties, and offered commercial information to businessmen (pp. 71–73).

- Paper and production advances made during the Industrial Revolution as well as a rising middle class set the stage for a more inclusive press, leading to the creation of **penny papers**— priced at an affordable one cent—which enabled papers to become a mass medium (pp. 73–74).

- The proliferation of penny papers caused many papers to begin accepting ads, which further expanded the industry and led six New York newspapers in 1848 to form the Associated Press, the first news **wire service**—a commercial and cooperative organization that relayed news stories and information around the country and the world using telegraph lines (pp. 75–76).

- In the late 1800s, a new brand of papers arose, ushering in an era of **yellow journalism**, which emphasized sensational stories and also laid the foundation for investigative journalism (pp. 76–78).

Track the Evolution of Modern Professional Journalism

- In the late 1800s, as readership expanded nationwide, many papers, such as the *New York Times*, began presenting so-called **objective journalism**, or factual, balanced coverage, via the **inverted-pyramid style**—a story form that packaged and presented reports based on answering who, what, when, and where (pp. 76, 78–79).

- As newspapers in the early twentieth century started moving toward the objective journalism model, universities started offering advanced journalism degrees, transforming journalism from a trade into a profession with values and established practices (p. 79).

- Amid the complex national and global events of the early 1900s, **interpretive journalism** grew out of the public's need to put events and issues in context, becoming more widespread in the 1950s and 1960s (p. 80).

- First with radio, and later with television, the culture of journalism grew from the printed page of newspapers and magazines to the airwaves, and later to the Internet. This brought a new speed to reporting, while also bringing new logistical and ethical dilemmas to journalism (pp. 85–86).

Journalism Evolves across Media

- As radio, television, and later the Internet entered the scene, the practice of journalism moved into each new realm, drawing upon and adapting earlier approaches (pp. 80–81).

- The coverage of Civil Right Movement in the 1960s, with the way televised news documented the plight of Southern blacks in evocative moving images, demonstrated the power of this visual medium to connect with audiences in new ways (pp. 81, 84).

- The rise of cable news in the 1980s amplified the need for a steady stream of content and led to major changes in what is considered news, with a growing reliance on "talking head" hosts and pundits (pp. 84–85).

Understand the Culture and Rituals of Reporting

- We define **news** as the process of gathering information and making reports that use a narrative framework. A key part of a journalist's job is determining what information is **newsworthy**—that is, what merits transformation into news stories (pp. 87–88).

- A number of values define the practice of American journalism. These include neutrality (which leads to greater credibility); newsroom diversity; the drive to get a good story, to get the story first, and to get the story right. In addition to professional standards, scholars have found a number of underlying values that influence journalists and the news, including **ethnocentrism** (which involves judging other countries and cultures according to how they live up to or imitate American practices and ideals), **responsible capitalism** (which assumes that businesspeople compete with one another to increase prosperity for all), **small-town pastoralism** (which causes journalists to favor the small over the large and the rural over the urban), and **individualism**

(which favors individual rights and responsibilities over group needs or institutional mandates) (pp. 88–93).

- Journalists face a variety of ethical dilemmas. For example, they must decide whether or not to use deception to gain information or whether to invade someone's privacy, all the while trying to avoid situations that present **conflicts of interest** or situations in which they may benefit personally. In an effort to resolve these dilemmas, journalists have developed guidelines based on ethical principles (pp. 93–95).

Discuss the Economics behind Journalism in the Twenty-First Century

- Whether traditional broadcast, cable, or print news, one all-too-common characteristic is that newsrooms are shrinking due to budget cuts and layoffs (pp. 95–96).

- The majority of newspapers' revenue comes from selling advertising space, which can take up as much as one-half to two-thirds of large newspapers' pages. The **newshole**,

which has shrunk in most newspapers today, refers to the space left over for news content after all the ads are placed (p. 96).

- Several news sites have switched to some form of a **paywall** system, which requires users to pay either to access news reports or to access more than a set number of articles per month (pp. 96–97).

Consider the Challenges Facing Journalism in the Information Age

- Journalists are trying to adjust to a rapidly changing news experience as they work in shrinking newsrooms and compete with,

or adapt to, social media, blogs, citizen journalism, and an ever-more-polarized political sphere (pp. 99, 102–105).

Explore How Newspapers' Existing Challenges Pose a Threat to Sustaining a Democratic Society

- As the fate of print journalism is called into question, we must ask ourselves where we will get the best information, based on strong reporting, that we need to make informed choices and receive multiple points of view (pp. 106–107).

STUDY QUESTIONS

1. How did newspapers emerge as a mass medium during the penny press era? How did content changes make this happen?
2. What different forms of journalism developed? What are their characteristics? What are their strengths and limitations?
3. What are some of the differences between the practices of print and broadcast journalism? How might the changes to journalism as it entered the broadcasting age be similar or different to the changes currently happening to journalism in the Information Age?
4. Describe and discuss some of the business challenges faced by newspapers today.
5. How might the "echo chamber" and "fake" news be changing the way the public views, and uses, the news?
6. What is journalism's role in a democracy?

MEDIA LITERACY PRACTICE

The toughest issue facing newspapers today is their survival—whether in print or online or both. To investigate this economic and social problem, consider a newspaper in your community.

DESCRIBE the current financial situation of your local newspaper, including its circulation and advertisers, and the online version of the paper. Ask others to comment on the current problems facing newspapers.

ANALYZE trends and patterns in the data. What problems are noted most often? What do people seem to like or dislike about your local paper? What are the main points people make about your local paper and its online edition?

INTERPRET what these patterns mean. For example, who is being best served by the newspaper in your community? Are there people in your community who are not served well by the newspaper?

EVALUATE what you have discovered. Which criticisms and ideas are good or bad, and why?

ENGAGE with your community on your findings. What problems and solutions are noted most often? What new business models are suggested? Brainstorm with the people you have been talking to about two or three specific ideas for improving the news in your community.

4

Magazines in the Age of Specialization

Considering that since the 1960s *Cosmopolitan* has been effectively marketing itself to single women ages eighteen to thirty-four, it shouldn't be surprising that even in the digital age, the publication is one of the most popular magazines among undergraduate college women. What might be surprising is that a college student reading today's *Cosmopolitan*, currently famous for revealing cover photographs and headlines like "67 New Sex Tricks," might have a subscription to the same magazine that her great-great-great grandmother subscribed to. Of course, other than the title, these two magazines don't have much in common.

The 1886 version of *Cosmopolitan* was also targeted at women—but more often married women, with articles on cooking, child care, and household decoration. When it did feature fashion, it was of the high-collared Victorian-era variety.[1] The magazine struggled until it was rescued by journalist and entrepreneur John Brisben Walker, who turned it into an illustrated literary and journalistic magazine.

The magazine grew in prestige and earnings until it was sold at a profit in 1905 to competitor and powerful newspaper publisher William Randolph Hearst. The new owner turned *Cosmopolitan* into a muckraking magazine

Chester Higgins Jr./The New York Times/Redux Pictures

113

focused on digging up dirt against big business and corrupt politicians. Although this work didn't boost Hearst's political ambitions in the way that he'd hoped, it did help the magazine continue to grow and thrive. Despite this success, the magazine continued to change alongside the tastes of its readership. After 1912, *Cosmopolitan* returned to its literary past, featuring short stories and serialized novels largely targeted toward a female audience. This worked for a while, but by the 1960s, this format seemed dated and was losing interest among subscribers.

In 1965, the Hearst Corporation hired Helen Gurley Brown, who had recently written the best-selling book *Sex and the Single Girl*. Brown modeled the magazine on the book's vision of strong, sexually liberated women. The new *Cosmopolitan*, following this fifth makeover, helped spark a sexual revolution and was marketed to the "Cosmo Girl": women ages eighteen to thirty-four with an interest in love, sex, fashion, and their careers.[2]

Brown's vision of *Cosmo* lives on in the magazine's "fun, fearless female" slogan. Today, it's the top-selling women's fashion magazine—surpassing competitors like *Glamour*, *InStyle*, and *Vogue*. It also maintains a popular Web site and a mobile version for reading on smartphones. *Cosmopolitan*'s ability to reinvent itself repeatedly over the last 129 years testifies to the remarkable power of magazines as a mass medium to both adapt to and shape American society and culture.

SINCE THE 1740s, magazines have played a key role in America, becoming a national mass medium even before newspapers, which at the time were mainly local and regional in scope. Magazines provided venues for political leaders and thinkers to offer their views on the broad issues and events of the day, including public education, abolition, women's suffrage, and the Civil War. Many leading literary figures also used magazines to gain public exposure for their essays or stories. Readers consumed the articles and fictional accounts offered in magazines, and snapped up the products and services advertised in each issue, hastening the rise of a consumer society. As consumerism grew, magazines themselves changed, with the most popular titles often focusing less on news and essays, and more on fashion, celebrities, advice, and entertainment.

Today, more than twenty thousand magazines are published in the United States annually. And just like newspapers, radio, movies, and television, these magazines—including *Cosmopolitan*—both reflect and create what's going on in American life.

In this chapter, we track the shifting role of magazines in the United States by:

- tracing the early history of magazines, including their highly politicized purpose in colonial and early America and their transformation into the country's first national medium

- examining turning points in the evolution of modern American magazines, such as the emergence of muckraking as a magazine-reporting style and the rise and fall of general-interest magazines

- taking stock of the many types of magazines specialized for particular audiences (including men, women, sports fans, young people, and minorities)

- discovering how magazines operate economically, including how they make money and what they spend money on to fulfill their mission and surmount challenges

- considering how magazines today are affecting the health of our democratic society

The Early History of Magazines

Magazines have changed extensively during their journey to mass medium status. They started out in Europe as infrequently published periodicals that looked like newspapers and contained mostly political commentary. They caught on slowly in colonial America and served mostly as vehicles for politicians (such as John Adams and Thomas Jefferson) and thinkers (including Thomas Paine) to convey their views. It wasn't until the nineteenth century that magazines really took off in America. During the 1800s, magazines took the form of specialized and general-interest periodicals that appealed to an increasingly literate populace, that could be published quickly through improved printing technologies, and that boasted arresting illustrations.

Today, the word **magazine** broadly refers to any collection of articles, stories, and advertisements published on a nondaily cycle (such as weekly or monthly) in the smaller tabloid style rather than the larger broadsheet newspaper style.

The First Magazines: European Origins

The first magazines appeared in seventeenth-century France in the form of bookseller catalogues and notices that book publishers inserted in newspapers. (In fact, the word *magazine* derives from the French term *magasin*, meaning "storehouse.") In Europe, magazines then became channels for political commentary and argument. They looked like newspapers of the time, but they were published less frequently. The first political magazine, called the *Review*, appeared in London in 1704 and was printed sporadically until 1713.

Regularly published magazines or pamphlets, such as the *Tatler* and the *Spectator*, also appeared in England around this time. Offering poetry, politics, and philosophy for London's elite, they served small readerships of a few thousand. The first publication to use the term *magazine* was *Gentleman's Magazine*, which appeared in London in 1731 and consisted of articles reprinted from newspapers, books, and political pamphlets.

Magazines in Eighteenth-Century America: The Voices of Revolution

Without a substantial middle class, widespread literacy, or advanced printing technology, magazines took root slowly in America. Like the partisan newspapers of the time, colonial magazines served politicians, the educated, and the merchant class. However, they also served the wider purpose of conveying colonial leaders' thoughts about the big questions percolating during the era—such as how taxation should work, how much self-rule the colonies should have, how Indians

---

CHAPTER 4 // TIMELINE

1741 Colonial Magazines
First appearing in Philadelphia and Boston, these magazines mainly reprinted material from London newspapers.

1821 National Magazines
The *Saturday Evening Post* is launched, becoming the first major magazine to appeal directly to women and the longest-running magazine in U.S. history.

1850s Engravings and Illustrations
Drawings, woodcuts, and other forms of illustration begin to fill the pages of magazines.

1879 Postal Act of 1879
Both postal rates and rail transportation costs plummet, allowing magazine distribution to thrive.

should be treated, and who should have access to public education. Magazines thus gave voice to the people who ultimately decided to break away from England and create a new, independent nation.

The first colonial magazines appeared in Philadelphia in 1741, about fifty years after the earliest newspapers. Andrew Bradford started it all with *American Magazine, or A Monthly View of the Political State of the British Colonies*. Three days later, Benjamin Franklin launched his *General Magazine, and Historical Chronicle*.

Though neither of these experiments was successful, they inspired other publishers to launch magazines in the remaining colonies, beginning in Boston in the 1740s. The most successful of these periodicals simply reprinted articles from leading London newspapers to keep readers abreast of European events.

Magazines in Nineteenth-Century America: Specialization and General Interest

As the nineteenth century dawned, the magazine industry remained somewhat unstable in the newly created United States. During 1800–1825, about five hundred such periodicals had cropped up and then withered. However, as the century progressed, the idea of specialized magazines devoted to certain categories of readers gained momentum—leading to the creation of religious magazines, literary periodicals publishing the works of important writers of the day, and magazines devoted to professions such as law and medicine.

The nineteenth century also saw the birth of the first general-interest magazine aimed at a large national audience: the *Saturday Evening Post*, launched in 1821. Like most magazines of the day, the early *Post* included a few original essays but reprinted many pieces from other sources. Eventually, however, the *Post* grew to incorporate news, poetry, essays, play reviews, and the writings of

Library of Congress

The first issue of Benjamin Franklin's *General Magazine, and Historical Chronicle* appeared in 1741. Although it lasted only six months, Franklin found success in other publications, like his annual *Poor Richard's Almanack*, starting in 1732 and lasting twenty-five years.

Early 1900s Muckraking Magazines
McClure's, Collier's, Ladies' Home Journal, and *Cosmopolitan* push progressive social reforms with their investigative reports.

1903 *Ladies' Home Journal*
The magazine reaches a circulation of one million.

1922 *Reader's Digest*
The pocket-size monthly will become the nation's most popular magazine by 1946.

1923 *Time*
Time is launched and develops a new brand of journalism, in which stories are written in narrative form, with greater reliance on the reporters' interpretations of events.

North Wind Picture Archives

Colorful illustrations first became popular in the fashion sections of women's magazines in the mid-1800s. The color for this fashion image from Godey's *was added to the illustration by hand.*

popular authors such as Nathaniel Hawthorne and Harriet Beecher Stowe.

The *Post* was also the first major magazine to appeal directly to women through its "Lady's Friend" advice column. This new device may have served as an inspiration; in 1828, Sarah Josepha Hale started the first magazine directed exclusively to a female audience: *Ladies' Magazine*. In addition to general-interest pieces, such as essays and criticism, the periodical advocated for women's education, work, and property rights. Other women's magazines—including the hugely successful *Godey's Lady's Book*—would soon follow.

Going National as the Twentieth Century Approaches

Thanks to increases in literacy and public education, the development of faster printing technologies, and improvements in mail delivery (through rail transportation), demand for national (versus local) magazines soared. Whereas in 1825 a mere one hundred magazines struggled for survival, by 1850 nearly six hundred magazines were being published regularly, many of them with national readerships. Magazines were on their way to becoming a mass medium. Significant national magazines of this era included *Graham's Magazine* (1840–1858), *Knickerbocker* (1833–1864), the *Nation* (1865–present), and *Youth's Companion* (1826–1929).

The advent of illustration further moved magazines toward mass medium status. By the mid-1850s, drawings, engravings, woodcuts, and other forms of illustration had become a major feature of magazines and greatly heightened their appeal for readers. During the 1890s, magazines (and newspapers) also began

CHAPTER 4 // TIMELINE continued

1936 *Life*
Life is launched and pioneers fashion spreads and advances in photojournalism.

1953 *TV Guide*
TV Guide becomes an overnight success as a niche publication.

1965 *Cosmopolitan*
Editor Helen Gurley Brown turns *Cosmopolitan* into a leading magazine by targeting women ages eighteen to thirty-four with an interest in love, sex, fashion, and careers.

1969–1972 Shutdowns
The *Saturday Evening Post*, *Look*, and *Life* shut down; competition from television is a chief factor.

including photographs with printed articles, helping to launch an entirely new profession: photojournalism.

The Evolution of Modern American Magazines

As the sun set on the nineteenth century, decreases in postage costs made it cheaper for publishers to distribute magazines, and improvements in production technologies lowered the costs of printing them. Now accessible and affordable to ever-larger audiences, magazines became a true mass medium. They also began reflecting the social, demographic, and technological changes unfolding within the nation as the twentieth century progressed. For example, a new interest in social reform sparked the rise of muckraking, or investigative journalism designed to expose wrongdoing. The growth of the middle class initially heightened receptivity to general-interest magazines aimed at broad audiences, but then television's rising popularity put many general-interest magazines out of business. Some magazines struck back by focusing their content on topics not covered by TV programmers and by featuring short articles heavily illustrated with photos.

Distribution and Production Costs Plummet

In 1870, about twelve hundred magazines were being produced in the United States; by 1890, that number had reached forty-five hundred. By 1905, the nation boasted more than six thousand magazines. Part of this surge in titles and readership was facilitated by the Postal Act of 1879, which assigned magazines lower postage rates—putting them on an equal footing with newspapers delivered by mail.

1974 *People*
The first successful mass market magazine in decades is published.

1998 *ESPN The Magazine*
The magazine launches, successfully capitalizing on the growing ESPN sports media empire.

2009 Recession
The economic recession leads to the closing of several leading magazines, including *Country Home*, *Domino*, *Nickelodeon Magazine*, *Gourmet*, *Modern Bride*, *Portfolio*, *Teen*, *Vibe*, and *Blender*.

2014 *AARP Bulletin* and *AARP The Magazine*
These subscription-only publications continue to boast the highest circulations of any magazines in the United States.

This vastly reduced distribution costs. Meanwhile, advances in mass-production printing, conveyor systems, assembly lines, and printing press speeds lowered production costs and made large-circulation national magazines possible.

This combination of reduced distribution and production costs enabled publishers to slash magazine prices. As prices dropped from thirty-five cents to fifteen and then to ten cents, people of modest means began subscribing to national publications. Magazine circulation skyrocketed, attracting new waves of advertising revenues. Even though publishers had dropped the price of an issue below the actual cost to produce a single copy, they recouped the loss through ad revenue—guaranteeing large readerships to advertisers eager to reach more customers. By the turn of the twentieth century, advertisers increasingly used national magazines to capture consumers' attention and build a national marketplace.

Muckrakers Expose Social Ills

The rise in magazine circulation coincided with major changes in American society in the early 1900s. Americans were moving from the country to the city in search of industrial jobs, and millions were immigrating to the United States hoping for new opportunities. Many newspaper reporters interested in writing about these and other social changes turned to magazines, for which they could write longer, more analytical pieces on such topics as corruption in big business and government, urban problems faced by immigrants, labor conflicts, and race relations. Some of these writers built their careers on crusading for social reform on behalf of the public good—often criticizing long-standing American institutions.

In 1906, President Theodore Roosevelt dubbed these investigative reporters **muckrakers**, because they were willing to crawl through society's muck to uncover a story. Although Roosevelt wasn't always a fan, muckraking journalism led to some much-needed reforms. For example, influenced in part by exposés at *Ladies' Home Journal* and *Collier's* magazines, Congress in 1906 passed the Pure Food and Drug Act and the Meat Inspection Act. Reports in *Cosmopolitan*, *McClure's*, and other magazines led to laws calling for increased government oversight of business, a progressive income tax, and the direct election of U.S. senators.

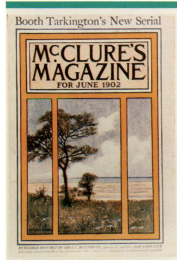

Muckraking magazines like *McClure's* were the first to publish investigative stories on American institutions.

Booth Tarkington's serial "The Two Vanrevels" enhances the value of this issue of "McClure's Magazine."

The New York Public Library/Art Resource, NY

General-Interest Magazines Hit Their Stride

The heyday of the muckraking era lasted into the mid-1910s, when America was drawn into World War I. During the next few decades and even through the 1950s, **general-interest magazines** gained further prominence. These publications covered a wide variety of topics aimed at a broad national audience—such as recent developments in government, medicine, or society. A key aspect of these magazines was **photojournalism**—the use of photographs to augment editorial content (see "Media Literacy Case Study: The Evolution of Photojournalism" on pages 124–125). High-quality photos gave general-interest magazines a visual advantage over radio, which was the most popular medium of the day. In 1920, about fifty-five magazines fit the general-interest category; by 1946, more than a hundred such magazines competed with radio networks for the national audience. Four giants dominated this magazine genre: the *Saturday Evening Post*, *Reader's Digest*, *Time*, and *Life*.

Saturday Evening Post

Although the *Post* had been around since 1821, it didn't become the first widely popular general-interest magazine until 1897. The *Post* printed popular fiction and romanticized American virtues through words and pictures. During the 1920s, it also featured articles celebrating the business boom of the decade. This reversed the journalistic direction of the muckraking era, in which magazines focused on exposing corruption in business. By the 1920s, the *Post* had reached two million in circulation, the first magazine to hit that mark.

Reader's Digest

Reader's Digest championed one of the earliest functions of magazines: printing condensed versions of selected articles from other magazines. With its inexpensive production costs, low price, and popular pocket-size format, the magazine saw its circulation climb to more than one million even during the depths of the Great Depression. By 1946, it was the nation's most popular magazine. By the mid-1980s, it was the most popular magazine in the world.

Margaret Bourke-White was a photojournalist of many firsts: first female photographer for *Life* magazine, first Western photographer allowed into the Soviet Union, first person to shoot the cover photo for *Life*, and first female war correspondent. Bourke-White was well known for her photos of World War II, including pictures of Nazi concentration camps.

Time

During the general-interest era, national newsmagazines such as *Time* also scored major commercial successes. Begun in 1923, *Time* developed a magazine brand of interpretive journalism, assigning reporter-researcher teams to cover newsworthy events, after which a rewrite editor would shape the teams' findings into articles presenting a point of view on the events covered. Newsmagazines took over photojournalism's role in news reporting, visually documenting both national and international events. Today, *Time*'s circulation stands at about 2.6 million.

Life

More than any other magazine of its day, *Life*, an oversized pictorial weekly, struck back at radio's popularity by advancing photojournalism. Launched in 1936, *Life* satisfied the public's fascination with

Margaret Bourke-White/Getty Images

images (invigorated by the movie industry) by featuring extensive photo spreads with its researched articles, lavish advertisements, and even fashion photography. By the end of the 1930s, *Life* had a **pass-along readership**—the total number of people who come into contact with a single copy of a magazine—of more than seventeen million. This rivaled the ratings of even the most popular national radio programs.

General-Interest Magazines Decline

In the 1950s, weekly general-interest magazines began to lose circulation after dominating the industry for thirty years. Following years of struggle, the *Saturday Evening Post* finally folded in 1969; *Look* (another oversized pictorial weekly), in 1971; and *Life*, in 1972. Oddly, all three at the time were in the Top 10 in paid circulation. Although some critics attributed the problem to poor management, general-interest magazines were victims of several forces: high production costs, increased postal rates, and—in particular—television. As families began spending more time gathered around their TVs instead of reading magazines, advertisers began spending more money on TV spots, which were less expensive than magazine ads and reached a larger audience.

TV Guide

Launched in 1953 to exploit the nation's growing fascination with television, *TV Guide*, which published TV program listings, took its cue from the pocket-size format of *Reader's Digest* and the supermarket sales strategy used by women's magazines. By filling a need (many newspapers were not yet listing TV programs), the magazine by 1962 had become the first weekly to reach a circulation of eight million. At that time, it had seventy regional editions. (See Table 4.1 for the circulation figures of the Top 10 U.S. magazines.)

When local newspapers began listing TV program schedules, they undermined *TV Guide*'s regional editions, and the magazine saw its circulation decline. In response, the magazine transformed itself to survive. Today, *TV Guide* is a full-size, single-edition, national magazine,

With large pages, beautiful photographs, and compelling stories on celebrities, *Look* entertained millions of readers from 1939 to 1971, emphasizing photojournalism to compete with radio. By the late 1960s, however, TV had lured away national advertisers, postal rates had increased, and production costs had risen, forcing *Look* to fold despite a readership of more than eight million.

The Advertising Archives

having dropped its smaller digest format and its 140 regional editions in 2005. It now focuses on entertainment and lifestyle news and carries only limited listings of cable and network TV schedules. The brand name also lives on in the TV Guide Network—an on-screen cable and satellite TV program guide—and TVGuide.com.

People

People (launched by Time Inc. in March 1974) capitalized on the celebrity-crazed culture that accompanied the rise of television. And, like *TV Guide*, it crafted a distribution strategy emphasizing supermarket sales. These moves helped it become the first successful mass market magazine to be introduced in decades. With an abundance of celebrity profiles and human-interest stories, *People* showed a profit in just two years and reached a circulation of more than two million within five years. Instead of using a bulky oversized format and relying on subscriptions, *People* downsized and generated most of its circulation revenue from newsstand and supermarket sales. To this day, it uses plenty of photos, and its articles are about one-third the length of those in a typical newsmagazine. *People*'s success has inspired the launching of similar magazines specializing in celebrities, human-interest stories, and fashion, such as *InStyle* and *Hello*, and has influenced competing Webzines like *TMZ* and *Wonderwall*.

TABLE 4.1 // THE TOP 10 MAGAZINES (RANKED BY PAID U.S. CIRCULATION AND SINGLE-COPY SALES, 1972 vs. 2014)

1972		2014	
Rank/Publication	Circulation	Rank/Publication	Circulation
1 *Reader's Digest*	17,825,661	1 *AARP The Magazine*	22,274,096
2 *TV Guide*	16,410,858	2 *AARP Bulletin*	22,244,820
3 *Woman's Day*	8,191,731	3 *Game Informer*	7,629,995
4 *Better Homes and Gardens*	7,996,050	4 *Better Homes and Gardens*	7,615,641
5 *Family Circle*	7,889,587	5 *Good Housekeeping*	4,348,641
6 *McCall's*	7,516,960	6 *Reader's Digest*	4,288,529
7 *National Geographic*	7,260,179	7 *Family Circle*	4,092,525
8 *Ladies' Home Journal*	7,014,251	8 *National Geographic*	4,029,881
9 *Playboy*	6,400,573	9 *People*	3,527,541
10 *Good Housekeeping*	5,801,446	10 *Woman's Day*	3,311,803

Data from: Alliance for Audited Media, www.auditedmedia.com/news/blog/2014/february/us-snapshot.aspx

MEDIA LITERACY

Case Study

The Evolution of Photojournalism
By Christopher R. Harris

What we now recognize as photojournalism started with the assignment of photographer Roger Fenton, of the *Sunday Times* of London, to document the Crimean War in 1856. Since then—from the earliest woodcut technology to halftone reproduction to the flexible-film camera—photojournalism's impact has been felt worldwide, capturing many historic moments and playing important political and social roles. For example, Jimmy Hare's photoreportage on the sinking of the battleship *Maine* in 1898 near Havana, Cuba, fed into growing popular support for Cuban independence from Spain and eventual U.S. involvement in the Spanish-American War; and the documentary photography of Jacob Riis and Lewis Hine at the turn of the twentieth century captured the harsh

Eddie Adams's Pulitzer Prize–winning photo of a general executing a suspected Vietcong terrorist during the Vietnam War is said to have turned some Americans against the war. Adams (1933–2004) later regretted the notoriety the image brought to the general, as the man he shot had just murdered eight people (including six children).

working and living conditions of the nation's many child laborers. Reaction to these shockingly honest photographs resulted in public outcry and new laws against the exploitation of children. In addition, *Time* magazine's coverage of the Roaring Twenties to the Great Depression and *Life*'s images from World War II and the Korean War changed the way people viewed the world.

With the advent of television, photojournalism continued to take on a significant role, bringing to the public live coverage of the assassination of President John F. Kennedy in 1963 and its aftermath as well as visual documentation of the turbulent 1960s, including aggressive photographic coverage of the Vietnam War and shocking images of the Civil Rights movement.

Into the 1970s and onward, the emergence of computer technologies has raised new ethical concerns about photojournalism. These new concerns deal primarily with the ability of photographers and photo editors to change or digitally alter the

Christopher R. Harris is a professor in the Department of Electronic Media Communication at Middle Tennessee State University.

macmillanhighered.com/mediaessentials3e

⊚ **Visit LaunchPad** to watch a clip about the power of photojournalism. How does it relate to the content of this box?

documentary aspects of a news photograph. By the late 1980s, computers could transform images into digital form, easily manipulated by sophisticated software programs. In addition, any photographer can now send images around the world almost instantaneously through digital transmission, and the Internet allows publication of virtually any image without censorship. Because of the absence of physical film, there is a resulting loss of proof, or veracity, of the authenticity of images. Digital images can be easily altered, but such alteration can be very difficult to detect.

A recent example of tampering with a famous image involved an Orthodox Jewish newspaper in Brooklyn that deleted then Secretary of State Hillary Clinton and counterterrorism director Audrey Tomason from a photograph of President Barack Obama and other White House staff monitoring the Navy Seals raid that killed Osama bin Laden. The paper does not publish images of women in accordance with Orthodox Jewish rules about modesty and ignored White House conditions that the supplied photo not be altered. They issued an apology shortly thereafter.

Have photo editors gone too far? Photojournalists and news sources are now confronted with unprecedented concerns over truth-telling. In the past, trust in documentary photojournalism rested solely on the verifiability of images as they were used in the media. Now, news sources have a variety of guidelines in place regarding image manipulations, ranging from vague requirements that the image not be changed in a misleading way to specific lists of acceptable Photoshop tools. Just as we must evaluate the words we read, at the start of a new century we must also view with a more critical eye these images that mean so much to so many.

APPLYING THE CRITICAL PROCESS

DESCRIPTION Select three types of magazines (e.g., national, political, and alternative) that contain photojournalistic images. Look through these magazines, taking note of what you see.

ANALYSIS Document the patterns in each magazine. What kinds of images are included? What kinds of topics are discussed? Do certain stories or articles have more images than others? Are the subjects generally recognizable, or do they introduce readers to new people or places? Do the images accompany an article or are they stand-alone, with or without a caption?

INTERPRETATION What do these patterns mean? Talk about what you think the orientation is of each magazine based on the images. How do the photos work to achieve this view? Do the images help the magazine in terms of verification or truth-telling? Or are the images mainly to attract attention? Can images do both?

EVALUATION Do you find the motives of each magazine to be clear? Can you see any examples in which an image may have been framed or digitally altered to convey a specific point of view? What are the dangers in this? Explain.

ENGAGEMENT If you find evidence that a photo has been altered or has framed the subject in a manner that makes it less accurate, e-mail the magazine's editor and explain why you think this is a problem.

Types of Magazines: Domination of Specialization

As television has commanded more of Americans' attention, magazines have had to switch tactics to remain viable. General-interest publications have given way to highly specialized magazines appealing to narrower audiences that can be guaranteed to advertisers seeking to tap into niche markets. These narrow groups of readers might be defined by profession (*CIO, Progressive Grocer*), lifestyle (*Dakota Farmer, Game Informer*), gender (*Men's Health, Woman's Day*), age (*AARP The Magazine, Highlights for Children*), or ethnic group (*Ebony, Latina*). There are even specialty magazines appealing to fans of specific interests and hobbies—such as hand-spinning, private piloting, antique gun restoration, and poetry. These niche markets can be categorized in a few broader areas of specialization.

Men's and Women's Magazines

One way the magazine industry competed with television was to reach niche audiences who were not being served by TV, including those interested in sexually explicit subject matter. *Playboy*, started in 1953 by Hugh Hefner, was the first magazine to address this audience by emphasizing previously taboo topics and featuring pornographic photos. But newer men's magazines have broadened their focus to include health (*Men's Health*) and lifestyle (*Details* and *Maxim*) in addition to titillating photos and stories.

Women's magazines had long demonstrated that targeting readers by gender was highly effective. Yet as the magazine industry grew more specialized, publishers stepped up their efforts to capture even more of this enormous market. *Better Homes and Gardens, Good Housekeeping, Ladies' Home Journal*, and *Woman's Day* focused on cultivating the image of women as homemakers and consumers in the conservative 1950s and early 1960s. As the women's movement advanced in the late 1960s and into the 1970s, such magazines began including articles on sexuality, careers, and politics—topics magazine editors previously associated primarily with men.

Entertainment, Leisure, and Sports Magazines

The television age spawned not only *TV Guide* but also a number of specialized entertainment, leisure, and sports magazines. Executives have developed

Specialized magazines target a wide range of interests, from mainstream sports to such hobbies as making model airplanes. Some of the more successful specialized magazines include *Rolling Stone*, *WWD*, and *National Geographic*.

multiple magazines for fans of everything from soap operas, running, tennis, golf, and hunting, to quilting, antiquing, surfing, and gaming. Within categories, magazines specialize further, targeting older or younger runners, men or women golfers, duck hunters or bird-watchers, and midwestern or southern antique collectors.

The most popular sports and leisure magazine is *Sports Illustrated*, which took its name from a failed 1935 publication. Launched in 1954 by Henry Luce's Time Inc., *Sports Illustrated*'s circulation held fairly steady in 2014 at about three million. It is now the most successful general sports magazine in history.

Another popular magazine type that fits loosely into this category comprises magazines devoted to music—everything from the *Source* (hip-hop) to *Country Weekly*. The all-time circulation champ in this category is *Rolling Stone*, begun in 1967. Once considered an alternative magazine, by 1982 *Rolling Stone* had become mainstream, with a circulation approaching 800,000. By 2014, that number had expanded to more than 1.4 million.

National Geographic is another successful publication in this category. Founded in 1888, it promoted "humanized geography" and began featuring color photography in 1910. *National Geographic*'s circulation reached one million in 1935 and ten million in the 1970s. Beginning in the late 1990s, its circulation of paid subscriptions began sliding, down to four million in 2014 (with an additional three million in international distribution). Still, many of *National Geographic*'s televised specials on nature and culture, which began airing back in 1965, rank among the most popular programs in the history of public TV.

Age-Specific Magazines

Magazines have sliced their target markets even more finely by appealing to ever-narrower age groups often ignored by mainstream television. For example, magazines such as *Boys' Life* (the Boy Scouts' national publication since 1912), *Highlights for Children*, and *Ranger Rick* have successfully targeted preschool and elementary-school children. The ad-free and subscription-only *Highlights for Children* topped the children's magazine category in 2014, with a circulation of more than two million.

Leading female teen magazines have also shown substantial growth; the top magazine for thirteen- to nineteen-year-olds is *Seventeen*, with a circulation of two million in 2014.

Maxim, launched in 1997, targeted young men in their twenties and was one of the fastest-growing magazines of the late 1990s. Its covers boast the magazine's obsession with "sex, sports, beer, gadgets, clothes, fitness." But by 2010, the "lad fad" had worn off; ad revenues declined, although *Maxim* still had about 2.5 million subscribers.

Magazines that have had the most success with targeting audiences by age have set their sights on readers over fifty, America's fastest-growing age demographic. These publications have tried to meet the interests of older Americans, whom mainstream culture has historically ignored. By 2014, *AARP The Magazine*—established in 1958 as *Modern Maturity*—had a circulation of more than 22 million, far surpassing that of any other magazine besides its sister publication, *AARP Bulletin*, which has nearly as many subscribers. *AARP The Magazine* articles cover a range of topics related to lifestyle, travel, money, health, and entertainment, such as the effects of Viagra on relationships, secrets for spectacular vacations, and how playing poker can sharpen your mind (see Table 4.1 on page 123).

Elite Magazines

Although they had long existed, *elite magazines* gained popularity as magazines began specializing. Elite magazines are characterized by their combination of literature, criticism, humor, and journalism and by their appeal to highly educated audiences, often living in urban areas. The most widely circulated elite magazine is the *New Yorker*. Launched in 1925 by Harold Ross, the *New Yorker* became the first city magazine aimed at a national upscale audience. Over the years, it featured many prominent biographers, writers, reporters, and humorists and introduced some of the finest literary journalism of the century. By the mid-1960s, the *New Yorker*'s circulation hovered around 500,000; by 2014, it stood at one million print-version subscribers.

Minority Magazines

Minority-targeted magazines, like newspapers, have existed since before the Civil War. One of the most influential early African American magazines, the *Crisis*, was founded by W. E. B. Du Bois in 1910 and is the official magazine of the National Association for the Advancement of Colored People (NAACP).

Since then, the major magazine publisher for African Americans has been John H. Johnson, a former Chicago insurance salesman. Johnson started *Negro Digest* in 1942, *Ebony* in 1945 (a picture-text magazine modeled on *Life* but serving black readers), and *Jet* in 1951 (*Jet* announced in 2014 it would switch to a digital-only format). *Essence*, the first major magazine geared toward African American women, debuted in 1969, and by 2014 had a circulation of more than one million.

Other magazines have served additional minority groups. For example, the *Advocate*, founded in 1967 as a twelve-page newsletter, was the first major magazine to address issues of interest to gay men and lesbians. Since its founding, it has published some of the best journalism on topics not covered by the mainstream press.

Magazines appealing to Spanish-speaking readers have proliferated since the 1980s, reflecting the growth of Hispanic populations in the United States. Today, *People en Español*, *Latina*, and *Vanidades* rank as the top three Hispanic magazines by ad revenue.

Although national magazines aimed at other minority groups were slow to arrive, there are now magazines targeting virtually every race, culture, and ethnicity, including *Asian Week*, *Native Peoples*, and *Tikkun* (published for Jewish readers).

Courtesy of Selecta Magazine

Selecta is an upscale fashion magazine targeted at Hispanic women. The magazine is published in Spanish, although it maintains Twitter and Instagram feeds in English. Other popular magazines aimed at this audience include *Latina* and *People en Espanol*.

Trade Magazines

Trade and professional magazines represent one of the most stable segments in the magazine industry. **Trade publications**—specialty magazines aimed at narrowly defined audiences—supply news; spot trends; share data; and disseminate expert insights relevant to specific manufacturing trades, professional fields, and business sectors. The trade press includes such diverse magazines as *Organic Matters* for organic farmers, *Packaging Machinery Technology* for packaging

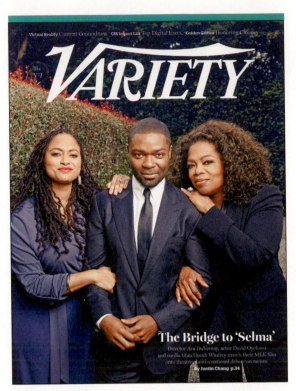

Variety © Variety Media, LLC

Variety, a trade magazine covering the entertainment industry, was founded in 1933 and remains a widely read source of news and reviews.

engineers, and *Coach and Bus Week*. Media industries, too, have relied on trade magazines like *Advertising Age* and *Variety*. In addition to narrowly targeted advertising content, trade publications provide an invaluable venue for job notices related to the specific field. The health of the trade press is evident in findings of a media usage study conducted by Readex Research and released in October 2011. According to the study, when professionals were asked which media they used regularly in their work, print trade magazines came in second (tied with e-newsletters) at 74 percent. Only search engines ranked higher.[4]

Alternative Magazines

About ninety of the almost twenty thousand American magazines now in existence reach circulations of one million or more. This means that most magazines serve relatively small groups of readers. Of these, many are alternative magazines. However, what constitutes an alternative magazine has broadened over time to include just about any publication considered "outside the mainstream," ranging from environmental magazines to alternative lifestyle magazines to punk zines—the magazine world's answer to punk rock. (**Zines**, pronounced "zeens," is a term used to describe self-published magazines.) Numerous alternative magazines have defined themselves in terms of politics—published either by the Left (the *Progressive*, *In These Times*, the *Nation*) or by the Right (the *National Review*, *American Spectator*, *Insight*). Though their circulations may be relatively small, they often exert significant influence on politics by stimulating public debate and affecting citizens' political choices.

Supermarket Tabloids

With headlines like "Angelina Walks in on Brad & Jen," "Extraterrestrials Follow the Teachings of Oprah Winfrey," and "Al-Qaeda Breeding Killer Mosquitoes," **supermarket tabloids** push the limits of credibility. Although they are published on newsprint, the Audit Bureau of Circulations—which checks newspaper and magazine circulation figures to determine advertising rates—counts weekly tabloids as magazines. Tabloids have their historical roots in newspapers' use of graphics and pictorial layouts in the 1860s and 1870s. But the modern U.S. tabloid began with the founding of the *National Enquirer* by William Randolph Hearst in

1926. Its popularity inspired the founding of other tabloids, like *Globe* (1954) and *Star* (1974), as well as the adoption of a tabloid style by some general-interest magazines, such as *People* and *Us Weekly*. Today, tabloid magazine sales are down from their peak in the 1980s. One of the more far-fetched of these supermarket tabloids, *Weekly World News*, ended its print version in 2007 but still exists online.

Online Magazines

With widespread high-speed Internet access, Wi-Fi systems, and a variety of phones, tablets, and e-readers available to consumers, the magazine industry increasingly relies on the Internet to connect with its niche audiences. For example, between 2010 and 2012, the number of U.S. consumer magazine iPad apps grew from 98 to 2,234.[5] Some magazines are now published in both print and online versions, whereas others moved to an online-only format after their print version ended. Still other magazines—**Webzines**—started up online and have remained there. Respected Webzines include *Slate* and *Salon* (which claims 17.6 million monthly unique visitors). These online-only publications have made the Web a legitimate arena for reporting breaking news and encouraging public debate about culture and politics. In some cases, what's old is new again in online magazine publishing. The publishing model of the popular *Huffington Post*, with its heavy reliance on sharing and abridging stories and essays from other sources, combined with content produced by *HuffPo* staff covering a broad number of topics, is reminiscent of the approach of the *Saturday Evening Post* a century ago.

At first observers viewed the Internet as the death knell for print magazines, but now the industry embraces it. Numerous magazines that have moved online now carry blogs, original video and audio podcasts, social networking features, and other interactive components that could never work in print. For example,

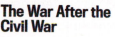

Online magazines like *Slate* (pictured) have made the Web their exclusive home. Since launching in 1996, *Slate* has won many awards, such as the National Magazine Award for General Excellence for Digital Media.

the online version of *Popular Mechanics* offers interactive 3-D models for do-it-yourself projects, such as constructing a piece of furniture by examining joints and parts from every angle.

In fact, new print magazines often publish with brand-extending synergies in mind. In 1998, for example, cable network ESPN launched *ESPN The Magazine*. The brand familiarity helped the new print periodical find readers in a segment already crowded with *Sports Illustrated*, the *Sporting News*, and dozens of niche sports publications. The magazine also drives cross-promotion of ESPN's growing business empire, including its cable channels, ESPN radio, the ESPN Web site, ESPN Zone restaurants, and the X Games. As magazines create apps for smartphones and tablets, editorial content will be even more tightly woven with advertising. Readers can now, for example, read *Entertainment Weekly*'s music recommendations on their devices and then click through to buy the song or album mentioned. The publication gets a cut of the sale, and the reader gets music almost instantly.

As more publications migrate over to digital and mobile platforms, these partnerships have become more important than ever, as have the brand identities of the magazines themselves. With so many magazines appearing in a variety of formats, publishers want to create the sense that names like ESPN, *Cosmopolitan*, and *Entertainment Weekly* can be trusted across the entire media landscape.

The Economics of Magazines

Whatever their circulation size, specialty, or format (print or online), magazines must bring in money (e.g., from advertising revenues and subscription fees) to fulfill their mission and compete with other media. For instance, to combat loss of ad dollars to TV, many magazines began publishing special editions, which guaranteed advertisers access to their target markets. These competitive strategies fueled the massive growth of magazines despite competition from television, but now magazines face new challenges from Web sites, blogs, and social media, all competing for audiences and ad dollars. Magazines must also invest money to carry out the business processes essential to their operations—such as content development, production, sales and marketing, and distribution. To extend their reach, lower their costs, and beef up their budgets, many magazines have merged into large chains, often backed financially by major media conglomerates. Even large chains, however, are not immune to the economic reality that many well-known magazine titles continue to cease production entirely.

Money In

Magazine publishers make money through two primary means: advertisers and newsstand/subscription sales.

Advertising

Consumer magazines rely heavily on advertising revenue. The more successful the magazine (that is, the higher its circulation), the more it can charge for ad space. A top-rated consumer magazine might charge as much as $320,000 for a full-page color ad and $89,000 for a one-third-page, black-and-white ad. The average magazine contains about 50 percent ad copy and 50 percent editorial content, a ratio that has remained fairly constant for the past twenty-five years.

In some cases, advertisers can strongly influence editorial content. For example, some companies have canceled their ads after a magazine printed articles that were unflattering toward or critical of the firm or its industry.[6] For editors, the specter of a major advertiser bringing its business elsewhere can present a dilemma: Should the magazine shift its editorial point of view to avoid offending advertisers and thus retain much-needed ad revenues? Or should it continue publishing the same types of articles, hoping that if some advertisers are driven away, others that agree with the magazine's viewpoint will come in and take their place?

In addition to grappling with this dilemma, magazines have developed innovative strategies for retaining advertisers. For instance, as television stations began generating more national ad revenues in the 1950s, magazines started introducing different editions to guarantee advertisers a specific audience—and thus win them back. There are several types of special editions:

- **Regional editions** are national magazines whose content is tailored to the interests of specific geographic areas. For example, *Sports Illustrated* often prints five regional versions of its College Football Preview and March Madness Preview editions, picturing a different local star on each of the five covers.
- In **split-run editions**, the editorial content remains the same, but the magazines include a few pages of ads purchased by local or regional companies. Most editions of *Time*, *Newsweek*, and *Sports Illustrated*, for instance, contain a number of pages reserved for regional ads.

CONVERGING MEDIA

Case Study

The Digital Pass-Along: Magazine Readers on Social Media

For a long time now, magazine publishers have been aware of pass-along readership, the practice of sharing a magazine with someone else when the reader is done with it. The idea of sharing magazine content has become even more important in courting digital readers, especially those eighteen to thirty-four years of age.

National magazine trade organization MPA (formerly the Magazine Publishers of America, now the Association of Magazine Media) conducted a survey in 2012 of traditional print-magazine readers who are also on social media. What they discovered about this age group (much desired by advertisers) reveals not only that there are multiple varieties of convergence but also that readers, especially avid readers, *like* this convergence.

It's no secret that eighteen- to thirty-four-year-olds spend a lot of time on social media, but the MPA survey paints a picture of readers who are far from abandoning magazines, with the vast majority of respondents (93%) having read either a print or a digital magazine article in the past sixty days. Over half of these people "Follow" a magazine on Twitter or "Like" its page on Facebook. Part of the survey also focused on those who said they were avid magazine readers. Of that group, almost two-thirds use Twitter or Facebook to follow at least one magazine.

Avid magazine readers are doing a lot more than just reading articles via social media. Over 60 percent of these readers share magazine articles on Facebook or tweet links to articles, reminiscent of the way readers would pass along printed copies of magazines to friends and family. What's more, half of those readers say it's important to them to be able to follow a magazine in a social media environment like Facebook and then share it quickly. In addition to the Facebook and Twitter platforms, Pinterest has been a popular way for readers to interact with magazine content, following and repinning content from magazines.

But the convergence of print and online doesn't stop with methods of sharing articles. Well over one-third of readers in the survey use social media

LaunchPad

macmillanhighered.com/mediaessentials3e

▶ **Visit LaunchPad** to watch a clip from *13 Going on 30* set in a magazine office. What has changed in the decade or so since this movie's release?

Data from: "Magazine Media Readers Are Social: Key Research Findings," MPA (Association of Magazine Media), www.magazine.org /sites/default/files/SOCIAL-f5%20website.pdf; and "MPA Releases Benchmark Social Media Study," www.magazine.org/insights-resources /research-publications/guides-studies/new-mpa-releases-benchmark-social-media

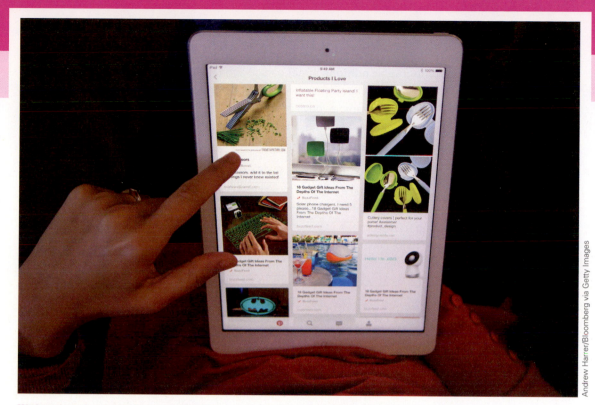

With its emphasis on home crafts, decorating, and recipes, Pinterest might seem a natural competitor to a magazine like *Better Homes and Gardens*. But far from competing, *Better Homes and Gardens* has a strong presence on Pinterest, with nearly 800,000 followers by 2014.

to talk back to the magazines they read or to the columnists they follow. This could take the form of leaving comments in response to articles, uploading their own content (recipes, for example), or posting photographs for possible use in future issues. What's more interesting is that the eighteen to thirty-four age group increasingly sees this kind of interaction as more than a novelty. Half of those in this survey said the ability to engage with favorite magazines, and in some cases the staff of those magazines, was more than just nice—it was *important* to them. This underscores the idea that successful convergence will be a key to success, if not survival, for the magazine industry.

- **Demographic editions** target particular groups of consumers. In this case, market researchers identify subscribers primarily by occupation, class, and zip code. Time Inc., for example, developed special editions of *Time* magazine for top management, high-income zip-code areas, and ultrahigh-income professional/managerial households.

Newsstand and Subscription Sales

Magazines also make money from single-copy sales at newsstands and from subscription sales. (Some online magazines charge a subscription fee in addition to making money from advertisers.) Toward the end of the general-interest magazine era in 1950, newsstand sales accounted for about 43 percent of magazine sales, and subscriptions constituted 57 percent. Today, newsstand sales have fallen to 12 percent, whereas subscriptions' contribution to sales has risen to 88 percent.

One tactic used by magazine circulation departments to increase subscription sales is to encourage consumers to renew well in advance of the date on which their subscription is set to expire. Another strategy is the **evergreen subscription**—which is automatically renewed on a credit card unless the subscriber requests that the automatic renewal be stopped.

Controlled circulations can boost revenue from ad sales. Here's how it works: A business or some other type of organization (such as an airline or a professional association) sponsors the magazine, and the published issues are given free to readers (such as airline passengers or members of the professional association). Advertisers are often interested in buying ad space in such magazines, attracted by the notion of a captive audience.

Money Out

To operate, magazines must spend money on resources essential to their business, such as development of content (including staff writers' salaries and freelance writers' fees), production (including desktop-publishing technology needed for designing and laying out each issue, and paper and printing costs for print versions of magazines), sales and marketing, and distribution (including postage for printed periodicals).

Content Development

The lifeblood of any magazine is the *editorial department*, which produces the periodical's content, excluding advertisements. Like newspapers, most magazines have a chain of command that begins with a publisher and extends down to the editor in chief, the managing editor, and a variety of subeditors. These subeditors oversee such editorial functions as photography, illustrations, reporting and writing, and copyediting. Magazine writers generally include contributing staff writers, who are specialists in certain fields, and *freelance writers*—self-employed professionals assigned to cover particular stories or regions. Many magazines—especially those with small budgets—also accept unsolicited articles from freelancers to fill their pages, often paying the writers a flat fee or an honorarium in return for their work.

Production

A magazine's *production and technology department* maintains the computer hardware and software necessary to design each issue of the magazine (that is, to select typefaces and styles) and to lay out each issue (place the text and graphics together on each page spread). Staff or freelance subeditors specializing in design and layout are often assigned to these tasks.

A small newsletter or magazine can be launched quite cheaply with the use of computer-based **desktop publishing**, which enables an aspiring publisher-editor to write, design, lay out, and print the publication or post it online. Yet despite the rise of inexpensive desktop publishing, most large commercial magazines still operate several departments, which employ hundreds of people.

Production costs also include paper and printing for those magazines published in print format. Because such magazines are on a weekly, monthly, or bimonthly publication cycle, rather than coming out daily, it is not economically practical for their publishers to maintain expensive print facilities. Instead, many national magazines digitally transport files containing their print-ready issues to regional printing sites for the insertion of local ads and for faster distribution.

Sales and Marketing

Magazine publishers must also maintain a sales force and a marketing staff to focus on increasing subscriptions and attracting more advertisers. These professionals' responsibilities often include gathering and analyzing subscriber data to see who's renewing their subscriptions (and why) and who's letting their subscriptions lapse (and why), as well as designing marketing campaigns to attract new readers.

Distribution

Magazines also have to spend money on distribution. This function encompasses maintenance of subscriber mailing lists, postage for shipping published issues of print-version magazines to subscribers, and possibly fees for displaying and selling published issues through newsstands or at supermarket checkout lines. This is an area in which online versions of magazines have an advantage,

Reprinted by permission of *Ms.* magazine, © 1972

Ms. magazine, founded in 1972 as the first magazine to take the feminist movement seriously, made another bold move when it stopped carrying advertisements in 1990—except for ads from nonprofit and cause-related organizations. Although that choice has allowed the magazine to publish more thought-provoking articles, it has unfortunately led to continued financial instability.

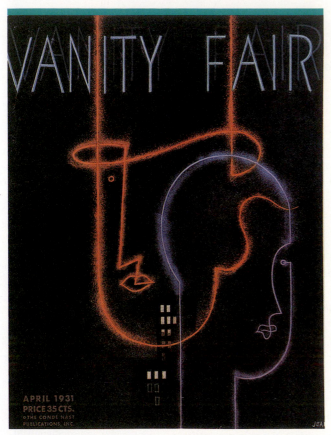

Illustration by Jean Corlu/Vanity Fair
© 1931, Conde Nast Publications, Inc.

Originally launched in the United States in 1914 by Condé Nast, *Vanity Fair* featured top writers such as Dorothy Parker and P. G. Wodehouse. Known for its mix of social and political commentary, celebrity profiles, fiction, and arts coverage, *Vanity Fair* today includes contributions by noted photographer Annie Leibovitz and writers James Wolcott and Bethany McLean.

although hosting, maintaining, and promoting an online magazine introduces its own set of distribution challenges.

Major Magazine Chains

To survive in an increasingly competitive marketplace, many magazines have merged into large, powerful chains, often backed by deep-pocketed media conglomerates. This strategy provides more funding for magazines and enables them to lower their costs—for example, by centralizing basic functions such as content development or production.

In the commercial magazine industry, large companies or chains have come to dominate the business. Condé Nast is one example. A division of Advance Publications, which operates the Newhouse newspaper chain, the Condé Nast group controls several upscale consumer magazines, including *Vanity Fair*, *GQ*, and *Vogue*. Time Warner, one of the world's largest media conglomerates, also runs a magazine subsidiary, Time Inc. This top player among magazine-chain operators boasts about thirty major titles, including *People* and *Sports Illustrated*.

Many large publishers—including the Hearst Corporation, the Meredith Corporation, Time Inc., and Rodale Press—have generated additional revenue by creating custom-publishing divisions that produce limited-distribution publications for client companies. These publications, sometimes called **magalogs**, combine the style of glossy magazines with the sales pitch of retail catalogues. For example, a large international corporation might pay a publisher to produce a magalog for its employees on how to manage their 401(k).

A number of major magazines (*Reader's Digest*, *Cosmopolitan*, *Newsweek*, and *Time* are good examples) have further boosted revenues by launching international editions in several languages. However, most U.S. magazines are local, regional, or specialized and therefore aren't readily exportable to other countries. Of the approximately twenty thousand magazines now published in the United States, only about two hundred circulate routinely in the world market. Moreover, even the best-known and most-circulated magazines, backed by the largest companies, may not survive in the marketplace. For example, Condé Nast shut down its popular

Gourmet and *Modern Bride* magazines at the end of 2009, though the *Gourmet* brand name continues to be used for occasional online and print publications.

Magazines in a Democratic Society

In the early days of the industry, individual magazines had a powerful national voice and united separate communities around important political and social issues, such as abolition and suffrage. Muckrackers promoted social reform in the pages of general-interest magazines. Today, with so many specialized magazines appealing to ever-narrower groups of consumers, magazines no longer foster such a strong sense of national identity.

To be sure, contemporary commercial magazines still provide essential information about politics, society, and culture. Thus, they help us form opinions about the big issues of the day and make decisions—key activities in any democracy. However, owing to their increasing dependence on advertising revenue, some publications view their readers as consumers first (viewers of displayed products and purchasers of material goods) and citizens second. To keep advertising dollars flowing in, editorial staffs may decide to keep controversial content out of their magazine's pages, which constrains debate and thus hurts the democratic process.

At the same time, magazines have arguably had more freedom than other media to encourage and participate in democratic debate. More magazines circulate in the marketplace than do broadcast or cable television channels. And many new magazines are uniting dispersed groups of readers by, for example, giving cultural minorities or newly arrived immigrants a sense of membership in a broader community.

In addition, because magazines are distributed weekly, monthly, or bimonthly, their publishers are less restricted by deadline pressure than are newspaper publishers and radio and television broadcasters. Journalists writing for magazines can thus take time to offer more rigorous and thoughtful analyses of the topics they cover. The biweekly *Rolling Stone*, for example, often mounts more detailed, comprehensive political pieces than you might find in a daily news source. However, this is changing in some cases, as online publications attempt to cover breaking news and face the kinds of constant deadline pressure that used to be associated only with daily newspapers and broadcasters.

Amid today's swirl of images, magazines and their advertisements certainly contribute to the commotion. But good magazines—especially those offering carefully researched, thoughtful, or entertaining articles and photos—have continued to inspire lively discussion among readers. And if they're also well designed, they maintain readers' connection to words—no small feat in today's increasingly image-driven world.

CHAPTER ESSENTIALS

Now that you have finished reading this chapter, you can use the following tools:

LaunchPad for *Media Essentials*

Go to **macmillanhighered.com/mediaessentials3e** for videos, review quizzes, and more.

LaunchPad for *Media Essentials* includes:

- **REVIEW WITH LEARNINGCURVE**
  LearningCurve uses gamelike quizzing to help you master the concepts you need to learn from this chapter.

REVIEW

Track Main Points of Magazines' Early History

- The first **magazines**—collections of articles, stories, and advertisements published on a nondaily cycle in a smaller tabloid style— were influenced by European newspapers of the seventeenth century. As the eighteenth century unfolded, a rising middle class, increased literacy, and advancements in printing technology helped magazines spread to America, where colonial leaders and thinkers used the medium to discuss important issues of the day (pp. 115–117).

- Due to even greater increases in literacy and education, faster printing technology, and improvements in mail delivery, the demand for national (as opposed to local) magazines soared in the mid to late nineteenth century. The advent of illustration in magazines—such as drawings, engravings, and woodcuts— heightened their appeal to readers. These factors helped move magazines toward mass medium status (pp. 117–119).

Understand Key Events in the Evolution of Modern American Magazines

- As distribution and production costs declined, magazines were able to reach a wider audience, and advertisers began to turn to them to capture consumer attention. The rise in magazine circulation caused the growth of different kinds of newspaper reporting, such as **muckraking**—inspired by an interest in advocating social reform and exposing wrongdoing (pp. 119–120).

- The growth of the middle class created a market for **general-interest magazines**, which covered a wide variety of topics aimed at a broad national audience, such as recent developments in government, medicine, or society. A key aspect of these magazines was **photojournalism**, the use of photographs to augment editorial content. The popularity of these magazines was marked by their high **pass-along readership**, the total number of readers of a single issue. Four of the most notable general-interest magazines of the twentieth century were the *Saturday Evening Post*, *Reader's Digest*, *Time*, and *Life* (pp. 120–122).

- Television's rising popularity put many general-interest magazines out of business in the 1950s. Some magazines fought back by focusing their content on topics not covered by TV programmers and by featuring short articles heavily illustrated with photos. Two early examples include *TV Guide* and *People* (pp. 122–123).

Outline the Many Different Types of Magazines

- General-interest magazines have now given way to highly specialized magazines appealing to narrower audiences and niche markets. Some areas of specialization include men's and women's magazines; entertainment, leisure, and sports magazines; age-specific magazines; elite magazines; minority magazines; trade magazines; and alternative magazines (pp. 126–130).

- Another type of magazine, the **supermarket tabloid**, features a more sensationalistic brand of story, which might include celebrity gossip or claims of UFO sightings (pp. 130–131).

- Recently, the Internet has become a place where specialized magazines can extend their reach to target audiences. Some magazines are published in both print and online versions; others have moved to online-only formats. Still others, **Webzines**, started up online and have remained there (pp. 131–132).

Explain How Magazines Operate Economically

- Magazine publishers make money through advertisers. As a result, many magazines have developed different editions to target specific audiences and guarantee advertising revenue. For example, **regional editions** are national magazines whose content is tailored to the interests of different geographic areas; **split-run editions** contain the same editorial content, but the magazines have a few pages of ads purchased by local or regional companies; **demographic editions** target particular groups of consumers (pp. 132–133, 136).

- Magazine publishers also take in revenue from newsstand and subscription sales. One subscription strategy, the **evergreen subscription**, automatically renews a consumer's subscription on a credit card unless the subscriber requests that the automatic renewal be stopped (p. 136).

- Magazine publishers spend money on the development of content, production (such as **desktop publishing**, which enables the publisher-editor to write, design, lay out, and print the publication or post it online), sales and marketing, and distribution (pp. 136–138).

- To survive in an increasingly competitive marketplace, many magazines have merged into large chains often backed by media conglomerates. This strategy provides more funding for magazines and enables them to lower their costs by centralizing basic functions. Many large publishers have also generated revenue by producing limited-distribution publications—**magalogs**—that combine glossy magazines with the sales pitch of retail catalogues (pp. 138–139).

Discuss the Effect of Magazines on Our Democratic Society

- Early magazines had a powerful national voice and united separate communities around significant political and social issues. Magazines provided an important venue for muckrakers in the early 1900s: Reporters investigated social problems, and their stories often led to much-needed reforms (p. 139).

- Today, with so much specialization, magazines no longer foster a strong sense of national identity, though they continue to have a strong influence on society (p. 139).

STUDY QUESTIONS

1. How did magazines become national in scope?
2. What role did magazines play in social reform at the turn of the twentieth century?
3. What triggered the move toward magazine specialization?
4. How have the Internet and convergence changed the magazine industry?
5. How do magazines serve a democratic society?

MEDIA LITERACY PRACTICE

An ongoing conflict in the magazine industry exists between the desire for editorial independence and the drive for advertising revenue. Investigate the so-called firewall between the editorial and business sides by comparing at least two magazines.

DESCRIBE the magazines by charting the placement and kinds of ads that appear in the magazines as well as the magazines' editorial content, including stories, photographs, and other features.

ANALYZE the information by looking for patterns: How similar are the ads and editorial content in style and subject matter? Are ads placed in proximity to content on related subjects (e.g., sunglasses advertised next to an article on beach vacations)? Are there ads at odds with the content (e.g., cigarette ads in youth-oriented magazines)?

INTERPRET what these patterns mean. Is there a clear firewall between editorial and business content, or do the ads seem to influence magazine content?

EVALUATE your findings, and consider whether there can be a desirable balance between ads and editorial content.

ENGAGE with the magazine industry by writing letters to the editors of magazines that seem to shape editorial copy for advertisers or ignore important issues that might offend advertisers.

U2 (featuring Bono, left) and Beyoncé (right) have both tried out new digital album–release strategies in recent years.

5

Sound Recording and Popular Music

In September 2014, rock band U2 teamed up with Apple to offer what it thought was going to be a successful promotion: giving away its new album, *Songs of Innocence*, for free to over 500 million iTunes subscribers. Instead, it set off a major backlash. Some users were upset that the album had automatically downloaded and was taking up space on their devices or in their cloud accounts. Some musicians worried that less-wealthy groups would suffer in a marketplace accustomed to free music. Before the controversy died down, Apple had to create an app with easy-to-follow instructions for those wanting to remove the album.

There is a note of irony to this backlash of consumer anger over free digital music, because it was the desire to download free music that kicked off the ongoing transformation of the sound recording industry. Shawn Fanning, John Fanning, and Sean Parker launched music-sharing site Napster in 1999. Although not the first service to let people share music files online, it combined the lure of free music with an easy-to-use interface that rapidly increased its popularity with users—and its unpopularity with music companies and many artists. Ultimately, the courts agreed with the record labels and artists who complained about copyright infringement, and shut down the service in 2001. Other file-sharing services sprang up, but the next big development was the launch of iTunes in 2003, an online music store from which people could buy individual songs instead of entire albums. Downloaded music sales from iTunes and other sources skyrocketed, only beginning to slow down recently due to competition from streaming services like Spotify and Pandora.

So with all of these changes in the business side of the music business, why did U2 decide to give away an album for free? In this case, U2 did get paid, but from Apple rather than from consumers. In addition to an undisclosed payment, Apple agreed to spend $100 million on a marketing campaign for the band, which could be especially lucrative for a big-name band capable of drawing big crowds willing to pay premium ticket prices.

U2's approach was the latest example of artists looking for ways to take advantage of convergence and the power of social media—that is, to make money in new ways. For example, Beyoncé dropped a surprise album in December 2013, using social media to create buzz, share music videos, and push pre-holiday sales. The band Radiohead took another approach in 2007, making songs from the album *In Rainbows* available online, asking fans to pay what they thought was fair (actual CDs were available a couple months later). Marketing also converged with the Internet (including YouTube and social media sites) to help launch the careers of less established artists like Justin Bieber and Iggy

Azalea, and help independent artists Macklemore & Ryan Lewis top the music charts.[1]

Although predictions about Napster ending the music industry haven't come true, the Internet age has seen music industry revenue cut in half (from $14.5 billion in 1998 to about $7 billion in 2013), and the growing popularity of music streaming services could mean that number will continue to fall. One prediction that is likely to come true is that the music industry will continue to search out new strategies. Taylor Swift, one of music's biggest stars, actually moved away from streaming when her album *1989* was released, going so far as to take all of her previous albums off of Spotify, arguing that artists should be paid more by streaming sites (where typically only the most successful artists, like Swift, can make substantial money). Artists with less leverage than Swift (which is to say, most of them) may soon use songs as loss leaders: products labels know up front will not make money on their own but will act as marketing for more lucrative licensing deals and concert tours (see also "Converging Media Case Study: 360 Degrees of Music," pages 172–173). However the music industry proceeds, it will continue to look very different from how it looked even just a few years ago.

THE INVENTION OF SOUND RECORDING TECHNOLOGY transformed our relationship with popular music and made sound recording a mass medium. Before recording, people had one way to listen to music: attend a live performance. With the advent of sound recording, people could also buy recordings and listen to their favorite music as often as they wanted in their own homes. As technological advances made it cheaper and easier for everyone to gain access to sound recordings, music began reshaping society and culture. But the recording industry itself has also changed with the times. Consider what happened in the 1950s after TV began capturing a bigger share of Americans' attention and time: Record labels and radio stations—previously adversaries—joined forces to create Top 40 (or "hit song") programming to attract more listeners and stimulate music sales. Many years later, the industry was forced to shift again in the face of technology, as the MP3 format made recorded music more accessible (and easier to duplicate) than ever.

In this chapter, we assess the full impact of sound recording and popular music on our lives by:

- examining the early history and evolution of sound recording, including the shift from analog to digital technology and the changing relationship between record labels and radio stations

- shining a spotlight on the rise of popular music (including jazz, rock, and country) in the United States

- tracing the changes in the American popular-music scene, such as rock's move into the mainstream and the proliferation of rock alternatives (including folk and grunge)

- analyzing the economics of the sound recording industry, including how music labels, artists, and other participants make and spend money

- considering sound recording's impact on our democratic society today by exploring such questions as whether the recording industry is broadening participation in democracy or constraining it

macmillanhighered.com /mediaessentials3e Use **LearningCurve** to review concepts from this chapter.

The Early History and Evolution of Sound Recording

Early inventors' work helped make sound recording a mass medium and a product that enterprising businesspeople could sell. The product's format changed with additional technological advances (e.g., moving from records and tapes to CDs, and then to online downloads and digital music streaming). Technology also enhanced the product's quality; for example, many people praised the digital clarity of CDs over "scratchy" analog recordings. However, the latest technology—online downloading and streaming of music—has drastically reduced sales of CDs and other physical formats, forcing industry players to look for other ways to survive.

From Cylinders to Disks: Sound Recording Becomes a Mass Medium

In the development stage of sound recording, inventors experimented with sound technology; and in the entrepreneurial stage, people sought to make money from the technology. Sound recording finally reached the mass medium stage when entrepreneurs figured out how to quickly and cheaply produce and distribute multiple copies of recordings.

The Development Stage

In the 1850s, French printer Édouard-Léon Scott de Martinville conducted the first experiments with sound recording. Using a hog's-hair bristle as a needle, he tied one end to a thin membrane stretched over the narrow part of a funnel. When he spoke into the wide part of the funnel, the membrane vibrated, and the bristle's free end made grooves on a revolving cylinder coated with a thick liquid. Although de Martinville never figured out how to play back the sound, his experiments ushered in the *development stage* of sound recording.

The Entrepreneurial Stage

In 1877, Thomas Edison helped move sound recording into its *entrepreneurial stage* by first determining how to play back sound, then marketing the machine that did it. He recorded his own voice by concocting a machine that played foil cylinders, known as the *phonograph* (derived from the Greek terms for "sound" and "writing"). Edison then patented his phonograph in 1878 as a kind of answering machine. In 1886, Chichester Bell and Charles Sumner Tainter patented an improvement on the phonograph, known as the *graphophone*, which played more durable wax cylinders.[2] Both Edison's phonograph and Bell and Tainter's graphophone had only marginal success as a voice-recording office machine. Yet these inventions laid the foundation for others to develop more viable sound recording technologies.

The Mass Medium Stage

Adapting ideas from previous inventors, Emile Berliner, a German engineer who had immigrated to America, made sound recording into a *mass medium*. Berliner developed a turntable machine that played flat disks, or "records," made of shellac. He called this device a *gramophone* and patented it in 1887. He also discovered how to mass-produce his records by making a master recording from which many copies could be easily duplicated. In addition, Berliner's records could be stamped in the center with labels indicating song title, performer, and songwriter.

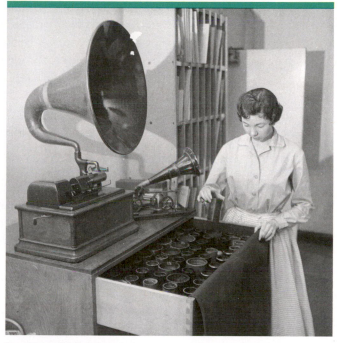

Russell Knight/BIPs/Getty Images

A graphophone and a collection of prerecorded wax cylinders.

By the early 1900s, record-playing phonographs were widely available for home use. Early record players, known as Victrolas, were mechanical and had to be primed with a crank handle. Electric record players, first available in 1925, gradually replaced Victrolas as more homes were wired for electricity.

Recorded music initially had limited appeal, owing to the loud scratches and pops that interrupted the music, and each record contained only three to four minutes of music. However, in the early 1940s, when shellac was needed for World War II munitions, the record industry began manufacturing records made of polyvinyl plastic. These vinyl records (called 78s because they turned at seventy-eight revolutions per minute, or rpms) were less noisy and more durable than shellac records. Enthusiastic about these new advantages, people began buying more records.

In 1948, CBS Records introduced the $33\frac{1}{3}$-rpm *long-playing record* (LP), which contained about twenty minutes of music on each side. This created a market for multisong albums and classical music, which was written primarily for ballet, opera, ensemble, or symphony, and continues to have a significant fan base worldwide. The next year, RCA developed a competing 45-rpm record, featuring a quarter-size hole in the middle that made these records ideal for playing in jukeboxes. The two new recording configurations could not be played on each other's machines; thus, a marketing battle erupted. In 1953, CBS and RCA compromised. The LP became the standard for long-playing albums, the 45 became the standard for singles, and record players were designed to accommodate both formats (as well as 78s, at least for a while).

From Records to Tapes to CDs: Analog Goes Digital

The advent of magnetic **audiotape** and tape players in the 1940s paved the way for major innovations, such as cassettes, stereophonic sound, and—most significantly—digital recording. Audiotape's lightweight magnetized strands made possible sound editing and multiple-track mixing, in which instrumentals or vocals could be recorded at one location and later mixed onto a master recording in a studio. This vastly improved studio recordings' quality and boosted sales, though recordings continued to be sold primarily in vinyl format until the late 1970s.

By the mid-1960s, engineers had placed miniaturized (reel-to-reel) audiotape inside small plastic cases and developed portable cassette players. Listeners could now bring recorded music anywhere, which created a market for pre-recorded cassettes. Audiotape also permitted home dubbing, which began eroding record sales.

Some people thought audiotape's portability, superior sound, and recording capabilities would mean the demise of records. However, vinyl's popularity continued, due in part to the improved fidelity that came with stereophonic sound. Invented in 1931 by Alan Blumlein, but not put to commercial use until 1958, **stereo** permitted the recording of two separate channels, or tracks, of sound. Using audiotape, recording-studio engineers could now record many instrumental or vocal tracks, which they would then "mix down" to two stereo tracks, creating a more natural sound.

The biggest recording advancement came in the 1970s, when electrical engineer Thomas Stockham made the first digital audio recordings on standard

CHAPTER 5 // TIMELINE

1850s de Martinville
The first experiments in sound recording are conducted using a hog's-hair bristle as a needle; de Martinville can record sound but is unable to play it back.

1877 Phonograph
Edison invents the phonograph as a way to play back sound.

1887 Flat Disk
Berliner invents the flat disk and the gramophone on which to play it. The disks are easily mass-produced, and sound recording becomes a mass medium.

1910 Victrolas
Music players enter living rooms.

computer equipment. In contrast to **analog recording**, which captures the fluctuations of sound waves and stores those signals in a record's grooves or a tape's continuous stream of magnetized particles, **digital recording** translates sound waves into binary on-off pulses and stores that information in sequences of ones and zeros as numerical code. Drawing on this technology, in 1983 Sony and Philips began selling digitally recorded **compact discs** (CDs), which could be produced more cheaply than vinyl records and even audiocassettes. By 2000, CDs had rendered records and audiocassettes nearly obsolete except among deejays, hip-hop artists (who still used vinyl for scratching and sampling), and some audiophile loyalists (see Figure 5.1). In a fairly recent development, however, vinyl albums, once nearly extinct, have been making a comeback. Still a relatively small part of the overall market in music sales, vinyl sales have jumped so much that many new albums are being pressed on vinyl. Some record-pressing plants have even reopened, and others have been built, just to keep up with demand. Whether this will be a lasting or a brief trend among a new wave of collectors (many of whom were born after the introduction of CDs) remains to be seen.

From CDs to MP3s: Sound Recording in the Internet Age

In 1992, the **MP3** file format was developed as part of a video compression standard. As it turns out, the format also enables sound, including music, to be compressed into small, manageable digital files. Combined with the Internet, the MP3 format revolutionized sound recording. By the mid-1990s, computer users were swapping MP3 music files online. These files could be uploaded and downloaded in a fraction of the time it took to exchange noncompressed music, and they used up less memory.

In 1999, Napster's now-infamous free file-sharing service brought MP3s to popular attention. By then, music files were widely available on the Internet—some for sale, some available legally for free downloading, and many traded

LaunchPad
macmillanhighered.com/mediaessentials3e

Recording Music Today
Composer Scott Dugdale discusses technological innovations in music recording.
Discussion: What surprised you the most about song production as shown in the video?

1925 Radio Threatens the Sound Recording Industry
Music can be heard over the airwaves, prompting ASCAP to establish fees for radio.

1940s Audiotape
Developed in Germany, audio-tape enables multitrack recording.

1950s Music Industry
As television threatens radio, radio turns to the music industry for salvation and becomes a marketing arm for the sound recording industry.

1950s Rock and Roll
This new music form challenges class, gender, race, geographic, and religious norms in the United States.

in violation of copyright laws. Losing countless music sales to free downloading, the music industry initiated lawsuits against file-sharing companies and individual downloaders.

In 2001, the U.S. Supreme Court ruled in favor of the music industry and against Napster, declaring free music file-swapping illegal because it violated music copyrights held by recording labels and artists. Yet even today, illegal swapping continues at a high level—in part because of how difficult it is to police the decentralized Internet. Music MP3s (some acquired legally, some not) are now played on computers, home stereo systems, car stereos, portable devices, and cell phones. In fact, MP3 is now the leading music format. (For more on music sales, see "Media Literacy Case Study: The Rise of Digital Music" on pages 156–157.)

The music industry, realizing that the MP3 format is not going away, has embraced services like iTunes (launched by Apple in 2003 to accompany the iPod), which has become the model for legal online distribution of music. By 2011, the music industry was making more money from digital downloads than from sales of CDs and other physical media. But new developments in the music industry might now undermine what had been a decade of steady growth in digital downloads. In 2013, the fastest-growing slice of the industry's revenue pie was made up of music subscription and streaming services like Pandora, Spotify, Grooveshark, and Last.fm. As with the advent of digital downloading of music, streaming services have generated some controversy and concern among artists and music labels, which will be discussed later in this chapter.

Paul J. Richards/AFP/Getty Images

Apple's iPod, the leading portable music and video player, began a revolution in digital music when it was released in 2001.

CHAPTER 5 // TIMELINE continued

1953 A Sound Recording Standard
This is established at $33\frac{1}{3}$ rpm for long-playing albums (LPs), 45 rpm for two-sided singles.

1960s Cassettes
This new format makes music portable.

Late 1970s Hip-Hop
This musical art form emerges.

1983 CDs
The first format to incorporate digital technology hits the market.

FIGURE 5.1 // THE EVOLUTION OF DIGITAL SOUND RECORDING SALES
Revenue in billions

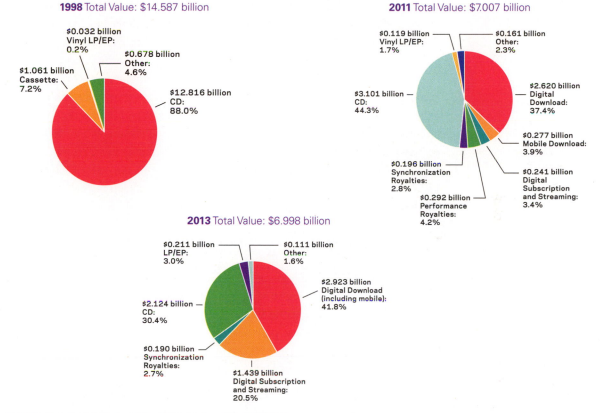

1998 Total Value: $14.587 billion

$0.032 billion
Vinyl LP/EP:
0.2%

$0.678 billion
Other:
4.6%

$1.061 billion
Cassette:
7.2%

$12.816 billion
CD:
88.0%

2011 Total Value: $7.007 billion

$0.119 billion
Vinyl LP/EP:
1.7%

$0.161 billion
Other:
2.3%

$3.101 billion
CD:
44.3%

$2.620 billion
Digital
Download:
37.4%

$0.277 billion
Mobile Download:
3.9%

$0.241 billion
Digital
Subscription
and Streaming:
3.4%

$0.196 billion
Synchronization
Royalties:
2.8%

$0.292 billion
Performance
Royalties:
4.2%

2013 Total Value: $6.998 billion

$0.211 billion
LP/EP:
3.0%

$0.111 billion
Other:
1.6%

$2.124 billion
CD:
30.4%

$2.923 billion
Digital Download
(including mobile):
41.8%

$0.190 billion
Synchronization
Royalties:
2.7%

$1.439 billion
Digital Subscription
and Streaming:
20.5%

Data from: Recording Industry Association of America, Annual Year-End Statistics

Note: The year 1998 is the year before Napster arrived and the peak year of industry revenue. In 2011, digital product revenue surpassed physical product revenue for the first time. In 2013, digital download revenue dropped for the first time, as digital subscriptions and streaming gained in popularity. Synchronization royalties are those from music being licensed for use in television, movies, and advertisements.

2000 Napster
A recently developed format that compresses music into digital files shakes up the industry as millions of Internet users share music files on Napster.

2001 File-Sharing
A host of new peer-to-peer Internet services make music file-sharing more popular than ever.

2008 Online Music Stores
Apple's iTunes becomes the No. 1 retailer of music in the United States.

Records and Radio: A Rocky Relationship

We can't discuss the development of sound recording without also discussing radio (covered in detail in Chapter 6). Though each industry developed independently of the other, radio constituted recorded sound's first rival for listeners' attention. This competition triggered innovations both in sound recording technology and in the business relationship between the two industries.

It all started in the 1920s, when, to the recording industry's alarm, radio stations began broadcasting recorded music without compensating the music industry. The American Society of Composers, Authors and Publishers (ASCAP), founded in 1914 to collect copyright fees for music publishers and writers, accused radio of hurting sales of records and sheet music. By 1925, ASCAP established music-rights fees for radio, charging stations between $250 and $2,500 a week to play recorded music. Many stations couldn't afford these fees and had to leave the air. Other stations countered by establishing their own live, in-house orchestras, disseminating music free to listeners. Throughout the late 1920s and 1930s, record sales continued plummeting as the Great Depression worsened.

In the early 1950s, television became popular and began pilfering radio's programs, advertising revenue, and audience. Seeking to reinvent itself, radio turned to the record industry. Brokering a deal that gave radio a cheap source of content and record companies greater profits, many radio stations adopted a new hit-songs format—dubbed "Top 40," for the number of records a jukebox could store. Now when radio stations aired songs, record sales soared.

In the early 2000s, though, the radio and recorded-music industries were in conflict again. Upset by online radio stations' decision to stream music on the Internet, the recording industry began pushing for high royalty charges, hindering the development of Internet radio. The most popular online streaming services developed separately from traditional radio stations.

U.S. Popular Music and the Rise of Rock

As sound recording became a mass medium, it fueled the growth of popular music, or **pop music**, which appeals to large segments of the general population or sizable groups distinguished by age, region, or ethnic background. Pop music today includes numerous genres—rock and roll, jazz, blues, country, Tejano, salsa, reggae, punk, hip-hop, and dance—many of which evolved from a common foundation.

For example, rock splintered off from blues (which originated in the American South), and hip-hop grew out of R&B, dance music, and rock. This proliferation of music genres created a broad range of products that industry players could package and sell—targeted to increasingly narrow listener groups.

It would be a mistake to think of the label "pop music" as an insult, somehow referring to music that is frivolous, unimportant, or unartistic. To be sure, some music is indeed just meant to entertain (or to separate consumers from their dollars). But from the folk music protests of Woody Guthrie to the blurring of racial lines in the development of rock music to the antiwar anthem "What's Going On" by Marvin Gaye, popular music has exerted a major influence on society, culture, and even politics.

The Rise of Pop Music

Though technological advancements made sound recording a mass medium and sparked the proliferation of pop music genres, this music had its earliest roots in something far less technical: sheet music. With mass production of sheet music in the nineteenth and early twentieth centuries, pop developed into a business fed by artists who set standards for the different genres—including jazz, rock, blues, and R&B.

Back in the late nineteenth century, a section of Broadway in Manhattan known as Tin Pan Alley began selling sheet music for piano and other instruments. (The name Tin Pan Alley referred to the way these quickly produced tunes supposedly sounded like cheap pans clanging together.) Songwriting along Tin Pan Alley helped transform pop music into big business. At the turn of the twentieth century, improvements in printing technology enabled song publishers to mass-produce sheet music for a growing middle class. Previously a novelty, popular music now became a major enterprise. With the emergence of the phonograph and recorded tunes, interest in and sales of sheet music soared. (These sales would eventually decline with the rise of radio in the 1920s, which turned audiences more into listeners of music than active participants playing instruments to sheet music in their living rooms.)

As sheet music gained popularity and phonograph sales rose, **jazz** developed in New Orleans. An improvisational and mostly instrumental musical form, jazz absorbed and integrated a diverse array of musical styles, including African rhythms, blues, and gospel. Groups led by Louis Armstrong, Tommy Dorsey, and

MEDIA LITERACY

Case Study

The Rise of Digital Music
By John Dougan

It is a success story that could have only happened in the hyperspeed of the digital age. Since its debut in April 2003, iTunes has gone from an intriguing concept to the number-one music retailer (surpassing retail giant Walmart) in the United States. Boasting a customer base of fifty million, a library of six million songs, and sales in excess of ten billion dollars, iTunes has conclusively proven that consumers, irrespective of age, have readily and happily adapted to downloading, preferring it to purchasing CDs. Frustrated by escalating CD prices and convinced that most releases contained only a few good songs and too much filler—not to mention the physical clutter created by CDs—many consumers have begun to shop on digital music sites, which offer them an à la carte menu with which

Inti St Clair/Blend Images/Jupiter Images

they can cherry-pick their favorite tracks and build a music library that is easily stored on a hard drive, transferable to an MP3 player, and, increasingly, accessible from other computers or devices via a cloud drive: a third-party server that stores files externally from personal devices.

The move toward digital music has also forever altered the way music fans locate and access nonmainstream music and recordings by unsigned bands. If iTunes resembles a traditional retailer with a deep catalogue, then a competitor such as eMusic is the online equivalent of a specialty record store,

John Dougan is a professor in the Department of Recording Industry at Middle Tennessee State University.

LaunchPad

macmillanhighered.com/mediaessentials3e

▶ **Visit LaunchPad** to watch a clip from a recent music video. How might music videos affect digital music sales today?

designed for connoisseurs who are uninterested in mass-marketed pop. The success of social networking sites and music blogs has made them important gathering places for virtual communities of fans for thousands of bands in dozens of genres. The Internet is changing not only how consumers are exposed to music but how record label A&R (artist and repertoire) departments scout talent. A&R reps, who no longer travel as much to locate talent, are searching for acts that do their own marketing and come with a built-in fan following.

The digital age has also made the album-length CD increasingly obsolete. And though digital downloading allows consumers greater and more immediate access to music, aesthetically it harks back to the late 1950s and early 1960s, when the 45-rpm single was dominant and the most reliable indicator of whether a song was a hit. Downloading a variety of tracks means that consumers build their own collection of virtual 45s that, when taken as a whole, becomes a personalized greatest-hits collection. Some artists imagine a future where they no longer release full albums but a series of individual tracks that consumers can piece together however they please.

But if the death knell has been sounded for the compact disc, what of the digital download? In 2010, there were those who claimed that after only seven years, iTunes was showing its age and would at some point face a stiff challenge from Google's Android mobile operating system. With Android, users are able to purchase music from any computer and have the files appear instantly on their phones. Users are able to send the music on their hard drive to the Internet, so they can access it on their phone as long as they have an Internet connection—a cloud drive that detaches music from a personal, physical device. However, in 2011 Apple developed a Web-based iTunes (iTunes in the Cloud) and went further with iTunes Match, which allows users to upload all their music (even if not purchased through iTunes) to the cloud and play it on all their devices. Perhaps, then, the future means accessing music from anywhere at any time.

APPLYING THE CRITICAL PROCESS

DESCRIPTION Arrange to interview four to eight friends or relatives about how they purchase music today. Where do they buy most of their music—online through sites like iTunes, or in a retail store? When is the last time they bought a CD from a retail store? Devise questions about what makes them decide where to purchase music.

ANALYSIS Chart and organize your results. Do you recognize any patterns emerging from the data? What influences your friends' purchasing behaviors? Have their actions changed over time?

INTERPRETATION Based on the patterns you have charted, determine what they mean. Over time, have the changes in buying been significant? Why or why not? Why do you think people's buying preferences developed as they did?

EVALUATION Do you think the influence of MP3 and other new digital technology forms helps or hurts musical artists? Why do so many contemporary musical performers differ in their opinions about the Internet?

ENGAGEMENT To expand on your findings and see how they match up with industry findings, go to your local retail store and speak with a customer service representative about the buying patterns in the store. Has he or she noticed a shift in retail buying in the last five years? Share your findings with the representative and discuss whether your data match. Speculate about ways retail stores can survive alongside the digital community.

Tom Copi/Michael Ochs Archive/Getty Images

Louis Armstrong (1901–1971) transformed jazz with astonishing improvised trumpet solos and scat singing.

others counted among the most renowned of the "swing" jazz bands, whose rhythmic sound dominated radio, recordings, and dance halls.

The first pop vocalists of the twentieth century came out of vaudeville—stage performances featuring dancing, singing, comedy, and magic shows. By the 1930s, Rudy Vallée and Bing Crosby had established themselves as the first "crooners" singing pop standards. Bing Crosby also popularized Irving Berlin's "White Christmas," which became one of the most covered songs in recording history. (A song recorded or performed by another artist is known as **cover music**.) Meanwhile, the bluesy harmonies of a New Orleans vocal trio, the Boswell Sisters, influenced the Andrews Sisters, whose boogie-woogie style sold more than sixty million records in the late 1930s and 1940s. Helped by radio, pop vocalists like Frank Sinatra in the 1940s were among the first singers to win the hearts of a large national teen audience. Indeed, Sinatra's early performances incited the kinds of audience riots that would later characterize rock-and-roll concerts.

Rock and Roll Arrives

Pop music's expanding appeal paved the way for **rock and roll** to emerge in the mid-1950s. Rock both reflected and shaped powerful societal forces (such as blacks' migration from the South to the North and the growth of youth culture) that had begun transforming American life. Rock also stirred controversy. Like the word *jazz*, the phrase *rock and roll* was a blues slang expression meaning "sex"— which offended some people with more conservative tastes in music and made them worry about their children's choice in music. Rock grew out of a blending of numerous musical styles. For instance, early rock combined the vocal and instrumental traditions of pop with the rhythm-and-blues sounds of Memphis and the country twang of Nashville. As rock and roll developed, that fusion of musical styles contributed to both racial progress and fears reflecting the social unease of the 1950s and 1960s.

Blues and R&B Set the Stage for Rock

The migration of southern blacks to northern cities in search of better jobs during the first half of the twentieth century helped disseminate different popular music styles to new places. In particular, **blues** music traveled north. Blues became the foundation of rock and roll and was influenced by African American spirituals, ballads, and work songs from the rural South.

Influential blues artists included Robert Johnson, Ma Rainey, Bessie Smith, Muddy Waters, Howlin' Wolf, and Charley Patton. After the introduction of the electric guitar in the 1930s, blues-based urban black music began to be marketed under the name **rhythm and blues (R&B)**. This new music appealed to young listeners fascinated by the explicit (and forbidden) sexual lyrics in songs like "Annie Had a Baby," "Sexy Ways," and "Wild Wild Young Men." Although banned on some stations, R&B continued gaining popularity into the early 1950s. Still, black and white musical forms were segregated, and trade magazines in the 1950s tracked R&B record sales on "race" charts, separate from the white "pop" charts.

Rock Reflects and Reshapes Racial Politics

As artists began to produce music that borrowed from what mainstream society thought of as "black" and "white" musical traditions, American society as a whole was entering a tumultuous time of social and political change that would help fuel rock's popularity. By the early 1950s, President Truman's 1948 executive order integrating the armed forces was fully in practice, bringing young men from very different ethnic and economic backgrounds together. Then, in 1954, the Supreme Court's *Brown v. Board of Education* decision declared unconstitutional the "separate but equal" laws that had segregated blacks and whites for decades. Mainstream America began to wrestle seriously with the legacy of slavery and the unequal treatment of its African American citizens. And so rock music reflected the complicated changes happening at the time while also helping to influence those changes. On the one hand, the fusion of musical traditions made rock music popular among young people across racial lines and could be understood as "desegregating" in its own right. On the other hand, sometimes the rock-and-roll business of the 1950s and 1960s (and beyond) perpetuated racial inequalities and denied artists of color the fruits of their artistic efforts. White producers would often give cowriting credit to white performers like Elvis Presley (who never wrote songs himself) for the tunes they covered. Many producers also bought the rights to potential hits from black songwriters, who seldom saw a penny in royalties or received songwriting credit.

By 1955, R&B hits regularly crossed over to the pop charts, but for a time the white cover versions were more popular and profitable. For example, Pat Boone's cover of Fats Domino's "Ain't That a Shame" shot to No. 1 and stayed on the Top 40 pop chart for twenty weeks. Domino's original made it only to No. 10. A turning point, however, came in 1962, when Ray Charles covered "I Can't Stop Loving You," a 1958 country song by the Grand Ole Opry's Don Gibson. This marked the first time that a black artist covering a white artist's song had notched a No. 1 pop hit.

© Bettmann/Corbis

A major influence on early rock and roll, Chuck Berry, born in 1926, scored big hits between 1955 and 1958, writing "Maybellene," "Roll Over Beethoven," "School Day," "Sweet Little Sixteen," and "Johnny B. Goode." At the time, he was criticized by some black R&B artists for sounding white and by some white conservative critics for his popularity among white teenagers. Berry's experience is another example of the complicated and sometimes contradictory nature of the relationship between race and popular music.

Fear Fuels Censorship

Rock's blurring of racial and other lines alarmed enough Americans that performers and producers alike worried that fans would begin defecting. They used various tactics to get people to accept the music. Cleveland deejay Alan Freed played original R&B recordings from the race charts and black versions of early rock on his program, while Philadelphia deejay Dick Clark took a different tactic—playing white artists' cover versions of black music. Still, problems persisted that further eroded rock's acceptance.

One particularly difficult battle rock faced was the perception among mainstream adults that the music caused juvenile delinquency. Such delinquency was statistically on the rise in the 1950s, owing to contributing factors such as parental neglect, the rising consumer culture, and the burgeoning youth population after World War II. But adults sought an easier culprit to blame. It was far simpler to point the finger at rock—especially artists who blatantly defied rules governing proper behavior. Authorities responded by censoring rock lyrics.

Rattled by this and other developments, the U.S. recording industry decided it needed a makeover. To protect the enormous profits the new music had been generating, record companies began practicing some censorship of their own. In the early 1960s, the industry introduced a new generation of clean-cut white singers, including Frankie Avalon, Connie Francis, Ricky Nelson, Lesley Gore, and Fabian. Rock's explosive violations of racial, class, and other boundaries gave way to simpler generation gap problems, and the music—for a time—developed a milder reputation.

Rock Blurs Additional Boundaries

Although rock and roll was molded by powerful social, cultural, and political forces, it also shaped them in return. As we've seen, rock and roll began by blurring the boundary between black and white, but it broke down additional divisions as well—between high and low culture, masculinity and femininity, country and city, North and South, and the sacred and the secular.

High and Low Culture

Rock challenged the long-standing distinction between high and low culture initially through its lyrics and later through its performance styles. In 1956, Chuck Berry's song "Roll Over Beethoven" merged rock and roll (which many people considered low culture) with high culture through lyrics that included references to classical music: "You know my temperature's risin' / And the jukebox's blowin' a fuse . . . Roll over Beethoven / And tell Tchaikovsky the news." Rock artists also defied norms governing how musicians should behave: Berry's "duck walk" across the stage, Elvis Presley's tight pants and gyrating hips, and Bo Diddley's use of the guitar as a phallic symbol shocked elite audiences—and inspired additional antics by subsequent artists.

Masculinity and Femininity

Rock and roll was also the first pop music genre to overtly challenge assumptions about sexual identity and orientation. Although early rock and roll largely attracted males as performers, the most fascinating feature of Elvis Presley, according to the Rolling Stones' Mick Jagger, was his androgynous appearance.[3] Little Richard (Penniman) took things even further, sporting a pompadour hairdo, decorative makeup, and feminized costumes during his performances.[4]

Country and City

Rock and roll also blended cultural borders between early-twentieth-century black urban rhythms and white country & western music. Early white rockers such as Buddy Holly and Carl Perkins combined country or hillbilly music, southern gospel, and Mississippi delta blues to create a sound called **rockabilly**. Conversely, rhythm and blues spilled into rock and roll. Many songs first popular on the R&B charts, such as "Rocket 88," crossed over to the pop charts during the mid to late 1950s, though many of these songs were performed by more widely known white artists.

Rock lyrics in the 1950s may not have been especially provocative or overtly political by today's standards, but soaring record sales and the crossover appeal of the music itself represented an enormous threat to long-standing racial and class divisions defined by geography. Distinctions at the time between traditionally rural white music and urban black music dissolved, as some black artists (such as Chuck Berry) strived to "sound white" to attract Caucasian fans, and some white artists (such as Elvis Presley) were encouraged by record producers to "sound black."

North and South

Not only did rock and roll blur the line between urban and rural, but it also mixed northern and southern influences together. As many blacks migrated north during the early twentieth century, they brought their love of blues and R&B with them. Meanwhile, musicians and audiences in the North had claimed blues music as their own, forever extending its reach beyond its origins in the rural South. Some white artists from the South—most notably Carl Perkins, Elvis Presley, and Buddy Holly—further carried southern musical styles to northern listeners.

Sacred and Secular

Many mainstream adults in the 1950s complained that rock and roll's sexual overtones and gender bending constituted an offense against God—even though

© Bettmann/Corbis

Although his unofficial title, King of Rock and Roll, has been challenged by Little Richard and Chuck Berry, Elvis Presley remains among the most popular solo artists of all time. From 1956 to 1962, he recorded seventeen No. 1 hits, from "Heartbreak Hotel" to "Good Luck Charm."

numerous early rock figures (such as Elvis Presley, Jerry Lee Lewis, and Little Richard) had strong religious upbringings. In the late 1950s, public outrage over rock proved so great that even Little Richard and Jerry Lee Lewis, both sons of southern preachers, became convinced that they were playing "the devil's music." Throughout the rock era and even today, boundaries between the sacred and the secular continue to blur through music. For example, some churches are using rock and roll to appeal to youth, and some Christian-themed rock groups are recording in seemingly incongruous musical styles, such as heavy metal.

The Evolution of Pop Music

As the volatile decade of the 1960s unfolded, pop music (including rock) changed to reflect additional social, cultural, and political shifts—while continuing to influence these aspects of American life as well. Authorities made further attempts to "tame" rock, concerned about its influence on teenagers. These attempts sparked resistance from defiant young people, many of whom embraced rock musicians from Great Britain who hadn't toned down their style. As pop music continued to adapt, it spun off into several genres, including soul, folk, and psychedelic, as well as country, punk, grunge, and hip-hop.

The British Are Coming!

Rock and roll proved so powerful that it transformed pop music across national borders. For instance, in England during the late 1950s, the young members of the Rolling Stones covered blues songs by American artists Robert Johnson and Muddy Waters. And the young Beatles imitated Chuck Berry and Little Richard.

Until 1964, rock-and-roll recordings had traveled on a one-way ticket to Europe. Even though American artists regularly reached the tops of charts overseas, no British performers had yet appeared on any Top 10 pop lists in the United States. This changed virtually overnight in 1964, when the Beatles came to America with their mop haircuts and delivered pop interpretations of American blues and rock. Within the next few years, more British bands—the Kinks, the Who, the Yardbirds—produced hits that climbed the American Top 40 charts. Ed Sullivan,

Photo by David Redfern/Redferns/Getty Images (left); Dave J Hogan/Getty Images (right)

British rock groups like the Beatles and the Rolling Stones first invaded American pop charts in the 1960s. Although the Beatles broke up in 1970, each member went on to work on solo projects. The Stones are still (mostly) together and touring more than fifty years later.

who booked the Beatles several times on his TV variety show in the mid-1960s, helped promote the group's early success.

With the British invasion, the rock industry split into two styles of music. The Rolling Stones developed a style emphasizing gritty, chord-driven, high-volume rock, which would influence later bands that created glam rock, hard rock, punk, heavy metal, and grunge. Meanwhile, the Beatles presented a more accessible, melodic, and softer sound, which would eventually inspire new genres, such as pop rock, power pop, new wave, and alternative rock. The British groups' success also demonstrated to the recording industry that older American musical forms, especially blues and R&B, could be repackaged as rock and exported around the world.

Motown: The Home of Soul

As rock attracted more and more devotees, it resurrected interest in the styles of music from which it had originated. Throughout the 1960s, black singers like James Brown, Aretha Franklin, Wilson Pickett, Otis Redding, and Ike and Tina Turner picked up on this interest, transforming the rhythms and melodies of older R&B, pop, and early rock and roll into what would become known as **soul**. These artists attracted large and racially diverse audiences, countering the British invaders with powerful vocal performances.

The most prominent independent label supporting black songwriters' and performers' work was Motown, started in 1959 by former Detroit autoworker and songwriter Berry Gordy. Motown signed many successful black artists and groups, including the Four Tops ("Baby I Need Your Loving"), the Marvelettes ("Please Mr. Postman"), Marvin Gaye ("What's Going On"), and the Jackson 5

© CBS/Landov

One of the most successful groups in rock-and-roll history, the Supremes recorded twelve No. 1 hits between 1964 and 1969, including "Where Did Our Love Go," "Baby Love," "Come See about Me," and "Stop! In the Name of Love." The group was inducted into the Rock and Roll Hall of Fame in 1988.

("I'll Be There"). But the label's most successful group was the Supremes, featuring Diana Ross, which scored twelve No. 1 singles between 1964 and 1969 (including "Where Did Our Love Go" and "Stop! In the Name of Love"). The Supremes' success showed Motown producers that songs emphasizing romance and featuring a danceable beat won far more young white fans than those trumpeting rebellion and political upheaval.

Folk and Psychedelic: Protest and Drugs

Popular music has always been both a product of and a shaper of its time. So it's not surprising that the social upheavals of the 1960s and early 1970s—over Civil Rights, women's rights, environmental protection, the Vietnam War, and the use of recreational drugs—found their reflections in rock music during these decades. By the late 1960s, many songwriters and performers spoke to their generation's social and political concerns through two music genres: folk and psychedelic rock.

Folk Inspires Protest

The musical genre that most clearly expressed pivotal political events of the time was folk, which had long served as a voice for social activism. **Folk music** exists in all cultures; it's usually performed by untrained musicians and passed down mainly through oral traditions. With its rough edges and amateur quality, folk is considered a democratic and participatory musical form. During the 1930s, the work of Woody Guthrie ("This Land Is Your Land") set a new standard for American folk music. Later, in the 1960s and 1970s, groups such as the Weavers, featuring labor activist and songwriter Pete Seeger, carried on Guthrie's legacy. These newer groups inspired yet another crop of singer-songwriters—Joan Baez; Arlo Guthrie; Peter, Paul, and Mary; Phil Ochs; Bob Dylan—who took a stand against worrisome developments of the day, including industrialization, poverty, racism, and war.

Rock Turns Psychedelic

With the increasing use of recreational drugs by young people and the availability of LSD (not illegal until the mid-1960s), more and more rock musicians experimented with and sang about drugs during rock's *psychedelic* era. Defining groups and performers of this era included newcomers like Jefferson Airplane, Big Brother and the Holding Company (featuring Janis Joplin), the Jimi Hendrix Experience, the Doors, and the Grateful Dead, as well as established artists like the Beatles and the Rolling Stones. These musicians believed they could enhance their artistic prowess by taking mind-altering drugs. They also saw the use of these drugs as a form of personal expression and an appropriate response to the government's failure to deal with social and political problems, such as racism and America's involvement in the Vietnam War.

© Andrew DeLory (left); © Christy Bowe/Corbis (right)

After a surge of optimism that culminated in the historic Woodstock concert in August 1969, the sun set on the psychedelic era. In particular, some of psychedelic rock's greatest stars died from drug overdoses, including Janis Joplin, Jimi Hendrix, and Jim Morrison of the Doors.

Punk, Grunge, and Alternative Rock: New Genres on the Horizon

As rock and roll moved from the edges of the American music scene into the mainstream, other genres arose to take its place on the fringes. While many people had considered rock a major part of the rebel counterculture in the 1960s, in the 1970s they increasingly viewed it as part of consumer culture. With major musical acts earning huge profits, rock had become just another product for manufacturers and retailers to promote, package, and profit from. According to critic Ken Tucker, this situation produced "faceless rock" performed by bands with "no established individual personalities outside their own large but essentially discrete audiences" of young white males.[5] To Tucker, these "faceless" groups—REO Speedwagon, Styx, Boston, Journey, Kansas—filled stadiums and entertained the maximum number of people while stirring up the minimum amount of controversy. It was only a matter of time before new types of music—punk, grunge, and

Born Robert Allen Zimmerman in Minnesota, Bob Dylan took his stage name from Welsh poet Dylan Thomas. He led a folk music movement in the early 1960s with engaging, socially provocative lyrics, but later infused folk with the electric sounds of rock. He continues recording and touring today, typically spending most of April through November on the road. He was awarded the Presidential Medal of Freedom in 2012.

Mark Metcalfe/Getty Images

Joan Jett, of the punk-rock group the Runaways and later Joan Jett and the Blackhearts, was influential in breaking down the boys' club mentality of rock and roll. She was inducted into the Rock and Roll Hall of Fame in 2015.

alternative rock—arose to challenge rock's mainstream once more. Concurrently, an older genre—country music—rose to greater prominence, crossing over to gain more mainstream acceptance.

Punk Revives Rock's Rebellious Spirit

Punk rock arose in the late 1970s to defy the orthodoxy and commercialism of the record business. Punk attempted to revive rock's basic defining characteristics: simple chord structures that anyone with a few guitar lessons could master, catchy melodies, and politically or socially defiant lyrics. Emerging in New York City around bands such as the Ramones, Blondie, and Talking Heads, punk quickly spread to England, where a soaring unemployment rate and growing class inequality ensured the success of socially critical rock. Groups like the Sex Pistols, the Clash, the Buzzcocks, and Siouxsie and the Banshees sprang up and even scored Top 40 hits on the U.K. charts. Despite their popularity, the Sex Pistols—one of the most controversial groups in rock history—was eventually banned for offending British decorum.

Punk didn't succeed commercially in the United States, in part because it was so hostile toward the commercialization of the mainstream music industry. However, it did help to break down the boys' club mentality of rock, launching unapologetic and unadorned front women like Patti Smith, Joan Jett, Debbie Harry, and Chrissie Hynde. It also introduced all-women bands whose members not only wrote but also performed their own music. Many of these female groups made it into the mainstream. Through these and other innovations, punk reopened the door to experimentation at a time when the industry had turned music into a purely commercial enterprise.

Grunge and Alternative Reinterpret Rock

Building on the innovative spirit of punk, the **grunge** genre further transformed rock in the 1990s. Grunge got its name from its often-messy guitar sound and the torn jeans and flannel shirts worn by its musicians and fans. Its lineage traced back to 1980s bands like Sonic Youth, the Minutemen, and Hüsker Dü. In 1992, after years of limited commercial success, this younger cousin of punk finally broke into the American mainstream with the success of Nirvana's "Smells Like Teen Spirit," the hit single from the album *Nevermind*.

Some critics view punk and grunge as subcategories or fringe movements of **alternative rock**, even though grunge was far more commercially successful than punk. This vague label encompasses many types of experimental rock music, which offered departures from the staged extravaganzas of 1970s glam rock. Such music appealed chiefly to college students and twentysomethings and set itself apart from the sounds of Top 40 and commercial FM radio. The same is true of **indie rock**, a broad category of independent-minded rock music usually distributed by smaller record labels. This genre, which can be traced to 1980s punk and post-punk acts, has achieved greater commercial success in recent years.

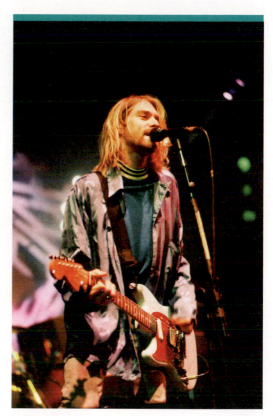

Pycha/DAPR/Zuma Press. © 1993 by DAPR

Hip-Hop Redraws Musical Lines

With the growing segregation of radio formats and the dominance of mainstream rock by white male performers, the place of black artists in the rock world diminished from the late 1970s onward. By the 1980s, few popular black successors to Chuck Berry or Jimi Hendrix had emerged in rock, with artists like Prince and Lenny Kravitz exceptions more than the rule. These trends, combined with the rise of "safe" dance disco by white bands (the Bee Gees), black artists (Donna Summer), and integrated groups (the Village People), created a space for a new sound to emerge starting in the late 1970s: **hip-hop**, a term for the urban culture that includes *rapping*, *cutting* (or *sampling*) by deejays, breakdancing, street clothing, poetry slams, and graffiti art.

Similar to punk's opposition to commercial rock, hip-hop music stood in direct opposition to the polished, professional, and often less political world of soul. Its combination of social politics, swagger, and confrontational lyrics carried forward long-standing traditions in blues, R&B, soul, and rock and roll.

Initially, the music industry saw it as a novelty destined to go nowhere. But by 1985, hip-hop had become a popular genre with the commercial successes of groups and artists like Run-DMC, the Fat Boys, LL Cool J, and Queen Latifah. Soon, white groups like the Beastie Boys and Linkin Park were combining hip-hop and hard rock, while some white artists (such as Eminem, Iggy Azalea, and Macklemore) were attracting huge followings by emulating black rap artists. This has not been without controversy, however, as some critics worry about a repeat of the appropriation of urban musical forms by white artists, robbing those original

Nirvana front man Kurt Cobain's vocal style, as well as a decidedly unglamorous look quite different from the much more theatrical "hair bands" of the 1980s, helped define the grunge genre in the early 1990s. The release of Nirvana's *Nevermind* in September 1991 bumped Michael Jackson's *Dangerous* from the top of the charts and signaled a new direction in popular music. Other grunge bands soon followed Nirvana on the charts, including Pearl Jam, Alice in Chains, Stone Temple Pilots, and Sound-garden.

© Aviv Small/ZUMA Press (left); Allen Berezovsky/WireImage/Getty Images (right)

Artists like Kanye West (*left*) and Nicki Minaj (*right*) have found a place in the world of hip-hop. West, born in Atlanta in 1977, is an American rapper, producer, and singer-songwriter who has received many awards and won critical acclaim for his work, often introducing controversy along the way. Born in Trinidad in 1982, Minaj began her career with mixtapes and guest appearances on other artists' songs before releasing her debut album, *Pink Friday*. Several more albums and guest appearances followed.

artists of both opportunities and their artistic voice. These concerns over race and cultural appropriation will likely continue to be a source of controversy.

Although hip-hop encompasses many different styles, its most controversial subgenre is probably **gangster rap**. In seeking to describe gang violence in America, gangster rap has been accused of inciting violence through its lyrics and the illegal activities of some of its performers. Gangster rap drew widespread condemnation in 1996 with the shooting death of Tupac Shakur, a rapper and convicted sex offender. Criticism mounted in 1997 after a drive-by shooter killed the Notorious B.I.G., who had dealt drugs as a youngster before becoming a rapper. Under pressure, the hip-hop industry softened its hard edges. Most prominently, artist Sean "Diddy" Combs developed a more danceable hip-hop that combined singing and rapping with musical elements of rock and soul. Today, hip-hop stars include artists such as 50 Cent, who emulates the gangster drama, and artists like Kanye West, Lupe Fiasco, Drake, and Talib Kweli, who often bring an old-school social consciousness to their performances.

From its origins in an urban American subculture, hip-hop has become a major part of mainstream global culture. Today, it's big business, and its most successful practitioners have diversified from record labels to clothing lines, restaurants, and movie production companies.

The Country Road

Country music has attracted enough loyal listeners in its various forms to survive as a profitable sector of the recording industry since the early days of pop music.

Though the many styles of **country** represent significant variations in the development of this musical form, they all share one element: the country voice, inflected by a twang or a drawl. In the late 1950s, the wilder honky-tonk sounds of country were tamed by a smoother style, inspired by the mellower songs of Elvis Presley. Replacing the fiddles, electric guitars, and nasal vocals of honky-tonk with symphonic strings, pitch-perfect background vocalists, and crooning stars like Jim Reeves and Patsy Cline, the emergent style would become known as the "Nashville sound." This laid-back and toned-down form of country music reigned throughout the 1960s.[6] In the 1970s, some singers and producers aimed for more mainstream acceptance. Lynn Anderson ("I Never Promised You a Rose Garden"), Charlie Pride ("Behind Closed Doors"), and Marie Osmond ("Paper Roses") belted out hits that made the country idiom well liked in suburban America.[7] By the late 1970s, this movement had spawned pop country, a form dedicated to generating hits that would score on both the pop and country charts, launching the careers of superstars Glen Campbell, John Denver, and Kenny Rogers. However, the genre would not peak until the 1990s, when "new country" attracted fresh throngs of fans. In 1989, Clint Black perfected the new country sound in his *Killin' Time* album, and in 1992, Billy Ray Cyrus followed up Black's triumph with the massive hit "Achy Breaky Heart." Shania Twain and Faith Hill went on to sell platinum country albums in the 1990s, but Garth Brooks would be the star to break sales and concert attendance records during the decade, establishing a huge country market for years to come.

Rich Polk/Getty Images for iHeartMedia

Kacey Musgraves became a hot country star in 2013 with songs featuring lyrics sometimes tagged as controversial, especially within the often-conservative country genre. Musgraves has spoken about wanting to try out other musical genres, and country does see a lot of entrances and exits: Taylor Swift started off as a country star before branching out into pop, while singer-songwriter Sheryl Crow gravitated to country music later in her career.

The Economics of Sound Recording

Sound recording is a complex business, with many participants playing many different roles and controlling numerous dimensions of the industry. Songwriters, singers, and musicians create the sounds. Producers and record labels sign up artists to create music and often own the artists' work. Promoters market artists' work, managers handle bands' touring schedules, and agents seek the best royalty deals for their artist-clients.

Ever since sound recording became a mass medium, there's been a lot of money to be had from the industry—primarily through sales of records and CDs. But with the increasing amount of music available for digital download, the traditional business model has broken down. The business has also changed though consolidation. In 1998, only six major labels remained; and by 2012, that number had dwindled to three: Universal Music Group, Sony Music Entertainment, and Warner Music Group. These three companies control about 65 percent of the recording industry market in the United States, have many music stars under contract, have the resources to promote those stars, and own catalogues of recordings to sell. But despite the oligopoly (few owners exerting great control over an industry), the biggest change in the music industry has been the rising market share of independent music labels.

A Shifting Power Structure

Over the years, the U.S. recording industry has experienced dramatic shifts in its power structure. From the 1950s through the 1980s, the industry consisted of numerous competing major labels as well as independent production houses, or **indies**. Over time, the major labels began swallowing up the indies and then buying each other. By 1998, only six big labels remained: Universal, Warner, Sony, BMG, EMI, and Polygram. That year, Universal acquired Polygram; in 2003, BMG and Sony merged; and in late 2011, EMI was auctioned off to Universal. Today, only three major music corporations exist: Universal Music Group, Sony Music Entertainment, and Warner Music Group. With their stables of stars, financial resources, and huge libraries of music to sell, these firms exert a great deal of control, at one time capturing about 85 percent of the market in the United States. Critics, consumers, and artists alike complain that this consolidation of power in the hands of a few resists new sounds in music that may not have traditional commercial appeal and supports only those major artists and styles that have large mainstream appeal. In 2013, the big three labels' control of the U.S. market had slipped to around 65 percent. And although this is still a major portion of the market, the bigger news is that this comes as a result of recent growth in independent labels (see Figure 5.2).

The Indies Grow with Digital Music

The rise of rock and roll in the 1950s and early 1960s showcased a rich diversity of independent labels—including Sun, Stax, Chess, and Motown—all vying for a share of the new music. That tradition lives on today. In contrast to the

FIGURE 5.2 // **U.S. MARKET SHARE OF THE MAJOR LABELS IN THE RECORDING INDUSTRY, 2013**

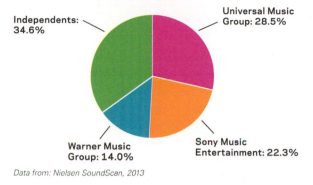

Independents: 34.6%

Universal Music Group: 28.5%

Sony Music Entertainment: 22.3%

Warner Music Group: 14.0%

Data from: Nielsen SoundScan, 2013

three global players, some five thousand large and small independent production houses—or indies—record less commercially viable music, or music they hope will become commercially viable. Often struggling enterprises, indies require only a handful of people to operate them. For years, indies accounted for 10–15 percent of all music releases. But with the advent of downloads and streaming, the enormous diversity of independent-label music became much more accessible, and the market share of indies more than doubled in size. Indies often still depend on wholesale distributors to promote and sell their music, or enter into deals with one of the three major labels to gain wider distribution for their artists (similar to independent filmmakers using major studios for film distribution). Independent labels have produced some of the best-selling artists of recent years: Big Machine Records (Taylor Swift, Rascal Flatts), Dualtone Records (the Lumineers), XL Recordings (Adele, Vampire Weekend), and Cash Money Records (Drake, Nicki Minaj). These companies can also release less commercially viable music or albums by established artists now ignored by the majors, who are also reluctant to invest in forgotten artists.

Often many of the year's most acclaimed albums are released by artists on independent labels—or artists who began on independent labels before jumping to a major. St. Vincent released three albums on indie labels like Beggars Banquet and 4AD before she put out her critically beloved self-titled fourth album through a division of Universal in 2014.

Making and Spending Money

Like most mass media, the recorded-music business consists of several components. Money today comes in as revenue earned mostly from sales of CDs, song downloads, and—increasingly—fees to the industry from online music subscription services. It goes out in forms such as royalties paid to artists, production costs, and distribution expenses.

Rick Kern/WireImage/Getty Images

CONVERGING MEDIA

Case Study

360 Degrees of Music

It used to be that recording labels made most or all of their money by receiving a percentage of the money generated by the sale of physical media, such as CDs, records, and tapes. But the era of digital downloads (both legal and illegal varieties) saw that revenue literally cut in half in little over a decade. In response, the recording industry is turning to something called 360-degree agreements. Defined by legal scholar Sara Karubian as "a legal contract between a musical artist and one company incorporating components of an artist's career that have traditionally been handled by separate contracts with different companies," the 360-degree deal gives a single corporation control over everything, from merchandising and publishing to endorsements and touring.[1]

What this means is that in addition to the money a record company would make from sales of recordings, the company would also get a cut of money from tours, concerts, publishing (if the artist is also the songwriter), merchandise, endorsements, even television and movie appearances, for the length of the contract. In theory, the recording company helps organize, market, and cover the up-front costs of those concert tours; merchandise production; and so on. The recording industry describes these deals as mutually beneficial, centralizing and maximizing revenue for the artist and the label at a time when both are suffering from the huge drop in music recording sales.

But in practice, critics worry that there may be significant downsides to these arrangements. For example, in some cases a record label might not automatically agree to provide support for the revenue stream it wants to share with the artist, meaning the artist essentially signs away a chunk of money at no benefit. These deals also shift power back to conglomerates at a time when more indie labels have gained traction in the industry. However, as these agreements have become more common in recent years, new artists may soon find they have little choice but to sign 360-degree contracts if they want to go with a major label.

Some artists may be content to become "middle-class" touring bands, making a little money off albums and singles but using them primarily to promote their live shows and accompanying merchandise. Media convergence has made this middle-class existence a more viable alternative for many acts that would have, in more label-dominated years, been forced to produce a huge hit or face obscurity.

LaunchPad

macmillanhighered.com/mediaessentials3e

▶ **Visit LaunchPad** to watch a clip from Katy Perry's *Prism* tour. How might an expensive tour bring in additional money for an artist like Perry?

Musical acts with large enough fan bases may follow the lead of British alternative rock group Radiohead, which handles its career without contracted label backing. (However, physical CD distribution is usually still handled through a third party; although Radiohead self-released its 2011 album *King of Limbs*, it was released as a CD via the label TBD Records). While few big artists can maintain a label-free career, many more of them offer fans the option of buying their music directly through the artist's or label's Web site, often selling exclusive packages that may include digital downloads, vinyl albums, T-shirts, concert tickets, or limited-edition releases. In these cases, artists are allowing multiple media to converge into their own hands. Whether through 360-degree deals, middle-class touring careers, or a self-releasing strategy, convergence is changing the way many musicians make money.

Money In

In the recording industry, the product that generates revenue is the music itself. However, selling in the music business has become more challenging than ever. Revenues for the recording industry started shrinking in 2000 as file-sharing began undercutting CD sales. By 2008, U.S. music sales had fallen to $8.5 billion—down from a peak of $14.5 billion in 1999.[8] CD sales fell between 2009 and 2010, as digital performance royalties increased at the same time.[9] In 2011, digital sales surpassed physical CD sales in the United States for the first time. By 2013, CDs accounted for a little less than a third of total sales, with digital downloads and streaming accounting for most of the other two-thirds of the market (see Figure 5.1).

In previous decades, the primary sales outlets for music were direct-retail music stores (independents or chains such as the now-defunct Tower) and general retail outlets like Walmart, Best Buy, and Target. Another 10 percent of recording sales came from music clubs, which operated like book clubs (see Chapter 2). But almost fifteen years of dropping CD sales (in the United States at least) has meant that direct-retail music stores have largely disappeared, and big retailers typically opt for stocking only top-selling CDs rather than offering a wide variety of choices.

Conversely, digital sales—which include digital downloads from online retailers (like iTunes and Amazon), subscription streaming services (like Rhapsody and the paid version of Spotify), free streaming services (like the ad-supported Spotify, Rdio, YouTube, and Vevo), streaming radio services (like Pandora and iHeartRadio), ringtones, and synchronization fees (payments for use of music in various media, such as film, TV, and advertising)—have grown to capture almost two-thirds of the U.S. market and 39 percent of the global market.[10] About 40 percent of all music recordings purchased in the United States are downloads, and iTunes is the leading retailer of downloads.

Subscription and streaming services have been a big growth area in the United States and now account for about 21 percent of U.S. music industry revenues. The difference between a streaming music service (e.g., Spotify) and streaming radio (e.g., Pandora) is that streaming music services enable listeners to stream specific songs, whereas streaming radio allows listeners to select only a genre or style of music.

The international recording industry is a major proponent of music streaming services because they are a new revenue source. Although **online piracy**—unauthorized online file-sharing—still exists, the advent of advertising-supported music streaming services has satisfied consumer demand for free music and weakened interest in illegal file-swapping. There are now about 450 licensed online music services worldwide.[11] Spotify, one of the leading services, has more than twenty million licensed songs to stream globally, with over twenty thousand songs added every day. Spotify carries so many songs that 20 percent of its songs have never been played.[12]

LaunchPad
macmillanhighered.com
/mediaessentials3e

Streaming Music Videos
On the Media Essentials LaunchPad, watch clips of recent music videos from Katy Perry.
Discussion: Music videos get less TV exposure than they did in their heyday, but they can still be a crucial part of major artists' careers. How do these videos help sell Perry's music?

Money Out

In the recording industry, major labels and indies must spend money to produce the product, including employing people with the right array of skills. They must also invest in the equipment and other resources essential for recording and duplicating songs and albums. The process begins with **A&R (artist and repertoire) agents**, who are the talent scouts of the music business. These agents work to discover, develop, and sometimes manage artists. A&R executives at the labels listen to demonstration tapes, or *demos*, from new artists, deciding what music to reject, whom to sign, and which songs to record.

Recording is complex and expensive. A typical recording session involves the artist, the producer, the session engineer, and audio technicians. In charge of the overall recording process, the producer handles most nontechnical elements of the session, including reserving studio space, hiring session musicians if neces-sary, and making final decisions about the recording's quality. The session engi-neer oversees the technical aspects of the recording session—everything from choosing recording equipment to managing the audio technicians.

Dividing the Profits

The complex relationship between artists and businesspeople in the recording in-dustry (including label executives and retailers) becomes especially obvious in the struggle over who gets how much money. To see how this works, let's consider the costs and profits from a typical CD that retails at $18.00. The wholesale price for that CD (the price paid by the store that sells it) is about $12.50, leaving the remainder as profit for the retailer. The more heavily discounted the CD, the less profit the retailer earns. The wholesale price represents the actual cost of produc-ing and promoting the recording plus the recording label's profits. The record com-pany reaps the highest profit (about $9.74 on a typical CD). But along with the artist, the record label also bears the bulk of the expenses: manufacturing costs, CD packaging design, advertising and promotion, and artists' royalties. The actual physical product—the CD itself—costs less than 25 cents to manufacture.

New artists usually negotiate a royalty rate of 8 to 12 percent on the retail price of a CD, although more established performers might bargain for 15 percent or higher. An artist who has negotiated a typical 11 percent royalty rate would earn about $1.93 for every CD sold at a price of $17.98. So, a CD that "goes gold"—sells 500,000 units—would net the artist around $965,000. But out of this amount, artists must repay the record company the money they have been advanced to cover the costs of recording, making music videos, and touring. Artists must also pay their band members, managers, and attorneys.

The profits are divided somewhat differently in digital download sales. A $1.29 iTunes download generates about $0.40 for iTunes (iTunes gets 30 percent of every song sale) and a standard $0.09 mechanical royalty for the song publisher and writer, leaving about $0.80 for the record company. Artists at a typical royalty rate of about 15 percent would get $0.20 from the song download. With no CD printing and packaging costs, record companies can retain more of the revenue on download sales.

Another venue for digital music is streaming services like Spotify and Rdio. Some leading artists initially held back their new releases from such services due to concerns that streaming eats into their digital download and CD sales, and that the compensation from streaming services wasn't sufficient. Spotify reports that (similar to Apple's iTunes) it pays out about 70 percent of its revenue to music-rights holders (divided between the label, performers, and songwriters), retaining about 30 percent for itself, and that on average each stream is worth about $0.007.[13] Depending on the popularity of the song, that could add up to a little or a lot of money—though even a play count of one million would still net only about $7,000. Songs played on Internet radio, like Pandora, Slacker, or iHeartRadio, have yet another formula for determining royalties. In 2000, the nonprofit group SoundExchange was established to collect royalties for Internet radio. SoundExchange charges fees of $0.002 per play, per listener.

Finally, video services like YouTube and Vevo have become sites to generate advertising revenue through music videos, which can attract tens of millions of views. For example, Beyoncé's 2014 video for "Drunk in Love" drew more than 166 million views in just five months. There aren't standard formulas for sharing ad revenue from music videos, but there is movement in that direction. In 2012, Universal Music Group and the National Music Publishers' Association agreed that music publishers would be paid 15 percent of advertising revenues generated by music videos licensed for use on YouTube and Vevo.

In addition to sales royalties, there are also performance and mechanical royalties that go to various participants in the industry. A *performance royalty* is paid to artists and music publishers whenever a song they created or own is played in any money-making medium or venue—such as on the radio, on television, in a film, or in a restaurant. Performance royalties are collected and paid out by the three major music performance rights organizations: ASCAP; the Society of European Stage Authors and Composers (SESAC); and Broadcast Music, Inc. (BMI). Songwriters also receive a *mechanical royalty* each time a

Solomon Linda (on far left, pictured with his singing group, the Original Evening Birds), the writer of the frequently covered hit song "The Lion Sleeps Tonight," signed over the copyright for the song for 10 shillings—the equivalent of 87 cents today—in 1952. After Linda's death in 1962, with only $22 to his name, his family fought for the royalties he should have received, resulting in a successful financial settlement for the family in 2006.

Naashon Falk/Full Frame

recording of their song is sold. The mechanical royalty is usually split between the music publisher and the songwriter. However, songwriters sometimes sell their copyrights to publishers to make a short-term profit. In these cases, they forgo the long-term royalties they would have received by retaining the copyright.

Sound Recording in a Democratic Society

Of all the developments that have unfolded since sound recording became a mass medium, controversies sparked by some forms of popular music have raised the most provocative questions about music's role in our democracy. Battles over what artists should be allowed to say in a song and how they should behave on stage or in a video speak to the heart of democratic expression. Are songs that express violent intent toward gay people, women, or ethnic or racial groups hate crimes? Are songs protected as free speech under the First Amendment of the U.S. Constitution? Moreover, will the ongoing consolidation of the industry by a few powerful music labels encourage them to "approve" lyrics and other forms of musical expression only if doing so will earn them maximum profits? Will the Internet continue to create more spaces for independent music to grow and for alternative voices to be heard? Popular musical forms that push at cultural boundaries face a dilemma: how to uphold the right to free expression while resisting control by companies bent on maximizing profits. Since the 1950s, forms of rock music have arisen to break through boundaries, then have been reined in to create a successful commercial product, then have reemerged as new agents of rebellion—and on and on, repeating the cycle.

Still, this dynamic between popular music's innovation and capitalism's profit motive seems like an ongoing dance that has sustained—at least until the age of the Internet—the economic structure of the music industry. The major labels need indies to identify and develop new and fresh talent. And talent is fresh only if it seems alternative or less commercial and comes from nonmainstream origins, such as ethnic communities, backyard garages, dance parties, and neighborhood clubs. For a long time, it was taken as a given that musicians need the major labels if they want to distribute their work widely, become famous, and reach large audiences. But examination of major label practices, both in terms of business and artist relations, may not reinforce this belief any longer, especially given the considerable success of several musical acts that have never been on a major label. A major component of media literacy as related to popular music involves evaluating the usefulness and pitfalls of the conglomerates that attempt to lead the industry. The interdependence of artists and businesses presents alluring opportunities (and potential trade-offs) for participants in the industry as well as those who watch and analyze it.

CHAPTER ESSENTIALS

Now that you have finished reading this chapter, you can use the following tools:

REVIEW

Trace the Early History and Evolution of Sound Recording

- In the development stage of sound recording, early inventors experimented with sound technology; in the entrepreneurial stage, people sought to make money from this technology; finally, in the mass medium stage, entrepreneurs learned how they could cheaply produce and distribute recorded music to large audiences (pp. 148–150).

- The introduction of magnetic **audiotape** (which made possible sound editing and multiple-track mixing, with vocals or instrumentals recorded at one location and later mixed onto a master recording in a studio) and tape players in the 1940s paved the way for innovations such as cassettes in the mid-1960s; the commercial use in the 1950s of **stereo** (more specifically, stereophonic sound, which created a more natural sound by improving on this 1930s invention); and **digital recording** in the 1970s, which stands in contrast to **analog recording**. Using digital technology, the first **compact discs** (CDs)—produced more cheaply than vinyl and audiocassettes—were first sold in 1983 (pp. 150–151).

- In 1992, the **MP3** file format was developed as part of a video compression standard, enabling sound to be compressed into small, manageable digital files. This allowed people to easily download music, thereby reducing sales of CDs and other physical formats, revolutionizing the sound recording industry, and shifting the rocky relationship between record labels and radio stations (pp. 151–154).

Understand the Rise of Popular Music and Rock in the United States

- As sound recording became a mass medium, it fueled the growth of **pop music**, which arose out of sheet-music sales. Pop music became a major enterprise, with numerous genres evolving from a common foundation, the first of which were blues and **jazz** (whose early artists often performed **cover music**) (pp. 154–155, 158).

- Pop music's appeal grew quickly, ushering in **rock and roll** in the mid-1950s. Rock's strongest influences can be traced back to **blues** (whose roots come from African American songs from the rural South) and **rhythm and blues**, or **R&B** (blues-based urban black music that emerged with the introduction of the electric guitar) (pp. 158–159).

- Rock both reflected and shaped powerful social forces, such as blacks' migration from the South to the North and the growth of youth culture. It also blurred the boundaries between black and white, and broke down divisions between high and low culture, masculinity and femininity, country and city (white rockers combined country or hillbilly music, southern gospel, and Mississippi delta blues to create a sound called **rockabilly**), North and South, and the sacred and the secular (pp. 159–162).

- Due to rock's social and cultural influence, it stirred controversies that eroded its acceptance. These controversies included black artists' frustration with being undermined by white cover music, and censorship by officials who thought rock turned young people into delinquents (pp. 159–160).

Explain the Evolution of Pop Music

- Despite authorities' attempts to "tame" rock, it would continue to grow even across national borders, influenced by the emergence of the Rolling Stones and the Beatles in the 1960s, all the while reflecting social, cultural, and political shifts of the time (pp. 162–163).

- As pop adapted to the times, it led to the creation of numerous genres over the next few decades, including **soul**, **folk music**, psychedelic music, and eventually **punk rock**, **grunge**, **alternative rock**, **indie rock**, **hip-hop**, **gangster rap**, and **country** (pp. 163–169).

Outline the Economics of the Sound Recording Industry

- Over the years, the recording industry has undergone a shift in its power structure—from numerous competing labels and independent production houses, or **indies**, to a few major labels swallowing up the indies and buying each other out (pp. 170–171).

- The recording industry makes money through music sales, though selling music has become increasingly challenging in the digital age as a result of file-sharing undercutting CD sales, and online retailers and digital downloading undermining music stores and cutting into the sale of CDs (pp. 171, 174).

- The recording industry spends money to produce the music, including employing people and investing in equipment and other resources to get the job done. The process begins with **A&R (artist and repertoire) agents**, who are the talent scouts of the business (pp. 174–175).

- Artists and businesspeople divide profits based on CD prices, manufacturing costs, CD packaging design, advertising and promotion, and artists' royalties. As of 2008, the rules for dividing digital download profits became more standardized (pp. 175–177).

Discuss the Sound Recording Industry's Impact on Our Democratic Society

- Popular music has raised many questions about music's role in our democracy, such as what people should be allowed to say in a song and whether or not they are protected under the First Amendment (p. 177).

- The challenge becomes how to support freedom of expression while resisting powerful control by companies whose profit motives are usually paramount (p. 177).

STUDY QUESTIONS

1. How did sound recording survive the advent of radio and the Great Depression?
2. How did rock and roll significantly influence two mass media industries?
3. Why did hip-hop and punk rock emerge as significant musical forms in the late 1970s and 1980s? What do their developments have in common, and how are they different?
4. What accounts for the cost of a typical CD recording? Where do the profits go? Where does the revenue from an iTunes download go?
5. Why do so many forms of alternative music become commercially successful? Explain this in economic terms.

MEDIA LITERACY PRACTICE

Investigate a recording company/music label—preferably a smaller one. Visit the label's Web site, send an e-mail, or call the company for information and background.

DESCRIBE what kind of music the label specializes in. Is the label limited to one genre or type of music? What/who are some of the groups or artists that the label produces? How does the label distribute its recordings to consumers?

ANALYZE the patterns. Does the variety of groups and artists the label produces suggest a type of fan the label is targeting? What methods does the label use to promote artists and reach its listeners? Is the label independent or part of a larger recording-industry company?

INTERPRET your research. What do you see as the major problems facing your label specifically and the industry in general? How do smaller labels overcome these problems?

EVALUATE the impact of the current industry system on the quality of music produced by your label (and by the industry in general).

ENGAGE with your community. Try to contact someone from the label—an artist, a producer, or an executive—and pose some of these questions to that person. From this exercise, you are trying to get a sense of the obstacles musicians and artists face in trying to make careers out of their talent and performances.

Taylor Swift performs at the 2014 iHeartRadio Music Festival.

6

Popular Radio and the Origins of Broadcasting

In radio, a "clear channel" refers to an AM signal that, by law, is set aside for just one station, which, when combined with a powerful transmitter, can cover a huge geographical area. This area gets even bigger at night, when upper layers of the atmosphere become more efficient at bouncing the signals back down to earth. Take, for example, clear channel WHO 1040 AM radio in Des Moines, Iowa. One of the nation's first powerhouse AM stations (it's so old it predates the practice of making the call letters of stations west of the Mississippi begin with the letter *K*), the station has a signal that can be heard across most of Iowa during the day, and most of the United States at night. In fact, it's not uncommon for the signal to reach other countries at night. Clear channel stations on the coasts can be picked up on the other side of the Atlantic and Pacific Oceans.

Up until late 2014, WHO 1040 wasn't just a clear channel station—it was also a Clear Channel station. Clear Channel was the name of a company that grew from a few stations in Texas to the largest radio chain in the United States, owning over twelve hundred stations at its peak. But in 2014, Clear Channel changed its name to iHeartMedia, rebranding that covered its iHeartRadio Music Festival, which has featured massive stars like Taylor Swift and Nicki Minaj.

Clear Channel has long been a poster child for the success—and the excess—of media consolidation following the Telecommunications Act of 1996. Not only a radio giant, the company has long been one of the biggest live-music-event promoters and outdoor billboard owners, among its other media and entertainment enterprises. But one of its biggest recent ventures has been into the online radio platform with its rapidly growing iHeartRadio service. Chairman and CEO Bob Pittman said in a press release announcing the change, "The opportunity for the new iHeartMedia is to use all of these industry-leading assets together in new ways—extending our massive reach and cultural influence across radio, outdoor, digital, social and live events."[1]

It is in part due to this extensive reach and cultural influence that Clear Channel has drawn a great deal of fire from critics both in and out of the radio industry. Tactics ranging from making drastic cuts to news and programming staffs at its local radio stations across the country to simulcasting much of the same programming (including pre-recorded announcers playing as if live) across multiple distant cities have made Clear Channel a target for those who say local news and other local content are a vital part of the public service required as part of a broadcasting license. Clear Channel has been a target of documentary films, books, and investigative news programs. This raises the possibility that the name change seeks to distance the company from bad public relations or the perception of being centered on an older technology rather than cutting edge.

Whatever the reason for Clear Channel's name change, the company's part in the recent history of radio raises profound questions about the entire industry: As radio has morphed from small, locally owned broadcasting to national networks and large radio conglomerates, what has happened to the economics driving this business? Do technological innovations like the Internet give more power to consumers, who can now listen to any format or message from any part of the world based on their preferences? Is localism still an important concept for the radio industry? Does nonprofit radio bring different kinds of voices to the airwaves (or Internet)? To find clues to possible answers, let's first trace how radio has evolved since its emergence as a full-blown mass medium.

THE STORY OF RADIO—from its invention in the late nineteenth century to its current incarnation as a multitechnology mass medium—is one of the most remarkable in media history. In the United States, the early days of network radio gave Americans "a national identity" and "a chance to share in a common experience."[2] Even with the arrival of television in the 1950s, the recent "corporatization" of broadcasting, and the demographic segmentation of radio today, this medium has continued to play a powerful role in our lives. Likewise, the ways in which legislators a century ago wrote the first laws governing radio set the stage for later laws written to cover all forms of electronic mass media, from television to cable to the Internet. For people throughout the nation, the music and talk emanating every day from their radios, PCs, and handheld devices powerfully shape their political opinions, social mores, and (owing to advertisements) purchasing decisions. In this chapter, we will explore these themes by:

LaunchPad
**macmillanhighered.com
/mediaessentials3e**
Use **LearningCurve** to review
concepts from this chapter.

- **examining radio's early history, including how its evolution from one-to-one to one-to-many communication led to new regulations and innovations in programming**

- **looking at how technological advances such as transistors and FM sparked the rise of format radio**

- **familiarizing ourselves with the array of characteristics defining radio today, such as format specialization, nonprofit business models, and digital radio technologies**

- **exploring the economics behind modern radio, including advertising and consolidation of ownership over the public airwaves**

- **considering radio's influence on American culture in an age when control of the public airwaves lies in fewer hands than ever**

The Early History of Radio

Radio did not emerge as a full-blown mass medium until the 1920s, though its development can be traced back to the introduction of the telegraph in the 1840s. As with most media, inventors tinkered in these earliest years with the technologies of the day to address practical needs. The telegraph and early experiments with wireless transmission set the stage for radio as a communication medium.

Inventors Paving the Way: Morse, Maxwell, and Hertz

The **telegraph**—the precursor of radio technology—was invented in the United States in the 1840s and was the first technology to enable messages to move faster than human travel. This meant that news and other messages could be transmitted from coast to coast within minutes, rather than the days required to physically carry information from place to place. American artist and inventor Samuel Morse initially developed this practical system of sending electrical impulses from a transmitter through a cable to a reception device. Telegraph operators used what became known as **Morse code**—a series of dots and dashes that stood for letters of the alphabet and interrupted the electrical current along a wire cable. By 1844, Morse had set up the first telegraph line, which linked Washington, D.C., and Baltimore, Maryland. By 1861, telegraph lines stretched from coast to coast. Just five years later, the first transatlantic cable, capable of transmitting about six words a minute, ran between Newfoundland and Ireland along the ocean floor.

Though revolutionary, the telegraph had significant limitations. For one thing, it couldn't transmit the human voice. Moreover, because it depended on wires, it was useless for anyone seeking to communicate with ships at sea. The world needed a telegraph *without* wires. In the mid-1860s, Scottish physicist James Maxwell theorized the existence of **radio waves**, which could be harnessed to send signals from one place to another without wires. In the 1880s, German physicist Heinrich Hertz tested

Guglielmo Marconi (1874–1937) transmitted the first radio signal across the Atlantic Ocean in 1901. He shared the 1909 Nobel Prize for Physics for his contributions to wireless telegraphy, soon required on all seagoing ships and credited with saving more than seven hundred lives when the *Titanic* sank in 1912.

SSPL-The Images Works

CHAPTER 6 // TIMELINE

1844 Samuel Morse
First telegraph line is set up between Washington, D.C., and Baltimore, Maryland.

1894 Guglielmo Marconi
The Italian inventor begins experiments on wireless telegraphy, seeing his invention as a means for point-to-point communication.

1906 Lee De Forest
American inventor develops the Audion vacuum tube for detecting and amplifying radio signals.

1910 Wireless Ship Act
Congress passes this act, requiring that all major ships be equipped with wireless radio.

1917 Amateur Radio Shutdown
At the request of the navy, the government closes down all amateur radio stations to ensure military security as the United States enters World War I.

Maxwell's theory by using electrical sparks that emitted **electromagnetic waves**, invisible electronic impulses similar to light. The experiment was the first recorded transmission and reception of radio waves, and would dramatically advance the development of wireless communication.

Innovators in Wireless: Marconi, Fessenden, and De Forest

As the nineteenth century unfolded, inventors building on the earlier technologies continued improving wireless communication. New developments took wireless from **narrowcasting** (person-to-person or point-to-point transmission of messages) to **broadcasting** (transmission from one point to multiple listeners; also known as one-to-many communication).

Marconi: The Father of Wireless Telegraphy

In 1894, a twenty-year-old, self-educated Italian engineer named Guglielmo Marconi read Hertz's work. He quickly realized that developing a way to send high-speed messages over great distances would transform communication, commercial shipping, and the military. The young engineer set out to make wireless technology practical. After successfully figuring out how to build a wireless communication device that could send Morse code from a transmitter to a receiver, Marconi traveled to England in 1896. There, he received a patent on **wireless telegraphy**, a form of voiceless *point-to-point communication*.

In London the following year, the Italian inventor formed the Marconi Wireless Telegraph Company, later known as British Marconi. He began installing wireless technology on British naval and private commercial ships. This left other innovators to explore the wireless transmission of voice and music, later known as **wireless telephony** and eventually **radio**. In 1899, Marconi opened a branch in the United States nicknamed American Marconi. That same year, he sent the first wireless

1922 Commercial Radio
The first radio advertisements cause an uproar as people question the right to pollute the public airwaves with commercial messages.

1926 David Sarnoff
NBC is created, the first lasting network of radio stations; connected by AT&T long lines, the network broadcasts nationally and plays a prominent role in unifying the country.

1927 Radio Act of 1927
Radio stations are required to operate in the service of "public interest, convenience, or necessity."

1928 William Paley
CBS is founded and becomes a competitor to NBC.

1930s The Golden Age of Radio
Living rooms are filled with music, drama, comedy, variety and quiz shows, weather forecasts, farm reports, and news.

Morse code signal across the English Channel to France. In 1901, he relayed the first wireless signal from Cornwall, England, across the Atlantic Ocean to St. John's, Newfoundland. History often cites Marconi as the "father of radio," but Russian scientist Alexander Popov accomplished similar feats in St. Petersburg at the same time, and Nikola Tesla, a Serbian Croatian inventor who had immigrated to the United States, invented a wireless electrical device in 1892.

Fessenden: The First Voice Broadcast

Marconi had taken major steps in London and the United States. But it was Canadian engineer Reginald Fessenden who transformed wireless telegraphy into *one-to-many communication*. Fessenden is credited with providing the first voice broadcast. Formerly a chief chemist for Thomas Edison, he went to work for the U.S. Navy and eventually for General Electric (GE), where he focused on improving the frequency of wireless signals. Both the navy and GE were interested in the potential for voice transmission. On Christmas Eve in 1906, after GE built Fessenden a powerful transmitter, he gave his first public demonstration, sending his violin performance of "O Holy Night" and a reading of a Bible passage through the airwaves from his station at Brant Rock, Massachusetts, to an unknown number of shipboard operators off the Atlantic Coast.

De Forest: Birthing Modern Electronics

American inventor Lee De Forest improved the usefulness of broadcasting by greatly increasing listeners' ability to hear dots and dashes, and later speech and music, on a receiver. In 1906, he developed the Audion vacuum tube, which detected and amplified radio signals. The device was essential to the development of voice transmission, long-distance radio, and (eventually) television. Although De Forest had the patent for the Audion, he was accused in court and by fellow

---

CHAPTER 6 // TIMELINE continued

1934 Federal Communications Act of 1934
This act allows commercial interests to control the airwaves.

1941 ABC
ABC is formed when RCA is forced to sell NBC-Blue.

1950s Radio Suffers
In the wake of TV's popularity, radio suffers but is resurrected via rock-and-roll music formats and transistor radios.

1960s FM
Invented by Edwin Armstrong in the 1920s and early 1930s, a new format finally gains national popularity.

1990 Talk Radio
Talk radio becomes the most popular format, especially on AM stations.

engineers of stealing others' ideas, even when the court ruled in his favor.[3] Many historians consider the Audion—which powered radios until the arrival of transistors and solid-state circuits in the 1950s—the origin of modern electronics.

In 1907, De Forest demonstrated his invention's power and practical value by broadcasting a performance by Metropolitan opera tenor Enrico Caruso to his friends in New York. The next year, he and his wife, Nora, played records into a microphone from atop the Eiffel Tower in Paris; the signals were picked up by receivers up to five hundred miles away.

Early Regulation of Wireless/Radio

By the turn of the twentieth century, radio had become a new force in American life. Recognizing radio's power to shape political opinion, economic dynamics, and military strategy and tactics, U.S. lawmakers moved to ensure U.S. control over the fledgling industry. With this goal in mind, legislators first defined radio as a shared resource for the public good. They then passed laws regulating how the public airwaves could be used and in what manner private businesses could take part in the industry.

Providing Public Safety

Because radio waves crossed state and national borders, legislators determined that broadcasting constituted a "natural resource"—a kind of interstate

The Everett Collection

Inventor Lee De Forest's (1873–1961) lengthy radio career was marked by incredible innovations, missed opportunities, and poor business practices. In the end, De Forest was upset that radio content had stooped, in his opinion, to such low standards. With a passion for opera, he had hoped radio would be a tool for elite culture.

1990s Internet Radio
In the second half of the decade, Internet radio—streaming either the content of an on-air station or a personalized radio station—takes hold.

1996 Telecommunications Act of 1996
This law effects a rapid, unprecedented consolidation in radio ownership across the United States.

2000 Pandora Internet Radio
Pandora Internet Radio launches in Oakland, California. Spotify, based in Europe, would start operating in the United States in 2011.

2002 Satellite Radio
A new format begins service.

2004 Podcasts
The combination of iPods and broadcasting creates podcasts, downloadable audio file programs posted to the Internet.

2014 Streaming Advances
According to ratings service Nielsen, Americans streamed over 70 billion songs in just the first half of 2014, well ahead of the same time period in 2013.

commerce—that should be regulated on the public's behalf in the public's best interests. Therefore, radio waves could not be owned, just licensed for use for a set period of time.

The first public safety rule came in 1910, when Congress passed the **Wireless Ship Act**. The law mandated that all major U.S. seagoing ships carrying more than fifty passengers and traveling more than two hundred miles off either coast be equipped with wireless equipment with a one-hundred-mile range. The importance of this act was underscored by the *Titanic* disaster in 1912, when over seven hundred passengers were saved by nearby ships responding to the passenger liner's radio distress signals. In the wake of the *Titanic* tragedy, Congress passed the **Radio Act of 1912**. It required all radio stations on land or at sea to be licensed and assigned special call letters. The act helped to bring some order to the airwaves, which had been increasingly jammed with amateur radio operators. This act also formally adopted the SOS Morse-code distress signal.

Ensuring National Security

By 1915, more than twenty American companies sold wireless point-to-point communication systems, primarily for use in ship-to-shore communication. American Marconi (a subsidiary of British Marconi) was the biggest of these companies. But with World War I erupting in Europe, the U.S. Navy questioned the wisdom of allowing a foreign-controlled company to wield so much power over communication. When the United States entered the war in 1917, the government closed down all amateur radio operations, took control of key radio transmitters, and blocked British Marconi from purchasing radio equipment from General Electric. These moves addressed concerns about national security. They also enabled the United States to reduce Britain's influence over communication and tightened U.S. control over the emerging wireless infrastructure.

RCA: The Formation of an American Radio Monopoly

Some members of Congress, along with some business leaders, opposed federal legislation granting the government or the navy a radio monopoly. To secure a place in the fast-evolving industry, GE proposed a plan by which it would create a *private-sector monopoly*—a privately owned company that would have the government's approval to dominate the radio industry. In 1919, the plan was accepted by the powers that be at both GE and the U.S. Navy—the

A radio operator at the controls in Minnesota in October 1923. In that year, only about a half million U.S. households had a radio receiver to hear the signals. Within two years, more than five million households would own radios.

© Minnesota Historical Society/Corbis

government branch most prominently fighting for control of the radio industry in America. GE founded the **Radio Corporation of America (RCA)** to purchase and pool patents from the navy, AT&T, GE, the former American Marconi, and other companies to ensure U.S. control over the manufacture of radio transmitters and receivers. Under the various agreements, AT&T made most transmitters; GE (and later Westinghouse) made radio receivers; and RCA administered patents, collected royalties, and redistributed them to the others.[4]

KDKA: The First Commercial Radio Station

With the advent of the United States' global dominance in mass communication, many people became intrigued by radio's potential. Amateur stations popped up in places like San Jose, California; Medford, Massachusetts; New York; Detroit; and Pierre, South Dakota. The best-known early station was begun by an engineer named Frank Conrad, who worked for GE's rival, Westinghouse Electric Company. In 1916, he set up a radio studio above his Pittsburgh garage by placing a microphone in front of a phonograph. Conrad broadcast music and news to his friends (whom he supplied with receivers) two evenings a week on experimental station 8XK. When a Westinghouse executive got wind of Conrad's activities in 1920, he established KDKA, generally regarded as the first commercial (profit-based) broadcast station. The following year, the U.S. Commerce Department officially licensed five radio stations for operation; by early 1923, more than six hundred commercial and noncommercial stations were operating. Just two years later, a whopping 5.5 million radio sets were in use across America—made by companies such as GE and Westinghouse and costing about $55 ($664 in today's dollars). Radio was officially a mass medium.

The Networks

With the establishment of the private sector's involvement in radio, the groundwork was laid for radio to take off as a business, which would enable commercial station owners (and the advertisers that funded them) to reach more listeners more efficiently than ever. The radio **network** arose: a cost-saving operation that links a group of affiliate or subsidiary broadcast stations that share programming produced at a central location. (At that time, stations were linked through special phone lines; today, they're linked through satellite relays.)

The network system enabled stations to control program costs and avoid unnecessary duplication of content creation. Simply put, it was cheaper to produce programs at one station and broadcast them simultaneously over multiple owned or affiliated stations than for each station to generate its own programs. Networks thus brought the best musical, dramatic, and comedic talent to one place, where programs could be produced and then distributed all over the country. This new business model concentrated control of radio in the hands of a few corporate players, all of whom jockeyed for additional power.

AT&T: Making a Power Grab

The shift toward networks began in 1922, when RCA's partnership with AT&T began to unravel. In a major power grab, AT&T, which already had a government-sanctioned monopoly in the telephone business, decided to break its RCA agreements in an attempt to monopolize radio. Identifying the new medium as the "wireless telephone," AT&T argued that broadcasting was merely an extension of its control over the telephone. The corporate giant complained that RCA had gained too much power. In violation of its early agreements with RCA, AT&T began making and selling its own radio receivers.

That same year, AT&T started WEAF (now WNBC) in New York, the first radio station to regularly sell commercial time to advertisers. Advertising, company executives reasoned, would ensure profits long after radio-set sales had saturated the consumer market. AT&T claimed that under the RCA agreements, it had the exclusive right to sell ads, which AT&T called *toll broadcasting*. Most people in radio at the time recoiled at the idea of using the medium for advertising, viewing the medium instead as a public information service. But executives remained riveted by the potential of radio ads to enhance profits.

Still, the initial motivation behind AT&T's toll broadcasting idea was to dominate radio. Through its agreements with RCA, AT&T retained the rights to interconnect the signals between two or more radio stations via telephone wires. By the end of 1924, AT&T had interconnected twenty-two stations in a network to air a talk by President Calvin Coolidge. Some of these stations were owned by AT&T, but most simply consented to become AT&T "affiliates," agreeing to air the phone company's programs.

Seeing AT&T's success, GE, Westinghouse, and RCA launched a competing network. AT&T promptly denied them access to its telephone wires, so the new network used inferior telegraph lines to connect its stations. In 1925, the Justice Department, irritated by AT&T's power grab, redefined patent agreements. AT&T received a monopoly on providing the wires, known as *long lines*, to interconnect stations nationwide. In exchange, AT&T agreed to sell its network to RCA for $1 million and promised not to reenter broadcasting for eight years.

NBC: RCA Forms a Network

The commercial rewards of the network and affiliate system continued to excite executives' imaginations. For example, after RCA bought AT&T's telephone line–based radio network, David Sarnoff, RCA's general manager, created a new subsidiary in September 1926 called the National Broadcasting Company (NBC). NBC's ownership

David Sarnoff, creator of NBC and network radio, demonstrated calculated ambition in the radio industry, which can easily be compared to Bill Gates's more recent drive to control the computer software and Internet industries.

© Topham/The Image Works

was shared by RCA (50%), General Electric (30%), and Westinghouse (20%). The former group of AT&T stations became known as NBC-Red. The network RCA, GE, and Westinghouse had already been building became NBC-Blue. By 1933, NBC-Red would have twenty-eight affiliates; NBC-Blue, twenty-four.

CBS: A Rival Network Challenges NBC

The network and affiliate system under RCA/NBC thrived throughout most of the 1920s and brought Americans together as never before to participate in the big events of the day. For example, when aviator Charles Lindbergh returned from the first solo transatlantic flight in 1927, an estimated twenty-five to thirty million people listened to his welcome-home party on the six million radio sets then in use. At the time, it was the largest shared audience experience in the history of any mass medium.

During this decade, competition stiffened further within the industry. For instance, in 1928, William Paley, the twenty-seven-year-old son of a Philadelphia cigar company owner, bought the Columbia Phonograph Company and built it into a network later renamed the Columbia Broadcasting System (CBS). Unlike NBC, which actually charged its affiliates up to $96 a week for the privilege of carrying its programming, CBS paid affiliates as much as $50 an hour to carry its programs. By 1933, Paley's efforts had netted CBS more than ninety affiliates, many of which had defected from NBC. Paley also concentrated on developing news programs and entertainment shows, particularly soap operas and comedy-variety series. To that end, CBS raided NBC not just for affiliates but also for top talent, such as comedian Jack Benny and singer Frank Sinatra. In 1949, CBS finally surpassed NBC as the highest-rated network on radio.

William S. Paley (*shown standing*), president of Columbia Broadcasting System for more than fifty years, activates the world's largest hookup of radio stations at that time in 1928. Known for his early support of quality programming and network news, Paley was also criticized for undermining his news division to sidestep controversy or to increase profits.

The Radio Act of 1927

The growing concentration of power in the network and affiliate system raised a red flag for government leaders. Throughout the 1920s to early 1940s, lawmakers would enact many regulations aimed at regaining control over the industry. In particular, by the late 1920s, the government had become alarmed by RCA/NBC's growing influence over radio content. Moreover, as radio moved from narrowcasting to broadcasting, battles among various players over such issues as more frequency space and less channel interference heated up. Manufacturers, engineers, station operators, network executives, and the listening public demanded action to address their conflicting interests. Many wanted more sweeping regulation than the simple licensing function granted under the Radio Act of 1912, which gave the Commerce Department little power to deny a license or to unclog the airwaves.

© Bettmann/Corbis

To restore order, Congress passed the **Radio Act of 1927**, which introduced a pivotal new principle: Licensees did not *own* their channels but could use them as long as they operated to serve the "public interest, convenience, or necessity." To oversee licenses and negotiate channel problems such as too many stations trying to air on too few frequencies, the 1927 act created the **Federal Radio Commission (FRC)**, whose members were appointed by the president.

Although the FRC was intended as a temporary committee, it grew into a powerful regulatory agency. With passage of the **Federal Communications Act of 1934**, the FRC became the **Federal Communications Commission (FCC)**. Its jurisdiction covered not only radio but also the telephone and the telegraph (and later television, cable, and the Internet). More significantly, by this time Congress and the president had sided with the already-powerful radio networks and acceded to a system of advertising-supported commercial broadcasting as best serving the "public interest, convenience, or necessity," overriding the concerns of educational, labor, religious, and citizen broadcasting advocates.

In 1941, an activist FCC set out to break up what it saw as overly large and powerful networks, which led to a Supreme Court ruling forcing RCA to sell NBC-Blue. The divested enterprise became the American Broadcasting Company (ABC). Such government crackdowns brought long-overdue reforms to the radio industry. However, they came too late to prevent considerable damage to noncommercial radio.

The Golden Age of Radio

From the late 1920s to the 1940s, radio basked in a golden age marked by a proliferation of informative and entertaining programs (such as weather forecasts, farm reports, news, music, dramas, quiz shows, variety shows, and comedies). This diversity of programming shaped—and was shaped by—American culture. It also paved the way for programs that Americans would later enjoy on television, as NBC, CBS, and ABC created television networks in the late 1940s and 1950s.

Early Radio Programming

In the early days of radio, only a handful of stations operated in most large radio markets. Through the networks they were affiliated with, these stations broadcast a variety of programs into listeners' homes (and in some cases, their cars). People had favorite evening programs,

This giant bank of radio network microphones makes us wonder today how President Franklin D. Roosevelt managed to project such an intimate and reassuring tone in his famous fireside chats. Conceived originally to promote FDR's New Deal policies amid the Great Depression, these chats were delivered between 1933 and 1944 and touched on national topics. Roosevelt was the first president to effectively use broadcasting to communicate with citizens.

© Bettmann/Corbis

usually fifteen minutes long. After dinner, families gathered around the radio to hear comedies, dramas, public service announcements, and more. Popular programs included *Amos 'n' Andy* (a serial situation comedy), *The Shadow* (a mystery drama), *The Lone Ranger* (a western), *The Green Hornet* (a crime drama), and *Fibber McGee and Molly* (a comedy), as well as the "fireside chats" regularly presented by President Franklin D. Roosevelt.

Variety shows featuring musical performances and comedy skits planted the seeds for popular TV variety shows that would come later, such as the *Ed Sullivan Show. Quiz shows* (including *The Old Time Spelling Bee*) introduced Americans to the thrill of competition. These radio programs set the stage for later competition-based TV shows, ranging from *The Price Is Right* and *Who Wants to Be a Millionaire* to reality-based shows such as *Survivor, Fear Factor, Project Runway,* and *Top Chef.*

Dramatic programs, mostly radio plays broadcast live from theaters, would inspire later TV dramas, including "soap operas." (The term came into use after Colgate-Palmolive began selling its soap products on dramas it sponsored.) Another type of program, the *serial,* introduced the idea of continuing story lines from one day to the next—a format soon adopted by soap operas and some comedy programs.

Radio as Cultural Mirror

Radio programs powerfully reflected shifts in American culture, including attitudes about race and levels of tolerance for stereotypes. For example, the situation comedy *Amos 'n' Andy* was based on the conventions of the nineteenth-century minstrel show and featured black characters stereotyped as shiftless and stupid. Created as a blackface stage act by two white comedians, Charles Correll and Freeman Gosden, the program was criticized as racist by some at the time; however, NBC and the program's producers claimed that *Amos 'n' Andy* was as popular among black audiences as it was among white listeners.[5]

Early radio research estimated that the program aired in more than half of all radio homes in the nation during the 1930–31 season, making it the most popular radio series in history. In 1951, *Amos 'n' Andy* made a brief transition to television, after Correll and Gosden sold the rights to CBS for $1 million. It became the first TV series to have an all-black cast. But amid a strengthening Civil Rights movement and a formal protest by the National Association for the Advancement of Colored People (NAACP), which argued that "every character is either a clown or a crook," CBS canceled the program in 1953.[6]

The Authority of Radio

In addition to reflecting evolving cultural beliefs, radio increasingly shaped them—in part by being perceived by listeners as the voice of authority. The adaptation of science-fiction author H. G. Wells's *War of the Worlds* (1898) on the radio series

On Halloween eve in 1938, Orson Welles's radio dramatization of *War of the Worlds* (*left*) created a panic up and down the East Coast, especially in Grover's Mill, New Jersey—the setting for the fictional Martian invasion, which many listeners assumed was real. A seventy-six-year-old Grover's Mill resident (*right*) guarded a warehouse against alien invaders.

Hulton Archive/Getty Images (left); © Bettmann/Corbis (right)

Mercury Theatre on the Air provides the most notable example of this. Considered the most famous single radio broadcast of all time, *War of the Worlds* was produced and hosted by Orson Welles, who also narrated it. On Halloween eve in 1938, the twenty-three-year-old Welles aired the Martian-invasion story in the style of a contemporary radio news bulletin. For people who missed the opening disclaimer, the program sounded like an authentic news report, with apparently eyewitness accounts of battles between Martian invaders and the U.S. Army.

The program triggered a panic among some listeners. In New Jersey, some people walked through the streets with wet towels wrapped around their heads for protection against deadly Martian heat rays. In New York, young men reported to their National Guard headquarters to prepare for battle. Across the nation, calls from terrified citizens jammed police switchboards. The FCC called for stricter warnings both before and during programs imitating the style of radio news.

The Evolution of Radio

In the 1950s, a new form of mass media—television—came on the scene. TV snatched radio's advertisers, program genres, major celebrities, and large evening audiences. The TV set even physically displaced the radio as the living room centerpiece around which families gathered. To survive, players in the radio industry transformed their business model so that they could provide new forms of value for listeners.

Transistors: Making Radio Portable

The portability of radio proved to be a major advantage in the medium's struggle for survival. In the late 1920s, car radios had existed but were considered a luxury. But when Bell Laboratories invented the transistor in 1947, radios became more accessible than ever before—and portable. **Transistors** were small electrical devices that, like vacuum tubes, could receive and amplify radio signals. However, they used less power and gave off less heat than vacuum tubes, and were more durable and less expensive. Best of all, they were tiny. The development of transistors let radio go where television could not—to the beach, to the office, into bedrooms and bathrooms, and into nearly all new cars.

The FM Revolution

To replace the shows radio had lost to TV, many people in radio switched the medium's emphasis to music, turning to the recording industry for content. However, making music sound better on radio required some technological innovation. Until then, radio technology had centered on **AM** (amplitude modulation). This type of modulation was sufficient for radio content such as talk, but it wasn't ideal for music. For that, radio needed **FM** (frequency modulation), which provided greater clarity as well as static-free radio reception.

FM radio had existed for decades. American inventor Edwin Armstrong had discovered and developed it during the 1920s and early 1930s. Between 1930 and 1933, Armstrong filed five patents on FM. The number of FM stations grew to 700 but then fell to 560 by the 1950s, as Armstrong was pulled into legal skirmishes over patents with such heavy hitters as David Sarnoff. (The RCA executive had initially supported Armstrong's explorations into FM but then opted to throw his weight behind the development of TV.) In 1954, weary from years of legal battles, Armstrong wrote a note apologizing to his wife, removed the air conditioner from his thirteenth-story New York apartment, and jumped to his death. It wasn't until the early 1960s, when the FCC opened up more spectrum space for the superior sound of FM, that FM began to grow into the preferred radio band for music.

The Rise of Format Radio

Once radio became portable and FM was introduced, music began to dominate the medium more than ever. This eventually led to the creation of **format radio**, in which station managers (rather than disc jockeys) controlled the station's hour-by-hour music programming. Of course, in the late 1930s, music had been radio's single biggest staple, accounting for 48 percent of all programming. However, most music was live, which many people considered superior to recorded music. The first disc jockeys demonstrated that recorded music could attract just as many listeners as live music.

As early as 1949, station owner Todd Storz and his program manager in Omaha, Nebraska, noticed that bar patrons and waitresses repeatedly played certain favorite songs from the forty records available in a jukebox. Drawing from jukebox culture, Storz hit on the idea of **rotation**: playing the top songs many times during the day. By the mid-1950s, the *Top 40 format* was born. Although the term *Top 40* derived from the number of records stored in a jukebox, this format came to refer to the forty most popular hits in a given week as measured by record sales.

As format radio grew, program managers combined rapid deejay chatter with the best-selling songs of the day and occasional oldies—popular songs from a few months earlier. Managers created a program log that deejays followed and sectioned off blocks of roughly four hours throughout the day and night. Each block tried to appeal to listeners' interests and thus attract more advertising dollars. For instance, a Top 40 station would feature its best deejays in the morning and afternoon periods, during listeners' commutes to school or work. Management also made savvy use of research. For example, if statistics showed that teenagers tended to listen to the radio mostly during evening hours and preferred music to news, then stations marketing to teens avoided scheduling news breaks during those hours.

The expansion of FM in the mid-1960s created room for stations to experiment, particularly with classical music, jazz, blues, and non–Top 40 rock songs. Many noncommercial stations broadcast from college campuses, where student deejays and managers rejected the commercialism associated with Top 40 tunes and began playing lesser-known alternative music and longer album cuts.

The Characteristics of Contemporary Radio

Contemporary radio differs markedly from its predecessor. In contrast to the few stations per market in the 1930s, most large markets today include more than forty stations that vie for listener loyalty.

With the exception of national network-sponsored news segments and nationally syndicated programs, most programming is locally produced (or made to sound like it) and heavily dependent on the music industry for content. In short, stations today are more specialized. Listeners are loyal to favorite stations, music formats, and even radio personalities, rather than to specific shows, and they generally listen to only four or five stations. About fifteen thousand radio stations now operate in the United States.

Format Specialization

Radio stations today use a variety of formats to serve diverse groups of listeners (see Figure 6.1). To please advertisers, who want to know exactly who is listening, formats usually target audiences according to their age, income, gender, or race/ethnicity. Radio's specialization enables advertisers to reach smaller target audiences at costs much lower than those for television. The most popular formats include the following:

- **Country.** The most popular format in the nation (except during morning drive time, when news/talk is number one), country is traditionally the default format for small communities with only one radio station. Country music has old roots in radio, starting in 1925 with the influential Grand Ole Opry program on WSM in Nashville.

- **News and talk radio.** As the second most popular format in the nation, news and talk radio has been buoyed by the popularity of personalities like Howard Stern, Tavis Smiley, and Rush Limbaugh. This format tends to cater to adults over age thirty-five (except for sports talk programs, which draw mostly male sports fans of all ages). Though more expensive to produce than a music format, it appeals to advertisers seeking to target working and middle-class adult consumers (see "Media Literacy Case Study: Host: The Origins of Talk Radio" on pages 202–203).

- **Top 40/contemporary hit radio (CHR).** Encompassing everything from rap to pop rock, this format appeals to many teens and young adults. Since the mid-1980s, however, these stations have lost ground steadily, as younger generations turned first to MTV and now to online sources for their music, rather than to radio.

- **Adult contemporary (AC).** This format, also known as middle of the road, or MOR, is among radio's oldest and most popular formats. It reaches about 7.3 percent of all listeners, most of them over the age of forty, with an eclectic mix of news, talk, oldies, and soft rock music. *Broadcasting* magazine describes AC as "not too soft, not too loud, not too fast, not too slow, not too hard, not too lush, not too old, not too new."

- **Urban adult contemporary.** In 1947, WDIA in Memphis was the first station to program exclusively for black listeners. This format targets a wide variety of African American listeners, primarily in large cities. Urban AC typically plays popular dance, rap, R&B, and hip-hop music (featuring performers like Rihanna and Tyga).
- **Spanish-language radio.** One of radio's fastest growing, this format is concentrated mostly in large Hispanic markets, such as Miami, New York, Chicago, Las Vegas, California, Arizona, New Mexico, and Texas. Besides talk shows and news segments in Spanish, this format features a variety of Spanish, Caribbean, and Latin American musical styles.

In addition, today there are other formats that are spin-offs from **album-oriented rock (AOR)**. Classic rock serves up rock favorites from the mid-1960s

FIGURE 6.1 // MOST POPULAR RADIO FORMATS IN THE UNITED STATES AMONG PERSONS AGE TWELVE AND OLDER, 2013

America's Top Formats in 2013 by Share of Total Listening (%)

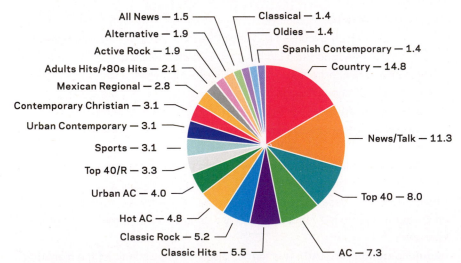

Data from: Nielsen report: "State of the Media: Audio Today 2014—How America Listens," February 2014

Note: Based on listener shares for primary AM and FM stations, plus HD stations and Internet streams of radio stations

through the 1980s to the baby-boom generation and other listeners who have out-grown Top 40. The oldies format originally served adults who grew up on 1950s and early 1960s rock and roll. As that audience has aged, oldies formats now target younger audiences with the classic hits format, featuring songs from the 1970s, 1980s, and 1990s. The alternative music format recaptures some of the experimental approach of the FM stations of the 1960s, although with much more controlled playlists, and has helped to introduce artists such as the Dead Weather and Cage the Elephant.

Research indicates that most people identify closely with the music they listened to as adolescents and young adults. This tendency partially explains why classic hits and classic rock stations combined have surpassed Top 40 stations today. It also helps explain the recent nostalgia for music from the 1980s and 1990s.

Nonprofit Radio and NPR

Although commercial radio dominates the radio spectrum, nonprofit radio maintains a voice. Two government rulings, both in 1948, aided nonprofit radio. Through the first ruling, the government began authorizing noncommercial licenses to stations not affiliated with labor, religion, education, or civic groups. The first license went to Lewis Kimball Hill, a radio reporter and pacifist during World War II who started the **Pacifica Foundation** to run experimental public stations. Pacifica stations have often challenged the status quo in both radio and government. In the second ruling, the FCC approved 10-watt FM stations. Before 1948, radio stations had to have at least 250 watts to get licensed. A 10-watt station with a broadcast range of only about seven miles took very little capital to operate, so the ruling enabled many more people to participate in radio. Many of these tiny stations became training sites for students interested in a broadcasting career.

During the 1960s, nonprofit broadcasting found a new friend in Congress, which proved sympathetic to an old idea: using radio and television as educational tools. In 1967, Congress created the first noncommercial networks: **National Public Radio (NPR)** and the **Public Broadcasting Service (PBS)**. Under the provisions of the **Public Broadcasting Act of 1967** and the **Corporation for Public Broadcasting (CPB)**, NPR and PBS were mandated to

Sarah Koenig, a producer on NPR's This American Life *program, garnered further attention for NPR by hosting and executive-producing* Serial, *a podcast spun off from* This American Life *that tells nonfiction stories over the course of multiple episodes.*

Andrew Toth/FilmMagic/Getty Images

MEDIA LITERACY
Case Study

© C.J.Burton/Corbis

Host: The Origins of Talk Radio
By David Foster Wallace

The origins of contemporary political talk radio can be traced to three phenomena of the 1980s. The first of these involved AM music stations getting absolutely murdered by FM, which could broadcast music in stereo and allowed for much better fidelity on high and low notes. The human voice, on the other hand, is midrange and doesn't require high fidelity. The eighties' proliferation of talk formats on the AM band also provided new careers for some music deejays—Don Imus, Morton Downey Jr.— whose chatty personas didn't fit well with FM's all-about-the-music ethos.

The second big factor was the repeal, late in Ronald Reagan's second term, of what was known as the Fairness Doctrine. This was a 1949 FCC rule designed to minimize any possible restrictions on free speech caused by limited access to broadcasting outlets. The idea was that, as one of the conditions for receiving an FCC broadcast license, a station had to "devote reasonable attention to the coverage of controversial issues of public importance," and consequently had to provide "reasonable, although not necessarily equal," opportunities for opposing sides to express their views. Because of the Fairness Doctrine, talk stations had to hire and program symmetrically: If you had a three-hour program whose host's politics were on one side of the ideological spectrum, you had to have another long-form program whose host more or less spoke for the other side. Weirdly enough, up through the mid-eighties it was usually the U.S. Right that benefited most from the doctrine.

Data from: Excerpted from David Foster Wallace, "Host: The Origins of Talk Radio," Atlantic, April 2005, 66–68.

LaunchPad
macmillanhighered.com/mediaessentials3e

▶ **Visit LaunchPad** to watch a clip of a talk radio host on television. How might he vary his broadcasting routine for a different medium?

The Fairness Doctrine's repeal was part of the sweeping deregulations of the Reagan era, which aimed to liberate all sorts of industries from government interference and allow them to compete freely in the marketplace. After 1987, though, just another industry is pretty much what radio became, and its only real responsibility now is to attract and retain listeners in order to generate revenue.

More or less on the heels of the Fairness Doctrine's repeal came the West Coast and then national syndication of *The Rush Limbaugh Show* through Edward F. McLaughlin's EFM Media. Limbaugh is the third great progenitor of today's political talk radio partly because he's a host of extraordinary, once-in-a-generation talent and charisma—bright, loquacious, witty, complexly authoritative—whose show's blend of news, entertainment, and partisan analysis became the model for legions of imitators. But he was also the first great promulgator of the Mainstream Media's Liberal Bias idea. This turned out to be a brilliantly effective rhetorical move, since the MMLB concept functioned simultaneously as a standard around which Rush's audience could rally, as an articulation of the need for right-wing (that is, unbiased) media, and as a mechanism by which any criticism or refutation of conservative ideas could be dismissed (either as biased or as the product of indoctrination by biased media). Boiled way down, the MMLB thesis is able both to exploit and to perpetuate many conservatives' dissatisfaction with extant media sources—and it's this dissatisfaction that cements political talk radio's large and loyal audience.

APPLYING THE CRITICAL PROCESS

DESCRIPTION Check your local listings and find a typical morning or late-afternoon hour of a popular right-wing talk-news radio station and an hour of a typical left-wing talk-news radio station from the same time period. Listen to each program over a two- to three-day period. Keep a log of what topics are covered and what news stories are reported.

ANALYSIS Look for patterns. What kinds of stories are covered? What kinds of topics are discussed? Create a chart to categorize the stories. How much time is given to *reporting* (clearly verified information) compared to time devoted to *opinion*? What kinds of interview sources are used?

INTERPRETATION What do these patterns mean? Is there a balance between reporting and opinion? Do you detect any bias, and if so, how did you determine this?

EVALUATION Do you agree with the 1949–1987 Fairness Doctrine rule that broadcasting should provide "reasonable, although not necessarily equal," attention to "controversial issues of public importance"? Why or why not? From which station did you learn the most, and which station did you find most entertaining? Explain. What did you like and dislike about each station?

ENGAGEMENT Contact the local general manager, program director, or news director at the stations you analyzed. Ask them what their goals are for their daily talk-news programming and what audience they are trying to reach. Incorporate their comments into a report on your findings. Finally, offer suggestions on how to make the programming at each station better.

provide alternatives to commercial broadcasting. With almost one thousand member stations, NPR draws thirty-two million listeners a week to popular news and interview programs like *Morning Edition* and *All Things Considered*. NPR and PBS stations rely on a blend of private donations, corporate sponsorship, and a small amount of public funding. Today, more than thirty-six hundred nonprofit radio stations operate in the United States.

Radio and Convergence

Like every other mass medium, radio has made the digital turn by converging with the Internet. Underscoring this trend, the largest owner of radio stations across the United States changed its name from Clear Channel to iHeartMedia in September 2014, clearly inspired by its recently established iHeartRadio Internet radio service.

Interestingly, the digital turn is taking radio back to its roots in some ways. Internet radio allows for much more variety, which is reminiscent of radio's earliest years, when nearly any individual or group with some technical skill could start a radio station. Moreover, *podcasts* have brought back such content as storytelling, instructional programs, and local topics of interest, which have largely been missing in corporate radio. And portable listening devices like the iPod and radio apps for the iPad and smartphones hark back to the compact portability that first came with the popularization of transistor radios in the 1950s. When we talk about these kinds of convergence, we are talking about the blurring of lines between categories. Even so, it's still possible to identify five particular ways radio is converging with digital technologies:

- **Internet radio.** Emerging in the 1990s with the popularity of the Web, Internet radio stations come in two types. The first involves an existing AM, FM, satellite, or HD station "streaming" a simulcast version of its on-air signal over the Web. According to StreamingRadioGuide.com, more than fifteen thousand radio stations stream their programming over the Web today.[7] iHeartRadio is one of the major streaming sites for broadcast and custom digital stations. The second kind of online radio station is one that has been created exclusively for the Internet. Pandora, 8tracks, Slacker, and Last.fm are some of the leading Internet radio services. In fact, services like Pandora allow users to have more control over their listening experience and the selections that are played. Listeners can create individualized stations based on a specific artist or song that they request. AM/FM radio is used by nearly eight out of ten people who like to learn about new music, but YouTube, Facebook, Pandora, iTunes, iHeartRadio, Spotify, and blogs are among the competing sources for new music fans.[8] (See "Converging Media Case Study: Streaming Music" on pages 208–209.)

- **Podcasting and portable listening.** Developed in 2004, podcasting (the term marries *iPod* and *broadcasting*) refers to the practice of making audio files available on the Internet so that listeners can download them to their computer and either transfer them to portable MP3 players or listen to the files from their computer. This popular distribution method quickly became mainstream as mass media companies created commercial podcasts to promote and extend existing content, such as news and reality TV, while independent producers kept pace with their own podcasts on niche topics like knitting, fly-fishing, and learning Russian. Podcasts led the way for people to listen to radio on mobile devices like smartphones. Satellite radio, Internet-only stations like Pandora and Slacker, sites that stream traditional broadcast radio like iHeartRadio, and public radio like NPR all offer apps for smartphones and touchscreen devices like the iPad, which has also led to a resurgence in portable listening. Traditional broadcast radio stations are becoming increasingly mindful that they need to reach younger listeners on the Internet, and that Internet radio is no longer tethered to a computer.

- **Convergence with mobile technology.** For the broadcast radio industry, portability used to mean listening on a transistor or car radio. But with the digital turn to iPods and mobile phones, broadcasters haven't been as easily available on today's primary portable audio devices. Hoping to change that, the National Association of Broadcasters (NAB) has been lobbying the FCC and mobile phone industry to include FM radio capability in all mobile phones. According to the NAB, adding an FM radio chip in the manufacturing of mobile phones would cost less than a dollar and add little bulk, with the chip just the size of a nail head. In a survey, about two-thirds of mobile phone users reported they would use a built-in radio.[9] The NAB argues that the radio chip would be most important for enabling listeners to access broadcast radio in times of emergencies and disasters. But the chip would also be commercially beneficial for radio broadcasters, putting them on the same digital devices as their nonbroadcast radio competitors, like Pandora.

- **Satellite radio.** Another alternative radio technology added a third band—satellite radio—to AM and FM. Two companies, XM and Sirius, completed their national introduction by 2002 and merged into a single provider in 2008. The merger was precipitated by their struggles to make a profit after building competing satellite systems and battling for listeners. SiriusXM offers about 165 digital music, news, and talk channels to the continental United States, with monthly prices starting at $14.49 and satellite radio receivers costing from $50 to $110. SiriusXM access is also available on mobile devices via an app. U.S. automakers (investors in the satellite radio companies) now equip most new cars with a satellite band, in addition to AM and FM, in order to promote further

© Shannon Stapleton/Reuters/Corbis

Howard Stern's broadcast radio show holds the record for FCC indecency fines, a fact that he and his cohost, Robin Quivers, used for material on the show. Stern avoided further indecency fines when he moved to satellite radio in 2006.

adoption of satellite radio. SiriusXM had more than twenty-five million subscribers by 2014.

- **HD radio.** Approved by the FCC in 2002, HD radio is a digital technology that enables AM and FM radio broadcasters to multicast two to three additional compressed digital signals within their traditional analog frequency. For example, KNOW, a public radio station at 91.1 FM in Minneapolis–St. Paul, runs its National Public Radio news format on 91.1 HD1, BBC News on 91.1 HD2, and the BBC Mundo Spanish-language news service on 91.1 HD3. About two thousand radio stations now broadcast in digital HD.

The Economics of Commercial Radio

Radio today remains one of the most used mass media, reaching 93 percent of all Americans age twelve or older every week.[10] Because of this continued broad reach, the airwaves are still desirable real estate for advertisers and content programmers, who want to target people in and out of their homes; for record labels, who want their artists' songs played; and for radio station owners, who want to attract large groups of diverse listeners to dominate multiple markets.

Money In and Money Out

As with any other enterprise, money flows both into and out of radio. Commercial stations take in money from advertisers and spend it on such assets as content programming, often purchasing programming from national network radio. Noncommercial stations are funded by donations, which are then used to cover expenses, including content.

Revenues from Local and National Advertising

About 10 percent of all U.S. spending on media advertising goes to radio stations. Like newspapers, radio generates its largest profits by selling local and regional ads. Thirty-second radio ads range from $1,500 in large markets to just a few dollars in the smallest markets. Today, gross advertising receipts for radio are about $17.6 billion (about 80 percent of the revenues are from local ad sales, with the remainder in national spot ads, network, and digital radio sales), up from about $16 billion in 2009 but down from an industry peak of $21.7 billion in 2006.[11] Nevertheless, the number of stations keeps growing, now totaling

15,406 stations (4,725 AM stations, 6,624 FM commercial stations, and 4,057 FM educational stations).[12]

Spending for Radio Content

Local radio stations get much of their music content free from the recording industry (although by 2009, the music industry—which has seen a shortfall in its own revenues—was proposing to charge radio for playing music on the air). Therefore, only about 20 percent of a typical radio station's budget goes to cover music programming costs. When radio stations want to purchase additional programming, they often turn to national network radio, which generates more than $1.1 billion in ad sales annually by offering dozens of specialized services (such as news features, entertainment programs, and music formats). The companies providing these programming services to local stations receive time slots for national ads in return.

Manipulating Playlists with Payola

In the world of radio, record labels play a central role in the relationship between money and content. Just as advertisers want to target specific audiences, record labels want specific people to hear their artists' songs. **Payola**, the questionable practice by which record promoters pay deejays to play particular records, was rampant during the 1950s as record companies sought to guarantee record sales. In response, radio management took control of programming. Managers argued that if individual deejays had less impact on which records were played, they would be less susceptible to bribery. Despite congressional hearings and new regulations, payola persisted. Record promoters showered their favors on a few influential, high-profile deejays, whose backing could make or break a record nationally, or on key program managers in charge of Top 40 formats in large urban markets. Recently, the FCC has stepped up enforcement of payola laws.

Radio Ownership: From Diversity to Consolidation

From the 1950s through the 1980s, the FCC tried to encourage diversity in broadcast ownership—and thus programming—by limiting the number of stations a media company could own. The **Telecommunications Act of 1996** introduced a new age of consolidation in the industry, as the FCC eliminated most ownership restrictions on radio. As a result, some twenty-one hundred stations and $15 billion changed hands that year alone. From 1995 to 2005, the number of radio station owners declined by one-third, from sixty-six hundred to about forty-four hundred.[13]

Radio: Yesterday, Today, and Tomorrow
Scholars and radio producers explain how radio adapts to and influences other media. **Discussion:** Do you expect that the Internet will be the end of radio, or will radio stations still be around decades from now?

Comedian Marc Maron hosts the popular podcast *WTF*, featuring detailed interviews with comedians like Amy Poehler, Conan O'Brien, Ben Stiller, and Sarah Silverman, as well as musicians and actors. He parlayed his podcast success into a TV comedy series called *Maron*, which has aired for three seasons on IFC.

Cassie Wright/WireImage/Getty Images

Streaming Music

In Chapter 5 (Sound Recording and Popular Music), we saw that streaming music is the biggest growth area for music consumption. Indeed, as sales of both CDs and digital downloads through places like iTunes slumped in 2013, the number of songs streamed grew around 30 percent to over 110 billion.[1] In just the first six months of 2014, the number of songs streamed in the United States was already over 70 billion.[2] This has implications not only for the music recording industry but also for radio.

For the past sixty years, a big part of the radio business model has been based on the ability to draw in an audience by playing recorded music, while exposing audience members to music they might then go out and buy. Online music streaming services challenge both parts of this long-standing relationship. First there are the on-demand services (Spotify, Rdio, Rhapsody), which act as a kind of online jukebox, allowing users to pick and play specific songs and artists. The other kind of service is the online radio station (Pandora), which puts a digital age spin on the usual listener–radio station interaction.

Pandora Radio, launched in 2000, provides an experience similar to that of broadcast and satellite radio but without a human deejay. Pandora selects songs based on an analysis of up to four hundred attributes that company employees index and categorize. Listeners can create personalized stations by entering key words (Alternative Coffee House Rock), artist or band names (Foo Fighters), or even a song ("All about That Bass"). After creating the station, Pandora streams music with characteristics that match the station's name. Like its broadcast counterparts, Pandora licenses its songs from music-rights organizations like ASCAP and BMI, and pays royalty fees on the songs it streams. With over seventy-six million active listeners, Pandora is the biggest online radio service in the United States.[3] However, it is getting more and more competition from both traditional radio and other Internet sites.

Leading radio corporation Clear Channel Communications (now iHeartMedia) unveiled its iHeartRadio service (www.iheart.com) in 2008, putting more than 850 of its stations from across the country on a free streaming service and allowing listeners to create their own custom stations by artist, song, or genre. In 2011, Clear Channel signed an agreement with Cumulus Radio to add its 570 stations to the

LaunchPad

macmillanhighered.com/mediaessentials3e

▶ **Visit LaunchPad** to watch a music video clip. What are some of the many ways a listener might seek out this track?

Fans of Meghan Trainor's song "All about That Bass" might create a streaming radio station based around that song's sound, rather than buy Trainor's full album.

iHeartRadio lineup. In 2014, after Grooveshark lost a federal copyright infringement case for songs it uploaded for its on-demand service, the company's owner said the company would regroup and launch as a radio service in 2015. All of these services are constantly releasing or updating their smartphone and tablet apps.

But even with music-playing competition from the Internet, radio does enjoy a few advantages over sites like Pandora. Radio remains the most local of broadcast media, allowing deejays to break into the playlist to provide live traffic, weather, and news updates, or broadcast live from a community event. At the same time, online streaming means a local station can have global reach. This is not to say, however, that the radio industry is content with the status quo. For several years, radio groups have been pushing for AM and FM receivers to be built into smartphones and tablets. Even the longest-standing type of radio isn't going away completely; it's converging into digital media alongside its competition.

The 1996 act allows individuals and companies to acquire as many radio stations as they want, with relaxed restrictions on the number of stations a single broadcaster may own in the same city. The larger the market or area, the more stations a company may own within that market. With few exceptions, for the past two decades the FCC has embraced the consolidation schemes pushed by the powerful NAB lobbyists in Washington, D.C., under which fewer and fewer owners control more and more of the airwaves.

This has reshaped the radio industry. Take, for example, the former Clear Channel Communications. It was formed in 1972 with one San Antonio station; in 1998, it swallowed up Jacor Communications, the fifth-largest radio chain, and became the nation's second-largest group, with 454 stations in 101 cities. Clear Channel continued its rapid expansion into the nation's largest radio owner, hitting a peak of 1,205 stations in 2005. As mentioned previously, Clear Channel changed its name to iHeartMedia in 2014, a rebranding the company says better reflects its diverse media businesses, especially those involving the Internet. Today, it owns 840 radio stations (still the largest) and has branched out into other areas, owning about 600,000 billboard and outdoor displays in over thirty countries across five continents, including 914 digital displays across thirty-seven U.S. markets. iHeartMedia also distributes many of the leading syndicated programs, including *The Rush Limbaugh Show*, *The Glenn Beck Program*, *On Air with Ryan Seacrest*, and *Delilah*. iHeartMedia is also an Internet radio source with its iHeartRadio, which has more than thirty million registered users.

Consider also the situation with the top five commercial radio groups: iHeartMedia (840 stations), Cumulus (525), Townsquare (312), CBS (126), and Entercom (103). Among them they own roughly 1,900 radio stations (more than 12 percent of all U.S. stations), dominate the fifty largest markets in the United States, and control at least one-third of the entire radio industry's $17.6 billion revenue. As a result of consolidations permitted by deregulation, in most American cities just a few corporations dominate the radio market.

When large corporations regained control of America's radio airwaves in the 1990s, activists in hundreds of communities across the United States protested by starting up their own noncommercial "pirate" radio stations, capable of broadcasting over a few miles with low-power FM signals of 1 to 10 watts. The major complaint of pirate radio station operators was that the FCC had long since ceased licensing low-power community radio stations. In 2000, the FCC responded to tens of thousands of inquiries about the development of a new local radio broadcasting service: It approved a new noncommercial **low-power FM (LPFM)** class of 10- and 100-watt stations to give voice to local groups lacking access to the public airwaves. LPFM station licensees included mostly religious groups but also high schools, colleges and universities, Native American tribes, labor groups, and museums. Then FCC chairman William E. Kennard, who fostered the LPFM initiative, explained: "This is about the haves—the broadcast industry—trying to prevent many have-nots—small community and educational organizations—from having just a little piece of the pie. Just a little piece of the airwaves which belong to all of the people."[14]

Bill Greene/The Boston Globe via Getty Images

Radio in a Democratic Society

As the first national electronic mass medium, radio has powerfully molded American culture. It gave us soap operas, situation comedies, and broadcast news, and it helped popularize rock and roll, car culture, and the politics of talk radio. Yet for all of its national influence and recent move toward consolidation, broadcast radio is still a supremely local medium. For decades, listeners have tuned in to hear the familiar voices of their community's deejays and talk-show hosts, and to enjoy music popular in their cultural heritage.

Though much mainstream radio programming is now managed by corporations, with many more specific voices opting to produce podcasts rather than traditional radio shows, local college and community stations can keep broadcasting locally.

The early debates over how radio should be used produced one of the most important and enduring ideas in communication policy for any democracy: a requirement to operate in the service of "public interest, convenience, or necessity." But as we've seen, the broadcasting industry has long chafed at this policy. Executives have maintained that because radio corporations invest heavily in technology, they should have more control over the radio frequencies on which they operate—as well as own as many stations as they want. Deregulation in the past few decades has moved the industry closer to that corporate vision. Today, nearly every radio market in the nation is dominated by a few owners, and those owners are required to renew their broadcasting licenses only every eight years.

This trend has begun moving radio away from its localism, as radio groups often manage hundreds of stations from afar. Given broadcasters' reluctance to openly discuss their own economic arrangements, public debate regarding radio as a natural resource has dwindled. Looking to the future, we face a big question: With a few large broadcast companies now permitted to dominate radio ownership nationwide, how much will the number and kinds of voices permitted to speak over the public airwaves be restricted? And if restrictions occur, what will happen to the democracy we live in, which is defined by local communities' having a say in how they're governed? To ensure that mass media, including radio, continue to serve democracy, we—the public—must play a role in developing the answers to these questions.

CHAPTER ESSENTIALS

Now that you have finished reading this chapter, you can use the following tools:

LaunchPad for *Media Essentials*

Go to **macmillanhighered.com/mediaessentials3e** for videos, review quizzes, and more.
LaunchPad for *Media Essentials* includes:

- **REVIEW WITH LEARNINGCURVE**
  LearningCurve uses gamelike quizzing to help you master the concepts you need to learn from this chapter.

REVIEW

Understand Key Aspects of Radio's Early History

- The **telegraph**, invented in the 1840s, sent electrical impulses from a transmitter through a cable to a reception point and was the first technology to enable communication to exceed the speed of human transportation. To send messages, telegraph operators used **Morse code**—a series of dots and dashes that stood for letters of the alphabet. The telegraph's limitations caused other inventors to experiment without wires, leading to the discovery of **radio waves** and **electromagnetic waves** (pp. 185–187).

- New developments in the nineteenth century improved wireless communication, taking it from **narrowcasting** (point-to-point communication) to **broadcasting** (one-to-many communication). Guglielmo Marconi is credited with developing **wireless telegraphy**, a form of voiceless point-to-point communication, in the 1890s, leaving others—such as Reginald Fessenden and Lee De Forest—to experiment with producing **wireless telephony** (voice transmissions) and amplifying **radio** sound (pp. 187–189).

- Early regulation of wireless/radio focused on providing public safety and national security; in 1910, Congress passed the **Wireless Ship Act**, which required all major ships to be equipped with wireless equipment, and two years later it passed the **Radio Act of 1912**, which required all radio stations on land or at sea to be licensed and assigned special call letters (pp. 189–190).

- Following World War I, radio moved into the private sector with the formation of the **Radio Corporation of America (RCA)**—a privately owned company that had the government's approval to acquire radio patents and dominate the radio industry (pp. 190–191).

- Radio's development as a business was solidified with the creation of the first lasting **network**, NBC, in 1926. Backed by David Sarnoff and connected by AT&T long lines, the network broadcast programs nationally and played a prominent role in unifying the country (pp. 191–193).

- The growth of the network and affiliate system alarmed government leaders, who banded together to pass the **Radio Act of 1927**, which began the process of issuing radio licenses and created the **Federal Radio Commission (FRC)** to oversee radio licenses and negotiate channel problems. The Radio Act introduced a pivotal new principle: Licensees did not *own* their channels but could use them as long as they operated to serve the "public interest, convenience, or necessity." With the passage of the **Federal Communications Act of 1934**, which allowed commercial interests to control the airwaves, the FRC became the **Federal Communications Commission (FCC)**, an independent U.S. government agency charged with regulating interstate and international communications (pp. 193–194).

- By 1930, the golden age of radio was in full force; living rooms were filled with music, drama, comedy, variety and quiz shows, weather forecasts, farm reports, and news (pp. 194–196).

Outline the Evolution of Radio

- In the wake of TV's development and massive popularity in the 1950s, radio suffered but was resurrected via portable **transistor** radios and the shift to music formats that relied on the recording industry for content (pp. 196–197).

- The rise of **FM** (frequency modulation) brought greater clarity and reception to radio, and became the dominant band for music by the 1980s. Until then, radio technology had centered on **AM** (amplitude modulation) (p. 197).

- The rise of **format radio**, in which station managers controlled the station's music programming, gearing it to specific listeners, solidified music as radio's single biggest staple and also introduced the idea of **rotation**: playing the top songs many times during the day (pp. 197–198).

Explain the Characteristics of Contemporary Radio

- Radio stations use a variety of formats to serve a diverse group of listeners, including **news and talk radio** (the most popular format of the 1990s, especially on AM stations) and music, which is often divided into specific categories: **country**, **Top 40/contemporary hit** radio (CHR), **adult contemporary (AC)**, **urban adult contemporary**, **Spanish-language radio** (sometimes in both talk and music formats), and **album-oriented rock (AOR)** (pp. 198–201).

- Nonprofit radio stations, such as those in the **Pacifica Foundation** network, and noncommercial networks, such as **National Public Radio (NPR)** and the **Public Broadcasting Service (PBS)**—both of which were mandated under federal provisions of the **Public Broadcasting Act of 1967** and the **Corporation for Public Broadcasting (CPB)**—were created to provide alternatives to commercial broadcasting (pp. 201, 204).

- Over the past decade or so, five alternative radio technologies have helped bring more diverse sounds and options for listening to radio audiences: **Internet radio, podcasting and portable listening, convergence with mobile technology, satellite radio**, and **HD radio** (pp. 204–206).

Discuss the Economics of Commercial Radio

- Commercial radio stations take in revenue from advertisers and spend money on assets such as content programming, often purchasing programming from national network radio (pp. 206–207).

- A radio station's musical content can be influenced by **payola**, the unethical practice of record promoters paying deejays or program managers to favor particular songs over others (p. 207).

- The **Telecommunications Act of 1996** introduced a new age of consolidation in radio ownership across the United States (pp. 207, 210).

- In response to large corporations' control over the airwaves, **low-power FM (LPFM)** was approved by the FCC in 2000 as a new class of noncommercial radio stations that aimed to give voice to local groups lacking access to the public airwaves (pp. 210–211).

Consider Radio's Influence on Our Democratic Society

- Radio has shaped trends in music, news, and entertainment while still remaining a supremely local medium, yet the trend has begun moving radio away from its localism, as radio groups often manage hundreds of stations from afar (p. 211).

- In an age when control of the public airwaves lies in fewer hands than ever, it is important to think about the impact this has on the number of voices permitted to speak and how this could affect our democracy (p. 211).

STUDY QUESTIONS

1. How did broadcasting, unlike print media, come to be federally regulated?
2. What is the significance of the Radio Act of 1927 and the Federal Communications Act of 1934?
3. How did radio adapt to the arrival of television?
4. What has been the main effect of the Telecommunications Act of 1996 on radio station ownership?
5. What is the relevance of localism to debates about ownership in radio?

MEDIA LITERACY PRACTICE

One of the most contentious issues in radio today involves diversity of ownership, which might influence diversity in sound and formats. To investigate this issue, explore the radio stations in your community.

DESCRIBE the ownership of stations in your (or a nearby) radio market and their formats.

ANALYZE the information in your list, looking for patterns and trends. How many stations attract the majority of the market's ratings? Are there multiple stations serving the same formats? What formats are missing?

INTERPRET what these patterns mean. For example, what does your market profile suggest about diversity in ownership and station formats? Are there people in your community who are underserved by all of the on-air options?

EVALUATE radio in your community. Do newer developments like Internet radio, satellite radio, podcasts, and HD radio offer better alternatives, or are they poor substitutes for broadcast radio?

ENGAGE with your community by writing to a local station. Tell the manager what the station is doing right or what could be done better to serve the community.

7

Movies and the Impact of Images

When Dr. Ryan Stone (Sandra Bullock) tumbles out of control farther and farther into space, knocked loose in a storm of debris that hits during a spacewalk, the camera follows her spinning course, displaying a stunning rush of images of Earth and the darkness of space across the screen. But whereas Bullock's character in Alfonso Cuarón's film *Gravity* was separated from her space shuttle, audiences watching the film in 3-D in the theater were anything but detached from the digital 3-D action on the screen. Though it's not quite the biggest success story among films taking advantage of the new and improved digital 3-D (2009's *Avatar* holds the top spot as the highest-grossing movie of all time), *Gravity* found unexpected blockbuster-level success with a combination of stunning visual effects, star power, and a compelling story, all while bucking the typical blockbuster movie formula.[1]

Another movie about space flight made over a century ago with what was then state-of-the-art technology and special effects also amazed audiences and captured imaginations. Georges Méliès's *A Trip to the Moon*, released in 1902, was an early example of how new techniques and technologies led filmmakers to make movies that heralded new eras in filmmaking. Warner Brothers' *The Jazz Singer* in 1927, Orson Welles's *Citizen Kane* in 1941, George Lucas's *Star Wars* in 1977, and James Cameron's *Avatar* in 2009 all mark such changes in the art, craft, and business of filmmaking. Méliès pioneered the use of fantasy in film, Warner Brothers ushered in the sound era,

Welles developed deep-focus cinematography and other technical milestones, Lucas helped create the modern blockbuster mentality and continued to lead the way in new special effects, and Cameron masterfully deployed the innovation of digital performance-capture technology to transform the 3-D movie from gimmick to potential art form. The movies, then, have always been a technological spectacle, a grand illusion that—like a magic act—uses smoke, light, and trickery to make marvelous illusions come to life. Since the early twentieth century, the movies have operated as one of the world's chief storytellers.

These movie narratives create community, too. We attend theaters or watch at home with family and friends. Movies distract us from our daily struggles: They evoke and symbolize universal themes of human experience (childhood, coming of age, family relations, growing older, coping with death); they help us understand and respond to major historical events and tragedies (for instance, the Holocaust and 9/11); and they encourage us to rethink contemporary ideas as the world evolves, particularly in terms of how we think about race, class, spirituality, gender, and sexuality. As with the experience of the main character in *Gravity*, the best films can untether us from the reality of our daily lives, only to challenge us to try to reconnect with our world in a new way.

Of course, as cultural products, movies are subject to the same economic constraints as are other mass media forms. For example, there is a tendency for the major studios to roll out standardized big-budget blockbusters in hopes of finding the next *Avatar*, while narratives that break the mold can sometimes languish for lack of major studio backing. But in the emerging terrain of digital video and Internet distribution, the ability of moviemakers to find audiences without major studio support is increasing.

GIVEN THE FILM INDUSTRY'S LENGTHY AND COMPLEX ROLE in Americans' lives, along with its steady transformation in response to new technologies, cultural change, and other developments, it's vital to take a closer look at this unique mass medium. In particular, we need to ask big questions about what purposes movies serve for us today, compared to the past; how strong an impact the U.S. film industry has on society and culture in our own country and in others; and where the film industry may be headed in the future.

To these ends, we use this chapter to examine the rich legacy and current role of movies by:

- considering film's early history, including the technological advances that made movies possible

- tracing the evolution of the Hollywood studio system, which arose to dominate the global film industry

- exploring how narrative styles developed in moviemaking, including the transition from silent film to "talkies" and the emergence of different camera techniques and movie genres

- examining the transformation of the Hollywood studio system in response to new forces, such as the birth of television and the rise of home entertainment

- analyzing the economics of the movie business—specifically, how it makes money and what it invests in to stay profitable

- weighing movies' role in our democracy today and in the diverse world around us

LaunchPad
macmillanhighered.com
/mediaessentials3e
Use **LearningCurve** to review concepts from this chapter.

The Early History of Movies

Filmmaking has passed through several stages on its way to mass medium status. In the following pages, we trace those stages— including development (when inventors first made pictures move), entrepreneurial (when experimenters conducted movie demonstrations for a small number of paid viewers), and finally true mass medium (when movies became widely accessible and began telling coherent stories with specific meanings for viewers). Throughout these stages, creative and bold innovators have worked together to continually advance the medium, revealing the strongly collaborative nature of this industry.

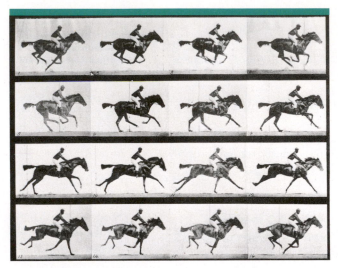

Eadweard Muybridge/Time Life Pictures/Getty Images

Eadweard Muybridge's studies of horses in motion, like the one shown, proved that a horse gets all four feet off the ground during a gallop. In his various studies of motion, Muybridge could use twelve cameras at a time.

Advances in Film Technology

The concept of film goes back as early as Leonardo da Vinci, who theorized in the late 1400s that a device could be created to reproduce reality. There were other early precursors to film as well. For example, in the 1600s, the *magic lantern* projected images painted on glass plates using an oil lamp as a light source. In 1824, the *thaumatrope* consisted of a two-sided card whose different images appeared to combine when the card was twirled. And the *zoetrope*, created in 1834, was a cylindrical device with slits cut into it that rapidly spun images on the inside, appearing to viewers as if the images were moving.

But the true development stage of filmmaking began when inventors discovered a process for making a series of photographs appear to move while projected on a screen.

Muybridge and Goodwin Make Pictures Move

Eadweard Muybridge, an English photographer living in America, is credited with being the first person to make images move. He studied motion by using multiple cameras to take successive photographs of humans and animals in motion. By 1880, he had developed a method for projecting the photographic images on a wall for public viewing.

Meanwhile, other inventors were also capturing moving images and projecting them. In 1884, George Eastman (founder of Eastman Kodak) developed the first roll

CHAPTER 7 // TIMELINE

1889 Celluloid
New Jersey minister Hannibal Goodwin develops celluloid, which enables motion pictures to be created.

1894 Kinetoscope Parlors
The first kinetoscope parlor of coin-operated machines opens in New York City.

1896 The Vitascope
Edison's vitascope popularizes large-screen film projection in the United States.

1907 Nickelodeons
Storefront movie theaters with a five-cent admission price begin to flourish in the United States.

1914 Movie Palaces
The first of a national trend of opulent movie palaces opens in New York.

film—a huge improvement over the heavy metal-and-glass plates previously used to make individual photos. Louis Aimé Augustin Le Prince, a Frenchman living in England, invented the first motion-picture camera using roll film. Le Prince, who disappeared mysteriously on a train ride to Paris in 1890, is credited with filming the first motion picture, *Roundhay Garden Scene*, in 1888. Recorded at twelve frames per second, the film depicts several people strolling on a lawn and runs for just a few seconds.

In 1889, a New Jersey minister, Hannibal Goodwin, improved Eastman's roll film by using thin strips of transparent, pliable material called **celluloid**, which could hold a coating of chemicals sensitive to light. Goodwin's breakthrough enabled a strip of film to move through a camera and be photographed in rapid succession, producing a series of pictures.

Edison and the Brothers Lumière Create Motion Pictures

The early developers of film laid the groundwork for the shift to the entrepreneurial stage. During this stage, inventors came up with new projection and distribution technologies, enabling people to come together in a public place to view movies. The action began in the late 1800s, when American inventor and businessman Thomas Edison (with the help of his assistant, William Kennedy Dickson) combined his incandescent light bulb, Goodwin's celluloid, and Le Prince's camera to create another early movie camera, the **kinetograph**, and a single-person viewing system, the **kinetoscope**. This small projection system required individual viewers to look through a small hole to see images moving on a tiny plate.

Meanwhile in France, brothers Louis and Auguste Lumière developed the *cinematograph*—a combined camera, film development, and projection system. The projection system was particularly important, as it enabled more than one person at a time to see the moving images on a large screen.

With inventors around the world now dabbling in moving pictures, Edison continued innovating in film. He patented several inventions and manufactured a new

1920s Movie Studio System
Movie studios solidify control of production, distribution, and exhibition of movies.

Late 1920s Big Five and Little Three
The Big Five studios and the Little Three form a powerful oligopoly.

1927 and 1928 Sound Comes to Movies
The Jazz Singer and *The Singing Fool*, both starring Al Jolson, bring sound to the screen.

1947 The Hollywood Ten
The House Un-American Activities Committee (HUAC) investigates ten unwilling witnesses on grounds of allegedly having communist sympathies.

1948 Paramount Decision
The Supreme Court forces studios to divest themselves of their theaters to end vertical integration.

Everett Collection

Kinetoscopes allowed individuals to view motion pictures through a window in a cabinet that held the film. The first kinetoscope parlor opened in 1894 in New York City and was such a hit that many others quickly followed.

large-screen system called the **vitascope**, through which longer filmstrips could be projected without interruption. This device hinted at the potential of movies as a future mass medium. Staged at a music hall in New York in April 1896, Edison's first public showing of the vitascope featured shots from a boxing match and waves rolling onto a beach. Some members of the audience were so taken with the realism of the images that they stepped back from the screen's crashing waves to avoid getting their feet wet.

At this point, movies consisted of movement recorded by a single continuous camera shot. Early filmmakers had not yet figured out how to move the camera itself or how to edit film shots together. Moreover, movies' content consisted simply of people or objects in motion, without conveying any story. Nonetheless, various innovators had spotted the commercial possibilities of film. By 1900, short movies had become a part of the entertainment industry, used as visual novelties in amusement arcades, traveling carnivals, wax museums, and vaudeville theaters.

Telling Stories: The Introduction of Narrative

With the introduction in the late 1890s of **narrative films**—movies that tell stories through the series of actions depicted (later matched with sound)—the industry advanced from the entrepreneurial stage to mass medium status. And film promised to offer a far richer experience than other storytelling media—specifically, books and radio. Unlike those media, narrative films provided realistic moving images and compelling stories in which viewers became so immersed that they sometimes forgot they were watching a fictional representation.

CHAPTER 7 // TIMELINE continued

1967 Ratings System
The Motion Picture Association of America initiates the first ratings system for age appropriateness.

1977 Video Transforms the Industry
VHS-format videocassette recorders (VCRs) hit the consumer market, creating the movie rental and purchase industry.

1990s The Rise of the Indies
Independent films become an important source for identifying new talent.

1995 Megaplex Mania
A wave of giant movie complexes are built.

1997 DVDs
The new format is quickly adopted as superior to the VHS cassette.

Some of the earliest narrative films (which were silent) were produced and directed by French magician and inventor Georges Méliès, who opened the first public movie theater in France in 1896. Méliès began producing short fantasy and fairy-tale films, including *The Vanishing Lady* (1896), *Cinderella* (1899), and *A Trip to the Moon* (1902). He increasingly used editing and unique camera tricks and techniques, such as slow motion and cartoon animation, which would become key ingredients in future narrative filmmaking.

The first American filmmaker to adapt Méliès's innovations to narrative film was Edwin S. Porter. Porter shot narrative scenes out of order (for instance, some in a studio and some outdoors) and reassembled, or edited, them to tell a story. In 1902, he made what is regarded as America's first narrative film, *The Life of an American Fireman*, which included the first recorded close-up. Porter also introduced the western genre and the first chase scene in *The Great Train Robbery* (1903).

Everett Collection

The Great Train Robbery (1903) may have introduced the western genre, but it was actually filmed in New Jersey. The still above shows a famous scene in which a bandit shoots his gun at the audience.

The Arrival of Nickelodeons

Another turning point in film's development as a mass medium was the 1907 arrival of **nickelodeons**—a type of movie theater whose name combines the admission price (five cents) with the Greek word for "theater." According to media historian Douglas Gomery, these small and uncomfortable makeshift theaters often consisted of converted storefronts redecorated to mimic vaudeville theaters.[2] Nickelodeons showed silent films, which typically transcended language barriers and provided workers and immigrants with an inexpensive escape from the challenges of urban life. Not surprisingly, nickelodeons flourished during the great European immigration at the dawn of the twentieth century. Between 1907 and 1909, the number of nickelodeons in the United States skyrocketed from five thousand to ten thousand. The craze peaked by 1910, when entrepreneurs began seeking more affluent spectators, attracting them with larger and more lavish movie theaters.

2000 Digital Film Production
The digital production and distribution format gains strength in Hollywood and with independents.

Early 2000s IMAX Experience
Select Hollywood films are digitally remastered and exhibited in the larger IMAX format.

2008 Blu-ray
Hollywood settles on the Blu-ray format to succeed the DVD, but home exhibition also moves toward Internet streaming.

2012 3-D
Over two dozen movies are released in digital 3-D, including several converted classics.

The Evolution of the Hollywood Studio System

By the 1910s, movies had become a major industry, and entrepreneurs developed many tactics for controlling it—including monopolizing patents on film-related technologies and dominating the "three pillars" of the movie business: production (making movies), distribution (getting films into theaters), and exhibition (playing films in theaters). Controlling those three parts of an industry achieves **vertical integration**. In the film business, it means managing the entire moviemaking process—from the development of an idea to the screening of the final product before an audience. The resulting concentration of power gave rise to the **studio system**, in which creative talent was firmly controlled by certain powerful studios. Five vertically integrated movie studios, sometimes referred to as the Big Five, made up this new film **oligopoly** (a situation in which an industry is controlled by just a few firms): Paramount, MGM, Warner Brothers, Twentieth Century Fox, and RKO. An additional three studios, sometimes called the Little Three— Columbia, Universal, and United Artists—did not own chains of theaters but held powerful positions in movie production and distribution.

Edison's Attempt to Control the Industry

Among the first to try his hand at dominating the movie business and reaping its profits, Thomas Edison formed the Motion Picture Patents Company, known as the Trust, in 1908. A cartel of major U.S. and French film producers, the company pooled film-technology patents, acquired most major film distributorships, and signed an exclusive deal with George Eastman, who agreed to supply stock film only to Trust-approved theater companies.

However, some independent producers refused to bow to the Trust's terms. These producers abandoned film production centers in New York and New Jersey and moved to Cuba; Florida; and ultimately Hollywood, California. In particular, two Hungarian immigrants—Adolph Zukor (who would eventually run Paramount Pictures) and William Fox (who would found the Fox Film Corporation, later named Twentieth Century Fox)—wanted to free their movie operations from the Trust's tyrannical grasp. Zukor's early companies figured out ways to bypass the Trust. A suit by Fox, a nickelodeon operator-turned-film distributor, resulted in the Trust's breakup for restraint-of-trade violations in 1917.

A Closer Look at the Three Pillars

Ironically, film entrepreneurs like Zukor who fought the Trust realized they could control the film industry themselves through vertical integration. The three pillars of vertical integration occur in a specific sequence: First, movies are produced. Next, copies are distributed to people or companies who get them out to theaters. Finally, the movies are exhibited in theaters. But even as power through vertical integration became concentrated in just a few big studios, other studios sought to dominate one or another of the three pillars. This competition sparked tension between the forces of centralization and those of independence.

Production

A major element in the production pillar is the choice of actors for a particular film. This circumstance created an opportunity for some studios to gain control using tactics other than Edison's pooling of patents. Once these companies learned that audiences preferred specific actors to anonymous ones, they signed exclusive contracts with big-name actors. In this way, the studio system began controlling the talent in the industry. For example, Adolph Zukor hired a number of popular actors and formed the Famous Players Film Company in 1912. One Famous Players performer was Mary Pickford, who became known as "America's Sweetheart" for her portrayal of spunky and innocent heroines. Pickford so elevated film actors' status that in 1919, she broke from Zukor to form her own company, United Artists. Actor Douglas Fairbanks (her future husband) joined her, along with comedian-director Charlie Chaplin and director D. W. Griffith.

Although United Artists represented a brief triumph of autonomy for a few powerful actors, by the 1920s the studio system had solidified its control over all creative talent in the industry. Pioneered by director Thomas Ince and his company, Triangle, the system constituted a kind of assembly line for moviemaking talent: Actors, directors, editors, writers, and others all worked under exclusive contracts for the major studios. Ince also designated himself the first studio head, appointing producers to handle hiring, logistics, and finances so that he could more easily supervise many pictures at once. The studio system proved so efficient that major studios were soon producing new feature films every week. Pooling talent,

With legions of fans, Mary Pickford became the first woman ever to make a salary of $1 million in a year and gained the freedom to take artistic risks with her roles. She launched United Artists, a film distribution company, with Douglas Fairbanks, Charlie Chaplin, and D. W. Griffith. No woman since has been as powerful a player in the movie industry. Here she is seen with Buddy Rogers in My Best Girl.

Everett Collection

rather than patents, turned out to be a more ingenious tactic for movie studios seeking to dominate film production.

Distribution

Whereas there were two main strategies for controlling the production pillar of moviemaking (pooling patents or pooling talent), studios seeking power in the industry had more options open to them for controlling distribution. One early effort to do so came in 1904, when movie companies provided vaudeville theaters with films and projectors on a *film exchange* system. In return for their short films, shown between live acts in the theaters, movie producers received a small percentage of the vaudeville ticket-gate receipts.

Edison's Trust used another tactic: withholding projection equipment from theater companies not willing to pay the Trust's patent-use fees. However, as with the production of film, independent film companies looked for distribution strategies outside of the Trust. Again, Adolph Zukor led the fight, developing **block booking**. Under this system, movie exhibitors who wanted access to popular films with big stars like Mary Pickford had to also rent new or marginal films featuring no stars. Although this practice was eventually outlawed as monopolistic, such contracts enabled the studios to test-market possible up-and-coming stars at little financial risk.

As yet another distribution strategy, some companies marketed American films in Europe. World War I so disrupted film production in Europe that the United States stepped in to fill the gap—eventually becoming the leader in the commercial movie business worldwide. After the war, no other nation's film industry could compete economically with Hollywood. By the mid-1920s, foreign revenue from U.S. films totaled $100 million. Even today, Hollywood dominates the world market for movies.

Exhibition

Companies could gain further control of the movie industry by finding ways to get more people to buy more movie tickets. Innovations in exhibition (such as construction of more inviting theaters) transformed the way people watched films and began attracting more middle- and upper-middle-class viewers.

Initially, Edison's Trust tried to dominate exhibition by controlling the flow of films to theater owners. If theaters wanted to ensure they had films to show their patrons, they had to purchase a license from the Trust and pay whatever price it asked. But after the Trust collapsed, emerging studios in Hollywood came up with their own ideas for controlling exhibition and making certain the movies they produced were shown. When industrious theater owners began forming film cooperatives to compete with block-booking tactics, producers like Zukor conspired to buy up theaters. Zukor and the heads of several major studios understood that they did not have to own all the theaters to ensure that their movies would be shown. Instead, the major studios needed to own only the first-run theaters (about 15% of the nation's theaters). First-run theaters premiered new films in major downtown areas in front of the largest audiences and generated 85 to 95 percent of all film revenue.

The studios quickly realized that to earn revenue from these first-run theaters, they would have to draw members of the middle and upper-middle classes to the movies. With this goal in mind, they built **movie palaces**, full-time single-screen theaters that provided a more enjoyable and comfortable movie-viewing environment. In 1914, the three-thousand-seat Strand Theatre, the first movie palace, opened in New York.

Another major innovation in exhibition was the development of *mid-city movie theaters*. These theaters—built in convenient locations near urban mass-transit stations—attracted city dwellers as well as the initial wave of people who had moved to city outskirts in the 1920s and commuted into work from the suburbs. This strategy is alive and well today, as **multiplexes** and **megaplexes** featuring many screens (often fourteen or more), upscale concession services, stadium-style seating, digital projection and sound, 3-D capabilities, and giant IMAX screens lure middle-class crowds to interstate highway crossroads (see "Converging Media Case Study: Movie Theaters and Live Exhibition" on pages 244–245).

© James Marshall/Corbis

The historic Fox Movie Palace, located in Detroit, was originally built in the late 1920s and restored in 1990.

Hollywood's Golden Age: The Development of Style

Once the Hollywood studio system was established as a profitable business model, studios had the luxury of developing a distinctive moviemaking style that ultimately marked Hollywood's Golden Age. This style began taking shape in 1915, characterized by the use of new narrative techniques (such as close-up camera shots and multiple story lines) in the silent era, the later introduction of sound, and the rise of movie genres. Hollywood's monopolization of this style produced numerous films that have since become treasured classics. Yet during Hollywood's Golden Age, other moviemaking models—including global cinema, documentaries, and independent films—provided alternatives to the classic style and shaped the medium just as powerfully.

Narrative Techniques in the Silent Era

Though telling stories in films occurred early on, moviemaking hit its stride as a viable art form when studios developed innovative narrative techniques, including the use of varied camera distances, close-up shots, multiple story lines, fast-paced editing, and symbolic imagery—even before sound was introduced. As these techniques evolved, making a movie became more than just telling a story; it became about *how* to tell the story. For example, the same sequence of events filmed from different camera angles could have totally different impacts on viewers.

D. W. Griffith, among the earliest "star" directors, used nearly all of these techniques at the same time in *The Birth of a Nation* (1915)—the first *feature-length film* (more than an hour long) produced in America. Although considered a technical masterpiece and an enormous hit, the film glorified the Ku Klux Klan and stereotyped southern blacks. The National Association for the Advancement of Colored People (NAACP) campaigned against the film, and protests and riots broke out at many screenings.

Other popular films created during the silent era were historical and religious epics, including *Napoleon*, *Ben-Hur*, and *The Ten Commandments*. But the era also produced pioneering social dramas, mysteries, comedies, horror films, science-fiction movies, war films, crime dramas, and westerns.

Al Jolson in *The Singing Fool* (1928). The film was the box-office champ for more than ten years, until it was dethroned by *Gone with the Wind* in 1939.

© Warner Bros./Photofest

Augmenting Images with Sound

Hollywood's Golden Age also saw the introduction of sound in 1927, which further established a distinctive narrative style and set new commercial standards in the industry. The availability of movies with sound pushed annual movie attendance in the United States from sixty million a week in 1927 to ninety million a week just two years later. By 1931, nearly 85 percent of America's twenty thousand theaters accommodated **talkies** (sound pictures). And by 1935, the rest of the world had adopted talking films as the commercial standard.

Earlier attempts at creating talkies had failed; however, technical breakthroughs in the 1910s at AT&T's research arm, Bell Labs, produced prototypes of loudspeakers and sound amplifiers. Experiments with sound continued during the 1920s, particularly at Warner Brothers. In 1927, the studio produced *The Jazz Singer*, a feature-length silent film interspersed with musical numbers and brief dialogue. Starring Al Jolson, a charismatic and popular vaudeville singer who wore blackface makeup as part of his act, the movie further demonstrated racism's presence in the film industry. Warner Brothers' 1928 release *The Singing Fool*, which also starred Jolson, became the real breakthrough for talkies. Costing $200,000 to make, the film raked in a whopping $5 million and "proved to all doubters that talkies were here to stay."[3]

Warner Brothers was not the only studio exploring sound technology. Five months before *The Jazz Singer* opened, Fox premiered sound-film **newsreels** (weekly ten-minute compilations of news events from around the world). Fox's newsreel company, Movietone, captured the first film footage with sound of the takeoff and return of Charles Lindbergh, who piloted the first solo, nonstop flight across the Atlantic Ocean in May 1927. The Movietone sound system eventually became the industry standard.

Inside the Hollywood System: Setting the Standard for Narrative Style

By the time talkies had transformed the film industry, Hollywood had established firm control over narrative style—the recognizable way in which directors told stories through the movies they made. Hollywood had set the example for most moviemaking style worldwide, and continues to dominate American filmmaking style today. The model it developed serves up three ingredients that give Hollywood movies their distinctive flavor: the narrative (story), the genre (type of story), and the author (director). The right blend of these ingredients—combined with timing, marketing, and luck—has enabled Hollywood to create a long string of movie hits, from 1930s and 1940s classics like *Gone with the Wind* and *Casablanca* to recent successes like *The Avengers* and *Gravity*.

Hollywood Narratives

As we've seen, storytelling had long existed in movies, even in the silent era. But it was Hollywood's Golden Age that saw the emergence of a distinctive narrative style that movie viewers soon associated with American filmmaking. *Narrative* always includes a story (what happens to whom) and discourse (how the story is told). Most movies feature a number of stories that play out within the film's larger, overarching narrative. These narratives also present recognizable character

LaunchPad
macmillanhighered.com
/mediaessentials3e

Storytelling in *Gravity*
Visit LaunchPad to view a short clip from the Oscar-winning movie *Gravity*.
Discussion: Based on this clip, how does the movie seem to use advanced technical tools in service of classical studio-system storytelling?

Hollywood genres help us categorize movies. The 1949 film *White Heat* is considered a film noir drama, Rob Reiner's *When Harry Met Sally* (1989) is a romantic comedy, and *Maleficent* (2014) is a fantasy film.

Everett Collection (left); © Columbia Pictures/Everett Collection (middle); © Walt Disney Studios Motion Pictures/Everett Collection (right)

types (protagonist, antagonist, romantic interest, sidekick) and have a clear beginning, middle, and end. The plot is usually propelled by the main character's decisions and actions to resolve a conflict by the end of the movie. Nowadays, filmmakers also use computer-generated imagery (CGI) or digital remastering to augment narratives with special effects—providing a powerful experience that satisfies most audiences' appetite for both the familiar and the distinctive.

Hollywood Genres

In addition to establishing a unique narrative style in its Golden Age, Hollywood gave birth to movie **genres**, categories in which conventions regarding characters, scenes, and themes recur in combination. Familiar genres include comedy, drama, romance, action/adventure, mystery/suspense, gangster, westerns, horror, fantasy/science fiction, musicals, and film noir (French for "black film")—a genre developed in the United States after World War II that explores unstable characters and the sinister side of human nature.

Grouping films by category enabled the movie industry to achieve both *product standardization* (a set of formulas for producing genres) and *product differentiation* (a diverse set of movie-watching experiences for viewers to choose from).

Hollywood "Authors"

As another defining characteristic of Hollywood's Golden Age, movie directors gained significant status. In commercial filmmaking, the director serves as the main "author" of a film. Sometimes called by the French term, *auteurs*, successful directors develop a particular cinematic style or an interest in specific topics that differentiates their narratives from those of other directors. During Hollywood's Golden Age, notable directors included Alfred Hitchcock, Howard Hughes, Sam Goldwyn, and Busby Berkeley—each famous for his defining moviemaking style. Today, directors are just as distinctive: When you hear that a new movie is a "Spielberg film," a "Tarantino project," or "the latest from the Coen brothers," you have a good idea of what to expect.

As the 1960s and 1970s unfolded, the films of Francis Ford Coppola (*The Godfather*), Brian De Palma (*Carrie*), William Friedkin (*The Exorcist*), George Lucas (*Star Wars*), Martin Scorsese (*Taxi Driver*), and Steven Spielberg (*Jaws*) signaled the start

Female directors have long struggled in Hollywood, but some, like Kathryn Bigelow (*shown*), have made big names for themselves. Winning the 2010 Academy Award for *The Hurt Locker*, Bigelow has also *Point Break* (1991) and *Zero Dark Thirty* (2012) among her film credits.

© Columbia Pictures/Everett Collection

of a period that Scorsese has called "the deification of the director." Through this development, a handful of talented directors gained the kind of economic clout and celebrity standing that had previously belonged to top movie stars. Though directors lost power in the 1980s and 1990s, the tradition carries on with well-known directors like Tim Burton, Quentin Tarantino, and Christopher Nolan.

Even today, most well-known film directors are white men. Only four women have ever received an Academy Award nomination for directing a feature film: Lina Wertmüller in 1976 for *Seven Beauties*, Jane Campion in 1994 for *The Piano*, Sofia Coppola in 2004 for *Lost in Translation,* and Kathryn Bigelow in 2010 for *The Hurt Locker* (she won). Directors from other groups have also struggled for recognition in Hollywood—and a few have become successful. Well-regarded African American directors include Kasi Lemmons (*Black Nativity*, 2013), John Singleton (*Abduction*, 2011), and Spike Lee (*Red Hook Summer*, 2012). (For more, see "Media Literacy Case Study: Breaking through Hollywood's Race Barrier" on pages 234–235.) Asian Americans M. Night Shyamalan (*After Earth*, 2013), Ang Lee (*Life of Pi*, 2012), and Wayne Wang (*Snow Flower and the Secret Fan*, 2011) have also built accomplished directing careers.

Outside the Hollywood System: Providing Alternatives

Despite Hollywood's dominance of the film industry, viewers have long had alternatives to the feature-length, hugely attended, big-budget movies offered by the studio system. These alternatives include global cinema, documentaries, and independent films.

Global Cinema

Films made in other countries constitute less than 2 percent of motion pictures seen in the United States today. Yet foreign films did well in 1920s America, especially in diverse neighborhoods in large cities. These films' popularity has waxed and waned since the Great Depression, in response to such developments as assimilation of immigrants, postwar prosperity, and the rise of the home-video market.

To be sure, the modern success in the United States of movies like *Crouching Tiger, Hidden Dragon* (Taiwan, 2000), *Amélie* (France, 2001), and *The Lives of Others* (Germany, 2006) suggests that American audiences are willing to watch subtitled films with non-Hollywood perspectives. But foreign films have continued losing screen space to the expanding independent American film market. Today, the largest foreign-film

LaunchPad
macmillanhighered.com
/mediaessentials3e

Breaking Barriers with 12 Years a Slave
Visit LaunchPad to view a short clip from the Oscar-winning movie from director Steve McQueen.
Discussion: How do you think *12 Years a Slave* differs from previous depictions of black history in America?

The Tale of Princess Kaguya, a Japanese animated film based on a folktale, was first released in Japan in 2013 and came to North America in 2014.

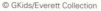
© GKids/Everett Collection

industry is in India, which aficionados call "Bollywood" (a play on words combining *Bombay* and *Hollywood*). Bollywood produces as many as one thousand films every year, most of them romances or adventure musicals displaying a distinct style.

There are other avenues for U.S. audiences seeking access to international cinema. The Global Film Initiative, for example, selects and distributes an annual film series—Global Lens—to more than thirty-five locations in the United States, including many college campuses. Global Lens 2014 included films from Cameroon, Croatia, Egypt, India, Morocco, Russia, Rwanda, Turkey, and Venezuela.

Documentaries

Documentaries, through which directors interpret reality by recording real people and settings, evolved from several earlier types of nonfictional movies: *interest films* (which contained compiled footage of regional wars, political leaders, industrial workers, and agricultural scenes), *newsreels*, and *travelogues* (depictions of daily life in various communities around the world).

Over time, documentaries developed a unique identity. As educational, noncommercial presentations, they usually required the backing of industry, government, or philanthropy to cover production and other costs. By the late 1950s and early 1960s, the development of portable cameras led to a documentary style known as **cinema verité** (French for "truth film"). Portable cameras enabled documentarians (such as Robert Drew, for *Primary*, 1960) to go where cameras could not go before and record fragments of everyday life unobtrusively.

Perhaps the major contribution of documentaries has been their willingness to tackle controversial subject matter or bring attention to issues about which the public might not be aware. For example, *Blackfish*, a documentary by Gabriela Cowperthwaite released in 2013, tracks the tragic life of Tilikum, a captive killer whale that attacked and killed his trainer. The documentary examines the controversial practice of training orca whales for entertainment venues like SeaWorld. In fact, *Blackfish*, which first screened at the Sundance Film Festival, sparked anti-SeaWorld protests across the country. American documentary filmmaker Michael Moore often targets corporations or the government in his films, which include *Fahrenheit 9/11* (2004), a critique of the Bush administration's Middle East policies and the Iraq War, and *Sicko* (2007), an investigation into the flaws of the U.S. health-care system.

Independent Films

The success of some documentary films dovetails with the rise of **indies**, another alternative to the Hollywood system. As opposed to directors who work within the Hollywood system, independent filmmakers typically operate on a shoestring budget and show their movies in campus auditoriums, small film festivals, and—if they're lucky—independent theaters. Successful independents like Kevin Smith (*Clerks*, 1994; *Tusk*, 2014), Darren Aronofsky (*Black Swan*, 2010; *Noah*, 2014), and Sofia Coppola (*Lost in Translation*, 2003; *The Bling Ring*, 2013) continue to find substantial audiences in theaters and through online services like Netflix, which promote work produced outside the studio system.

The rise of independent film festivals in the 1990s also helped Hollywood rediscover low-cost independent films as alternatives to the standard big-budget blockbuster types of movies. Big studios looked to these festivals as ways to find new talent, which sometimes led them to purchase independent film companies or set up deals to help with distribution for a cut of the profit. This feeder system has since declined due to a poor economy, waning interest by major studios, and indies taking greater advantage of digital distribution models, though many indie directors of the 1990s—such as David O. Russell (*American Hustle*, 2013) and Alexander Payne (*Nebraska*, 2013)—have also found success at the big studios.

The Transformation of the Hollywood Studio System

Starting in the late 1940s, a number of forces began reshaping how people viewed movies and what they expected to see when they watched a film. These forces stemmed from new regulations seeking to break up studios' hold over the film industry, social developments (e.g., massive migrations of city dwellers to the suburbs), and competing mass media (namely, the increasing popularity of TV). Together, these changes forced the Hollywood studio system to adapt in an effort to remain viable and profitable, even after national weekly movie attendance peaked in 1946.

The Paramount Decision

An important force reshaping the Hollywood system took form in the wake of the **Paramount decision.** This 1948 court ruling (fueled by the government's discomfort with the movie industry's power) forced the big, vertically integrated studios to break up their ownership of movie production, distribution, and exhibition. As a result, the studios eventually gave up their theater businesses.

The ruling never really changed the oligopoly structure of the Hollywood film industry, because it failed to weaken the industry's control over movie

Breaking through Hollywood's Race Barrier

Despite inequities and discrimination, a thriving black cinema existed in New York's Harlem district during the 1930s and 1940s. Usually bankrolled by white business executives who were capitalizing on the black-only theaters fostered by segregation, independent films featuring black casts were supported by African American moviegoers, even during the Depression. But it was a popular Hollywood film—*Imitation of Life* (1934)—that emerged as the highest-grossing film in black theaters during the mid-1930s. The film told the story of the friendship between a white woman and a black woman whose young daughter denied her heritage and passed for white, breaking her mother's heart.

Despite African Americans' long support of the film industry, their moviegoing experience has not been the same as that of whites. From the late 1800s until the passage of Civil Rights legislation in the mid-1960s, many theater owners discriminated against black patrons. In large cities, blacks often had to attend separate theaters, where new movies might not appear until a year or two after white theaters had shown them. In smaller towns and in the South, blacks were often only allowed to patronize local theaters after midnight. In addition, some theater managers required black patrons to sit in less desirable areas of the theater.[1]

Changes took place during and after World War II, however. When the "white flight" from central cities began during the suburbanization of the 1950s, many downtown and neighborhood theaters began catering to black customers in order to keep from going out of business. By the late 1960s and early 1970s, these theaters had become major venues for popular commercial films such as *Guess Who's Coming to Dinner?* (1967) and *In the Heat of the Night* (1967).

Based on the popularity of these films, black photographer-turned-filmmaker Gordon Parks, who'd directed *The Learning Tree* (1969), adapted from his own novel, went on to make commercial action/adventure films, including *Shaft* (1971), remade by John Singleton in 2000. Popular in urban theaters, especially among black teenagers, the movies produced by Parks and his son—Gordon Parks Jr. (*Super Fly*, 1972)—spawned a number of commercial imitators, labeled blaxploitation movies. These films were the subjects of heated cultural debates in the 1970s; like some rap songs today, they were both praised for their realistic depictions of black urban life and criticized for glorifying violence. Nevertheless, these films reinvigorated urban movie attendance, reaching an audience that had not been well served by the film industry until the 1960s.

Although opportunities for black film directors expanded in the 1980s and 1990s, mainstream Hollywood is still a formidable place for outsiders to crack. Even acclaimed director Spike Lee has had

LaunchPad

macmillanhighered.com/mediaessentials3e

▶ **Visit LaunchPad** to watch a clip from a Tyler Perry film. How does Perry establish a clear and distinctive voice in his work?

© Variance Films/Everett Collection (left);
© Lions Gate/Everett Collection (right)

Spike Lee (*left*) and Tyler Perry (*right*)

difficulty securing large budgets from the studios, despite several critical and commercial successes. For example, in making *Get on the Bus* (1996), Lee asked a number of wealthy black men to bankroll $2 million for the film, which depicted the October 1995 Million Man March on Washington, D.C., celebrating the kind of black self-reliance that Lee's own moviemaking has long illustrated. In 2013, Lee again sought creative freedom by raising $1.4 million on crowd-source fundraising Web site Kickstarter. That effort resulted in the 2015 release of *Da Sweet Blood of Jesus*, a project inspired by 1973's *Ganja and Hess*, a film by black director Bill Gunn that used vampires as a metaphor for assimilation of black identity in the post–Civil Rights era.[2] And in 2004, director and playwright Tyler Perry split the $5.5 million budget with Lionsgate Films for *Diary of a Mad Black Woman*, which went on to gross more than $50 million. Its success allowed Perry to become an industry unto himself, writing, directing, and producing a series of successful films. These films consistently demonstrate the appeal of themes and narratives brought to the screen by black directors.

APPLYING THE CRITICAL PROCESS

DESCRIPTION Consider a list of the all-time highest-grossing movies in the United States, such as the one on the Internet Movie Database, http://us.imdb.com /boxoffice/alltimegross.

ANALYSIS Note patterns in the list. For example, of the top fifty or so, pay attention to how many films are from African American directors or have major roles with African American actors. Note what the most popular genres are.

INTERPRETATION What do the patterns mean? Economically, it's clear why Hollywood likes to have successful blockbuster movie franchises. But what kinds of films and representations get left out of the mix?

EVALUATION It is likely that we will continue to see an increase in youth-oriented, animated/action movie franchises that are heavily merchandised and intended for wide international distribution. Indeed, Hollywood does not have a lot of motivation to put out movies that don't fit these categories. Is this a good thing?

ENGAGEMENT Watch a film by an African American director and consider what's missing from most theater marquees. Visit aafca.com or browse imdb.com to find more films that feature African American directors and actors. See if Netflix, Hulu Plus, or your campus libraries carry any of these titles, and request them if they don't. Spread the word on notable African American films by reviewing them online or in a college newspaper.

distribution. However, it did open up opportunities in the exhibition pillar of the industry for new players outside Hollywood. For instance, art houses began showing more documentaries or foreign films, and thousands of new drive-in theaters sprang up in farmers' fields—all of which offered alternative fare to moviegoers.

Flight to the Suburbs

After World War II, waves of Americans experienced a severe case of pent-up consumer demand after years of wartime frugality. Thus, they migrated from cities to the suburbs to purchase their own homes and spend their much-increased discretionary income on all manner of newly available luxuries. These changes badly hurt the Hollywood studio system: Suburban neighborhoods were located far from downtown movie theaters, and people's leisure-time preferences had shifted from watching movies to shopping for material goods, such as cars, barbecue grills, and furniture.

To make matters worse for studios, the average age of couples entering marriage dropped from twenty-four to nineteen after the war. Thus, there were significantly fewer young couples going to the movies on dates.

Television

As Hollywood responded to the political, regulatory, and social changes transforming 1940s and 1950s America, it also sought to strike back at the major technological force emerging at that time: television. Studios used several strategies in their efforts to compete with TV.

When the current ratings system was created in 1967, it did not include the now-popular PG-13 rating. That rating was introduced in 1984, following an outcry over violence in the PG-rated *Indiana Jones and the Temple of Doom* and *Gremlins*.

First, with growing legions of people gathering around their living-room TV sets, studios shifted movie content toward more serious themes—including alcoholism (*The Lost Weekend*, 1945), racism (*Pinky*, 1949), sexuality (*Peyton Place*, 1957; *Butterfield 8*, 1960; and *Lolita*, 1962), and other topics from which television stayed away. Ironically, such films challenged the authority of the industry's own Motion Picture Production Code, adopted in the early 1930s to restrict film depictions of violence, crime, drug use, and sexual behavior. (For more on the Code, see Chapter 13.) In 1967, the Motion Picture Association of America initiated

© Amblin/Warner Bros./Photofest

the current ratings system, which rates films for age appropriateness rather than censoring all adult content.

Second, the film industry introduced a host of technological improvements designed to lure Americans away from their TV sets. These innovations included Technicolor, a series of color film processes (alluring in a world where TV screens showed only black-and-white images). Movie theaters also began offering wide screens, stereophonic sound, and extra-clear film, which was a huge improvement over previously fuzzy images. But although these developments may have drawn some people back to downtown movie theaters, they weren't enough to surmount the studios' core problem: the middle-class flight to the suburbs, away from downtown movie theaters.

Home Entertainment

Things got even more challenging for the studio system in the 1970s, when the introduction of cable television and the videocassette gave rise to the home-entertainment movement. Despite some worries that this trend would be a blow to the studios, Hollywood managed to adapt, developing a new market for renting and selling movies—first on VHS, then on DVD, and more recently on the Blu-ray format.

Studios and indies alike are looking toward Internet distribution for the future of the video business. Currently, movie fans can download or stream movies and television shows for rent or for purchase from services like Netflix, Amazon, Hulu, Google, and the iTunes store to their television sets through devices like Roku, Apple TV, TiVo Premiere, video game consoles, and Internet-ready TVs. As people invest in wide-screen TVs (including 3-D televisions) and sophisticated sound systems, home entertainment is getting bigger and keeping pace with the movie theater experience. Interestingly, home entertainment is also getting smaller—movies are increasingly available to stream and download on portable devices like tablets, laptop computers, and smartphones.

The Economics of the Movie Business

Despite the many changes transforming the movie business, the Hollywood studio system continues to make money, whether it's through producing movies, distributing them (through such channels as movie theaters and home-video sales), or exhibiting them (for example, in theaters or through downloads from the Internet). But to remain profitable, industry players must also invest money—in creative talent, postproduction tasks such as editing, and construction of theaters.

Money In

Film-industry players make money through a variety of means. In the commercial film business, these **Big Six** players are Warner Brothers, Paramount, Twentieth Century Fox, Universal, Columbia Pictures, and Disney—all owned by large parent conglomerates (see Figure 7.1). Together, the Big Six account for about 80 percent of the revenue generated by commercial films. They also control more than half the movie market in Europe and Asia.

Nevertheless, the cost of producing films has risen, and studios have had to find ways to generate more revenues to produce movies profitably. On top of that, with 80 to 90 percent of newly released films failing to make money at the domestic box office, studios need a couple of major hits each year to make money through one of the six main revenue sources:

1. **Box-office sales.** Studios get about 40 percent of the theater box-office take in this first "window" for movie exhibition (the theater gets the rest). Studios have recently found that they can often reel in bigger box-office receipts for 3-D films and their higher ticket prices.
2. **DVD/video sales and rentals.** Sales to the home-video market (video-on-demand, subscription streaming, Blu-ray, DVD sales and rentals) typically start about three to five months after a theatrical release and generate more revenue than domestic box-office income for major studios.
3. **Cable and television outlets.** This includes premium cable (such as HBO and Showtime), and network and basic cable showings. The syndicated TV market also pays the studios on a negotiated film-by-film basis.
4. **Foreign distribution.** Studios earn profits from distributing films in foreign markets. In fact, at $25 billion in 2013, international box-office gross revenues are more than double U.S. and Canadian box-office receipts, and they continue to climb annually, even as other countries produce more of their own films.
5. **Independent-film distribution.** Studios make money by distributing the work of independent producers and filmmakers, who hire the studios to gain wider circulation. Independents pay the studios 30–50 percent of the box-office and home-video revenue they make from their movies.
6. **Licensing and product placement.** Studios earn revenue from merchandise licensing (for example, licensing sales of action figures representing characters

FIGURE 7.1 // MARKET SHARE OF U.S. FILM STUDIOS AND DISTRIBUTORS, 2014 (IN MILLIONS)

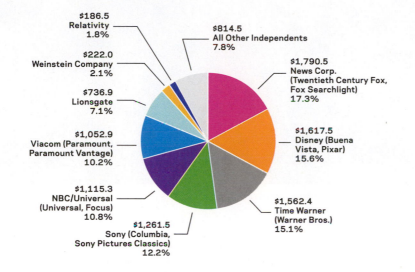

$186.5
Relativity
1.8%

$222.0
Weinstein Company
2.1%

$736.9
Lionsgate
7.1%

$1,052.9
Viacom (Paramount,
Paramount Vantage)
10.2%

$1,115.3
NBC/Universal
(Universal, Focus)
10.8%

$1,261.5
Sony (Columbia,
Sony Pictures Classics)
12.2%

$814.5
All Other Independents
7.8%

$1,790.5
News Corp.
(Twentieth Century Fox,
Fox Searchlight)
17.3%

$1,617.5
Disney (Buena
Vista, Pixar)
15.6%

$1,562.4
Time Warner
(Warner Bros.)
15.1%

Note: Based on gross box-office revenue, January 1, 2014–December 31, 2014. Overall gross for period: $10.360 billion.

Data from: Box Office Mojo, Studio Market Share, www.boxofficemojo.com/studio/?view=company&view2=yearly&yr=2014&p=.htm

from a particular movie) to retailers. Companies that make cars, snacks, and other products also pay studios to place their products in movies, so that actors and characters will be shown using those products. Famous product placements include Reese's Pieces in *E.T.: The Extra-Terrestrial* (1982), Pepsi-Cola in *Back to the Future II* (1989), and *The Lego Movie* (2014)—an entire movie built around the popular toy line. The Superman movie *Man of Steel* (2013) reportedly features a record amount of product placement, and was singled out for Sears and IHOP logos having prominent places during big action sequences.

Synergy—the promotion and sale of a product throughout the various subsidiaries of a media conglomerate—has further driven revenues in the film industry. Companies like Disney promote not only the new movies produced by its studio division but also books, soundtracks, calendars, T-shirts, and toys based on these movies.

Blockbusters like *Guardians of the Galaxy* (2014) are sought after despite large budgets because they can potentially bring in twice that much in box-office sales, DVDs, merchandising, licensing fees, and international distribution.

© Walt Disney Studios Motion Pictures/Everett Collection

Money Out

Just as film-industry participants generate revenues through an array of sources, they must also spend money on various expenditures to provide the kinds of moviegoing experiences viewers want. Major expenditures include the following:

- **Production**, including fees paid to stars, directors, and other personnel, and costs associated with special-effects technology, set design, and musical-score composition. In recent years, production costs have amounted to about 65 percent of the cost of making a movie.
- **Marketing, advertising, and print** costs. For typical Hollywood films, these expenses can amount to 35 percent of a movie's overall cost.[4] Heavy advance promotion can double the cost of a commercial film.
- **Postproduction** activities, such as film editing and sound recording.
- **Distribution** expenses, such as screening a movie for prospective buyers representing theaters.
- **Exhibition** costs, such as the significant expenses involved in constructing theaters and purchasing projection equipment.
- **Acquisitions.** Many big studios buy up other media-related companies (such as firms making media equipment that consumers use in their homes, or enterprises providing animation services) to gain the technologies and competencies needed to stay in business. For example, Disney bought its animation partner, Pixar, in 2006, and signed a long-term distribution deal with Steven Spielberg's DreamWorks Studios in 2009. Likewise, Time Warner's purchase of basic and

premium cable channels like TBS and HBO has enabled it to distribute its own films on cable channels for home viewing.

To cut costs, many professional filmmakers have begun seeking less expensive ways of producing movies. **Digital video** has become a major alternative to celluloid film, allowing filmmakers to replace expensive and bulky 16-mm and 35-mm film cameras with cheaper, lightweight digital video cameras. Digital video also lets filmmakers see the results of their camera work immediately, rather than having to wait until the film is developed. Moreover, filmmakers can capture additional footage cheaply, compared with costlier film stock and processing expenses. In fact, very few film cameras are being manufactured in the United States, as they recede in favor of the digital models.

Chuck Zlotnick/@ Focus Features/Everett Collection

Digital video is now common in Hollywood films. One of the latest digital cameras, the Red, is considered affordable at $17,500, making digital equipment more accessible to new or lower-budget filmmakers.

With digital video equipment and computer-based desktop editors, people can now make movies for just a few thousand dollars—a tiny fraction of what the cost would be on film. Every year, more and more films are being made digitally. And nonprofessionals are jumping into the action—producing their own films through accessible tools such as Final Cut Pro and posting them on venues such as YouTube and Vimeo.

Convergence: Movies Adjust to the Digital Turn

The biggest challenge the movie industry faces today is the Internet. After witnessing the difficulties that illegal file-sharing brought on the music labels (some of which share the same corporate parent as film studios), the movie industry has more quickly embraced the Internet for movie distribution through outlets like Apple's iTunes store and Netflix.

The popularity of Netflix's streaming service (added in 2008 to its DVD-rental-by-mail service) opened the door to other similar services. Hulu—a joint venture by NBC Universal (Universal Studios), News Corp. (Twentieth Century Fox), and Disney—was created as the studios' attempt to divert attention from YouTube and get viewers to watch free, ad-supported streaming movies and television shows online or subscribe to Hulu Plus, Hulu's premium service. Others, such as Comcast (Xfinity TV), Google (YouTube), Walmart (Vudu), and Amazon (Amazon Instant Video), have also gotten into online digital movie distribution.

Movies are also increasingly available to stream or download on mobile phones and tablets. Several companies, including Netflix, Hulu, Amazon, Google, Apple, Redbox, and Blockbuster, have developed distribution to mobile devices (see Figure 7.2).

The year 2012 marked a turning point: For the first time, movie fans accessed more movies through digital online media than physical copies, like DVDs or Blu-rays.[5] For the movie industry, this shift to Internet distribution has mixed consequences. On the one hand, the industry needs to offer movies where people want to access them, and digital distribution is a growing market. On the other hand, although streaming is less expensive than producing physical DVDs, the revenue is still much lower compared to DVD sales, which had a larger impact on the major studios that had grown reliant on healthy DVD revenue.

The digital turn creates two long-term paths for Hollywood. One path is that studios and theaters will lean even more heavily toward making and showing big-budget blockbuster film franchises with a lot of special effects, since people will want to watch those on the big screen (especially IMAX and 3-D) for the full effect (see also "Converging Media: Case Study: Movie Theaters and Live Exhibition"

FIGURE 7.2 // ONLINE VIDEO STREAMING MARKET SHARE RANKING, 2013

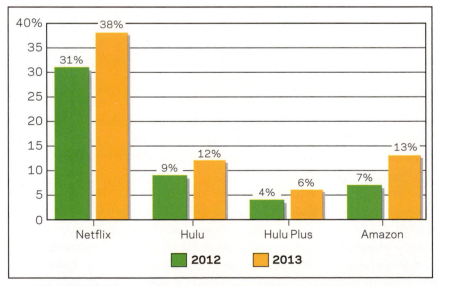

Data from: Nielsen Newswire, "'Binging' Is the New Viewing for Over-the-Top Streamers," September 18, 2013, www.nielsen.com/us/en/newswire/2013/binging-is-the-new-viewing-for-over-the-top-streamers.html

on pages 244–245); plus, they are easy to export for international audiences. The other path features inexpensive digital distribution for lower-budget documentaries and independent films, which likely wouldn't get wide theatrical distribution anyway, but could find an audience in those who watch at home.

The Internet has also become an essential tool for movie marketing—one that studios are finding less expensive than traditional methods, like television ads or billboards. Films regularly have Web pages, but many studios also now use a full menu of social media to promote films in advance of their release.

The Movies in a Democratic Society

In 1947, in the wake of the unfolding Cold War with the Soviet Union, some members of Congress began investigating Hollywood for alleged subversive and communist ties. During the investigations, the House Un-American Activities Committee (HUAC) coerced prominent people from the film industry to declare their patriotism and to give up the names of colleagues suspected of having politically unfriendly tendencies. Upset over labor union strikes and outspoken writers, many film executives were eager to testify and provide names. For instance, Jack L. Warner of Warner Brothers suggested that whenever film writers made fun of the wealthy or America's political system in their work, or if their movies were sympathetic to "Indians and the colored folks,"[11] they were engaging in communist propaganda. Many other prominent actors and directors also "named names," either out of a belief it was their patriotic duty or out of fear of losing their jobs.

Eventually, HUAC subpoenaed ten unwilling witnesses who were questioned about their memberships in various organizations. The so-called **Hollywood Ten**—nine screenwriters and one director—refused to discuss their memberships or to identify communist sympathizers. Charged with contempt of Congress in November 1947, they were eventually sent to prison. Although jailing the Hollywood Ten clearly violated their free-speech rights, in the atmosphere of the Cold War many people worried that "the American way" could be sabotaged via unpatriotic messages planted in films. Upon release from jail, the Hollywood Ten found themselves blacklisted, or boycotted, by the major studios, and their careers in the film industry were all but ruined. The national fervor over communism continued to plague Hollywood well into the 1950s.

When HUAC made sure to include the film industry in its communist witch hunts, they were reacting to the way they saw film as a powerful cultural tool

CONVERGING MEDIA

Case Study

Movie Theaters and Live Exhibition

Adaptation or extinction: This Darwinian law has helped the business of movie exhibition survive into the twenty-first century. Since the arrival of the nickelodeon—the first permanent locations devoted to screening motion pictures—the exhibition branch has witnessed several profound transformations, from the development of drive-ins in the 1950s to the proliferation of multiplex screens in the 1970s and 1980s. As home viewing becomes an increasingly viable option, movie theaters are still on the lookout for opportunities to fill seats—especially on weeknights, when business is slow.

Media convergence has provided just such an opportunity. In 2011, the transition to digital cinema reached what industry analysts consider a tipping point. With more than sixty thousand screens converted to digital projection technology (roughly half the exhibition facilities worldwide), movie exhibition is taking the next step in its technological evolution: the addition of live programming. Until recently, the use of theaters for the presentation of live events

© Donald Cooper/Photostage

was limited but not unheard of. According to legend, the *Amos 'n' Andy* radio show was so popular in the 1930s that many theaters halted their screenings for fifteen minutes to play the program over loudspeakers to the gathered audience.[1] But until recently, television and radio have been the media devoted to the presentation of live events.

The repurposing of movie theaters, enabled by the conversion to digital projection, began as early as 2002, but it did not attract national attention until December 2006, when National CineMedia's programming division, NCM Fathom, presented *The Magic Flute*, the first installment of its *Metropolitan Opera: Live in HD* series.[2] Fathom now boasts a network of five hundred screens. Cinedigm, another player in this fledgling field, specializes in distributing live 3-D sporting events to its eighty-eight-theater network.[3] Cinedigm's 3-D presentation of the 2009 BCS National Championship football game sold out nineteen of the eighty theaters then in its network and generated four times the per-screen revenue of any film that night. And in 2010, more than a hundred thousand people paid $20 a ticket to

LaunchPad

macmillanhighered.com/mediaessentials3e

▶ **Visit LaunchPad** to watch a clip from one of Peter Jackson's *Hobbit* films. How might theatrical exhibition change this experience?

watch Fathom's live operatic broadcast of *Carmen* at theaters nationwide.[4]

In addition to using this technology for sports, concerts, and opera, Fathom is also exploring and cultivating corporate and religious markets. This convergence may help movie theaters survive, even as more people opt to watch movies at home; just as audiences have a greater range of choices in how, when, and where they watch a movie, movie theaters can offer a greater range of choices in communal experiences than just new films. The movie theater of the twenty-first century could potentially be the destination for professional conventions, worship services, political rallies, and electronic gaming tournaments, as well as for watching movies in the dark with strangers. Digitizing movies for the big screen has posed additional challenges for studios. As Hollywood began making more 3-D films (the latest form of product differentiation), studios had to subsidize theater chains' installation of new projection systems. By 2012, more than 12,620 3-D screens had been installed in theaters across the United States.[5] Some theaters have also begun to experiment with high-frame-rate (HFR) projection, which Peter Jackson has championed for his trilogy of *Hobbit* films, and which offers images with greater clarity, particularly in 3-D.

However, the increasing number of 3-D and HFR screens isn't always preferable. The ultra-clarity of HFR can sometimes disrupt the audience's suspension of disbelief if the setting of the movie suddenly looks too much like a soundstage, rather than the imaginary world the filmmakers are trying to create. On the other hand, HFR technology might be a boon for live events, which tend to have a less "cinematic" look. It's possible that whatever will be shown in movie theaters of the future won't look much like movies as we know them today.

that could threaten the status quo. That's because movies function as **consensus narratives**—popular cultural products that provide us with shared experiences. Whether they are dramas, romances, westerns, or mysteries, movies communicate values, hopes, and dreams through accessible language and imagery that can reinforce some cultural norms, challenge others, and even bridge cultural differences. This can be a double-edged sword.

As the American film industry has continued to dominate the movie-watching experience in many other nations, observers have begun questioning this phenomenon. Some have wondered whether American-made films are helping to create a kind of global village, where people around the world share a universal culture. Others have asked whether these films stifle local cultures worldwide.

With the rise of international media conglomerates, public debate over such questions has ebbed. This is worrisome, as movies exert a powerful impact on people's beliefs, values, and even actions. As other nations begin to view the American film industry as an interloper in their people's culture, they may develop a resentment against the United States overall.

Likewise, the continuing power of the movie industry within our own nation raises questions about movies' role in our democracy. It's vital that those of us who consume movies do so with a critical eye and a willingness to debate these larger questions about this mass medium's cultural, political, and social significance. The political significance of film is easy to see in movies that strike political chords with many members of the audience, such as Michael Moore's *Capitalism: A Love Story* (a director and film that surely would have drawn the wrath of HUAC) or Clint Eastwood's *American Sniper.* But that's not to say viewers only need to watch serious, issue-based films closely or critically. If anything, a consensus narrative is more powerful when audiences accept it without even really knowing that's what they are doing.

For instance, most mainstream audiences see Disney's movies as harmless forms of entertainment. But a critical look at the images of femininity in Disney films, from *Snow White* to *Pirates of the Caribbean*, reveals a consistent view of beauty that hews close to a Barbie-doll ideal. What's more, inner beauty is typically reflected by an attractive outward appearance. Other Disney films (like the *Lion King* and *Pocahontas*) verge on racial stereotyping or xenophobia, as when the heroes of *Aladdin* look less Middle Eastern than the villains. A media-literate viewer, then, must recognize that part of the cultural power of broad entertainments like Disney movies is bound up in packaging potentially questionable messages about gender, race, and class in stories that seem transparently wholesome. Given the expanded viewing options and the increasing access to independent, foreign, and otherwise nonmainstream films, viewers can seek out various alternatives to mass-marketed Hollywood films. With an entity as large as the U.S. film industry producing compelling messages about what we should value, how we should live, and how we should act, it's vital for those of us who consume movies to do so with a critical, media-literate eye—and to seek out other cinematic voices.

CHAPTER ESSENTIALS

Now that you have finished reading this chapter, you can use the following tools:

LaunchPad for *Media Essentials*

Go to **macmillanhighered.com/mediaessentials3e** for videos, review quizzes, and more.

LaunchPad for *Media Essentials* includes:

- **REVIEW WITH LEARNINGCURVE**
  LearningCurve uses gamelike quizzing to help you master the concepts you need to learn from this chapter.

- **VIDEO:** *CLUELESS*
  Watch a clip from the classic 1995 teen comedy and discuss how it works as a consensus narrative.

REVIEW

Understand Main Events in Movies' Early History

- Major advances in film technology took place in the late nineteenth century, when Eadweard Muybridge created a method for making images move while George Eastman developed the first roll film, capable of capturing moving images and projecting them. Soon after, Hannibal Goodwin improved roll film by using strips of transparent, pliable material called **celluloid**, enabling a strip of film to move through a camera and be photographed in rapid succession, producing a series of pictures (pp. 220–221).

- Film moved to the entrepreneurial stage when inventors such as Thomas Edison created the **kinetograph**, an early movie camera; the **kinetoscope**, a single-person viewing system; and the **vitascope**, a new large-screen system through which longer film strips could be projected without interruption. During this time, others dabbled in film development, and movies first began to be seen by the public—although they consisted of movement recorded by a single continuous camera shot (pp. 221–222).

- Movies advanced to the mass medium stage in the late 1890s with the introduction of **narrative films**—movies that tell stories through a series of actions, offering audiences a realistic movie experience. In addition, the arrival of **nickelodeons**—a type of movie theater whose name combines the admission price with the Greek word for "theater"— made movies accessible to everyone, including workers and immigrants (pp. 222–223).

Trace the Evolution of the Hollywood Studio System

- By the 1910s, movies had become a major industry due to the creation of monopolies and entrepreneurs jockeying for power over the "three pillars" of the film business: production (making movies), distribution (getting films into theaters), and exhibition (playing films in theaters). Controlling these three parts achieved **vertical integration**. The resulting concentration of power gave rise to the **studio system**, in which creative talent was firmly controlled by studios. Five film studios made up this new film **oligopoly**—a situation in which industry is dominated by just a few firms (p. 224).

- By pooling film-technology patents, inventor Thomas Edison tried to dominate the business by forming in 1908 the Motion Picture Patents Company, known as the Trust, to the dismay of many early film producers. Edison's monopoly was later broken up, but movie studios emerged and gained power through a variety of tactics, including **block booking**—pressuring theater operators to accept marginal films with no stars in order to get access to films with the most popular stars—and drawing in members of the middle and upper-middle classes with **movie palaces** and later city dwellers with **multiplexes** and modern **megaplexes** (pp. 224–227).

Discuss the Development of Style in Hollywood's Golden Age

- Once the Hollywood studio system established itself as a profitable business, it ushered in a Golden Age beginning in 1915, whereby distinct moviemaking styles were developed and standards were set, including narrative techniques like innovative use of camera angles to tell stories; the introduction of sound pictures (**talkies**) and later sound-film **newsreels**; a Hollywood narrative style with recognizable plots and character types; movie **genres**, or categories in which conventions regarding characters, scenes, and themes recur in combination; and the rise in status of the movie director, who developed a particular cinematic style or an interest in specific topics (pp. 227–231).

- Outside the Hollywood system, many alternatives to the feature-length film exist, such as global cinema, **documentaries** (sometimes developed with portable cameras in a style known as **cinema verité**), and independent films (or **indies**) (pp. 231–233).

Explain the Transformation of the Hollywood Studio System

- Beginning in the 1940s, a number of political, social, and cultural forces reshaped how people viewed movies, forcing the Hollywood studio system to adapt. For example, the **Paramount Decision** in 1948—a court ruling forcing the big, vertically integrated studios to break up their ownership of the three pillars—and the migration of Americans from the cities to the suburbs (and away from movies to new luxuries) changed the way movies were consumed (pp. 233, 236).

- Although many people thought the introduction of television and home entertainment (such as the rise of cable and the videocassette) would be the end of film, studios used several strategies to compete, such as covering more serious themes in movies and using technological improvements like Technicolor in film, while also capitalizing on video/DVD sales and rentals (pp. 233, 236–237).

Analyze the Economics of the Movie Business

- In the commercial film business, players such as the **Big Six** (Warner Brothers, Paramount, Twentieth Century Fox, Universal, Columbia Pictures, and Disney) make money from box-office sales, DVD/video sales and rentals, cable and television outlets, foreign distribution, independent-film distribution, and licensing and product placement. **Synergy**—the promotion and sale of a product throughout the various subsidiaries of a media conglomerate—further drives revenue (pp. 237–239).

- The film industry spends money on production; marketing, advertising, and print; postproduction; distribution; exhibition; and acquisitions. To cut costs, many filmmakers have sought less expensive ways of producing movies with **digital video**. However, the dawn of the digital age presents new uncertainties and is forcing studios to rethink their business models (pp. 240–242).

Consider How Movies Function in Our Democratic Society

- Movies act as **consensus narratives**—popular cultural products that provide us with shared experiences and communicate values, hopes, and dreams (pp. 243, 246).

- The continuing power of the movie industry raises questions about movies' role in society—both internationally and within the United States. Therefore, it's vital to consume movies with a critical eye (pp. 246–247).

STUDY QUESTIONS

1. How did film go from the novelty stage to the mass medium stage?
2. Why did Thomas Edison and the Trust fail to shape and control the film industry, and why did Adolph Zukor of Paramount succeed?
3. Why are genres and directors important to the film industry?
4. What political and cultural forces changed the Hollywood system in the 1950s?
5. What are the various ways in which major movie studios make money from the film business?
6. Do films contribute to a global village in which people throughout the world share a universal culture? Or do U.S.-based films overwhelm the development of other cultures worldwide? Discuss.

MEDIA LITERACY PRACTICE

Although American-made films may create a kind of global village, in which people around the world share a universal culture, there has long been concern about whether American films stifle local cultures worldwide, creating a cultural imperialism in which U.S. stories and images dominate. But what do *we* learn from American movies about people outside our own borders? Consider a few movies to investigate this question.

DESCRIBE the representations of foreign people and places in the ten U.S. films you have seen most recently.

ANALYZE the representations. Do the movie narratives treat the foreigners as friends or foes, fellow humans or strange curiosities? How are foreign environments treated—as friendly, alienating, or otherwise?

INTERPRET what these patterns mean. For example, does the language, skin color, or gender of the foreign characters make a difference? Is a foreign love interest "exotic," but a foreign official "threatening"?

EVALUATE the portrayal of international characters and places in American movies. Do American movies enable us to see the foreign characters as they might see themselves, or do we interpret them through an "American" gaze (or, more specifically, a white, middle-class, American male gaze)?

ENGAGE with your community by reviewing the portrayal of foreign people and places for an online site or a college newspaper, and submitting your review for online posting or publication.

8

Television, Cable, and Specialization in Visual Culture

Matt Dinnerstein/© Fox/Everett Collection

It wasn't all that long ago when television critics worried that reality television shows like *The Bachelor*, *Jersey Shore*, and *Celebrity Apprentice* would kill off scripted television programs. Reality television, so named because of its supposed lack of scripting and ability to capture spontaneous "real life" (though it often employs contrived situations and conflict), is much cheaper to produce than programs that require higher-paid writers and actors, and more elaborate sets and scripts. As these types of shows grew more popular, there was a fear that networks and production companies would shift their focus and abandon the more expensive scripted shows.

But since 2010, high-concept scripted television comedy and dramas have enjoyed a comeback in popularity. Some of these commercial or critical hits have come from the Big Four broadcast networks, such as *Scandal* on ABC or *Empire* on Fox (pictured at left), but many have come from other outlets. For example, premium cable channel HBO, whose hit series *The Sopranos* ran from 1999 to 2007, hit it big again in 2011 when it tackled the epic fantasy novel series with the TV adaptation *Game of Thrones*. Cable channel AMC, once home to replays of theatrical films, captured its share of critical, commercial, and pop culture success with series like *Mad Men*, *Breaking Bad*, and *The Walking Dead*.

Perhaps even more revolutionary, though, has been the success of television that never existed as a cable or broadcast network series. Video-streaming giant Netflix has received critical and audience attention with programs like *House of Cards* and *Orange Is the New Black*, releasing an entire season's worth of episodes at the same time. Viewers no longer need a cable subscription or even a television set to watch these programs (although over 90% of U.S. homes do have a TV set). Thanks to technological convergence, services like Netflix and Hulu can be watched on laptops, tablets, and smartphones as well. Responding to this success, other nontraditional sources of programming have been looking into creating their own productions, such as Yahoo! Screen picking up the canceled NBC series *Community* for another season. Reality shows still flourish, too—there's more space than ever before for new shows of any genre. It turns out, then, that fears about one type of show dominating the medium were unfounded. Viewers want good stories across genres, channels, and platforms.

FOR A LONG TIME AFTER ITS INCEPTION, television brought millions of American viewers together to share major turning points in U.S. history. For example, people gathered around their sets to watch coverage of Civil Rights struggles, the moon landing, the Watergate scandal, the explosion of a space shuttle, the 9/11 attacks, Hurricane Katrina, and the wars in Iraq and Afghanistan. Television also united people around more enjoyable activities, like movie, television, and music awards shows (the Oscars, the Emmys, or the CMA Awards), or major sporting events like the Super Bowl. Throughout the country, Americans watched the latest episode of their favorite TV comedy or drama at home, then discussed it with friends and colleagues the next day.

With the invention of cable and then satellite television, we now have more channels and programming options than ever to choose from, each of them appealing—like magazines—to narrow niches of viewers. New platforms keep attracting more users as the ways we experience television continue to change. In 1977, only 14 percent of all American homes received cable service (which at that time carried just twelve channels). In 1999, that number had grown to 70 percent (with many times more channels). However, by 2011 it dipped below 50 percent because of competition from Internet-based streaming and direct broadcast satellite (DBS) services—and "cord-cutting" has only become more popular since. Even traditional cable television customers no longer rely on the same services, with digital cable, DVR, and video-on-demand giving us more options for what we watch and how we watch it.

These technologies and business models, then, have changed the way we watch television and modified the role it plays in our lives. It's become easier to watch only what we want—when and where we want. But it's also harder to capture that sense of community that comes from watching a program together in our living rooms and talking about it with others afterward.

In this chapter, we examine television's impact on American life—yesterday, today, and tomorrow—by:

- considering television's early history, including its foundational technological innovations, the development of program content, and the arrival of cable

- tracing turning points in the evolution of network programming, such as the development of daily news broadcasts, the arrival of new entertainment forms (comedy, drama, reality television), and the creation of public television

- exploring the evolution of cable and satellite programming, including the emergence of basic and premium services

- assessing the regulatory challenges network television and cable have faced, such as the government's attempts to decrease networks' control over content and limit cable's growth

- examining network television and cable in the digital age, including the impact of home video; the Internet, cell phones, and mobile video; and direct broadcast satellite

- analyzing the economics of television by considering how industry players make money and what they spend it on to stay in business

- raising questions about television's role in our democratic society, such as whether it is uniting us or fragmenting us and whether it's giving a greater or fewer number of people a voice

The Early History of Television

In 1948, only 1 percent of American households had a television set. By 1953, more than 50 percent had one, and by the early 1960s, the number had risen past 90 percent. During these early years, several major developments shaped television and helped turn it into a dominant mass medium. Others, especially an infamous scandal over corrupt TV quiz shows, brought its potential and promise into question.

Becoming a Mass Medium

Inspired by the ability to transmit audio signals from one place to another, inventors had long sought to send "tele-visual" images. For example, in the 1880s, German inventor Paul Nipkow developed the *scanning disk*, a large flat metal disk perforated with small holes organized in a spiral pattern. As the disk rotated, it separated pictures into pinpoints of light that could be transmitted as a series of electronic lines. Subsequent inventors improved on this early electronic technology. Their achievements pushed television from the development stage to the entrepreneurial stage and then to the mass medium stage—complete with technical standards, regulation, and further innovation (such as the move from black-and-white to color television).

The Development Stage: Establishing Patents

Television's development and commercialization were fueled by a battle over patents between two independent inventors—Vladimir Zworykin and Philo Farnsworth—each seeking a way to send pictures through the air over long

CHAPTER 8 // TIMELINE

Late 1880s Cathode Ray Tube
The cathode ray tube—forerunner of the TV picture tube—is invented.

1927 First TV Transmission
Philo Farnsworth transmits the first TV picture electronically.

1934 First Public TV Demo
Farnsworth conducts the first public demonstration of television in Philadelphia.

1940s Cable Television
CATV systems originate in Oregon, Pennsylvania, New York City, and elsewhere to bring in TV signals blocked by mountains and tall buildings.

1951 *I Love Lucy*
I Love Lucy becomes the first TV program filmed in front of a live studio audience.

1952–54 *Today* and the *Tonight Show*
NBC introduces *Today* and the *Tonight Show*, helping to wrest control of programming away from advertisers.

distances. In 1923, after immigrating to America and taking a job at RCA, the Russian-born Zworykin invented the *iconoscope*, the first TV camera tube to convert light rays into electrical signals. He received a patent for his device in 1928.

Around the same time, Farnsworth—an Idaho teenager—transmitted the first electronic TV picture by rotating a straight line scratched on a square of painted glass by 90 degrees. RCA accused Farnsworth of patent violation. But in 1930, after his high school teacher provided evidence of his original drawings from 1922, Farnsworth received a patent for the first electronic television and later licensed his patents to RCA and AT&T, which used them to commercialize the technology. He also conducted the first public demonstration of television at the Franklin Institute in Philadelphia in 1934—five years before RCA's much more famous public demonstration at the 1939 World's Fair.

© Bettmann/Corbis

Philo Farnsworth, one of the inventors of television, experiments with an early version of an electronic TV set.

The Entrepreneurial Stage: Setting Technical Standards

Turning television into a business required creating a coherent set of technical standards for product manufacturers. In the late 1930s, the National Television Systems Committee (NTSC), a group representing engineers, inventors, network executives, and major electronics firms, began outlining industry-wide manufacturing practices and defining technical standards. In 1941, the Federal Communications Commission (FCC) adopted an **analog** standard (a 525-line image) for all U.S. TV sets (which at that time could show only black-and-white

---

1954 Color TV Standard
RCA's color system is approved by the FCC as the industry standard.

1958–59 Quiz-Show Scandal
Investigations into rigged quiz shows force networks to cancel twenty programs.

1960 Telstar
The first communication satellite relays telephone and television signals.

1967 PBS
The passing of the Public Broadcasting Act creates the Corporation for Public Broadcasting, which establishes PBS and begins funding nonprofit radio and public TV stations.

1968 *60 Minutes*
CBS premieres *60 Minutes*, establishing the standard for TV newsmagazines.

1975–76 Consumer VCRs
Beta and VHS videocassette recorders begin to be sold to consumers.

images). About thirty countries adopted this system, though most of Europe and Asia eventually adopted a system with slightly better image quality and resolution.

The Mass Medium Stage: Assigning Frequencies and Introducing Color

TV signals are part of the same electromagnetic spectrum that carries light waves and radio signals. In the early days of television, and before the advent of cable, the number of TV stations a city or region could support was limited because airwave frequencies interfered with one another (so you could have a Channel 5 but not a Channel 6 in the same market). In the 1940s, the FCC began assigning certain channels in specific geographic areas to prevent interference. In 1952, after years of licensing freezes due to World War II, the FCC created a national map and tried to distribute all available channels evenly throughout the country. By the mid-1950s, the nation had more than four hundred television stations in operation. Television had become a mass medium.

Television's new status led to additional standards. In 1952, the FCC tentatively approved an experimental color system developed by CBS; however, its signal could not be received by black-and-white sets. In 1954, RCA's color system, which sent TV images in color but allowed older sets to receive the images as black-and-white, became the color standard.

Controlling TV Content

As a mass medium, television had become big business, and broadcast networks began jockeying for increased control over its content. As in radio during the 1930s and 1940s, early television programs were developed, produced, and

CHAPTER 8 // TIMELINE continued

1975 HBO Uplinks to Satellite
The first premium channel is launched in the United States.

1976 Cable Takes Off
Ted Turner beams a signal from WTBS, his Atlanta broadcast station, creating the first superstation.

Late 1970s Franchising Frenzy
Cable companies rush to win local cable franchises across the United States.

1979 *Midwest Video Case*
A U.S. Supreme Court decision grants cable companies the power to select the content they carry.

1980 CNN
Ted Turner's 24-hour news network premieres and grows to revolutionize the news business.

1981 MTV
Warner Communications launches the influential music television channel, which is acquired by Viacom in 1985.

supported by a single sponsor—often a company, such as Goodyear, Colgate, or Buick. This arrangement gave the companies that controlled brand-name products extensive power over what was shown on television. But then newly emerging broadcast networks wanted more control and, using several strategies, set out to diminish sponsor and ad agency control.

One strategy involved lengthening program times. Sylvester "Pat" Weaver, president of NBC, took the lead. A former advertising executive used to controlling radio content for his clients, Weaver increased TV program length from fifteen minutes (standard for radio programs) to thirty minutes and even longer. This substantially raised program costs for advertisers, discouraging some from sponsoring programs.

In addition, NBC introduced two TV program types to gain more control over content. The first type—the magazine format—featured multiple segments, including news, talk, comedy, and music. These early 1950s programs—*Today* and the *Tonight Show*—are still attracting morning and late-evening audiences. By running daily rather than weekly, they made studio production costs much more prohibitive for a single sponsor. Instead of sponsoring, an advertiser paid the network for thirty- or sixty-second time slots during the show. The network, not the sponsor, now owned such programs or bought them from independent producers. In the second new program type—the "television spectacular"—networks bought

Newhouse News Service/Landov

On the assembly line, this 1954 RCA CT-100 was the first mass-produced electronic color TV set. Only affluent customers could afford these early sets, priced at $1,000 or more.

1987 Fox Debuts
The Australian media giant News Corp. launches the Fox network, the first network launch in more than thirty-five years.

1994 DBS
The direct broadcast satellite (DBS) industry offers full-scale service, growing at a rate faster than cable.

1996 Telecommunications Act of 1996
The act abolishes most TV ownership restrictions, paving the way for consolidation. Cable is again deregulated.

2008 Digital Streaming Boost
Netflix starts offering subscribers unlimited viewing of movies and programs in its online catalogue.

2009 Digital TV Standard
The FCC ends a TV set's ability to receive analog broadcast signals through the airwaves with an antenna.

2013 Comcast/NBC Merger
General Electric sells control of NBC and Universal Studios to Internet giant Comcast.

programs on special topics from producers and sold ad spots to multiple advertisers. Early spectaculars (which came to be called "specials") included decades of Bob Hope Christmas shows and the 1955 TV version of *Peter Pan*, which drew over sixty-five million viewers—more than triple the audience for one episode of *American Idol*.

Staining Television's Reputation

In the late 1950s, corruption in an increasingly popular TV program format—quiz shows—tainted television's reputation and further altered the power balance between broadcast networks and program sponsors. Quiz shows had become huge business. By the end of the 1957–58 TV season, twenty-two of them aired on network television. They were (and remain) cheap to produce, with inexpensive sets and amateurs as guests. For each show, the corporate sponsor—such as Revlon or Geritol—prominently displayed its name on the set throughout the program.

But as it turned out, many quiz shows were rigged. To heighten the drama and get rid of unappealing guests, sponsors pressured TV executives to give their favorite contestants answers to the quiz questions and allow them to rehearse their responses. The most notorious rigging occurred on *Twenty-One*, a quiz show owned by Geritol, whose profits had climbed by a whopping $4 million a year after it began sponsoring the program in 1956.

When investigations exposed the rigging, the networks further decreased their use of sponsors to create programming. Even more important, the fraud undermined Americans' belief in television's democratic promise—to bring inexpensive, honest information and entertainment into every household. The scandals had magnified the separation between the privileged, powerful few (wealthy companies) and the general public. For the next forty years, the broadcast networks kept quiz shows out of **prime time**—the block of time (7–11 P.M. EST) with large viewer audiences.

Introducing Cable

Despite the quiz-show scandals, broadcast television continued to grow in popularity in the late 1950s; however, some communities remained unable to receive traditional over-the-air TV signals, often because of their isolation or because

Everett Collection

In 1957, the most popular contestant on the quiz show *Twenty-One* was college professor Charles Van Doren (*left*). Congressional hearings on rigged quiz shows revealed that Van Doren had been given some answers that helped him defeat opponents that the show's producers and sponsors deemed less appealing than Van Doren.

FIGURE 8.1 // A BASIC CABLE TELEVISION SYSTEM

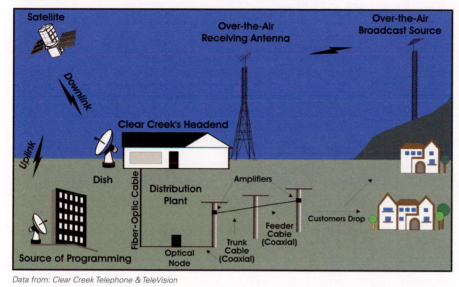

Data from: *Clear Creek Telephone & TeleVision*

mountains or tall buildings blocked transmission. The first small cable systems—
called **CATV**, or community antenna television—originated in Oregon, Pennsylvania,
and New York City in the late 1940s as an early attempt to solve this problem. New
cable companies ran wires from relay towers that brought in broadcast signals
from far away. The cable companies then strung wire from utility poles and
sent the signals to individual homes, stimulating demand for TV sets in those
communities.

These early systems served only about 10 percent of the country and usually
contained only twelve channels because of early technical and regulatory limits.
Yet cable offered big advantages. First, it routed each channel in a separate wire,
thereby eliminating the over-the-air interference that sometimes happened with
broadcast transmissions. Second, it ran signals through *coaxial cable*, a core of
aluminum wire encircled by braided wires that provided the option of adding more
channels. Initially, many small communities with CATV received twice as many
channels as were available over the air in much larger cities. Eventually, the cable
industry would pose a major competitive threat to conventional broadcast television. But cable would also encounter new challenges (and opportunities) with
the invention of satellite television, which uses large dishes to "downlink" signals
from communication satellites in order to transmit cable TV services like HBO and
CNN (see Figure 8.1).

The Evolution of Network Programming

Even with the emergence of mostly small-town cable operations, broadcast networks still controlled most TV programming in the 1950s. They began specializing in many types of programming (much of it "borrowed" from radio), including early-evening newscasts, variety shows, sitcoms, and soap operas. Eventually, additional genres and services emerged, including talk shows, newsmagazines, reality television, and public television.

Information: Network News

Over time, many Americans abandoned their habit of reading an afternoon newspaper and began following the network evening news to catch coverage of the latest national and international events. By the 1960s, NBC, CBS, and ABC offered their thirty-minute versions of the evening news and dominated national TV news coverage until the emergence of CNN and the 24/7 cable news cycle in the 1980s. The network news divisions have been responsible for a number of milestones. The *CBS-TV News*, which premiered on CBS in May 1948, became in 1956 the first news show videotaped for rebroadcast in central and western time zones on **affiliate stations** (local TV stations that contract with a network to carry its programs; each network has roughly two hundred affiliates around the country), while NBC's weekly *Meet the Press* (1947–) remains the oldest show on television.

As with entertainment programming, the ever-broadening competition from cable and online sources of news has siphoned off network viewers. In 1980, the Big Three evening news programs had a combined audience of more than fifty million on a typical weekday evening. That audience now hovers around twenty million.[1] Nonetheless, all three network newscasts often draw more viewers than do many prime-time programs.

Entertainment: Comedy

Originally, many new programs on television were broadcast live and are therefore lost to us today. The networks did sometimes manage to save early 1950s shows through poor-quality

In 1968, after the popular CBS news anchor Walter Cronkite visited Vietnam, CBS produced the news special "Report from Vietnam by Walter Cronkite." Most political observers said that Cronkite's opposition to the war—along with his reputation as "the most trusted man in America"—influenced President Lyndon Johnson's decision not to seek reelection.

CBS Photo Archive/Getty Images

kinescopes, made by using a film camera to record live TV shows off a studio monitor (which today would be like saving a *Big Bang Theory* episode by shooting the TV screen in our living room with a video camera). However, the producers of *I Love Lucy* decided to preserve their comedy series by filming each episode, like a movie. This produced a high-quality version of each show that could be played back as a rerun. In 1956, videotape was invented, and many early comedies were preserved this way, allowing networks to create a rerun season in late spring and summer, thereby reducing the number of episodes produced each year from thirty-nine live broadcasts to about twenty-four taped programs.

In capturing *I Love Lucy* on film for future generations, the program's producers understood the enduring appeal of comedy. Although a number of comedy programs and ideas were stolen from radio, television eventually developed its own history with comedy, which became a central programming strategy for both the networks and cable. TV comedy has been delivered to audiences through sketch comedy and situation comedy (sitcom).

Sketch Comedy

Most current audiences are familiar with **sketch comedy** thanks to NBC's long-running *Saturday Night Live* (1975–). In the early days of television, variety shows drew heavily from vaudeville-style performers, such as singers, dancers, acrobats, animal acts, stand-up comics, and ventriloquists. Typically, these shows required new ideas for sketches and other acts, with new characters and new sets, each week. This is still somewhat true of *Saturday Night Live* (many *SNL* alums have written about the all-consuming demands of working on the show), but today other sketch comedy is often pretaped and delivered without variety elements, on shows like *Key and Peele* and *Inside Amy Schumer*, which offer more diverse and specific viewpoints than the earlier mass-appeal variety shows.

The comedy series Seinfeld started slow in the ratings but placed in the top three for its last five seasons on the air, and influenced other shows, such as Friends and It's Always Sunny in Philadelphia.

© NBC/Photofest

Situation Comedy

In contrast, **situation comedy (sitcom)** is at least in some ways a simpler story form than sketch comedy. In sitcoms, you have the same characters in the same places from week to week, dealing with an increasingly complicated situation (often at home or at work),

which is usually resolved in some way at the end of the half-hour program.[2] From early hits like *I Love Lucy* and *The Honeymooners* to *How I Met Your Mother*, *Modern Family*, and *The Big Bang Theory*, the programs developed from favoring to mixing in more grounded character development. Other shows take this development further, adding more serious elements to create a *dramedy*. *M*A*S*H* was an early example of this form, which has become more common with cable shows like *Louie* and *Weeds*.

Entertainment: Drama

Television's drama programs, which also came from radio, developed as another key genre of entertainment programming. Because production of TV entertainment was centered in New York in its early days, many of the sets, technicians, actors, and directors came from the New York theater world. Young stage actors often worked in the new television medium if they couldn't find stage work. The TV dramas that grew from these early influences fit roughly into two categories: anthology dramas and episodic series.

Anthology Drama

Although the subject matter, style, and storytelling are very different, **anthology dramas** share some of the same challenges as sketch comedy. Both essentially start from scratch each week, requiring new stories, new characters, and new sets. And like the variety programs of early television, the anthology dramas of the early 1950s borrowed heavily from live theater, first with stage performances and later with *teleplays* (scripts written for television).

But by the 1960s, networks were moving away from anthologies. This shift was due not only to the demands of producing a completely new story each week but also to the fact that anthologies brought from the stage the tradition of dealing with heavy, complicated, and controversial topics. This increasingly contrasted with the goal of less challenging programming and also with advertising, which tended to claim products could offer quick and easy fixes to life's problems. These factors combined to make the programs less appealing to advertisers, and thus to networks, regardless of the artistic, cultural, and social contributions anthologies could make. Despite having virtually disappeared from network television, anthology drama's legacy continues on American public television, especially with the imported British program *Masterpiece Theatre* (1971–), now known as *Masterpiece Classic*, *Masterpiece Mystery!*, and *Masterpiece Contemporary*.

Episodic Series

Abandoning anthologies, network producers and writers developed **episodic series**, first used on radio in the late 1920s. In this format, main characters continue from week to week, sets and locales remain the same, and technical crews stay with the program. Story concepts are broad enough to accommodate new adventures each week, establishing ongoing characters with whom viewers can regularly identify. Such episodic series come in two general types: chapter shows and serial programs.

Chapter shows are self-contained stories that feature a problem, a series of conflicts, and a resolution. Often reflecting Americans' hopes, fears, and values, this structure has been used in a wide range of dramatic genres, including network westerns like *Gunsmoke*; medical dramas like *ER* and *Grey's Anatomy*; police/crime network shows like *CSI: Crime Scene Investigation* and cable's *The Closer*; family dramas like *Little House on the Prairie*; and fantasy/science fiction like network's *Sleepy Hollow*. **Serial programs** are open-ended episodic shows; that is, most story lines continue from episode to episode. Among the longest-running and most familiar serial programs in TV history are daytime *soap operas*, which typically run five days a week and are cheaper to produce than their more prestigious prime-time counterparts, such as *Scandal* on ABC.

But the lines between traditionally separate chapter and serial approaches have blurred over the past two decades. Although many dramas are written to tell a more-or-less self-contained story in each episode, they also commonly incorporate serial elements, with story arcs that carry over several episodes, or even from season to season. Many dramas today somewhat resemble the television *miniseries*, a form that is less common now but has a notable place in broadcast television history. A miniseries typically ran during prime time over a few nights or perhaps over a week or two and then was over. Perhaps the most famous example was when ABC turned Alex Haley's novel *Roots: The Saga of an American Family* into an award-winning miniseries in 1977. Current shows like HBO's *True Detective* and FX's *Fargo* have positioned themselves as a hybrid of miniseries and serial drama, with a season covering a full serialized story before starting over with a new (if sometimes related) set of characters in subsequent seasons.

© Fox Broadcasting Company/Photofest

Serial programs like Fox's popular comics-based series *Gotham* (which follows various characters and events in fictional Gotham City before the emergence of Batman) feature continuing story lines over many episodes, though they may feature chapter elements as well, like *CSI*-style crimes that can be solved by the end of an episode.

Talk Shows and TV Newsmagazines

Many other programming genres have arisen in television's history, both inside and outside prime time. Talk shows like the *Tonight Show* (1954–) emerged to satisfy viewers' curiosity about celebrities and politicians, and to offer satire on politics and business. Game shows like *Jeopardy* (which has been around in some version since 1964) provide people with easy-to-digest current events fare and history quizzes that families can enjoy together. Variety programs like the *Ed Sullivan Show* (1948–1971) have introduced new comedians as well as music artists, including Elvis Presley and the Beatles. **TV newsmagazines** like CBS's long-running *60 Minutes* usually feature three stories per episode, alternating hard-hitting investigations of corruption or political intrigue with softer feature stories about Hollywood celebrities and cultural trends.

Reality Television

Reality television dominated television from the late 1990s through much of the first decade of the twenty-first century. Inspired by MTV's longest-running program, *The Real World* (1992–), the genre's biggest success was probably Fox's *American Idol*, which was the nation's top-rated show from 2004 to 2009. The popularity of the genre meant variations showed up on many of the niche channels up and down the broadcast and cable lineups. One could (and largely still can) find offerings ranging from network programs like *The Bachelor* and *Celebrity Apprentice* to cooking-based shows like the Food Network's *Hell's Kitchen* to backwoods shows like A&E's *Duck Dynasty*.

Featuring non-actors, cheap sets, and limited scripts, reality shows (like quiz shows) are much less expensive to produce than are sitcoms and dramas. For a time, critics worried the combination of popularity with cheap overhead would spell the doom of scripted television programs (see chapter opening). However, only two reality programs made it into the 2013–14 Top 10 rated shows (*Dancing with the Stars* at No. 8 and *The Voice* at No. 10).[3]

Public Television

In the 1960s, public television was created by Congress to serve viewers whose interests were largely ignored by ad-driven commercial television. Much of this noncommercial television was targeted to children, older Americans, and the well educated. Under President Lyndon Johnson, Congress passed the

The most influential children's show in TV history, *Sesame Street* (1969–) has been teaching children their letters and numbers for more than forty-five years.

© PBS/Photofest

Public Broadcasting Act of 1967. The act created the Corporation for Public Broadcasting (CPB), which in 1969 established the Public Broadcasting Service (PBS). The act led to the creation of children's series like *Mister Rogers' Neighborhood*, *Sesame Street*, and *Barney*. Public television also broadcasts more adult fare, such as *Masterpiece Theatre* and other imported British programs.

In the early 2000s, despite the continued success of such staples as *Sesame Street*, government funding of public television was slashed. The Obama administration restored some of it, but with the rise of cable and satellite, people who have long watched PBS now often get their favorite kinds of content from sources other than network and public television. For example, the BBC—historically a major provider of British programs to PBS—also sells its shows to cable channels (including its own BBC America) and to streaming video services, such as Netflix. In 2015, Sesame Workshop reached a deal with cable channel HBO to produce more new episodes of *Sesame Street*, to air exclusively on HBO for six months before being provided to PBS stations for free. Though some were upset by HBO's exclusive window, money from HBO will keep *Sesame Street* on the air (and at a lower cost to PBS stations) for the foreseeable future.

The Evolution of Cable Programming

As network programming evolved, so did cable programming, offering a greater variety of content and services thanks in part to satellite technology. For instance, in 1975, the HBO (originally called Home Box Office) premium cable service began delivering uncut, commercial-free movies and exclusive live coverage of major boxing matches via satellite for a monthly fee. The following year, WTBS—an independent Atlanta broadcast station then owned by future media mogul Ted Turner—was uplinked to a satellite and made available to cable companies, becoming the first cable "superstation." In 1980, Turner, who had become a major player in cable, established CNN (originally the Cable News Network) as a 24/7 news operation. Such efforts gave more people greater and more convenient TV access to movies, news, sports, and other content—presenting a direct challenge to traditional over-the-air broadcast TV.

With the advent of satellite TV, cable companies could excel at **narrowcasting**—the delivery of specialized programming, such as the History Channel or the Food Network, for niche viewer groups—which cut into broadcasting's large mass audience. Narrowcasting gave rise to different types of cable stations offering various content and cable providers various service options: Viewers could choose basic cable services with just a few channels for a modest monthly fee or add more niche channels and premium cable services for a higher monthly or per-use fee (see "Media Literacy Case Study: The United Segments of America: Niche Marketing in Cable" on pages 270–271).

Basic Cable

Basic cable offers numerous channels appealing to specific audiences' interests that the broadcast networks don't offer—such as ESPN (sports), CNN (news), MTV and VH1 (music), Nickelodeon (new children's programs and older TV series reruns), Lifetime (movies), BET (Black Entertainment Television), the Weather Channel, and QVC (home shopping). Basic cable also traditionally offers **superstations** (independent broadcast TV stations uplinked to a satellite), such as WPIX (New York) and WGN (Chicago), although in 2014 WGN the superstation became WGN America, a regular entertainment-based cable channel with higher-profile original programming.

Typically, local cable companies pay each satellite-delivered service anywhere from less than $1 per month per subscriber for low-cost, low-demand channels to as much as $3 or $4 per month per subscriber for high-cost, high-demand channels like ESPN, which is available in two hundred countries worldwide. A standard basic cable channel may negotiate a fee somewhere between $.25 and $1.00 per subscriber per month, usually demanding more in areas serving larger populations. That fee is passed along to consumers as part of their basic monthly fee.

In 1992, eighty-seven cable networks were in business. By 2014, that number had grown to over eight hundred.[4] With the advent of high-bandwidth fiber-optic cable and *digital cable* in the late 1990s, cable systems could expand their offerings beyond the basic analog channels. Digital cable typically used set-top cable boxes to offer on-screen program guides and dozens of additional premium, pay-per-view, and audio music channels, increasing total cable capacities to between 150 and 500 channels. Even more than broadcast network programming, cable services evolved far beyond the old limited categories of news information and fictional entertainment. Satisfied with smaller niche audiences, cable became much more specialized than its broadcast counterpart.

Specialized Information: CNN

CNN, the first 24/7 cable TV news channel, quickly mastered continuous coverage of breaking news events and, early on, avoided presenting news anchors as celebrities (like network anchors). With around-the-clock programming, it began delivering up-to-the-minute news in great detail and featuring live, unedited coverage of news conferences, press briefings, and special events. Although it has since cut many of its international bureaus, CNN today dominates international TV news coverage. It operates in more than two hundred territories and countries where many viewers use it to practice their English; more than two billion people have access to a CNN service. Spawning a host of competitors in the United States and worldwide, CNN now battles for viewers with other twenty-four-hour news providers, including the Fox News Channel; MSNBC; CNBC; EuroNews; Britain's Sky Broadcasting; Al Jazeera; and thousands of Web and blog sites, such as *Politico*, the *Huffington Post*, the *Drudge Report*, and *Salon*. (See Chapter 3 for more on cable news, news satire, and "fake news" programs.)

Specialized Entertainment: MTV

Started in 1981, MTV (originally the Music Television Network) and its global offspring reach more than 400 million homes worldwide. MTV initially played popular music videos from mainstream white artists for white suburban teens; however, the popularity of Michael Jackson's *Thriller* album in late 1982 opened MTV up to black artists and more diverse music forms. Then, in the late 1980s and early 1990s, MTV began providing more original programming with shows like *The Real World* and *Beavis and Butt-head* and more recently *Jersey Shore* and *MADE*. Since MTV's inception, critics have worried that much of its programming has encouraged vulgarity and overt sexism. Advocates maintain that MTV (and cable overall) has created a global village by giving people around the world a common language and cultural bond. They also applaud MTV's special programs on important social issues, such as drug addiction, racism, and social/political activism, especially with its Rock the Vote campaigns that encourage young people to participate in national elections.

Anderson Cooper has been the primary anchor of *Anderson Cooper 360°* since 2003. Although the program is mainly taped and broadcast from his New York City studio and typically features reports of the day's main news stories with added analyses from experts, Cooper is one of the few talking heads who still report live fairly often from the field for major news stories. Most notably, he has done extensive coverage of the 2010 BP oil spill in the Gulf of Mexico (*below*), the February 2011 uprisings in Egypt, and the devastating earthquake in Japan in 2011. In 2013, he won a Gay and Lesbian Alliance Against Defamation (GLAAD) Media Award for openly gay media professionals, after coming out the previous year.

Zuma Press/Newscom

MEDIA LITERACY

Case Study

The United Segments of America: Niche Marketing in Cable

Individually, most cable television programs don't generate very impressive audience numbers. A top network television program like *The Big Bang Theory* on CBS delivers about twenty-three million television viewers per episode. For the 2013–14 season, only three of the Top 50 most-watched television programs had their home on a cable channel (AMC's *Walking Dead* at No. 4 with more than 18 million viewers, ESPN's *Monday Night Football* at No. 15 with almost 14 million viewers, and A&E's *Duck Dynasty* at No. 33 with just over 11 million viewers).[1] With the exception of these three programs, many cable hits draw closer to three or four million.

Yet taken together, cable television now attracts a larger total audience than the traditional television networks (ABC, CBS, NBC, Fox, and the CW). Moreover, a number of top advertisers, such as General Motors, are putting the majority of their

MGM/The Kobal Collection

television advertising budgets into cable, rather than broadcast network television. The key to cable's success is its ability to attract highly specific audiences, which might explain why some cable shows are gaining in popularity despite competition from the Internet and other media, while network shows continue to dip. Cable can still offer advertisers attractive demographics that may not be as focused on a particular network series or online program.

For example, Bravo, home of *The Real Housewives* and *Top Chef*, bills itself as the best cable network to reach adult viewers ages twenty-five to fifty-four who have a household income greater than $150,000, hold top management positions, and have a graduate degree. Also, the Food Network is a top choice for reaching what it calls "upscale" women in this age bracket. These viewers are likely to be working women with a household income of $75,000 or more who have a Visa or MasterCard Gold card. Even news

LaunchPad

macmillanhighered.com/mediaessentials3e

▶ **Visit LaunchPad** to view a clip from the MTV series *Teen Wolf*. How does the show seem to position itself in regard to the MTV "brand"?

channels have niche audiences—Fox News Channel is known for being politically to the right of CNN and draws more male viewers, whereas CNN draws slightly more female viewers.

MTV offers itself to advertisers as the one channel that "owns the young adult demographic." MTV says that it is the "best way to connect" with the twelve to thirty-four age group, which at ninety-one million strong and growing represents 33 percent of the population and more than $250 billion in spending power. The median age of MTV's viewers is 20.4. Similarly, Black Entertainment Television (BET) markets itself as the best way to reach African Americans, who spend more than $500 billion on consumer products annually. BET's main focus, especially in prime time, is the demographic of African Americans ages eighteen to thirty-four.

Where do you find the older demographics? Flip between the History Channel and the Weather Channel (median age forty-six). To reach children, advertisers can look to the Cartoon Network, where the audience is composed of 70 percent kids and teens. However, Nickelodeon is the king of this demographic, delivering more children under the age of twelve than any other basic cable network. Even more specifically, Nickelodeon claims to deliver more women ages eighteen to forty-nine who have children under the age of twelve than any other basic cable network (apparently, the moms are watching with their children).

For women, Lifetime (with an audience of 76% women) is the top cable network, with Oxygen, Bravo, and HGTV competing for the same audience. For men, ESPN (with an audience of 75% men) is the leader, and it claims more high-income male viewers than any other ad-supported network. Other cable networks that skew heavily male include the Speed Channel (85% men), the Golf Channel (74.5% men), ESPN2 (72.3% men), and Comedy Central.

An interesting twist to the niche audience approach is that many stations have drifted away from their original niche over time. For example, MTV (Music Television) used to spend most of its time showing music videos. Similarly, the Learning Channel (now shortened to TLC) was founded in part and run by NASA in the 1970s, and when it became a staple of basic cable packages in the 1980s, it was focused on educational content, especially documentaries relating to things like science and nature. One can only guess at what those early founders and programmers thought when they flipped on TLC a couple decades later and got *Toddlers and Tiaras* and later *Here Comes Honey Boo Boo*.

APPLYING THE CRITICAL PROCESS

DESCRIPTION Arrange to interview four to eight friends or relatives about their cable program tastes, devising questions about the shows they watch. Note how their preferences have changed over time. Be sure to collect demographic and consumer information: age, gender, occupation, educational background, place of birth, and current place of residence.

ANALYSIS Compose a chart comparing the viewing preferences among these people. Do you recognize any patterns emerging from the data? What kinds of shows do people of different ages and genders watch?

INTERPRETATION Based on what you have discovered and the patterns you have charted, determine what the patterns mean. Does age, gender, education, or geographic location matter in programming tastes? Why or why not? Why do you think various people's television preferences developed as they did?

EVALUATION Determine how your interview subjects came to like the particular programs. What constitutes "good" and "bad" shows for them? Did their ideas change over time? How? Do you think their criteria are a valid way for cable companies to target audiences?

ENGAGEMENT To expand on your findings and see how they match up with industry findings, track down a cable company representative and ask whom the company is trying to target with its shows. How does the company find out about the program tastes of its consumers? Share your findings with the representative and discuss whether they match those of the company.

Premium Cable

Besides basic programming, cable offers special **premium channels** featuring recent and classic Hollywood movies as well as original movies and popular series—such as HBO's *Girls* and Showtime's *Homeland*—all with no advertising. Premium services have also proved innovative. They include pay-per-view (PPV) programs; video-on-demand (VOD); and interactive services through which consumers can bank, shop, play games, and access the Internet. Subscribers pay fees in addition to charges for basic cable.

Innovative Content: HBO

HBO—the oldest premium cable channel—pioneered original, uncut movies and series on cable. Its most successful and acclaimed shows include *The Sopranos*, *True Detective*, *Curb Your Enthusiasm*, and *Game of Thrones*. Since the late 1990s, HBO has regularly garnered more Emmy nominations each year for its original programs than any of the traditional networks. Its widespread appeal and acclaim have even inspired basic cable services to produce original programming, such as Bravo's *Project Runway*, USA's *Burn Notice*, TNT's *The Closer*, and AMC's *Mad Men*. HBO remains the dominant premium channel.

Innovative Viewing Options: Pay-per-View and Video-on-Demand

In addition to presenting fresh types of programming, premium cable has introduced innovative viewing options to customers. **Pay-per-view (PPV)** channels came first. These offered recently released movies or special one-time sporting events (such as a championship boxing match) to subscribers who paid a designated charge to their cable company. In the early 2000s, U.S. cable companies introduced a new pay-per-view option for their digital customers: **video-on-demand (VOD)**. Through VOD, customers choose among hundreds of titles, then download a selection from the cable operator's server onto their cable TV box hard drive either for free (for access to older TV series or movies) or for any amount up to four dollars (for more popular recent movies). They watch the movie the same way they would watch a video, pausing and fast-forwarding when desired. Today, the largest cable companies and DBS services also offer digital video recorders (DVRs) to their customers.

Girls follows the life of Hannah Horvath as the aspiring young writer and her friends navigate life and work in New York City. Lena Dunham, who plays Hannah in the program, created and is one of the producers of the show, which started its run on HBO in 2012.

© HBO/Everett Collection

Regulatory Challenges Facing Television and Cable

Though cable cut into broadcast TV's viewership, both types of programming came under scrutiny from the U.S. government. Initially, thanks to extensive lobbying efforts, cable growth was suppressed to ensure that ad-revenue streams of local broadcasters and traditional TV networks were not harmed by the emergence of cable. Later, as cable developed, FCC officials worried that power and profits were growing increasingly concentrated in fewer and fewer industry players' hands. Therefore, the commission set out to mitigate the situation through the implementation of a variety of rules and regulations.

Restricting Broadcast Networks' Control

From the late 1950s to the end of the 1970s—the **network era**—CBS, NBC, and ABC dominated prime-time TV programming. By the late 1960s, the FCC, viewing the three networks as a quasi-monopoly, passed a series of regulations to undercut their power. The Prime Time Access Rule (PTAR), introduced in April 1970, reduced networks' control of prime-time programming from four to three hours in an effort to encourage more local news and public affairs programs, usually slated for the 6–7 P.M. EST time block. However, most stations simply ran thirty minutes of local news at 6 P.M. and then acquired syndicated quiz shows (*Wheel of Fortune*) or **infotainment** programs (*Entertainment Tonight*) to fill up the remaining half hour.

In 1970, the FCC also created the Financial Interest and Syndication Rules—called **fin-syn**—which banned the networks from running their own syndication companies and thus reduced their ability to reap profits from syndicating old TV series. Five years later, the Department of Justice limited the networks' production of non-news shows, requiring them to seek most of their programming from independent production companies and film studios.

With the rise of cable and home video in the 1990s, the FCC gradually phased out fin-syn, arguing that by then the TV market had grown more competitive. Beginning in 1995, the networks were once again allowed to syndicate and profit from rerun programs, but only those they had produced in-house.

Major merger deals, such as Disney's acquisition of ABC in 1995, have caused many independent companies to argue that a few corporations have too much control over broadcast content.

Robert Sullivan/AFP/Getty Images

Buoyed by the spirit of deregulation in the 1980s and 1990s, the elimination of fin-syn and other rules opened the door for major merger deals (such as Disney's acquisition of ABC in 1995) that have constrained independent producers from creating new shows and competing for prime-time slots. Many independent companies and TV critics complain that the corporations that now own the networks—Disney, CBS, News Corp., and Comcast—have historically exerted too much power and control over broadcast television content.

Reining in Cable's Growth—for a While

Throughout the 1950s and 1960s (before the broadcast networks accumulated extensive power), the FCC blocked cable companies from bringing distant TV stations into cities and towns that had local channels. The National Association of Broadcasters (NAB), the main trade organization for over-the-air television, lobbied Congress to restrict cable's growth so that it would not interfere with broadcast station interests and local TV ad sales. However, by the early 1970s, particularly with the advent of communication satellites, cable had the capacity for more channels and better reception—and the potential to expand beyond small, isolated communities. In 1972, new FCC rules began to allow cable to start expanding while still protecting broadcasters.

Through the **must-carry rules**, the FCC required all cable operators to carry all local TV broadcasts on their systems. This ensured that local network affiliates, independent stations (those not carrying network programs), and public television channels would benefit from cable's clearer reception. The FCC also mandated **access channels** in the nation's top one hundred TV markets, requiring cable systems to provide free nonbroadcast channels for local citizens, educators, and governments to use. In addition, the FCC called for **leased channels**, on which citizens could buy time and produce longer programs or present controversial views.

Because the Communications Act of 1934 had not anticipated cable, the industry's regulatory status was unclear at first. As a result, there was uncertainty in the 1970s about whether cable should be treated like print and broadcast media (with cable receiving First Amendment protections of its content choices). Cable operators argued that they should be considered **electronic publishers**, able to choose which channels and content to carry. However, some FCC officials and consumer groups maintained that cable systems were really more like **common carriers**—services, like phone companies, that do not get involved in monitoring channel content. Thus, access to content should be determined by whoever paid the money to lease or use the channel (like a telephone company that does not interfere with the content of a phone call). In 1979, this debate ended in the landmark *Midwest Video* case, in which the U.S. Supreme Court upheld cable companies' right to dictate their own content and defined the industry as a form of electronic publishing.[5] With cable's regulatory future secured, competition to obtain franchises to supply local cable services intensified.

Through the 1980s and early 1990s, Congress approved several cable acts until rewriting the nation's communications laws in the **Telecommunications Act of 1996**, which took away a number of ownership restrictions from radio and television and also brought cable fully under federal oversight, treating the industry like broadcasting. In its most significant move, Congress used the Telecommunications Act to knock down regulatory barriers. By allowing regional phone companies, long-distance carriers, and cable companies to enter one another's markets, lawmakers hoped to spur competition and lower rates for consumers. Instead, cable and phone companies have merged operations in many markets, keeping prices at a premium. In fact, broadcast networks now own or co-own cable services. As the broadcast TV audience eroded throughout the 1990s and 2000s, the major networks also began acquiring or developing cable channels to recapture viewers. Thus, what appears to be competition between TV and cable is sometimes an illusion. NBC, for example, operates cable news services MSNBC (with Microsoft), CNBC, and entertainment channel Bravo. ABC owns the successful ESPN sports franchise, along with portions of Lifetime, A&E, History, and E! CBS was the slowest to develop cable holdings. Its once successful TNN (now Spike TV) and CMT (Country Music TV) channels are now controlled by its former parent company, Viacom. Such business practices and ownership combinations have continued in the digital era, as broadcast TV and cable seek to maintain their position in the face of new technologies that are changing the way Americans view and use TV content.

The emergence of home recording technology, such as Sony's Betamax VCR in 1975, changed American viewing. Today's home recording is dominated by the use of DVRs, which store saved or recorded TV shows in digitized computer form rather than on the cassette tapes required by VCRs.

Television in the Digital Age

Thanks to new technologies—home video, the Internet, smartphones, mobile video, and DBS—Americans can now watch the visual content they want (whether it's movies, broadcast TV shows, or cable programming) when they want and where they want (on a TV set, on their laptop, on a handheld mobile device).

WATCH WHATEVER WHENEVER.

SONY BETAMAX
THE LEADER IN VIDEO RECORDING

The Advertising Archives

Home Video and Recording

Home video technologies have evolved over the past few decades. In 1975–76, the introduction of videocassettes and **videocassette recorders (VCRs)** enabled viewers to tape-record TV programs and play them back later. The VHS (Video Home System) introduced by JVC quickly became the consumer standard, whereas Sony's Beta system became the industry and news standard. By the end of the twentieth century, DVDs were rapidly replacing the VHS format, and now Blu-ray discs are becoming the **high-definition** replacement for DVDs.

By 2012, more than 90 percent of American homes were equipped with DVD players. At the same time, more than 50 percent of U.S. homes also had **DVRs (digital video recorders)**, which let users download onto the DVR's computer memory specific shows or even types of shows appearing on any channel. The newest versions of DVRs are also recordable—like VCRs—and allow users to make DVD collections of their favorite shows. While offering greater flexibility for viewers, DVRs also provide a means to "watch" the watchers, giving advertisers information about what each household views. This kind of technology has raised concerns among some lawmakers and consumer groups about having our personal viewing and buying habits tracked by marketers.

The impact of home video has been enormous, especially in two key ways: video rentals and time shifting. Video rental, formerly the province of walk-in video stores like Blockbuster, has given way to mail services like Netflix (which started as a mail service and later added online streaming), movie rental vending machines like Redbox, or online services like iTunes, Hulu, and Amazon. **Time shifting**, which began during the VCR era, occurs when viewers record shows and watch them at a later, more convenient time. Video rentals and time shifting, however, have threatened the TV industry's advertising-driven business model; when viewers watch DVDs and DVRs, they often aren't watching the ads that normally accompany network or cable shows.

The Internet, Smartphones, and Mobile Video

The way traditional television has converged across so many digital platforms is perhaps one of the most striking examples in this book of how fast these changes can take place—and how dramatic they can be. The first part of this picture is the Internet, which has fueled convergence with other technologies as high-speed connections and Wi-Fi have become more common.

Many new TV sets are Internet ready out of the box. For those that aren't or for older-model televisions, there are a wide variety of options for consumers who want to connect their TV to the Internet, from laptops and high-end video game consoles to dedicated devices such as the Roku box. The advantage is the ability to watch streaming content on what often has the biggest screen and best sound in a home (see also the Chapter 7 discussion of home entertainment).

On the other end of the screen-size spectrum, consumers can take their TV viewing with them using smartphones and tablets capable of accessing the Internet via Wi-Fi systems or with faster cellular technology commonly called 4G LTE (Long-Term Evolution, which beat out WiMax technology as the common standard for telephone and mobile broadband).

Once consumers have the hardware in place, the next piece of the picture is the service they will use to find whatever show they want to watch. Some programs will stream episodes directly from their Web sites (like Comedy Central's *The Daily Show*) or make segments available via YouTube (like HBO's *Last Week Tonight with John Oliver*). Other programs and networks keep tighter control of their programs, and try to earn money by selling them via services like Apple's iTunes Store or on Amazon.com, or through fee-based streaming services such as Hulu Plus or Netflix. Some sites, like Hulu.com, allow viewers to watch some programs for free but with commercials.

The final piece of the convergence puzzle is understanding that the streaming services can also link all of an audience member's devices together. So, for example, using a combination of apps for smartphones and tablets as well as devices like a Roku box at home, a person might use the same Netflix account on any of these devices anywhere there is Internet service (see also "Converging Media Case Study: Shifting, Bingeing, and Saturday Mornings" on pages 278–279).

DBS

Of all the emerging technologies, **direct broadcast satellite (DBS)** has had the biggest impact on cable in particular. In its early days, DBS transmission was especially efficient in regions with rugged terrain or isolated farm regions, where it's difficult or cost prohibitive to install cable wiring. DBS differs from cable in that it allows individual consumers to downlink satellite-transmitted signals into their homes without having them relayed through cable companies, which process these same signals and then send them out to homes via wires.

Japanese companies launched the first DBS system in Florida in 1978, but the early receiving dishes, which used to dot the rural landscape in the 1980s, were ten to twelve feet in diameter and expensive ($3,000). By 1994, however, full-scale DBS service was available, and consumers could soon buy satellite dishes the size of a large pizza. Today, there are two U.S.-based DBS companies: DirecTV,

CONVERGING MEDIA

Case Study

Shifting, Bingeing, and Saturday Mornings

When kids woke up on the morning of Saturday, October 4, 2014, for the first time in a half century there was no commercial broadcast network offering Saturday morning cartoons. That was the date the last holdout, the CW, ended its string of Saturday morning cartoons, replacing it with family-oriented but non-animated programs; the other networks had begun phasing out Saturday morning cartoons as early as the 1990s. What is unclear is whether or not any kids noticed the difference (although their parents and grandparents might have felt a pang of nostalgia at the news).[1]

So what finally killed off the broadcasters' weekend morning kid cartoons? There are likely several contributing factors (from cable channels dedicated to cartoons to FCC requirements for more educational programming), but perhaps the most relevant is the ongoing shift in the way audiences consume television programming of all kinds, and the biggest of those changes involve the *time shifting* and *binge watching* that come with online video streaming.

Indeed, the end of Saturday morning cartoons will not deny kids the experience of shows like *Scooby Doo!*, *Teenage Mutant Ninja Turtles*, and *Transformers*. Video streaming has made these titles—and many more—available at any time, rendering programming blocks somewhat obsolete. Although not many comprehensive studies have been done on these viewing patterns, there's room for some observations. For example, say children in a household watched two hours of cartoons on a Saturday morning in the 1980s. They would likely have seen four different cartoon programs (each with a half-hour time slot) with around a half hour of commercials mixed throughout. Today, if the household has an Internet-based streaming service like Netflix, that same two hours could just as easily start at 6 o'clock on a Thursday night (an example of time shifting) and would include five cartoons, each about twenty minutes long, without commercials. There's also a good chance that the kids would be watching the same cartoon the whole time if they were binge viewing, which is often defined as watching two or more episodes of a program in one sitting.

This change in what was once a staple of television programming and weekly viewing is just one example of the way the digital world is transforming the way we interact with and consume our entertainment. A 2014 survey found that 50 percent of adults consider themselves binge viewers,

LaunchPad

macmillanhighered.com/mediaessentials3e

▶ **Visit LaunchPad** to view a clip from the old *Transformers* cartoon. How do you think today's audiences would react to the show?

and 55 percent of those binge viewers said they did more binge watching in 2014 than they had in 2013. Binge viewing is even more prevalent among college-age adults (18–24), 53 percent of whom said they binge-view on a daily or weekly basis.[2]

Another study commissioned by Netflix had similar results, showing not only that binge viewing is growing in popularity but also that when a season of a popular TV show is released, an increasing number of users will watch the entire season—even twenty-two episodes—within a week. Both studies found that almost two-thirds of those who identified themselves as binge viewers use their mobile phones (or another second screen) while bingeing, and that the use complements their viewing instead of competing with it.[3] For that matter, smartphones and tablets have meant that binge watching can happen practically anywhere.

But beyond ushering in the end of Saturday morning cartoons, what are the larger implications when one steps back and considers the combination of on-demand streaming video, time shifting, binge viewing, and engaging social media while watching a program? Answering these questions will likely be a big focus for years to come for networks, production companies, cable companies, and media scholars and researchers. But we do have a few tantalizing clues as to what the future of television entertainment may hold.

On the business side of television and cable, the ability to stream video content has led to a growing trend of *cord-cutting*—consumers getting rid of cable and watching only content available online (see also the opening of Chapter 1). Premium cable channel HBO, which has long resisted having any of its programs appear in the Netflix lineup, has announced that it was looking into offering its own streaming service. Major media giants like Comcast (which provides Internet and cable services as well as owns NBC and Universal Studios), who want to charge Web sites more for faster Internet connections, are butting heads with net neutrality advocates and companies like Netflix who feel the Comcast proposal of a tiered Internet system amounts to a shakedown (see also the section on net neutrality in Chapter 9, pages 306–307).

On the creative side of the television business, some critics note a positive trend with more high-quality dramatic and comedic television programs, which they see as a welcome change after reality television meant less demand for scripted productions. The surveys mentioned earlier support this idea—that consumers are demanding higher-quality and complex shows like *Breaking Bad* and *Mad Men*, and will reward those programs with near-fanatical following. It also means quirky programs like *Portlandia*, which might have struggled to find a big enough audience on a less widespread cable network like IFC, can build a bigger following after episodes become available on Netflix.

The social implications of time-shifted binge viewing will likely be the subject of some debate. Some critics worry that binge watching might lead to loss of productivity or social interaction for students and workers alike, while others feel that the flexibility offered by streaming video (and DVRs) makes it easier to be productive because being a devoted fan of a particular TV program doesn't mean having to adjust personal schedules to accommodate TV schedules. Still others point out that simultaneous engagement with social media can encourage conversations that might not have happened in years past. Kids won't get the Saturday morning cartoon blocks their parents experienced, but they may be learning to engage with television more actively than ever before.

with close to twenty million U.S. customers, and the DISH Network (formerly known as EchoStar Communications), which has around fourteen million subscribers. These companies offer consumers most of the same channels and tiers of service that cable companies carry, often at a slightly lower monthly cost.

DBS systems can carry between 350 and 500 basic, premium, and pay-per-view channels, which customers can purchase in various packages. In addition, DBS gives subscribers nationwide access (in packages that cost between $10 and $40 per month) to more professional sports leagues—including hockey, football, baseball, soccer, and men's and women's basketball—than do most premium cable services, providing games that aren't carried locally on broadcast networks or basic cable channels. Finally, DBS systems have the same ability as cable to bundle high-speed Internet and telephone service with their video programming, so that consumers pay one bill for phone, TV, and Internet needs.

The Economics of Television and Cable

The economics of TV and cable differ in certain ways, as we'll see in the pages that follow. However, like all other industries, both TV and cable must bring in revenue from specific sources and then invest that money in the business processes that are crucial to their operations.

Money In

Sources of revenue differ in some respects between TV and cable. Both broadcast network and cable programming make money from syndication, deals with online streaming services, and advertising, but only cable makes money from subscriptions—monthly fees charged to consumers for different tiers of service.

Syndication

Syndication—leasing TV stations the exclusive right to air older TV series—is a critical source of revenue for broadcast networks and cable companies. Early each year, executives from thousands of local TV stations gather at the world's largest "TV supermarket" convention, the National Association of Television Program Executives (NATPE), to acquire programs that broadcast networks (and, more recently, cable channels) have put up for syndication. Networks might make cash deals—selling shows to the highest-bidding local station—or give a program to a local station in exchange for a split in the advertising revenue—usually called a

barter deal, as no money changes hands. Through this process, the stations obtain the exclusive local market rights, usually for two- or three-year periods, to network-created game shows, talk shows, and **evergreens**—popular reruns, such as the *Andy Griffith Show*, *I Love Lucy*, or *Seinfeld*. Buying syndicated programs is usually cheaper for local TV stations than producing their own programs, and it provides a familiar lead-in show to the local news.

AMC/Everett Collection

The highest-rated cable series in history, *The Walking Dead* is the rare basic-cable series that attracts as many viewers as the highest-rated network shows.

Many local stations show syndicated programs during **fringe time**—immediately before the evening's prime-time schedule and following the local evening news or the network's late-night talk show. Syndicated shows filling these slots are either "off-network" or "first-run." In **off-network syndication**, older programs that no longer run during network prime time, such as *Everybody Loves Raymond*, are made available as reruns to local stations, cable operators, online services, and foreign markets. **First-run syndication** is any non-network program specifically produced for sale only into syndication markets, such as the *Oprah Winfrey Show* or *Wheel of Fortune*.

Advertising

Advertising is another major source of revenue for the industry. TV shows live or die based on how satisfied advertisers are with the quantity and quality of the viewing audience. Since 1950, the major organization tracking and rating prime-time viewing has been Nielsen, which estimates what viewers are watching in the nation's major markets. Ratings services provide advertisers, networks, and local stations with considerable detail about viewers—from race and gender to age, occupation, and educational background.

In TV measurement, a **rating** is a statistical estimate based on a random sample, expressed as the percentage of households tuned to a program in the total market being sampled. Another audience measure is the **share**, which gauges the percent of homes tuned to a program compared with those actually using their sets at the time of the sample. Prime-time advertisers want to reach relatively affluent eighteen- to forty-nine-year-old viewers, who account for most consumer spending. If a show is attracting those viewers, advertisers will compete to buy time during that program (see Figure 8.2). Traditionally, shows

FIGURE 8.2 // PRIME-TIME NETWORK TV PRICING

The top-earning television shows in 2014 and 2013 based on the average cost of a thirty-second ad.

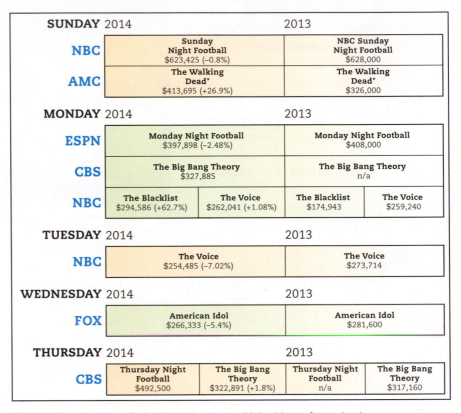

	2014		**2013**	
SUNDAY				
NBC	Sunday Night Football $623,425 (–0.8%)		NBC Sunday Night Football $628,000	
AMC	The Walking Dead* $413,695 (+26.9%)		The Walking Dead* $326,000	
MONDAY				
ESPN	Monday Night Football $397,898 (–2.48%)		Monday Night Football $408,000	
CBS	The Big Bang Theory $327,885		The Big Bang Theory n/a	
NBC	The Blacklist $294,586 (+62.7%)	The Voice $262,041 (+1.08%)	The Blacklist $174,943	The Voice $259,240
TUESDAY				
NBC	The Voice $254,485 (–7.02%)		The Voice $273,714	
WEDNESDAY				
FOX	American Idol $266,333 (–5.4%)		American Idol $281,600	
THURSDAY				
CBS	Thursday Night Football $492,500	The Big Bang Theory $322,891 (+1.8%)	Thursday Night Football n/a	The Big Bang Theory $317,160

Price is for a package of ads that run across multiple airings of an episode.

Data from: Brian Steinberg, "TV Ad Prices: Football, 'Walking Dead,' 'Big Bang Theory,' 'Blacklist' Top the List," *Variety*, September 26, 2014, http://variety.com/2014/tv/news/tv-ad-prices-football-walking-dead-big-bang-theory-blacklist-top-the-list-1201314484

that did not reach enough of the "right" viewers wouldn't attract advertising dollars and thus risked being canceled. But in the age of niche markets and Internet competition, smaller audience ratings and shares are tolerated, especially in cable programming.

Advertising also brings in money for cable. Most basic cable channels block out time for local and regional ads from, for example, restaurants, clothing stores, or car dealerships in the area. These ads are cheaply produced compared with national network ads, and they reach a smaller audience.

Subscriptions

In addition to making money from syndication, deals with streaming services, and from selling local ads, cable companies also earn revenue through monthly subscriptions for basic service, pay-per-view programming, and premium movie channels. Cable companies charge the customer a monthly fee—on average between $40 and $50 per month in 2009—and then pay cable channels like CNN and ESPN anywhere from $.35 to more than $3.00 per customer per month for these basic cable services. Whereas a cable company might pay HBO or Showtime $4 to $6 per month per subscriber to carry one of these premium channels, the company can charge each customer $10 or more per month—reaping a nice profit. Consumers also buy subscriptions to streaming sites like Netflix, which must negotiate with whomever holds the rights to the programs in order to offer them in their catalogues.

Money Out

For both TV and cable, primary costs include production (creation of programming). TV networks also invest heavily in distribution (airing of the programs they've created) by paying affiliate stations a fee to show their content. Cable operators distribute their programs most often by downlinking them from communication satellites and transmitting them to their various communities.

Production

Key players in the TV and cable industry—networks, cable stations, producers, and film studios—spend fortunes creating programs that they hope will keep viewers captivated for a long time. Roughly 40 percent of a new program's production budget goes to "below-the-line" costs, such as equipment, special effects, cameras and crews, sets and designers, carpenters, electricians, art directors, wardrobe, lighting, and transportation. The remaining 60 percent covers the creative talent—or "above-the-line" costs—such as actors, writers, producers, editors, and directors. In highly successful long-running series, actors' salary demands can drive these above-the-line costs from 60 percent to more than 90 percent.

Many prime-time programs today are developed by independent production companies owned or backed by a major film studio, such as Sony or Disney. In addition to providing and renting production facilities, these studios serve as a bank, offering enough capital to carry producers through one or more seasons. In television, after a network agrees to carry a program it's kept on the air through **deficit financing**: The production company leases the show to a network for a license fee that is less than the cost of production, assuming it will recoup this loss later in lucrative rerun syndication.

To save money and control content, many networks and cable stations create their own programs, including TV newsmagazines and reality programs. For example, NBC's *Dateline* requires only about half the outlay (between $600,000 and $800,000 per episode) demanded by a new hour-long drama. In addition, by producing projects in-house, the networks avoid paying license fees to independent producers.

Distribution

Whereas cable companies rely on subscriptions to fund distribution of content, the broadcast networks must pay their affiliate stations a fee to show the programs the networks have either created or licensed from independent production companies. In return for this fee, networks have the right to sell the bulk of advertising time (and run promotions of its own programs) during the shows—which helps them recoup their investments in these programs. Through this arrangement, local stations not only receive income but also get national programs that attract large local audiences to the local ad slots they retain as part of their affiliation contracts with the networks.

The networks themselves don't usually own their affiliated stations, except in major markets like New York, Los Angeles, and Chicago. Instead, they sign contracts with local stations (one each from the two-hundred-plus top regional TV markets) to rent time on these stations to air their network programs.

Ownership and Consolidation

Despite their declining reach and the rise of cable, the traditional networks have remained attractive business investments. In 1985, General Electric, which once helped start RCA/NBC, bought back NBC. In 1995, Disney bought ABC for $19 billion; in 1999, Viacom acquired CBS for $37 billion (Viacom and CBS split in 2005, but Viacom's CEO remains CBS's main stockholder). And in January 2011, the FCC and the Department of Justice approved Comcast's purchase of NBC Universal from GE—a deal valued at $30 billion and completed in early 2013.

In the late 1990s, cable became a coveted investment, not so much for its ability to carry television programming as for its access to households connected with high-bandwidth wires. Today, there are about 5,200 U.S. cable systems, down from 11,200 in 1994. Since the 1990s, thousands of cable systems have been bought by large **multiple-system operators (MSOs)**, corporations like Comcast and Time Warner Cable that own many cable systems. The industry for years called its major players **multichannel video programming distributors (MVPDs)** and included DBS providers like DirecTV and DISH Network. By 2014, cable's main trade organization, the National Cable & Telecommunications

TABLE 8.1 // TOP 10 VIDEO SUBSCRIPTION SERVICES

Rank	Video Subscription Service	Subscribers (in millions)
1	Netflix	39.1
2	Comcast Corporation	22.4
3	DirecTV	20.4
4	Dish Network Corporation	14.0
5	Time Warner Cable	10.8
6	Hulu	6.0
7	AT&T, Inc.	5.9
8	Verizon FiOS	5.6
9	Charter Communications, Inc.	4.5
10	Cox	4.2

Data from: National Cable & Telecommunications Association, www.ncta.com/industry-data

Association (NCTA), moved away from the MVPD classification and started using the term **video subscription services**, which now also includes Netflix and Hulu (see Table 8.1 above).

Comcast, AT&T, and Time Warner

In cable, the industry behemoth today is Comcast, especially after its takeover of NBC and move into network broadcasting. Back in 2001, AT&T had merged its cable and broadband industry in a $72 billion deal with Comcast, then the third-largest MSO. The new Comcast instantly became the cable industry leader. In 2014, Comcast also owned E! Entertainment, NBCSN, the Golf Channel, Universal Studios, Fandango (the online movie ticket site), and a 32 percent stake in Hulu (with Fox and Disney). In 2014, there were about 660 companies still operating cable systems. Along with Comcast, the other large MSOs included Time Warner Cable (formerly part of Time Warner, Inc.), Cox Communications, Charter Communications, and Cablevision Systems. Comcast announced in early 2014 that it planned to buy Time Warner Cable for more than $45 billion, but dropped those plans in 2015 in the face of vocal public opposition, threats of regulatory delays, and antitrust investigations from the FCC and the Department of Justice.

DirecTV and DISH Network

In the DBS market, DirecTV and DISH Network control virtually all of the DBS service in the continental United States. In 2008, News Corp. (which owns Fox) sold DirecTV to cable service provider Liberty Media, which also owned the Encore and Starz movie channels. The independently owned DISH Network was founded as EchoStar Communications in 1980. In 2014, to counter the proposed merger talks between cable giants Comcast and TWC (later dropped), DirecTV began investigating deals with both DISH and AT&T. Over the last few years, TV services (combined with existing voice and Internet services) offered by telephone giants AT&T (U-verse) and Verizon FiOS have developed into viable competitors for cable and DBS.

Television in a Democratic Society

The development of cable, VCRs and DVD players, DVRs, the Internet, and smartphone services has fragmented television's audience by appealing to viewers' individual and special needs. These changes and services, by providing more specialized and individual choices, also alter television's former role as a national unifying cultural force, potentially de-emphasizing the idea that we are all citizens who are part of a larger nation and world. Moreover, many cable channels have survived mostly by offering live sports or recycling old television shows and movies. Although cable and on-demand service like Netflix are creating more and more original quality programming, they rarely reach even the diminished audience numbers commanded by the traditional broadcast networks. In fact, given that the television networks and many leading cable channels are now owned by the same media conglomerates, cable has evolved into something of an extension of the networks. And even though cable audiences are growing and network viewership is contracting, the division between the two is blurring. New generations that grow up on cable and the Internet rarely make a distinction between a broadcast network, a cable service, or an on-demand program. In addition, tablets, smartphones, and Internet services that now offer or create our favorite programs are breaking down the distinctions between mobile devices and TV screens. Today, the promise that cable once offered as a place for alternative programming and noncommercial voices is now being usurped by the Internet, where all kinds of TV experiments are under way.

A show like *Broad City*, with its offbeat, edgy sensibility and jokes about the specificity of twentysomething women in New York City, might not have made it to air ten or fifteen years ago. But the show's devoted audience has made it into a hit for cable's Comedy Central.

© Comedy Central/Everett Collection

The bottom line is that television, despite the audience fragmentation, still provides a gathering place for friends and family at the same time that it provides access anywhere to a favorite show. Like all media forms before it, television is adapting to changing technology and shifting economics. As the technology becomes more portable and personal, television-related industries continue to search for less expensive ways to produce stories and more channels on which to deliver them. But what will remain common ground on this shifting terrain is that television continues as our nation's chief storyteller, whether those stories come in the form of news bulletins, sporting events, cable dramas, network sitcoms, or YouTube vignettes.

TV's future will be about serving smaller rather than larger audiences. As sites like YouTube develop original programming and as niche cable services like the Weather Channel produce reality TV series about storms, no audience seems too small and no subject matter too narrow for today's TV world. For example, in 2013, *Duck Dynasty* had become a hit series on A&E—a program about an eccentric Louisiana family that got rich making products for duck hunters. The program averaged a cable-record 12.4 million viewers in 2012–13, but then lost half those numbers in 2013–14, as many viewers grew weary of the series. An overwhelming number of programming choices like this now exist for big and small TV screens alike. How might this converged TV landscape, with its volatile ups and downs in viewer numbers, change how audiences watch—and pay for—television? With hundreds of shows available, will we adopt à la carte viewing habits, in which we download or stream only the shows that interest us, rather than pay for cable (or DBS) packages with hundreds of channels we don't watch?

CHAPTER ESSENTIALS

Now that you have finished reading this chapter, you can use the following tools:

REVIEW

Trace the Early History of Television

- In the development stage of television, early inventors (Zworykin and Farnsworth) competed to establish a patent for the first electronic television. In the entrepreneurial stage, television developed technical standards and turned into a business; the FCC adopted **analog** (broadcast signals made of radio waves) for all U.S. TV sets. In the mass medium stage, the FCC began assigning channels throughout the country and later introduced the color standard (pp. 256–258).

- Television soon became a big business, and broadcast networks competed for control over its content, mainly by setting out to diminish sponsors' influence on and ownership of programming. With the advent of magazine-format programs and the TV spectacular, spot advertising developed (pp. 258–260).

- In the late 1950s, the rigging of quiz shows, in particular *Twenty-One*, tainted television's reputation and caused networks to further minimize the control of sponsors. For the next forty years, quiz shows were kept out of **prime time**, the 7–11 P.M. (EST) time slot with the largest audiences (p. 260).

- The introduction of cable provided access for communities that couldn't receive airwave-based broadcast signals, but it also posed a major competitive threat to broadcast television. The first small cable systems—**CATV,** or community antenna television—originated in the late 1940s (pp. 260–261).

Consider the Evolution of Network Programming

- In the 1950s, broadcast networks began specializing in different types of programming. Information, in the form of news, became popular with the major networks: ABC, NBC, and CBS (the first to run a news show videotaped for rebroadcast on **affiliate stations**, which contract with a network to carry its programs) (p. 262).

- The networks also experimented with entertainment programming—sometimes preserving shows with **kinescopes**, made by using a film camera to record live shows off a monitor. Comedies became popular and came in two varieties: **sketch comedy** and **situation comedy (sitcom)** (pp. 262–264).

- Drama arose as another genre of entertainment programming. **Anthology dramas** brought live dramatic theater to viewers; **episodic series** showed central characters appearing every week. Episodic series come in two types: **chapter shows** and **serial programs** (pp. 264–265).

- Other programming genres that have arisen in television's history include talk shows, **TV newsmagazines**, reality television, and public television (pp. 265–267).

Discuss the Evolution of Cable Programming

- With the advent of satellite TV, cable companies could excel at **narrowcasting**—the delivery of specialized programming for niche viewer groups (thereby cutting into broadcasting's large audiences) (pp. 267–268).

- **Basic cable** is composed of local broadcast signals, nonbroadcast access channels, a few regional PBS stations, and a variety of cable channels (including **superstations**—independent broadcast stations uplinked to a satellite). **Premium channels** include movie channels and interactive services, such as **pay-per-view (PPV)** and **video-on-demand (VOD)** (pp. 268–269, 272).

Explain the Regulatory Challenges Facing Television and Cable

- From the late 1950s to the end of the 1970s—the **network era**—CBS, NBC, and ABC dominated prime-time TV programming. To undercut the networks' power, the FCC passed a series of regulations, such as the **fin-syn** rules in 1970 that banned the networks from running their own syndication companies. (This was in response to the networks' acquisition of syndicated shows and **infotainment programs**—those that package human-interest and celebrity stories.) These rules have since been eliminated (pp. 273–274).

- Through the **must-carry rules**, the FCC required all cable operators to assign channels to and carry all local TV broadcasts on their systems. It also mandated **access channels**, requiring cable systems to provide free nonbroadcast channels for education, local government, and the public, and **leased channels**, on which citizens could buy time. In response, cable operators maintained that they operated like **electronic publishers** (and, as such, should carry whatever channels and content they wanted); however, some FCC officials claimed cable should be treated like **common carriers**—services like traditional phone companies that do not get involved in channel content. The *Midwest Video* case settled this in 1979, declaring that cable operated like electronic publishers. Congress eventually rewrote the nation's laws in the **Telecommunications Act of 1996**, bringing cable fully under federal jurisdiction (pp. 274–275).

Describe Television in the Digital Age

- Home video technologies challenged traditional television, starting with the introduction of **videocassette recorders (VCRs)** in 1975–76. Today, viewers turn to DVDs, **high-definition** Blu-ray players, and **DVRs (digital video recorders)**, which let users download specific shows to the DVR's computer memory (p. 276).

- Traditional television has converged across multiple platforms, fueled by the Internet, allowing content to be streamed on TV sets as well as such devices as tablets and smartphones (pp. 276–277).

- **Direct broadcast satellite (DBS)** allows individual consumers to downlink hundreds of satellite channels and services for a monthly fee (pp. 277, 278).

Outline the Economics of Television and Cable

- Both broadcast networks and cable programmers make money from **syndication**—leasing rights to air reruns or **first-run** programs during **fringe time**. The networks and cable programmers also make money from advertising, which is based on **ratings** and **shares**; other services like cable providers and video streaming earn revenue from subscriptions (pp. 280–283).

- Broadcast networks and cable companies spend money on production and distribution of programs. This often involves **deficit financing**, in which the company leases the show to a network for a license fee that is less than the cost of production (pp. 283–284).

- Cable systems have been bought up by **multiple-system operators (MSOs)**—large corporations eager to cash in on the infrastructure of high-bandwidth wires connecting households across the country; this trend suggests a move toward oligopoly, in which a handful of megafirms control programming. Cable systems are now classified as **video** **subscription services**, which also include streaming services like Netflix (pp. 284–286).

Answer Questions about Television's Role in Our Democratic Society

- Many people argue that cable hasn't fully realized its potential and that its specialization has frayed the common shared experiences network programs once offered. Questions of access emerge as cable giants control content and cost (p. 286).

- Regardless, television provides a forum where people gather to participate in cultural or sociological events like the Super Bowl, which can have both positive and negative effects on broadcasting and society (p. 287).

STUDY QUESTIONS

1. What were the major factors that shaped the early history of television?
2. Why did cable and its programming pose a challenge to broadcasting?
3. What role has the FCC taken in regulating networks and cable?
4. What are the technological challenges that network television and cable face?
5. How has television served as a national cultural center or reference point?

MEDIA LITERACY PRACTICE

Interview two or three people who are a generation or two ahead of you about their experiences with television and cable news.

DESCRIBE the impact televised news has had on their lives. What network and cable news shows do they watch? Have their attitudes toward TV news changed?

ANALYZE the patterns and common themes that emerge from your interviews. What kinds of TV news experiences stick with your interview subjects?

INTERPRET what these patterns mean. What does it say about TV news if your subjects have shifted in their attitudes toward it? What does it say about TV and cable that your subjects remember certain news events?

EVALUATE what they think about the quality of news on traditional networks (ABC, NBC, CBS) versus cable news programs (Fox, MSNBC, CNN) versus print forms of news.

ENGAGE with your peers by comparing your findings. Is there any common ground? Look for a place to publish your findings in an online forum.

9

The Internet and New Technologies: The Media Converge

It was meant to be a raunchy comedy with a far-fetched plot: Two American journalists admired by North Korean leader Kim Jong-un are invited to come to his country to interview him, resulting in the CIA recruiting the two (played by Seth Rogen and James Franco) to assassinate the dictator. But in the final months of 2014, the events surrounding the release of *The Interview* made it seem more like an international drama or high-tech geopolitical spy thriller than a comedy. In a span of two months, there was a massive online attack on a major corporation and its employees, another cyber attack on an entire country, threats of a terrorist attack, the canceling of the movie's theatrical release, and international sanctions.

On November 24, 2014, a group calling themselves the Guardians of Peace hacked Sony Pictures Entertainment—the distributor of *The Interview*—and released embarrassing personal e-mails of employees as well as digital copies of some unreleased films.[1] Speculation began that North Korea, upset about *The Interview*, was behind the attacks. A few weeks later, the Guardians of Peace threatened attacks on movie theaters showing the film that Christmas. Sony announced that theaters not wishing to show the film could be released from bookings, and then briefly canceled the release entirely.

The Department of Homeland Security did not consider the warnings from the Guardians of Peace a credible terrorist threat, and President Barack Obama said the movie's release should not have been curtailed. Meanwhile, the FBI announced it believed the hackers were indeed operating out of North Korea, although Kim Jong-un's government maintained its denial of any involvement. On January 2, 2015, President Obama signed an executive order increasing sanctions on North Korea, citing the Sony attack as the reason.

Eventually, Sony executives decided to release *The Interview* as scheduled online, on demand, and in some independent movie theaters.[2] But the real importance of this dramatic series of events surrounding a comedy film was summed up by Director of National Intelligence James Clapper, who in early 2015 called the Sony hack the "most serious" cyber attack up to that point on a U.S. interest.[3] While notable in its scale, this wasn't a completely isolated incident in a period that's seen stories about massive data theft from major retailers and medical institutions, and the constant threat of phishing and identify theft (discussed later in this chapter) in the online world.

The Internet revolutionizes and encompasses all forms of mass communication—not replacing them but converging them. It connects people across great distances almost instantly and offers access to boundless information, entertainment, and more. But as the Sony hacking incident demonstrates, the interconnectivity comes with some risks and raises profound questions about security, privacy, and freedom of speech on the Internet. As you consider these issues, think about the ways in which you balance convenience and connectivity with caution and security as you go online— and the ways governments and corporations may do the same.

THE INTERNET—the vast network of telephone and cable lines, wireless connections, and satellite systems that link and carry computer information worldwide— was described early on as the *information superhighway*. This description suggests that people envisioned a new system for conveying information that would replace the old one (books, newspapers, television, and radio). Created in the 1950s, the Internet was a government-sponsored technology enabling military and academic researchers in different locations to share information and findings by computer. Drawing on the technology used to build the first computer (the ENIAC, invented in 1946), the Internet exploited the power of digitization. Through **digitization**, information in analog form (such as text or pictures) is translated into binary code—a series of ones and zeros that can be encoded in software and transmitted between computers.

In many ways, the original description of the Internet has turned out to be accurate: This medium has expanded dramatically from its initial incarnation to a vast entity that encompasses all other media today (video and audio content in addition to text). Since becoming a mass medium in the mid-1990s, the Internet has transformed the way we do business, communicate, socialize, entertain ourselves, and get information—in short, it has profoundly touched the way most of us interact with media across all aspects of our lives.

Unlike other mass media, the Internet seems to have no limits: More and more content is being made accessible on it, more and more people are gaining access to it, and more and more types of media are converging on it. But one thing *is* certain: As governments, corporations, and public and private interests vie to shape the Internet so that it suits their needs, the questions of who will have access to it and who will control it are taking on more urgency.

In this chapter, we explore these questions, along with the Internet's impact on various aspects of our lives, by:

- examining the early history of the Internet, including its initial uses as a military-government communication tool

- tracing the evolution of the Internet to a mass medium with multimedia capability

- analyzing the economics of the Internet, including the new business models it has inspired as well as the noncommercial entities that use it

- considering concerns that have arisen regarding the security of personal information on the Internet and the appropriateness of content now accessible through this medium

- weighing the negative and positive implications of the Internet for our democratic society

The Early History of the Internet

After World War II, the United States entered the Cold War against the Soviet Union, pitting the two great powers in a decades-long battle of military and economic superiority. The space race was a symbolic part of the Cold War, and when the Soviet spacecraft *Sputnik* became the first to orbit the earth in 1957, the United States was shocked at being beaten. The event ushered in a new era of U.S. government spending on technological, scientific, and military developments. The United States would later make its first successful rocket launch with *Explorer* in 1958, but perhaps more important to our world today was the creation that same year of a new U.S. Defense Department research agency that would eventually develop the Internet. In the decades that followed, new technology like microprocessors and fiber-optic cable increased the commercial viability of data transmission, paving the way for the Internet to become a mass medium.

Unveiled on April 7, 1964, the IBM 360 was considered one of the most influential computer rollouts. Programmers could use the special typewriter to talk to the mainframe.

© Charles E. Rotkin/Corbis

Military Functions, Civic Roots

Created in 1958, the U.S. Defense Department's Advanced Research Projects Agency (ARPA) assembled a team of computer scientists around the country to develop and test technological innovations. Computers were relatively new at this time, and there were only a few expensive mainframe computers, each big enough to fill an entire room. Yet the scientists working on ARPA projects wanted access to these computers.

CHAPTER 9 // TIMELINE

1960s ARPAnet
U.S. Defense Department begins research on a distributed network—ARPAnet—the groundwork for the Internet.

1971 E-mail
E-mail is invented, revolutionizing modes of communication.

1971 Microprocessors
These circuits enable personal computers (PCs) to be born.

1980s Fiber-Optic Cable
These thin bundles of glass enable the transmission of thousands of messages at once.

A solution to the problem was proposed: First, share computer-processing time by creating a wired network system in which users from multiple locations could log onto a computer whenever they needed it. Second, to prevent logjams in data communication, the network used a system called packet switching, which broke down messages into smaller pieces to easily route through the network, and reassembled them on the other end. This system provided multiple paths linking computers to one another, thereby allowing communication to continue if one of the paths got clogged or disrupted—much like the national highway system supported by President Dwight Eisenhower. This computer network became the original Internet—called **ARPAnet** and nicknamed the Net—and it enabled military and academic researchers to communicate on a distributed network system (see Figure 9.1).

With only a few large, powerful research computers in the country, many computer scientists were suddenly able to access massive (for that time) amounts of computer power. The first Net messages ever were sent in 1969, when ARPAnet connections linked four universities: the University of California–Los Angeles, the University of California–Santa Barbara, Stanford, and the University of Utah. By 1970, another terminal was in place in Cambridge, Massachusetts, at the computer research firm Bolt, Beranek and Newman (BBN), and by late 1971, there were twenty-three Internet hosts at university and government research centers across the United States. This same year, Ray Tomlinson of BBN came up with an essential innovation to help researchers communicate— **e-mail**—and decided to use the "@" sign to separate the user's name from the computer name, a convention that has been used ever since.

This advertisement for the Commodore 64, one of the first home PCs, touts the features of the computer. The Commodore was heralded in its time, but today's PCs far exceed its abilities.

The Advertising Archives

1980s Hypertext
This data-linking feature enables users to link one Web page to another, creating the World Wide Web.

1985 AOL
The company is launched, becoming the most successful ISP over the next decade.

1986 NSF
The National Science Foundation sponsors a high-speed communications network, connecting computers across the country.

1993 Web Browsers
The Internet becomes navigable and user-friendly.

FIGURE 9.1 // DISTRIBUTED NETWORKS

Paul Baran, a computer scientist at the Rand Corporation during the Cold War era, worked on developing a national communications system. Centralized networks (*a*) lead all the paths to a single nerve center. Decentralized networks (*b*) contain several main nerve centers. In a distributed network (*c*), which resembles a net, there are no nerve centers; if any connection is severed, information can be immediately rerouted and delivered to its destination. But is there a downside to distributed networks when it comes to the circulation of network viruses?

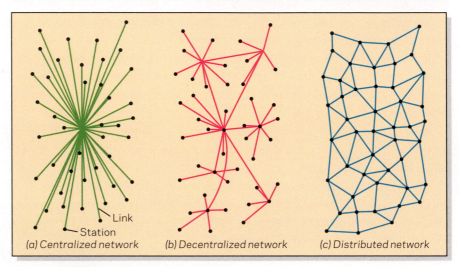

Link
Station
(a) Centralized network (b) Decentralized network (c) Distributed network

Data from: Katie Hafner and Matthew Lyon, Where Wizards Stay Up Late *(New York: Simon & Schuster, 1996)*

During this development stage, the Internet (still called ARPAnet at this time) was used primarily by universities, government research labs, and corporations involved in computer software and other high-tech products. These users exchanged e-mail and posted information on computer *bulletin boards*—sites that listed information about particular topics, such as health, technology, or employment services.

CHAPTER 9 // TIMELINE continued

1999 Blogging
Blogging software is created, helping to popularize this form of communication.

2000 Cookies
Information profiles on users enable data mining to flourish.

2000s Broadband
Users switch from dial-up to broadband with cable modem or DSL connections.

2001 Instant Messaging
Instant messaging becomes the fastest-growing area of the Internet.

The Net Widens

From the early 1970s to the late 1980s, the Internet moved from the development stage to the entrepreneurial stage, in which it became a marketable medium. The first signal of the Net's imminent marketability came in 1971 with the introduction of **microprocessors**—miniature circuits that could process and store electronic signals. This led to the introduction of the first *personal computers* (*PCs*), which were smaller, cheaper, and more powerful than the bulky systems that had occupied entire floors of buildings during the 1960s. In 1986, the National Science Foundation sponsored the development of a high-speed communications network (NSFNET) and established supercomputer centers on the campuses of Princeton, the University of Illinois, the University of California–San Diego, and Cornell, and a fifth in Pittsburgh—jointly operated by Carnegie Mellon, the University of Pittsburgh, and Westinghouse—which were designed to speed up access to research data and encourage private investment in the Net. This government investment triggered a dramatic rise in Internet use and opened the door to additional commercial possibilities.

Also in the mid-1980s, **fiber-optic cable**, thin bundles of glass capable of transmitting thousands of messages simultaneously (via laser light), became the standard for conveying communication data speedily—making the commercial use of computers even more viable than before. Today, thanks to this increased speed, the amount of information that digital technology can transport is nearly limitless.

In 1990, ARPAnet officially ended; and in 1991, the NSF opened its network fully to commercial use. By this time, a growing community of researchers, computer programmers, amateur hackers, and commercial interests had already tapped into the Internet. These tens of thousands of participants in the network became the initial audience for the Internet's emergence as a mass medium.

2002 Social Networking
Friendster is founded as the first major social networking site, inspiring MySpace (2003) and Facebook (2004).

2007 Smartphones
The iPhone is introduced, creating a trend toward Internet-accessing smartphones.

2010 iPad
Apple releases a multipurpose touchscreen tablet.

The Evolution of the Internet: From Web 1.0 to Web 2.0 and Beyond

During the 1990s and early 2000s, the Internet's primary applications were e-mail (one-to-one communication) and Web page display (one-to-many communication). By 2005, it had evolved into a far more powerful social network. In other words, the Web became a many-to-many tool, as an increasing number of applications on it led to the creation of new content and navigational possibilities for users. While doing so, it continued to change our relationship with the Internet. Through social networks, users can engage in real-time conversations with others; write, read, and comment on blogs and wikis; share photos and videos; and interact within virtual 3-D environments. People commonly describe these first two phases in the Internet's evolution as Web 1.0 and Web 2.0, even as elements of Web 3.0 (or the Semantic Web) become more common.

The GUI (graphical user interface) of the World Wide Web changed overnight with the release of Mosaic in 1993. As the first popular Web browser, Mosaic unleashed the multimedia potential of the Internet. Mosaic was the inspiration for the commercial browser Netscape, which was released in 1994.

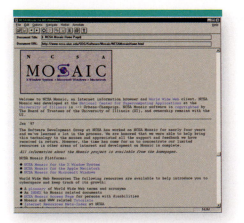

Courtesy of the National Center for Supercomputing Applications and the Board of Trustees of the University of Illinois

Web 1.0

Internet use before the 1990s mostly consisted of people transferring files, accessing computer databases from remote locations, and sending e-mails through an unwieldy interface. The **World Wide Web** (or the Web) changed all of that. Developed in the late 1980s by software engineer Tim Berners-Lee at the CERN particle physics lab in Switzerland to help scientists better collaborate, the Web enabled users to access texts through clickable links rather than through difficult computer code. Known as *hypertext*, the system allowed computer-accessed information to associate with, or link to, other information on the Internet— no matter where it was located. **HTML (HyperText Markup Language)**, the written code that creates Web pages and links, can be read by all computers. Thus, computers with different operating systems (Windows, Macintosh, Linux) can communicate easily through hypertext. After CERN released the World Wide Web source code into the public domain in 1993, many people began to build software to further enhance the Internet's versatility.

The release of **Web browsers**—software applications that help users navigate the Web—brought the Web to mass audiences for the first time. Computer programmers led by Marc Andreessen at the University of Illinois (a supercomputer center that was part of NSFNET) released Mosaic in 1993, the first user-friendly browser to load text and graphics together in a magazine-like layout. With its attractive fonts and easy-to-use navigation buttons, Mosaic was a huge improvement over previous technology. In 1994, Andreessen joined investors in California's Silicon Valley to introduce another major advance—a commercial browser called Netscape. Together, the World Wide Web, Mosaic, and Netscape gave the Internet basic multimedia capability, enabling users to transmit pictures, sound, and video.

Web 2.0

The shift to Web 2.0 encouraged a deeper trend toward *media convergence*: different types of content (video, text, audio) created by all sorts of sources (users, corporations, nonprofit organizations) coming together and accessed on a variety of devices (personal computers, smartphones, tablets). Whereas the Internet was primarily a medium for computer-savvy users to deliver text-and-graphic content during its Web 1.0 stage, it has been transformed into a place where people can access and share all manner of media content: music on Spotify, video on YouTube, journalism on Blogspot, eBooks on Amazon, mountains of collective intelligence on *Wikipedia*, gossip on Twitter, and relationships on Facebook. Whereas the signature products of Web 1.0 were increased content access and accompanying dot-com consumerism, the iconic achievement of Web 2.0 is social networking.

Types of Social Media

In less than a decade, a number of different types of social media have evolved, with multiple platforms for the creation of user-generated content. European researchers Andreas M. Kaplan and Michael Haenlein identify six categories of social media on the Internet: social networking sites, blogs, collaborative projects, content communities, virtual game worlds, and virtual social worlds.[4]

Social Networking Sites

Social networking sites—including Facebook, Twitter, Google+, Tumbler, and Pinterest—have become among the most popular places on the Internet. The largest of these sites, Facebook, started at Harvard in 2004 as an online substitute to the printed facebooks the school created for incoming first-year students. Ten years later, it had become a global phenomenon, with over a billion active users and available in more than seventy languages. Facebook empowers users to create personal profiles; upload photos; create lists of their favorite movies, books, and music; and post messages to connect with old friends and meet new

Etsy is principally a commerce site, but the way it connects crafters with potential buyers has a social component, creating a sense of community even in the business of buying and selling goods.

ones. A subcategory of social networking sites contains sites more specifically devoted to professional networking, such as LinkedIn. The popularity of social media combined with an explosion in mobile devices has altered our relationship with the Internet. Two trends are noteworthy: (1) Apple now makes more than five times as much money selling iPhones, iPads, iPods, and accessories as it does selling computers, and (2) the number of Facebook users (1.23 billion in 2014) keeps increasing. The significance of these two trends is that through our Apple devices and Facebook, we now inhabit a different kind of Internet—what some call a closed Internet or a walled garden.[5]

In the world in which the small screens of smartphones are becoming the preferred medium for linking to the Internet, we don't typically get the full open Internet, one represented by the vast searches brought to us by Google. Instead, we get a more managed Internet, brought to us by apps or platforms that carry out specific functions via the Internet. Are you looking for a nearby restaurant? Don't search on the Internet—use this app especially designed for that purpose. The distributors of these apps act as gatekeepers; Apple has more than 1.15 million apps in its App Store, and Apple approves every one of them. The competing Android app stores on Google Play and Amazon have a similar number of apps (with many fewer apps in the Windows Store), but Google and Amazon exercise less control over approval of apps than Apple does.

Blogs

Years before there were status updates or Facebook, **blogs** (short for Weblogs) enabled people to easily post their ideas to a Web site. Popularized with the release of Blogger (now owned by Google) in 1999, blogs contain articles or posts in chronological, journal-like form, often with reader comments and links to other sites. Blogs can be personal or corporate multimedia sites, sometimes with photos, graphics, podcasts, and video. Some blogs have developed into popular news and culture sites, such as the *Huffington Post*, *TechCrunch*, *Mashable*, *Gawker*, *HotAir*, *ThinkProgress*, and *TPM (Talking Points Memo)*.

Some blogs are simply an individual's online journal or personal musings. Others provide information, analysis, or commentary that isn't presented in the more traditional news media. Although some are written by journalists, the vast majority of the Web's approximately 200 million blogs are written by individuals who don't use established editorial practices to check their facts.

Some of the leading platforms for blogging include Blogger, WordPress, Tumblr, Weebly, and Wix. But by 2013, the most popular form of blogging was microblogging, with about 241 million active users on Twitter, sending out 500 million tweets (a short message with a 140-character limit) per day.[6] In 2013, Twitter introduced an app called Vine that enabled users to post short video clips. A few months later, Facebook's Instagram responded with its own video-sharing service.

Courtesy of Talking Points Memo. Photo by Michael P. King/ AP Photo

Talking Points Memo began in 2000 and has grown into one of the most popular political blogs, with an average of twenty-one million page views per month.

Collaborative Projects

Probably the most common examples of projects in which users build something together, often with anyone able to edit or add information, are Web sites called **wikis** (*wiki* means "quick" in Hawaiian). Large wikis include Wikitravel (a global travel guide); Wikimapia (combining Google Maps with wiki comments); and, of course, *Wikipedia*, the online encyclopedia that is constantly being updated by interested volunteers.

Although *Wikipedia* has become one of the most popular resources on the Web, some people have expressed concern that its open editing model compromises its accuracy.[7] When accessing any wiki, the user may not know for certain who has contributed which parts of the information found there, who is changing the content, and what the contributors' motives are. (For example, politicians and other well-known individuals who are particularly concerned about their public image may distort information in their *Wikipedia* entries to improve their image—or their supporters may do the same.) This worry has led *Wikipedia* to lock down topic pages that are especially contested, which has inevitably led to user protests about information control. At the same time, *Wikipedia* generally offers a vibrant forum where information unfolds, debates happen, and controversy over topics can be documented. And just like a good term paper, the best *Wikipedia* entries carefully list their sources, allowing a user to dig deeper and have some way of judging the quality of information in a given listing.

But wikis aren't the only way in which Internet users collaborate. Kickstarter is a popular fund-raising tool for creative projects such as books, recordings, and films. InnoCentive is a crowd-sourcing community that offers award payments for people who can solve business and scientific problems. And Change.org has become an effective petition project to push for social change. For example, in 2014, Lucien Tessier of Maryland began a campaign to petition the Boy Scouts of America (BSA) to drop its ban against openly gay Scouts. Nearly 130,000 people signed the Change.org petition, and after additional lobbying, the BSA dropped its ban on gay Scouts under the age of eighteen.[8]

Content Communities

Content communities are the best examples of the many-to-many ethic of social media. **Content communities** exist for the sharing of all types of content, from text (Fanfiction.net) to photos (Flickr, Photobucket) and videos (YouTube, Vimeo). YouTube, created in 2005 and bought by Google in 2006, is the most well-known content community, with hundreds of millions of users around the world uploading and watching amateur and professional videos. YouTube gave rise to the viral video—a video that becomes immediately popular by millions sharing it through social media platforms. The most popular video of all time—a fifty-six-second home video titled "Charlie bit my finger—again!" had more than 815 million views as of April 2015. By 2014, YouTube reported that one hundred hours of video are uploaded to the site every minute, and it has more than one billion unique users each month.

Virtual Game Worlds and Virtual Social Worlds

Virtual game worlds (covered in greater detail in Chapter 10) and virtual social worlds invite users to role-play in rich 3-D environments, in real time, with players throughout the world. In virtual game worlds (also known as massively multi-player online role-playing games, or MMORPGs) such as *World of Warcraft* and *Elder Scrolls Online*, players can customize their online identity, or avatar, and work with others through a game's challenges. Community forums for members extend discussion and shared play outside the game. Virtual social worlds, like *Second Life*, enable players to take their avatars through simulated environments and even make transactions with virtual money.

Social networking sites have given a huge boost to one-to-many communication. However, they've also raised some thorny privacy questions: Should we post highly personal information about ourselves, including pictures and messages about our political views? (Potential—or current—employers routinely visit these sites to examine job candidates' or employees' profiles.) Should information in our profiles be considered public for some eyes but off-limits to others?

macmillanhighered.com
/mediaessentials3e

The Internet in 1995
In a clip from the 1995 thriller *The Net*, Sandra Bullock's character communicates using her computer.
Discussion: How does this movie from over two decades ago portray online communication? What does it get right, and what seems outdated now?

Web 3.0: The Semantic Web

Although we have drawn a relatively clear line between Web 1.0 and Web 2.0, the boundaries between 2.0 and 3.0 are fuzzier. But hypertext inventor Tim Berners-Lee and two coauthors published an influential article in *Scientific American* in which they described a "Semantic Web." Semantics is the study of meaning, so a Semantic Web refers to a more meaningful—or organized—Web. Essentially, this involves a continuing evolution in our relationship with the

© Warner Bros. Pictures/Everett Collection

In the Spike Jonze film *Her*, a man played by Joaquin Phoenix falls in love with his lifelike operating system, voiced by Scarlett Johansson. Though the film takes place in the future and uses elements of science fiction and fantasy, it has been acclaimed for its reflections on modern technology, such as Apple's voice recognition assistant, Siri.

Internet, more than just major changes in what is on the Internet. Berners-Lee and his colleagues explain, "The Semantic Web is not a separate Web but an extension of the current one, in which information is given well-defined meaning, better enabling computers and people to work in cooperation."[9]

The best example of the Semantic Web is Apple's voice recognition assistant, Siri, first shipped with its iPhone 4S in 2011. Siri uses conversational voice recognition to answer questions, find locations, and interact with various iPhone functionalities, such as the calendar, reminders, the weather app, the music player, the Web browser, and the maps function. Some of its searches get directed to Wolfram Alpha, a computational search engine that provides direct answers to questions, rather than the traditional list of links for search results. Other Siri searches draw on the databases of external services, such as Yelp! for restaurant locations and reviews, and StubHub for ticket information. Another example is the Siemens refrigerator (available in Europe) that takes a photo of the interior every time the door closes. The owner may be away at the supermarket but can call up a photo of the interior to be reminded of what should be on the shopping list.[10]

The Economics of the Internet

One of the unique things about the Internet is that no one owns it— but that hasn't stopped some corporations from trying to control it. Companies have realized the potential of dominating the Internet through access to phone and broadband wires, browser software,

MEDIA LITERACY

Case Study

Net Neutrality

For more than a decade, the debate over net neutrality has framed the potential future of the Internet. Far from being any closer to a final resolution, the debate has become even more heated recently, and has begun to expand into areas that include the overall Internet speed and access being provided by the infrastructure owned by various Internet service providers (ISPs). **Net neutrality** refers to the principle that every Web site and every user—whether a multinational corporation or a private citizen—has the right to the same Internet network speed and access. The idea of an open and neutral network has existed since the origins of the Internet, but as we will see, making those ideals into lasting rules has been a battle that is far from finished.

The dispute over net neutrality and the future of the Internet is dominated by some of the biggest communications corporations. These major telephone and cable companies—including Comcast,

President Obama has spoken out as a proponent of net neutrality, saying in 2014: "An open Internet is essential to the American economy, and increasingly to our very way of life. By lowering the cost of launching a new idea, igniting new political movements, and bringing communities closer together, it has been one of the most significant democratizing influences the world has ever known."

Jeremy Hogan/Polaris/Newscom

AT&T, Time Warner Cable, Verizon, and Cox—control 98 percent of broadband access in the United States through DSL and cable modem service. They want to offer faster connections and priority to clients willing to pay higher rates, and provide preferential service for their own content or for content providers who make special deals with them—in other words, to eliminate net neutrality. For example, tiered Internet access might mean that these companies would charge customers more for data-heavy services like Netflix, YouTube, Hulu, or iTunes. These companies argue that the profits they could make with tiered Internet access would allow them to build expensive new networks, benefiting everyone.

But supporters of net neutrality—mostly bloggers, video gamers, educators, religious groups, unions, and small businesses—argue that the cable and telephone giants actually have incentive to rig their services and cause net congestion in order to force customers to pay a premium for higher-speed connections. They claim that an Internet without net neutrality would hurt small businesses, non-profits, and Internet innovators, who might be stuck in the "slow lane" and not be able to afford the fastest connections that large corporations can

afford. Large Internet corporations like Google, Yahoo!, Amazon, eBay, Microsoft, Skype, and Facebook also support net neutrality because their businesses depend on their millions of customers having equal access to the Web.

In late 2010, the FCC adopted rules on net neutrality, noting it as "an important step to preserve the Internet as an open platform for innovation, investment, job creation, economic growth, competition, and free expression."[1] But the big telecom companies filed lawsuits in protest, and the FCC's first attempts at net neutrality rules were twice rejected by federal courts.

In late 2014, the Obama administration started advocating stronger net neutrality rules, asking the FCC to follow suit—which they did in February of 2015, voting to reclassify broadband Internet service as a public utility, with FCC Chairman Tom Wheeler saying Internet access was "too important to let broadband providers be the ones making the rules."[2] The move doesn't transform private companies into public entities, but does grant the public (via the FCC) clearer jurisdiction over Internet rules. It also brings mobile wireless broadband under the same jurisdiction, and tries to make it easier for communities to encourage competition by creating their own municipal telecoms. Specifically, the FCC has put into place rules that disallow **blocking** (broadband providers prohibiting access to legal content and services), **throttling** (the act of intentionally impairing or degrading Internet performance based on content or source), and **paid prioritization** (favoring some Internet traffic over other lawful traffic in exchange for payment, creating "fast lanes").[3]

The FCC action doesn't mean the issue is now settled; less than two months after the ruling, lawsuits challenging the ruling had already been filed, including one by USTelecom, a trade group that represents several large telecommunications corporations.[4] If the past is any indication, these lawsuits will take months or even years to move through the courts.

Supporters of the FCC's new regulations say that the large private ISPs, which largely operate as monopolies in their areas, have been more focused on profits than customer service and technological advancement, making intervention necessary. Wheeler argued that the overall Internet speed in the United States is too slow, in part after a number of studies showed the U.S. system lagging far behind systems in other countries. For example, customers in South Korea, Japan, and most of Europe are paying less for much faster service.[5] Companies like Comcast say paid prioritization would help pay for a faster Internet, but some studies on Internet service find that the U.S. communities with the fastest service are those that have systems owned and operated by local governments without a tiered fee structure, found in places like Chattanooga, Tennessee, and Cedar Falls, Iowa.[6]

Despite the new FCC rules, it's clear that this issue isn't settled. The fight will continue in the court system as well as the political arena. The FCC members are appointed by the sitting president and confirmed by the Senate for five-year terms. The vote that approved the new rules in 2015 was 3–2, along party lines. This will likely be a consideration for major telecommunication groups as they write checks to lobbyists and political campaigns.

APPLYING THE CRITICAL PROCESS

DESCRIPTION Interview a sample of people about their views on net neutrality. Would they be willing to pay higher rates for faster connections? Do they think every Web site should have the same network speed and access?

ANALYSIS What sorts of patterns emerge from your interviews? Are there common views on the way the Internet should be accessed? Do your interviewees seem to be concerned or unconcerned about the issue of net neutrality? Do your questions make them think about this issue for the first time?

INTERPRETATION What do these patterns mean? Is the idea of net neutrality better or worse for democracy? Would eliminating net neutrality undercut the usefulness and accessibility of the medium?

EVALUATION Is net neutrality a benefit of the Internet? What should the standards of speed and access to it be? How should they be enforced?

ENGAGEMENT Learn about and take action for or against net neutrality. Visit SavetheInternet.com to learn how to prevent net neutrality's elimination. Share your knowledge with your peers.

search engines, and—perhaps most important—advertising. However, throughout the Internet's relatively short history, several companies have risen and fallen trying to control a medium characterized by few regulations and a strong entrepreneurial ethic.

Internet Businesses

The business of the Internet, as we've seen in other chapters, often involves adapting existing businesses or forms of mass media to an increasingly online world. But there are some elements that are unique to the Internet, and success in one of these areas can give a company a huge advantage—and a certain measure of control—over how others use the Internet. Three such examples are Web browsers, directories and search engines, and, to a lesser extent, e-mail.

Web Browsers

In the early 1990s, as the Web became the most popular part of the Internet, digital companies like Microsoft thought that Web browsers—the most common interface of the Internet—would be the key to their commercial success.

Beginning in 1995, Microsoft—at that time with a near monopoly over computer operating systems with its Windows software—achieved a near monopoly over the Internet by strategically bundling its Windows 95 operating system with its new Internet Explorer browser software. The release of Windows 95, which made Internet Explorer the preferred browser for computers using Windows, devastated Netscape, the most popular browser at the time. Alarmed by the company's growing power, the U.S. Department of Justice brought an antitrust lawsuit against Microsoft in 1997, arguing that it had used its operating system dominance to sabotage competing browsers. In 2001, the Department of Justice dropped its efforts to break Microsoft into two independent companies. In Europe, however, the European Union ruled that Microsoft had committed antitrust violations and fined Microsoft a total of about $2.5 billion.[11] Web browsers never became huge revenue-generating portals, and today companies like Microsoft, Apple, and Google release free browsers as a way to familiarize users with their other software. (Firefox, a nonprofit open-source browser, is an exception.) Although Internet Explorer dominated Web browsers for years, Microsoft recently replaced it with the Edge browser, which faces increasing competition from Firefox, Google Chrome, and Safari.

Directories and Search Engines

As Web sites rapidly proliferated on the Internet throughout the early 1990s, entrepreneurs seized the opportunity to help users navigate this vast amount of information. Two types of companies emerged—directories and search engines.

Directories rely on people to review and catalogue Web sites, creating categories with hierarchical topic listings that can be browsed. Yahoo! was one of the first companies to successfully provide such a service. Established in 1994, Yahoo!'s directory quickly dominated the Web-directory market by acting as an all-purpose entry point, or **portal**, to the Internet.

Andrew Cowie/EPA/Landov

Search engines offer a different route for finding content on the Web: a complicated algorithm and an enormous database of Web pages compiled and regularly updated by the search engine company. Users type in key words, and the algorithm is then applied to the company's massive database, gleaning a list of Web pages ranked in order of relevance. Beyond its directory, Yahoo! began syndicating with the search engine service Inktomi to bring algorithmic search to its very popular portal.

In 1998, Google introduced the first algorithm to mathematically rank a page's popularity based on how many other pages link to it—and immediately became the megastar search engine. Even Yahoo! switched to Google, along with many other portals, as its main search provider. However, search engine syndication provided only so much revenue. The application that made search engines (and Google especially) such important Web properties in the early 2000s was the ability to connect advertisers to the same key words users were typing into the search box. Ad sites soon appeared alongside (and in some cases, within) an algorithmic search list—an advertising strategy that was far more effective than banner ads. Google transformed almost overnight from a syndicated search engine service to an advertising firm. Yahoo! and Microsoft have heavily invested in competing search engine initiatives to reap some of the advertising profits but have not been able to match Google's superior search engine. Google now claims about 70 percent of the search engine market in the United States, with Yahoo! and Microsoft's Bing search engines trailing far behind. This has helped Google not only make a great deal of money on advertising (discussed later in the chapter) but also branch out into other areas. The company now offers other Internet services, including shopping (Froogle), mapping (Google Maps), e-mail

Google has grown from a popular search engine into a major digital conglomerate with a variety of holdings and well over fifty thousand full-time employees. They have toyed with the idea of opening a retail store akin to Apple's high-traffic storefronts, but the plans have not yet been finalized.

(Gmail), blogging (Blogger), and browsing (Chrome), and has begun to experiment with behavioral advertising and the placement of TV ads. Google has even begun challenging Microsoft's Office programs with Google Apps software. In its most significant investments to date, Google acquired YouTube for $1.64 billion and purchased DoubleClick, one of the Internet's leading advertising placement companies.

E-mail

Because sending and receiving e-mail is still one of the most popular uses of the Internet, major Web corporations such as Yahoo!, AOL, Google, and Microsoft continue to offer free e-mail accounts to draw users to their sites; even Facebook introduced e-mail accounts in 2010. Each of these companies, some with millions of users, generates revenue through advertisements in subscribers' e-mail messages, with Google's Gmail ads tailored to key words contained in a message.

Money In and Money Out

The Internet's quick commercialization in the 1990s led to battles between corporations vying to attract the most users. In the beginning, commercial entities like AOL (America Online) and Microsoft sought to capture business as Internet service providers and Web browser software companies, respectively. What no one anticipated was the emergence of search engines, such as Google, as a key advertising force, and the influence of the sharp rise in the use of mobile devices. We discuss throughout this book how other forms of mass media have changed their business models because of the Internet, and certainly that gives us part of the economic impact and performance of the Internet. The Internet is a big place, with many layers and different approaches to making money. The economic model of the Internet can be broken into four main areas: infrastructure (ISPs), paid Web services (such as Netflix), direct sales (such as Amazon), and advertising.

Infrastructure

Since the early 1990s, **Internet service providers (ISPs)** have competed to provide consumers with access to the Internet. The earliest ISPs offered dial-up access through a traditional telephone line. Today, the preferred access method is through **broadband** connections, which are much faster than dial-up. These systems incorporate the hardware of the Internet—fiber-optic cables, computer servers, routers, cellular towers, and mobile data systems—and individual connections with homes and businesses. The primary income for ISPs comes from the people who sign up for the service, usually a subscription with a monthly fee. In some instances, that fee is based on the volume of data a user downloads or uploads, but more often it is a flat fee per month, commonly bundled with cable television and telephone services. In fact, if this sounds similar to the business model of cable television companies, that's because the largest ISPs are also the largest telephone and cable companies. These companies—including Verizon, Comcast, AT&T, Time Warner Cable, and Cox—control 98 percent of broadband DSL and cable modem services in the United States. Other providers include cities, which provide telecommunication services in the same way they provide other municipal utilities (see also "Media Literacy Case Study: Net Neutrality" on pages 306–307).

Paid Web Services

Another way companies make money on the Internet is by offering services for which a customer can pay by amount of use or by monthly subscription. These services might be tied to other media businesses, such as Hulu (a joint venture between several broadcasters), or might be accessible only on the Internet, such as the video-streaming service provided by Netflix (which, according to some sources, accounts for up to a third of Internet traffic[12]). But these services are not limited to video streaming; in fact, this has become an area of entrepreneurial explosion on the Internet. A few examples of this array of services include paid sites (or premium options on otherwise free sites) for dating (Match.com, e-Harmony), data storage (Dropbox), computer security (Norton, McAfee), music (Pandora, Spotify), and even karaoke (KaraFun). Another example would be a news organization like the *New York Times* or publications like *Consumer Reports*, which have taken their traditional paper or magazine subscription models online.

Direct Sales

Some businesses rely in whole or in part on the Internet to sell products to consumers. This is distinct from the category of Web services because direct sales, or **e-commerce**, involves sales of physical objects (or, in the case of such things as music downloads, computer files). For consumers, buying items online or through mobile devices has the advantage of convenience. For sellers, the Internet can offer access to customers from different cities or even different countries. This can be a double-edged sword for some retailers. A small mom-and-pop business might now be able to sell to customers that would never have found it otherwise, but that same business might also lose local customers to a massive online retailer like Amazon. No matter the business doing the selling, online retail has indeed become big business. Online sales in the United States were around $300 billion in 2014 and are projected to be well over $400 billion by 2018. What's more, a fast-growing percentage of that e-commerce is happening through mobile devices, though the projections don't even include mobile transactions on apps like Uber or using mobile accounts to pay for consumer goods like coffee and pizza.[13]

Advertising

In the early years of the Web, advertising consisted of traditional display ads placed on pages. These reached small, general audiences and thus weren't very profitable. In the late 1990s, Web advertising began shifting to search engines. Paid links now appear as "sponsored links" at the top, bottom, and side of a search engine result list. Every time a user clicks on a sponsored link, the advertiser pays the search engine for the click-through. However, even though search engines insist on the relevance of their search results, the increasingly commercial nature of the Web and the ability of commercial sites to buy advertisements on popular sites (thus making more links) mean that search engine results are biased toward commercial sites. A site like Google is today making billions of dollars in revenue from these pay-per-click advertisements.

More than just attaching ads to searches for certain key words, Google has become a model of how to generate dollars through **targeted advertising**, or ads targeted to a consumer based on information the various Web sites have gathered about that individual. For example, Google's e-mail program, Gmail, has an automatic search function that "reads" e-mails and then, based on key words it finds, selects ads to show users. This is one example of **data mining**, a system of collecting information about consumers, of which consumers are largely unaware.

Another common method that commercial interests use to track the browsing habits of computer users is **cookies**, or information profiles that are automatically collected and transferred between computer servers whenever users access Web sites.[14] The legitimate purpose of a cookie is to verify that a user has been cleared for access to a particular Web site, such as a library database that is open only to university faculty and students. However, cookies can also be used to create marketing profiles of Web users to target them for advertising. Many Web sites require the user to accept cookies in order to gain access to the site.

Facebook is another site that has had success with targeted advertising, though it has gotten itself into some trouble as a result of aggressive data-mining efforts. With over a billion Facebook users across the globe, the massive social media service keeps track of what we "Like," where we live, what we read, and what we want. Because typical Facebook users reveal so much about themselves in their profiles and messages, Facebook can offer advertisers exceptionally tailored ads. But in 2011, the Federal Trade Commission (FTC) accused Facebook of taking information it had told users would be private and sharing it with advertisers and third-party applications. Facebook CEO Mark Zuckerberg ended up settling with the FTC, admitting to "a bunch of mistakes," and agreeing to submit to privacy audits.[15]

The rise in smartphone use has contributed to extraordinary growth in mobile advertising, which jumped from $3.4 billion in 2012 to $7.1 billion in 2013, accounting for 17 percent of the $42.8 billion in total Internet advertising that year.[16]

Overhead: Building the Infrastructure

We've just explored ways in which companies make money by attracting users—and thus advertisers—to the Internet. But what about money they have to spend to build their Internet businesses? "Money out" takes the form of investments in infrastructure needed for the Internet to operate. This infrastructure includes software, facilities, and equipment, such as fiber-optic networks and bandwidth. Whereas giants like Amazon and Google certainly have a great deal of overhead—often related to keeping warehouses (for shipping of products or housing of dedicated servers)—the investments required by ISPs, and how they are allowed to capitalize on those expenditures, has become a part of public debate over the future of Internet regulation and control (see also "Media Literacy Case Study: Net Neutrality" on pages 306–307).

The Noncommercial Web

Despite powerful commercial forces dictating much of the content we access online, the pioneering spirit of the Internet's independent early days endures; the Internet continues to be a participatory medium where anyone can be involved. Two of the most prominent areas in which alternative voices continue to flourish are in open-source software and digital archiving.

Open-Source Software

Microsoft has long dominated the software industry—requiring users to pay for both its applications and its upgrades, and keeping its proprietary code protected from changes by outsiders. Yet independent software creators persist in making alternatives through **open-source software**, in which code can be updated by anyone interested in modifying it. One example is the open-source operating system Linux, introduced in 1991 by Linus Torvalds and shared with computer programmers and hobbyists around the world who have avidly participated to improve it. Today, even Microsoft acknowledges that Linux is a credible alternative to expensive commercial programs.

AP Photo/Paul Sakuma

Linus Torvalds, the Finnish software developer, holds a license plate bearing the name of his invention, the Linux computer operating system. Since Torvalds's first version of Linux in 1991, hundreds of other developers around the world have contributed improvements to this open-source software rival of Microsoft's Windows.

Digital Archiving

Librarians have worked tirelessly to build digital archives that exist outside of any commercial system. One of the biggest and most impressive digital-preservation initiatives is the Internet Archive (www.archive.org), established in 1996. The Internet Archive aims to ensure that researchers, historians, scholars, and all U.S. citizens have access to digitized content. This content comprises all the text, moving images, audio, software, and more than eighty-five billion archived Web pages reaching back to the earliest days of the Internet.

The Internet Archive has also partnered with the Open Content Alliance to digitize every book in the public domain (generally, those published before 1922). This book-scanning effort is the nonprofit alternative to Google's Library Project, which has the colossal goal of digitizing every book ever printed. Working with the Boston Public Library, several university and international libraries, and a few corporate sponsors, the Open Content Alliance aims to keep as much online information as possible in the "commons"—a term that refers to the collective ownership of certain public resources, such as the broadcast airwaves, the Internet, and public parks. The alliance's concern is that online content like digital books might otherwise become solely the property of commercial entities.

Security and Appropriateness on the Internet

When we watch television, listen to the radio, read a book, or go to a movie, we don't need to provide personal information to get access to the media content we're consuming. However, when we use the Internet—whether it's to sign up for an e-mail account, comment on a blog, or shop online—we give away personal information, even if we don't mean to. This has raised concerns about the security of information, personal safety, and the appropriateness of content available on the Web.

Information Security: What's Private?

Government surveillance, online fraud, and unethical data-gathering methods have become common, making the Internet a potentially treacherous place.

• *Government Surveillance.* Since the inception of the Internet, government agencies around the world have obtained communication logs, Web browser histories, and the online records of users who thought their Internet activities were private. In the United States, for example, the USA PATRIOT Act (which became law about a month after the September 11 attacks in 2001 and was renewed in 2006, with several provisions later extended further) grants sweeping powers to law-enforcement agencies to intercept individuals' online communications, including e-mail messages and browsing records. The act was intended to allow the government to more easily uncover and track potential terrorists and terrorist organizations, but many now argue that it is too vaguely worded, allowing the government to unconstitutionally probe the personal records of citizens without probable cause and for reasons other than preventing terrorism. Moreover, searches of the Internet permit law-enforcement agencies to gather huge amounts of data, including the communications of people who are not the targets of an investigation. Documents leaked to the news media in 2013 by former CIA employee and former National Security Agency (NSA) contractor Edward Snowden revealed that the NSA had continued its domestic spying program for more than a decade, collecting bulk Internet and mobile phone data on millions of Americans.

- *Online Fraud.* The Internet has increasingly become a conduit for online robbery and *identity theft*, the illegal obtaining of someone's credit and identity information to fraudulently spend his or her money. One particularly costly form of Internet identity theft is **phishing**. Through this tactic, scammers send phony e-mail messages that appear to be from official Web sites—eBay, PayPal, Chase—asking customers to enter or update their credit card details and other personal information (such as bank account numbers). Once scammers have this information, they can go on a shopping spree using the victim's credit card or siphon funds out of the victim's bank account.

- *Unethical Data Gathering.* As discussed in the earlier section about the business of the Internet, companies use cookies to collect information and tailor marketing messages. Even more frustrating is **spyware**, information-gathering software that is often secretly bundled with free downloaded software and that sends pop-up ads to users' computer screens. Spyware has also made it possible for unauthorized parties (such as hackers) to collect personal or account information about users and to plant viruses and malicious click-fraud programs on computers.

Online crimes can include massive data breaches, like the one that resulted in the stolen credit- and debit-card information of more than forty million Target customers at the end of 2013. The settlement of a lawsuit against Target on behalf of victims of the breach may cost the company as much as $10 million.

George Frey/Landov

In 1998, the FTC developed fair information principles to combat the unauthorized collection of personal data online. Unfortunately, the FTC has no power to enforce these principles, and most Web sites either don't self-enforce them or say they do when they really don't.[17] Consumer and privacy advocates are calling for stronger regulations, such as requiring Web sites to adopt opt-in policies. **Opt-in policies** require a Web site to obtain explicit permission from consumers before it can collect their browsing-history data.

Personal Safety: Online Predators

In some cases, predators have used access to Internet users to cause harm. For instance, child molesters have used social networking sites to pose as friendly people, with the goal of forming relationships with naïve underage youngsters. Once a relationship takes root online, the predator suggests a face-to-face meeting, with the intent of exploiting the youngster sexually. These incidents have provoked an outcry from parents and demands for better mechanisms for protecting Internet users' safety.

Appropriateness: What Should Be Online?

The question of what constitutes appropriate content has been part of the story of every mass medium, from debates over the morality of lurid pulp-fiction books in the nineteenth century to arguments over the appropriateness of racist, sexist, and homophobic content in films and music. But the biggest topic of debate has centered on sexually explicit content.

Public objection to indecent and obscene Internet content has led to various legislative efforts to tame the Web. For example, the Children's Internet Protection Act of 2000 was passed and upheld in 2003. This act requires schools and libraries that receive federal funding for Internet access to use software that filters out any visual content deemed obscene, pornographic, or harmful to minors, unless disabled at the request of adult users. Yet regardless of laws, pornography continues to flourish on commercial sites, individuals' blogs, and social networking pages.

Although these back alleys of the Internet have caused considerable public concern, sites that carry potentially dangerous information (such as bomb-building instructions and hate speech) have also incited calls for Internet censorship. The terrorist attacks of September 11, 2001, along with tragic incidents in which armed and disturbed high school students massacred fellow students, have intensified debate about whether such information should be available on the Net.

The Internet in a Democratic Society

Despite concerns over some online content, many tout the Internet as the most democratic social network ever conceived. But this same medium has also presented threats to our democracy—in the form of a division between people who can afford to use the Internet and those who can't, and the Internet's increasing commercialization.

Access: Closing the Digital Divide

Coined to echo the term *economic divide* (the disparity of wealth between the rich and the poor), the term **digital divide** refers to the contrast between the information haves (those who can afford to pay for Internet services) and the information have-nots (those who can't).

Although about 87 percent of U.S. households are connected to the Internet, there are big gaps in access. For example, a 2014 study by the Pew Research Center found that only 57 percent of Americans over the age of sixty-five go online, compared with 88 percent of Americans ages fifty to sixty-four, 93 percent of Americans ages thirty to forty-nine, and 97 percent of Americans ages eighteen to twenty-nine. Education has an even more pronounced effect: Only 76 percent of people with a high school education or less have Internet access, compared with 91 percent of people with some college and 97 percent of college graduates.[18]

The rising use of smartphones is helping to narrow the digital divide, particularly along racial lines. In the United States, African American and Hispanic families have generally lagged behind whites in home access to the Internet, which requires a computer and broadband access. However, another Pew Research Center survey reported that African Americans and Hispanics are active users of mobile Internet devices. Thus, the report concluded, "While blacks and Latinos are less likely to have access to

Access to electronics that some in the United States may take for granted can help close the digital divide in other parts of the world. In this photo, schoolchildren in Vietnam learn through the use of a laptop computer.

Chau Doan/LightRocket via Getty Images

CONVERGING MEDIA

Case Study

Activism, Hacktivism, and Anonymous

Even if you aren't very familiar with the loosely organized group of *hacktivists*—those who hack computer systems in the name of being activists for a cause—known as Anonymous, you may be familiar with the stylized Guy Fawkes mask often used as a symbol of the group. Masks of Fawkes (a member of a 1605 plot to assassinate King James I of England) have been a part of Guy Fawkes Day celebrations in England for centuries. The mask became even more internationally recognizable as a result of the Alan Moore graphic novel *V for Vendetta* and the 2006 film of the same name, in which the main character—part terrorist or part freedom fighter, depending on how you view him—is never seen without this mask. But it might be a different Moore novel (also made into a film) called *Watchmen* that best captures the conundrum of Anonymous as it quotes the Latin phrase, "*Quis custodiet ipsos custodies?*" which can be translated to "Who watches the watchmen?"

Anonymous first came to widespread public attention in 2008 after a video of a fervent Tom Cruise, meant for only internal promotional use by the Church of Scientology, was leaked to the Web site *Gawker*. The church tried to suppress the video through copyright claims, and Anonymous retaliated. It launched a DDoS (distributed denial of service) attack (a flood of outside requests that can slow down or crash a server or network) on the Scientology Web site, inundated the church with prank calls and faxes, and "doxed" the church by stealing and then publishing sensitive internal documents. Since then, targets of Anonymous have ranged from the Indian government (protesting plans to block certain Web sites) to Monsanto (protesting malicious lawsuits and dominance of the food industry) to KKK members (revealing member identities and taking over the KKK's Twitter account because of threats of violence against protesters in Ferguson, Missouri) to jihadists (crashing Web sites in the wake of the attack at the *Charlie Hebdo* magazine in Paris that left twelve dead).

Anonymous is more than an online presence. Real life sometimes converges with the virtual world when live protests feature people wearing the Guy Fawkes mask and refusing to be identified even when they do speak to members of the media. The anonymity is part of the group's ethos. The group has a general agenda of sorts (distrust of governments, protection of a free and open Internet, opposition to child pornography, and a distaste for corporate conglomerates) and has championed causes (both online and with live demonstrators) ranging from the Occupy movement to the Arab Spring. But otherwise, there isn't much organization to the group. Rather, it is made up of individual hackers who act independently without expecting recognition. A reporter from the *Baltimore City Paper* aptly characterized Anonymous as "a group, in the sense that a flock of birds is a group. How do you know they're a

LaunchPad

macmillanhighered.com/mediaessentials3e

MERCEDES HAEFER
"INTERNET DENIZEN"

▶ **Visit LaunchPad** to watch a portion of *We Are Legion: The Story of the Hacktivists*. How does this film seem to portray the practice of hacktivism?

group? Because they're traveling in the same direction. At any given moment, more birds could join, leave, peel off in another direction entirely."[1]

It's often easy to see the moral high ground the group members are taking. But it's also true that members of the group are violating a number of laws when they hack into private systems, cause those systems to crash, and expose the information on those systems. Certainly other hackers have caused serious harm through things like identity theft and the stealing of personal information. This sets up an ethical quandary, perhaps best exemplified when a hacker working under the Anonymous banner was identified and arrested. Deric Lostutter, a twenty-six-year-old programmer from Kentucky, helped to expose the cover-up of a rape of a sixteen-year-old girl in Steubenville, Ohio, by two high school football players in 2012. Lostutter posted a video taken by the rapists and their friends that showed that the girl was unconscious during the sexual violence. For some, Lostutter was a hero, shedding light on a cover-up that ultimately led to indictments against the school superintendent, coaches, and others. But for others, Lostutter was a criminal.

His house was raided by the FBI, and by 2013 he was facing more than ten years in jail for his hacking work. *Rolling Stone* magazine pointed out the cruel irony: "Now he's facing more jail time than the convicted rapists." (One rapist received a minimum sentence of one year; the other got two years.)[2]

In essence, then, Anonymous sets itself up as a sort of vigilante watching over (and sometimes avenging) the deeds of powerful groups or other people guilty of serious crimes who might otherwise go unpunished. Because the members of Anonymous are indeed anonymous, the very flexibility that allows them their form of hacktivism also means that there is no oversight or accountability. Such oversight would likely silence or at least diminish the group, an outcome that runs counter to the ethos of fighting for the widest possible access and freedom of speech on the Internet. And so this leaves us with some profound questions: Do we need anonymous groups like Anonymous to serve as a kind of conscience or "watchman" over the Internet, because governments, corporations, and others in power can't be trusted? And if Anonymous is the watchman, who, then, is watching the watcher?

home broadband than whites, their use of smartphones nearly eliminates that difference."[19]

Other ways of bridging the digital divide include greater public access through libraries and other public facilities, and for cities and other municipalities to offer inexpensive **Wi-Fi**—wireless Internet access—which enables users of laptops, tablets, and other devices to connect to the Internet wherever they are.

Globally, though, the have-nots face an even greater obstacle in crossing the digital divide. Although the Web claims to be worldwide, the most economically powerful countries—such as the United States, Sweden, Japan, South Korea, Australia, and the United Kingdom—account for much of its activity and content. In nations such as Jordan, Saudi Arabia, Syria, and Myanmar (Burma), the government permits limited or no access to the Web. In other countries, an inadequate telecommunications infrastructure hampers access to the Internet. And in underdeveloped countries, phone lines and computers are almost nonexistent. For example, in Sierra Leone—a nation of about six million people in western Africa, with poor public utilities and intermittent electrical service—only about ten thousand people (about 0.16% of the population) are Internet users.[20] However, as mobile phones become more popular in the developing world, they could provide one remedy to the global digital divide.

Ownership and Customization

Some people have argued that the biggest threat to democracy on the Internet is its increasing commercialization (see "Media Literacy Case Study: Net Neutrality" on pages 306–307). Similar to what happened with radio and television, the growth of commercial "channels" on the Internet has far outpaced the emergence of viable nonprofit channels, as a few corporations have gained more control over this medium. Although there was much buzz about lucrative Internet start-ups in the 1990s, it was the largest corporations (Microsoft, Yahoo!, Google) that weathered the crash of the dot-coms in the early 2000s and maintained their dominance.

As we've seen, the Internet's booming popularity has tempted commercial interests to gain even more control over the medium. It has also sparked debate between defenders of the digital age and those who want to regulate the Net. Defenders argue that newer media forms—digital music files, online streaming of films and TV shows, blogs—have made life more satisfying and enjoyable for Americans than has any other medium. Further, they maintain that **mass customization**, whereby individual consumers can tailor a Web page or other

LaunchPad
macmillanhighered.com
/mediaessentials3e

The Rise of Social Media
Media experts discuss how social media are changing traditional media.
Discussion: Some consider the new social media an extension of the very old oral form of communication. Do you agree or disagree with this view? Why?

media form, has enabled us to express our creativity more easily and conveniently than ever. For example, if we use a service like Facebook, we get the benefits of creating our own personal Web space without having to write the underlying code. On the other hand (dissenters point out), we're limited to the options, templates, and automated RSS feeds provided by the media company. So (the dissenters ask), how free are we, really, to express our true creative selves? And how much are we being controlled by the big Internet firms?

CHAPTER ESSENTIALS

Now that you have finished reading this chapter, you can use the following tools:

LaunchPad for *Media Essentials*

Go to **macmillanhighered.com/mediaessentials3e** for videos, review quizzes, and more.

LaunchPad for *Media Essentials* includes:

- **REVIEW WITH LEARNINGCURVE**
  LearningCurve uses gamelike quizzing to help you master the concepts you need to learn from this chapter.

- **VIDEO: USER-GENERATED CONTENT**
  Editors, producers, and advertisers discuss the varieties of user-generated content and how it can contribute to the democratization of media.

REVIEW

Understand Key Points about the Internet's Early History

- The **Internet**—the vast central network of telephone and cable lines, wireless connections, and satellite systems designed to link and carry computer information worldwide—was initially modeled after the highway system. Begun in the late 1960s, the original Internet, **ARPAnet**, was created by the U.S. Defense Department's Advanced Research Projects Agency (ARPA) and used as a military-government communication tool. **E-mail** enabled researchers to communicate with ease from separate locations (pp. 296–298).

- Innovations in the 1970s and 1980s took the Internet from the development stage to the entrepreneurial stage, as a growing community of researchers, computer programmers, amateur hackers, and commercial interests tapped into the Net. **Microprocessors**—miniature circuits that could process and store electronic signals—led to the introduction of the first personal computers (PCs); **fiber-optic cable**—thin bundles of glass capable of transmitting thousands of messages at once—helped make the commercial use of computers even more viable (p. 299).

Outline the Evolution of the Internet

- Though limited to text browsing (content only) and e-mailing capabilities (Web 1.0), the Internet reached the masses for the first time in the late 1980s with the creation of the **World Wide Web**—a free and open data-linking system for organizing and standardizing information on the Internet. Information is made accessible through **HTML (HyperText Markup Language)**, the written code that connects Web pages and links, and **Web browsers**, software that helps users navigate the Web (pp. 300–301).

- The rise of faster microprocessors, high-speed broadband networks, and the proliferation of digital content in the 2000s have pushed the Internet into a new phase (Web 2.0), whereby multimedia, interactive, user-generated functions and media convergence abound. People use the Web for a variety of social media, of which six categories have been identified: **social networking sites**, **blogs**, collaborative projects, **content communities**, virtual game worlds, and virtual social worlds (pp. 301–304).

- The next phase (Web 3.0) centers around a Semantic Web, which reflects the continuing evolution in our relationship with the Internet (p. 305).

Explain the Economics of the Internet

- Commercial entities on the Web strive to bring in money by selling access to the Internet, services for fees, goods via the Internet, and advertising. **Internet service providers (ISPs)** compete to provide consumers with Web access via **broadband** connections, **Web browsers** make it easy for users to navigate the Web, **directories** and **search engines** make money by providing users access and allowing advertisers to engage in **targeted advertising**, online retailers take a larger share each year of the retail market, and an increasing portion of those online sales are taking place through mobile devices (pp. 308–313).

- Noncommercial entities on the Web do not make a profit from the Internet but still strive to innovate in their operations. **Open-source software** is shared freely and developed collectively on the Internet, whereas digital archiving aims to ensure that data is stored and preserved digitally, so that all people have access to it (pp. 313–314).

Discuss Issues of Security and Appropriateness on the Internet

- Government surveillance, online fraud (such as **phishing** or sending phony e-mail messages that appear to be from official Web sites), and unethical data gathering via **cookies** (information profiles that are collected and transferred between computer servers) and **spyware** have raised questions of information security on the Web and what should be considered private (pp. 314–316).

- At the same time, the issues of protecting people from online predators and figuring out what constitutes appropriate content on the Web, particularly regarding sexually explicit material, have sparked public concern (pp. 316–317).

Consider the Internet's Influence on Our Democratic Society

- The Internet has made it easier for more people to voice opinions and become involved in a wide range of topics, but it has also revealed a **digital divide** regarding those who have access to information and those who do not. Mobile technology is helping to bridge the divide, and some cities are looking into inexpensive public access **Wi-Fi**, or wireless Internet access, allowing users to connect wherever they are (pp. 317, 320).

- Questions over commercial ownership and **mass customization**, whereby individual consumers can tailor a Web page or other media form, have raised doubts about the true participatory nature of the Internet (pp. 320–321).

STUDY QUESTIONS

1. How did the Internet originate? What does its development have in common with earlier mass media?
2. Trace the evolution of the Internet from Web 1.0 to Web 2.0. What are the key differences between these two phases of Internet growth?
3. How have major companies tried to control the Internet? Which failed, and why?
4. What are the central concerns about the Internet regarding security and appropriateness?
5. How can the Internet make democracy work better? What are the key challenges to making the Internet itself more democratic?

MEDIA LITERACY PRACTICE

As media consumers, we are virtually anonymous to the people who make the television we watch; the films we see; the music and radio we listen to; and the books, magazines, and newspapers we read. But on the Internet, all of that has changed. How much do media companies follow our habits as we navigate the Web? To help figure this out, look at the computer you regularly use. Go to the Web browser and select "Preferences." Find where the cookies are stored (depending on your browsing software, it might be under "Privacy" or "Security"). Have the browser show the cookies.

DESCRIBE what you see. Set the browser preferences to always ask you if you wish to accept cookies or, alternately, to never accept cookies. Then, when you use your computer, note how often you need a cookie to advance to the next Web page.

ANALYZE your findings by looking for patterns. Can you identify which companies set cookies on your browser? What is the expiration date for most cookies? In your "cookie-less" browser run, how often did you get stopped because the site wanted to set cookies?

INTERPRET what all of this means. Were you aware that so many cookies were tracking your visits to certain sites? Did you give those sites explicit permission? Do you have any idea what the cookie information was being used for? What does this say about privacy and ethics on the Web?

EVALUATE whether this kind of data collection is good or bad.

ENGAGE with your community by writing to the FCC (see the "FCC Complaints" Web page) to register your concerns, or ask someone at one of the Web sites about what kind of information the site is collecting.

10

Digital Gaming and the Media Playground

There is a popular image of digital game enthusiasts (gamers) as being mostly young and male, and spending countless hours either in front of a computer or on a couch in front of a television and game console. But if that ever defined the majority of gamers, it doesn't anymore. Digital games have escaped the confines of living rooms, parents' basements, and arcades. And today, the average age of gamers—almost half of which are female—is thirty-one, with 39 percent over the age of thirty-five, and 29 percent under eighteen.[1]

There are probably several reasons for this, but one of them is certainly the rise in *casual* games: games that tend to feature very little in the way of story lines, focusing instead on repeating games and puzzles of increasing difficulty. Some examples of these kinds of games include *Tetris*, *Minesweeper*, *Angry Birds*, *Candy Crush*, and *Plants vs. Zombies*. An even bigger change is that all of these games—from strategy games like *SimCity* and *Minecraft* to first-person shooters like *Contract Killer: Zombies* and *Call of Duty* (various titles)—have mobile app versions. Whereas portable games like the Game Boy have been around since the 1980s, the sheer convenience of gaming on a device like a smartphone makes gaming a very different, and more common, experience. New games can be searched for, downloaded, and played on devices also used for social media, e-mail, and photos.

That's not to say that traditional console-based gaming, using systems like Wii or PlayStation, is in danger of disappearing. In fact, Facebook—already home to many successful casual and social games, such as *Candy Crush*, *Bejeweled*, and *Farmville*—recently spent $2 billion to buy Oculus VR.[2] The company is responsible for Oculus Rift, a virtual reality headset developed with money from Kickstarter .com. This move by Facebook is somewhat reminiscent of Microsoft's move into the gaming business when it released the Xbox.

As more people play more games in more places, some scholars and critics have started to look more closely at the role digital games play in society and culture. Although concerns about violence have been around for a long time, in just the past few years the growing recognition of the cultural and economic importance of digital games has meant more press coverage (see "Media Literacy Case Study: Writing about Games" on pages 352–353) as well as a growing critique on what the games say about women and minorities. Given that about half of gamers are women, it perhaps shouldn't be surprising that there is an increasing demand for games that aren't designed specifically for young males. Yet there has also been a troubling backlash aimed at critics, especially female critics, who have called for more diversity in games, with less misogyny in games and gaming culture (see also "Converging Media Case Study: Anita Sarkeesian, #GamerGate, and Convergence" on pages 342–343).

Of course, many gamers just want to have fun, whether it be with more "serious" games on their computers and game consoles, or with more casual games on their mobile devices. But with dedicated fandoms rivaling those for books and films in an earlier era, billions of dollars in gaming-related sales, and a confirmed place in popular culture, digital gaming has become more than simple play.

DIGITAL GAMES offer play, entertainment, and social interaction. Like the Internet, they combine text, audio, and moving images. But they go even further than the Internet by enabling players to interact with aspects of the medium in the context of the game—from deciding when an on-screen character jumps or punches to controlling the direction of the story in games such as *World of Warcraft*. This creates an experience so compelling that vibrant communities of fans have cropped up around the globe. And the games have powerfully shaped the everyday lives of millions of people worldwide.

Players can now choose from a massive range of games designed to satisfy almost any taste. Today, digital gaming and the media playground encompass classic video games like *Super Mario Bros.*, virtual sports-management games like ESPN's *Fantasy Football*, and more physically interactive games like those found on *Wii Fit*—to say nothing of massively multiplayer online role-playing games and casual games like *Angry Birds*. Indeed, for players around the world, digital gaming has become a social medium—as compelling and distracting as other social media. The U.S. Supreme Court has even granted digital gaming First Amendment freedom of speech rights, ensuring its place as a mass medium.

In this chapter, we take a look at the evolving mass medium of digital gaming by:

- examining the early history of digital gaming, including its roots in penny arcades

- tracing the evolution of digital gaming from arcades and bars to living rooms and hands

- discussing the rise of gaming as a social medium that forms communities of play

- analyzing the economics of gaming, including the industry's various revenue streams

- raising questions about the role of digital gaming in our democratic society

LaunchPad
macmillanhighered.com
/mediaessentials3e
Use **LearningCurve** to review concepts from this chapter.

The Early History of Digital Gaming

When the Industrial Revolution swept Western civilization two centuries ago, the technological advances involved weren't simply about mass production. They also promoted mass consumption and the emergence of *leisure time*—both of which created moneymaking opportunities for media makers. By the late nineteenth century, the availability of leisure time sparked the creation of mechanical games like pinball. Technology continued to grow, and by the 1950s, computer science students in the United States had developed early versions of the video games we know today.

Mechanical Gaming

In the 1880s, the seeds of the modern entertainment industry were planted via a series of coin-operated contraptions devoted to cashing in on idleness. First appearing in train depots, hotel lobbies, bars, and restaurants, these leisure machines (also called "counter machines") would find a permanent home in the first thoroughly modern indoor playground: the **penny arcade**.[3]

Arcades were like nurseries for fledgling forms of amusement, which would mature into mass entertainment industries during the twentieth century. They offered fun even as they began shaping future media technology. For example, automated phonographs used in arcade machines evolved into the jukebox, and the kinetoscope (see Chapter 7) set the stage for the coming wonders of the movies. But the machines most relevant to today's digital gaming were more interactive and primitive than the phonograph and kinetoscope. Some were strength testers, which dared young men to show off their muscles by punching a boxing bag or arm-wrestling a robotlike Uncle Sam. Others required more refined skills and sustained play, such as those that simulated bowling, horse racing, and football.[4]

Another arcade game, the bagatelle, spawned the **pinball machine**, the most prominent of the mechanical games. In pinball, players score points by manipulating the path of a metal ball on a play field enclosed in a glass case. In the 1930s and 1940s, players could control only the launch of the ball. For this reason, pinball was considered a sinister game of chance, which—like the slot machine—fed the coffers of the gambling underworld. As a result, pinball was banned in most

---

CHAPTER 10 // TIMELINE

1880s Penny Arcades
Penny arcades become popular, showing off automated phonographs; kinetoscopes; and mechanical games, such as strength testers and sports simulations.

1931 Pinball Machines
The first coin-operated pinball machine is invented by Automatic Industries.

1947 Flipper Bumpers
The flipper bumper is introduced by the D. Gottlieb Company, giving pinball players more control.

1948 First Video Game Patent
Thomas T. Goldsmith and Estle Ray Mann patent a "Cathode-Ray Tube Amusement Device," featuring the cathode ray tube (CRT).

1972 First Home Television Gaming Console
Magnavox releases Odyssey, sold for $100 and featuring a twelve-game inventory.

American cities, including New York, Chicago, and Los Angeles.[5] However, pinball gained mainstream acceptance and popularity after World War II with the addition of the **flipper bumper**, which enables players to careen the ball back up the play table. This innovation transformed pinball into a challenging game of skill, touch, and timing—all of which would become vital abilities for video game players years later.

Ken Reid/Getty Images

The modern pinball machine with flipper bumpers.

The First Video Games

The postwar popularity of pinball set the stage for the emergence of video games; the first video game patent was issued on December 14, 1948. It went to Thomas T. Goldsmith and Estle Ray Mann for what they described as a "Cathode-Ray Tube Amusement Device." The invention, which was never marketed or sold, featured the key component of the first video games: the **cathode ray tube (CRT)**.

CRT-type screens provided the images for analog television and for early computers' displays, on which the first video games appeared a few years later. Computer science students developed these games as novelties in the 1950s and 1960s, but because computers consisted of massive mainframes at the time, the games were not readily available to the general public.

However, more and more people owned televisions, and this development provided a platform for video games. Ralph Baer, a German immigrant and television engineer, developed the first home television gaming console, a system called Odyssey. Released by Magnavox in 1972 and sold for a whopping $100, Odyssey used player controllers that moved dots of light around the screen in

---

1972 *Pong*
Atari releases the first commercially successful arcade video game.

1977 8-bit
Processing and
Cartridge System
The Atari 2600, using an 8-bit processor and interchangeable game cartridges, is introduced.

1983 Nintendo
The first Nintendo Entertainment System is released in Japan.

1984 Atari's
Demise
Warner Communications shuts down its Atari division.

1989 16-bit
Processing
Sega releases the Genesis, the first 16-bit console.

The Advertising Archives

A later model of the Odyssey console, the Odyssey², was released in 1978 and featured a full keyboard that could be used for educational games.

a twelve-game inventory of simple aiming and sports games. From 1972 until Odyssey's replacement by a simpler model (the Odyssey 100) in 1975, Magnavox sold roughly 330,000 of the consoles.[6]

In the next decade, a ripped-off version of one of the Odyssey games brought the delights of video gaming into modern **arcades**, establishments gathering multiple coin-operated games together in a newer version of the penny arcade. The same year that Magnavox released the Odyssey console, a young American computer engineer named Nolan Bushnell and a friend formed a video game development company called **Atari**. The enterprise's first creation was *Pong*, a simple two-dimensional tennis-style game with two vertical paddles that bounced a white dot back and forth. Unlike the Odyssey version, *Pong* made blip noises when the ball hit the paddles or bounced off the sides of the court. *Pong* quickly became the first video game to hit it big in arcades.

In 1975, Atari began successfully marketing a home version of *Pong* through an exclusive deal with Sears. The arrangement established the home video game market. Just two years later, Bushnell (who also started the Chuck E. Cheese pizza-arcade restaurant chain) sold Atari to Warner Communications for an astounding $28 million. Although Atari folded in 1984, plenty of companies—including Nintendo, Sony, and Microsoft—followed its early lead, transforming the video game business into a full-fledged industry.

CHAPTER 10 // TIMELINE continued

1989 Handheld Consoles
Nintendo releases the Game Boy, a popular handheld console.

1993 Entertainment Software Rating Board
The ESRB institutes a rating system for video games.

1995 PlayStation
With its CD-ROM technology and emphasis on 3-D gaming, the PlayStation becomes the first console to ship 100 million units.

1999 Online Consoles
Sega Dreamcast becomes the first home console to feature a built-in modem, boosting online play.

2001 Xbox
Microsoft enters the console market, providing new competition for Sony and Nintendo.

The Evolution of Digital Gaming

In their most basic form, digital games involve users in an interactive computerized environment where they strive to achieve a desired outcome. These days, most digital games go beyond a simple competition like *Pong*; they often entail sweeping narratives and offer imaginative and exciting adventures, sophisticated problem-solving opportunities, and multiple possible outcomes.

But the boundaries were not always so varied. Digital games evolved from their simplest forms in the arcade into four major formats: television, handheld devices, computers, and finally the Internet. As these formats evolved and graphics advanced, distinctive types of games emerged and became popular. These included classically structured games played in arcades and on consoles and mobile devices, online role-playing games, computerized versions of card games, fantasy sports leagues, and virtual social environments. Together, these varied formats constitute an industry that now generates more than $45 billion in annual revenues worldwide— and that has become a socially driven mass medium.

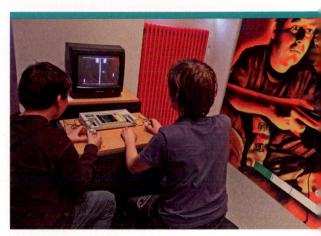

Sean Gallup/Getty Images

Gaming has undergone enormous changes since the days of Atari and *Pong*.

2004 Rise of the MMORPG
Blizzard releases *World of Warcraft*, eventually bringing the MMORPG to a mass audience of more than eleven million.

2006 Motion Controllers
Nintendo's Wii reinvents video gaming with an innovative motion controller.

2010 Kinect
Microsoft unveils Kinect, which reads body movement and voice commands for the Xbox.

2011 First Amendment Protection
The U.S. Supreme Court grants digital gaming freedom of speech protections.

2014 GamerGate
A gaming-based controversy highlights deep misogyny in video game culture.

Marilyn K Yee/The New York Times/Redux Pictures

Though home consoles have become widespread, some gaming fans still enjoy playing in arcades, which have evolved from their earliest counterparts and provide a different social experience from today's Internet-enabled home systems.

Arcades and Classic Games

By the late 1970s and early 1980s, games like *Asteroids*, *Pac-Man*, and *Donkey Kong* filled arcades and bars, competing with traditional pinball machines. In a way, arcades signaled digital gaming's potential as a social medium, because many games allowed players to compete with or against each other, standing side by side. To be sure, arcade gaming has been superseded by the console and computer. But the industry still attracts fun-seekers to amusement parks, malls, and casinos, as well as to businesses like Dave & Buster's—a gaming/restaurant chain operating in more than fifty locations.

To play the classic arcade games, as well as many of today's popular console games, players use controllers like joysticks and buttons to interact with graphical elements on a video screen. With a few notable exceptions (puzzle games like *Tetris*, for instance), these types of video games require players to identify with a position on the screen. In *Pong*, this position is represented by an electronic paddle; in *Space Invaders*, it's an earthbound shooting position. After *Pac-Man*, the **avatar** (a graphic interactive "character" situated within the world of the game) became the most common figure of player control and position identification. In the United States, the most popular video games today assume a first-person perspective, in which the player "sees" the virtual environment through the eyes of an avatar. In contrast, players in South Korea often favor real-time strategy games with an elevated three-quarters perspective, which affords a grander and more strategic vantage point on the field of play.

Consoles and Advancing Graphics

Today, many digital games are played on home **consoles**, devices people use specifically to play video games. These systems have become increasingly more powerful since the appearance of the early Atari consoles in the 1970s. One way of charting the evolution of consoles is to track the number of bits (binary digits) they can process at one time. The bit rating of a console is a measure of its power at rendering computer graphics. The higher the bit rating, the more detailed and sophisticated the graphics. The Atari 2600, released in 1977, used an 8-bit processor, as did the wildly popular Nintendo Entertainment System, first released in Japan in 1983. Sega Genesis, the first 16-bit console, appeared in 1989. In 1992, 32-bit computers appeared on the market; the following year, 64 bits became the new standard. The 128-bit era dawned with the marketing of Sega Dreamcast in 1999. With the current generation of consoles, 256-bit processors are the standard.

But more detailed graphics have not always replaced simpler games. Nintendo, for example, offers many of its older, classic games for download onto its newest consoles even as updated versions are released, for nostalgic gamers as well as new fans. Perhaps the best example of enduring games is the *Super Mario Bros.* series. Created by Nintendo mainstay Shigeru Miyamoto in 1983, the original *Mario Bros.* game began in arcades. The 1985 sequel—*Super Mario Bros.*, developed for the 8-bit Nintendo Entertainment System—became the best-selling video game of all time. It held this title until as recently as 2009, when it was unseated by Nintendo's *Wii Sports*. Graphical elements from the *Mario Bros.* games, like the "1-Up" mushroom that gives players an extra life, remain instantly recognizable to gamers of all ages. Some even appear on nostalgic T-shirts, as toys and cartoons, and in updated versions of newer games.

Through decades of ups and downs in the digital gaming industry (Atari closing down, Sega no longer making video consoles), three major home console makers emerged: Nintendo, Sony, and Microsoft. Nintendo has been making consoles since the 1980s; Sony and Microsoft came later, but both companies were already major media conglomerates and thus well positioned to support and promote their interests in the video game market. Veteran digital manufacturer Sony has the second most popular console, its PlayStation series, introduced in 1994. Its current console, the PlayStation 4 (PS4), boasts more than one hundred million users on its online PlayStation Network. Microsoft's first foray into video game consoles was the Xbox, released in 2001 and linked to the Xbox LIVE online service in 2002. Xbox LIVE allows its nearly fifty million subscribers to play online and enables users to download new content directly to the console—the Xbox One. In 2015, this was the world's third most popular console.

Nintendo released its most recent console, the Wii, in 2006. The device supports traditional video games like the *New Super Mario Bros.* However, its unique wireless motion-sensing controller takes the often-sedentary nature out of video gameplay. Games like *Wii Sports* require the user to mimic the full-body motion of bowling or playing tennis, while *Wii Fit* uses a wireless balance board for interactive yoga, strength, aerobic, and balance games. Although the Wii has lagged behind Xbox and PlayStation in establishing an online community, it is now the best selling of the three major console systems.

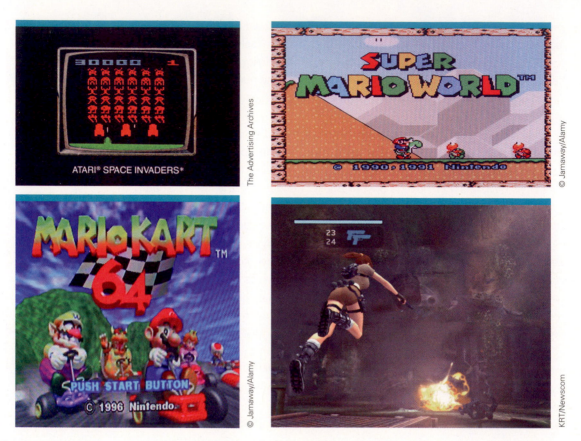

ATARI® SPACE INVADERS®

The Advertising Archives

© Jamaway/Alamy

© Jamaway/Alamy

KRT/Newscom

These images trace gaming graphics from 8 bits (*Space Invaders*) to 16 bits (*Super Mario World*) to 64 bits (*Mario Kart 64*) to a modern 256-bit entry in the *Tomb Raider* series.

Advances in graphics and gameplay have also enhanced smaller handheld consoles. Nintendo's Game Boy, a two-color handheld console introduced in 1989, was one early success, selling far more than the competing Sega Game Gear and Atari Lynx, even though those two systems included full-color graphics. For many players, cutting-edge graphics on handheld consoles were—and remain—second in importance to convenience and simplicity. Nonetheless, the early handhelds gave way to later generations of devices, offering more advanced graphics and wireless capabilities. These include the Nintendo DS and the PlayStation PSP, as well as simpler games played on smartphones and other mobile devices. Handheld video games have made the medium more accessible and widespread. Even people who wouldn't identify themselves as gamers may kill time between classes or waiting in line by playing *Words with Friends* on their phones.

Computers and Related Gaming Formats

Early home computer games, like the early console games, often mimicked (and sometimes ripped off) popular arcade games like *Frogger*, *Centipede*, *Pac-Man*, and *Space Invaders*. But for a time in the late 1980s and much of the 1990s, personal computers held some clear advantages over console gaming. The versatility of keyboards, compared with the relatively simple early console controllers, allowed for ambitious puzzle-solving games like *Myst*. Moreover, faster processing speeds gave some computer games richer, more detailed three-dimensional (3-D) graphics. Many of the most popular, early first-person shooter games (like *Doom* and *Quake)* were developed for home computers rather than traditional video game consoles. As consoles caught up with greater processing speeds and disc-based games in the late 1990s, elaborate computer games attracted less attention.

But computer-based gaming survives in the form of certain genres not often seen on consoles. Examples include the digitization of card and board games. In video games, players identify with a playing position on the screen; in digital versions of card and board games, players remain positioned outside the field of play.

The early days of the personal computer saw the creation of digital versions of *Solitaire*; digital versions of games like *Hearts*, *Spades*, and *Chess* followed. Currently, players can build their skills by playing against the computer and then test their skills by competing in online matches with other people. Sometimes players start online and then transfer their skills to traditional environments. For example, in 2003, Chris Moneymaker (his real name), an accountant from Tennessee, paid $39 to enter a qualifying tournament at PokerStars.com. He then moved from online poker to the face-to-face gaming tables of Las Vegas, where he ended up taking home the $2.5 million grand prize at the World Series of Poker. One of the largest and most vibrant types of digital gaming performs the reverse action, transferring real-world action into a gaming environment: online fantasy sports. Fantasy sports games eventually became a key component of Internet-connected social gaming.

The Internet and Social Gaming

With the introduction of the Sega Dreamcast in 1999, the first console to feature a built-in modem, game playing emerged as an online, multiplayer social activity. The Dreamcast didn't last, but online connections are now a normal part of console video games. Internet-connected players oppose one another in combat, fight together against a common enemy, or team up to achieve a common goal (like sustain a medieval community). With multiple players joining in digital games via the Internet, this form of gaming has become a contemporary social medium.

Some of the biggest social gaming titles have been first-person shooter games like *Counter-Strike*, an online spin-off of the popular *Half-Life* console game. Each player views the game from the first-person perspective but also plays on a team, as either a terrorist or counterterrorist. The ability to play online has added a new dimension to other, less combat-oriented games, too. For example, football and music enthusiasts playing already-popular console games like *Madden NFL* and *Rock Band* can now engage with others in live, online, multiplayer play. And young and old alike can compete against teams in other locations in Internet-based bowling tournaments using the Wii.

The increasingly social nature of video games has made them a natural fit for social networking sites. Many online games—like *Lexulous* (inspired by the board game *Scrabble*) and *Farmville*—are now embedded in these sites. **Online fantasy sports** games also reach a mass audience with a major social component. Players—real-life friends, virtual acquaintances, or a mix of both—assemble teams and use actual sports results to determine scores in their online games. But rather than experiencing the visceral thrills of, say, *Madden NFL 11*, fantasy football participants take a more detached, managerial perspective on the game—a departure from the classic video game experience. Fantasy sports' managerial angle makes it even more fun to watch almost any televised game. That's because players focus more on making strategic investments in individual performances scattered across the various professional teams than they do in rooting for local teams. In the process, players become statistically savvy aficionados of the game overall, rather than rabid fans of a particular team. According to the Fantasy Sports Trade Association, in 2014, nearly forty-two million Americans and Canadians played fantasy sports, spending around three and a half billion dollars in the process.[7]

This kind of online community building has also enabled a fairly recent form of gaming: **massively multiplayer online role-playing games (MMORPGs)**. These games are set in virtual worlds that require users to play through an avatar of their own design. The fantasy adventure game *World of Warcraft* made a big splash when it launched just in time for the 2004 holiday season, growing steadily until membership peaked at around twelve million active subscribers globally in 2010, before those numbers dropped a bit to ten million by 2014.[8] Users can select from ten different types of avatars, including dwarves, gnomes, night elves, orcs, trolls, and humans. To succeed in the game, many players join with other players to form guilds or tribes, working together toward in-game goals that can be achieved only through teams. *Second Life*, a 3-D social simulation set in real time, also features social interaction. Players build human avatars, selecting from an array of physical characteristics and clothing. They then use real money to buy virtual land and to trade in virtual goods and services.

Simulations like *Second Life* and MMORPGs like *World of Warcraft* are aimed at teenagers and adults. But one of the biggest areas in online gaming is the children's market. Club Penguin, a moderated virtual world purchased by Disney, enables kids to play games and chat as colorful penguins. Similarly, the toy maker Ganz developed the online Webkinz World to revive its stuffed animal sales. Each Webkinz stuffed animal comes with a code that lets players access the online world, play games, and care for the virtual version of their plush pets.

Online games have further fostered media convergence. *World of Warcraft*, for instance, is now a comic-book series, a quarterly magazine, and a feature film in development with director Duncan Jones. The "massively multiplayer" aspect of MMORPGs also indicates that digital games—once designed for solo or small-group play—have expanded to reach large groups, similar to traditional mass media.

Consoles, Portables, and Entertainment Centers

In the earlier days of video games, their most prominent media crossovers came when a movie or perhaps a TV cartoon was derived from a popular game. Increasingly, though, games can be consumed the same way so much music, television, and film are consumed: just about anywhere, in a number of shapes, sizes, and styles. Video game consoles, once used exclusively for games, now work as part computer, part cable box. They've become powerful entertainment centers, with multiple forms of media converging in a single device. For example, Xbox 360 and PS3 can function as DVD players and digital video recorders (with hard drives of up to 250 gigabytes) and offer access to Twitter, Facebook, blogs, and video chat. PS3 can also play Blu-ray discs, and all three console systems offer connections to stream Netflix movies. Portable players like the top-selling Nintendo DS, released in 2004, and PlayStation Portable (PSP), released in 2005, are additional examples of converged gaming devices. Both are Wi-Fi capable, so players can interface with other DS or PSP users to play games or even browse the Internet.

Portable players remain immensely popular; Nintendo DS sold more than 154 million units through 2014. However, they face competition from the widespread use of smartphones and touchscreen tablets. These devices are not typically designed principally for games, but their capabilities bring casual gaming to customers who might not have been interested in the handheld consoles of the past. Manufacturers of these devices are catching on to their converged gaming potential: After years of relatively little interest in video games, Apple introduced Game Center in 2010. This social gaming network allows users to invite friends or find others for multiplayer gaming, track their scores, and view high scores on

MAJOR VIDEO GAME CONVENTIONS

Innovation	Description	Examples	
Avatars	On-screen figures of player identification	Pac-Man, the Mario Bros. (right), Sonic the Hedgehog, Link from *Legend of Zelda*	© Jamaway/Alamy
Bosses	Powerful enemy characters that represent the final challenge in a stage or the entire game	Bowser from the *Mario* series, Hitler in *Castle Wolfenstein*, *Donkey Kong* (right)	© Jamaway/Alamy
Vertical and Side Scrolling	As opposed to a fixed screen, scrolling that follows the action as it moves up, down, or sideways in what is called a "tracking shot" in the cinema	Platform games like *Jump Bug*, *Jungle King*, and *Super Mario Bros.*; also integrated into the design of *Angry Birds* (right)	© lifestyleUK/Alamy
Isometric Perspective (also called Three-Quarters Perspective)	An elevated and angled perspective that enhances the sense of three-dimensionality by allowing players to see the tops and sides of objects	*Zaxxon* (right), real-time strategy games like *StarCraft*, god games like *Civilization* and *Populous*	© ArcadeImages/Alamy

Innovation	Description	Examples	
First-Person Perspective	Presents the gameplay through the eyes of your avatar	First-person shooter (FPS) games like *Castle Wolfenstein*, *Doom* (right), *Halo*, and *Call of Duty*	Jonathan Alcorn/Bloomberg via Getty Images
Third-Person Perspective (or Over-the-Shoulders Perspective)	Enables you to view your heroic avatar in action from an external viewpoint	*Tomb Raider* (right), *Assassin's Creed*, and the default viewpoint on *World of Warcraft*	Square Enix
Cut Scenes (also called In-Game Cinematic or In-Game Movie)	Narrative respite from gameplay, providing cinematic scenes that advance the story; often appear at the beginning of games and between levels	Well-known early example appears in *Maniac Mansion* (1987); cut scenes from games like the *Grand Theft Auto* series (right) have become increasingly vivid and complex	The Advertising Archives

Anita Sarkeesian, #GamerGate, and Convergence

Anita Sarkeesian has a well-documented love of playing video games, from *Mario Kart* and *Rock Band* to *Plants vs. Zombies* and *Half-Life 2*. But that hasn't stopped her from becoming one of the most outspoken, and targeted, critics of how video games depict and treat women. In 2012, a successful Kickstarter campaign helped her launch her *Tropes vs Women in Video Games* video series. As Sarkeesian explains, she was moved to examine video games because she saw, as a girl growing up and playing the games, that so many of the troubling stereotypes about women were enmeshed in games and gaming culture.

"The games often reinforce a similar message, overwhelmingly casting men as heroes and relegating women to the roles of damsels, victims or hypersexualized playthings," Sarkeesian explains in a 2014 *New York Times* op-ed. "The notion that

gaming was not for women rippled out into society, until we heard it not just from the games industry, but from our families, teachers and friends. As a consequence, I, like many women, had a complicated, love-hate relationship with gaming culture."[1]

"Love-hate" is probably also a good way to describe the reaction to Sarkeesian's critique of games. On the one hand, she has gained critical acclaim and visibility for her videos and writing, appearing in the *New York Times*, *Businessweek*, and *Rolling Stone*, as well as on *The Colbert Report*. On the other hand, since she began releasing her videos on digital games, she has been the target of incredibly graphic and violent threats of rape, torture, and murder on social media. This ongoing online harassment reached a new low in the fall of 2014, when another of her Feminist Frequency video releases coincided with the #GamerGate controversy.

The story surrounding the event that ostensibly touched off the #GamerGate firestorm started when a computer programmer, Eron Gjoni, had a bad breakup with game designer Zoe Quinn. Gjoni then went online with their breakup, claiming that Quinn had had an affair with a writer at Kotaku, an influential gamers' Web site that features information about a variety of games. #GamerGate supporters pointed to this as indicative of a larger trend of shady journalistic ethics in the gaming press, and also complained that more inclusive indie games were getting too much good press (see also "Case Study: Writing about Games" on pages 352–353). Very quickly, however, the attacks on journalistic ethics were overshadowed by those focused on "slut-shaming" Quinn, as well as anonymous

LaunchPad

macmillanhighered.com/mediaessentials3e

▶ **Visit LaunchPad** to view one of Sarkeesian's videos. Do you agree with her analysis? Why or why not?

threats of rape, torture, and death. Soon the #GamerGate controversy became the name for some of the worst elements of the gaming community.[2]

It was at this point that Sarkeesian (and other critics) spoke up and pointed out that the deeply disturbing threats that Quinn, Sarkeesian, and many other female gamers and critics were experiencing proved her point about a deeper problem in the gaming culture, which in turn reflected broader cultural misogyny. In response to this criticism, many supporters of #GamerGate started behaving even worse.

Soon Sarkeesian and others weren't just receiving anonymous and graphic threats in places like Twitter, disturbing enough on its own, but found themselves victims of doxing and SWATing. To *dox* someone means to steal private or personal information (from addresses and personal phone numbers to social security and credit card information in some cases) and make it public. To *SWAT* someone means to call in an anonymous tip to a police department where a victim lives in an attempt to provoke a raid—particularly by an armed SWAT team—on the person's home. In one such incident, approximately twenty Portland police officers were dispatched to the scene of a supposed armed-hostage situation when the target of the hoax saw someone bragging about it on a message board and called the police before the situation could escalate.[3]

In another case, before a scheduled speech by Sarkeesian at Utah State University, an anonymous person threatened to carry out the biggest school shooting ever if the video game critic spoke. Sarkeesian canceled her speech after campus police said Utah's gun laws prohibited them from turning away any audience member who showed up with a gun. Sarkeesian went into hiding for a time, afraid to return to her home because of the various threats. Her *Wikipedia* page has been vandalized from time to time with pornographic pictures, and her Feminist Frequency Web site has been the target of denial of service (DoS) attacks.

But Sarkeesian is far from giving up. In an ironic twist, the hatred leveled at the critic has brought many supporters her way as well. For example, in the first quarter of 2014, her crowd-funded Feminist Frequency Web site received $1,500 in donations. In the last quarter of 2014 (after #GamerGate really started heating up), donors sent almost $400,000 to Feminist Frequency, which is now officially a nonprofit organization dedicated to providing commercial-free videos critiquing the portrayal of women in video games and mass media. Sarkeesian also quadrupled Feminist Frequency's followers on Twitter to a quarter of a million by the end of 2014.[4]

For a student of mass media, one of the interesting things about the #GamerGate controversy and protests is that they couldn't exist without digital media convergence. Digital game players learn of criticism by reading it from any number of print or online sources or through social media links, or they watch it on YouTube, then they discuss and coalesce as a community (and build anger) on Reddit or in 4chan or 8chan discussion boards, then they lash out again on social media, and then the targets of that harassment take their story back to their followers via social media as well as traditional media outlets. Some gamers take it even further, making death threats and using various computer hacking techniques to attack the targets of their anger (see also the discussion of hacktivism in the previous chapter). Meanwhile, as mainstream journalists began noticing the controversy over #GamerGate, the conversation spread beyond discussion boards to newspaper op-ed pages, cable news and comedy shows, and college classrooms. And as with every other form of media we've discussed in this book, being able to navigate that convergence is essential.

a leader board—which the DS and PSP do as well. With more than 500 million iPhones and more than 210 million iPads sold worldwide by 2014 (and millions more iPod Touch devices in circulation), plus more than 260,000 games like *Blek* and *Minecraft: Pocket Edition* available in its App Store, Apple has all the elements in place to transform the portable video game business.[9] Gaming on smartphones will gather steam as well, especially with Xbox LIVE access on Microsoft's Windows Phone 7.

This convergence is changing the way people look at video games and their systems. The games themselves are no longer confined to arcades or home television sets, while the systems have gained power as entertainment tools, reaching a wider and more diverse audience. Many phones and PDAs operate as de facto handheld consoles, and many home consoles serve as comprehensive entertainment centers. Thus, gaming has become an everyday form of entertainment, rather than the niche pursuit of hard-core enthusiasts.

With its increased profile and flexibility across platforms, the gaming industry has achieved a mass medium status on par with that of film or television. This rise in status has come with stiffer and more complex competition, not just within the gaming industry but also across media. Rather than Sony competing with Nintendo, or TV networks competing among themselves for viewers, or new movies facing off at the box office, media must now compete against other media for an audience's attention.

The Media Playground

To fully explore the larger media playground, we need to look beyond digital gaming's technical aspects and consider the human faces of gaming. The attractions of this interactive playground validate digital gaming's status as one of today's most powerful social media. Players can interact socially within the games themselves; they can also participate in communities outside of the games, organized around gaming-related interests.

Communities of Play: Inside the Game

Virtual communities often crop up around online video games and fantasy sports leagues. Indeed, players may get to know one another through games without ever meeting in person. They can interact in two basic types of groups. PUGs (short for "Pick-Up Groups") are temporary teams usually assembled by matchmaking programs integrated into the game. The members of a PUG may range from elite players to noobs (clueless beginners) and may be geographically and generationally diverse. PUGs are notorious for harboring ninjas and trolls—two universally despised player types (not to be confused with ninja or troll avatars). Ninjas are players who snatch loot out of turn and then leave the group; trolls are players who delight in intentionally spoiling the gaming experience for others.

Because of the frustration of dealing with noobs, ninjas, and trolls, most experienced players join organized groups called guilds or clans. These groups can be small and easygoing or large and demanding. Guild members can usually avoid PUGs and team up with guildmates to complete difficult challenges requiring coordinated group activity. As the terms *ninja*, *troll*, and *noob* suggest, online communication is often encoded in gamespeak—a language filled with jargon, abbreviations, and acronyms relevant to gameplay. The typical codes of text messaging (OMG, LOL, ROFL, and so forth) form the bedrock of this language system.

Players communicate in two forms of in-game chat—voice and text. Xbox LIVE, for example, uses three types of voice chat that allow players to socialize and strategize, either in groups or one-on-one. Other in-game chat systems, like that in *World of Warcraft*, are text-based, with chat channels for trading in-game goods or coordinating missions within a guild. These methods of communicating with fellow players who may or may not know one another outside the game create a sense of community around the game's story. Some players have formed lasting friendships or romantic relationships through game playing. Avid gamers have even held in-game ceremonies, like weddings or funerals—sometimes for game-only characters, sometimes for real-life events.

Sean Gallup/Getty Images

The first *Warcraft* game was released in 1994; the first MMORPG version, *World of Warcraft*, followed in 2004. In this version, players can compete and cooperate within an online game; they can also participate in text-based chatting. A film version arrived in 2016, though the game was surpassed in popularity by *League of Legends* in 2012.

Communities of Play: Outside the Game

Communities also form outside games, through Web sites and even face-to-face gatherings dedicated to digital gaming in its many forms. This is similar to when online and in-person groups form to discuss other mass media, such as movies, TV shows, and books. These communities extend beyond gameplay, enhancing the social experience gained through the game. Sites that cater to communities of play fit into three categories. Some collect and share user-generated **collective**

John Tlumacki/The Boston Globe via Getty Images

The annual Penny Arcade Expo (PAX)—first held in Washington State in 2004— has expanded to include festivals on the East Coast (2010–), Australia (2013–), and Texas (2015–).

intelligence on gameplay.[10] Others are independent sites that operate as community organizers for gamers. Still others are maintained by the industry and focus on distributing promotional material provided by hardware manufacturers and game publishers.

Collective Intelligence

Gamers looking for tips and cheats provided by fellow players need only Google what they want. The largest of the sites devoted to sharing **collective intelligence** is the *World of Warcraft* wiki (http://wowwiki.com). Similar user-generated sites are dedicated to a range of digital games, including *Age of Conan*, *Assassin's Creed*, *Grand Theft Auto*, *Halo*, *Super Mario Bros.*, *Metal Gear*, *Pokémon*, *Sonic the Hedgehog*, and *Spore*.

Independent Sites

Penny-arcade.com is perhaps the best known of the independent community-building sites. Founded by Jerry Holkins and Mike Krahulik, the site started out as a Web comic focused on video game culture. It has since expanded to include forums and a Webcast called PATV, which documents behind-the-scenes work at Penny Arcade. Penny Arcade organizes a live festival for gamers called the Penny Arcade Expo (PAX), a celebration of gamer culture, and a children's charity called Child's Play.

Industry Sites

GameSpot.com and IGN.com are apt examples of the giant industry sites. GameSpot serves all the major gaming platforms and provides reviews, news, videos, cheats, and forums. It also has a culture section that features interviews with game designers and other creative artists. In 2011, GameSpot launched Fuse, a social networking service for gamers. IGN.com has most of the same services, as well as its *Daily Fix*—a regular Webcast about games.

Immersion and Addiction

As games and their communities have grown more elaborate and alluring, many players have spent more and more time immersed in them—a situation that can feed addictive behavior in some people. These deep levels of involvement are not always considered negative, however, especially within the media playground, but they are nonetheless issues to consider as gaming continues to evolve.

Immersion

For better or worse, gaming technology of the future promises experiences that will be more immersive, more portable, and more inclusive. As gaming matures as a mass medium, the industry will use its potential for immersion to attract different audiences seeking diverse experiences.

For example, the Wii's system has successfully harnessed user-friendly motion-control technology to open up gaming to nontraditional players—women, senior citizens, and technophobes of all ages. More motion-controlled gaming is expected, with wireless controls to detect more of players' body movements and even facial expressions. One version of this technology is Microsoft's Kinect system, which uses a sensor camera to capture full-body player motion. The Kinect will also recognize players' voices and faces, making on-screen avatars more accurate likenesses of the players. Used with Xbox LIVE, players can interact in full video or avatar form with friends online.

Another form of immersion has been imported from an older mass medium: In light of Hollywood's great success with 3-D movies, television set production and video games have moved toward 3-D experiences. PlayStation rolled out 3-D games in the summer of 2010, followed shortly by Nintendo's release of its 3DS—a 3-D version of its popular handheld console that doesn't require special glasses.

These technological enhancements are being applied to existing entertainment brands, but video games in the future will also continue to move beyond entertainment. Games are already being used in workforce training, in military recruiting, for social causes, in classrooms, and as part of multimedia journalism. For instance, to accompany related news stories, the *New York Times* developed an interactive game called *Gauging Your Distraction*. The game demonstrates how distractions like cell phones affect a person's driving ability. All of these developments continue to make games an ever-larger part of our media experiences—even for people who may not consider themselves avid gamers.

Addiction

No serious—and honest—gamer can deny the addictive qualities of digital gaming. In a 2011 study of more than three thousand third through eighth graders in Singapore, one in ten were considered pathological gamers, meaning that their gaming addiction was jeopardizing multiple areas of their lives, including school, social and family relations, and psychological well-being. Children with stronger addictions were more prone to depression, social phobias, and increased anxiety, which led to poorer grades in school. Singapore's high percentage of pathological youth gamers is in line with studies from other countries, including the United States (8.5%), China (10.3%), and Germany (11.9%).[11] Gender is a factor in game addiction: A 2013 study found that males are much more susceptible. This makes sense, given that the most popular games—action and shooter games—are heavily geared toward males.[12]

These findings are not entirely surprising, given that many digital games are not addictive by accident but rather by design. Just as "habit formation" is a primary goal of virtually every commercial form of digital media, from newspapers to television to radio, cultivating obsessive play is the aim of most game designs. From recognizing high scores to offering a variety of difficulty settings (encouraging players to try easy, medium, and hard versions) to embedding levels that gradually increase in difficulty, designers provide constant in-game incentives for obsessive play. This is especially true of multiplayer online games—such as *Halo*, *Call of Duty*, and *World of Warcraft*—which make money from long-term engagement by selling expansion packs or charging monthly subscription fees. These games have elaborate achievement systems with hard-to-resist rewards, including military ranks like "General" or fanciful titles like "King Slayer," as well as special armor, weapons, and mounts (creatures your avatar can ride, including bears, wolves, and even dragons), all aimed at turning casual players into habitual ones.

This strategy of promoting habit formation may not differ from the cultivation of other media obsessions, like watching televised sporting events. Even so, real-life stories, such as that of the South Korean couple whose three-month-old daughter died of malnutrition while the negligent parents spent ten-hour overnight sessions in an Internet café raising a virtual daughter, bring up serious questions about video games and addiction. South Korea, one of the world's most Internet-connected countries, is already sponsoring efforts to battle Internet addiction.[13] Meanwhile, industry executives and others cite the positive impact of digital games, such as the learning benefits of games like *SimCity* and the health benefits of *Wii Fit*.

The Economics of Digital Gaming

Today, about 72 percent of households play computer or video games. The entire U.S. video game market, including portable and console hardware and accessories, adds up to about $20.8 billion annually and over $90 billion globally.[14] Thanks largely to the introduction of the Wii and mobile games, today's audience for games extends beyond the young-male gamer stereotype.

Though the obsessive gamers who frequent GameSpot and IGN.com are largely youthful and male, the population of casual gamers has grown much more diverse. These numbers speak to the economic health of the digital gaming industry, which has proven to be recession-proof this far. Digital gaming companies can make money selling not just consoles and games but also online subscriptions, companion books, and movie rights.

Money In

Traditionally, the primary source of revenue in the digital gaming industry is the sale of games and the consoles on which they can be played. But just as the digital turn has altered the distribution relationships between other mass media and their audiences, it has also transformed the selling of electronic games. Although the selling of $60 AAA (top of the line) console games at retail stores is an enduring model, many games are now free (with opportunities for hooked players to pay for additional play features), and digital stores are making access to games almost immediate.

Pay Models

There are three main pay models in the electronic game industry: the boxed game/retail model, the subscription model, and the free-to-play model. Of these, the *boxed game/retail model* is the most traditional, dating back to the days of cartridges on Atari, Sega, and Nintendo console systems from the 1970s to the 1990s. By the 1990s, games began to be released on CD-ROMs and later DVDs, to better handle the richer game files. Many boxed games are now sold with offers of additional downloadable content, known as DLC in gaming circles.

Some of the most popular games are also sold via *subscription models*, in which gamers pay a monthly fee to play. Notable subscription games include *World of Warcraft* and *Star Wars: The Old Republic*. Subscriptions can generate enormous revenue for game publishers. At its height of popularity, *World of Warcraft* earned more than $1 billion a year for Activision Blizzard.[15] Players first buy the game (either boxed or as a download, at $19.99, with expansions costing $29.99–$39.99), and then pay a subscription from $12.99 to $14.99 a month.

Free-to-play (sometimes called *freemium*) is the latest pay model, and is common with casual and online games, such as *100 Balls*. Free-to-play games are offered online or downloadable for free to gain or retain a large audience. These games make money by selling extras, like power boosters (to aid in gameplay), or in-game subscriptions for upgraded play. In addition to free casual games (e.g., *Angry Birds Seasons*, *Clash of Clans*, and *Temple Run*), popular MMORPG games—like Sony Online Entertainment's *EverQuest* and *DC Universe Online*—also offer free-to-play versions.

Video Game Stores vs. Digital Distribution

Several brick-and-mortar stores sell boxed game titles (Walmart, Best Buy, Target), but there is only one major video game store chain—GameStop, which operates more than 6,600 stores in the United States and fourteen other countries, often in shopping or strip malls. The biggest challenge to gaming stores, regardless of size, is digital distribution. All three major consoles are Wi-Fi capable, and each has its own digital store—Xbox LIVE Marketplace, Wii Shop Channel, and PlayStation Store. Using these platforms, customers can purchase and download games, get extra downloadable content, and buy other media—such as television shows and movies—as the consoles compete to be the sole entertainment center of people's living rooms.

Although the three major console companies control digital downloads to their devices, several companies compete for the download market in PC games. The largest is Steam, which carries more than three thousand games from a variety of game publishers. Of course, the most ubiquitous digital game distributors are Apple's App Store and Google Play, where users can purchase games on mobile devices. Although Google's Android system has surpassed the iPhone in market penetration, Apple customers are more likely to purchase apps, including games—a situation that has drawn more independent developers to work in the Apple operating system.

Digital Gaming Tie-ins and Licensing

Beyond the immediate industry, digital games have had a pronounced effect on media culture. Fantasy league sports have spawned a number of draft specials on ESPN as well as a regular podcast, *Fantasy*

Milla Jovovich stars as Alice in the popular *Resident Evil* film series, including *Resident Evil: Afterlife* (2010) and *Resident Evil: Retribution* (2012). However, not all game adaptations have been so successful; film versions of *Super Mario Bros.*, *Doom*, and *Prince of Persia* disappointed at the box office—though gaming companies were still paid for the rights.

© Screen Gems/Everett Collection

Focus, on ESPN Radio. On FX, fantasy football has even inspired an adult comedy called *The League*, while the Web series *The Guild* follows the on- and off-line lives of a group of gamers. Like television shows, books, and comics before them, digital games have inspired movies, such as *Super Mario Bros.* (1993), *Lara Croft: Tomb Raider* (2001), and the *Resident Evil* series (2002–present, including a sixth installment in 2016). For many Hollywood blockbusters today, a video game spin-off is a must-have item. Recent box-office hits like *Avatar* (2009), *Transformers: Dark of the Moon* (2011), *Frozen* (2013), and *Godzilla* (2014) have companion video games for consoles and portable players. Japanese manga and anime (comic books and animation) have also inspired video games, such as *Akira*, *Astro Boy*, and *Naruto*.

Whereas game adaptations of other media can serve partly as advertising for a cross-media franchise, some games also include direct advertising. In-game advertisements are ads for companies and products that appear as billboards or logos on products in the game environment, or as screen-blocking pop-up ads. In-game ad specialist agency IGA claims to put "hundreds of millions of impressions per week" in video games played on PS3, Wii, and Xbox 360 for clients like McDonald's, T-Mobile, Geico, AT&T, and Red Bull.[16]

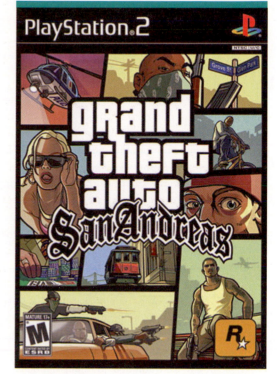

Handout/KRT/Newscom

One of many games in the *Grand Theft Auto* series, *Grand Theft Auto: San Andreas* (2004) takes place in a fictional state based on both California and Nevada.

Money Out

AAA game titles (games that represent the current standard for technical excellence) can cost as much as a blockbuster film to make and promote. With a budget of $100 million, *Grand Theft Auto 4* (*GTA4*) currently ranks as the most expensive console game ever made. During three and a half years of production, more than one thousand people worked on the game. Just obtaining rights for the hundreds of music tracks in *GTA4* involved contacting more than two thousand people.[17]

Development, licensing, and marketing constitute the major expenditures in game publishing. The largest part of the **development budget**—the money spent designing, coding, scoring, and testing a game—goes to paying talent, digital artists, and game testers. Each new generation of gaming platforms doubles the number of people involved in designing, programming, and mixing digitized images and sounds.

macmillanhighered.com /mediaessentials3e

Video Games at the Movies Alice, the hero of the game-based *Resident Evil* film series, fights zombies in this clip. **Discussion:** In what ways does this clip replicate the experience of gameplay? In what ways are films inherently different?

Writing about Games

A host of opportunities await talented writers interested in pursuing a career in gaming journalism. Gaming publications provide information on news, games, and peripherals associated with a popular platform. Some, like *PlayStation: The Official Magazine* and the *Official Xbox Magazine*, are sanctioned by console manufacturers. Others, like *Edge* and *Game Informer*, report on a broader spectrum of the digital gaming industry. Almost all follow a reveal/preview/review cycle, whereby periodicals announce, promote, and evaluate new consoles and games.

Whereas the origins of gaming journalism were dominated by manufacturer publications and fanzines (magazines written by gamers for other gamers), in recent years the gaming press has grown to include more traditional journalism practices, such as those on online sites like *Kotaku*, *Gamasutra*, and *Eurogamer*. Like other forms of journalism, the relationship between reporter and subject can affect credibility as well as create some complicated ethical situations. For example, some independent gaming artists rely on the site *Patreon* (like a Kickstarter site for patrons of the arts) for financial support, and then release material first to their backers from the site. As some gaming journalism sources create policies preventing writers from donating, others have to balance this principle with the journalistic goal of getting the story first (see also Chapter 3's discussion of journalism values and ethics on pages 88–95).

Another problem some gaming journalists have experienced is pushback from gamers who have seemingly grown used to the more fan-based style of reporting, which was less likely to include any critique of gaming culture. As *Vox* writer Todd VanDerWerff suggests, this has led to a "fundamental disconnect between what those who *read* gaming media believe journalism to be and what it actually is."[1] This disconnect probably helped contribute to the #GamerGate controversy, as some gamers responded to criticism of the treatment of women and minorities in games and gaming culture by launching deeply disturbing attacks on journalists and critics (see also "Converging Media Case Study: Anita Sarkeesian, #GamerGate, and Convergence" on pages 342–343).

Another new trend in the gaming press is New Games Journalism. An article published in *PC Gamer*, a British magazine, provided the inspiration for the movement. In the piece, Ian Shanahan (who uses the screen name always_black) relates the story of how a random online opponent opened

LaunchPad

macmillanhighered.com/mediaessentials3e

⊙ **Visit LaunchPad** to watch a video representing a form of New Games Journalism. What problems with video game journalism might this form solve? What problems might it exacerbate?

a lightsaber duel with a racial slur because he assumed Shanahan to be a player of color. Shanahan then transports the reader into a fleeting gaming moment when, for him, winning a routine match carried special meaning and significance beyond the fantasy of the game he was playing at the time of the challenge, *Jedi Knight II*.[2]

Kieron Gillen, a fellow British writer, found Shanahan's article so compelling that he wrote a widely read blog post calling for the establishment of New Games Journalism—an intensely personal form of game writing that would embrace the human side of gaming. The idea of writing about games in the manner of the New Journalism of the 1960–1970s attracted the attention of game writers on both sides of the Atlantic. Citing the examples of Tom Wolfe, Truman Capote, Norman Mailer, and Hunter S. Thompson, Gillen argued that "the worth of a videogame lies not in the game, but in the gamer." If done correctly, New Games Journalism would resemble travel journalism, but would take readers to imaginary places instead of real ones. "Our job is to describe what it's like to visit a place that doesn't exist outside of the gamer's head," writes Gillen, and to "go to a place, report on its cultures, foibles, distractions and bring it back to entertain your readers."[3]

Video game fans may be prepared to write professional articles that follow the reveal/preview/review rituals of traditional games journalism. However, all media students have something to say about their own experiences with digital gaming and the digital playground. New Games Journalism thus counts as a provocative development. With its focus on the player experience, it gives a voice to anyone who wants to comment on this emergent medium.

APPLYING THE CRITICAL PROCESS

DESCRIPTION Investigate New Games Journalism by reading some well-known examples of the movement at http://www.theguardian.com/technology/gamesblog/2005/mar/03/tenunmissable. For purposes of comparison, also read a game review posted on GameSpot or IGN.com.

ANALYSIS Does always_black address you as a consumer, a citizen, or a fellow gamer? What part of the gaming dynamic is important to always_black? How does the standard game review address the reader? What part of the gaming dynamic is emphasized at GameSpot or IGN.com? What type of reader would be attracted to New Games Journalism? What type of reader would be alienated by it? Why?

INTERPRETATION Which form of games journalism—traditional or new—seeks to discover what it means to play digital games? Which form is devoted to reporting information about digital games?

EVALUATION Discuss the strengths and weaknesses of New Games Journalism.

ENGAGEMENT Write your own New Games Journalism article. Report on a particularly meaningful experience you had with digital gaming, or go to a video arcade on a busy night and record your opinions about what arcade gaming means today.

Independent gamemakers must also deal with two types of licensing. First, they have to pay royalties to console manufacturers (Nintendo, Sony, or Microsoft) for the right to distribute a game using their system. These royalties vary from $3 to $10 per unit sold. The other form of licensing involves **intellectual properties**— stories, characters, personalities, and music that require licensing agreements. In 2005, for instance, John Madden reportedly signed a $150 million deal with EA Sports that allowed the company to use his name and likeness for the following ten years.[18]

The marketing costs of launching a game often equal or exceed the development costs. The successful launch of a game involves online promotions, banner ads, magazine print ads, in-store displays, and the most expensive of all: television advertising. In many ways, the marketing blitz associated with introducing a major new franchise title, including cinematic television trailers, resembles the promotional campaigns surrounding the debut of a blockbuster movie. Just as avid fans line up for the midnight release of a new *Avengers* or *Jurassic Park* movie, devoted gamers mob participating retail outlets during the countdown to the midnight launch of a hotly anticipated new game.

Digital Gaming in a Democratic Society

Though many people view gaming as a simple leisure activity, the digital gaming industry has sparked controversy. Parents and politicians have expressed concern about the content of some games, whereas other critics say the portrayal of women and minorities in games is either nonexistent or troubling. Meanwhile, the gaming industry has argued that it qualifies for free-speech protection, and that its ratings and regulations should not necessarily bear the force of law.

Self-Regulation

Back in 1976, an arcade game called *Death Race* prompted the first public outcry over violence in digital gaming. The primitive graphics of the game depicted a blocky car running down stick-figure gremlins that, if struck, turned into grave markers. Described as "sick and morbid" by the National Safety Council, *Death Race* inspired a *60 Minutes* report on the potential psychological damage of playing video games. Since then, violent video games have prompted citizens' groups and politicians to call for government regulation of digital game content.

In 1993, after the violence of *Mortal Kombat* and *Night Trap* attracted the attention of religious and educational organizations, U.S. Senator Joe Lieberman conducted a hearing that proposed federal regulation of the gaming industry. Following a pattern established in the movie and music industries, the gaming industry implemented a self-regulation system enforced by an industry panel. The industry founded the **Entertainment Software Rating Board (ESRB)** to institute a labeling system designed to inform parents of sexual and violent content that might not be suitable for younger players. Currently, the ESRB sorts games into six categories: EC (Early Childhood), E (Everyone), E 10+ (Everyone 10+), T (Teen), M (Mature 17+), and AO (Adults Only 18+).[19]

© ArcadeImages/Alamy

Though unrealistic by today's standards, the violence in *Mortal Kombat* attracted the ire of some parents in the early 1990s.

Free Speech and Video Games

Though 80 percent of retail outlets voluntarily chose to observe the ESRB guidelines and not sell M- and AO-rated games to minors, the ratings did not have force of law. That changed in 2005, when California tried to make renting or selling an M-rated game to a minor an offense enforced by fines. The law was immediately challenged by the industry and struck down by a lower court as unconstitutional. California petitioned the Supreme Court to hear the case. In a landmark decision handed down in 2011, the Supreme Court granted digital games speech protections afforded by the First Amendment. According to the opinion written by Justice Antonin Scalia, video games communicate ideas worthy of such protection:

> Like the protected books, plays, and movies that preceded them, video games communicate ideas—and even social messages—through many familiar literary devices (such as characters, dialogue, plot, and music) and through features distinctive to the medium (such as the player's interaction with the virtual world).[20]

Scalia even mentions *Mortal Kombat* in footnote 4 of the decision:

> Reading Dante is unquestionably more cultured and intellectually edifying than playing *Mortal Kombat*. But these cultural and intellectual differences are not constitutional ones. Crudely violent video games, tawdry TV shows, and cheap novels and magazines are no less forms of speech than *The Divine Comedy*. . . . Even if we can see in them "nothing of any possible value to society" . . . they are as much entitled to the protection of free speech as the best of literature.[21]

However, as in the music, television, and film industries, First Amendment protections will not make the rating system for the gaming industry go away. Parents continue to have legitimate concerns about the games their children play. Game publishers and retailers understand it is still in their best interests to respect those concerns, even though the ratings cannot be enforced by law.

Alternate Voices

While historically much of the concern over video games has focused on portrayals of general violence, in recent years there has been a growing criticism about the portrayals of women and minorities in gaming and gaming culture. As discussed in the opening of this chapter, about half of gamers are female and are increasingly skewing older. This has prompted pointed questions from gaming critics, including avid female gamers: Why aren't more games created to appeal to women? Why don't more heroic female avatars exist? Why are some portrayals of women so deeply disturbing? For example, critics often point out the popular game series *Grand Theft Auto*, which in one of its versions made it so that a character could build up health by having sex with a prostitute, and then get his money back by killing the woman. Other critics also point to the lack of heroic representations of nonwhite characters.

That's not to say there aren't games being written from other perspectives. Online funding sites like Kickstarter and Patreon are helping independent game artists write and develop their own games. Some examples include *Depression Quest*, a nontraditional game that uses a multiple-choice text adventure to simulate the experience of having depression, or *Gone Home*, which engages LGBT issues.[22] These games, although nowhere near as well known as top-tier box games or casual games, have received good reviews in the gaming press.

Decades ago, groundbreaking critical cultural scholar Stuart Hall wrote that even though popular television wasn't considered "high culture" by many social critics and academics of the time, it was still very important to study and understand the cultural messages contained in television because so many people spent so much time engaged with it. He argued that when looking at an entire nation, relatively few people in a society had the time or resources required to frequent museums or attend the opera. But they did own and watch televisions.[23]

Perhaps a similar argument can be made about digital games. In one form or another, they are growing in popularity across ages and genders. Gamers both serious and casual spend many hours engaging with these virtual worlds, absorbing what they see and hear. Once considered a distraction, they're now a prominent part of the mass media landscape.

CHAPTER ESSENTIALS

Now that you have finished reading this chapter, you can use the following tools:

LaunchPad for *Media Essentials*

Go to **macmillanhighered.com/mediaessentials3e** for videos, review quizzes, and more.

LaunchPad for *Media Essentials* includes:

- **REVIEW WITH LEARNINGCURVE**
  LearningCurve uses gamelike quizzing to help you master the concepts you need to learn from this chapter.

- **VIDEO: TABLETS, TECHNOLOGY, AND THE CLASSROOM**
  Tech experts discuss the use of handheld electronic devices like tablets in the classroom.

REVIEW

Track the Main Points of Digital Gaming's Early History

- In the 1880s, the seeds of the modern entertainment industry were planted via coin-operated contraptions. First appearing in train depots, hotel lobbies, bars, and restaurants, these leisure machines would find a permanent home in the **penny arcade** (p. 330).

- The most prominent of the mechanical machines, **pinball**, gained mainstream acceptance and popularity after World War II with the addition of the **flipper bumper**, an innovation that transformed it into a challenging game of skill, touch, and timing (pp. 330–331).

- **Cathode ray tube (CRT)** screens provided the images for analog television as well as the displays for early computers, on which the earliest video games appeared. Computer science students developed these games as

novelties in the 1950s and 1960s, but because computers were massive mainframes at the time, distributing the games was difficult (p. 331).

- Magnavox released Odyssey, the first home gaming system, in 1972. That same year, computer engineer Nolan Bushnell formed a video game development company called **Atari**. Atari's first creation was *Pong*, a simple two-dimensional tennis-style game with two vertical paddles bouncing a white dot back and forth. *Pong* quickly became the first big **arcade** video game. In 1975, Atari began successfully marketing a home version of *Pong* through an exclusive deal with Sears, thus establishing the home video game market (pp. 331–332).

Understand Key Events in the Evolution of Digital Gaming

- By the late 1970s and early 1980s, games like *Asteroids*, *Pac-Man*, and *Donkey Kong* filled arcades and bars, competing with traditional pinball machines. After *Pac-Man*, the **avatar** became the most popular figure of player control in a video game. Though the console and the computer have superseded arcade gaming, the industry still attracts fun-seekers to chains, malls, and casinos (p. 334).

- Through decades of ups and downs in the digital gaming industry, three major **console** makers emerged: Nintendo, Sony, and Microsoft. Nintendo's Wii is now the best selling of the three major console systems (pp. 334–335).

- With multiple players joining in digital gaming through the Internet, gaming has become a contemporary social medium. The social dimension of gaming is especially apparent in **online fantasy sports** and **massively multiplayer online role-playing games (MMORPGs)**. In fantasy sports leagues, real-life friends, virtual acquaintances, or a mix of both draft teams and use actual sports results to determine team standings. *World of Warcraft*, the most popular MMORPG, counts more than eleven million players around the globe (pp. 337–339).

Map the Media Playground

- Many players get to know one another without ever meeting in person. Most online games facilitate player interaction by enabling two types of groups: PUGs (short for "Pick-Up Groups") and guilds or clans (pp. 344–345).

- Sites that cater to communities of play fit into three categories. Some collect and share user-generated **collective intelligence** on gameplay. Others are independent and operate as community organizers for gamers. Still others are maintained by the industry and are primarily devoted to distributing promotional material provided by hardware manufacturers and game publishers (pp. 345–346).

- As gaming technology continues to develop, future experiences will likely be more immersive, portable, and inclusive. Games are still largely considered entertainment, but they are also being used in workforce training, in military recruiting, for social causes, in classrooms, and as part of multimedia journalism (pp. 346–347).

- In a 2011 study of third through eighth graders in Singapore, one in ten were considered pathological gamers, which is in line with statistics from other countries. These findings are not entirely surprising, given that many digital games are addictive by design. Just as habit formation is a primary goal of virtually every commercial form of digital media, cultivating obsessive play is the aim of most game designs (pp. 347–348).

Explain How Digital Gaming Operates Economically

- There are three main pay models for the video game industry: the boxed game/retail model (relying on brick-and-mortar stores and online retailers), the subscription model (gamers pay a monthly fee for downloaded games and access to games played online), and the free-to-play model (offering free casual games on mobile devices but charging for extras) (pp. 349–351).

- Development, licensing, and marketing constitute the major expenditures in game publishing. The largest part of the **development budget** (the money spent designing, coding, scoring, and testing a game) goes to paying talent, digital artists, and game testers (p. 351).

- Independent gamemakers deal with two types of licensing. First, they must pay royalties to console manufacturers (Nintendo, Sony, or Microsoft) for the right to distribute a game that uses the manufacturers' systems. They also pay licenses for **intellectual properties**— stories, characters, personalities, and music used in their games (p. 354).

- The marketing costs of launching a digital game often equal or exceed the development costs. The successful launch of a game involves online promotions, banner ads, magazine print ads, in-store displays, and the most expensive of all: television advertising (p. 354).

Discuss the Place of Digital Gaming in Our Democratic Society

- In 1993, Senator Joe Lieberman conducted a hearing that proposed federal regulation of the gaming industry. In response to this threat, the industry founded the **Entertainment Software Rating Board (ESRB)** to institute a labeling system designed to inform parents of sexual and violent content that might not be suitable for younger players (pp. 354–355).

- Though most retail outlets voluntarily chose to observe the ESRB guidelines, the ratings did not have force of law until 2005, when California tried to make renting or selling an M-rated game to a minor an offense enforced by fines. The law was immediately challenged by the industry and struck down by a lower court as unconstitutional. California petitioned the Supreme Court to hear the case. In a landmark decision handed down in 2011, the Supreme Court granted digital games First Amendment freedom of speech protections (pp. 355–356).

- As more critics and gaming journalists spoke about the need for improvement in the portrayal of women and minorities in games and gaming culture, a building backlash came to a head, beginning in 2014 under the name #GamerGate (pp. 342–343, 356–357).

STUDY QUESTIONS

1. Why were the first video games developed at major research universities?
2. Why is bit rate useful for charting the evolution of gaming consoles?
3. How does online fantasy football differ from the classic video game?
4. What is an example of a Web site that addresses gamers as citizens of a virtual community?
5. On what grounds did the Supreme Court grant video games First Amendment protection?

MEDIA LITERACY PRACTICE

Can you judge a video game by its cover? Game covers, like book covers, serve the important function of informing customers about the content and the pleasures of the entertainment experience. In short, game covers tell players what to expect. They can also tell a potential customer that "this game is not for you."

DESCRIBE the treatment of female figures on the covers of the top ten best-selling video game titles at your local gaming store.

ANALYZE the information by looking for patterns: Do the game covers represent an invitation or a warning to potential female gamers? Which consoles seem more female friendly? Female neutral? Female hostile?

INTERPRET these patterns' meaning. What do these images say about gamers' values and attitudes?

EVALUATE your findings. Consider how problems with the treatment of women on game covers might be addressed. Who is to blame for troubling depictions of women?

ENGAGE with the media playground. Participate in blogs and forums on gender relations in the gaming community. Share what you discovered in your study of gaming covers.

11

Advertising and Commercial Culture

A recent success story of viral online marketing is a product that gets a lot of attention despite rarely appearing on-screen. The product isn't staying behind the camera; the product *is* the camera. Nick Woodman founded GoPro in 2002 after being disappointed in the quality of pictures and videos he and other amateur photographers could capture of activities they enjoyed, like surfing. He set out to develop a good-quality camera that was affordable to amateur photographers, but also durable and versatile enough to capture professional-looking pictures and video. Easily attached to a helmet, a bike, or a skateboard, GoPro videos shared on YouTube started getting millions of views and have become recognizable by their clear fish-eye lens point of view. When the company went public in 2014, it was valued at over $3 billion. The brand has become so successful that the name GoPro is often used to describe any brand of body-mounted camera, similar to the way Kleenex or Band-Aid (both brand names) are often used to refer to any tissues or self-adhesive bandages.[1]

GoPro has a distinct advantage in the age of social media because it's a product that can produce stunning and easily shareable videos, like an eagle-POV shot as the bird soars over an alpine valley (over nine million views) or a firefighter rescuing a kitten (over twenty-five million views). Successful marketing through the Internet and mobile and social media is a rapidly growing part of the advertising industry, as is the risk of making splashy public mistakes (see also "Converging Media Case Study: Marketing, Social Media, and Epic Fails" on pages 388–389). GoPro videos can be entertaining pieces of media on their own, but they're all arguably pieces of advertising or marketing for the brand.

Building ads into TV shows and movies has long been a standard practice, so the convergence of advertising into the digital realm is not surprising. But as advertising has proliferated and become a standard part of our daily lives, it has come to look very different than it did in its infancy. In the digital age, advertising is everywhere, from billboards to T-shirt logos to the beginnings of three-minute YouTube videos.

Regardless of its changing forms, advertising has long played a prominent role in contemporary life. For consumers, ads shape our purchasing decisions. For companies, savvy advertising can drive sales, putting a firm far ahead of its competitors. Advertising has also given rise to whole new industries and lucrative business models—from the Madison Avenue ad agencies that produce slick campaigns for high-end clients to the most basic classified ads created by individuals on craigslist to the search engine industry now led by Google and fueled by online ads. With social media playing such a prominent part in our everyday lives, more companies are hoping to imitate successes like GoPro, finding ways to benefit not only from traditional ad content it creates but also from materials created by the consumers themselves.

ADVERTISING COMES IN MANY FORMS—from classifieds to business-to-business ads to those providing detailed information on specific consumer products. However, in this chapter, we concentrate on the more conspicuous consumer advertisements that shape product images and brand-name identities. So much of consumer advertising intrudes into daily life, causing many people to routinely complain about it. And people are increasingly finding ways to avoid ads—for example, by using digital DVRs to zip through them or by blocking pop-ups with Web browsers. However, because advertising shows up in most media—the Internet, TV, radio, books, newspapers, magazines, movies—it serves as a kind of economic glue holding these industries together. Without consumer advertisements, most media businesses would cease to function in their present forms.

In this chapter, we take a close look at advertising's evolving role in our lives by:

- **examining the early history of American advertising, including the rise of ad agencies, brand-name recognition, advertising's power to create new markets and build a consumer culture, and regulation to control that power**

- **tracing the evolution of U.S. advertising, including the shift to emphasizing visual design in ads, specialization and restructuring of advertising agencies, and the impact of the Internet on this medium**

- **assessing persuasive techniques in contemporary advertising, such as using testimonials, playing on people's fears, and placing products on movie sets or on TV shows**

- **considering the nature of "commercial speech" and regulation of such speech—for example, to combat deception in advertising**

- **exploring advertising's impact on our democracy**

LaunchPad
**macmillanhighered.com
/mediaessentials3e**
Use **LearningCurve** to review concepts from this chapter.

The Early History of American Advertising: 1850s to 1950s

Before the Industrial Revolution, most Americans lived in isolated areas and produced much of what they needed—tools, clothes, food—themselves. There were few products for sale, other than by merchants who offered additional goods and services in their own communities, so anything like modern advertising simply wasn't necessary.

All that began changing in the 1850s with the Industrial Revolution and the linking of American villages and towns through railroads, the telegraph, and new print media. Merchants (such as patent medicine makers and cereal producers) wanted to advertise their wares in newspapers and magazines, giving rise to advertising agencies that managed these deals. These first national ads introduced the notion that it was important for sellers to differentiate their product from competing goods—which inspired more and more businesspeople to adopt advertising to drive sales.

Over the coming decades, all this fueled the growth of a consumer culture, in which Americans began desiring specific products and giving their loyalty to particular brands. Critics began decrying advertising's power to seemingly dictate values and create needs in people—triggering the formation of watchdog organizations and careful consumers.

The First Advertising Agencies

The first American advertising agents were newspaper **space brokers**: individuals who purchased space in newspapers and then sold it to various merchants. Newspapers, accustomed to advertisers' not paying their bills (or paying late), welcomed the space brokers, who paid up front. Brokers usually received discounts of 15 to 30 percent, then sold the space to advertisers at the going rate. In 1841, Volney Palmer opened the first ad agency in Philadelphia; for a 25 percent commission from newspaper publishers, he sold space to advertisers.

The first full-service modern ad agency, N. W. Ayer, introduced a different model: Instead of working for newspapers, the agency worked primarily for companies—or clients—that manufactured consumer products. Opening in 1869 in Philadelphia, N. W. Ayer helped develop, write, produce, and place ads in selected newspapers and magazines for its clients.

Originally called the Joseph A. Campbell Preserve Company back in 1869, the Campbell Soup Co. introduced its classic red-and-white soup can labels in 1897. Today, the label is updated, but Campbell's red-and-white cans remain one of the most recognized brands in the country.

© Richard B. Levine/Newscom

CHAPTER 11 // TIMELINE

1704 First Newspaper Ad
The first newspaper ads in colonial America run in the *Boston News-Letter*.

1841 First Ad Agency
Representing newspaper publishers, Volney Palmer opens the first ad agency in Philadelphia.

1869 First Modern Agency
The N. W. Ayer agency, working for advertisers and product companies rather than newspaper publishers, opens in Philadelphia.

1906 Food and Drugs Act
To monitor misleading patent medicine claims in newspaper and magazine ads, the Federal Food and Drugs Act is passed.

The agency collected a fee from its clients for each ad placed, which covered the price that each media outlet charged for placement of the ad, plus a 15 percent commission. According to this model, the more ads an agency placed, the larger its revenue. Today, while the commission model still dominates, some advertising agencies now work for a flat fee, and some are paid on how well the ads they create drive sales for the client.

Retail Stores: Giving Birth to Branding

During the mid-1800s, most manufacturers sold their goods directly to retail store owners, who usually set their own prices by purchasing products in large quantities. Stores would then sell these loose goods—from clothing to cereal—in large barrels and bins, so customers had no idea who made them. This arrangement shifted after manufacturers started using newspaper advertising to create brand names—that is, to differentiate their offerings and their company's image from those of their competitors in the minds of consumers and retailers—even if the goods were basically the same. For example, one of the earliest brand names, Quaker Oats (the first cereal company to register a trademark in the 1870s), used the image of William Penn, the Quaker who founded Pennsylvania in 1681, in its ads to project a company image of honesty, decency, and hard work.

Consumers, convinced by the ads, began demanding certain products. And retail stores felt compelled to stock the desired brands. This enabled manufacturers, not the retailers, to begin setting the prices of their goods—confident that they'd prevail over the stores' anonymous bulk items. Indeed, product differentiation in brand-name packaged goods represents advertising's single biggest triumph.

The Advertising Archives

Unregulated patent medicines, such as the one represented in this ad for Armour's Vigoral, created a bonanza for nineteenth-century print media in search of advertising revenue. After several investigative (or "muckraking") magazine reports about deceptive patent medicine claims, Congress created the Food and Drug Administration (FDA) in 1906.

1914 FTC
The Federal Trade Commission (FTC) is established by the federal government to help monitor advertising abuses.

1940s The War Advertising Council
A voluntary group of ad agencies and advertisers organizes war bond sales, blood donor drives, and scarce-goods rationing.

1971 TV Tobacco Ban
Tobacco ads are banned on TV following a government ruling.

1988 Joe Camel
Joe Camel is revived as a cartoon character from an earlier print media campaign; the percentage of teens smoking Camels rises.

Though most ads don't trigger a large jump in sales in the short run, over time they create demand by leading consumers to associate particular brands with qualities and values important to them.

Patent Medicines: Making Outrageous Claims

As the nineteenth century marched on, patent medicine makers, excited by advertising's power to differentiate their products, invested heavily in print ads developed and placed by ad agencies. But many patent medicines (which consisted of mostly water and high concentrations of ethyl alcohol) made outrageous claims about the medical problems they could cure. The misleading ads spawned public cynicism. As a result, advertisers began to police their own ranks and developed industry codes to restore consumers' confidence. Partly to monitor patent medicine claims, Congress passed the Federal Food and Drugs Act in 1906.

Department Stores: Fueling a Consumer Culture

Along with patent medicine makers, department stores began advertising heavily in newspapers and magazines in the late nineteenth century. By the early 1890s, more than 20 percent of ad space in these media was devoted to department stores.

By selling huge volumes of goods and providing little individualized service, department stores saved a lot of money—and passed these savings on to customers in the form of lower prices (as Target and Walmart do today). The department stores thus lured customers away from small local stores, making even more money that they could reinvest in advertising. This development further fueled the growth of a large-scale consumer culture in the United States.

Transforming American Society

By the dawn of the twentieth century, advertising had become pervasive in the United States. As it gathered force, it began transforming American society. For

CHAPTER 11 // TIMELINE continued

1989 Channel One
Channel One is introduced into thousands of schools, offering "free" equipment in exchange for ten minutes of news programming and two minutes of commercials.

1998 Billboard Tobacco Ban
The tobacco industry agrees to a settlement with several states, and tobacco ads are banned on billboards.

1990s Beer Ads on TV
Budweiser uses cartoon-like animal characters to appeal to young viewers.

one thing, by stimulating demand among consumers for more and more products, advertising helped manufacturers create whole new markets. The resulting brisk sales also enabled companies to recover their product-development costs quickly. In addition, advertising made people hungry for technological advances by showing how new machines—vacuum cleaners, washing machines, cars—might make daily life easier or better. All this encouraged economic growth by increasing sales of a wide range of goods.

Advertising also began influencing Americans' values. As just one example, ads for household-related products (mops, cleaning solutions, washing machines) conveyed the message that "good" wives were happy to vanquish dirt from their homes. By the early 1900s, business leaders and ad agencies believed that women, who constituted as much as 70 to 80 percent of newspaper and magazine readerships, controlled most household purchasing decisions. Agencies developed simple ads tailored to supposedly feminine characteristics—ads featuring emotional and even irrational content. For instance, many such ads portrayed cleaning products and household appliances as "heroic" and showed grateful women gushing about how the product "saved" them from the shame of a dirty house or the hard labor of doing laundry by hand.

Early Regulation of Advertising

During the early 1900s, advertising's growing clout—along with revelations of fraudulent advertising claims and practices—catalyzed the formation of the first watchdog organizations. For example, advocates in the business community in 1913 created the nonprofit Better Business Bureau, whose mission included keeping tabs on deceptive advertising. The following year, the government established the Federal Trade Commission (FTC), in part to help monitor advertising abuses. Alarmed by government's willingness to step in, players in the advertising industry urged self-regulation to keep government interference at bay.

2007 TV Ad Time
Fifteen minutes of each hour of prime-time network TV contains ads.

2013 Mega-Agencies
Four international mega-agencies—Omnicom, Interpublic, WPP, and Publicis—control more than half of the world's ad revenues.

2015 Super Bowl Record
The average cost of a thirty-second spot during the Super Bowl reaches $4.5 million.

© Bettmann/Corbis

During World War II, government offices around the world engaged the advertising industry to create messages supporting the war effort. Advertisers promoted the sale of war bonds, conservation of natural resources such as tin and gasoline, and even saving of kitchen waste so that it could be fed to farm animals.

At the same time, advertisers recognized that a little self-regulation could benefit them in other ways as well. They especially wanted a formal service that tracked newspaper and magazine readership, guaranteed accurate audience measures, and ensured that newspapers didn't overcharge agencies and their clients. To that end, publishers formed the Audit Bureau of Circulation (ABC) in 1914 to monitor circulation figures. In 2012, the group changed the name of its North American operations to Alliance for Audited Media, a rebranding partly aimed at staying relevant in a time of emerging digital newspaper and magazine business.

But it wasn't until the 1940s that the industry began to deflect the long-standing criticisms that advertisers created needs that consumers never knew they had, dictated values, and had too strong a hand in the economy. To promote a more positive self-image, the ad industry developed the War Advertising Council. This voluntary group of ad agencies and advertisers began organizing war bond sales, blood donor drives, and scarce-goods rationing. Known today by a broader mission and its postwar name, the Ad Council chooses a dozen worthy causes annually and produces pro bono *public service announcements* (PSAs) aimed at combating social problems, such as illiteracy, homelessness, drug addiction, smoking, and AIDS.

With the advent of television in the 1950s, advertisers had a brand-new visual medium for reaching consumers. Critics complained about the increased intrusion of ads into daily family life. They especially decried what was then labeled **subliminal advertising**. Through this tactic, TV ads supposedly used hidden or disguised print and visual messages (often related to sex, like the shape of a woman's body in an ice cube for a vodka ad) that allegedly register only in viewers' subconscious minds, fooling them into buying products they don't need. However, research has reported over the years that subliminal ads are no more powerful than regular ads. Demonstrating a willingness to self-regulate, though, the National Association of Broadcasters banned the use of anything resembling a subliminal-type ad in 1958.

The Evolution of U.S. Advertising: 1950s to Today

As the twentieth century progressed, U.S. advertising changed in several ways. Visual design began to play a more prominent role in ads, reflecting people's growing interest in imagery. This trend helped spark the growth of new types of ad agencies that began dominating the field—large global firms serving a broad range of clients, and small companies working for a select group of clients. Ad agencies of all types developed a distinctive organizational structure, which included specialized departments responsible for such activities as account planning and creative development. But that, too, began changing with the advent of the Internet in the 1990s. The new medium presented fresh possibilities for designing and placing ads, giving rise to entirely new types of players in the advertising sector, including search engine giant Google.

Visual Design Comes to the Fore

Visual design began playing a more central role in advertising during the 1960s and 1970s. This revolution was influenced in part by overseas design schools and European designers—whom agencies hired as art directors and who were not tied to word-driven print and radio advertising. The new emphasis on imagery also drew inspiration from changes in television and cable content. By the early 1970s, agencies had developed teams of writers and visual artists, thus granting equal status to images and words in the creative process. Video-style ads featuring prominent performers (Ray Charles, Michael Jackson, Madonna) soon saturated TV.

Today, thanks to technologies such as mobile phones, tablet computers, and incredibly crisp digital displays, visual design has reached new levels of sophistication. For example, ads on mobile phones feature full-motion 3-D animation and high-quality audio. At the same time, designers have had to simplify the imagery they create, so that ads and logos can show up clearly and scroll vertically on small digital screens. Finally, to appeal to the global audience, many ad agencies are hiring graphic designers who can capture a diversity of visual styles from around the world.

New Breeds of Advertising Agencies Are Born

The increasing prominence of visual design in advertising led to the development of two specialized types of advertising agencies: **mega-agencies**, large firms that are formed from the merging of several individual agencies and that maintain worldwide regional offices, and **boutique agencies**, smaller companies that devote their talents to just a handful of select clients. Both types of agencies wield great control over the kinds of advertising we see daily.

Mega-Agencies

Mega-agencies provide a full range of services—from handling advertising and public relations to operating their own in-house radio and TV production studios.

FIGURE 11.1 // GLOBAL REVENUE FOR THE WORLD'S LARGEST AGENCIES (IN BILLIONS OF DOLLARS)

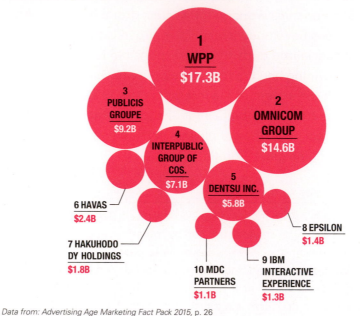

1
WPP
$17.3B

3
PUBLICIS
GROUPE
$9.2B

2
OMNICOM
GROUP
$14.6B

4
INTERPUBLIC
GROUP OF
COS.
$7.1B

5
DENTSU INC.
$5.8B

6 HAVAS
$2.4B

7 HAKUHODO
DY HOLDINGS
$1.8B

10 MDC
PARTNERS
$1.1B

9 IBM
INTERACTIVE
EXPERIENCE
$1.3B

8 EPSILON
$1.4B

Data from: Advertising Age Marketing Fact Pack 2015, p. 26

The five largest mega-agencies are WPP, Omnicom Group, Publicis Groupe, the Interpublic Group of Companies, and Dentsu, with a combined revenue in 2013 of about $54 billion.[2] In 2013, Omnicom and Publicis announced plans to merge, which might have made them the biggest ad agency, but the deal fell apart in 2014 and the merger was called off (see Figure 11.1).

The mega-agency trend has stirred debate among consumer and media watchdog groups. Some have considered large agencies a threat to the independence of smaller firms, which were slowly bought up in the 1990s. Others warn against having a few firms control much of the distribution of advertising dollars globally. According to these critics, with such concentration of power, the cultural values depicted in U.S. and European ads (such as an obsession with youth or appearance) could unduly influence people in developing countries or regions with markedly different values. Such critics decry the intrusion of American culture into these areas.

Boutique Agencies

The visual revolutions in advertising during the 1960s elevated the standing of the creative side of the ad business, particularly the designers, writers, and graphic artists who became closely identified with the look of specific ads. Breaking away from bigger agencies, many of these individuals formed small boutique agencies. Offering more personal services, the boutiques prospered—thanks to the innovative ad campaigns they developed to popularize brands like Nike, ESPN, and Target.

Throughout the 1980s and 1990s, large agencies bought up many of the boutiques. Nevertheless, some boutiques continue to operate as fairly independent subsidiaries of multinational corporations. Due to the economic crisis, both types of ad agencies suffered revenue declines in 2008 and 2009 but slowly improved in 2010 and 2011.

Ad Agencies Develop a Distinctive Structure

Regardless of type (mega or boutique), most ad agencies have a similar organizational structure, comprising four main functions: account planning, creative development, media buying, and account management.

Account Planning

The account planner's role is to develop an effective advertising strategy by combining the views of the client, creative team, and consumers. Consumers' views are the most difficult to understand, so account planners coordinate **market research** to assess consumers' behaviors and attitudes regarding particular products long before the agency develops any ads. Researchers might test consumers' preferences regarding a wide range of things—including possible names for a new product, size of text in a possible print ad, and potential features of a product in development.

Agencies have increasingly employed scientific methods to study consumer behavior. The earliest type of market research, **demographics**, mainly documented audience members' age, gender, occupation, ethnicity, education, and income—and then looked for patterns between these characteristics and consumers' purchasing choices. (For example, what types of clothing and skin-care products do high-earning women over forty years of age generally purchase?) Today, demographic data have become even more specific, enabling marketers to identify consumers' economic status and geographic location (usually by zip code) and compare their consumption behaviors, lifestyles, and attitudes.

By the 1960s and 1970s, advertisers and agencies began using **psychographics**, a research approach that attempts to categorize consumers according to their attitudes, beliefs, interests, and motivations. Psychographic analysis often relies on **focus groups**, a small-group interview technique in which a moderator leads

© Image by Anheuser-Busch/Splash News/Corbis

Budweiser, a heavy spender on ads during the Super Bowl and throughout the year, came under fire in 2015 for advertising on a Bud Light bottle calling it "the perfect beer for removing 'no' from your vocabulary"—a tagline that, as many pointed out, carried connotations of coercion, ignoring consequences of actions, and even sexual assault.

a discussion about a product or an issue, usually with six to twelve participants. For instance, a focus group moderator may ask participants what they think of several possible names for a new brand of beer, why they like or dislike particular names proposed, and what role beer plays in their lives.

In 1978, this research grew even more sophisticated when Strategic Business Insights (formerly SRI International) developed its **Values and Lifestyles (VALS)** strategy. Using questionnaires, VALS researchers today divide respondents into eight types—thinkers, innovators, achievers, strivers, survivors, believers, makers, experiencers—associated with certain behaviors and preferences of interest to clients. For example, an automaker considering which vehicle models to advertise during which types of TV shows might be told that *achievers* watch a lot of sports programs and prefer luxury cars, whereas *thinkers* enjoy TV dramas and documentaries and like minivans and hybrids.

VALS research assumes that not every product suits every consumer, and encourages advertisers to pitch various sales slants to particular market niches. VALS (and similar research techniques) ultimately provides advertisers with microscopic details suggesting which consumers may be most likely to buy which products, but it also stereotypes people as consumers, reduced to eight manageable categories.

Creative Development

Teams of writers and artists—many of whom regard ads as a commercial art form—make up the nerve center of the advertising business. They outline the rough sketches for print and online ads and then develop the words and graphics. For radio, "creatives" prepare a working script, generating ideas for everything from choosing the narrator's voice to determining background sound effects. For television, they develop a **storyboard**, a roughly drawn comic-strip version showing each scene in the potential ad. For digital media, the creative team may develop Web sites, interactive tools, games, downloads, social media campaigns, and **viral marketing**—short videos or other forms of content that they hope will swiftly capture an ever-widening circle of attention as users share the content with friends online or by word of mouth.

FIGURE 11.2 // TOP U.S. ADVERTISERS IN 2013 (IN BILLIONS OF DOLLARS)

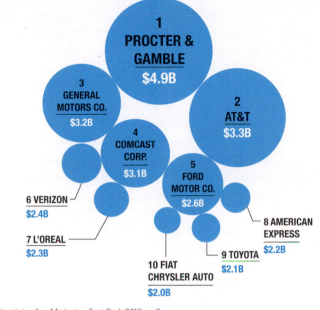

1
PROCTER & GAMBLE
$4.9B

3
GENERAL MOTORS CO.
$3.2B

2
AT&T
$3.3B

4
COMCAST CORP.
$3.1B

5
FORD MOTOR CO.
$2.6B

6 VERIZON
$2.4B

7 L'OREAL
$2.3B

8 AMERICAN EXPRESS
$2.2B

9 TOYOTA
$2.1B

10 FIAT CHRYSLER AUTO
$2.0B

Data from: Advertising Age Marketing Fact Pack 2015, p. 8

Creatives often lock horns with researchers over what will appeal most to consumers and how best to influence target markets. However, both sides acknowledge that they can't predict with absolute certainty which ads will succeed, especially in a competitive economy in which eight out of ten products introduced to market typically fail. Agencies say ads are at their best if they slowly create and then hold brand-name identities by associating certain products over time with quality and reliability in the minds of consumers. Famous brands like Coca-Cola, Budweiser, Toyota, and Microsoft spend millions of dollars each year just to maintain their brand-name aura. However, some economists believe that much of the money spent on advertising, especially to promote new products, is ultimately wasted, since it just encourages consumers to change from one well-known brand name to another (see Figure 11.2).

Media Buying

An ad agency's media coordination department is staffed by media planners and **media buyers**: people who choose and purchase the types of media that are best suited to carry a client's ads and reach the targeted audience. For instance, a company like Procter & Gamble, always among the world's top purchasers of

Lemon.

This Volkswagen missed the boat.
The chrome strip on the glove compartment is blemished and must be replaced. Chances are you wouldn't have noticed it, Inspector Kurt Kroner did.

There are 3,389 men at our Wolfsburg factory with only one job: to inspect Volkswagens at each stage of production. 3000 Volkswagens are produced daily; there are more inspectors than cars.)

Every shock absorber is tested (spot checking won't do), every windshield is scanned. VWs have been rejected for surface scratches barely visible to the eye.

Final inspection is really something! VW inspectors run each car off the line onto the Funktionsprüfstand (car test stand), tote up 189 check points, gun ahead to the automatic brake stand, and say "no" to one VW out of fifty.

This preoccupation with detail means the VW lasts longer and requires less maintenance, by and large, than other cars. (It also means a used VW depreciates less than any other car.)

We pluck the lemons; you get the plums.

The New York ad agency Doyle Dane Bernbach created a famous series of print and television ads for Volkswagen beginning in 1959 and helped to usher in an era of creative advertising that combined a single-point sales emphasis with bold design, humor, and apparent honesty.

advertising, displays its hundreds of major brands—most of them household products like Crest toothpaste, Ivory soap, and Pampers diapers—on TV shows viewed primarily by women, who still do the majority of household cleaning.

Client companies usually pay an ad agency a commission or fee for its work. But they might also add incentive clauses to their contracts with the agency. For example, they may pay a higher fee if sales reach a specific target after an ad is aired—or pay a lower fee if sales fall short of the target. Incentive clauses can sometimes encourage agencies to conduct repetitive **saturation advertising**, by which they inundate a variety of media with ads aimed at target audiences. The initial Miller Lite beer campaign ("Tastes great, less filling"), which used humor and retired athletes to reach its male audience, ran from 1973 to 1991 and became one of the most successful saturation campaigns in media history.

Of course, such efforts are expensive. And indeed, the cost of advertising—especially on network television— increases each year. The Super Bowl remains the most expensive program for purchasing television advertising, but running a thirty-second ad during a national prime-time TV show can cost from $100,000 to more than $600,000, depending on the program's popularity and ratings. Cost thus strongly influences where and when media buyers place ads.

Account Management

An agency's **account executives** are responsible for bringing in new business. For example, if a potential new client has requested bids for an upcoming ad campaign, the account executive might coordinate the presentation of a proposed campaign, complete with cost estimates. Account executives also manage relationships with established clients, including overseeing project budgets, market research, creative work, and media planning done on their campaigns. Account executives thus function as liaisons between the client firm and the agency's creative team.

The advertising business is volatile, and account-management departments are especially vulnerable to upheavals. Clients routinely conduct **account reviews**— assessing an existing ad agency's campaign or inviting several new agencies to submit new campaign strategies. If clients are dissatisfied, they may switch agencies, something that has occurred more and more frequently since the late 1980s.[3]

Online and Mobile Advertising Alter the Ad Landscape

When the Internet made its appearance as a new mass medium in the 1990s, it presented a host of new decisions for companies to grapple with—such as what kinds of ads to invest in and where to place them. It also opened the door for new giants (such as Google) to dominate the online-advertising industry. Building on the popularity of smartphones and tablets, mobile advertising is the latest trend in advertising.

The Rise of Web Advertising

The earliest form of Web advertising showed up in the mid-1990s and featured banner ads, the printlike display ads that load across the top or side of a Web page. Since that time, Web advertising has grown in sophistication. Other formats have emerged, including pop-up ads, pop-under ads, multimedia ads, and—ironically—the classic thirty-second video ad. Internet advertising now also includes classified ads—the most prominent is craigslist—and unsolicited e-mail ads known as **spam**. In fact, a number of companies have emerged in the past few years, several in India, devoted simply to producing spam ads for various clients.

Today, paid search advertising dominates sites such as Google, Yahoo!, and Bing. These search engines have quietly morphed into online advertising companies, selling sponsored links associated with search terms and distributing online ads to affiliated Web pages.[4] This type of advertising is far more precise than the earlier Web ads, enabling companies to reach target customers defined in ever-narrower terms, such as where they live and what key words they use while searching the Web. Some observers claim that clients in the near future will pay only for highly targeted ads and proven results. This targeting is even more precise with mobile advertising, as ads can be tailored not only to what a person has bought in the past but to where that individual is at a particular moment.

Currently, online companies pose a real threat to traditional advertising agencies. Google, as the top search engine, has surpassed the traditional mega-agencies in revenue, earning $59 billion in 2013, with almost all of that coming from advertising. Facebook, the top social networking site, is not yet in Google's league but remains poised to become a bigger advertising threat, with an audience of over 1.3 billion users worldwide in 2014. Facebook earned $7.8 billion in 2013, most of that also coming from ads.[5]

How Online Ads Work

Online ads are generally placed by advertising agencies and served to hundreds of client sites by the agencies' computers. The agencies track **ad impressions** (how often ads are seen) and **click-throughs** (how often users land briefly on a

© CJG-Technology/Alamy

Online ads are mostly placed with large Internet companies like Google, Yahoo!, Facebook, and Twitter. Such services have allowed small businesses access to more customers than traditional advertising ever has because the online ads are cheaper and only shown to targeted users. Social media sites have become particularly popular for advertisers.

site before clicking through to the next site). They also develop consumer profiles that direct targeted advertisements to Web site visitors. Online agencies gather information about Internet users through "cookies" (code that tracks users' activity on the Web) and online surveys.

Mobile phones and tablets have provided a "third screen" (in addition to TV and personal computers) for online advertisers. These devices present the possibility for advertisers to tailor ads to phone users' specific geographic location. For example, a restaurant chain can display a special promotional ad on the mobile phone of someone driving a car or walking in the area of its nearest location. Google has also developed unique applications for mobile advertising and search. For example, the Google Goggles smartphone app enables users to take a photo of an object—such as a book cover, a landmark, or a logo—and then have Google return related search results. Google's Voice Search app lets users speak their search terms. Such apps are designed to maintain Google's dominant Web search engine position (which generates most of its profits) on the increasingly important mobile platform. Other mobile ad technologies include **QR (Quick Response) codes**, square bar codes that link to videos and Web pages when scanned by mobile phone cameras. Smartphone cameras can also be used to launch "augmented reality" views (not unlike the effect of the digital "first down" line in football television broadcasts), which can layer advertising and other sorts of information over a camera's real-time image of a product or shopping district. Google has put that same augmented reality technology into eyeglasses, which have small cameras that "see" what we see, then layer information (and ultimately advertising) in the small screens for each eye. The company rolled out its prototype model in 2013 and made it available to the public in 2014 (with a price tag of about $1,500), but it failed to catch on with the public. Google announced in early 2015 that it was going to quit marketing the glasses for a while so it could develop an updated version.

Advertising Invades Social Media

Social media, such as Facebook, Twitter, and Foursquare, provide a wealth of data for advertisers to mine. These sites and apps create an unprecedented public display of likes, dislikes, locations, and other personal information; advertisers use such information to further refine their ability to send targeted ads. Facebook and other sites like Hulu go even further by asking users if they liked the ad or not. The information users provide goes straight back to advertisers so they can revise their advertising and better engage their viewers. Most social media also encourage advertisers to create their own online identity, with a Facebook page that users can "Like" and share with one another. Despite appearances, such profiles and identities still constitute advertising and serve to promote products to an online audience for virtually no cost.

Companies and organizations also buy traditional paid advertisements on social media sites. A major objective of their paid media is to get earned media, or to convince online consumers to promote products on their own. If you "Like" a particular ad or product on Facebook, your friends may view it, knowing that you like it. Social media are helping advertisers use such personal endorsements to further their own products and marketing messages.

Web Advertising's Growing Power

The leading Internet companies aggressively expanded into the advertising market by acquiring smaller Internet advertising agencies. For example, in the past few years Google bought DoubleClick, the biggest online ad server, and AdMob, a mobile advertising company. Yahoo! purchased Right Media, which auctions online ad space. Apple purchased Quattro Wireless, a mobile ad company, while Facebook bought Relation, another mobile advertising firm. Amazon.com didn't purchase an ad agency but partnered with San Francisco–based online advertiser Triggit to sell ads to Amazon users based on their browsing history. This kind of micro-targeted advertising—based on the data mining of browsing or buying history, social media contacts, and other personalized information—is becoming ever more common as mass media (and other aspects of life) converge on the Internet.

With their deep pockets and broad reach, these companies also began to move beyond the multibillion-dollar Internet ad market and have become ad brokers for other mass media. Meanwhile, the traditional advertising agencies have struck back by expanding their Internet capabilities.

Persuasive Techniques in Contemporary Advertising

In addition to using a similar organizational structure, most ad agencies employ a wide variety of persuasive techniques in the ad campaigns they create for their clients. Indeed, persuasion—getting consumers to buy one company's products and services and not

Matthew McConaughey appeared in a series of ads for the Lincoln Motor Company shortly after his Academy Award win for Best Actor in 2014.

another's—lies at the core of the advertising industry. Persuasive techniques take numerous forms, ranging from conventional strategies (such as having a famous person endorse a product) to not-so-conventional strategies (for instance, showing video game characters using a product).

Do these tactics work—that is, do they boost sales? This is a tough question, because it's difficult to distinguish an ad's impact on consumers from the effects of other cultural and social forces. But companies continue investing in advertising on the assumption that without the product and brand awareness that advertising builds, consumers just might go to a competitor.

Using Conventional Persuasive Strategies

Advertisers have long used a number of conventional persuasive strategies.

1. **Famous-person testimonial:** A product is endorsed by a well-known person. For example, Serena Williams has become a leading sports spokesperson, having appeared in ads for such companies as Nike, Kraft Foods, and Procter & Gamble.
2. **Plain-folks pitch:** A product is associated with simplicity. For instance, General Electric ("Imagination at work") and Microsoft ("Your potential. Our passion") have used straightforward slogans stressing how new technologies fit into the lives of ordinary people.
3. **Snob appeal:** An ad attempts to persuade consumers that using a product will maintain or elevate their social status. Advertisers selling jewelry, perfume, clothing, and luxury automobiles often use snob appeal.
4. **Bandwagon effect:** The ad claims that "everyone" is using a particular product. Brands that refer to themselves as "America's favorite" or "the best-selling" imply that consumers will be "left behind" if they ignore these products.

5. **Hidden-fear appeal:** A campaign plays on consumers' sense of insecurity. Deodorant, mouthwash, and shampoo ads often tap into people's fears of having embarrassing personal hygiene problems if they don't use the suggested product.

6. **Irritation advertising:** An ad creates product-name recognition by being annoying or obnoxious. (You may have seen one of these on TV, in the form of a local car salesman loudly touting the "UNBELIEVABLE BARGAINS!" available at his dealership.)

Associating Products with Values

In addition to the conventional persuasive techniques just described, ad agencies draw on the **association principle** in many campaigns for consumer products. Through this technique, the agency associates a product with a positive cultural value or image—even if that value or image has little connection to the product. For example, many ads displayed visual symbols of American patriotism in the wake of the 9/11 terrorist attacks in an attempt to associate products and companies with national pride.

Yet this technique has also been used to link products with stereotyped caricatures of targeted consumer groups, such as men, women, or specific ethnic groups. For example, many ads have sought to appeal to women by portraying men as idiots who know nothing about how to use a washing machine or how to heat up leftovers for dinner. The assumption is that portraying men as idiots will make women feel better about themselves—and thus be attracted to the advertised product (see "Media Literacy Case Study: Idiots and Objects: Stereotyping in Advertising" on pages 382–383).

Another popular use of the association principle is to claim that products are "real" and "natural"—possibly the most common adjectives used in advertising. For example, Coke sells itself as "the real thing." The cosmetics industry offers synthetic products that make us look "natural." And "green" marketing touts products that are often manufactured and not always environmentally friendly.

In the 1950s and 1960s, Philip Morris used the association principle to transform the image of its Marlboro filtered cigarette brand (considered a product for women in the 1920s) into a product for men. Ad campaigns featured images of active, rugged males, particularly cowboys. Three of the men who appeared in these ad campaigns eventually died of lung cancer caused by cigarette smoking. But that apparently hasn't blunted the brand's impact. By 2014, the branding consultancy BrandZ had named Marlboro the world's ninth "most powerful

Idiots and Objects: Stereotyping in Advertising

Over the years, critics and consumers alike have complained about stereotyping in mainstream advertising. *Stereotyping* refers to the process of assigning people to abstract groups whose members are assumed to act as a single entity—rather than as individuals with distinct identities—and to display shared characteristics, which often have negative connotations.

Today, particularly in beer ads, men are often stereotyped as inept or stupid, incapable of negotiating a routine day or a normal conversation unless fortified—or dulled—by the heroic product. Throughout advertising history, men have often been portrayed as doofuses and idiots when confronted by ordinary food items or a simple household appliance.

On the other hand, in the early history of product ads on television, women were often stereotyped as naïve or emotional, needing the experienced voice of a rational male narrator to guide them around their own homes. Ads have also stereotyped women as brainless or helpless or offered them as a man's reward for drinking a particular beer, wearing cool jeans, or smoking the right cigarette. Worst of all, women, or even parts of women—with their heads cut from the frame—have been used as objects, merely associated with a particular product (e.g., a swimsuit model holding a new car muffler or wrapped around a bottle of Scotch). Influenced by the women's movement and critiques of advertising culture, such as Betty Friedan's *The Feminine Mystique* (1963), ads depicting women have changed in some cases. Although many sexist stereotypes still persist in advertising, women today are portrayed in a variety of social roles.

In addition to ads that have stereotyped men and women, there is also invisible stereotyping. This occurs when whole segments of the population are ignored—particularly African, Arab, Asian, Latin, and Native Americans. Advertising—especially in its early history—has often faced criticism that many segments of the varied and multicultural U.S. population have been missing or underrepresented in the ads and images that dominate the landscape.

In the last several years, however, conscious of how diverse the United States has become, some ad campaigns have been making changes. One example of this is a series of ads for the breakfast cereal Cheerios (a brand owned by General Mills). In the summer of 2013, the company released an ad that featured a white mom, an African American father, and a biracial daughter. The ad received praise from some advertising critics but garnered so many racist comments on YouTube (where the company

LaunchPad
macmillanhighered.com/mediaessentials3e

⊙ **Visit LaunchPad** to watch a *Saturday Night Live* ad that parodies football-themed snack ads. What do you think the ad is saying about stereotyping in advertisements?

also posted the ad) that it had to disable the commenting function. In early 2014, Cheerios debuted an ad during the Super Bowl featuring the same mother and father telling the little girl she was going to get a little brother; later that year, the company started another ad campaign that included two gay white dads from Quebec talking in a heartfelt way about the adoption of their black daughter. In all of these cases, some groups hailed them as progress while others ripped them apart, often with racist or homophobic slurs.[1]

Italian clothing manufacturer Benetton has a long history of tackling controversial topics, ranging from interracial relationships to kissing politicians, in its United Colors of Benetton advertisements. The most famous of these do not actually show any of the clothes the company makes—just a small logo somewhere in the photograph. More than the tame domestic scenes presented in the Cheerios ads, the photos in the Benetton marketing campaigns are much more provocative—and controversial on multiple levels.

In both cases, some media critics have praised the companies for presenting more diversity and social awareness in their advertising while remaining skeptical of the motives behind the ads. After all, they say, the first goal of advertising is to boost sales.

APPLYING THE CRITICAL PROCESS

DESCRIPTION Gather four to six advertisements from various newspapers, magazines, or Internet sites that feature individuals (and not just products).

ANALYSIS Examine the content of each ad: What product is being sold? What are the profiles of the people who appear in the ad, or what are they doing? Note the publication or Web site each ad comes from. What patterns emerge, and what do these patterns suggest to you?

INTERPRETATION What do the patterns mean? How are the people in each ad helping to sell the product? What is the message that each ad is trying to portray? Why did the advertiser choose the specific newspaper, magazine, or Internet site to advertise the product?

EVALUATION Do any of the ads foster existing stereotypes? Explain how they do or do not. Do you think these ads are effective? How might the stereotypes in these ads convey a distorted or mixed message to the consumer?

ENGAGEMENT Choose one ad from your selection to revise. How might you redesign this ad to remove existing stereotypes? Compose a draft. Do you think your ad is more or less effective than the original? Explain your answer.

TABLE 11.1 // THE TOP 10 GLOBAL BRANDS

Rank	Brand	Brand Value ($Millions)	Brand Value Change, 2014 vs. 2013 (%)
1	Google	158,843	40
2	Apple	147,880	−20
3	IBM	107,541	−4
4	Microsoft	90,185	29
5	McDonalds	85,706	−5
6	Coca-Cola*	80,683	3
7	Visa	79,197	41
8	AT&T	77,883	3
9	Marlboro	67,341	−3
10	Amazon.com	64,255	41

Coca-Cola includes Diet Coke, Coke Light, and Coke Zero.

Data from: "BrandZ Top 100 Most Powerful Brands 2014," Millward Brown Optimor, www.millwardbrown.com/brandz /2014/Top100/Docs/2014_BrandZ_Top100_Chart.pdf

[memorable] brand," having an estimated worth of $67.3 billion. (Google, Apple, and IBM were the top three rated brands; see Table 11.1.)

Telling Stories

Many ads also tell stories that contain elements found in myths (narratives that convey a culture's deepest values and social norms). For example, an ad might take the shape of a mini-drama or sitcom, complete with characters, settings, and plots. Perhaps a character experiences a conflict or problem of some type. The character resolves the situation by the end of the ad, usually by purchasing or using the product. The product and those who use it emerge as the heroes of the story.

For instance, in the early 2000s, ads for GEICO car insurance featured TV commercials that looked like thirty-second sitcoms. The ad's plot lines told the story of cavemen trying to cope in the modern world but who found themselves constantly ridiculed—for being cavemen ("so easy a caveman can do it"). The point of the ads included associating the product with humor, making the audience feel superior to dim-witted prehistoric guys. The ads were funny and popular, and ABC actually commissioned a short-lived sitcom called *Cavemen* based on the ads' characters.

Although most of us realize that ads telling stories create a fictional world, we often can't help but get caught up in them. That's because they reinforce our values and assumptions about how the world works. And they reassure us that by using familiar brand names—packaged in comforting mini-stories—we can manage the everyday tensions and problems that confront us.

Placing Products in Media

Product placement—strategically placing ads or buying space in movies, TV shows, comic books, and video games so that they appear as part of a story's set environment—is another persuasive strategy ad agencies use. For example, the 2010 movie *Iron Man 2* features product placements from over sixty brands, almost triple the number shown in the original 2008 film, which included prominent use of brands like Burger King, Audi, and LG mobile. The NBC sitcom *30 Rock* even made fun of product placement, satirizing how widespread it had become. In one scene, the actors talk about how great Diet Snapple is. Then an actual commercial for Snapple appears.

Many critics argue that product placement has gotten out of hand. In 2005, watchdog organization Commercial Alert asked both the FTC and the FCC to mandate that consumers be warned about product placement in television shows. The FTC rejected the petition, and by 2008 the FCC had still made no formal response to the request. Most defenders of product placement argue that there is little or no concrete evidence or research that this practice harms consumers. The 2011 documentary *POM Wonderful Presents: The Greatest Movie Ever Sold* takes a satirical look at product placement—and filmmaker Morgan Spurlock financed the film's entire budget using that very strategy.

Commercial Speech and Regulating Advertising

Advertisements are considered **commercial speech**—defined as any print or broadcast expression for which a fee is charged to organizations and individuals buying time or space in the mass media. Though the U.S. Constitution's First Amendment protects freedom of speech and of the press, it doesn't specify whether advertisers can say anything they want in their commercial speech; thus, the question of whether commercial speech is protected by the Constitution is tricky. In some critics' view, certain forms of advertising can have destructive consequences and therefore should be regulated. These

LaunchPad

macmillanhighered.com
/mediaessentials3e

**Advertising and Effects
on Children**
Scholars and advertisers
analyze the effects of
advertising on children.
Discussion: In the video,
some argue that using cute,
kid-friendly imagery in alcohol ads can lead children
to begin drinking; others
dispute this claim. What do
you think, and why?

include ads that target children, that tout unhealthy products (such as alcohol and tobacco), that prompt people to adopt dangerous behaviors (such as starving themselves to look like models in magazines), and that hawk prescription medications directly to consumers instead of to doctors.

To be sure, no one has figured out just how much power such ads have to actually influence target consumers. Indeed, studies have suggested that 75 to 90 percent of new consumer products fail because the buying public doesn't embrace them—suggesting that advertising isn't as effective as some critics might think.[6] Nevertheless, serious concerns over the impact of advertising persist.

Targeting Children and Teens

Because children and teenagers may influence billions of dollars each year in family spending—on everything from snacks to cars—advertisers have increasingly targeted them, often viewing young people as "consumers in training." When ads influence youngsters in a good way (for example, by getting them interested in reading books), no one complains about advertising's power. It's when ads influence kids and teens in what is perceived as a dangerous way (such as tempting them with unhealthy foods) that concerns arise.

For years, groups such as Action for Children's Television (ACT) worked to limit advertising aimed at children (especially ads promoting toys associated with a show). In addition, parent groups have pushed to limit the heavy promotion of unhealthy products like sugar-coated cereals during children's TV programs. Congress has responded weakly, hesitant to question the First Amendment's protection of commercial speech and pressured by determined lobbying from the advertising industry. The Children's Television Act of 1990 mandated that networks provide some educational and informational children's programming, but the act has been difficult to enforce and has done little to restrict advertising aimed at kids.

In addition to trying to control TV advertising aimed at young people, critics have complained about advertising that has encroached on school property. The introduction of Channel One into thousands of schools during the 1989–90 school year has been one of the most controversial cases of in-school advertising. The brainchild of advertising firm Whittle Communications, Channel One offered free video and satellite equipment (tuned exclusively to Channel One) in exchange for a twelve-minute package of current events programming that included two minutes of commercials.

Over the years, the National Dairy Council and other organizations have also used schools to promote products—for example, by providing free filmstrips, posters, magazines, folders, and study guides adorned with member companies' logos. Many teachers, especially in underfunded districts, have been grateful for these free materials. However, many parent and teacher groups have objected to Channel One (now in about eight thousand middle and high schools in the United States), which in their view requires teens to watch commercial messages in a learning environment.

Triggering Anorexia and Overeating

Some critics accuse ads of contributing to anorexia among girls and women; others, of contributing to obesity among young and adult Americans. To be sure, companies have long marketed fashions and cosmetics by showing ultrathin female models using their products. Through such campaigns, advertising strongly shapes standards of beauty in our culture. Many girls and women apparently feel compelled to achieve those standards—even if it means starving themselves or having repeated cosmetic surgeries.

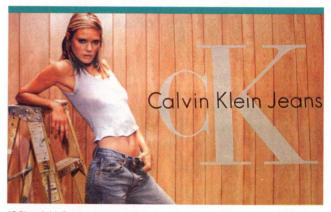

AP Photo/L.M. Otero

Critics argue that toothpick-sized models set unattainable standards that can lead to eating disorders among women.

At the same time, advertising has been blamed for the tripling of obesity rates in the United States since the 1980s. Corn-syrup-laden soft drinks, fast food, junk food, and processed food are the staples of media advertising. Critics maintain that advertisements for fattening products have directly contributed to widespread obesity in the United States. The food and restaurant industry has denied this connection. Industry advocates claim that people have the power to decide what they eat—and many individuals are making poor choices, such as eating too much fast food.

Promoting Smoking

One of the most sustained criticisms of advertising is its promotion of tobacco consumption. Each year, an estimated 400,000 Americans die from diseases related to nicotine addiction and poisoning. Still, for a long time tobacco companies kept cranking out ad campaigns designed to win over new customer segments, which often included teenagers.

The government's position regarding the tobacco industry began changing in the mid-1990s. At that time, new reports revealed that tobacco companies had

Case Study

Marketing, Social Media, and Epic Fails

In the fall of 2014, things were going well for the New England Patriots football team, not only on the field but also on social media; by November, the team was up to one million followers on Twitter. When it hit that number, the marketers running the team's Twitter account tweeted a thank-you, which they asked their fans to RT (retweet). Fans who did that would see another tweet from the Patriots' account, with a picture of their Twitter handle digitally printed on the back of a Patriots jersey. It seemed to go well until the team inadvertently posted a picture, visible to all one million of its followers, of a jersey with a blatantly offensive racial slur on the back. Many people complained, and the offensive tweet was deleted from the Patriots' account—but not before the image was captured, leading to plenty of news coverage over the next few days.

In addition to using the more traditional method of paid advertising to promote a product, brand, or person online, the holy grail of online marketing is the kind that receives massive and mostly free exposure by going *viral*—that is, marketing that's shared and reshared on social media, spreading across the Internet. Although a company might pay a great deal of money for a social media campaign, whether or not it will go viral on Twitter, Tumblr, and so on, is out of its hands. But if a piece of advertising catches on, it can be a very powerful way to spread a marketing message. Not only that, but sharing between friends on social media is the digital equivalent of a word-of-mouth recommendation—also highly prized by marketers. But this kind of accessibility can be a double-edged sword; just as social media can amplify a marketing message, it can also amplify a mistake.

Some social media catastrophes, like the situation with the Patriots, are the result of a group attempting to start something positive, only to see it backfire once control of the message switches to the public. Other cases can offer a chance for social commentary. For example, in the spring of 2014, the New York Police Department's Twitter page, @NYPDnews, asked users to tweet photos of members of the public interacting with NYPD officers. Clearly, the department was hoping for positive pictures. What they also got were a number of pictures showing what looked like police abusing their power—and members of the public. For example, one tweet showed a picture of an officer kneeling on the neck and upper torso of a man lying on the ground, accompanied by the words: "You might not have known this, but the NYPD can help you with the kink in your neck. #myNYPD."

A fake ad made by the comedy program Saturday Night Live *parodies the use of stereotypes in advertising and the negative reactions they engender. Watch the parody on LaunchPad for* Media Essentials.

Other social media disasters are simply mistakes that are corrected relatively quickly—but not fast enough to outrun the speed of the Internet. An employee at U.S. Airways found this out the hard way after responding to a customer service complaint on Twitter by tweeting back a graphically pornographic picture. An internal investigation later determined it had been unintentional.

Two other ways brands get into trouble in the social media world include ill-conceived attempts at humor or latching on to a trending hashtag. Frozen pizza company DiGiorno found itself in the hot seat in 2014 when it decided to tweet: "#WhyIStayed You had pizza." The problem: At that time, the hashtag #WhyIStayed was trending on Twitter as survivors of domestic abuse explained why they stayed in abusive relationships. The pizza company quickly apologized, saying it hadn't read what the hashtag was about before posting.

Experts in marketing and advertising are always watching cases like this and hoping to learn how to get the most positive social media buzz (see also the chapter introduction on GoPro) while avoiding a social media fail. As we've discussed throughout this chapter (and this book), online and social media advertising continues to be a rapidly growing part of the mass media industry. Companies, brands, and ad agencies that learn to successfully navigate the social media waters will have a big advantage.

known that nicotine was addictive as far back as the 1950s and had withheld that information from the public. Settlements between the industry and states have put significant limits on advertising and marketing of tobacco products. For example, ads cannot use cartoon characters such as Joe Camel, because such characters appeal to young people. And companies can't show ads on billboards or in subway or commuter trains, where young people might be vulnerable to them. In June 2009, President Obama, himself a professed addicted smoker since his teen years, signed the Family Smoking Prevention and Tobacco Control Act. The act allows the Food and Drug Administration (FDA) to lessen the nicotine in tobacco products and block misleading cigarette-packaging labels that say "low tar" and "light." Despite these restrictions, tobacco companies still spend about $9 billion annually on U.S. advertisements—more than twenty times the amount spent on anti-tobacco public service spots.

Promoting Drinking

In 2013, 88,000 people in the United States died from alcohol-related diseases; another 10,000 lost their lives in car crashes involving drunk drivers. Many of the same complaints regarding tobacco advertising are also being leveled at alcohol ads. For example, critics have protested that one of the most popular beer campaigns of the late 1990s—featuring a trio of frogs croaking *Budweis-errrr*—used cartoon-like animal characters to appeal to young viewers. Some alcohol ads, such as Pabst Brewing Company's ads featuring Snoop Dogg for Blast by Colt 45 (a strong flavored malt beverage that the Massachusetts attorney general called "binge-in-a can"), have targeted young minority populations specifically.

The alcohol industry has also heavily targeted college students with ads, especially for beer. The images and slogans in alcohol ads often associate the products with power, romance, sexual prowess, or athletic skill. In reality, though, alcohol is a depressant: It diminishes athletic ability and sexual performance, triggers addiction in as much as 10 percent of the U.S. population, and factors into many domestic-abuse cases. Thus, many ads present a false impression of what alcohol products can do for consumers.

Hawking Drugs Directly to Consumers

New advertising tactics by the pharmaceutical industry—such as marketing directly to consumers instead of to doctors—have also drawn fire from critics worried about vulnerable groups of consumers. According to a study by the Kaiser Family Foundation, from 1994 to 2007, spending on direct-to-consumer advertising for prescription drugs soared from $266 million to $5.3 billion. About two-thirds of such ads are shown on television, and they've proved effective for the pharmaceutical companies that invest in and use them. A survey found that nearly one in three adults has talked to a doctor about a particular drug after seeing an ad for it on TV, and one in eight subsequently received a prescription. The tremendous growth of prescription drug ads brings with it the potential for misleading or downright false claims. That's because a brief TV advertisement can't effectively communicate all of the cautionary information consumers need to know about these medications.

Monitoring the Advertising Industry

Worried about advertising's power over vulnerable consumers, a few nonprofit watchdog and advocacy organizations, such as Commercial Alert and the American Legacy Foundation, have emerged. Such groups strive to compensate for some of the shortcomings of the FTC and other government agencies in monitoring false and deceptive ads and the excesses of commercialism. At the same time, the FTC is still trying to combat the negative impact of advertising, though its effectiveness remains questionable, especially in light of cutbacks at the agency that have been going on since the 1980s.

Commercial Alert

Since 1998, Commercial Alert has worked to "limit excessive commercialism in society." Founded in part with help from longtime consumer advocate Ralph Nader, Commercial Alert became a project of Public Citizen, a nonprofit consumer protection organization based in Washington, D.C. In addition to its efforts to check commercialism, Commercial Alert has challenged specific marketing tactics that allow corporations to intrude into civic life. In 2012, Commercial Alert objected to the state of Kentucky's proposal to sell advertising on school buses. The group argued that "children need a sanctuary from a world where everything seems to be for sale." In constantly questioning the role of advertising in our democracy, Commercial Alert has aimed to strengthen noncommercial culture and limit the amount of corporate influence on publicly elected government officials and organizations.

The American Legacy Foundation

Some nonprofit organizations have used innovative advertising of their own to offset the effects of ads for dangerous products. In 2000, the American Legacy Foundation launched an anti-smoking/anti–tobacco industry ad campaign called "Truth." The campaign's mission has been to counteract tobacco marketing and

Courtesy truth®/Legacy

In 2005, "Truth," the national youth smoking prevention campaign, won an Emmy Award in the National Public Service Announcement category.

reduce tobacco use among young people. The "Truth" project uses print and television ads that contradict the images that have long been featured in cigarette ads. For example, one of their early spots showed a giant rat expiring on a city sidewalk, clutching a cardboard sign saying that cigarettes contain the same chemical found in rat poison. All "Truth" spots prominently reference the foundation's Web site, www.thetruth.com, which offers statistics, discussion forums, and outlets for teen creativity, such as games.

The FTC

Through its truth-in-advertising rules, the FTC has played an investigative role in substantiating the claims of various advertisers. Thus, the organization contributes to some regulation of the ad industry. The FTC usually permits a certain amount of *puffery*—ads featuring hyperbole and exaggeration—particularly when an ad describes a product as "new and improved." However, the FTC defines ads as deceptive when they are likely to mislead reasonable consumers through statements made, images shown, or omission of certain information. (For example, in some Campbell Soup ads once featuring images of a bowl of soup, marbles had been placed in the bottom of the bowl to push bulkier ingredients to the surface. This was deceptive advertising because it made the soup look less watery than it really was.) Moreover, when an advertiser makes comparative claims for a product, such as it's "the best," "the greatest," or "preferred by four out of five doctors," FTC rules require statistical evidence to back up the claims.

When the FTC discovers deception in advertising, it usually requires advertisers to change or remove the ads from circulation. The FTC can also impose monetary civil penalties, which are paid to consumers. And it occasionally requires an advertiser to run spots correcting the deceptive ads.

Advertising in a Democratic Society

Advertising has had both creative and destructive impacts on our democratic society. With its ability to "produce" not products but actual consumers, it became the central economic support system for American mass media industries, powerfully fueling our economy. Yet in creating a consumerist society, the ad industry has also widened divisions between those who can afford to buy all the alluring products it promotes and those who cannot (or, alternately, those who go into debt buying the alluring products on credit). When some people can participate in an economy and others are unable to, democracy is undermined. Moreover, advertising's ubiquity intrudes on our privacy and subjects us to corporate efforts to gather our personal information (such as income and spending habits).

J.D. Pooley/Getty Images

During the 2008 presidential campaign, Barack Obama logos, like this one, provided his campaign with a successful way to brand itself.

Equally worrisome, fewer and fewer large media conglomerates are controlling an increasing amount of commercial speech, especially in mainstream, traditional media. This raises the question of whether we're getting all the information we need to make well-reasoned choices—a key characteristic of any democratic society.

Advertising's role in politics offers an apt example. Since the 1950s, political consultants have adopted market-research and advertising techniques to "sell" their candidates to the electorate. **Political advertising**, the use of ad techniques to promote a candidate's image and persuade the public to adopt a particular viewpoint, is the most popular form of this. Many political ads are shown on television in the form of thirty-second spots paid for by candidates from the two main parties (or largely unregulated political action committees and Super PACs, made legal by the 2010 Supreme Court case *Citizens United v. Federal Elections Commission*). The *Citizens United* decision is already having a huge impact on political ad spending, which topped $6.28 billion in all races in 2012.[7] Even more disturbing, the political network run by Charles and David Koch, conservative oil tycoons and longtime opponents of campaign disclosure laws, promised in early 2015 they would spend almost a billion dollars on the 2016 elections (they spent $400 million in 2012), which is on par with the spending of the national Republican and Democratic parties.[8]

One result of this is that only very wealthy candidates, or those with the wealthiest patrons, can typically afford these expensive promotional strategies. Thus, citizens who rely on television for their information don't get a complete picture of the options available and may never learn about obscure but qualified third-party candidates who can't afford to pay for TV spots. The present political environment, in which the most affluent can flood the commercial media with their paid messages, has become a situation in which free speech really isn't free.

Moreover, critics have raised probing questions about the unintended consequences of political ads aired on television. For example, can serious information about complex political issues really be conveyed in a thirty-second spot? If not, viewers aren't getting a full understanding of the issues and can't make informed voting decisions. And do repeated attack ads, which assault another candidate's character, undermine citizens' confidence in the electoral process? If so, people may stop voting entirely—a *really* bad thing for a democracy. As it is, about 62 percent of eligible voters turned out in the 2008 national election, which means that 38 percent of us chose not to vote, and that was the best turnout for decades. But that didn't help in 2014, when only about 36 percent of voters turned up for the midterm (no presidential race) election, the lowest turnout for a national election since 1942.[9]

Political ads most often appear during traditional televised commercial breaks, but other forms of advertising can be more subtle, especially in the digital world of promotion-paid Twitter accounts, product placement, and ads woven into search engine results. As advertising becomes more niche targeted, it's important for citizens to remain media literate about how and when they're being targeted as consumers. Thus, we need to be aware that simple activities in our daily lives—such as clicking "Like" on a Facebook page, searching on Google, or shopping on Amazon—are also part of the data-collection system that profiles our behavior and targets us with ever more advertising.

Despite these and other concerns about advertising's potential negative consequences for our democracy, it maintains its hold on American culture—for several reasons. Without advertising, many mass media industries—television, the Internet, movies, magazines—would have to entirely reinvent their business models, as newspapers and magazines are doing right now in the face of losing so much of their ad revenue sources over the last decade. Leaders in these industries continue to embrace advertising as an economic necessity. Consumers themselves hold conflicting views of the ad industry: Some dismiss advertising as trivial and ineffective. These individuals don't typically support strong monitoring of the industry. Others find ads entertaining, decorating their rooms or clothing with their favorite product posters or company logos and happily identifying with the images certain products convey. They, too, remain oblivious to advertising's less-than-positive effects on our society. Advertising can be enjoyable—think of the viewers who watch the Super Bowl to see new ads that are often hyped just as heavily as the products they hawk, or even the game itself—but if we consider it just entertainment, we misunderstand its ultimate purpose.

What does all this mean for advertising's future in the United States? As with any other mass medium, it's important that we all remember what advertising's purpose is, understand how it both benefits and costs our society, and "consume" commercial culture and its ads with a critical eye.

Think about it: In what ways are our own behaviors, values, and decisions—in all aspects of our life—affected by advertising? How might we consume and respond to ads more critically? And in what ways could we all participate in efforts to monitor the advertising landscape?

CHAPTER ESSENTIALS

Now that you have finished reading this chapter, you can use the following tools:

REVIEW

Outline the Early History of American Advertising

- The first American advertising agents were newspaper **space brokers**, individuals who purchased space in newspapers and then sold it to various merchants. The first modern ad agencies worked mainly for companies that manufactured consumer products, not for the newspapers (pp. 366–367).

- As a result of manufacturers using newspaper stories and ads to create brand names, consumers began demanding specific products and retail stores started stocking desired brands, ushering in product differentiation (pp. 367–368).

- Patent medicine makers in the nineteenth century embraced advertising as a way to differentiate their products, sometimes making outrageous claims or covering up a product's harmful effects. Such behaviors sparked cynicism and the development of industry codes. At the same time, department stores began advertising heavily in newspapers and magazines, luring people away from small local stores (p. 368).

- By the twentieth century, advertising had transformed American society, creating new markets, shaping values, and influencing the rising consumer culture. This influence catalyzed the first watchdog organizations, such as the Better Business Bureau and the Federal Trade Commission (FTC). To create a more positive image, the advertising industry developed the War Advertising Council, known today as the Ad Council, to support worthy causes. However, with the advent of television in the 1950s, the industry faced criticism again for its use of **subliminal advertising** (pp. 368–370).

Track the Evolution of U.S. Advertising

- Beginning in the 1960s and 1970s, visual design played a more prominent role in advertising. This trend sparked the growth of new types of advertising agencies: **mega-agencies**—large firms that are formed from the merging of several individual agencies and that maintain worldwide regional offices—and **boutique agencies**—smaller companies that devote their talents to just a handful of select clients (pp. 371–373).

- Regardless of the type of ad agency, most have similar organizational structures, consisting of departments for account planning (where planners coordinate **market research** to assess consumer behaviors and attitudes by studying **demographics** and **psychographics**—often relying on **focus groups**—and conducting **Values and Lifestyles [VALS]** research); creative development (where writers and artists develop **storyboards** that show each scene of a potential ad or a **viral marketing** campaign to be shared online); media buying (staffed by media planners and **media buyers** who choose and purchase the types of media that are best suited to carry a client's ads and reach the targeted audience, sometimes by engaging in repetitive **saturation advertising**); and account management (staffed with **account executives** who are responsible for bringing in new business and are most vulnerable to **account reviews** or client assessments of an existing ad campaign) (pp. 373–376).

- The growth of the Internet in the 1990s has changed the advertising industry considerably. New forms of Internet advertising include pop-up ads and ad **spam**. Internet ad companies pose a threat to traditional advertising agencies. Ad agencies can track **ad impressions** and **click-throughs** and develop consumer profiles. Mobile ad technologies include **QR (Quick Response) codes** (pp. 377–379).

Explain Persuasive Techniques in Contemporary Advertising

- Ad agencies use a number of persuasive strategies, such as **famous-person testimonial** (a product endorsed by a well-known person); **plain-folks pitch** (a product associated with simplicity); **snob appeal** (an ad that claims using a product will elevate one's status); **bandwagon effect** (an ad that claims "everyone" is using it); **hidden-fear appeal** (a campaign that plays on a consumer's insecurities); and **irritation advertising** (an ad that creates product-name recognition by being annoying or obnoxious) (pp. 380–381).

- In addition, advertisers draw on the **association principle**, in which a product is linked with a positive cultural value or image. Others tell stories or narratives that convey a culture's deepest values and social norms.

Still others focus on **product placement**—strategically placing ads or buying space in movies, TV shows, comic books, and video games so that they appear as part of a story's environment (pp. 381, 384–385).

Discuss Commercial Speech and the Regulation of Advertising

- Advertisements consist of **commercial speech**, any print or broadcast expression for which a fee is charged to organizations and individuals buying time or space in the mass media. The question of whether advertisers are fully protected by the First Amendment remains controversial (pp. 385–386).

- Serious concerns exist over the impact of advertising on children; teens; and people susceptible to eating disorders, smoking, alcoholism, or inappropriate prescription-drug use, leading to the creation of nonprofit watchdog and advocacy organizations such as Commercial Alert and the American Legacy Foundation (pp. 386–387, 390–392).

Consider Advertising's Impact on Our Democratic Society

- Advertising has helped fuel the economy while also creating a consumer society with divisions between those who can afford to buy and those who cannot. It has also raised concerns about the impact of a handful of large media conglomerates controlling commercial speech. **Political advertising**—the use of ad techniques to promote a candidate's image and persuade the public to adopt a particular viewpoint—makes us question whether or not we're getting unbiased information (pp. 392–394).

- Despite these issues, without advertising, many mass media industries would not survive. Given its pervasiveness, it's important for the public to be critical consumers of advertising (pp. 394–395).

STUDY QUESTIONS

1. What role did advertising play in transforming the United States into a consumer society?
2. What are the major divisions at most ad agencies? What is the function of each department?
3. How do the common persuasive techniques used in advertising work?
4. What are four serious contemporary issues regarding health and advertising? Why is each issue controversial?
5. What are the effects of advertising on a democratic society?

MEDIA LITERACY PRACTICE

TV advertising functions to promote an advertiser's goods or services, but ads always mean more than advertisers intend. Investigate this issue by examining some familiar ads.

DESCRIBE ads from similar product categories—clothing or accessories, automobiles, computers or cell phones—that run during your favorite shows, whether on television or streamed via the Internet. Take notes on the stories told and the techniques used to make the products appealing, and write up your notes in a three- to four-page paper. .

ANALYZE the patterns. What kinds of stories are the ads telling to sell their products? Are there any product placement ads that also coincide with the "regular" TV spots from your category?

INTERPRET what these ads mean and the values or attitudes being sold. What does it mean if product placement ads are prevalent during your TV program?

EVALUATE whether you think your ads do a good job or a poor job of selling their products. If there are product placement ads, how effective are they?

ENGAGE with your community by contacting someone from one of the companies that advertised the products you studied. What is that person's general view of the ad industry and product placement?

12

Public Relations and Framing the Message

About a hundred years ago, in the second decade of the twentieth century, media stardom emerged as both the subject of public fascination and a human resource to be exploited by the movie business. Interest in the private lives of stars spawned gossip columns and fan magazines that usually relayed information provided by press agents employed by the stars' studios. Today, Hollywood's public relations (PR) machinery continues to construct images, often emphasizing the ordinary aspects of its extraordinary people; stars are depicted as regular folks who enjoy sports, love their children and pets, and go grocery shopping. However, even the most visible stars have traditionally been insulated from direct contact with their adoring fans by armies of bodyguards, publicists, and other industry functionaries.

For many popular performers, the layers of PR professionals protecting them from both their fans and themselves have been peeled away by the social networking site Twitter. Twitter, which began in 2006, is a "micro-blogging" site where users can post status updates and follow feeds that display the updates of friends, acquaintances, and, increasingly, celebrities—a converged form of mass communication that can be used to reach dozens of friends or thousands (or millions) of fans. As of early 2015, Katy Perry had the most followers (over 72 million), followed by Justin Bieber (65 million), President Barack Obama (62 million), Taylor Swift (60 million), and video site YouTube (53 million).[1] These enormous followings allow stars and politicians to engage in public relations beyond magazines like *Us Weekly* or gossip shows like *Entertainment Tonight*—or, in the case of President Obama, beyond traditional news outlets. For celebrities and politicians, this can allow them to share messages directly with their followers.

In some cases, celebrities themselves tweet out to their fans, bypassing the usual layers of handlers and media professionals and creating the illusion of personal connection. But others, perhaps fearing an embarrassing mistake, hire public relations firms to run their Twitter and other social media accounts, which of course risks turning off fans who want to hear from celebrities directly, not one of their employees. The experience of actor Ashton Kutcher gives an idea of the public relations paradox celebrities can face on Twitter. Kutcher was an early adopter of Twitter, and the spontaneous and unfiltered style of his tweets resonated with fans. Soon he had a huge Twitter following, bigger than many more-prominent stars. But the

tweets that helped him get followers became a liability when he reacted to the firing of Joe Paterno, the head football coach at Penn State. He lambasted the decision without fully understanding that it was connected to the coach's implication in the cover-up of a child sex-abuse scandal. Kutcher later deleted the tweet, but not before prompting a flood of responses that attacked the star for supporting the disgraced football legend. The event so rattled Kutcher that he issued a statement announcing that he was turning the management of his account over to his PR team at Katalyst Media as a "secondary editorial measure."[2]

Clearly, much of the popularity of stars like Katy Perry, Taylor Swift, and Ashton Kutcher has been cultivated and nurtured by Twitter-based connections with their publics. But it seems likely that this newfound interactivity will actually increase the need for PR professionals, be it for formal approvals—like those of Kutcher's media team—or for less regulated consulting for celebrities who want to keep control of their feed. With media platforms converging and stars becoming more accessible than ever, public relations work will continue to expand beyond traditional events, comments, and press releases.

AS THE STORY OF CELEBRITY TWITTER ACCOUNTS REVEALS, the field of public relations continues to grow and change with the media industries it depends on. An effective public relations effort involves numerous activities, including shaping the public image of a product (or a person or an organization), establishing or restoring communication between consumers and companies, and promoting particular individuals or organizations. Broadly defined, **public relations** refers to the total communication strategy conducted by a person, a government, or an organization attempting to reach an audience and persuade it to adopt a point of view.[3] Or, in the brief definition offered by the Public Relations Society of America (PRSA), "Public relations helps an organization and its publics adapt mutually to each other."

Although public relations may sound very similar to advertising, which also seeks to persuade audiences, it differs in important respects. Advertising uses discrete, simple, and fixed messages ("Our appliance is the most efficient and affordable"), transmitted directly to the public through the purchase of ads for specific products or services. Whereas advertising focuses mainly on sales, public relations develops or reshapes an image for a person, an organization, a product, a service, or an issue to make it more marketable, popular, important, compelling, or accessible, among other desired outcomes. In doing so, public relations creates more complex messages that may evolve over time (for example, a political campaign, or a long-term strategy to dispel unfavorable reports about "fatty processed foods"). PR may be transmitted to the public indirectly, often through articles and reports in the news media. Finally, public relations messages often reflect larger trends and ideas that are percolating through society—such as the notion that it is good to recycle, or that smoking is bad for you. Even broad ideas like "liberty" or "fairness" often take on connotations based on public relations efforts. PR thus shapes and is shaped by what is going on in society at large.

Since its inception, PR has exerted a huge influence on American society and culture. For example, after the Industrial Revolution, when people began purchasing (rather than making) many of the goods they needed, manufacturers used PR to emphasize how various industries benefited consumers. By helping to drive economic activity, the public relations profession thus contributed to an improvement in standards of living in the United States. PR also set the tone for the corporate image-building that characterized the twentieth century—and for the debates over today's environmental, energy, labor, and other public policy issues. However, PR's most significant impact is probably on the political process:

Politicians and organizations hire PR professionals to shape their image in the media, which influences how people vote. No matter what issue you care about, there is undoubtedly someone doing PR on its behalf, on all sides.

Today, there are more than twenty-nine hundred PR firms worldwide, including nineteen hundred in the United States. Many organizations also have in-house departments devoted to PR. Moreover, since the 1980s, the formal study of public relations has grown significantly at colleges and universities. By 2015, the Public Relations Student Society of America (PRSSA) boasted more than eleven thousand student members and more than three hundred chapters in colleges and universities.

In this chapter, we examine the workings and the impact of public relations in more detail by:

- **looking at the early days of public relations, including the emergence of press agents and the birth of modern PR**

- **considering how the PR profession has evolved in terms of the structure of public relations firms and the functions that PR practitioners perform (such as formulating messages about their clients and conveying those messages to the public)**

- **exploring the tensions that have arisen between public relations professionals and the press, and the causes behind those tensions**

- **considering the role PR plays in our democratic society by focusing on the impact of public relations on the political process in particular**

CHAPTER 12 // TIMELINE

1840–1880 Early Promotions through Media
Theatrical agent P. T. Barnum employs early PR tactics to promote his many acts.

1880 The Railroads
The PR practice of bribing reporters for positive news stories and deadheading reaches its height.

1914 "Poison Ivy" Lee
After opening one of the first PR firms in New York in the early 1900s, "Poison Ivy" Lee works for the wealthy Rockefeller family.

1923 Edward Bernays
Bernays teaches the first public relations course at New York University and writes the first PR textbook.

1948 PRSA
To better its standing among the public and the news media, the PR industry forms the Public Relations Society of America (PRSA) to function as an internal watchdog.

Early History of Public Relations

Public relations traveled an interesting path in its journey toward becoming a profession. The first PR practitioners were **press agents**, people who conveyed favorable messages to the public about their clients, often by staging stunts that reporters described in newspapers. As the United States became industrialized and people began purchasing more goods and services, larger companies—impressed by press agents' power to shape public opinion—began hiring these early practitioners to further their interests. Some PR tactics proved deceitful, but when journalists and citizens complained, PR agencies began policing themselves to foster more ethical practices in the profession.

Age of the Press Agent: P. T. Barnum and Buffalo Bill

The earliest press agents excelled at **publicity**—a type of PR communication that uses various media messages to spread information and interest (or buzz) about a person, a corporation, an issue, or a policy. The most effective publicity efforts not only excited people's imagination but also helped establish enduring national values.

In the 1800s, some publicity tactics could also border on outrageous. Consider press agent Phineas Taylor (P. T.) Barnum, who used gross exaggeration, fraudulent stories, and staged events to secure newspaper coverage for his clients, for

LaunchPad
macmillanhighered.com/mediaessentials3e
Use **LearningCurve** to review concepts from this chapter.

1982 Tylenol Scare
After it is determined that Tylenol capsules have been laced with cyanide, Johnson & Johnson responds with rapid and ethical PR crisis management, saving the Tylenol brand.

1989 *Exxon Valdez* Disaster
Exxon's initial denials of responsibility and slow response to the *Exxon Valdez* oil spill severely damage its reputation.

1996 Walmart and Sweatshop Labor
Human-rights groups bring attention to sweatshop labor when they expose the production conditions of Walmart's Kathie Lee Gifford clothing line.

2005 Video News Releases (VNRs) draw FCC action
Responding to citizen pressure, the FCC mandates that the source of a video news release (VNR) must be clearly disclosed when broadcast.

Library of Congress Prints and Photographs Division

"Buffalo Bill's Wild West and
Congress of Rough Riders of
the World" show, depicted
here, was internationally
popular as a touring show for
more than thirty years.

his American Museum, and (later) for his circus, which he dubbed "The Greatest Show on Earth."

William F. Cody was another notorious publicity hound. From 1883 to 1916, Cody, who once killed buffalo for the railroads, used press agents to promote himself and his traveling show: "Buffalo Bill's Wild West and Congress of Rough Riders of the World." The show employed sharpshooter Annie Oakley and Lakota holy man Sitting Bull, whose legends were partially shaped by Cody's press agents. These agents were led by John Burke, one of the first to use an array of media channels to generate publicity. Burke promoted Cody's show through a heady mix of newspaper stories, magazine articles and ads, dime novels, theater marquees, poster art, and early films. Burke and Buffalo Bill fired up Americans' love of rugged individualism and frontier expansion—a national mythology that later showed up in books, radio programs, and Hollywood films about the American West.

Business Adopts Press Agent Methods

The successes enjoyed by P. T. Barnum, Buffalo Bill, John Burke, and others demonstrated that publicity could not only stimulate business but also help any individual or organization (such as not-for-profit groups and government agencies) spread the word about its value and fulfill its mission. For businesses, press agentry became an important mechanism for generating the profits and (in some cases) bringing in the government funding needed to achieve their mission. However, in the early days of press agents, some of the tactics used were especially deceptive.

Around 1850, for example, the railroads began hiring press agents to help them obtain federal funds, which hinged on positive public perceptions of the railroads' value. These agents' tactics included bribing reporters to write favorable news stories about the railroads. Agents also engaged in **deadheading**—giving journalists free rail passes with the tacit understanding that they would write glowing reports about traveling by rail. Finally, the larger railroads used **lobbyists**—professionals who seek to influence lawmakers' votes—to gain federal subsidies and establish policies (such as rate reductions) that made it harder for smaller regional lines to compete. Thanks to such efforts, a few large rail companies gained dominance over the industry.

Utility companies such as Chicago Edison and AT&T also used press agent strategies in the late 1800s for similar ends. Again, some of their tactics were deceptive. For instance, they, too, bought votes of key lawmakers, and they hired third-party editorial services to produce written pieces in their favor. For example, these services sent articles touting the utilities to newspapers, produced ghost-written articles lauding the utilities' value, and influenced textbook authors to write historical accounts that put the utilities in a positive light.[4]

Professional Public Relations Emerges

By the early 1900s, some journalists began investigating and reporting on the questionable promotional practices businesses were using, which helped increase awareness of these tactics among the public. Facing a more informed citizenry, businesses were finding it harder to buy favorable press and use it to mislead people. Two PR pioneers—Ivy Ledbetter Lee and Edward Bernays—realized that public relations needed to be more professional. To that end, they ushered in new approaches that emphasized honesty, directness, and an understanding of psychology and sociology.

Ivy Ledbetter Lee: Two Sides to Every Story

Press agent Ivy Ledbetter Lee counseled his corporate clients that honesty and directness were better PR devices than the deceptive practices of the 1800s, which had given big business a bad name. Lee opened one of the first PR firms in the early 1900s with George Parker. Following a rail accident in late 1906, the Pennsylvania Railroad hired the firm to help downplay the resulting unfavorable publicity. Lee advised the railroad to admit its mistake, vow to do better, and let newspapers in on the story, rather than trying to cover up the accident or deny responsibility. In 1912, Lee quit the firm to work for the Pennsylvania Railroad.

In 1914, Lee went to work for John D. Rockefeller Jr., who by the 1880s controlled 90 percent of the nation's oil industry. Rockefeller and his Standard Oil Company already had image problems, beginning when journalists published a powerful muckraking series about his business tactics in 1902–1904. In 1913–14, strikebreakers at one of Rockefeller's mining companies and members of the state militia battled striking coal miners trying to win recognition for their union. Fifty-three workers and their family members were killed in Ludlow, Colorado. The oil magnate hired Lee to contain the damaging publicity fallout. Lee immediately distributed a series of "fact sheets" to the press, telling the company's side of the story and discrediting the tactics of the United Mine Workers, who had organized the strike. Lee clearly recognized that there are several sides to every story,

Ivy Lee, a founding father of public relations, did innovative crisis work with John D. Rockefeller Jr., staging photo opportunities at the Ludlow mines.

© Bettmann/Corbis

Courtesy of the Rockefeller Archive Center

and that decisions about which facts to present to the public, and which to leave out, could strongly shape public perceptions. Lee also brought in the press and staged photo opportunities at Rockefeller's company, which helped rehabilitate the Rockefeller family's image. While certainly effective, his efforts earned him the nickname "Poison Ivy" Lee from his enemies.

Edward Bernays: Public Relations Counselor

Edward Bernays opened his own PR office in 1919. He was the first person to apply the findings of psychology and sociology to the public relations profession. Bernays described the shaping of public opinion through PR as the "engineering of consent." That is, he believed that skilled experts, leaders, and PR professionals could shape messages and ideas in ways people could rally behind.[5]

Indeed, Bernays referred to himself as a "public relations counselor" rather than a "publicity agent." Over the years, his client list included such big-name companies as the American Tobacco Company (now R. J. Reynolds Tobacco), General Electric, and General Motors. Bernays also worked for the Committee on Public Information (CPI) during World War I. In that role, he developed propaganda that supported the U.S. entry into the war and promoted the image of President Woodrow Wilson as a peacemaker.

Bernays also demonstrated that women could work in the PR profession. His business partner and later his wife, Doris Fleischman, collaborated with

© Bettmann/Corbis   The New York Public Library/Art Resource, NY

Edward Bernays and his business partner and wife, Doris Fleischman, creatively influenced public opinion. Bernays worked on behalf of a client, the American Tobacco Company (who owned Lucky Strike and other brands), to make smoking socially acceptable for women.

him on many of his campaigns as a researcher and coauthor. PR later became one of the few professions accessible to women who chose to work outside the home. Today, women outnumber men by more than three to one in the profession.

The Evolution of Public Relations

As the PR profession evolved, two major types of public relations organizations took shape: PR agencies and in-house PR services. Practitioners in this field began excelling at specific functions, such as researching target audiences and formulating messages conveyed to them.

PR Agencies and In-House PR Services

Almost two thousand U.S. companies identify themselves as public relations agencies today. Many of the largest companies are owned by, or are affiliated

World War II was a time when the U.S. government used propaganda, such as Uncle Sam, and other PR strategies to drum up support for the war.

with, multinational communications holding companies, such as WPP, Omnicom, and Interpublic (see Figure 12.1). For example, two of the largest PR agencies—Burson-Marsteller and Hill & Knowlton—together generated over a half billion dollars in PR revenue for their parent corporation, the WPP Group, in 2013. Other PR firms are independent. These companies tend to be smaller than the conglomerate-owned ones and have just local or regional operations. New York and Chicago–based Edelman, the largest independent PR agency, is an exception, boasting global operations and clients around the world.

Many corporations, professional organizations, and nonprofit entities retain PR agencies to provide a range of services. Large organizations of all types—particularly in the manufacturing and service industries—often have their own in-house PR staffs as well. These departments handle numerous tasks, such as writing press releases, managing journalists' requests for interviews with company personnel, and staging special events.

A Closer Look at Public Relations Functions

Regardless of whether they work at a PR agency or on staff at an organization's in-house PR department, public relations professionals pay careful attention to the needs of their clients and to the perspectives of their targeted audiences. They provide a multitude of services, including developing publicity campaigns and formulating messages about what their clients are doing in such areas as government relations, community outreach, industry relations, diversity initiatives, and product or service development. Some PR professionals also craft **propaganda**. This is communication that is presented as advertising or publicity and that is intended to gain (or undermine) public support for a special issue, program, or policy—such as a nation's war effort (see "Converging Media Case Study: Military PR in the Digital Age" on pages 412–413). In addition, PR practitioners might produce employee newsletters, manage client trade shows and conferences, conduct historical tours, appear on news programs, organize damage control after negative publicity, or analyze complex issues and trends affecting a client's future.

FIGURE 12.1 // THE PUBLIC RELATIONS FIRMS, 2013 (BY WORLDWIDE REVENUE IN MILLIONS OF U.S. DOLLARS)

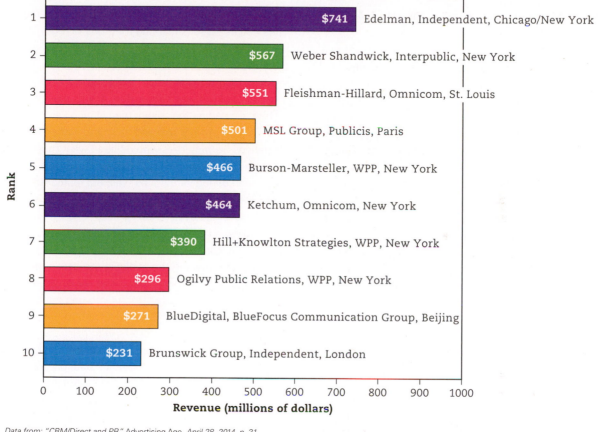

Rank (y-axis) | Revenue (millions of dollars) (x-axis)

1 — $741 — Edelman, Independent, Chicago/New York
2 — $567 — Weber Shandwick, Interpublic, New York
3 — $551 — Fleishman-Hillard, Omnicom, St. Louis
4 — $501 — MSL Group, Publicis, Paris
5 — $466 — Burson-Marsteller, WPP, New York
6 — $464 — Ketchum, Omnicom, New York
7 — $390 — Hill+Knowlton Strategies, WPP, New York
8 — $296 — Ogilvy Public Relations, WPP, New York
9 — $271 — BlueDigital, BlueFocus Communication Group, Beijing
10 — $231 — Brunswick Group, Independent, London

Data from: "CRM/Direct and PR," Advertising Age, April 28, 2014, p. 31.

Research: Formulating the Message

Like advertising, PR makes use of mail, telephone, and Internet surveys, as well as focus groups, to get a fix on an audience's perceptions of an issue, a policy, a program, or a client's image. This research also helps PR firms focus their campaign messages. For example, the Liz Claiborne Foundation has tried to combat domestic violence (specifically, teen dating abuse) by using survey results from 683 teens to develop its "Love Is Not Abuse" campaign.

CONVERGING MEDIA

Case Study

Military PR in the Digital Age

Public relations has a long connection with the military and wartime communication. After all, father of modern public relations Edward Bernays got his start developing propaganda promoting U.S. military involvement in World War I. Gaining and keeping public support has long been a key to any military endeavor, and public relations and wartime propaganda have played a major role in shaping public opinion. But as media technology has changed and converged over the last century, so have the PR efforts of governments looking for support for various wars.

Many historians point to Vietnam as an important turning point for the way the media covered war, and a wake-up call for military image handlers hoping to control that flow of information: the relatively unfiltered images of death and destruction broadcast into American living rooms via television fueled a growing antiwar sentiment. This was an early form of convergence, in which stark journalism was now appearing on television, and the military learned its lesson, adapting methods to regain control of information coming out of war zones. For example, when President Ronald Reagan ordered troops to invade the small Caribbean island of Grenada in 1983, it was days before any journalists were allowed on the island, many being kept offshore on a navy ship and having to settle for briefings from officers who decided what they could—and couldn't—know. (Official briefings were common during Vietnam as well, but journalists also had greater freedom of movement and could augment coverage beyond the "official" line.)

Following Grenada, journalists and others accused Reagan of trying to shield himself from criticism by keeping the public in the dark about the outcome of major policy decisions. When President George H. W. Bush sent troops into Iraq during the First Gulf War, the military had turned to the practice of "embedding" reporters with particular units. Although this certainly gave reporters greater access than the deck of a ship miles offshore, complaints about media control being placed in the hands of military image handlers persisted. But by the time of the Afghanistan and Iraq invasions in 2002 and 2003, the convergence of nearly all aspects of communication with the Internet had changed the game again—and it's still changing.

For example, the U.S. Army faced a public relations nightmare when military police personnel took digital photographs documenting torture of prisoners held at the Abu Ghraib prison in Iraq. Before being seized by military authorities, these photos were believed to have circulated via e-mail—something that could not have happened in earlier wars. Photos like these, and the January 2012 video documenting four U.S. Marines urinating on Taliban corpses in Afghanistan, have

LaunchPad

macmillanhighered.com/mediaessentials3e

▶ **Visit LaunchPad** to watch a clip of soldiers in Afghanistan dancing to Lady Gaga. How might this affect a viewer's thoughts about the war?

complicated U.S. efforts at winning the trust and respect of the population in that war-torn part of the globe. And though both of these examples deal with scandalous behavior of soldiers in the line of duty, media is making the private or personal moments and thoughts of soldiers part of the public conversation, for good or ill.

As with the celebrities we talked about in the opening of this chapter, public relations in a social media world is a complex place, with opportunities as well as pitfalls. In recent years, troops and their families have used social media to stay in touch with each other, an important way to boost morale in a war zone and at home. Some of these messages home became public and even went viral, including a 2010 YouTube video of soldiers in Afghanistan blowing off steam by dancing to a Lady Gaga song. The much-viewed video was praised by the military for demonstrating a good sense of humor. Military bloggers also helped connect the home front with the front lines in a way that carried more authenticity than any press release.

On the other hand, some of the videos, photographs, and messages posted and shared by soldiers on social media have had the opposite effect. From pictures of inappropriate or dishonorable behavior while in uniform to ideological rants against the commander in chief of the military (the president) to sites that make crude sexual and threatening posts about female soldiers, the military has struggled for years to come up with a useful and enforceable social media policy. Complicating the task even further are social media sites by former military members or civilians, whom the Department of Defense has no control over or ability to punish.[1]

Still another dimension to converged military public relations is that it's a tool that anyone can use—including your enemies. Terrorist groups have taken advantage of the inexpensive global reach of the Internet to post videos ranging from propaganda statements to executions. This new reality of waging war in the face of converged media was the subject of a 2009 report by Cori E. Dauber, published by the

© Tammy Hanratty/Corbis

Strategic Studies Institute of the U.S. Army War College. Titled *YouTube War: Fighting in a World of Cameras in Every Cell Phone and Photoshop on Every Computer*, the report argues that "terrorist attacks ought to be understood as consciously crafted *media events*": "Their true target is not that which is blown up—that item or those people—for that is merely a stage prop. The goal, after all, is to have a psychological effect (to terrorize), and it isn't possible to have such an effect on the dead."[2] The report finds that mainstream television journalism often uses footage released by insurgents because of the visual power of the imagery—even though this practice actually expands the audience for the enemy propaganda, essentially encouraging more attention-getting "newsworthy" actions.

The U.S. military's public relations effort, then, must contend with the way converged and viral media makes its job trickier and more difficult to control. Part of fighting a war in an era of global and converged media involves recognizing that public perceptions matter—and because of this, images matter. And these images are more accessible and easier to disseminate than ever before. Soldiers and military leaders need to be made aware of a major consequence of the inevitable spread of these images: It undermines their terrorism-fighting mission.

Communication: Conveying the Message

Once a PR group has formulated a message, it conveys that message through a variety of channels. With advances in digital technology, these channels have become predominantly Internet based in recent years. **Press releases**, or news releases, are announcements written in the style of news reports that provide new information about an individual, a company, or an organization, now typically issued via e-mail. In issuing press releases, PR agents hope that journalists will pick up the information and transform it into news reports about the agents' clients.

Since the introduction of portable video equipment in the 1970s, PR agencies and departments have also been issuing **video news releases (VNRs)**—thirty- to ninety-second visual press releases designed to mimic the style of a broadcast news report. Although networks and large TV news stations do not usually broadcast VNRs, news stations in small TV markets regularly use material from these releases, which can also be sent to editors of well-trafficked blogs and other Web sites, or displayed independently online. As with press releases, VNRs give PR firms some control over what constitutes "news" and a chance to influence the public's opinion about an issue, a program, or a policy, although the FCC requires that the source of a VNR be disclosed if video from the VNR is broadcast in a news program.

PR firms can also bring attention to nonprofits by creating **public service announcements (PSAs)**: usually fifteen- to sixty-second audio or video reports that promote government programs, educational projects, volunteer agencies, or social reform.

Public Relations in the Internet Age

Historically, public relations practitioners have tried to earn news media coverage (as opposed to buying advertising) to communicate their clients' messages to the public. Although that is still true, the Internet, with its instant accessibility, offers public relations professionals a number of new routes for communicating with the public.

A company's or an organization's Web site has become the home base of public relations efforts. Companies and organizations can upload and maintain their media kits (including press releases, VNRs, images, executive bios, and organizational profiles), giving the traditional news media access to the information at any time. And because everyone can access these corporate Web sites, the barriers between the organization and the groups that PR professionals ultimately want to reach are broken down.

The Web also enables PR professionals to have their clients interact with audiences on a more personal, direct basis through social media tools like Facebook, Twitter, YouTube, *Wikipedia*, and blogs. Now people can be "friends" and "followers" of companies and organizations. Corporate executives can share their professional and personal observations and seem downright chummy through a blog (e.g., Whole Foods Market's blog by co-CEO John Mackey). Executives, celebrities, and politicians can seem more accessible and personable through a Twitter feed. But social media's immediacy can also be a problem, especially for those who send messages into the public sphere without considering the ramifications.

Another concern about social media is that sometimes such communications appear without complete disclosure, which is an unethical practice. Some PR firms have edited *Wikipedia* entries for their clients' benefit, a practice *Wikipedia* founder Jimmy Wales has repudiated as a conflict of interest. A growing number of companies also compensate bloggers to subtly promote their products, unbeknownst to most readers. Public relations firms and marketers are particularly keen on working with "mom bloggers," who appear to be an independent voice in discussions about consumer products but may receive gifts in exchange for their opinions. In 2009, the Federal Trade Commission instituted new rules requiring online product endorsers to disclose their connections to companies.

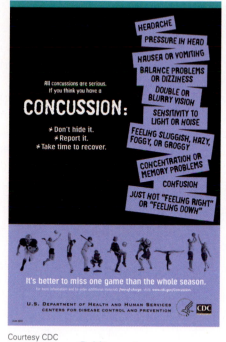

Courtesy CDC

Public service announcements also include print and Web components (not just TV or radio ads).

Managing Media Relations

Some PR practitioners specialize in media relations. These specialists promote a client or an organization by securing publicity or favorable coverage in the various news media. In an in-house PR department, media-relations specialists will speak on behalf of their organization or direct reporters to experts inside and outside the company who can provide information about whatever topic the reporter is writing about.

Media-relations specialists may also recommend advertising to their clients when it seems that ads would help focus a complex issue or enhance a client's image. In addition, they cultivate connections with editors, reporters, freelance writers, and broadcast news directors to ensure that their press releases or VNRs are favorably received (see "Media Literacy Case Study: Improving the Credibility Gap" on pages 416–417).

Improving the Credibility Gap

In the 1990s, a growing number of Americans focused on the problems of outsourcing: using the production, manufacturing, and labor resources of foreign companies to produce American brand-name products, sometimes under deplorable working conditions. Outsourcing was pushed into the public eye in 1996 after major media attention focused on morning talk-show host Kathie Lee Gifford when investigations by the National Labor Committee (now the Institute for Global Labour and Human Rights) revealed that part of her clothing line, made and distributed by Walmart, came from sweatshops in New York and Honduras. The sweatshops paid less than minimum wages, and some employed child laborers. Human-rights activists claimed that in overseas sweatshops in particular, children were being exploited in violation of international child-labor laws.

Many leading clothing labels and retailers continue to ignore pressure from consumer and labor groups and still tolerate sweatshop conditions in which workers take home minimal pay. Gap Inc.—one of the world's largest clothing retailers, with more than thirty-one hundred Gap, Banana Republic, Old Navy, and Athleta stores, made a huge statement in the industry by publicizing its efforts to watch over labor conditions at its overseas factories with its first Social Responsibility Report back in 2004. Yet while Gap's reputation has arguably improved following these efforts, human-rights issues still arise with many major clothing companies, including some owned by Gap Inc.

That 2004 report and the reports that followed have comprised Gap's efforts at improved transparency and better communication with its employees, its shareholders, and those concerned about garment industry operations. The company now employs a team of more than ninety people to inspect and improve working conditions in its approximately three thousand contracted garment factories in fifty countries, and continues to issue progress reports. Typical violations include lack of compliance with child-labor laws, pay below minimum wages, workweeks in excess of sixty hours, psychological coercion and verbal abuse, locked or inaccessible exits, and lack of access to potable water.

But while Gap and other companies have become more efficient and public in the way that they deal with these problems, the improved public relations doesn't always mean that the problems have gone away. Gap and other major clothing brands received new criticism after a garment factory collapsed in Bangladesh, killing over eleven hundred workers and injuring twenty-five hundred more. Workers' advocates say pressure by major brands like Gap have pushed unscrupulous factory

LaunchPad
macmillanhighered.com/mediaessentials3e

▶ **Visit LaunchPad** to see a clip from John Oliver's piece on clothing companies. How is Oliver's satire at odds with the Gap's image?

AP Images

owners to cut corners on safety and workers' rights. After the collapse (and a major fire the previous year), Gap and other companies signed agreements calling for better and safe conditions, although critics note that Gap wasn't among the companies that supported the right of Bangladeshi garment workers to organize. A 2015 segment on the satirical news program *Last Week Tonight*, hosted by John Oliver, called out more of the ongoing problems in the garment industry. As Oliver explains, major labels look the other way when the "official" local clothing manufacturers farm out much of the actual labor to subcontractors with poor working conditions and a lack of oversight.

APPLYING THE CRITICAL PROCESS

DESCRIPTION Select three clothing retailers—for example, chains like Target, Macy's, Dillard's, JCPenney, J. Crew, Ann Taylor, L Brands, or Abercrombie & Fitch.

ANALYSIS Go to each retailer's corporate Web site, and (often under investor relations) find its social responsibility statement or guidelines. (If there is not a category like this, look for its code of ethics or business practices.) Look for the patterns—similarities and differences—among the three. Do their ethics apply to only the corporate environment of the company, or do they also consider the environmental impact and labor conditions of their suppliers in the United States and developing countries?

INTERPRETATION How comprehensive and transparent should a corporation's ethical and social responsibility guidelines be? (In other words, how broadly should a corporation define its "publics"—its employees, its customers, the local communities, the entire world—and what should the corporation promise to do?)

EVALUATION Which of the three retailers has the most comprehensive and transparent corporate social responsibility policy? What made it the best of the three?

ENGAGEMENT Engage directly with the business you were most impressed with by writing or e-mailing and telling it why. Contact one of the other businesses and tell it how it could improve its policy. You can also connect with a number of other groups, such as the Institute for Global Labour and Human Rights, to learn more about corporate labor records.

Hurricane Katrina slammed into the Gulf Coast on August 29, 2005, creating the worst natural disaster in the nation's history and an unimaginable opportunity for crisis communications. The Japanese tsunami in 2011 and Hurricane Sandy in 2012 further show that crisis management continues to be a global concern.

Courtesy of R. Eliot Fagley

If a client company has had some negative publicity (for example, one of its products has been shown to be defective or dangerous, or a viral video on the Internet has spread disinformation about the company), media-relations specialists also perform damage control or crisis management. In fact, during a crisis, these specialists might be the sole source of information about the situation for the public. How PR professionals perform this part of their job can make or break an organization. The handling of the *Exxon Valdez* oil spill and Tylenol tampering deaths in the 1980s offer two contrasting examples.

In 1989, the *Exxon Valdez* oil tanker spilled eleven million gallons of crude oil into Prince William Sound. The accident contaminated fifteen hundred miles of Alaskan coastline and killed countless birds, otters, seals, and fish. In one of the biggest PR blunders of that century, Exxon reacted to the crisis grudgingly and accepted responsibility slowly. Although the company's PR advisers had recommended a quick response, Exxon failed to send any of its chief officers immediately to the site—a major gaffe. Many critics believed that Exxon was trying to duck responsibility by laying the burden of the crisis on the shoulders of the tanker's captain. Even though the company changed the name of the tanker to *Mediterranean* and implemented other strategies intended to salvage the company's image, the public continued to view Exxon in a negative light. BP had a similar public relations failure following a deadly oil rig explosion and massive oil leak in the Gulf of Mexico in 2010.

A decidedly different approach was taken in the 1982 tragedy involving Tylenol pain-relief capsules. Seven people in the Chicago area died after consuming capsules that someone had laced with poison. The parent company,

Johnson & Johnson, and its PR representatives discussed whether to pull all Tylenol capsules from store shelves. Some participants in these discussions worried that this move might send the message that corporations could be intimidated by a single deranged person. Nevertheless, Johnson & Johnson's chairman and the company's PR agency, Burson-Marsteller, opted to fully disclose the tragedy to the media and to immediately recall all Tylenol capsules across the nation. The recall cost the company an estimated $100 million and cut its market share in half.

Burson-Marsteller tracked public opinion about the crisis and about its client nightly through telephone surveys. It also organized satellite press conferences to debrief the news media. In addition, it set up emergency phone lines to take calls from consumers and health-care providers who had questions about the crisis. When the company reintroduced Tylenol three months later, it did so with tamper-resistant bottles that almost every major drug manufacturer soon copied. According to Burson-Marsteller, which received PRSA awards for its handling of the crisis, the public thought Johnson & Johnson had responded admirably to the situation and did not hold Tylenol responsible for the deaths. In fewer than three years, Tylenol recaptured its dominant share of the market.

Hubert Boesl/DPA /Landov

The intense media coverage at awards shows drums up ad revenue for broadcasts and seemingly endless magazine coverage. Can we consider the Oscars or Golden Globes a pseudo-event?

Coordinating Special and Pseudo-Events

Another public relations practice involves coordinating *special events* to raise the profile of corporate, organizational, or government clients. Through such events, a corporate sponsor aligns itself with a cause or an organization that has positive stature among the public. For example, John Hancock Financial has been the primary sponsor of the Boston Marathon since 1986 and provides the race's prize money.

In contrast to a special event, a **pseudo-event** is any circumstance created for the sole purpose of gaining coverage in the media. Pseudo-events may take the form of press conferences, TV and radio talk-show appearances, or any other staged activity aimed at drawing public attention and media coverage. Clients and sometimes paid performers participate in these events, and their success is strongly determined by how much media attention the event attracts. For example, during the 1960s, antiwar and Civil Rights activists staged protest events only if news media were assembled.

Fostering Positive Community and Consumer Relations

Another responsibility of PR practitioners is to sustain goodwill between their clients and the public. Many public relations professionals define "the public" as consisting of two distinct audiences: communities and consumers. Thus, they carefully manage relations with both groups.

PR specialists let the public know that their clients are valuable members of the communities in which they operate by designing opportunities for them to demonstrate that they are good citizens. For example, they arrange for client firms to participate in community activities, such as hosting plant tours and open houses, making donations to national and local charities, participating in local parades and festivals, and allowing employees to take part in community fund-raising drives for good causes.

PR strategists also strive to show that their clients care about their customers. For example, a PR campaign might send the message that the business has established product-safety guarantees, or that it will answer all calls and mail from customers promptly. These efforts result in satisfied customers, which translates into repeat business and new business, as customers spread the word about their positive experiences with the organization.

Cultivating Government Relations

PR groups working for or in corporations also cultivate connections with the government agencies that have some say in how companies operate in a particular community, state, or nation. Through such connections, these groups can monitor the regulatory environment and determine new laws' potential implications for the organizations they represent. For example, a new regulation might require companies to provide more comprehensive reporting on their environmental safety practices, which would represent an added responsibility.

Government PR specialists monitor new and existing legislation, look for opportunities to generate favorable publicity, and write press releases and direct-mail letters to inform the public about the pros and cons of new regulations. In many industries, government relations has developed into **lobbying**: the process of trying to influence lawmakers to support legislation that would serve an organization's or industry's best interests. In seeking favorable legislation, some lobbyists contact government officials on a daily basis. In Washington, D.C., alone, there are about twelve thousand registered lobbyists, and lobbying expenditures targeting the federal government rose to $3.24 billion in 2013, up from $2.06 billion ten years earlier (see Figure 12.2).[6]

FIGURE 12.2 // TOTAL LOBBYING SPENDING AND NUMBER OF LOBBYISTS* (1998–2014)

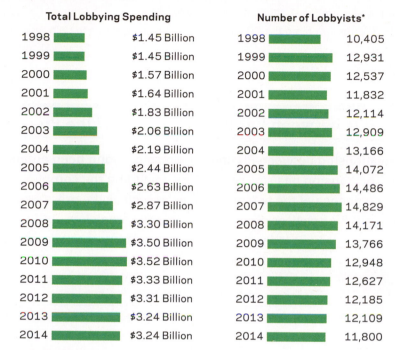

Total Lobbying Spending		Number of Lobbyists*	
1998	$1.45 Billion	1998	10,405
1999	$1.45 Billion	1999	12,931
2000	$1.57 Billion	2000	12,537
2001	$1.64 Billion	2001	11,832
2002	$1.83 Billion	2002	12,114
2003	$2.06 Billion	2003	12,909
2004	$2.19 Billion	2004	13,166
2005	$2.44 Billion	2005	14,072
2006	$2.63 Billion	2006	14,486
2007	$2.87 Billion	2007	14,829
2008	$3.30 Billion	2008	14,171
2009	$3.50 Billion	2009	13,766
2010	$3.52 Billion	2010	12,948
2011	$3.33 Billion	2011	12,627
2012	$3.31 Billion	2012	12,185
2013	$3.24 Billion	2013	12,109
2014	$3.24 Billion	2014	11,800

Note: Figures are calculations by the Center for Responsive Politics based on data from the Senate Office of Public Records, accessed June 5, 2015, www.opensecrets.org/lobby.

*The number of unique registered lobbyists who have actively lobbied

The millions of dollars that lobbyists inject into the political process—treating lawmakers to special events and making campaign contributions in return for legislation that accommodates their clients' interests—is viewed by many as unethical. Another unethical practice is **astroturf lobbying**, which consists of phony grassroots public affairs campaigns engineered by unscrupulous public relations firms. Through this type of lobbying, PR firms deploy blogs, social media campaigns, massive phone banks, and computerized mailing lists to drum up support and create the impression that millions of citizens back their client's side of an issue—even if the number is much lower.

Just as corporations use PR to manage government relations, some governments have used PR to manage their image in the public's mind. For example, following the September 11, 2001, terrorist attacks on the United States, the Saudi Arabian government hired the PR firm Qorvis Communications to help repair its image with American citizens after it was revealed that many of the 9/11 terrorists were from Saudi Arabia.[7]

Tensions between Public Relations and the Press

The relationship between PR and the press has long been antagonistic. This tension has several sources, including the complex interdependence of the two professions as well as the press's skepticism about PR practices. Some of the press's complaints about PR have led public relations practitioners to take steps to enhance their profession's image.

Elements of Interdependence

Journalists have historically viewed themselves as independent professionals providing a public service: gathering and delivering the facts about current events to the public. Some have accused PR professionals of distorting the facts to serve their clients' interests. Yet journalists rely heavily on public relations practitioners to provide the information used in creating news reports. Many editors, for instance, admit that more than half of their story ideas each day originate from PR work, such as press releases. In the face of newspaper staff cutbacks and television's growing need to cover local news events, professionals in the news media need PR story ideas more than ever. This doesn't sit comfortably with some journalists.

As another example of the two professions' interdependence, PR firms often raid news media's workforces for new talent. Because most press releases are written in the style of news reports, the PR profession has always sought skilled writers who are well connected to sources and knowledgeable about the news business. But although many reporters move into the PR profession, few public relations

The manipulation of scientific facts by "experts" trying to promote a specific agenda is addressed in a series of books by John Stauber and Sheldon Rampton.

Trust Us, We're Experts! by Sheldon Rampton and John Stauber © 2002

practitioners—especially those who started their careers as journalists—move back into journalism.

PR practitioners, for their part, maintain that they make reporters' jobs easier—supplying the kinds of information reporters used to gather themselves. Some members of the news media criticize their own ranks for being lazy. Others, grateful for the help, have hesitated to criticize a particular PR firm's clients—which brings up questions of journalistic ethics.

Journalists' Skepticism about PR Practices

In addition to the uncomfortable interdependence characterizing the journalism and PR professions, several specific complaints about PR from journalists have heightened the tension between the two groups. Specifically, some journalists maintain that PR professionals undermine the facts and block reporters' access to information. Journalism's most prevalent criticism of public relations is that it counters the truths reporters seek to bring to the public by selectively choosing which facts to communicate or by delivering deceptive information. To be sure, outright deception is unethical, and the PR profession has worked to eradicate it in its own ranks. But deciding which facts to present is something that journalists do, too. After all, a reporter cannot say everything about a particular event, so he or she must choose which information to include and which to leave out. Journalists have also accused PR professionals of blocking the press's access to business leaders, political figures, and other newsworthy people. This strategy, reporters explain, attempts to manipulate reporters by giving exclusives to those most likely to write a favorable story, or cutting off a reporter's access to a newsworthy client if the reporter has written unfavorably about that person.

Others dislike the PR field's tendency to present publicity as news. Journalists critical of the PR profession claim that PR thus takes media space and time away from organizations and individuals who do not have the money or sophistication required to attract the public eye. These critics also complain that by presenting client information in a journalistic context, PR gains credibility for its clients that the purchase of advertising does not offer.

Shaping PR's Image

Questionable PR moves in the past and journalism's hostility toward PR prompted some public relations practitioners to direct their skills toward improving their profession's image. In 1948, the PR industry formed its own professional organization, the PRSA (Public Relations Society of America). The PRSA functions as an

LaunchPad

macmillanhighered.com
/mediaessentials3e

Give and Take: Public Relations and Journalism
This video debates the relationship between public relations and journalism.
Discussion: Are the similarities between public relations and journalism practices a good thing for the public? Why or why not?

TABLE 12.1 // PUBLIC RELATIONS SOCIETY OF AMERICA ETHICS CODE

In 2000, the PRSA approved a completely revised Code of Ethics, which included core principles, guidelines, and examples of improper conduct. Here is one section of the Code.

PRSA Member Statement of Professional Values

This statement presents the core values of PRSA members and, more broadly, of the public relations profession. These values provide the foundation for the Member Code of Ethics and set the industry standard for the professional practice of public relations. These values are the fundamental beliefs that guide our behaviors and decision-making process. We believe our professional values are vital to the integrity of the profession as a whole.

Advocacy

We serve the public interest by acting as responsible advocates for those we represent. We provide a voice in the marketplace of ideas, facts, and viewpoints to aid informed public debate.

Honesty

We adhere to the highest standards of accuracy and truth in advancing the interests of those we represent and in communicating with the public.

Expertise

We acquire and responsibly use specialized knowledge and experience. We advance the profession through continued professional development, research, and education. We build mutual understanding, credibility, and relationships among a wide array of institutions and audiences.

Independence

We provide objective counsel to those we represent. We are accountable for our actions.

Loyalty

We are faithful to those we represent, while honoring our obligation to serve the public interest.

Fairness

We deal fairly with clients, employers, competitors, peers, vendors, the media, and the general public. We respect all opinions and support the right of free expression.

Data from: The full text of the PRSA Code of Ethics is available at www.prsa.org.

Note: Adherence to the PRSA Code of Ethics is voluntary; there is no enforcement mechanism.

Alexander Tamargo/Getty Images

Leslie Ryan (left) and John Wentworth (right) are Vice President and Executive Vice President, respectively, for the Communications department of CBS Television Distribution. This essentially means they are big-name publicists whose "clients" include syndicated television shows like *Jeopardy!*, *Entertainment Tonight*, and *Judge Judy*.

internal watchdog group that accredits PR agents and firms, maintains a code of ethics, and probes its own practices, especially those pertaining to its influence on the news media. In addition to the PRSA, independent organizations devoted to uncovering shady or unethical public relations activities publish their findings in periodicals like *PR Week* and *PR Watch*. In particular, the Center for Media and Democracy's *PR Watch* seeks to serve the public by discussing and investigating PR practices. Indeed, ethical issues have become a major focus of the PR profession (see Table 12.1).

PR practitioners have also begun using different language—such as *strategic communication*, *institutional relations*, *corporate communications*, *crisis communications*, and *news and information services*—to describe what they do. Their hope is that the new language will signal a more ethically responsible industry. Public relations' best strategy, however, may be to point out the shortcomings of the journalism profession itself. Journalism organizations only occasionally examine their own practices, and journalists have their own vulnerability to manipulation by public relations. Thus, by not publicly revealing PR's strategies to influence their news stories, many journalists have allowed PR professionals to interpret "facts" to their clients' advantage.

Public Relations in a Democratic Society

PR's most significant impact on our democracy may be its involvement in the political process, especially when organizations hire public relations specialists to favorably shape or reshape a candidate's image. As with military propaganda (see also "Converging Media Case Study: Military PR in the Digital Age" on pages 412–413), the history of modern public relations goes hand in hand with political campaigns. In fact, Edward Bernays, who literally wrote the book on propaganda in 1928, is believed to have staged the first presidential publicity stunt: a pancake breakfast for Calvin Coolidge with vaudevillian performers.

The need to handle a candidate's image has become increasingly important, as technology has allowed images of the candidates to be broadcast into America's living rooms. In 1952, President Dwight D. Eisenhower became the first presidential candidate to hire a marketing agency to produce his "Eisenhower Answers America" television commercials, whereas President John F. Kennedy set the bar for future presidential candidates with his ease and charisma on-screen.[8]

By the end of the twentieth century, no president or major presidential candidate could exist without an immense PR effort. Sometimes things go well; other times, they don't. For example, in the 2008 presidential contest, Democratic nominee Barack Obama's team was headed by David Axelrod, founder of Chicago-based political and media consulting firm AKPD Message and Media, who smoothly guided Obama to the White House. By contrast, Republican nominee John McCain and his running mate, Sarah Palin, went through numerous campaign and PR strategists in their more tumultuous bid for the Oval Office.

Political public relations efforts don't end after an election, however. PR is in play when candidates take office, govern, or participate in or react to political movements—like the Tea Party or Occupy Wall Street. Just as many journalism outlets cover the news in permanent twenty-four-hour cycles, so must PR agencies stay involved with political, social, and media processes.

As discussed earlier in the chapter, the role of public relations efforts and lobbying is about more than presidential candidates and other politicians. From railroad companies looking for money from federal, state, and local governments to the explosion in the lobbying profession (see Figure 12.2 on page 421), outside groups wanting to influence the government's actions have an enormous and not always easy-to-understand impact on how our democracy functions.

Though public relations often provides political information and story ideas, the PR profession bears only part of the responsibility for "spun" news; after all, it is the job of a PR agency to get favorable news coverage for the individual or group it represents. PR professionals to some extent police their own ranks for unethical or irresponsible practices, but the news media should also monitor the public relations industry, as they do other government and business activities. Journalism also needs to be more conscious of how its own practices play into the hands of spin strategies. As a positive example of change on this front, many major newspapers and TV networks now offer regular assessments of the facts and falsehoods contained in political advertising. This media vigilance should be on behalf of citizens, who are entitled to robust, well-rounded debates on important social and political issues.

Like advertising and other forms of commercial speech, PR campaigns that result in free media exposure raise a number of questions regarding democracy and the expression of ideas. Large companies and PR agencies, like well-financed politicians, have money to invest in figuring out how to obtain favorable publicity. The question is not how to prevent that but how to ensure that other voices—those less well financed and less commercial—also receive an adequate hearing. To that end, journalists need to become less willing conduits in the distribution of publicity. PR agencies, for their part, need to show clients that participating as responsible citizens in the democratic process can serve them well and enhance their image. But in the end, all citizens bear the responsibility of understanding that the public relations industry surrounds us, regardless of what issues or sides we favor. It is a part of the media experience and, as such, part of our daily lives. Therefore, media literacy must also include awareness and knowledge of PR, and all of the ways it can affect us.

CHAPTER ESSENTIALS

Now that you have finished reading this chapter, you can use the following tools:

LaunchPad for *Media Essentials*

Go to **macmillanhighered.com/mediaessentials3e** for videos, review quizzes, and more.

LaunchPad for *Media Essentials* includes:

- **REVIEW WITH LEARNINGCURVE**
  LearningCurve uses gamelike quizzing to help you master the concepts you need to learn from this chapter.

- **VIDEO: GOING VIRAL: POLITICAL CAMPAIGNS AND VIDEO**
  Online video has changed political campaigning forever. In this video, Peggy Miles of Intervox Communications discusses how politicians use the Internet to reach out to voters.

REVIEW

Understand the Early History of Public Relations

- **Public relations** refers to the total communication strategy conducted by a person, a government, or an organization attempting to reach and persuade its audience to adopt a point of view. The first PR practitioners in the 1800s were **press agents**, such as P. T. Barnum and John Burke, who conveyed favorable messages to the public about their clients, often by staging stunts that reporters described in newspapers. These agents focused on **publicity**, using various media messages to spread information and interest about a person, a corporation, an issue, or a policy (pp. 403–406).

- As the United States became more industrialized and moved toward a consumer society, larger companies, such as railroads and utility organizations like AT&T, began hiring press agents to generate profits and spread the word on whatever they were promoting. However, in these early days of press agents, some of the tactics used were deceptive. Agents bribed journalists to write favorable stories and engaged in **deadheading**, or giving reporters free rail passes. Larger **railroads** and utility companies used **lobbyists**, professionals who seek to influence lawmakers' votes—to gain federal subsidies and establish policies that made it harder for smaller lines to compete (pp. 406–407).

- By the early 1900s, journalists began investigating some of the questionable PR practices being used, precipitating the professionalization of public relations. This effort was spear-headed by two pioneers of PR, Ivy Ledbetter Lee and Edward Bernays. Lee, who counseled his clients that honesty and directness were better PR devices than deceit, later worked with John D. Rockefeller. Bernays was the first to apply the findings of psychology and sociology to the PR profession (pp. 407–409).

Track the Evolution of Public Relations

- As the PR profession grew, two major types of public relations organizations took shape: PR agencies and in-house PR services (p. 409).

- Many large PR agencies are owned by or affiliated with multinational holding companies, such as WPP, Omnicom, and Interpublic. Other firms are independent and have local or regional operations, such as Edelman (pp. 409–410).

- Both PR agencies and in-house services have many functions. They sometimes craft **propaganda**, or communication that is presented as advertising or publicity intended to gain or undermine public support for a certain issue, program, or policy (p. 410).

- In addition, PR professionals research or formulate the message for a given product, policy, program, or issue. They are responsible for conveying the message, often via **press releases** (news releases), **video news releases (VNRs)**, or **public service announcements (PSAs)**, which are press releases for nonprofits (pp. 411, 414).

- Some PR practitioners manage media relations. This includes responding to negative images or crisis situations (pp. 415, 418–419).

- PR agents may also coordinate special and **pseudo-events** (staged activities aimed at drawing public attention and media coverage) in an effort to raise the profile of corporate, organizational, or business clients (p. 419).

- PR practitioners foster positive community and consumer relations and cultivate government relations, which is sometimes accomplished via **lobbying** (the process of trying to influence lawmakers to support legislation that would serve an organization's or industry's best interests). **Astroturf lobbying** is a kind of lobbying that consists of phony grassroots public affairs campaigns engineered by unscrupulous PR firms (pp. 420–422).

Discuss the Tensions between Public Relations and the Press

- The tense relationship between PR and the press consists of a complex interdependence of the two professions as well as journalists' skepticism about PR practices (pp. 422–423).

- PR practitioners maintain that they make journalists' jobs easier by supplying information, whereas journalists argue that PR agents selectively choose which facts to bring forward (p. 423).

- Some of the complaints from the press about PR have led some public relations practitioners to take steps to improve the profession's image. The industry formed its own professional organization (the Public Relations Society of America) in 1948, which functions as a watchdog group. PR practitioners have also begun using different language to describe what they do (pp. 423–425).

Explain the Role of Public Relations in Our Democratic Society

---

- PR's impact on the political process is significant, as many organizations hire public relations specialists to shape or reshape a candidate's image (p. 426).

- The fact that most affluent people and corporations can afford the most media exposure through PR raises questions about whether this restricts the expression of ideas from other, less affluent sources (p. 427).

STUDY QUESTIONS

1. Who were the individuals who conducted the earliest type of public relations in the nineteenth century? How did they contribute to the development of modern public relations in the twentieth century?

2. What are the two organizational structures for a PR firm? What are some of the ways these structures conduct business for their clients?

3. Explain the antagonism between journalism and public relations. Can and should the often hostile relationship between the two be mended? Why or why not?

4. In what ways does the profession of public relations serve the process of election campaigns? In what ways can it impede such campaigns?

MEDIA LITERACY PRACTICE

As noted earlier, public relations and journalism are extremely interdependent. To investigate this relationship, examine the public relations practices of an organization that interests you.

DESCRIBE the most recent ten or twelve press releases from a local/regional business or organization large enough to have its own PR department (your own college or university might be a worthy subject). Then pick a local news organization and see how many stories seem to have come about as a result of those press releases.

ANALYZE the resulting patterns: What kinds of press releases got picked up by your local news organization? Were the releases published in the newspaper verbatim, or were the stories just loosely based on the press releases?

INTERPRET what these patterns mean. For example, do press releases from this organization make an impact in the local news? Do you think the size of the newspaper and its staff makes a difference in how press releases are handled?

EVALUATE the relationship between public relations and journalism in your community. Based on this case study, is the level of the newspaper's reliance on public relations a good thing or a bad thing for the people in your community? Are the press releases promoting a healthy dialogue in the community or trying to publicize something not worthy of the news?

ENGAGE with the community by writing to the newspaper's editor and letting her or him know about your case study and conclusions.

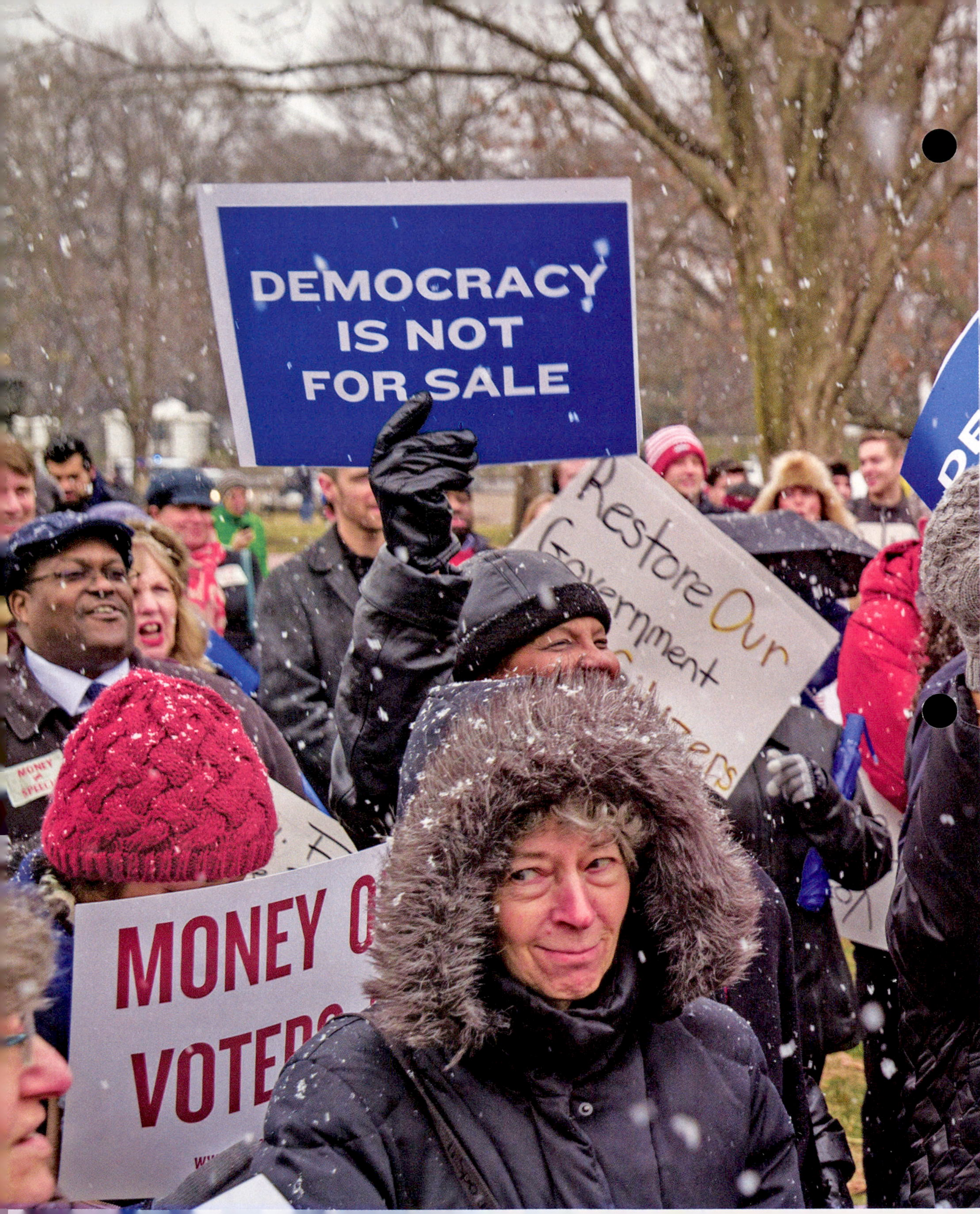
DEMOCRACY IS NOT FOR SALE
Restore Our Government
MONEY

13

Legal Controls and Freedom of Expression

Politicians and their constituents can talk, but money speaks much louder. Some aspects of the current U.S. political system amount to a legal pay-to-play system in which the wealthiest can wield indirect influence over elections (manipulating issues by buying lots of advertising) and more direct influence over legislation (manipulating politicians who desperately want money to pay for campaign advertising).[1] Although unpopular with a majority of Americans, this influence through campaign contributions has been defended on First Amendment grounds. Here is what the First Amendment (adopted in 1791) says about money as speech in political campaigns:

> Congress shall make no law respecting an establishment of religion, or prohibiting the free exercise thereof; or abridging the freedom of speech, or of the press; or the right of the people peaceably to assemble, and to petition the Government for a redress of grievances.

In other words, it says nothing explicitly about money. Yet money now counts as speech, protected by the First Amendment. So how did we end up here?

Ironically, it started with Congress's intention to *control* the amount of money in elections. In 1974, Congress amended federal election law to further limit campaign contributions. Two years later, in *Buckley v. Valeo* (1976), the U.S. Supreme Court suggested for the first time that political contributions count as speech. The court argued that restrictions on campaign money "necessarily reduce[d] the quantity of expression by restricting the number of issues discussed, the depth of the exploration, and the size of the audience reached. This is because virtually every means of communicating ideas in today's mass society requires the expenditure of money."[2]

Over the ensuing years, Congress has tried to again rein in campaign finance with new laws, but federal courts, beholden by the idea that money equals speech, have always struck them down. This brings us to the current state of our national elections. For the 2012 election, the two main political parties and their supporters spent an estimated $6 billion on campaign advertising, more than doubling the previous record. The main explanation for this new record was the unlimited amount that corporations and rich individuals could now spend, thanks to another decision by the Supreme Court: *Citizens United v. Federal Election Commission* (2010). The 5–4 decision said that it was a violation of First Amendment free-speech rights for the federal government to limit corporate or union spending for TV and radio advertising, usually done through organized "Super PACs" (political action committees) that are most often sponsored by corporate interests or super-rich donors.

Although not the only important factor, a candidate with access to lots of money for things like campaign ads has a clear advantage. But as Harvard Law School professor Lawrence Lessig explains, the threat to democracy and freedom of speech isn't just about the messages audiences hear during election time. Lessig argues that it's also about whom politicians listen to after an election: "Politicians are dependent upon 'the funders'—spending anywhere from 30 percent to 70 percent of their time raising money from these funders," he writes. "But 'the funders' are not 'the People': .26 percent of Americans give more than $200 in a congressional campaign; .05 percent give the max to any congressional candidate; .01 percent—the 1 percent of the 1 percent—give more than $10,000 in an election cycle; and .0000063 percent have given close to 80 percent of the super PAC money spent in this election so far. That's 196 Americans."[3] Given the *Citizens United* ruling, what can be done to give all citizens a voice in the campaign finance system and make them "patrons" of the political process?

SUCH DEBATES OVER WHAT CONSTITUTES "FREE SPEECH" or "free expression" are intricately tied together with questions of politics and economics. In addition to the growing involvement of money in politics, money is central to another set of laws affecting free speech: copyright law. For example, arguments about what constitutes copyright violation revolve around who should be allowed to make money from the creation, distribution, and ownership of media content— and who should shoulder the expense of enforcing copyright law. Meanwhile, debates about the particular messages in a piece of media content raise questions about legality, which we turn to politicians and lawmakers to answer. For instance, do teenagers have a right to use social media to bully a person because of his or her sexual orientation? Do military secrets published on the Internet prevent the government from protecting the citizenry?

Such arguments also raise questions regarding the variation in regulatory standards that has evolved across different mass media. For example, print media have the least regulation, as the First Amendment clearly protects freedom of the press. Broadcast has the strictest regulation, as lawmakers have defined the airwaves as a shared public resource. And regulation regarding the Internet is contested, as the technology (and the different ways in which people and organizations use it) is still relatively new.

In this chapter, we examine these themes more closely by:

- exploring the origins of free expression and a free press, identifying four models of free expression, taking a closer look at the First Amendment to the U.S. Constitution, tracing the emergence of censorship, and comparing the First Amendment with the Sixth Amendment

- shining a spotlight on film and the First Amendment, assessing social and political pressures affecting moviemaking, self-regulation in the film industry, and the emergence of the film rating system

- taking stock of free expression in the broadcast and online media, including examining the Federal Communications Commission (FCC) regulation of broadcasting, definitions and regulation of indecent speech, laws governing political broadcasts, the impact of the Fairness Doctrine, and communication policy regarding the Internet

- considering the First Amendment's role in our democracy today, including such questions as who (journalists? citizens? both?) should fulfill the civic role of watchdog

The Origins of Free Expression and a Free Press

In the United States, freedom of speech and freedom of the press are protected by the First Amendment in the Bill of Rights, developed for our nation's Constitution. Roughly interpreted, these freedoms suggest that anyone should be able to express his or her views, and that the press should be able to publish whatever it wants, without prohibition from Congress. But there's always been a tension between the notion of "free expression" and the idea that some expression (such as sexually explicit words or images) should be prohibited or censored. Many people have wondered what free expression really means.

In this section, we examine several aspects of free speech and freedom of the press. We explore the roots of the First Amendment and different interpretations of *free expression* that have arisen in modern times. We look at evolving notions of censorship and forms of expression that are not protected by the U.S. Constitution. And we consider ways in which the First Amendment has clashed with the Sixth Amendment, which guarantees accused individuals the right to speedy and public trials by impartial juries.

A Closer Look at the First Amendment

To understand how the idea of free expression has developed in the United States, we must understand how the notion of a free press came about. The story goes back to the 1600s, when various national governments in Europe controlled the circulation of ideas through the press by requiring printers to obtain licenses from them. Their goal was to monitor the ideas published by editors and writers and swiftly suppress subversion. However, in 1644, English poet John Milton published his essay *Areopagitica*, which opposed government licenses for printers and defended a free press. Milton argued that in a democratic society, all sorts of ideas—even false ones—should be allowed to circulate. Eventually, he maintained, the truth would emerge. In 1695, England stopped licensing newspapers, and most of Europe followed suit. In many democracies today, publishing a newspaper, magazine, or newsletter requires no license.

Less than a hundred years later, the writers of the U.S. Constitution were ambivalent about the idea of a free press. Indeed, the version of the Constitution ratified in 1788 did not include such protection. The states took a different tack, however. At that time, nine of the original thirteen states had charters defending freedom of the press. These states pushed to have federal guarantees of free speech and the press approved at the first session of the new Congress. Their efforts paid off: The Bill of Rights, which contained the first ten amendments to the Constitution, won ratification in 1791.

However, commitment to freedom of the press was not yet tested. In 1798, the Federalist Party, which controlled the presidency and the Congress, passed the Sedition Act to silence opposition to an anticipated war against France. The act was signed into law by President John Adams and resulted in the arrest and conviction of several publishers. However, after failing to curb opposition, the Sedition Act expired in 1801, during Thomas Jefferson's presidency. Jefferson, a Democratic-Republican who had challenged the act's constitutionality, pardoned all defendants convicted under it.[4] Ironically, the Sedition Act—the first major attempt to constrain the First Amendment—ended up solidifying American support behind the notion of a free press.

Interpretations of Free Expression

Americans are not alone in debating what constitutes free expression and whether constraining expression is ever appropriate. Over time, four models have emerged that capture the widely differing interpretations of what "free expression" means.[5] We can think of these as the authoritarian, state, social responsibility, and libertarian models. These models are distinguished by the degree of freedom their proponents advocate, and by ruling classes' attitudes toward the freedoms granted to average citizens.

The Authoritarian Model

The **authoritarian model** developed around the time the printing press first arrived in sixteenth-century England. Under this model, criticism of government and public dissent were not tolerated, especially if such speech undermined "the common good"—an ideal that elites and rulers defined. The government actively censored any expression it found threatening, and it issued printing licenses only to those publishers willing to say positive things about the government. Today, this model persists in many developing countries that have authoritarian governments. In these nations, journalism's job is to support government and business efforts to foster economic growth, minimize political dissent, and promote social stability.

AREOPAGITICA
A
SPEECH
OF
Mr JOHN MILTON
For the Liberty of UNLICENSED
PRINTING
To the PARLIAMENT of ENGLAND

Τοὐλεύθερον δ᾽ ἐκεῖνο· εἴ τις θέλει πόλει
Χρηστόν τι βούλευμ᾽ εἰς μέσον φέρειν ἔχων.
Καὶ ταῦθ᾽ ὁ χρῄζων λαμπρός ἐσθ᾽, ὁ μὴ θέλων
Σιγᾷ. τί τούτων ἐστ᾽ ἰσαίτερον πόλει;
Euripid. Hicetid.

This is true Liberty when free born men
Having to advise the public may speak free,
Which he who can, and will, deserves high praise,
Who neither can nor will, may hold his peace ;
What can be juster in a State than this?
Euripid. Hicetid.

THEY who to states and governors of the commonwealth direct their speech, high court of parliament, or wanting such access in a private condition, write that which they foresee may advance the public good; I suppose them, as at the beginning of no mean endeavour, not a little altered and moved inwardly in their minds; some with doubt of what will be the success, others with fear of what will be the censure; some with hope, others with confidence of what they

M.   1

The Print Collector/Print Collector/Getty Images

John Milton's *Areopagitica* is one of the most significant early defenses of freedom of the press.

© Oscilloscope Laboratories/Everett Collection

Government control of the press under the state model has led to protests like that of this Burmese monk and others like him.

The State Model

Under the **state model**, the government controls the press and what it reports. Leaders believe that the press should serve the goals of the state. Although the government tolerates some criticism, it suppresses ideas that challenge the basic premises of state authority. Today, a few countries use this model, including Myanmar (Burma), China, Cuba, and North Korea.

The Social Responsibility Model

The **social responsibility model** captures the ideals of mainstream journalism in the United States and most other democracies. The concepts and assumptions behind this model were outlined in 1947 by the Hutchins Commission, which was formed to examine the press's increasing influence. The commission's report called for the development of press watchdog groups, on the assumption that the mass media had grown too powerful. The report also concluded that the press needed to take more responsibility for improving American society by providing services like news forums for the exchange of ideas and better coverage of social groups and society's range of economic classes.

The social responsibility model has roots in revolutionary Europe. This model calls for the press to be privately owned, so that newspapers operate independently of government. By doing so, the press functions as a **Fourth Estate**—an unofficial branch of government that watches for abuses of power by the legislative, judicial, and executive branches. The press supplies information about such abuses to citizens, so they can make informed decisions about political and social issues.

The Libertarian Model

The **libertarian model** is the flip side of both the state and the authoritarian models and an extension of the social responsibility model. This model encourages vigorous criticism of government and supports the highest degree of individual and press freedoms. Proponents of the libertarian model argue that *no* restrictions should be placed on the mass media or on individual speech. In North America and Europe, many alternative newspapers and magazines operate on such a model. They often emphasize the importance of securing rights for sidelined populations (such as gay men and lesbians), and follow an ethic that absolute freedom of expression is the best way to fight injustice and arrive at the truth.

The Evolution of Censorship

In the United States, the First
Amendment theoretically prohibits
censorship. Over time, Supreme
Court decisions have defined
censorship as **prior restraint**—
meaning that courts and governments cannot block any publication
or speech before it actually occurs.
The principle behind prior restraint
is that a law has not been broken
until an illegal act has been committed. However, the Court left
open the idea that the judiciary
could halt publication of news in
exceptional cases—for example, if such publication would threaten national security. In the 1970s, two pivotal court decisions tested the idea of prior restraint.

© Bettmann/Corbis

In 1971, Daniel Ellsberg, a
former Pentagon researcher,
turned against America's
military policy in Vietnam
and leaked information to the
press. The federal case against
him was dropped in 1973 when
illegal government-sponsored
wiretaps of Ellsberg's psycho-
analyst came to light during
the Watergate scandal.

The Pentagon Papers Decision

In 1971, with the Vietnam War still raging, Daniel Ellsberg, a former Defense
Department employee, stole a copy of the forty-seven-volume report "History of
U.S. Decision-Making Process on Vietnam Policy." A thorough study of U.S. involvement in Vietnam since World War II, the report was classified by the government
as top secret. Ellsberg and a friend leaked the report—nicknamed the Pentagon
Papers—to the *New York Times* and the *Washington Post*. In June 1971, the *Times*
began publishing excerpts of the report. To block any further publication, the Nixon
administration applied for and received a federal court injunction against the *Times*
to halt publication of the documents, arguing that it posed "a clear and present
danger" to national security by revealing military strategy to the enemy.

In a 6–3 vote, the Supreme Court sided with the newspaper. Justice Hugo
Black, in his majority opinion, attacked the government's attempt to suppress publication: "Both the history and language of the First Amendment support the view
that the press must be left free to publish news, whatever the source, without
censorship, injunctions, or prior restraints."[6]

The *Progressive* Magazine Decision

The conflict between prior restraint and national security surfaced again in 1979,
when the U.S. government issued an injunction to block publication of the
Progressive, a national left-wing magazine. The editors had planned to publish an

article titled "The H-Bomb Secret: How We Got It, Why We're Telling It." The dispute began when the magazine's editor sent a draft to the Department of Energy to verify technical portions of the article. Believing that the article contained sensitive data that might damage U.S. efforts to halt the proliferation of nuclear weapons, the department asked the magazine not to publish it. When the magazine said it would proceed anyway, the government sued the *Progressive* and asked a federal district court to block publication.

In an unprecedented action, Justice Robert Warren sided with the government, deciding that "a mistake in ruling against the United States could pave the way for thermonuclear annihilation for us all. In that event, our right to life is extinguished and the right to publish becomes moot."[7] Warren was seeking to balance the *Progressive*'s First Amendment rights against the possibility that the article, if published, would spread dangerous information and undermine national security. During appeals, several other publications printed their own stories about the H-bomb, and the U.S. government eventually dropped the case. None of the articles, including one ultimately published by the *Progressive*, contained precise details on how to design a nuclear weapon. But Warren's decision represented the first time in American history that a prior-restraint order imposed in the name of national security stopped initial publication of a news report.

Unprotected Forms of Expression

Despite the First Amendment's provision that "Congress shall make no law" restricting speech and the press, the federal government, state laws, and even local ordinances have on occasion curbed some forms of expression. And over the years, the U.S. court system has determined that some kinds of expression do not merit protection under the Constitution. These forms include sedition, copyright infringement, libel, obscenity, and violation of privacy rights.

Sedition

For more than a century after the Sedition Act of 1798, Congress passed no laws prohibiting the articulation or publication of dissenting opinions. But sentiments that fueled the Sedition Act resurfaced in the twentieth century, particularly in times of war. For instance, the Espionage Acts of 1917 and 1918—enforced during the two world wars—made it a federal crime to utter or publish "seditious" statements, defined as anything expressing opposition to the U.S. war effort.

For example, in the landmark *Schenck v. United States* (1919) appeal case, taking place during World War I, the Supreme Court upheld the conviction of a Socialist Party leader, Charles T. Schenck, for distributing leaflets urging American men to protest the draft. Justices argued that Schenck had violated the recently passed Espionage Act.

In supporting Schenck's sentence—a ten-year prison term—Justice Oliver Wendell Holmes noted that the Socialist leaflets were entitled to First Amendment protection, but only during times of peace. In establishing the "clear and present danger" criterion for expression, the Supreme Court demonstrated the limits of the First Amendment.

Copyright Infringement

Appropriating a writer's or an artist's words, images, or music without consent or payment is also a form of expression not protected by the First Amendment. A **copyright** legally protects the rights of authors and producers to their published or unpublished writing, music, lyrics, TV programs, movies, or graphic art designs. Congress passed the first Copyright Act in 1790, which gave authors the right to control their published works for fourteen years, with the opportunity to renew copyright protection for another fourteen years. After the end of the copyright period, the work would enter the **public domain**, which would give the public free access to the work. (For example, a publisher could reprint a written work that had entered the public domain.) The idea was that a period of copyright control would give authors financial incentive to create original works, and that moving works into the public domain would give others incentive to create works derived from earlier accomplishments.

But in time, artists, as they began to live longer, and corporations, which could also hold copyrights, wanted to prolong the period in which they could profit from creative works. In 1976, Congress extended the copyright period to the life of the author plus fifty years (seventy-five years for a corporate copyright owner). In 1998 (as copyrights on works such as Disney's Mickey Mouse were set to expire), Congress again extended the copyright period for an additional twenty years.

Today, nearly every innovation in digital culture creates new questions about copyright law. For example, is a video remix that samples copyrighted sounds and images a copyright violation or a creative accomplishment protected under the concept of *fair use* (the same standard that enables students to legally quote attributed text in their research papers)? One of the laws that tips the debates toward stricter enforcement of copyright is the Digital Millennium Copyright Act of 1998, which outlaws technology or actions that circumvent copyright systems.

Janette Beckman/Getty Images

In a 1994 landmark case, the Supreme Court ruled that the rap group 2 Live Crew's 1989 song "Pretty Woman" was a legitimate parody of the 1964 Roy Orbison song and was thus covered by the fair-use exception to copyright.

In other words, it may be illegal merely to create or distribute technology that enables someone to make illegal copies of digital content, such as a movie DVD.

SOPA and PIPA

In general, the copyright lobby has enjoyed success getting lawmakers to pass favorable legislation. But this has not always been the case. Starting in 2011, U.S. lawmakers were considering two proposals: the Stop Online Piracy Act (SOPA) in the House, and the Protect Intellectual Property Act (PIPA) in the Senate. The proposals were spurred by concerns over illegally copied movies, music, games, and so on, that were being dubbed in foreign countries, outside the reach of U.S. law enforcement, and distributed globally via the Internet. Supporters said that PIPA and SOPA would attack the pirates by getting at the flow of pirated material online. But opponents saw it as an unprecedented power grab for Internet control by the U.S. government and raised cries of censorship and concerns about other ways the laws would threaten free speech. They argued that the laws would allow copyright holders to block Web sites, censor search results, and cut off advertising revenue without even going through a judge. Others feared the language was too vague and would reduce fair-use protections. Joining the protests were major Internet companies like Google, Mozilla, *Wikipedia*, and Reddit, who were among over 115,000 Web sites that held a "blackout" in protest on January 18, 2012. *Wikipedia*, for example, displayed a message to all visitors that said "Imagine a world without free knowledge" instead of the usual encyclopedic entries. The massive online protest resulted in three million e-mails to Congress to oppose the bills.[8] The protests went international, with the European Union Parliament weighing in by adopting a resolution that stressed the "need to protect the integrity of the global internet and freedom of communication by refraining from unilateral measures to revoke IP addresses or domain names."[9]

Although the SOPA and PIPA proposals have been dropped (at least for now), it's notable that in addition to the important questions about free speech in a digital era, this conflict also represented a fight between "old" media and "new" media. The groups pushing for the bills were made up of people from the Motion Picture Association of America and the Recording Industry Association of America, whereas some of the highest-profile opponents were Internet groups like *Wikipedia* and Google. In addition to broader concerns over copyright versus free speech, the opposition effort probably got a boost from the public by portraying SOPA and PIPA as destructive to the more freewheeling and open culture of the Internet.

Libel

The biggest legal worry haunting editors and publishers today is the possibility of being sued for libel, a form of expression that, unlike political speech, is not protected under the First Amendment. **Libel** is defamation of someone's character in written or broadcast form. It differs from **slander**, which is spoken defamation. Inherited from British common law, libel is generally defined as a false statement that holds a person up to public ridicule, contempt, or hatred, or that injures a person's business or livelihood. Examples of potentially libelous statements include falsely accusing someone of professional incompetence (such as medical malpractice); falsely accusing a person of a crime (such as drug dealing); falsely stating that someone is mentally ill or engages in unacceptable behavior (such as public drunkenness); and falsely accusing a person of associating with a disreputable organization or cause (such as being a member of the Mafia or a neo-Nazi military group) (see "Media Literacy Case Study: A False *Wikipedia* 'Biography'" on pages 444–445).

Since 1964, *New York Times v. Sullivan* has served as the standard for libel law. The case stems from a 1960 full-page advertisement placed in the *New York Times* by the Committee to Defend Martin Luther King and the Struggle for Freedom in the South. Without naming names, the ad criticized the law-enforcement tactics used in southern cities to break up Civil Rights demonstrations. The city commissioner of Montgomery, Alabama, L. B. Sullivan, sued the *Times* for libel, claiming the ad defamed him indirectly. Alabama civil courts awarded Sullivan $500,000, but the *Times'* lawyers appealed to the Supreme Court. The Court reversed the ruling, holding that Alabama libel law violated the *Times'* First Amendment rights.[10]

Private individuals (such as city sanitation employees, undercover police informants, or nurses) must prove three things to win a libel case: (1) that the public statement about them was false; (2) that damages or actual injury occurred (such as loss of a job or mental anguish); and (3) that the publisher or broadcaster was negligent in failing to determine the truthfulness of the statement.

In the *Sullivan* case, the Supreme Court asked future civil courts to distinguish whether plaintiffs in libel cases are "public officials" or "private individuals." To win libel cases, the Court said, public officials (such as movie or sports stars, political leaders, or lawyers defending a prominent client) are held to a tougher standard and must prove falsehood, damages, negligence, and **actual malice** on the part of the news media. *Actual malice* means that the reporter or editor either knew the statement was false and printed or broadcast it anyway, or acted with a reckless disregard for the truth. Because actual malice against a public official is hard to prove, it is difficult for public figures to win libel suits.

Historically, the best defense against libel in American courts has been the truth. In most cases, if libel defendants can demonstrate that they printed or broadcast true statements, plaintiffs will not recover any damages—even if their reputations were harmed. There are other defenses against libel as well. For

A False *Wikipedia* "Biography"
By John Seigenthaler

> "John Seigenthaler Sr. was the assistant to Attorney General Robert Kennedy in the early 1960's. For a brief time, he was thought to have been directly involved in the Kennedy assassinations of both John, and his brother, Bobby. Nothing was ever proven."
>
> *–Wikipedia*

This is a highly personal story about Internet character assassination. It could be your story. I have no idea whose sick mind conceived the false, malicious "biography" that appeared under my name for 132 days on *Wikipedia*, the popular, online, free encyclopedia whose authors are unknown and virtually untraceable.

At age 78, I thought I was beyond surprise or hurt at anything negative said about me. I was wrong. One sentence in the biography was true. I was Robert Kennedy's administrative assistant in the early 1960s.

At my request, executives of the Web site have removed the false content about me. I phoned Jimmy Wales, *Wikipedia*'s founder, and asked, "Do you . . . have any way to know who wrote that?"

"No, we don't," he said. Naturally, I want to unmask my "biographer." But searching cyberspace for the identity of people who post spurious information can be frustrating. I traced the registered IP (Internet Protocol) number of my "biographer" to a customer of BellSouth Internet and left two e-mails with the company's "Abuse Team."

After three weeks, hearing nothing further about the Abuse Team investigation, I phoned BellSouth's Atlanta corporate headquarters, which led to conversations between my lawyer and BellSouth's counsel. My only remote chance of getting the name, I learned, was to file a "John or Jane Doe" lawsuit against my "biographer." Major communications Internet companies are bound by federal privacy laws that protect the identity of their customers, even those who defame online. Only if a lawsuit resulted in a court subpoena would BellSouth give up the name.

Federal law also protects online corporations—BellSouth, AOL, MCI, *Wikipedia*, etc.—from libel

Note: In 2006, Seigenthaler, with the help of some intrepid reporters, tracked down the man who posted the libelous content. Seigenthaler, however, chose not to sue him, deciding instead to speak out about the experience and to call on Wikipedia to require those who post entries to sign their names and take responsibility for their work. The controversy is now a part of his online Wikipedia bio and also has its own entry (pictured).

Source: Excerpted from John Seigenthaler, "A False Wikipedia *'Biography,'" USA Today, November 30, 2005, p. 11A.*

John Seigenthaler Sr. Wikipedia biography controversy

From Wikipedia, the free encyclopedia

The **John Seigenthaler Sr. Wikipedia biography controversy** arose when contributor Brian Chase anonymously posted a hoax in the Wikipedia entry for John Seigenthaler, Sr., a well known writer and journalist. The post was not discovered and corrected until more than four months later. This incident received publicity and led to critical examination into the credibility of the information that Wikipedia offers and to policy changes within the Wikimedia Foundation.[1]

Contents [hide]

1 Hoax
2 Detection and correction
3 Anonymous editor identified
4 Seigenthaler's public reaction
5 Other reactions
6 Wikimedia Foundation reaction
7 See also
8 Notes
9 External links
   9.1 News articles

John Seigenthaler Sr. on CNN, 5 December 2005.

Hoax   [edit]

Brian Chase was an operations manager of Rush Delivery, a delivery service company in Nashville, Tennessee. As a prank on a colleague, Chase modified Seigenthaler's Wikipedia biography to suggest that Seigenthaler may have had a role in the assassinations of both John F. Kennedy and Robert F. Kennedy. While at his workplace on May 26, 2005, Chase added the false texts:

---

lawsuits. Under the Communications Decency Act, passed in 1996—and unlike print and broadcast companies—online service providers cannot be sued for disseminating defamatory attacks on citizens posted by others.

    Wikipedia's Web site acknowledges that it is not responsible for inaccurate information, but Wales, in a C-Span interview with Brian Lamb, insisted that his Web site is accountable and that his community of thousands of volunteer editors (he said he has only one paid employee) corrects mistakes within minutes.

    My experience refutes that. My "biography" was posted May 26 [2005]. For four months, *Wikipedia* depicted me as a suspected assassin before Wales erased it from his Web site's history Oct. 5. And so we live in a universe of new media with phenomenal opportunities for worldwide communications and research—but populated by volunteer vandals with poison-pen intellects. Congress has enabled them and protects them.

APPLYING THE CRITICAL PROCESS

DESCRIPTION Go to *Wikipedia* and look up entries for three topics with which you are familiar. (For example, they could be entries on movies, a musical act, or your hometown.)

ANALYSIS Look for patterns: Are the entries accurate, with sufficient footnoted sources for verification? Is there significant information missing from the entries? When was each entry last updated (see the bottom of the entry page)? Is there an active debate about each topic?

INTERPRETATION What makes a good *Wikipedia* entry? Why might some topics receive more editing attention than others?

EVALUATION Is the mostly open editing process of *Wikipedia* a good thing or a bad thing?

ENGAGEMENT Become a registered user of Wikipedia and correct or update a *Wikipedia* entry yourself.

example, prosecutors (who would otherwise be vulnerable to accusations of libel) are granted *absolute privilege* in a court of law, so they can freely make accusatory statements toward defendants—a key part of their job. Reporters who print or broadcast statements made in court are also protected against libel.

Another defense against libel is the rule of **opinion and fair comment**, the notion that libel consists of *intentional* misstatements of factual information, not expressions of opinion. However, the line between fact and opinion is often blurry. For instance, one of the most famous tests of opinion and fair comment came with a case pitting conservative minister and political activist Jerry Falwell against Larry Flynt, publisher of *Hustler*, a pornographic magazine. The case developed after a spoof ad in the November 1983 issue of *Hustler* suggested that Falwell had had sex with his mother. Falwell sued for libel, demanding $45 million in damages. The jury rejected the libel suit but found that Flynt had intentionally caused Falwell emotional distress—and awarded Falwell $200,000. Flynt's lawyers appealed, and the U.S. Supreme Court overturned the verdict in 1988, explaining that the magazine was entitled to constitutional protection.

Libel laws also protect satire, comedy, and opinions expressed in reviews of books, plays, movies, and restaurants. However, such laws do not protect malicious statements in which plaintiffs can prove that defendants used their free-speech rights to mount an uncalled-for, damaging personal attack.

Obscenity

For most of this nation's history, legislators have argued that **obscenity** is not a form of expression protected by the First Amendment. However, experts have not been able to agree on what constitutes an obscene work, especially as definitions of obscenity have changed over the years. For example, during the 1930s, novels (such as James Joyce's *Ulysses*) were judged obscene if they contained "four-letter words."

The current legal definition of *obscenity*, derived from the 1973 *Miller v. California* case, states that obscene materials meet three criteria: (1) the average person, applying contemporary community standards, finds that the material as a whole appeals to prurient interest (that is, incites lust); (2) the material depicts or describes sexual conduct in a patently offensive way; and (3) the material as a whole lacks serious literary, artistic, political, or scientific value. The *Miller* decision acknowledged that different communities and regions of the country have different standards with which to judge obscenity. It also required that a work be judged *as a whole*. This was designed to keep publishers from simply inserting a political essay or literary poem into pornographic materials to demonstrate that their publication contained redeeming features.

Since the *Miller* decision, major prosecutions of obscenity have been rare, and most battles now concern the Internet, for which the concept of community standards has been eclipsed by the medium's global reach. The most recent incarnation of the Child Online Protection Act—originally conceived in 1998 to make it illegal to post "material that is harmful to minors"—was found unconstitutional in 2007 because it infringed on the right to free speech online. The presiding judge in this decision also stated that the act would be ineffective, as it wouldn't apply to pornographic Web sites from overseas, which account for up to half of such sites. The ruling suggested that parents and software filters offer the best protection for children against harmful content on the Web.

Violation of Privacy Rights

Whereas libel laws safeguard a person's character and reputation, the right to privacy protects an individual's peace of mind and personal feelings. In the simplest terms, the **right to privacy** addresses a person's right to be left alone, without his or her name, image, or daily activities becoming public property. The most common forms of privacy invasion are unauthorized tape recording, photographing, and wiretapping of someone; making someone's personal records, such as health and phone records, available to the public; disclosing personal information, such as religious or sexual activities; and appropriating (without authorization) someone's image or name for advertising or other commercial purposes.

In general, the news media have been granted wide protections under the First Amendment to do their work, even if it approaches or constitutes violation of privacy. For instance, journalists can typically use the names and pictures of private individuals and public figures without their consent in their news stories. Still, many local municipalities and states have passed "anti-paparazzi" laws protecting public individuals from unwarranted scrutiny and surveillance on their private property. A number of laws also protect regular citizens' privacy. For example, the Privacy Act of 1974 protects individuals' records from public disclosure unless they give written consent. In some cases, however, private citizens become public figures— for example, rape victims who are

Right to privacy is different for public as opposed to private individuals. However, the recent trend of oppressive paparazzi has led to laws protecting some personal activities for celebrities.

Gilles Mingason/Getty Images

covered in the news. In these situations, reporters have been allowed to record these individuals' quotes and use their images without permission.

The Electronic Communications Privacy Act of 1986 extended the law regarding private citizens to include computer-stored data and the Internet, such as employees' e-mails composed and sent through their employer's equipment. However, subsequent court decisions ruled that employees have no privacy rights in electronic communications conducted on their employer's equipment. The USA PATRIOT Act of 2001 further weakened the earlier laws, giving the federal government more latitude in searching private citizens' records and intercepting electronic communications without a court order. Following leaks from Edward Snowden about the domestic spying program of the NSA (National Security Agency), we learned that these interceptions and invasions of privacy were much more widespread than most people had guessed.

Congress took a step toward bringing more Internet privacy to Americans by proposing the Do Not Track Me Online Act of 2011. If passed, it would give consumers the ability to opt out of having their online activity collected by private companies without their permission. But in a society that is both fiercely defensive of its privacy and widely engaged in sharing more personal information than in any other period in history, it remains unclear how individual privacy will be legally controlled in the digital age.

First Amendment versus Sixth Amendment

First Amendment protections of speech and the press have often clashed with the Sixth Amendment, which guarantees an accused individual in "all criminal prosecutions . . . the right to a speedy and public trial, by an impartial jury." Gag orders, shield laws, and laws governing the use of cameras in a courtroom all put restrictions on speech and other forms of expression for the sake of Sixth Amendment rights.

Gag Orders

In recent criminal cases, some lawyers have used the news media to comment publicly on cases that are pending or in trial. This can make it difficult to assemble an impartial jury, thus threatening individuals' Sixth Amendment rights. In the 1960s, the Supreme Court introduced safeguards for ensuring fair trials in heavily publicized cases. These included placing speech restrictions, or **gag orders**, on lawyers and witnesses. In some countries, courts have issued gag orders to prohibit the press from releasing information or giving commentary that might prejudice jury selection or cause an unfair trial. But in the United States, especially

since a Supreme Court review in 1976, gag orders have been struck down as a prior-restraint violation of the First Amendment.

Shield Laws

Shield laws state that reporters do not have to reveal the sources of the information they use in news stories. The news media have argued that protecting sources' confidentiality maintains reporters' credibility, protects sources from possible retaliation, and serves the public interest by providing information citizens might not otherwise receive. Thirty-five states and the District of Columbia now have some type of shield law. However, there is no federal shield law in the United States, leaving journalists exposed to subpoenas from federal prosecutors and courts.

Laws Governing the Use of Cameras in a Courtroom

Debates over limiting electronic broadcast equipment and photographers in courtrooms date back to the Bruno Hauptmann trial in the mid-1930s. Hauptmann was convicted and executed for the kidnap-murder of the nineteen-month-old son of Anne and Charles Lindbergh (the aviation hero who made the first solo flight across the Atlantic Ocean in 1927). During the trial, Hauptmann and his attorney complained that the circus atmosphere fueled by the presence of radio and flash cameras prejudiced the jury and turned the public against him. After the trial, the American Bar Association amended its professional ethics code, stating that electronic equipment in the courtroom detracted "from the essential dignity of the proceedings." For years after the Hauptmann trial, almost every state banned photographic, radio, and TV equipment from courtrooms.

But as broadcast equipment became more portable and less obtrusive, and as television became the major news source for most Americans, courts gradually re-evaluated the bans. In the early 1980s, the Supreme Court ruled that the presence of TV equipment did not make fair trials impossible. The Court then left it up to each state to implement its own system. Today, all states allow television coverage of some cases (some just trial courts, some just appellate courts, some both), though most also allow presiding judges to place

An early 1980s Supreme Court ruling opened the door for the debut of court TV in 1991 and the televised O. J. Simpson trial in 1994 (the most publicized case in history).

Vince Bucci/AFP/Getty Images

certain restrictions on coverage of courtrooms. The state courts are now dealing with questions about the use of other electronic devices, such as smartphones and tablets, and whether or not to allow reporters to tweet or send blog posts live from the courtroom. The United States Supreme Court continues to ban TV from its proceedings, although it broke its anti-radio rule in 2000 by permitting delayed broadcasts of the hearings on the Florida vote recount case that determined the winner of the 2000 presidential election.

The First Amendment beyond the Printed Page: Film and Broadcasting

Back when the Bill of Rights was ratified, our nation's founders could not have predicted the advent of visual media. Film, which came into existence in the late 1890s, presented new challenges for those seeking to determine whether expression in film should be protected. The First Amendment said nothing explicit about film, so lawmakers, courts, society, and industry began an ongoing struggle over exactly how to apply it. As new communication technologies emerged, so did concerns over the impact of films and broadcast sounds and images on the values and morals of the public—especially children. It's useful to understand how these ongoing battles over the limits of free speech have played out over the last century, as the model of self-regulation and self-censorship developed in the movie industry is often invoked in discussions of the regulation of video games, the Internet, and similar technologies (see also discussions about regulation in technology-specific chapters).

Jack Johnson (1878–1946) was the first black heavyweight boxing champion, from 1908 to 1914. His stunning victory over white champion Jim Jeffries in 1910 resulted in race riots across the country and led to a ban on the interstate transportation of boxing films.

© Bettmann/Corbis

Citizens and Lawmakers Control the Movies

During the early part of the twentieth century, civic leaders in individual towns and cities formed local *review boards*, which screened movies to determine their moral suitability for the community. By 1920, more than ninety cities in the United States had such boards, which were composed of vice squad officers, politicians, or other citizens. By 1923, twenty-two states had such boards.

Meanwhile, lawmakers seeking to please their constituencies introduced legislation to control films. For example, after African American heavyweight champion Jack Johnson defeated white champion Jim Jeffries in 1910, the federal government outlawed transportation of boxing movies across state lines. The move reflected racist attitudes (a fear of images of a black man defeating a white man) more than distaste for violent imagery, as legislators pandered to white constituents who saw Johnson as a threat.

The idea of film as free speech took a big hit in 1915, when the Supreme Court decided in the *Mutual v. Ohio* case that films were "a business pure and simple" and thus not protected by the First Amendment. The Court further described the film industry as a circus, a "spectacle" for entertainment with "a special capacity for evil."[11]

Everett Collection

Roberto Rossellini's *The Miracle* (1948), a 40-minute Italian film, is about a peasant woman who mistakenly thinks she has experienced a virgin pregnancy. When it was shown in New York City with two other short films under the group title *The Way of Love*, Catholic groups protested. The attempt to ban the film in New York led to a landmark Supreme Court decision placing movies with books and newspapers in terms of First Amendment protection.

The Movie Industry Regulates Itself

In the early 1920s, a series of scandals—including the rape and murder of an aspiring actress at a party thrown by silent-film comedian Fatty Arbuckle—rocked Hollywood and pressured the movie industry to regulate itself before public review boards or the government could force regulations on them (or before audiences were driven away from movie theaters by the scandals). So over the next few decades, the industry set up its own way of policing not only the content of films but also the personal lives of actors, directors, and others involved in the moviemaking process.

The Motion Picture Producers and Distributors of America

In the 1920s, industry leaders hired Will Hays, a former Republican National Committee chair, as president of the Motion Picture Producers and Distributors of

America (MPPDA). Under Hays, promising actors or movie extras who had even minor police records were **blacklisted**, meaning they were put on a list of people who would subsequently not be hired by any of the movie studios. Hays also developed a public relations division for the MPPDA, which promptly squelched a national movement to create a federal law censoring movies.

The Motion Picture Production Code

In the early 1930s, the Hays Office established the Motion Picture Production Code. The code stipulated that "no picture shall be produced which will lower the moral standards of those who see it. Hence the sympathy of the audience shall never be thrown to the side of crime, wrong-doing, evil or sin." The code also dictated which phrases, images, and topics producers and directors had to avoid. For example, "excessive and lustful kissing" and "suggestive postures" were not allowed. The code also prohibited negative portrayals of religion or religious figures. Anyone who broke these rules was blacklisted.

Almost every executive in the industry adopted the code, viewing it as better than regulation coming from the government, and it influenced most commercial movies for the next twenty years. The level of self-censorship and control Hays and his organization achieved under this "voluntary" self-censorship and blacklisting was arguably greater than the government could have achieved on its own. Not only did this stifle creativity and critique, but it spread with anticommunist hysteria in the mid-twentieth century, when individuals could get blacklisted for the merest suspicion of communist sympathies.

This ideologically based blacklisting, inherently a violation of a citizens First Amendment rights, hit its peak in the 1950s, just as the grip of Hays's motion picture code was about to crumble. In 1952, the Supreme Court decided in *Burstyn v. Wilson* that New York could not ban the Italian film *The Miracle* under state regulations barring "sacrilegious" films. The Court had decided that movies were an important vehicle for public opinion, putting American movies on the same footing as books and newspapers in terms of protection under the First Amendment.

The Rating System and Forced Self-Censorship

In the wake of the 1952 *Miracle* case and the demise of the production code, renewed discontent over sexual language and imagery in movies pushed the MPPDA (renamed the Motion Picture Association of America, or MPAA) in the late 1960s to establish a movie-rating system to help concerned viewers avoid offensive material. Eventually, G, PG, R, and X ratings (X isn't used by the MPAA but as a promotional tool by adult filmmakers) emerged as guideposts for films' suitability for various age groups. In 1984, the MPAA added the PG-13 rating to distinguish slightly higher levels of violence or adult themes in movies that might

TABLE 13.1 // THE VOLUNTARY MOVIE RATING SYSTEM

Rating	Description
G	**General Audiences:** All ages admitted; contains nothing that would offend parents when viewed by their children.
PG	**Parental Guidance Suggested:** Parents urged to give "parental guidance," as it may contain some material they may not find suitable for their young children.
PG-13	**Parents Strongly Cautioned:** Parents should be cautious because some content may be inappropriate for children under the age of 13.
R	**Restricted:** The film contains some adult material. Parents/guardians are urged to learn more about it before taking children under the age of 17 with them.
NC-17	**No one 17 and under admitted:** Adult content. Children are not admitted.

Data from: Motion Picture Association of America, "Understanding the Film Ratings," accessed April 22, 2015, www.mpaa.org/film-ratings

otherwise qualify as PG, and later the NC-17 rating (no children under 17) for films with strong content that nevertheless aren't pornographic (see Table 13.1).

Ratings have an important relationship to the ability of a film to make money. An R can sometimes have a negative effect, but an NC-17 in most cases is seen as a kiss of death, not least because several major theater chains refuse to screen films rated NC-17, and many outlets won't run ads for them. Critics have attacked the system for being secretive (in theory, the identities of ratings board members is kept anonymous) and for applying standards arbitrarily and unequally. For example, violence is generally more acceptable than nudity or sexual content, and often similar sex scenes can earn films wildly different ratings, depending on the scene's point of view. Critics say this forces directors and producers to re-edit films in ways that silence the voices of certain groups in order to avoid an NC-17 rating—and probable bankruptcy. This raises important free-speech questions not only for movies but also for the industries that look to the film industry as a model of self-regulation (and self-censorship).

The First Amendment, Broadcasting, and the Internet

As the film industry developed, the lack of clarity regarding the First Amendment's protection of expression in movies prompted the

© Bettmann/Corbis

The sexual innuendo of an "Adam and Eve" radio sketch between sultry film star Mae West and dummy Charlie McCarthy (voiced by ventriloquist Edgar Bergen) enraged many listeners. The networks banned West from further radio appearances for what was considered "indecent" speech.

industry to regulate itself. And with the rise of additional new media that our nation's founders could not have envisioned— namely, broadcasting and the Internet— legislators and industry players once again began debating the question of how free these media are under the First Amendment. Different types of protections and levels of regulation developed in broadcast and cyberspace. Whereas film received protections similar to print in the 1952 Supreme Court ruling, broadcast is subject to fewer protections, and the Internet is so relatively new that people are still debating how First Amendment rights might apply to it.

Two Pivotal Court Cases

Drawing on the argument that limited broadcast signals constitute a scarce national resource, Congress passed the Communications Act of 1934 (see Chapter 6 on radio). The act mandated that radio broadcasters operate in "the public interest, convenience, or necessity," suggesting that they were not free to air whatever they wanted. Since that time, station owners have challenged the "public interest" statute and argued that because the government is not allowed to dictate newspaper content, it similarly should not be permitted to control licenses or mandate broadcast programming. But the U.S. courts have outlined major differences between broadcast and print—as demonstrated by two cases.

The first case—*Red Lion Broadcasting Co. v. FCC* (1969)—began when WGCB, a small-town radio station in Red Lion, Pennsylvania, refused to give airtime to author Fred Cook. Cook wrote a book criticizing Barry Goldwater, the Republican Party's presidential candidate in 1964. On a syndicated show WGCB aired, a conservative radio preacher and Goldwater fan verbally attacked Cook on the air. Cook asked for response time from the stations that carried the attack. Most complied, but WGCB snubbed him. He appealed to the FCC, which ordered the station to give Cook free time. The station refused, claiming the First Amendment gave it control over its programming content. The Supreme

Court sided with the FCC and ordered the station to give Cook airtime, arguing that the public interest—in this case, the airing of differing viewpoints—outweighs a broadcaster's rights.

The second case—*Miami Herald Publishing Co. v. Tornillo* (1974)—centered on the question of whether the newspaper in this case, the *Miami Herald*, should have been forced to give political candidate Pat Tornillo Jr. space to reply to an editorial opposing his candidacy. In contrast to the *Red Lion* decision, the Supreme Court sided with the paper. The Court argued that forcing a newspaper to give a candidate space violated the paper's First Amendment right to decide what to publish. Clearly, print media had more freedom of expression than did broadcasting.

Dirty Words, Indecent Speech, and Hefty Fines

Like the Supreme Court's rulings in the *Red Lion* and *Miami Herald* cases, regulators' actions regarding indecency in broadcasting reflected the idea that broadcasters had less freedom of expression than did print media. In theory, communication law says that the government cannot censor (prohibit before the fact) broadcast content. However, the government may punish broadcasters *after* the fact for **indecency**.

© Ted Streshinsky/Corbis

The current precedent for indecency is based on a complaint about comedian George Carlin's sketch about the "seven dirty words" that could not be aired.

Concerns over indecent broadcast programming cropped up in 1937, when the FCC scolded NBC for airing a sketch featuring sultry comedian-actress Mae West. After the sketch, which West peppered with sexual innuendos, the networks banned her from further radio appearances for "indecent" speech. Since then, the FCC has periodically fined or reprimanded stations for indecent programming, especially during times when children might be listening. For example, after an FCC investigation in the 1970s, several stations lost their licenses or were fined for broadcasting *topless radio*, which featured deejays and callers discussing intimate sexual subjects in the afternoon. (Topless radio would reemerge in the 1980s, this time with doctors and therapists, rather than deejays, offering intimate counsel to listeners.)

The current precedent for regulating broadcast indecency stems from a complaint to the FCC that came in 1973. In the middle of the afternoon, WBAI, a nonprofit Pacifica network station in New York, aired George Carlin's famous comedy sketch about the "seven dirty words" that can't be said on TV. A man riding in a car with his fifteen-year-old son heard the program and complained to the FCC, which sent WBAI a letter of reprimand. Although no fine was issued, the station challenged the warning on principle—and won its case in court. The FCC promptly appealed to the Supreme Court. Though no court had legally defined indecency (which remains undefined today), the Supreme Court sided with the FCC in the 1978 *FCC v. Pacifica Foundation* case. The decision upheld the FCC's authority to require broadcasters to air adult programming only at times when children were not likely to be listening. The FCC banned indecent programs from most stations between 6:00 A.M. and 10:00 P.M.

Political Broadcasts and Equal Opportunity

In addition to indecency rules, another law affecting broadcasting but not the print media is **Section 315** of the Communications Act of 1934. The section mandates that during elections, broadcast stations must provide equal opportunities and response time for qualified political candidates. In other words, if broadcasters give or sell time to one candidate, they must give or sell the same opportunity to others. Local broadcasters and networks have fought this law for years, claiming that because no similar rule applies to newspapers or magazines, the law violates their First Amendment right to control content. Many stations decided to avoid political programming entirely, ironically reversing the rule's original intention. The TV networks managed to get the law amended in 1959 to exempt newscasts, press conferences, and other events—such as political debates—that qualify as news. For instance, if a senator running for office appears in a news story, opposing candidates cannot invoke Section 315 and demand free time.

Supporters of the equal opportunity law in broadcasting argue that it enables lesser-known candidates representing views counter to those of the Democratic and Republican parties to add their perspectives to political dialogue. It also gives less-wealthy candidates a more affordable channel than newspaper and magazine ads for getting their message out to the public.

Fair Coverage of Controversial Issues

Considered an important corollary to Section 315, the **Fairness Doctrine** was to controversial issues what Section 315 is to political speech. Initiated in 1949, this FCC rule required stations to air programs about controversial issues affecting their communities and to provide competing points of view during the programs. Broadcasters again protested that the print media did not have to obey these requirements. And once more, many stations simply avoided airing controversial issues. The Fairness Doctrine ended with little public debate in 1987 after a federal court ruled that it was merely a regulation, not an extension of Section 315 law.

Since 1987, however, support for reviving the Fairness Doctrine has surfaced periodically. Its advocates argue that broadcasting is fundamentally different from—and more pervasive than—print media. Thus, it should be more accountable to the public interest. The end of the Fairness Doctrine might have contributed to a more polarized political climate, fed in part by news networks unburdened by the requirement to provide different points of view. On the other hand, the lack of requirement could allow the dissemination of other views that might not otherwise garner much attention.

Communication Policy and the Internet

Because the Internet is not regulated by the government, is not subject to the Communications Act of 1934, and has done little self-regulating, many people see it as the one true venue for unlimited free speech under the First Amendment. Its current global expansion is comparable to the early days of broadcasting, when economic and technological growth outstripped law and regulation.

Early debates about what forms of expression should be allowed on the Internet typically revolved around such issues as civility and pornography. Those discussions have continued (see "Converging Media Case Study: Bullying Converges Online" on pages 458–459), but the debate has expanded to issues like government surveillance and how traditional means like wiretapping and search warrants can be expanded to include the turning over of Internet browsing histories and other data. As this medium continues to expand rapidly, we will need to consider some important questions: Will the Internet remain free of government attempts to contain it, change it, and monitor who has access to it? Can the Internet continue to serve as a democratic forum for regional, national, and global interest groups? Many global movements use this medium to fight political oppression. Human Rights Watch, for example, encourages free-expression advocates to use blogs "for disseminating information about, and ending, human rights abuses around the world." [12]

Supporters of WikiLeaks founder Julian Assange feel he is essentially a political prisoner, having been granted political asylum by Ecuador in 2012 and unable to leave the Ecuadorian embassy in London since then. Sexual assault charges await Assange in Sweden, but his defenders say that the charges are little more than political cover to allow the U.S. government to nab him as retribution for WikiLeaks publishing documents related to national security.

Carl Court/Getty Images

CONVERGING MEDIA

Case Study

Bullying Converges Online

Throughout this book, we have discussed the important and interesting ways in which people have merged their real worlds with the digital world online. As we've seen, these digital frontiers can also have troubling consequences, perhaps the most disturbing of which is when harassment and bullying go online.

Bullying in particular has received attention for the effects it has on digital natives—people who have grown up with converged, digital technology. The Web site stopbullying.gov offers some helpful explanations of bullying and cyberbulling, defining bullying as aggressive behavior that exploits a power imbalance—physical strength, access to embarrassing information, or popularity—to repeatedly make threats, spread rumors, attack physically or verbally, expose to ridicule, or exclude from a social group as a means of torment.[1] Cyberbullying, then, is defined as bullying that takes place using electronic technology, and can range from mean text messages or Snapchats, to posts on social media sites sharing embarrassing photos and videos, to the creation of false online profiles. The site lists three important ways cyberbullying is different from regular bullying, most of which revolve around the difficulty to escape the bullying:

- Cyberbullying can happen at any time.
- Messages and images can be posted anonymously and distributed quickly to a very wide audience. It can be difficult and sometimes impossible to trace the sources.
- Deleting inappropriate or harassing messages, texts, and pictures is extremely difficult after they have been posted or sent.[2]

Government researchers say that because of rapidly changing technology, it's hard to get a precise picture of how many kids are victims of cyberbullying, but a 2013 survey showed around 20 percent of high school students reporting that they were bullied, with 15 percent saying the bullying had been electronic.[3]

Convergence means that many people no longer need to stay in front of a computer screen to access e-mail, Twitter, Facebook, and other social media; bullies, then, can follow their victims virtually anywhere. Though some of this harassment depends on anonymity, the most devastating form of cyberbullying is committed by people who know the victim. This was certainly the case in a series of widely reported teen suicides over the last ten years. In one case, thirteen-year-old Megan Meier ended her life after receiving an online message: "The world would be a better place without you." Megan thought the message was from a cute boy named Josh Evans. But Josh Evans turned out to be the invention of a forty-seven-year-old woman named Lori Drew, who lived down the street from Megan. Megan had recently ended her friendship with Drew's daughter, a decision that prompted Drew to create the Josh Evans account and, as she put it to another neighbor, "mess with Megan." The problem is not limited to high school students. A Rutgers University undergraduate committed suicide after his roommate secretly used his computer's Webcam to record and tweet about a private romantic encounter between the student and another man.

In both of these cases (and many others), prosecutors struggled to find laws that applied. In the first example, Drew was convicted of a misdemeanor violation of the Computer Fraud and Abuse Act, a conviction that was later overturned. In the second example, the roommate was convicted of invasion of privacy and some other minor felonies and was sentenced to a month in jail and probation (he is appealing the conviction). High-profile cases like these have prompted lawmakers from several states to attempt to pass an anti-bullying law, some mentioning cyberbullying specifically (the stopbullying .gov Web site includes a state-by-state map of anti-bullying laws).[4]

But passing laws targeting bullying, especially cyberbullying, can be tricky. As with the Child Online Protection Act (COPA) of 1998, laws with the best of intentions can be worded too vaguely and also outlaw other, nonbullying, speech. For example, under the proposed Megan Meier Cyberbullying Prevention Act, which would make it a felony to transmit messages with intent to cause emotional distress, it might be hard to distinguish between bullying and a particularly spirited political debate on Facebook, during which it's easy to imagine someone feeling harassed.

Online bullying demonstrates another way in which the virtual world and the "real" world have converged, and that while some might still see online harassment as less real than its in-person counterparts, it can have equally dire consequences. As such, the ubiquity of the Internet makes it subject to the same tough questions regarding freedom of speech as other media, and raises even more difficult questions about what is considered allowable free speech and what constitutes harassment or hate speech. Hateful forms of speech may indeed be the acid test of a vibrant democracy—a test with such paradoxical implications as tolerating intolerance and defending the indefensible. Such contradictions are at the heart of living as an informed, media-literate citizen in a diverse and conflicted democracy.

The First Amendment in a Democratic Society

Ultimately, questions about the First Amendment's implications for freedom of expression in mass media are really about democracy. And when it comes to our democracy, the news media—whether print, TV, radio, or the Internet—play a particularly important role. For most of our nation's history, citizens have counted on journalists to alert them to abuses in government and business. But today, news stories tend to address us more as consumers than as citizens, focusing, for example, on how a business merger affects the immediate price of a product rather than the long-term social and economic impact on workers and communities. Moreover, as newspapers, TV stations, radio stations, and Internet corporations are merged into larger entertainment corporations, and as media workers' jobs are threatened by outsourcing and consolidation, it has become more difficult for journalists to adequately cover and lead critical discussions about media ownership, media regulation, and business practices in general.

For these reasons, it has become more important than ever for citizens to share the watchdog role with journalists. Citizen action groups like Free Press, the Media Access Project, and the Center for Digital Democracy have worked to bring media ownership issues into the mainstream. These groups remind us that the First Amendment protects not only the news media's free-speech rights but also the rights of all of us to speak out. Mounting concerns over who can afford access to the media go to the heart of free expression. As we struggle to determine the future of converging print, electronic, and digital media and to broaden the democratic spirit underlying media technology, we need to take part in spirited public debates about media ownership and control, about the differences between commercial speech and free expression. As citizens, we must pay attention to who is included and excluded from opportunities not only to buy products but also to voice their views and thereby shape our nation's cultural and political landscape. To accomplish this, we must challenge government and business leaders—rather than assuming that journalists will do so.

In this regard, the Web site WikiLeaks represents the most extreme, controversial, and effective of the organizations attempting to provide reliable information on an Internet often cluttered with just the opposite. Officially launched in 2007, WikiLeaks is known for generating headlines by publishing sensitive corporate communications and secret government documents provided by anonymous sources. For example, in November 2010, the organization supplied five newspapers with the first of 250,000 leaked diplomatic cables from 274

U.S. embassies around the world. Cables addressing the corruption of Tunisian President Ben Ali reportedly helped rally activists in the first of the successful Arab Spring revolutions.[13]

But the site's most celebrated and notorious work to date attracted worldwide attention with a "data spill" of classified U.S. military documents. The most sensational of this material was the release in April 2010 of video taken from one of two helicopters firing on a crowd of both armed and unarmed people in Baghdad. Eighteen were killed in the attack, including two reporters from the Reuters news agency. Later in 2010, Julian Assange, the "editor in chief" of WikiLeaks, worked with journalists at the *New York Times*, the *Guardian*, and *Der Spiegel* to publish more classified material, though care was taken to redact names and not print information that might put lives at risk.[14]

WikiLeaks continues to release classified and sensitive documents acquired from anonymous sources. It also raises a number of troubling questions about freedom of speech in the age of convergent media. Are there limits to the public's right to know? Under what conditions do secrecy and confidentiality serve the public interest? Who benefited from the release of military footage of the helicopter attack in Baghdad? Who suffered? What ultimately was accomplished by this release of footage?

Regardless of views on WikiLeaks, the health of our democracy demands an informed electorate, not one that is kept in the dark about who we really are, what we stand for, why we go to war, and how those wars are fought. We need not approve of the methods employed by WikiLeaks in order to recognize the worth of such watchdog groups devoted to keeping the government—and the press—honest.

CHAPTER ESSENTIALS

Now that you have finished reading this chapter, you can use the following tools:

LaunchPad for *Media Essentials*

Go to **macmillanhighered.com/mediaessentials3e** for videos, review quizzes, and more.

LaunchPad for *Media Essentials* includes:

- **REVIEW WITH LEARNINGCURVE**
  LearningCurve uses gamelike quizzing to help you master the concepts you need to learn from this chapter.

- **VIDEO: THE FIRST AMENDMENT AND STUDENT SPEECH**
  Legal and newspaper professionals explain how student newspapers are protected by the First Amendment.

REVIEW

Track the Origins of Free Expression and a Free Press

- In the United States, freedom of speech and freedom of the press are protected by the First Amendment in the Bill of Rights. However, Americans have long debated what constitutes "free expression." Around the globe, four different interpretations of free expression have emerged: the **authoritarian model** (which tolerates little criticism of government or public dissent), the **state model** (in which the government controls the press), the **social responsibility model** (in which the press is privately owned and functions as a **Fourth Estate**—an unofficial branch of government that watches for abuses of power by the legislative, judicial, and executive branches), and the **libertarian model** (which encourages vigorous criticism of government and supports the highest degree of individual and press freedoms) (pp. 436–438).

- Though the First Amendment prohibits censorship, which is defined as **prior restraint**—meaning that courts and governments cannot block any publication or speech *before* it actually occurs—two pivotal court cases have tested this idea: the Pentagon Papers case and the *Progressive* magazine case (pp. 439–440).

- Some forms of expression are not protected under the Constitution. These forms include sedition, copyright infringement (a **copyright** legally protects the rights of the authors and producers to their published or unpublished writing, music, lyrics, TV programs, movies, or graphic art designs for a specified period of time, after which the work enters the **public domain**, allowing the public free access to the work), and **libel**—or defamation of someone's character in written or broadcast form (which differs from **slander**, or spoken defamation). To win a libel case, public officials must prove falsehood, damages, negligence, and **actual malice** (meaning that a reporter or an editor knew the statement was false and printed it anyway, or acted with a reckless disregard for the truth). Defenses against libel include the truth and the rule of **opinion and fair comment**—the notion that opinions, unlike statements of factual information, are protected from libel. Other forms of expression not protected by the Constitution are **obscenity**, which people have had difficulty defining over the years, and violation of privacy rights (the **right to privacy** addresses a person's right to be left alone, without personal information becoming public property) (pp. 440–443, 446–448).

- The First Amendment has clashed with the Sixth Amendment, which guarantees accused individuals the right to speedy and public trials by impartial juries. **Gag orders** (speech restrictions) and laws governing the use of cameras in the courtroom put restrictions on speech and other forms of expression for the sake of Sixth Amendment rights, whereas **shield laws** protect reporters from revealing confidential sources of information used in news stories (pp. 448–450).

Discuss the Relationship between the First Amendment and Film

- The advent of film presented new challenges for those seeking to determine whether expression in film should be protected. For the first half of the twentieth century, citizen groups and the Supreme Court failed to recognize movies as protected speech. The movie industry began regulating itself to safeguard its profits and avoid further government oversight (pp. 450–453).

Explain the Relationship between the First Amendment, Broadcasting, and the Internet

- Because it uses the public airwaves, broadcasting receives fewer protections than film and print. Although the government cannot censor broadcast content, it may punish broadcasters after the fact for **indecency** or profanity. In addition, **Section 315** of the Communications Act of 1934 mandates that during elections, broadcast stations must provide equal opportunities and response time for qualified political candidates. From 1949 to 1987, the **Fairness Doctrine**—an important corollary to Section 315—required stations to air programs about controversial issues affecting their communities and to provide competing points of view during the programs (pp. 453–456).

• Since the Internet is not regulated by the government, is not subject to the Communications Act of 1934, and has done little self-regulating, many consider it a true venue for free speech, though debates exist about what forms of expression should be allowed (p. 457).

Understand the Role of the First Amendment in Our Democratic Society

• Questions about the First Amendment's influence over freedom of expression in mass media are centered on democracy (p. 460).

• As journalism becomes compromised by the business of media, sites like WikiLeaks have become de facto watchdog groups, raising questions about the public's right to know sensitive information (pp. 460–461).

STUDY QUESTIONS

1. What is the basic philosophical concept that underlies America's notion of free expression?
2. How did both the Motion Picture Production Code and the current movie rating system come into being?
3. How does the Supreme Court view print and broadcasting as different forms of expression?
4. Why is the future of watchdog journalism in jeopardy?

MEDIA LITERACY PRACTICE

Broadcasters are required to operate in "the public interest, convenience, or necessity." But these days, renewing a radio or TV station license is a relatively easy thing and can be done via postcard every eight years. Work in groups of three or four to explore how well broadcasters serve your area. Ask each person to visit a radio or TV station during business hours to view its FCC file. (These businesses are required by law to let you read it.)

DESCRIBE the content of the files of each station, noting what activities have been in the public interest over several years. Share your descriptions with the group.

ANALYZE the patterns in the public files. Do some stations contribute in a greater capacity than others?

INTERPRET what these patterns mean. Do the activities constitute operations in "the public interest, convenience, or necessity"? Are these things the station would likely be doing anyway, or do the federal requirements compel it to do more extraordinary things?

EVALUATE the stations' commitment to the public interest. Do they do enough in the public interest to merit their broadcast license?

ENGAGE with the community by writing to the stations to criticize or commend them on their commitment to public interest in your community. Make sure to send a copy to the FCC, since your letter will become part of the stations' public record.

14

Media Economics and the Global Marketplace

Some of today's biggest mass media players have long histories, which they've built on and adapted through various technological changes, including history's recent digital turn. Columbia Records (now part of the Sony empire) was founded in 1888. The Warner Brothers piece of the current Time Warner conglomerate got its start in 1903, when three brothers bought their first movie theater. Walt Disney Studios began in the back of a small L.A. real estate office in 1923. NBC started out in 1926 as a radio network formed by RCA (founded in 1919) and is currently part of NBC Universal, which is a subsidiary of cable and broadband giant Comcast. Comcast itself started out with just over one thousand cable subscribers in 1963. There can be big advantages to having the resources, name recognition, and established political connections that come with being a longtime member of the mass media. But in the age of the Internet and the Internet start-up, the explosive growth of a new media business can happen at a breathtaking pace. Two prime examples of this are Google and YouTube.

Google traces its origins to 1995, when Stanford student Sergey Brin was assigned to show prospective student Larry Page around campus. A year later the pair were collaborating on a prototype search engine, and in 1997 they registered the domain name "Google.com," a play on the mathematical word *googol* (the number written out as a one followed by a hundred zeros). In 1998, the pair officially registered the company as an entity and hired their first employee. The company proceeded to grow at a startling pace, adding more and more services and features every few months—including AdWords in 2000, Images in 2001, Froogle (now Google Shopping) in 2002, Gmail in 2004, and Google Maps and a mobile search app in 2005—soon becoming one of the top American media companies[1] (see also Table 14.1 on page 489).

If anything, YouTube is even more of a digital age success story. The three founders, Chad Hurley, Steve Chen, and Jawed Karim, say they got the idea for a video-sharing site during a dinner party, and on Valentine's Day 2005 they registered the trademark, name, and logo for YouTube. The first video (of Karim at the zoo) was posted on April 23, and by September the site got its first million-hit video (a Nike ad). By December, the company was getting major investment attention, and the site was more widely available after upgrading bandwidth and servers. Google bought YouTube in October 2006, a little more than a year after the first video was posted, for $1.65 billion. Since then, YouTube has been run as a subsidiary of Google and continues to grow in popularity. The economic impact of a video-sharing and social media site like YouTube goes well beyond the video and banner ads it can sell. The site has launched dozens of homegrown stars (including Ryan Higa, Jenna Marbles, and Pewdie Pie) and has become a source for breaking news (such as the posts of mobile phone videos that have been the basis for news stories about police abuse).

The logistics of the rise of digital conglomerates like Google and YouTube may be different from those of traditional mass media companies like Sony or Disney, especially in their speed. But their enormous flow of money and substantial power over the media landscape make the economics of these relative newcomers just as important when studying the media.

COMPARING GOOGLE TO TIME WARNER AND DISNEY, WE SEE TWO TYPES OF MEDIA SUCCESS, one based on an idea that could have happened only in the Internet age (a need for a better search engine), and the other, legacy entertainment conglomerates that have survived years of leadership changes and power struggles to enter the twenty-first century with massive resources. But not all of the mergers, takeovers, and acquisitions that have swept through the global media industries in the last twenty years have capitalized on the histories and reputations of the corporations involved. Take, for instance, the ill-timed purchase of

MySpace by News Corp. in 2005. Paying $580 million for what was then the world's most popular social media site, Rupert Murdoch would watch a newcomer named Mark Zuckerberg (and his site Facebook) reduce the value of MySpace to $35 million, the price Justin Timberlake and Specific Media, Inc., paid for the service in 2011. Despite such spectacular exceptions, many cases of ownership convergence have provided even more economic benefit to the massive multinational corporations that dominate the current media landscape. As a consequence, we currently find ourselves enmeshed and implicated in an immense media economy characterized by consolidation of power and corporate ownership in just a few hands. This phenomenon, combined with the advent of the Internet, has made our modern media world markedly distinct from that of earlier generations—at least in economic terms. Not only has a handful of media giants—from Time Warner to Google—emerged, but the Internet has permanently transformed the media landscape. The Internet has dried up newspapers' classified-ad revenues; altered the way music, movies, and TV programs get distributed and exhibited; and forced almost all media businesses to rethink the content they will provide—and how they will provide it.

In this chapter, we explore the developments and tensions shaping this brave new world of mass media by:

- examining the transition our nation has made from a manufacturing to an information economy by considering how the media industries' structures have evolved, the impact of deregulation, the rise of media powerhouses through consolidation, trends that shape and reshape media industries, and theories about why U.S. citizens tend not to speak up about the dark side of mass media

- analyzing today's media economy, including how media organizations make money and formulate strategies, and how the Internet has changed the rules of the media game

- assessing the specialization and use of synergy currently characterizing media, using the history of the Walt Disney Company as an example

- taking stock of the social challenges the new media economy has raised, such as subversion of antitrust laws, consumers' loss of control in the marketplace, and American culture's infiltration into other cultures

- evaluating the media marketplace's role in our democracy by considering such questions as whether consolidation of media hurts or helps democracy, and what impact recent media-reform movements might have

The Transition to an Information Economy

In the first half of the twentieth century, the U.S. economy was built on mass production, the proliferation of manufacturing plants, and intense rivalry with businesses in other nations. By midcentury, this manufacturing-based economy began transitioning into an economy fueled by information (which new technologies made easier to generate and exchange anywhere) and by cooperation with other economies. Offices displaced factories as major work sites; centralized mass production declined in the United States and other developed nations; and American firms began outsourcing manufacturing work to developing countries, where labor was cheap and environmental standards were lax.

Mass media industries seized the opportunity to expand globally. They began marketing music, movies, television programs, and computer software overseas. And the media mergers-and-acquisitions (M&A) drive that had begun in the United States in the 1960s expanded into global media consolidation by the 1980s.

This transition from a manufacturing-based to an information-based economy had several defining points: Early regulation designed to break up monopolies in manufacturing-related industries such as oil, railroads, and steel gave way to deregulation, which ultimately catalyzed the M&A drive that created media powerhouses. These

CHAPTER 14 // TIMELINE

1923 Disney Founded
Disney begins as a small animation studio in Hollywood.

1952 News Corp.
Rupert Murdoch inherits two Australian newspapers from his father, beginning what will grow into the News Corp. media empire.

1980s AT&T
AT&T, a telephone monopoly approved and regulated by the government for more than a hundred years, is broken up.

1985 GE Buys NBC
The merger marks the start of an era of media consolidation.

1994 NAFTA and WTO
NAFTA in 1994 and the WTO in 1995 further encourage trade and the export of certain jobs.

1995 Disney Empire
Disney buys ABC.

information-based corporations in turn fueled new trends in the industry (including a decline of unionized labor and a growing wage gap). Soon a new society took shape—one in which the biggest media companies defined the values that dominated culture not only in the United States but also around the globe.

How Media Industries Are Structured

Most industries that make up the media economy have one of three common structures: monopoly, oligopoly, and limited competition.

Monopoly

A **monopoly** arises when a single firm dominates production and distribution in a particular industry—nationally or locally. For example, at the national level, AT&T ran a rare government-approved and government-regulated monopoly—the telephone business—for more than a hundred years before the government broke it up in the mid-1980s. And Microsoft dominates the worldwide market for business computer operating systems.

On the local level, monopolies have proved more plentiful, arising in any city that has only one newspaper or one cable company. The federal government has encouraged owner diversity since the 1970s by prohibiting a newspaper from operating a broadcast or cable company in the same city.

© Bettmann/Corbis

In 1911, John D. Rockefeller Sr., considered the richest man in the world, saw his powerful monopoly, Standard Oil, busted into more than thirty separate companies.

1996 Time Warner
The company buys Turner Broadcasting.

1996 Media Merger
The Telecommunications Act of 1996 unleashes a wave of media mergers.

2001 AOL and Time Warner
AOL, the largest Internet service provider at the time, merges with Time Warner, the largest media corporation.

2009 More Cable Deregulation
A U.S. federal court strikes down the FCC's regulation limiting a cable company's holdings to not more than 30 percent of the U.S. cable market.

2011 Comcast Buys NBC
Cable giant Comcast completes a deal to buy a majority share of NBC Universal.

But since 2003, the Federal Communications Commission (FCC) has made several efforts to relax cross-ownership rules, arguing that the Internet and cable and satellite television provide sufficient informational diversity for citizens. Media activists have countered that the large traditional media are still the dominant news media in any market, and that when they merge, it results in fewer independent media voices.

Oligopoly

In an **oligopoly**, just a few firms dominate an industry. For example, in the late 1980s, the production and distribution of the world's music was controlled by only six corporations. By 2004, after a series of acquisitions, the "big six" had been reduced to the "big four"—Time Warner (U.S.), Sony (Japan), Universal (France), and EMI (Great Britain). In late 2011, Universal purchased EMI at auction, and by 2012 three companies controlled nearly two-thirds of the recording industry market. The Internet is also changing the music game, enabling companies like Apple to gain new dominance with innovative business models such as the iTunes store. Time will reveal whether the "big three" maintain their status as an oligopoly.

Firms that make up an oligopoly face little economic competition from small independent firms. However, many oligopolies choose to purchase independent companies in order to nurture the fresh ideas and products those companies generate. Without the financial backing of an oligopoly, many of those ideas and products could have a tough time making it to market.

Limited Competition

Limited competition characterizes a media market that has many producers and sellers but only a few products within a particular category.[2] For instance, hundreds of independently owned radio stations operate in the United States. However, most of these commercial stations feature just a few formats—such as country, classic rock, news/talk, or contemporary hits. Fans of other formats—including blues, alternative country, and classical music—may not be able to find a radio station that matches their interests. Of course, as with music, the Internet is changing radio, too, enabling companies like Pandora and Spotify to offer streaming audio for a huge array of formats.

Deregulation Trumps Regulation

Beginning in the early twentieth century, Congress passed several acts intended to break up corporate trusts and monopolies, which often fixed prices to force competitors out of business. But later in the century, many business leaders began complaining that such regulation was restricting the flow of capital

FIGURE 14.1 // MEDIA INDUSTRY STRUCTURES

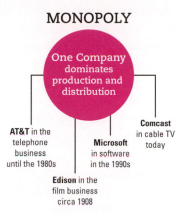

MONOPOLY

One Company dominates production and distribution

AT&T in the telephone business until the 1980s

Microsoft in software in the 1990s

Comcast in cable TV today

Edison in the film business circa 1908

On the local level, monopoly situations have been more plentiful, occurring in any city that has only one newspaper or cable company. Although the federal government has encouraged owner diversity since the 1970s by prohibiting a newspaper from operating a broadcast or cable company in the same city, many individual local media monopolies have been purchased by national and international firms.

OLIGOPOLY

A Few Firms dominate an industry

Advertising/PR
WPP
Omnicom
Publicis
Interpublic

Internet
Google
Amazon
Apple
Facebook

Book Retail
Amazon
Apple
Google Play

Internet Streaming
Pandora
Spotify
Deezer

Music
Sony
Universal
Warner

Video Games
Nintendo
Microsoft
Sony
Activision
Blizzard

Film/TV
Sony
Viacom
Time Warner
Disney
News Corp.
NBC Universal
Netflix
Google/YouTube

Theaters
Regal
AMC Entertainment
Cinemark
Carmike
Cineplex
Marcus

LIMITED COMPETITION
(sometimes called "monopolistic competition")

In limited competition, there are many producers and sellers but only a few products, as in the example of radio.

Contemporary Hits stations
News/Talk stations
Country stations

Because commercial broadcast radio is a difficult market to enter, requiring an FCC license and major capital investment, most stations play one of the few formats that attract sizable audiences. Under these circumstances, fans of blues, jazz, or classical music may not be able to find a radio station. That is changing, though, with the Internet.

---

essential for funding business activities. President Jimmy Carter (1977–1981) initiated deregulation, and President Ronald Reagan (1981–1989) dramatically weakened most controls on business (e.g., environmental and worker safety rules). Many corporations in a wide range of industries flourished in this new pro-commerce climate. Deregulation also made it easier for companies to merge, to diversify, and—in industries such as the airlines, energy, communications, and financial services—to form oligopolies.[3]

In the broadcast industry, the Telecommunications Act of 1996 (under President Bill Clinton) lifted most restrictions on how many radio and TV stations one corporation could own. The act further permitted regional telephone companies to buy cable firms. In addition, cable operators regained the right to raise their rates with less oversight and to compete in the local telephone business. What prompted this shift to deregulation in the communications industry? With new cable channels, DBS, and the Internet, lawmakers no longer saw broadcasting as a scarce resource—once a major rationale for regulation as well as government funding of noncommercial and educational stations.

Not surprisingly, the 1996 act unleashed a wave of mergers in the industry, as television, radio, cable, telephone, and Internet companies fought to become the biggest corporations in their business sector and acquire new subsidiaries in other media sectors. The act also revealed legislators' growing openness to make special exemptions for communications companies. For example, in 1995, despite complaints from NBC, News Corp. received a special dispensation from the FCC and Congress that allowed it to continue owning and operating the Fox network and a number of local TV stations.

Today, regulation of the communications industry is even looser. In late 2007, the FCC relaxed its rules further when it said that a company located in a Top 20 market (ranging in size from New York to Orlando, Florida) could own one TV station and one newspaper as long as there were at least eight TV stations in that market. Previously, a company could not own a newspaper and a broadcast outlet (a TV or radio station) in the same market. In 2009, a U.S. federal court struck down the FCC's regulation limiting a cable company's holdings to not more than 30 percent of the U.S. cable market, opening the possibility for a new round of unlimited cable mergers and acquisitions.

The Rise of Media Powerhouses

Into the 1980s, antitrust rules attempted to ensure diversity of ownership among competing businesses. In the mid-1980s, for instance, the Justice Department broke up AT&T's century-old monopoly, creating competition in the telephone industry. But as politicians eroded those laws, the overall result has been much more consolidation and much less competition in the world of mass media.

Not only were some rules relaxed, but the antitrust laws have been unevenly applied in media industries, forcing competition in some industries while allowing consolidation in others. For example, as the Justice Department broke up AT&T to create competition in the telephone industry, it also authorized several mass media mergers that concentrated power in the hands of a few behemoths. These included General Electric's purchase of RCA/NBC in the 1980s, Disney's acquisition of ABC for $19 billion in 1995, and Time Warner's purchase of Turner Broadcasting for $7.5 billion in 1996. In 2001, AOL acquired Time Warner for $106 billion—the largest media merger in history at the time. In 2011, cable giant Comcast purchased a majority share of NBC Universal, once the deal was approved by regulatory agencies.

As traditional mass media corporations have grown, we've also seen the rise of new media powerhouses in the twenty-first century. Companies like Apple, Google, Amazon, and Facebook aren't experts at creating media programming, but they've envisioned new ways for us to experience media content: by buying content from their retail stores (e.g., the iTunes store and Amazon.com), consuming content on their innovative devices (e.g., the iPad, the Kindle Fire, the Android mobile phone), and being linked to other media content (via Google search and our friends on Facebook). Imagine experiencing the mass media without using a product or service of one of these companies and you begin to understand how this "digital turn," with these four companies leading the way, has transformed the mass communication environment in less than a decade (see "Converging Media Case Study: Shifting Economics" on pages 476–477).

Analyzing the Media Economy

The immense reach and heft of the mass media economy raises some complicated questions, beginning with the role government should play in regulating media ownership. Should citizens step up demands for more accountability from media? Is American culture, expressed through our mass media, hurting other cultures? And is concentration of ownership in the media damaging our democracy? To explore possible answers to these questions, we examine how media industries are structured, how companies in these industries operate, and how the Internet is transforming the media economy.

How Media Companies Operate

In analyzing how media companies operate, economists pay attention to several things—including how these firms make money, and how they formulate strategies for establishing their prices, marketing their offerings, and meeting stakeholders' expectations and demands.

Making Money

Media companies bring in money from two sources: direct and indirect payments. **Direct payments** come from consumers who buy media products, such as books, movies, and Internet or cable TV services. **Indirect payments** derive from advertisers—companies that purchase ads in various media to attract specific consumers of those media. Over-the-air radio and TV broadcasting, daily newspapers, consumer magazines, and most Web sites rely on indirect payments for most of their revenue. But many media companies generate revenue through

LaunchPad
macmillanhighered.com
/mediaessentials3e

The Impact of Media Ownership
Media critics and professionals debate the pros and cons of media conglomerates. **Discussion:** This video argues that it is the drive for bottom-line profits that leads to conglomerates. What solution(s) might you suggest to make the media system work better?

Shifting Economics

The advent of the Internet has brought about a number of major economic changes, and as media continue to converge, we can expect the status quo to keep shifting. For example, when the Internet was first emerging as a mass medium in the early 1990s, one of the most popular ways of accessing it was through a subscription to America Online (AOL). AOL offered a simple, easy-to-use interface, with its own e-mail, chat, and other content, as well as early Web browsing, making the Web manageable for newcomers. But as the Internet became less mysterious and more commonplace, that model of access became less relevant. Although AOL's 2001 merger with Time Warner failed, Time Warner found success with another telecommunication spin-off, Time Warner Cable, which began to offer high-speed Internet access in the late 1990s. This type of access—getting Internet service from a cable or phone company—has become the dominant model.

This development has, in turn, changed the way many people pay for media content. Before the converged Internet, the easiest way to gain constant access to a particular song, album, or movie was to buy it, on discs or cassettes. Some consumers still buy physical CDs, vinyl LPs, or Blu-ray discs, of course, but those particularly conscious of clutter, budget, or their own shifting tastes may instead opt to stream their music online on services like Spotify, watch TV shows on Hulu, or, it must be said, download media illegally. All of this requires a high-speed Internet connection, meaning that money that might have gone to music labels or movie studios now heads toward telecommunication providers.

Authors and owners of media content are still trying to figure out how best to navigate this altered economic landscape, experimenting with different methods of generating revenue. Cable television, for example, so often packaged with high-speed Internet, could eventually become outmoded like AOL as more people subscribe to services like Netflix or Hulu Plus, where programming is less bound by particular channels or airtimes—and fees don't equal those charged by cable companies. These services also pay studios to license their programming, which could be a path to traditional profitability for individual movies and TV shows. Of course, in the current converged media world, some of those groups creating the programming are also owned by the video-streaming services, such as NBC Universal and Hulu.com. In many homes across the country, the company that provides broadband Internet is Comcast, which owns NBC Universal.

© Richard Levine/Demotix/Corbis

Mobile technology also plays a big part in the shifting economics of convergence. Mobile phone companies compete with one another and with cable and broadband companies to sell Internet access to consumers. Most of those mobile phones and tablets operate on one of two dominant operating systems: the Apple iOS system and the Android system developed by Google.

Whichever operating system a mobile device uses, it represents a still relatively new convergence between person-to-person communication, mass communication (often via social media and video- and photo-sharing sites), and a staggering amount of commerce. Device owners can download books, music, movies, and games directly from the iStore or Google Play. Popular apps for sites like Pandora, Spotify, Hulu, and Netflix bring together mobile technology and online streaming of music and video. Consumers can choose from thousands of other apps that boost the potential

usefulness of a mobile device exponentially. And, of course, many businesses—from pizza chains and coffee shops to retailers like Amazon—have apps that allow consumers to buy goods directly from their smartphones. Apps also allow for easier access to social media sites, which collectively represent one of the main hubs of convergence.

It's important to remember that part of the shifting economic landscape in the digital age is related to the unpredictability of what will succeed, what will fail, and what will be replaced by the "next big thing." It wasn't terribly long ago, for example, that MySpace was the biggest social media network and wildly popular sites like YouTube and Facebook didn't even exist. What *is* predictable is that consumers will continue to spend money on mass media content and ways to access and use that content, and a great deal of effort will be expended by a lot of groups to get a piece of that pie.

both direct *and* indirect payments. These include newspapers, magazines, online services, and cable systems, which charge subscription fees in addition to selling commercial space and time to advertisers.

Increasingly, new media products must blur the line between the two forms of payment. Sales and rentals of physical media, such as CDs and DVDs, are declining (though legal downloads contribute to direct payments), whereas streaming services for music, TV, and movies are becoming more popular. This leads to consumers making direct payments for access to services like Netflix, Hulu, and Spotify, as well as to telecommunication companies who provide the Internet service needed to use those services, rather than direct payments to the companies who produce the content itself. Indirect payments are then made to the content producers by the various services and telecommunication companies.

Formulating Business Strategies

Media companies formulate strategies governing all their business processes. For instance, a local newspaper determines how high it can raise its monthly print or digital subscription price before enough disgruntled readers will drop their subscriptions and offset any profits made from the price increase. Or a book publisher tries to achieve **economies of scale** by increasing production levels to reduce the cost for each book printed.

Expectations of stakeholders—including customers, investors, and regulators—also strongly shape media companies' business strategies. For example, economists, media critics, and consumer organizations have asked the mass media to meet certain performance criteria. These criteria include meeting profit goals, introducing new technologies to the marketplace, making media products and services available to less-affluent people, facilitating free expression and robust political discussion, watching for wrongdoing in government and business, monitoring crises, playing a positive role in education, and maintaining the quality of culture.[4]

Media companies are living up to some of these expectations better than others. To illustrate, news executives may trim budgets and downsize staff to improve profit margins, but those actions may also undermine the newsroom's ability to adequately cover crucial topics and work as watchdogs of society.

How the Internet Is Changing the Game

Historically, media companies have operated in separate industries. That is, the newspaper business functioned separately from book publishing, which operated differently from radio, which in turn worked totally unlike the film industry.

The Internet has changed all that. This medium has not only provided a whole new portal through which people can consume older media forms but also pressured virtually all older media companies to establish an online presence. Today, newspapers, magazines, book publishers, music companies, radio and TV stations, and film studios all have Web sites or mobile apps marketing digital versions and ancillaries of their products.

This development has presented new opportunities for some media organizations. For example, it enables noncommercial public broadcasters to bring in ad revenue. Public radio and TV stations, which are prohibited by FCC regulations from taking advertising, face no such prohibitions online. Many have begun raising money by posting advertisements on their Web sites.

However, the Internet has also posed new challenges for some older media companies, who must navigate territory with less-established payment models. For instance, when Internet sites like YouTube display content from traditional broadcast and cable services, the companies selling those services lose direct-payment revenue every time someone consumes that content on the Internet rather than paying for services. But this availability may also create exposure for media companies' offerings. Traditional companies must then ask whether that new awareness translates into an increase in *paying* customers. Internet-based companies like Hulu are already offering different levels of access: free, ad-supported, but limited versions of their services alongside pay models with greater libraries of media offerings and more versatile formats.

Business Trends in Media Industries

Consolidation and digitization are not the only trends redefining the mass media business landscape. Additional trends shaping business overall have further affected the media economy. These include the growth of flexible markets and the decline of labor unions, as well as downsizing and a growing wage gap.

Flexible Markets and the Decline of Labor Unions

In today's economy, markets are flexible—that is, business and consumer needs and preferences change continuously and quickly. Companies seeking to increase profitability alter their products, services, and production processes as needed to satisfy specialized, ever-shifting demands. Making niche products for specialized markets is expensive, and most new products fail in the marketplace. To offset their losses from product failures, companies need to score a few major successes—such as a blockbuster movie or a game-changing handheld device. Large companies with access to the most capital—such as media powerhouses—can more easily absorb losses than can small businesses with limited capital. Thus, the powerhouses stand the best chance of surviving in today's flexible markets.

Justin Sullivan/Getty Images

As many U.S. companies export manufacturing work and rely on other sources of labor, American workers' power and membership in labor unions have decreased.

To lower their costs and earn back their investments in product development, companies have begun relying heavily on cheap labor—sometimes exploiting poor workers in domestic and international sweatshops—and on quick, high-volume sales. Many U.S. companies now export manufacturing work, such as production of computers, CD players, TV sets, VCRs, and DVDs, to avoid the more expensive unionized labor at home. (Today, many companies outsource even technical and customer support services for their products.) As U.S. firms have gained access to alternative sources of labor, American workers' power has decreased. Since the early 1980s, membership in labor unions has declined dramatically. Since the 1980s, real wages (wages adjusted for things like inflation) have stagnated for most American workers. This means that as productivity has increased, pay for many effectively has not. Consider also that the pay of chief executives of major companies grew from about twenty times the pay of the average worker in 1965 (a peak time for union membership and overall economic prosperity) to almost three hundred times the pay of the average worker in 2013.[5] Chief executive officers of major media companies like CBS, Viacom, Comcast, and Walt Disney often show up in annual lists of the highest-paid CEOs.

Downsizing and the Wage Gap

With the advantage to large companies in this age of flexible markets, the disadvantaged are the many workers who have lost their jobs as companies have downsized to become "more productive, more competitive, [and] more flexible."[6] Many people today scramble for paid work, often working two or three part-time and low-wage jobs. In his 2006 book *The Disposable American*, Louis Uchitelle noted unintended side effects of downsizing, including companies' difficulty in developing innovative offerings after gutting their workforces. In the news media, reporting staffs have been downsized by more than 25 percent since the early 1990s. As a result, traditional news reporting has given way to other forms—such as online news sites and blogs.

The Age of Hegemony

As media corporations have grown larger, they have also been able to manage public debate and dissent about their increasing power. How? One explanation is their ability to exercise **hegemony** in our society. In hegemony, society's least powerful members are persuaded (often without realizing any persuasion has taken place) to accept the values defined by its most powerful members.

In his 1947 article "The Engineering of Consent," Edward Bernays, the father of modern public relations (see Chapter 12), expressed the core concept behind hegemony: Companies cannot get people to do what they want until the people consent to what those companies are trying to do—whether it is getting more people to smoke cigarettes, or persuading more of them to go to war. To win people's consent to his clients' goals, Bernays tried to convince Americans that his clients' interests were "natural" and "common sense."

Framing companies' goals in this way makes it unlikely that anyone will challenge or criticize those goals. After all, who is going to argue with common sense? Yet definitions of common sense change over time. For example, it was once common sense that the world was flat and that women and others who did not own property shouldn't be allowed to vote. When people buy uncritically into common sense, they inadvertently perpetuate the divisions that some common sense can create, and they shut out any viewpoints suggesting that these divisions are *not* natural.

The mass media—through the messages they convey in their products—play a powerful role in defining common sense and therefore setting up hegemony in society. Every time we read an article in a newspaper; read a book or magazine; or watch a movie, TV show, or video clip on YouTube, we absorb messages suggesting what is important and how the world works. If we consume enough of these "stories," we might conclude that what we are seeing in these media products is just the way things are. And if we believe this is "just the way things are," we probably won't challenge these trends or come up with other, better possibilities.

The reason the narratives work is that they identify with a culture's dominant values. In the United States, Middle American virtues dominate our culture, and include allegiances to family, honesty, hard work, religion, capitalism, health, democracy, moderation, and loyalty. These Middle American virtues are the ones that our politicians most frequently align themselves with in the political ads that tell their stories.

These virtues lie at the heart of powerful American Dream stories that for centuries have told us that if we work hard and practice such values, we will triumph and be successful. Hollywood, too, distributes these shared narratives, celebrating characters and heroes who are loyal, honest, and hardworking. Through this process, the media (and the powerful companies that control them) provide the commonsense narratives that keep the economic status quo relatively unchallenged, leaving little room for alternatives. In the end, hegemony helps explain why we sometimes support economic plans and structures that may not be in our best interest.

American Dream stories are distributed through our media. Early television shows in the 1950s like *The Adventures of Ozzie and Harriet* idealized the American nuclear family as central to the American Dream.

© ABC/Photofest

Specialization and Global Markets

The outsourcing and offshoring of many jobs and the breakdown of global economic borders were bolstered by trade agreements made among national governments in the mid-twentieth century. These included NAFTA (North American Free Trade Agreement) in 1994 and the WTO (World Trade Organization) in 1995. Such agreements enabled the emergence of transnational media corporations and stimulated business deals across national borders. Technology helped, too, making it possible for consumers around the world to easily swap music, TV shows, and movies on the Internet (legally and illegally). All of this has in turn accelerated the global spread of media products and cultural messages.

As globalization gathered momentum, companies began specializing to enter the new, narrow markets opening up to them in other countries. They also began seeking ways to step up their growth through synergies—opportunities to market different versions of a media product.

The Rise of Specialization and Synergy

As globalization picked up speed, several mass media—namely, the magazine, radio, and cable industries—sought to tap specialized markets in the United States and overseas, in part to counter television's mass appeal. For example, cable channels such as Nickelodeon and the Disney Channel serve the under-eighteen market, History draws older viewers, Lifetime and Bravo go after women, and BET targets young African Americans.

In addition to specialization, media companies sought to spur growth through **synergy**—the promotion and sale of different versions of a media product across a media conglomerate's various subsidiaries. An example of synergy is Time Warner's HBO cable special about "the making of" a Warner Brothers movie reviewed in *Time* magazine. Another example is Sony's buying up movie studios and record labels and playing their content on its electronic devices (which are often prominently displayed in their movies). But of all the media conglomerates, the Walt Disney Company perhaps best exemplifies the power of both specialization and synergy.

Disney: A Postmodern Media Conglomerate

After Walt Disney's first cartoon company, Laugh-O-Gram, went bankrupt in 1922, Disney moved to Hollywood and found his niche. He created Mickey Mouse

© Walt Disney Pictures/Everett Collection

Released in the fall of 2013, the animated hit film *Frozen* provided a big boost for Disney. Not only did it break records at the box office, but it also boosted company profits through all of 2014 and into 2015 with *Frozen*-themed toys, DVDs, soundtracks, and a *Frozen*-themed *Disney On Ice*, which was itself poised to break records for ticket sales.

(originally named Mortimer) for the first sound cartoons in the late 1920s. He later began development on the first feature-length cartoon, *Snow White and the Seven Dwarfs*, which he completed in 1937.

For much of the twentieth century, the Disney Company set the standard for popular cartoons and children's culture. Nonetheless, the studio barely broke even because cartoon projects took time (four years for *Snow White*) and commanded the company's full array of resources. Moreover, the market for the cartoon film shorts that Disney specialized in was drying up, as fewer movie theaters were showing the shorts before their feature films.

Driving to Diversify

With the demise of the cartoon film short in movie theaters, Disney expanded into other specialized areas. The company's first nature documentary short, *Seal Island*, came in 1949; its first live-action feature, *Treasure Island*, in 1950; and its first feature documentary, *The Living Desert*, in 1953. Also in 1953, Disney started Buena Vista, a distribution company. This was the first step in the studio's becoming a major player in the film industry.

Disney also counted among the first film studios to embrace television. In 1954, the company launched a long-running prime-time show, and television became an even more popular venue than theaters for displaying Disney products. Then, in 1955, the firm added another entirely new dimension to its operations: It opened its Disneyland theme park in Southern California. (Walt Disney World in Orlando, Florida, would begin operation in 1971.) Eventually, Disney's theme parks would produce the bulk of the company's revenues.

Capturing Synergies

Walt Disney's death in 1966 triggered a period of decline for the studio. But in 1984, a new management team, led by Michael Eisner, initiated a turnaround. The company's newly created Touchstone movie division reinvented the live-action/animation hybrid for adults and children in *Who Framed Roger Rabbit?* (1988). A string of hand-drawn animated hits followed, including *The Little Mermaid* (1989) and *Beauty and the Beast* (1991). In a rocky partnership with Pixar Animation Studios, Disney also distributed a series of computer-animated blockbusters, including *Toy Story* (1995) and *Finding Nemo* (2003).

Since then, Disney has come to epitomize the synergistic possibilities of media consolidation. It can produce an animated feature or regular film for theatrical release and DVD distribution. Characters and stories from blockbuster films like *The Avengers*, *Thor*, and the *Iron Man* franchises can become series on the network ABC (Disney owns Marvel and ABC), like the programs *Agents of SHIELD* and *Agent Carter*, with storylines that intersect with the movies. Disney can release a book version of a movie through its publishing arm, Hyperion, and air "the-making-of" versions on cable's Disney Channel or ABC Family. It can also publish stories about the movie's characters in *Disney Adventures*, the company's popular children's magazine. Indeed, characters have become attractions at Disney's theme parks, which themselves have spawned lucrative Hollywood blockbusters, like the *Pirates of the Caribbean* series. Some Disney films have had as many as seventeen thousand licensed products—from clothing to toys to dog food bowls. And in New York City, Disney even renovated several theaters and launched versions of *Mary Poppins*, *The Lion King*, and *Aladdin* as successful Broadway musicals.

Expanding Globally

Building on the international appeal of its cartoon features, Disney extended its global reach by opening a successful theme park in Japan in 1983. Three years later, the company started marketing cartoons to Chinese television—attracting an estimated 300 million viewers per week. Disney also launched a magazine in Chinese and opened several Disney stores and a theme park in Hong Kong. Disney continued its international expansion in the 1990s with the opening of EuroDisney (now called Disneyland Paris). In 1997, Orbit—a Saudi-owned satellite relay station based in Rome—introduced Disney's twenty-four-hour cable channel to twenty-three countries in the Middle East and North Africa. Disney also expanded its products globally, adding a fourth ship to its international cruise line and a new nationwide Disney channel in Russia, and starting construction on the Shanghai Disney Resort in China, scheduled for a 2015 opening.

Facing Challenges and Seizing Opportunities

From 2000 to 2003, Disney grew into the world's second-largest media conglomerate. Yet the cartoon pioneer encountered major challenges as well as new opportunities presented by the digital age. Challenges included a recession, failed films and Internet ventures, declining theme-park attendance, and damaged relationships with a number of partners and subsidiaries (including Pixar and Miramax).

By 2005, Disney had fallen to No. 5 among movie studios in U.S. box-office sales—down from No. 1 in 2003. A divided and unhappy board of directors forced Eisner out in 2005, after he had served twenty-one years as CEO.[7] The following year, new CEO Robert Iger repaired the relationship between Disney and Pixar: He merged the companies and made Steve Jobs, founder of Pixar and Apple Computer, a Disney board member.

The Pixar deal showed that Disney was ready to seize the opportunities presented by the digital age. The company decided to focus on television,

© Walt Disney Studios Motion Pictures/Photofest

Disney now owns a variety of well-established families of characters, many of which used to compete with Disney characters: Marvel Comics, *Star Wars*, and the Muppets.

movies, and its new online initiatives. To that end, it sold its twenty-two radio stations and the ABC Radio Network to Citadel Broadcasting for $2.7 billion in 2007. Disney also made its movies and TV programs (and ABC's content) available for download at Apple's iTunes store, revamped its Web site as an entertainment portal, and joined News Corp. and NBC Universal as a partner in the video-streaming site Hulu.com in 2009. Disney made another big investment that year by purchasing Marvel Entertainment for $4 billion, which brought Spider-Man, Iron Man, the X-Men, and other superheroes into the Disney pool of characters, providing additional financial assets even when its other projects—such as underperforming movies *Mars Needs Moms* and *John Carter*—grossed less than anticipated. Disney mourned the death of Steve Jobs in 2011 but continued producing animated movies from Pixar and its in-house studios, scoring an enormous Marvel-branded hit with *The Avengers* in 2012, followed by more hit films based on Marvel characters, and then the animated hit *Frozen* in late 2013. In 2012, Disney purchased Lucasfilm and, with it, the rights to the *Star Wars* and *Indiana Jones* movies and characters; a new *Star Wars* film, *The Force Awakens*, followed in 2015. This means that Disney now has access to whole casts of "new" characters—not just for TV programs, feature films, and animated movies but also for its multiple theme parks.

The Growth of Global Audiences

As Disney's story shows, international expansion has afforded media conglomerates key advantages, including access to profitable secondary markets and opportunities to advance and leverage technological innovations. As media technologies have become cheaper and more portable (from the original Walkman to the iPad), American media have proliferated both inside and outside U.S. boundaries.

Today, greatly facilitated by the Internet, media products easily flow into the eyes and ears of people around the world. And thanks to satellite transmission, North American and European television is now available at the global level. Cable services such as CNN and MTV have taken their national acts to the international stage, delivering their content to more than two hundred countries.

This growth of global audiences has permitted companies that lose money on products at home to profit in overseas markets. Roughly 80 percent of American movies, for instance, do not earn back their costs in U.S. theaters; they depend on foreign circulation as well as home-video formats to make up for early losses. The same is true for the television industry.

Social Issues in Media Economics

Mergermania has sparked criticism in some quarters (see "Media Literacy Case Study: From Fifty to a Few: The Most Dominant Media Corporations" on pages 488–489). Some opponents lament the limits of antitrust laws. Others decry consumers' loss of control in the marketplace when just a few companies determine what messages and media content are produced. Still others warn against the infiltration of American culture and media messages into every corner of the globe.

The Limits of Antitrust Laws

Despite the intent of antitrust laws to ensure diversity of corporate ownership, companies have easily avoided these laws since the 1980s by diversifying their holdings and by forming local monopolies—especially in newspapers and cable. To accomplish this local control combined with megamedia mergers, media corporations developed well-polished and effective public relations and lobbying campaigns to get the public and lawmakers to back wave after wave of deregulation, thus weakening or stripping antitrust protections. These efforts have resulted in fewer voices in the marketplace and less competition among industry players.

Expanding through Diversification

Diversification, consolidation, and media partnerships promote oligopolies in which a few large companies control the majority of production and distribution of media content. Most media companies diversify among different media products (such as television stations and film studios), never fully dominating one particular media industry. Time Warner, for example, spreads its holdings among television programming, film, publishing, cable channels, and its Internet divisions. However, Time Warner competes directly with only a few other big companies, such as Disney, Viacom, and News Corp. And Comcast, following a series of mergers, not only has become the cable and broadband company that controls the path by which so many media products are streamed into the home but

From Fifty to a Few: The Most Dominant Media Corporations

When Ben Bagdikian wrote the first edition of *The Media Monopoly*, published in 1983, he warned of the chilling control wielded by the fifty elite corporations that owned most of the U.S. mass media. By the publication of the book's seventh edition in 2004, the number of corporations controlling most of America's daily newspapers, magazines, radio, television, books, and movies had dropped from fifty to five. Today, most of the leading corporations have a high profile in the United States, particularly through ownership of television networks: Time Warner (CW), Disney (ABC), News Corp. (Fox), CBS Corporation (CBS and CW), and Comcast-owned NBC Universal (NBC).

The creep of consolidation over the past few decades requires us to think differently about how we experience the mass media on a daily basis. Potential conflicts of interest abound. For example, should we trust how NBC News covers Comcast or how ABC News covers Disney? Should we be wary if *Time* magazine hypes a Warner Brothers film? More important, what actions can we take to ensure that the mass media function not just as successful businesses for stockholders but also as a necessary part of our democracy?

APPLYING THE CRITICAL PROCESS

DESCRIPTION To help you get a better understanding of how our media landscape is changing, look at Table 14.1, which lists the Top 10 media companies for 1980, 1996, and 2012.

ANALYSIS What patterns do you notice?

INTERPRETATION Based on what you have discovered, what do these patterns mean? How do they reflect larger trends in the media? That is, seven of the major companies in 1980 were mostly print businesses, but in 2012, none were. Why?

EVALUATION Although the subsidiaries of these companies often change, the charts demonstrate the wide reach of large conglomerates. Are these large media corporations good or bad for the economy? How do they affect democracy?

ENGAGEMENT Think about how much of your daily media consumption is owned by the Top 10 corporations and about the influence they have on your news and entertainment intake. Ask two or three people around you to do the same, and compare your responses.

LaunchPad

macmillanhighered.com/mediaessentials3e

Mickey Huff
Project Censored

© Bedford / St. Martin's

▶ **Visit LaunchPad** to watch a video of media professionals discussing the money behind the media. How do corporations affect the media we consume and how we consume it?

TABLE 14.1 // TOP 10 U.S. MEDIA COMPANIES, 1980, 1996, 2012*

1980 Rank	Company	Revenue in $ billions	1996 Rank	Company	Revenue in $ billions
1	American Broadcasting Co.	$2.204	1	Time Warner	$11.851
2	CBS Inc.	2.001	2	Walt Disney Co.	6.555
3	RCA Corp.	1.521	3	Tele-Communications Inc.	5.954
4	Time Inc.	1.348	4	NBC TV (General Electric Co.)	5.230
5	S.I. Newhouse & Sons	1.250	5	CBS Corp.	4.333
6	Gannett Co.	1.195	6	Gannett Co.	4.214
7	Times Mirror Co.	1.128	7	News Corp.	4.005
8	Hearst Corp.	1.100	8	Advance Publications	3.385
9	Knight-Ridder Newspapers	1.099	9	Cox Enterprises	3.075
10	Tribune Co.	1.048	10	Knight-Ridder	2.851

2012 Rank	Company	Revenue in $ billions
1	Comcast Corp.	$45.0
2	DirecTV Group	22.3
3	Walt Disney Co. (owns ABC)	21.5
4	Time Warner	19.9
5	Time Warner Cable	18.1
6	News Corp.	17.3
7	DISH Network Corp.	13.0
8	Cox Enterprises	12.0
9	Google	11.9
10	CBS Corp.	11.4

Data from: Ad Age's 100 Leading Media Companies *report, December 7, 1981;* "100 Companies by Media Revenue," Advertising Age, *August 18, 1997;* "Media 100," Advertising Age, *December 31, 2012.*

*Note: The revenue in $ billions is based on total net U.S. media revenue and does not include nonmedia and international revenue.

also, after buying NBC Universal, controls a big portion of the media products on that path.

One prime example of a media partnership is Hulu.com, a joint venture of NBC Universal TV (Comcast), Fox Broadcasting, and Disney-ABC Television. Not only do these three owners of the video-streaming service offer content from the pantheon of networks they own, but they have several other "content partners" as well, including the CW and BBC networks.

This kind of economic arrangement makes it difficult for companies outside the oligopoly to compete in the marketplace. For example, an independent film production company may be unable to attract enough investors to get its movies distributed nationwide.

Building Local Monopolies

Antitrust laws aim to curb *national* monopolies, so most media monopolies today operate locally. Nearly every cable company has been granted monopoly status in its local community. These firms alone decide which channels are made available and what rates are charged. Independent voices have little opportunity or means to raise the questions that regulatory groups—such as the Justice Department and the FCC—need to hear in order to shape the laws.

A Vast Silence

Despite the concerns expressed by some critics, there has been little public debate overall about the tightening oligopoly structure of international media. Experts have identified two forces behind this vast hegemonic silence: citizens' reluctance to criticize free markets because they equate them with democracy, and the often unclear distinction between how much choice and how much control consumers have in the marketplace.

Equating Free Markets with Democracy

Throughout the Cold War period in the 1950s and 1960s, many Americans refused to criticize capitalism, which they saw as synonymous with democracy. Any complaints about capitalism were viewed as an attack on the free marketplace, and attacks on the free marketplace in turn sounded like criticism of free speech. This was in part because business owners saw their right to operate in a free marketplace as an extension of their right to buy commercial speech in the form of advertising. This line of thinking, which originated in corporate efforts to equate capitalism with democracy, still casts a shadow over American culture today, making it difficult for many people to openly question the advertising-supported economic structure of the mass media.

Debating Consumer Choice versus Consumer Control

In discussing free markets, economists distinguish between *consumer control* over marketplace goods and freedom of *consumer choice:* "The former requires that consumers participate in deciding what is to be offered; the latter is satisfied if [consumers are] free to select among the options chosen for them by producers."[8] Most Americans and the citizens of other economically developed nations clearly have *choice*: options among a range of media products. Yet the choices sometimes obscure the fact that consumers have limited *control*: power in deciding what kinds of media get created and circulated. Consumers thus have little ability to shape the messages conveyed through media products about what is important and how the world should work. Instead, they can only react to those messages.

Yet independent and alternative producers, artists, writers, and publishers have provided a ray of hope. When their work becomes even marginally popular, big media companies often capitalize on these innovations by acquiring it—which enables these works to get out to the public. Moreover, business leaders "at the top" depend on independent ideas "from below" to generate new product lines. Fortunately, a number of transnational corporations encourage the development of promising local artists.

Cultural Imperialism

The increasing dominance of American popular culture around the world has sparked heated debate in international circles. On the one hand, people in other countries seem to relish the themes of innovation and rebellion expressed in American media products, and the global spread of access to media (particularly the ease of digital documentation via mobile devices) has made it harder for political leaders to secretly repress dissident groups. On the other hand, American styles in fashion and food, as well as media fare, dominate the global market—a situation known as **cultural imperialism**. Today, numerous international observers contend that consumers in countries inundated by American-made movies, music, television, and images have even less control than American consumers. Even the Internet has a distinctively American orientation. The United States got a head start in deploying the Internet as a mass medium and has been the dominant force ever since. Although the Internet is worldwide and in many languages, the majority of the Web's content is still in English; the United States controls the top domains, including .com and .org (without the requirement of having a nation-identifying domain name, such as .jp for Japan or .fr for France); and leading global sites like Google, Facebook, Amazon, YouTube, and *Wikipedia* are all American in design.

布萊德利庫柏 席安娜米勒

AMERICAN SNIPER
美國狙擊手
美國史上最致命神槍手

© Warner Bros. Pictures/Everett Collection

Ever since Hollywood gained an edge in film production and distribution, U.S. movies have dominated the box office in Europe, Asia, and the rest of the world. Worldwide grosses are in turn more important to Hollywood than ever.

Defenders of American popular culture's dominance argue that a universal culture creates a *global village* and fosters communication and collaboration across national boundaries. Critics, however, point out that two-thirds of the world's population cannot afford most of the products advertised on American, Japanese, and European television. Yet they see, hear, and read about consumer abundance and middle-class values through TV and other media, including magazines and the Internet. Critics worry that the obvious disparities in economic well-being and the frustration that must surely come from not having the money to buy advertised products may lead to social unrest.

The Media Marketplace in a Democratic Society

Multinational giants are controlling more and more aspects of production and distribution of media products. This is particularly worrisome when it comes to news media: Media conglomerates that own news companies have the capacity to use those resources to promote their products and determine what news receives national coverage. When news coverage is determined by fewer decision makers, citizens cannot be certain they are receiving sufficient information with which to make decisions. That's bad news for any democracy.

Media powerhouses are also increasingly shaping the regulatory environment. Politicians in Washington, D.C., regularly accept millions of dollars from media conglomerates and their lobbying groups to finance their campaigns. Companies that provide such financial support stand a better chance of influencing regulatory decisions. Indeed, they have successfully pushed for more deregulation, which has enabled them to grow even more and come under fewer constraints. This is also bad news for our democracy, especially because the journalism subsidiaries of major media conglomerates are not completely independent of the powerful corporate and political forces on which they report. Who will tell us the news about big media and their political allies?

Despite the forces we have examined that are discouraging energetic debate about these realities, some grassroots organizations have arisen to challenge the power and reach of media behemoths. Such movements—like the annual National Conference for Media Reform—are usually united by geographic ties, common political backgrounds, or shared concerns about the state of the media. The Internet has also enabled media reform groups to form globally, uniting around such efforts as fostering independent media, contesting censorship, or monitoring the activities of multinational corporations.

This development is encouraging news: It suggests that we consumers—whether in America or elsewhere—might be willing to look more closely at the media marketplace's impact on our lives. And we may start demanding that media companies take more responsibility for fulfilling one of their key missions: making democratic life better for those of us consuming their products and absorbing their messages.

Jeremy Montemagni/Sipa Press/Newscom

Amy Goodman is cohost of *Democracy Now!*, a radio/TV newscast airing daily on more than eight hundred public and college radio stations, satellite television, and the Internet. *Democracy Now!* argues that it maintains editorial independence by accepting funding only from listeners, viewers, and foundations, and rejecting government funding, corporate underwriting, and advertisers.

CHAPTER ESSENTIALS

Now that you have finished reading this chapter, you can use the following tools:

LaunchPad for *Media Essentials*

Go to **macmillanhighered.com/mediaessentials3e** for videos, review quizzes, and more.

LaunchPad for *Media Essentials* includes:

- **REVIEW WITH LEARNINGCURVE**
  LearningCurve uses gamelike quizzing to help you master the concepts you need to learn from this chapter.

REVIEW

Discuss the Transition to an Information Economy

- By the mid-twentieth century, the U.S. shifted from a manufacturing-based economy to one fueled by information and cooperation with other economies, causing mass media industries to expand globally. Although early regulation was designed to break up monopolies, deregulation of the industries won out, leading to a growth of mergers and acquisitions (pp. 470–471).

- Media industries have one of three common structures: **monopoly** (when a single firm dominates production and distribution in a particular industry), **oligopoly** (when a few firms dominate an industry), or **limited competition** (when there are many producers and sellers but only a few products within a particular category) (pp. 471–472).

- Today's media powerhouses avoid monopoly charges by purchasing diverse types of media rather than controlling just one medium (pp. 474–475).

Explain the Media Economy

- Media companies make money from **direct payments**, which come from consumers who buy media products, and **indirect payments**, which come from advertisers and companies that purchase ads to attract specific customers. Companies also come up with specific business strategies to maximize profits. For example, many try to achieve **economies of scale**, the economic process of increasing production levels so as to reduce the overall cost per unit (pp. 475, 478).

- Historically, media companies have operated in separate industries; however, the Internet has changed the way people consume media. This development has presented new opportunities for some media organizations while posing challenges for some older media companies (pp. 478–479).

- Other trends that have affected the media economy include flexible markets and the decline of unionized labor, as well as downsizing and a growing wage gap (pp. 479–480).

- All these trends take place, in part, because mass media play a powerful role in establishing **hegemony**, in which a society's least powerful members are persuaded to accept the values defined by its most powerful members (pp. 480–481).

Analyze Specialization and Global Markets

- As globalization increased, companies began specializing to enter the new, narrow markets in other countries. They also sought to spur growth through **synergy**—the promotion and sale of different versions of a media product across a media conglomerate's various subsidiaries (p. 483).

- The Walt Disney Company is an example of a media conglomerate that has excelled at specialization and synergy. The company has also had success with its global expansion (pp. 483–486).

- Following Disney's model, many media conglomerates look to international expansion as a way to access markets and to provide opportunities to advance (pp. 486–487).

Trace the Social Issues in Media Economics

- Critics of mergers and media consolidation argue that antitrust laws are too limited, resulting in fewer voices in the marketplace and less competition among industry players (p. 487).

- Others decry consumers' loss of control in the marketplace when just a few companies determine what messages and media content are produced (pp. 490–491).

- Still others warn against the infiltration of American culture and media messages into every corner of the globe—a situation known as **cultural imperialism** (pp. 491–492).

Talk about the Media Marketplace's Role in Our Democratic Society

• Democracy suffers when news coverage is determined by fewer decision makers and when media powerhouses increasingly shape the regulatory environment. Grassroots organizations and the Internet have enabled media reform groups to form globally, suggesting that consumers might be willing to look more closely at the media marketplace's impact on our lives (pp. 492–493).

STUDY QUESTIONS

1. How are the three basic structures of mass media organizations— monopoly, oligopoly, and limited competition—different from one another? How is the Internet changing everything?

2. Why has the federal government emphasized deregulation at a time when so many media companies are growing so large? How have media mergers changed the economics of mass media?

3. How do global and specialized markets factor into the new media economy? Using the Walt Disney Company as an example, what is the role of synergy in the current climate of media mergers?

4. What are the differences between freedom of consumer choice and consumer control over marketplace goods? What is cultural imperialism, and what does it have to do with the United States?

5. What do critics and activists fear most about the concentration of media ownership? What are some promising signs regarding the relationship between media economics and democracy?

MEDIA LITERACY PRACTICE

One of the most difficult things to comprehend about the largest media corporations is their sheer size and synergies. To investigate this topic, explore examples of such synergies.

DESCRIBE the various subsidiaries and synergies of one media corporation—try Time Warner, Disney, or News Corp. You can begin by looking at the corporate Web site and *Columbia Journalism Review*'s ownership site, www.cjr .org/resources. Also, read corporate press releases and news stories about the media corporation's businesses.

ANALYZE the patterns in the synergies. Which subsidiaries work with other subsidiaries? Are there any divisions that operate independently? Which kinds of products have the most extensive synergies: News? Prime-time television? Comic-book characters?

INTERPRET what these patterns mean. For example, do the synergies result in higher quality or more profitable media content? Do the synergies result in overexposure of some media content?

EVALUATE the media corporation's business structure. Is synergy a good thing or a bad thing? Can journalism function well in a large media corporation?

ENGAGE with the community by writing a letter to a local newspaper or an online publication (or a journalism outlet within the media corporation itself) that reveals the good and bad about synergies within corporate media.

15

Social Scientific and Cultural Approaches to Media Research

In 2010, soon after widely publicized stories attributing fifteen-year-old Billy Lucas's suicide to antigay bullying, commentator and author Dan Savage launched the It Gets Better Project with a YouTube video created to inspire hope for young people enduring homophobic harassment at school and online. His idea snowballed into a worldwide movement, generating over thirty thousand user-created videos as well as submissions from celebrities, politicians, and media personalities. But despite the barrage of positive, inspiring messages, there are still stories like that of fourteen-year-old Jamey Rodemeyer, who had posted a video on Savage's YouTube channel but ended up taking his own life the following year. Rodemeyer had been bullied at school since the fifth grade—and had endured online messages like "I wouldn't care if you died. No one would. So just do it :) It would make everyone WAY more happier!"[1]

In 2012, twelve people were killed and seventy wounded in Aurora, Colorado. The attack took place in a movie theater during a midnight showing of *The Dark Knight Rises*. The attack, amid a number of mass shootings in public places, prompted calls for stiffer gun control laws, and Warner Brothers, the studio behind *The Dark Knight Rises*, delayed the release of its film *Gangster Squad* to replace a sequence in which gangsters shoot up a movie theater. Another theater shooting occurred in the summer of 2015 at a showing of the comedy *Trainwreck*.

In 2012, the blogging site Tumblr announced a ban on blogs that "actively promote self-harm," including those facilitating or glorifying suicide, self-mutilation, anorexia, bulimia, or other eating disorders. Before launching the policy, Tumblr's staff considered continuing to allow users to publish such material but posting public service messages warning users of the content and providing information about helplines and other support services. Ultimately, the staff adopted the ban after deciding that "sometimes Tumblr gets used for things that are just wrong."[2]

These and other similar events have raised important questions: What power do the mass media have over individuals and society, and how do the media contribute to social problems like homophobia, bullying, suicide, self-mutilation, and eating disorders? And what should we do about it?

THE IDEA THAT MEDIA HAVE A SIGNIFICANT IMPACT on society has fueled the development of two types of research in the study of mass communication: social scientific and cultural studies.

Social scientific research attempts to understand, explain, and predict the impact of mass media on individuals and society. The main goal of this type of research is to define the problem with a testable hypothesis, collect data through one of various methodologies, and draw conclusions based on the data. Researchers who focus on **cultural studies** explore how people make meaning, understand reality, articulate values, and interpret their experiences through use of cultural symbols in media. Cultural studies scholars also examine how groups such as corporate and political elites use media to circulate their messages and serve their interests. Such research focuses on daily cultural experience, examining the subtle intersections among mass communication, history, politics, and economics.

In this chapter, we look at how these two forms of media research have evolved over time by:

- examining early media research methods, including propaganda analysis, public opinion research, social psychology studies, and marketing research

- assessing social scientific media research, including theories about how media influence people's behaviors and attitudes, and the benefits and limitations of such research

- taking stock of cultural approaches to media research, including early and contemporary cultural studies theories and the strengths and limitations of such research

- considering the role of media research in our democracy and exploring how effectively such research addresses real-life problems

LaunchPad
**macmillanhighered.com
/mediaessentials3e**
Use **LearningCurve** to review concepts from this chapter.

Early Media Research Methods

During most of the nineteenth century, philosophers such as Alexis de Tocqueville based their analysis of news and print media on moral and political arguments.[3] More scientific approaches to mass media research did not emerge until the late 1920s and 1930s. In 1920, Walter Lippmann's *Liberty and the News* called on journalists to operate more like scientific researchers in gathering and analyzing facts. Lippmann's next book, *Public Opinion* (1922), was the first to apply the principles of psychology to journalism. Considered by many academics to be "the founding book in American media studies,"[4] *Public Opinion* deepened Americans' understanding of the effect of media, emphasizing data collection and numerical measurement. According to media historian Daniel Czitrom, by the 1930s "an aggressively empirical spirit, stressing new and increasingly sophisticated research techniques, characterized the study of modern communication in America."[5] Czitrom traces four trends between 1930 and 1960 that contributed to the rise of modern media research: propaganda analysis, public opinion research, social psychology studies, and marketing research.

Propaganda Analysis

Propaganda analysis was a major early focus of mass media research. After World War I, some researchers began studying how governments used propaganda to advance the war effort. They found that during the war, governments routinely relied on propaganda divisions to spread "information" to the public. Though propaganda was considered important for mobilizing public support during the war, these postwar researchers criticized it as "partisan appeal based on half-truths and devious manipulation of communication channels."[6] Harold Lasswell's 1927 study *Propaganda Technique in the World War* defined propaganda as "the control of opinion by significant symbols, . . . by stories, rumors, reports, pictures and other forms of social communication."[7]

Public Opinion Research

After the second world war, researchers went beyond the study of wartime propaganda and began examining how the mass media filter information and shape public attitudes. Social scientists explored these questions by conducting *public opinion research* through citizen surveys and polls.

Public opinion research on diverse populations has provided insights into how different groups view major national events, such as elections, and how those views affect their behavior. Journalists, however, became increasingly dependent on polls, particularly for political insight.

Today, some critics argue that this heavy reliance on measured public opinion adversely affects Americans' participation in the political process. For example, people who read poll projections and get the sense that few others are voting for their favored candidate may not bother casting a ballot. "Why should I vote," they tell themselves, "if my vote isn't going to make a difference?" Some critics of incessant polling argue that polls mainly measure opinions on topics of interest to business, government, academics, and the mainstream news media. The public responds passively to polls, without getting anything of value in return. Professional pollsters object to **pseudo-polls**—typically call-in, online, or person-in-the-street polls that the news media use to address a "question of the day." Such polls, which do not use a random sample of the population and are therefore not representative of the population as a whole, nevertheless persist on news and entertainment Web sites, radio, and television news programs.

Social Psychology Studies

Whereas opinion polls measure public attitudes, *social psychology studies* measure the behavior, attitudes, and cognition of individuals. The Payne Fund

Studies—the most influential early social psychology media studies—comprised thirteen research projects conducted by social psychologists between 1929 and 1932. Named after the private philanthropic organization that funded the research, the Payne Fund Studies were a response to a growing national concern about the effects of motion pictures on young people. The studies, which some politicians later used to attack the movie industry, linked frequent movie attendance to juvenile delinquency, promiscuity, and other problematic behaviors, arguing that movies took "emotional possession" of young filmgoers.[8]

The conclusions of this and other Payne Fund Studies contributed to the establishment of the Motion Picture Production Code, which tamed movie content from the 1930s through the 1950s (see Chapter 13). As forerunners of today's research into TV violence and aggression, the Payne Fund Studies became the model for media research, although social psychology is also used to study the mass media's relationship to body image, gender norms, political participation, and a wide range of other topics. (See Figure 15.1 on page 506 for one example of a contemporary policy that has developed from media research. See also "Media Literacy Case Study: The Effects of Television in a Post-TV World" on pages 504–505.)

Library of Congress Prints and Photographs Division

Propaganda analysis researchers studied the impact of war posters and other government information campaigns to determine how audiences could be persuaded through stirring media messages about patriotism and duty.

Marketing Research

Marketing research emerged in the 1920s, when advertisers and consumer product companies began conducting surveys on consumer buying habits and other behaviors. For example, rating systems arose that measured how many people were listening to commercial radio on a given night. By the 1930s, radio networks, advertisers, large stations, and advertising agencies all subscribed to ratings services. However, compared with print media, whose circulation departments kept track of customers' names and addresses, radio listeners were more difficult to trace. The problem prompted experts to develop increasingly sophisticated market-research methods to determine consumer preferences and media use, such as direct-mail diaries, television meters, phone surveys, telemarketing, and eventually Internet tracking. In many instances, product companies paid consumers a small fee to take part in these studies.

The Effects of Television in a Post-TV World

Since television's emergence as a mass medium, there has been persistent concern about the effects of violence, sex, and indecent language seen in television programs. The U.S. Congress had its first hearings on the matter of television content in 1952 and has held hearings in every subsequent decade. In its coverage of congressional hearings on TV violence in 1983, the *New York Times* accurately captured the nature of these recurring public hearings: "Over the years, the principals change but the roles remain the same: social scientists ready to prove that television does indeed improperly influence its viewers, and network representatives, some of them also social scientists, who insist that there is absolutely nothing to worry about."[1]

© ABC/Photofest

One of the central focuses of the TV debate has been television's effect on children. In 1975, the major broadcast networks (then ABC, CBS, and NBC) bowed to congressional and FCC pressure and agreed to a "family hour" of programming in the first hour of prime-time television (8–9 P.M. Eastern, or 7–8 P.M. Central). Shows such as *Happy Days* and *Little House on the Prairie* flourished in that time slot. By 1989, Fox had arrived as a fourth major network and successfully counter-programmed in the family hour with daringly dysfunctional family shows like *Married . . . with Children.*

Since then, the most prominent watchdog monitoring prime-time network television's violence, sex, and indecent language has been the Parents Television Council (PTC), formed in 1995. As part of its primary mission, the lobbying group "promotes and restores responsibility and decency to the entertainment industry in answer to America's demand for positive, family-oriented television programming. The PTC does this by fostering changes in TV programming to make the early hours of prime time family-friendly and suitable for viewers of all ages."[2] Through its Web campaign of inundating the FCC with complaints, the PTC played a

leading role in getting the FCC to approve a steep increase in its fines for broadcast indecency.

Yet for the ongoing concerns of parent groups and Congress, it's worth asking: What are the effects of television in what researchers are now calling a "post-TV" world? In just the past few years, digital video recorders have become common, and services like Hulu, YouTube, Netflix, iTunes, and on-demand cable viewing mean that viewers can access TV programming of all types at any time of the day. Although Americans are watching more television than ever before, it's increasingly time-shifted programming. Should we still be considering the possible harmful effects of prime-time network television, given that most American families are no longer watching during the appointed broadcast network prime-time hours? Does the American public care about such media effects in this post-TV world?

These days, the PTC still releases its weekly "Family Guide to Prime Time Television" on its Web site. A sample of the guide from summer 2014, for example, listed no shows as being "family friendly," while shows as diverse as *The Big Bang Theory*, *Person of Interest*, *America's Got Talent*, and *Arrow* received a red-light designation for sexual content, language, and violence. Of course, as television viewers move away from broadcast networks and increasingly watch programming from multiple sources on a range of devices, the PTC's traditional concern about prime-time network viewing can seem outdated. In May 2012, the PTC announced it was awarding its seal of approval to the Inspiration Network cable channel "for programming that embraces time-honored values."[3] The channel's lineup features shows like *The Waltons; Dr. Quinn, Medicine Woman; Little House on the Prairie*; and *Happy Days*—all shows from an era decades before our post-TV world.

APPLYING THE CRITICAL PROCESS

DESCRIPTION Keep track of your TV viewing habits for one week. Devise a chart and create categories for the types of shows you watch (sitcoms, dramas, reality programs), how you watch each show (on television, laptop, smartphone), and if you are watching the shows when aired or are time-shifting in some way. If you are time-shifting, what time is it normally aired, and on what network or from what source?

ANALYSIS Take note of the content of each program—what topics are covered, and whether or not there is violence. What shows seem to feature more violence than others, and what kind of violence? How much violence do you find overall?

INTERPRETATION What do your findings mean? Are you surprised by the appearance of violence in any seemingly nonviolent shows? Do broadcast network shows (on ABC, CBS, NBC, Fox, the CW) feature more, similar amounts of, or less violent programming than cable, satellite, or streaming-only television shows?

EVALUATION How does exposure to violence in these shows affect you? Do you agree with the FCC statement that "exposure to violence in the media can increase aggressive behavior in children, at least in the short term"? Why or why not?

ENGAGEMENT Aside from TV shows, examine other forms of entertainment that you enjoy, such as your collection of movies or video games, for the presence of violent content. Are the rating systems for these products effective? File your comments or concerns online with the FCC (www.fcc.gov).

FIGURE 15.1 // TV PARENTAL GUIDELINES

The TV industry continues to study its self-imposed rating categories, promising to fine-tune them to ensure that the government keeps its distance. These standards are one example of a policy that was shaped in part by media research.

The following categories apply to programs designed solely for children:

 All Children
This program is designed to be appropriate for all children. Whether animated or live-action, the themes and elements in this program are specifically designed for a very young audience, including children from ages 2–6. This program is not expected to frighten young children.

 Directed to Older Children — Fantasy Violence
For those programs where fantasy violence may be more intense or more combative than other programs in this category, such programs will be designated **TV-Y7-FV**.

 Directed to Older Children
This program is designed for children age 7 and above. It may be more appropriate for children who have acquired the developmental skills needed to distinguish between make-believe and reality. Themes and elements in this program may include mild fantasy violence or comedic violence, or may frighten children under the age of 7. Therefore, parents may wish to consider the suitability of this program for their very young children.

The following categories apply to programs designed for the entire audience:

 General Audience
Most parents would find this program suitable for all ages. Although this rating does not signify a program designed specifically for children, most parents may let younger children watch this program unattended. It contains little or no violence, no strong language and little or no sexual dialogue situations.

Parental Guidance Suggested
This program contains material that parents may find unsuitable for younger children. Many parents may want to watch it with their younger children. The theme itself may call for parental guidance and/or the program may contain one or more of the following: some suggestive dialogue (D), infrequent coarse language (L), some sexual situations (S), or moderate violence (V).

Parents Strongly Cautioned
This program contains some material that many parents would find unsuitable for children under 14 years of age. Parents are strongly urged to exercise greater care in monitoring this program and are cautioned against letting children under the age of 14 watch unattended. This program may contain one or more of the following: intensely suggestive dialogue (D), strong coarse language (L), intense sexual situations (S), or intense violence (V).

 Mature Audiences Only
This program is specifically designed to be viewed by adults and therefore may be unsuitable for children under 17. This program may contain one or more of the following: crude indecent language (L), explicit sexual activity (S), or graphic violence (V).

Data from: TV Parental Guidelines Monitoring Board, www.tvguidelines.org, July 10, 2006

Social Scientific Research

Concerns about public opinion measurements, propaganda, and the impact of media on society intensified just as journalism and mass communication departments gained popularity in colleges and universities. As these forces dovetailed, media researchers looked increasingly to behavioral science as the basis of their work. Between 1930 and 1960, "who says what to whom with what effect" became the key question "defining the scope and problems of American communications research."[9] To address this question, researchers asked more specific questions, such as, If children watch a lot of TV cartoons (stimulus or cause), will this influence their behavior toward their peers (response or effect)? New social scientific models arose to measure and explain such connections—which researchers referred to as *media effects*.

Early Models of Media Effects

Between the 1930s and the 1970s, media researchers developed several paradigms about how media affect individuals' behavior. These models were known as hypodermic needle, minimal effects, and uses and gratifications.

Hypodermic Needle

The notion that powerful media adversely affect weak audiences has been labeled the **hypodermic-needle** (or **magic bullet**) **model**. It suggests that the media "shoot" their effects directly into unsuspecting victims.

One of the earliest challenges to this model came from a study of Orson Welles's legendary October 30, 1938, radio broadcast of *War of the Worlds*. The broadcast presented H. G. Wells's Martian-invasion novel in the form of a news report, which frightened millions of listeners who didn't realize it was fictional (see Chapter 6). In 1940, radio researcher Hadley Cantril wrote a book-length study of the broadcast and its aftermath, titled *The Invasion from Mars: A Study in the Psychology of Panic*. Cantril argued that contrary to what the hypodermic-needle model suggested, not all listeners thought the radio program was a real news report. In fact, the relatively few listeners who thought there was an actual invasion from Mars were those who not only tuned in late and missed the disclaimer at the beginning of the broadcast but also were predisposed (because of religious beliefs) to think that the end of the world was actually near. Although social scientists have since disproved the hypodermic-needle model, many people still subscribe to it, particularly when considering the media's impact on children.

Minimal Effects

Cantril's research helped lay the groundwork for the **minimal-effects** (or *limited effects*) **model** proposed by some media researchers. With the rise of empirical

© Bettmann/Corbis

Early media researchers concerned about Adolf Hitler's use of national radio to indoctrinate the German people in the 1930s found his international broadcasts to be failures. Because so many media messages competed with Nazi propaganda in democratic countries, Hitler's radio programs had little impact there.

research techniques, social scientists began discovering and demonstrating that media alone do not cause people to change their attitudes and behaviors. After conducting controlled experiments and surveys, researchers argued that people generally engage in **selective exposure** and **selective retention** with regard to media. That is, people expose themselves to media messages most familiar to them, and retain messages that confirm values and attitudes they already hold. Minimal-effects researchers have argued that in most cases, mass media *reinforce* existing behaviors and attitudes rather than change them.

Indeed, Joseph Klapper, in his 1960 research study *The Effects of Mass Communication*, found that mass media influenced only those individuals who did not already hold strong views on an issue. Media, Klapper added, had a greater impact on poor and uneducated audiences. Solidifying the minimal-effects argument, Klapper concluded that strong media effects occur largely at an individual level and do not appear to have large-scale, measurable, and direct effects on society as a whole.[10]

Uses and Gratifications

The **uses and gratifications** model arose to challenge the notion that people are passive recipients of media. This model holds that people instead actively engage in using media to satisfy various emotional or intellectual needs—for example, turning on the TV in the house not only to be entertained but also to create an "electronic hearth," making the space feel more warm and alive. Researchers supporting this model use in-depth interviews to supplement survey questionnaires. Through these interviews, they study the ways in which people use media. Instead of asking, "What effects do media have on us?" these researchers ask, "Why do we use media?"

Although the uses and gratifications model addresses the *functions* of the mass media for individuals, it does not address important questions related to the impact of the media on society. Consequently, the uses and gratifications model has never become a dominant or enduring paradigm in media research. But the rise of Internet-related media technologies has brought a resurgence of uses and gratifications research to understand why people use new media.

Conducting Social Scientific Media Research

As researchers investigated various theories about how media affect people, they also developed different approaches to conducting their research. These approaches vary depending on whether the research originates in the private or the public sector. *Private research*, sometimes called *proprietary research*, is generally conducted for a business, a corporation, or even a political campaign. It typically addresses some real-life problem or need. *Public research* usually takes place in academic and government settings. It tries to clarify, explain, or predict—in other words, to theorize about—the effects of mass media rather than to address a consumer problem.

Most media research today focuses on media's impact on human characteristics such as learning, attitudes, aggression, and voting habits. This research employs the **scientific method**, which consists of seven steps:

Mario Tama/Getty Images

The uses and gratifications model discusses media as being an "electronic hearth" that people gather around to share experiences. Here, we see people uniting in a sports bar to cheer on their favorite team.

1. Identify the problem to be researched.
2. Review existing research and theories related to the problem.
3. Develop working hypotheses or predictions about what the study might find.
4. Determine an appropriate method or research design.
5. Collect information or relevant data.
6. Analyze results to see whether they verify the hypotheses.
7. Interpret the implications of the study.

The scientific method relies on *objectivity* (eliminating bias and judgments on the part of researchers), *reliability* (getting the same answers or outcomes from a study or measure during repeated testing), and *validity* (demonstrating that a study actually measures what it claims to measure).

A key step in using the scientific method is posing one or more **hypotheses**: tentative general statements that predict either the influence of an *independent variable* on a *dependent variable*, or relationships between variables. For example, a researcher might hypothesize that frequent TV viewing among adolescents (independent variable) causes poor academic performance (dependent variable). Or a researcher might hypothesize that playing first-person-shooter video games (independent variable) is associated with aggression in children (dependent variable).

Researchers using the scientific method may employ experiments or survey research in their investigations.

Experiments

Like all studies that use the scientific method, **experiments** in media research isolate some aspect of content; suggest a hypothesis; and manipulate variables to discover a particular medium's impact on people's attitudes, emotions, or behavior. To test whether a hypothesis is true, researchers expose an *experimental group*—the group under study—to selected media images or messages. To ensure valid results, researchers also use a *control group*, which is not exposed to the selected media content and thus serves as a basis for comparison. Subjects are picked for each group through **random assignment**, meaning that each subject has an equal chance of being placed in either group.

For instance, suppose researchers wanted to test the effects of violent films on preadolescent boys. The study might take a group of ten-year-olds and randomly assign them to two groups. The experimental group then watches a violent action movie that the control group does not see. Later, both groups are exposed to a staged fight between two other boys, and researchers watch how each group responds. If the control subjects try to break up the fight but the experimental subjects do not, researchers might conclude that the violent film caused the difference in the groups' responses (see the "Bobo doll" experiment photos on page 511).

When experiments carefully account for independent variables through random assignment, they generally work well to substantiate cause-effect hypotheses. Although experiments are sometimes conducted in field settings, where people can be observed using media in their everyday environments, researchers have less control over variables in these settings. Conversely, a weakness of more carefully controlled experiments is that they are often conducted in the unnatural conditions of a laboratory environment, which can affect the behavior of the experimental subjects.

Survey Research

Through **survey research,** investigators collect and measure data taken from a group of respondents regarding their attitudes, knowledge, or behavior. Using random sampling techniques that give each potential subject an equal chance to be included in the survey, this research method draws on much larger populations than those used in experimental studies. Researchers can conduct surveys through direct mail, personal interviews, telephone calls, e-mail, and Web sites, thus accumulating large quantities of information from diverse cross sections of people. These data enable researchers to examine demographic factors in addition to responses to questions related to the survey topic.

Surveys offer other benefits as well. Because the randomized sample size is large, researchers can usually generalize their findings to the larger society as well as investigate populations over a long period of time. In addition, they can use the extensive government and academic survey databases now widely available to conduct **longitudinal studies**, in which they compare new studies with those conducted years earlier.

But like experiments, surveys also have several drawbacks. First, they cannot show cause-effect relationships. They can only show **correlations**— or associations—between two variables. For example, a random survey of ten-year-old boys that asks about their behavior might demonstrate that a correlation exists between acting aggressively and watching violent TV programs. But this correlation does not identify the cause and the effect. (Perhaps people who are already aggressive choose to watch violent TV programs.) Second, surveys are only as good as the wording of their questions and the answer choices they present. Thus, a poorly designed survey can produce misleading results.

Content Analysis

As social scientific media researchers developed theories about the mass media, it became increasingly important to more precisely describe the media content being studied. As a corrective, they developed a method known as **content analysis** to systematically describe various types of media content.

These photos of the "Bobo doll" experiments show that the children who observed an adult punching and kicking the Bobo dolls were more likely to imitate the adult model's behavior when returned to a room with many toys.

© Albert Bandura

Content analysis involves defining terms and developing a coding scheme so that whatever is being studied—acts of violence in movies, representations of women in television commercials, the treatment of political candidates in news reports—can be accurately judged and counted. One annual content analysis study is conducted by GLAAD each year to count the quantity, quality, and diversity of lesbian, gay, bisexual, and transgender (LGBT) characters on television. In 2014, GLAAD's content analysis found that MTV led all networks, with 49 percent of its primetime programming hours featuring LGBT characters (followed by FX, ABC Family, and NBC). On the other end of the GLAAD list, only 9 percent of TNT's prime-time programming included LGBT characters; A&E had 6 percent, and the History Channel came in last with no LGBT representations at all in its prime-time programming. The report also noted that some of the most "groundbreaking and fully realized depictions" of transgender characters was happening on new online content creators like Netflix and Amazon, with shows like *Orange Is the New Black* and *Transparent*.[11] Content analysis has its own limitations. For one thing, this technique does not measure the effects of various media messages on audiences or explain how those messages are presented. Moreover, problems of definition arise. For instance, how do researchers distinguish slapstick cartoon aggression from the violent murders or rapes shown during an evening police drama?

Contemporary Media Effects Theories

By the 1960s, several departments of mass communication began graduating Ph.D.-level researchers (the first had been at the University of Iowa in 1948) schooled in experiment and survey research techniques as well as content analysis. These researchers began developing new theories about how media affect people. Five particularly influential contemporary theories emerged. These are known as social learning theory, agenda-setting theory, the cultivation effect theory, the spiral of silence theory, and the third-person effect theory.

Social Learning Theory

Some of the best-known studies suggesting a link between mass media and behavior are the "Bobo doll" experiments, conducted on children by psychologist Albert Bandura and his colleagues at Stanford University in the 1960s. Although many researchers criticized the use of Bobo dolls as an experimental device (since the point of playing with Bobo dolls is to hit them), Bandura argued that the experiments demonstrated a link between violent media programs, such as those on television, and aggressive behavior. Bandura developed **social learning theory**, which he believed involved a four-step process: *attention* (the subject must attend to the media and witness the aggressive behavior), *retention* (the subject must retain the memory of what he or she saw for later retrieval), *motor reproduction* (the subject must be able to physically imitate the behavior), and *motivation* (there must be a social reward or reinforcement to encourage modeling of the behavior).

Supporters of social learning theory often cite real-life imitations of aggression depicted in media (such as the Columbine massacre) as evidence that the theory is correct. Critics argue that real-life violence actually stems from larger social problems (such as poverty or mental illness), and that the theory makes mass media the scapegoats for those larger problems.

© Susan Meiselas/Magnum Photos

A consequence of agenda-setting is that the stories that don't get attention from the mass media don't make it onto the public and political agendas. Some groups try to overcome this barrier. Human Rights Watch works hard to publicize the high maternal mortality rate in rural India so that this important issue gets on the media agenda.

Agenda-Setting Theory

Researchers who hold the **agenda-setting theory** believe that when mass media focus their attention on particular events or issues, they determine—that is, set the agenda for—what people discuss and what they pay attention to. Media thus do not so much tell us *what* to think as what to think *about*.

The first investigations into the possibility of agenda-setting began in the late 1960s, when scholars Maxwell McCombs and Donald Shaw compared issues cited by undecided voters on election day with issues covered heavily by the media. Since then, researchers exploring this theory have demonstrated that the more stories the news media do on a particular subject, the more importance audiences attach to that subject. For instance, the extensive news coverage of Hurricane Katrina in fall 2005 sparked a corresponding increase in public concern about the disaster. Today, with national news coverage of the aftereffects of Katrina almost nonexistent, public interest in the impact of Katrina has ebbed—even though many of the areas affected by the hurricane still lie in ruins.

The Cultivation Effect Theory

The **cultivation effect theory** holds that heavy viewing of TV leads individuals to perceive the world in ways consistent with television portrayals. The major research into this hypothesis grew from the TV violence profiles of George Gerbner and his colleagues, who attempted to make broad generalizations about the impact of televised violence. Beginning in the late 1960s, these social scientists categorized and counted different types of violent acts shown on network television. Using a methodology that combines annual content analyses of TV violence with surveys, the cultivation effect suggests that the more time individuals spend viewing television and absorbing its viewpoints, the more likely their views of social reality will be "cultivated" by the images and portrayals they see on television.[12] For example, Gerbner's studies concluded that although fewer than 1 percent of Americans are victims of violent crime in any single year, people who watch a lot of television tend to overestimate that percentage.

Some critics have charged that cultivation research has provided limited evidence to support its findings. In addition, some have argued that the cultivation effects recorded by Gerbner's studies have been minimal. When compared side by side, these critics argue, perceptions of heavy television viewers and nonviewers regarding how dangerous the world is are virtually identical.

The Spiral of Silence Theory

Developed by German communication theorist Elisabeth Noelle-Neumann in the 1970s and 1980s, the **spiral of silence theory** links mass media, social psychology, and public opinion formation. The theory proposes that those who believe that their views on controversial issues are in the minority will keep their views to themselves for fear of social isolation. The theory is based on social psychology studies, such as the classic conformity studies of Solomon Asch in 1951. In Asch's study on the effects of group pressure, he demonstrated that a test subject is more likely to give clearly wrong answers to questions about line lengths if everyone else in the room (all secret confederates of the experimenter) unanimously state an incorrect answer. Noelle-Neumann argued that this effect is exacerbated by mass media, particularly television, which can quickly and widely communicate a real or presumed majority public opinion.

Noelle-Neumann acknowledges that not everyone keeps quiet if they think they hold a minority view. In many cases, "hard-core nonconformists" exist and remain vocal even in the face of possible social isolation. These individuals can even change public opinion by continuing to voice their views.

The Third-Person Effect Theory

Identified in a 1983 study by W. Phillips Davison, the **third-person effect theory** suggests that people believe others are more affected by media messages than they are themselves. In other words, this theory posits the idea that "we" can escape the worst effects of media while still worrying about people who are younger, less educated, less informed, or otherwise less capable of guarding against media influence.

Under this theory, we might fear that other people will, for example, take tabloids seriously, imitate violent movies, or get addicted to the Internet, while dismissing the idea that any of those things could happen to us. It has been argued that the third-person effect is instrumental in censorship, as it would allow censors to assume immunity to the negative effects of any supposedly dangerous media they must examine.

Evaluating Social Scientific Research

Media effects research has deepened our understanding of the mass media. This wealth of research exists partly because funding for studies on media's impact on young people remains popular among politicians and has drawn ready government support since the 1960s. But funding restricts the scope of some media effects research, particularly if the agendas of government agencies, businesses, or other entities do not align with researchers' interests. Moreover, because media effects research operates best in examining media's impact on individual behavior, few of these studies explore how media shape larger community and social life. Some research has begun to address these deficits, as well as to explore the impact of media technology on international communication.

Cultural Approaches to Media Research

In the 1960s, cultural approaches to media research emerged to challenge social scientific media effects theories and to compensate for those theories' limitations. In contrast to social scientific media research, the *cultural studies* mode of media research involves interpreting written and visual "texts" or artifacts as symbols that contain cultural, historical, and political meanings. For example, researchers might argue that the wave of police and crime shows that flooded the TV landscape in the mid-1960s was a response to Americans' fears about urban unrest and income disparity. A cultural approach thus offers interpretations of the stories, messages, and meanings that circulate throughout society.

Like social scientific media research, cultural studies media research has evolved in the decades since it first appeared.

Early Developments in Cultural Studies Media Research

In Europe, media studies have always favored interpretive rather than scientific approaches. Researchers there have approached the media from the perspective of literary or cultural critics rather than experimental or survey researchers. These approaches were built on the writings of political philosophers such as Karl Marx and Antonio Gramsci, who investigated how mass media support existing hierarchies in society.

In the United States, early criticism of media effects research came from the Frankfurt School, a group of European researchers who emigrated from Germany to America to escape Nazi persecution in the 1930s. Under the leadership of Max Horkheimer, T. W. Adorno, and Leo Lowenthal, this group advocated augmenting experimental approaches with historical and cultural approaches to investigate mass media's long-range effects on audiences.

Since the time of the Frankfurt School, criticisms of the media effects tradition and its methods have continued, with calls for more interpretive studies of the rituals of mass communication. Academics who have embraced a cultural approach to media research try to understand how media and culture are tied to the actual patterns of communication in daily life. For example, in the 1970s, Stuart Hall and his colleagues studied the British print media and the police, who were dealing with an apparent rise in crime and mugging incidents. Arguing that the close relationship between the news and the police created a form of urban surveillance, the authors of *Policing the Crisis* demonstrated that the mugging phenomenon was exacerbated, and in part created, by the key institutions assigned the social tasks of controlling crime and reporting on it.[13]

Contemporary Cultural Studies Approaches

Cultural research investigates daily experiences, especially through the lenses of race, gender, class, sexuality, and imbalances of power and status in society. Such research emphasizes how some groups have been marginalized and ignored throughout history, particularly African Americans, Native Americans, Asians and Asian Americans, Arabic peoples, Latinos, Appalachians, gay men and lesbians, immigrants, and women. Cultural studies researchers also seek to recover these lost or silenced voices. The major approaches they use are textual analysis, audience studies, and political economy studies.

Textual Analysis

Textual analysis entails a close reading and interpretation of cultural messages, including those found in books, movies, and TV programs—such as portrayals of Arab and Arab American characters in popular films.[14] Whereas social

Media critic Jack Shaheen analyzes the cultural messages behind portrayals of Arabs and Arab Americans in film and TV, such as the Bugs Bunny cartoon shown here.

From the film "Reel Bad Arabs: How Hollywood Vilifies a People" produced and distributed by the Media Education Foundation

scientific research approaches media messages with the principles of modern science in mind—replicability, objectivity, and data—textual analysis looks at rituals, narratives, and meaning.

Although textual analysis has a long and rich history in film and literary studies, it gained new significance for mass media in the early 1970s with the work of Stuart Hall in the U.K., who theorized about how messages were sent and understood (encoded and decoded) via television, and with the publication of American Horace Newcomb's *TV: The Most Popular Art*—the first academic book to analyze television shows. Newcomb studied why certain TV programs and formats, such as the *Beverly Hillbillies*, *Bewitched*, and *Dragnet*, became popular. Trained as a literary scholar, Newcomb argued that content analysis and other social scientific approaches to popular media often ignored artistic traditions and social context.

Both Newcomb and Hall felt that textual analysis, which had largely focused on "important," highly regarded works of art—debates, film, poems, and books—should also be applied to popular culture. As Hall argued, things like television and popular music were important because they were what most people were using or experiencing most of the time. By the end of the 1970s, a new generation of media studies scholars, who had grown up on television and rock and roll, began studying less elite forms of culture. By shifting the focus to daily popular culture, such studies shone a spotlight on the more ordinary ways that "normal" people (not just military, political, or religious leaders) experience and interpret their daily lives through messages in media.

Audience Studies

Audience studies differ from textual analysis in that the subject being researched is the audience for the text, not the text itself. For example, in her book *Reading the Romance: Women, Patriarchy, and Popular Literature*, Janice Radway studied a group of midwestern women who enjoyed romance novels. Using her training in literary criticism and employing interviews and questionnaires, Radway investigated the meaning of romance novels to these women. She argued that reading romance novels functions as personal time for some women. The study also suggested that these particular romance-novel fans identified with the active, independent qualities of the romantic heroines they most admired.

As a cultural study, Radway's work did not claim to be scientific, and her findings cannot be generalized to all women. Rather, Radway investigated and interpreted the relationship between reading popular fiction and ordinary life for a specific group of women.[15] Such studies help define culture as comprising both the *products* a society fashions (such as romance novels) and the *processes* that forge those products.

Converging Methods for Studying Mass Media: Qualitative, Quantitative, and Mixed Methods

When making our most important decisions—where to go to school, what classes to take, where to live, who to vote for, what kind of car to buy—most of us would like to make the best choices possible. For each of these decisions there is a wealth of information available—either right in front of us or through a quick search online. But how do we know what information to believe? What methods can we use to test various claims of truth, and how can we separate justifiable conclusions from mere opinion? These are *epistemological* questions, questions about *how* we know what we think we know—questions that are of the utmost importance to anyone doing scholarly research.

A full discussion of the philosophy of how we know what we know could take up volumes; for our purposes in discussing mass communication research, it's helpful to keep two things in mind. The first is that some kind of rigorous method is necessary for research to be taken seriously by other experts. The second is that these research methods typically fall into one of two categories: quantitative and qualitative.

Quantitative methods, as one might guess, tend to make use of tools like statistical analysis and sampling techniques or controlled experiments to understand the place of mass media in the world. Quantitative methods, such as surveys, tend to be used most often in social scientific types of media research. Supporters say this method helps remove researcher bias from the data-collection process, making the results more "objective." **Qualitative** methods tend to align with a critical cultural approach to media research and employ methods like *ethnography* (interviews, observing people in their daily lives) and textual analysis (see also pages 516–517). Supporters say this allows researchers to consider things like history, economics, and culture in ways that are not quantifiable but are still observable parts of the human condition.

Historically, scholars tended to gravitate toward one of these two approaches of understanding mass media. Questions over which approach is epistemologically superior are still the subject of lively debate, as are claims of objectivity and cultural relevance, as well as discussions of the pros and cons of social scientific and critical cultural approaches to research, discussed earlier in this chapter. Researchers are, after all, human, and these debates can get very heated. At the same time, many scholars welcome the intellectual challenge of weighing the advantages and drawbacks of different approaches and grappling with profound questions about objectivity, validity, reliability, and even truth.

LaunchPad
macmillanhighered.com/mediaessentials3e

Jeff Goodby
Co-Chairman, Goodby, Silverstein & Partners

⊚ **Visit LaunchPad** to watch a video of experts discussing how media effects research informs media development. Why do you think this question has become such a constant concern?

One solution to this intellectual challenge is another kind of convergence: the convergence of methods of media study. A third trend among those studying journalism and mass communication is sometimes called **mixed methods**, which combines quantitative and qualitative methods in the same research project. The idea is that looking at mass media from different viewpoints allows for a kind of "triangulation," a concept borrowed from surveying that uses two or more points to observe a distant object in order to get a better fix on its exact position. For example, researchers might combine surveys (with their ability to collect and compare data from a much larger number of people) and interviews (with their ability to evoke greater depth and understanding from a smaller number of people).

This entire book is another example of how research from both traditions might converge to (hopefully) paint a richer picture of the mass media landscape. Key facts—such as how people (and how many people) use various mass media—are often based on survey research. Placing those facts within a historical, economic, cultural, or political context represents an approach at home within the qualitative tradition.

Part of living in modern society involves receiving a ton of information not only *from* mass media but also *about* mass media. From textbooks to political pundits, we are flooded with claims about who and what is to be believed, and these claims don't always agree. How might a discussion of epistemology and research methods help weigh and evaluate these various claims? How might it boost our ability to think critically about competing messages about media? In short, how can understanding these things help us make the best possible choice of what to believe?

Political Economy Studies

A focus on the production of popular culture and the forces behind it is the topic of **political economy studies**, which examine interconnections among economic interests, political power, and ways in which that power is used. Major concerns of such studies include the increasing consolidation of media ownership. With this consolidation, the production of media content is being controlled by fewer and fewer organizations, investing those for-profit companies with more and more power to dominate public discourse. The theory is that money—not democratic expression—is now the driving force behind public communication and popular culture.

Political economy studies work best when combined with textual analysis and audience studies to provide fuller context for understanding a media product: the cultural content of the media product, the economics and politics of its production, and audiences' responses to it.

Evaluating Cultural Studies Research

A major strength of cultural studies research is that researchers can more easily examine the ties between media messages and the broader social, economic, and political world, since such research is not bound by precise control variables. For instance, social scientific research on politics has generally concentrated on election polls and voting patterns. But cultural research has broadened the discussion to examine class, gender, and cultural differences among voters and the various uses of power by individuals and institutions in positions of authority.

Yet just as social scientific media research has its limits, so does cultural studies media research. Sometimes cultural studies have focused exclusively on the meanings of media programs or "texts," ignoring their effect on audiences. Some cultural studies have tried to address this deficiency by incorporating audience studies. Both social scientists and cultural studies researchers have begun to look more closely at the limitations of their work and to borrow ideas from each other to better assess media's meaning and impact.

Media Research in a Democratic Society

One charge frequently leveled at academic studies is that they don't address the everyday problems of life and thus have little practical application. To be sure, media research has built a growing knowledge base and dramatically advanced what we know about mass media's effect on individuals and societies. But the larger public has had little access to the research process, even though cultural studies research tends to identify with marginalized groups. Any scholarship is self-defeating if its complexity removes it from the daily experience of the groups it examines. Researchers themselves have even found it difficult to speak to one another because of differences in the discipline-specific language they use to analyze and report their findings.

In addition, increasing specialization in the 1970s began isolating many researchers from life outside the university. Academics were criticized as being locked away in their ivory towers, concerned with seemingly obscure matters to which the general public could not relate. However, academics across many fields moved to mitigate this isolation, becoming increasingly active in political and cultural life in the 1980s and 1990s. For example, essayist and cultural critic Barbara Ehrenreich has written frequently about labor and economic issues for such magazines as *Time* and the *Nation* and has written several books on such issues.

In recent years, public intellectuals have also encouraged discussion of the new challenges posed by media production in a digital world. Stanford University law professor Lawrence Lessig has been a leading advocate of efforts to rewrite the nation's copyright laws to enable noncommercial "amateur culture" to flourish on the Internet. He publishes his work in print and online. American University's Pat Aufderheide, longtime media critic for the alternative magazine *In These Times*, worked with independent filmmakers to develop the *Documentary Filmmakers' Statement of Best Practices in Fair Use.* The statement calls for documentary filmmakers to have reasonable access to copyrighted material for their work.

Like journalists, public intellectuals based on campuses help advance the conversations taking place in larger society. They actively circulate the most important new ideas of the day—including those related to mass media—and serve as models for how to participate in public life.

CHAPTER ESSENTIALS

Now that you have finished reading this chapter, you can use the following tools:

LaunchPad for *Media Essentials*

Go to **macmillanhighered.com/mediaessentials3e** for videos, review quizzes, and more.

LaunchPad for *Media Essentials* includes:

- **REVIEW WITH LEARNINGCURVE**
  LearningCurve uses gamelike quizzing to help you master the concepts you need to learn from this chapter.

REVIEW

Explain Early Media Research Methods

- Scientific approaches to mass media research did not emerge until the late 1920s and 1930s (p. 501).

- Four trends that contributed to the rise of modern media research include **propaganda analysis** (the study of propaganda's effectiveness in influencing and mobilizing public opinion), public opinion research (which uses social scientific methods to conduct surveys and polls to examine how the mass media filter and shape public attitudes), social psychology studies (which measure the behavior and thinking processes of individuals), and marketing research (which conducts surveys on consumer buying habits and other behaviors) (pp. 502–503).

- Professional public opinion researchers object to the use of **pseudo-polls**—typically call-in, online, or person-in-the-street polls—which do not represent the population as a whole (p. 502).

Evaluate Social Scientific Research

- Between the 1930s and the 1970s, media researchers developed several models about how media affect individuals' behavior. These models include the **hypodermic needle** or **magic bullet** (whose model suggests that powerful media adversely affect weak audiences), **minimal effects** or **limited effects** (whose model attempts to understand, explain, and predict the impact—or effects—of the mass media on individuals in society and argues that people generally engage in **selective exposure** and **selective retention**, exposing themselves to media messages most familiar to them), and **uses and gratifications** (which holds that people actively engage in using media to satisfy various emotional or intellectual needs) (pp. 507–508).

- At the same time, researchers developed different approaches to conducting their research. Most media research today focuses on media's impact and employs the **scientific method**, whose key step includes posing one or more **hypotheses** (general statements that predict the influence of an independent variable on a dependent variable). Researchers using the scientific method may conduct **experiments** (which isolate some aspect of content by using a control group picked through **random assignment**) or **survey research** (which is a method of collecting and measuring data taken from a group of respondents) (pp. 508–511).

- Researchers can use extensive government and academic survey databases now widely available to conduct **longitudinal studies**, in which they compare new studies with those conducted years earlier. Surveys can show only **correlations**—or associations—between two variables, not demonstrable causes and effects. Another method researchers can use is **content analysis** (which describes media content and its elements by systematically categorizing and coding it) (pp. 510–512).

- By the 1960s, researchers began developing new theories about how media affect people, such as **social learning theory** (which suggests a link between mass media and subjects who learn and then model media behavior), **agenda-setting theory** (which states that when the mass media pay attention to particular events or issues, they determine the major topics of interest for individuals and society), the **cultivation effect theory** (which suggests that heavy television viewing leads individuals to perceive reality in ways that are consistent with the portrayals they see on television), the **spiral of silence theory** (which links the mass media, social psychology, and the suppression of public opinion), and the **third-person effect theory** (which suggests that people believe others are more affected by media messages than they are themselves) (pp. 512–515).

Discuss Cultural Studies Approaches to Media Research

- In the 1960s, cultural studies approaches to media research emerged to challenge mainstream media effects theories. Early cultural studies research was built on the writings of political philosophers such as Karl Marx and Antonio Gramsci and the criticisms of media effects research from the Frankfurt School (pp. 515–516).

- Contemporary cultural studies approaches focus on **textual analysis** (a close reading and interpretation of cultural messages), **audience studies** (which differ from textual analysis in that the subject being researched is the audience for the text, not the text itself), and **political economy studies** (which examine interconnections among economic interests, political power, and ways in which that power is used) (pp. 516–517, 520).

Assess the Role of Media Research in Our Democratic Society

- Although media research has advanced what we know about mass media's effect on individuals and society, most people do not have access to the actual research process, which makes it hard to connect scholarship to the daily experience of the groups such research examines (pp. 520–521).

- We rely on public intellectuals to help advance the conversations taking place in larger society and culture. These individuals encourage discussion of the new challenges posed by media (p. 521).

STUDY QUESTIONS

1. What are ways in which the mass media might be implicated in social problems like bullying, gun violence, and vitriolic political speech, and how might the social scientific and cultural studies research traditions respond differently to them?
2. What are pseudo-polls, and what about them makes them less reliable than social scientific polls and surveys?
3. What are the main ideas behind social learning theory, agenda-setting theory, the cultivation effect theory, the spiral of silence theory, and the third-person effect theory?
4. Why did cultural studies develop in opposition to social scientific media research?
5. What role do media researchers play in public debates about the mass media?

MEDIA LITERACY PRACTICE

In the beginning of this chapter, three stories suggested relationships between the media and (a) antigay bullying, (b) gun violence, and (c) "self-harm" behaviors. Working in groups of three, investigate one of these topics through a content analysis.

DESCRIBE the nature of the problem, and define coding categories for identifying content (e.g., accounts of homophobic or other bullying, stories associated with gunplay, or images glorifying unhealthy bodies) in certain types of media (e.g., the teen blogosphere, social media sites, action movies, or fashion advertisements). Then, have the other two members of your group individually apply your coding scheme to the same media content. (If this is an effective coding scheme, their answers should agree at least 80 percent of the time. If not, rethink your definitions and coding scheme.)

ANALYZE the patterns in the data.

INTERPRET what these patterns mean. For example, do social media posts and blogs describing behaviors hurtful to oneself or others make those behaviors seem more acceptable? Do action movies suggest that surviving deadly gun battles makes one a hero? Do images of fashion models represent a limited range of body types?

EVALUATE the effectiveness of content analysis as a method. Do your original definitions affect the outcome of the analysis? How far does the content data go in proving any kind of media effects or impact?

ENGAGE with the community by presenting your conclusions to your class for feedback. If your research is strong enough, consult with your instructor and consider presenting your paper at an academic conference.

Notes

1 Mass Communication: A Critical Approach

1. National Cable and Telecommunications Association (NCTA), Industry Data, June 2014, www.ncta.com/industry-data.
2. Pricewaterhouse Coopers (PwC), Consumer Intelligence Series: Video content consumption, 2014, www.pwc.com /us/en/industry/entertainment-media/publications/consumer -intelligence-series/assets/pwc-consumer-intelligence-series -product-services-innovation.pdf.
3. For a historical discussion of culture, see Lawrence Levine, *Highbrow/Lowbrow: The Emergence of Cultural Hierarchy in America* (Cambridge, Mass.: Harvard University Press, 1988).
4. For overviews of this position, see Neil Postman, *Amusing Ourselves to Death: Public Discourse in the Age of Show Business* (New York: Penguin Books, 1985), 19; and Stuart Ewen, *Captains of Consciousness: Advertising and the Social Roots of the Consumer Culture* (New York: McGraw-Hill, 1976).
5. See James W. Carey, *Communication as Culture: Essays on Media and Society* (Boston: Unwin Hyman, 1989).
6. Tasha N. Dubriwny, "Constructing Breast Cancer in the News: Betty Ford and the Evolution of the Breast Cancer Patient," *Journal of Communication Inquiry* 33, no. 2 (2009): 104–125.
7. Charles K. Atkin, Sandi W. Smith, Courtnay McFeters, and Vanessa Ferguson, "A Comprehensive Analysis of Breast Cancer News Coverage in Leading Media Outlets Focusing on Environmental Risks and Prevention," *Health Communication* 13 (January/February 2008): 3–19.
8. Brooks Barnes, "Lab Watches Web Surfers to See Which Ads Work," *New York Times*, July 26, 2009, www .nytimes.com/2009/07/27/technology/27disney.html.
9. See Jon Katz, "Rock, Rap and Movies Bring You the News," *Rolling Stone*, March 5, 1992, 33.

CONVERGING MEDIA CASE STUDY: Comcast Extends Its Reach, p. 12

1. Comcast, "Time Warner Cable to Merge with Comcast Corporation to Create World-Class Technology and Media Company," February 13, 2014, http://corporate.comcast .com/news-information/news-feed/time-warner-cable -to-merge-with-comcast-corporation.
2. American Customer Satisfaction Index (ACSI), Benchmarks by Industry: Internet Service Providers, 2014, www.theacsi.org/index.php?option=com_content&view =article&id=147&catid=&Itemid=212&i=Internet Service Providers.

3. OpenSecrets.org, Center for Responsive Politics, "Comcast Corp.," 2014, www.opensecrets.org/orgs /summary.php?id=D000000461.

MEDIA LITERACY CASE STUDY: Football, *Fútbol*, and Soccer, p. 26

1. John Haydon, "America's Love-Hate Relationship with Soccer," *Newsweek*, July 9, 2014, www.newsweek.com /americas-love-hate-relationship-soccer-258089.

2 Books and the Power of Print

1. Amazon.com, Inc., 2013 Annual Report, Form 10-K, http://phx.corporate-ir.net/phoenix.zhtml?c=97664&p =irol-reportsannual.
2. Jeremy Greenfield, "How the Amazon-Hachette Fight Could Shape the Future of Ideas," *Atlantic*, May 28, 2014, www.theatlantic.com/business/archive/2014/05/how-the -amazon-hachette-fight-could-shape-the-future-of-ideas /371756/.
3. Leslie Kaufman and Elizabeth A. Harris, "J. K. Rowling's 'The Silkworm' a Boon for Other Booksellers as Hachette and Amazon Brawl," *New York Times*, June 18, 2014, www.nytimes.com/2014/06/19/business/media/jk-rowlings -the-silkworm-a-boon-for-other-booksellers-as-hachette -and-amazon-brawl.html.
4. "Authors United's Next Move: DOJ," *Publishers Weekly*, September 24, 2014, www.publishersweekly.com/pw/by -topic/industry-news/bookselling/article/64129-authors -united-s-next-move-doj.html.
5. Ryan Mac, "With New E-Book Service Amazon Plays Waiting Game with Publishers, Competition," *Forbes*, July 22, 2014, www.forbes.com/sites/ryanmac/2014/07/22 /with-new-e-book-service-amazon-plays-waiting-game -with-publishers-competition/.
6. See Elizabeth Eisenstein, *The Printing Press as an Agent of Change* (Cambridge: Cambridge University Press, 1980).
7. For a comprehensive historical overview of the publish-ing industry and the rise of publishing houses, see John A. Tebbel, *A History of Book Publishing in the United States*, 4 vols. (New York: R. R. Bowker, 1972–81).
8. National Association of College Stores, "FAQ on College Textbooks," May 2008, http://nacs.org/common/research /faq_textbooks.pdf.
9. Jim Milliot, "Book Sales Dipped in 2013," *Publishers Weekly*, June 27, 2014, www.publishersweekly.com/pw /by-topic/industry-news/publisher-news/article/63131 -book-sales-dipped-in-2013.html; see also Laura Hazard

Owen, "PwC: The U.S. Consumer Ebook Market Will Be Bigger Than the Print Book Market by 2017," PaidContent, June 4, 2013, http://paidcontent.org/2013/06/04/pwc-the-u-s-consumer-ebook-market-will-be-bigger-than-the-print-book-market-by-2017/.

10. Jim Milliot, "BEA 2014: Can Anyone Compete with Amazon?" *Publishers Weekly*, May 28, 2014, www.publishersweekly.com/pw/by-topic/industry-news/bea/article/62520-bea-2014-can-anyone-compete-with-amazon.html.

CONVERGING MEDIA CASE STUDY: Self-Publishing Redefined, p. 54

1. David Streitfeld, "Amazon Signs Up Authors, Writing Publishers out of Deal," *New York Times*, October 16, 2011, www.nytimes.com/2011/10/17/technology/amazon-rewrites-the-rules-of-book-publishing.html.

2. David Streitfield, "After Dispute, Novelist Gets Amazon Deal," *New York Times*, March 8, 2012, http://bits.blogs.nytimes.com/2012/03/08/after-dispute-novelist-gets-amazon-deal/?_php=true&_type=blogs&_r=0.

3. Betty Kelly Sargent, "Surprising Self-Publishing Statistics," *Publishers Weekly*, July 28, 2014, www.publishersweekly.com/pw/by-topic/authors/pw-select/article/63455-surprising-self-publishing-statistics.html

4. Kevin Bloom, "Analysis: If Amazon Ruled Book Publishing, Too . . ."*Daily Maverick*, October 19, 2011, http://dailymaverick.co.za/article/2011-10-19-analysis-if-amazon-ruled-book-publishing-too.

5. Sargent, "Surprising Self-Publishing Statistics."

3 Newspapers to Digital Frontiers: Journalism's Journey

1. See Brooke Kroeger, *Nellie Bly: Daredevil, Reporter, Feminist* (New York: Times Books/Random House, 1994).

2. See David T. Z. Mindich, "Edwin M. Stanton, the Inverted Pyramid, and Information Control," *Journalism Monographs* 140 (August 1993).

3. Michael Schudson, *Discovering the News: A Social History of American Newspapers* (New York: Basic Books, 1978), 23.

4. Enn Raudsepp, "Reinventing Journalism Education," *Canadian Journal of Communication* 14, no. 2 (1989): 1–14.

5. Curtis D. MacDougall, *The Press and Its Problems* (Dubuque, Iowa: William C. Brown, 1964), 143, 189.

6. Walter Lippmann, *Liberty and the News* (New York: Harcourt, Brace and Howe, 1920), 92.

7. For another list and an alternative analysis of news criteria, see the Missouri Group, *News Reporting and Writing,* 10th ed. (New York: Bedford/St. Martin's, 2011), 5–6.

8. For a full discussion of the *New York Times* and mainstream journalism's treatment of the LGBTQ community and the early days of the AIDS epidemic, see Edward Alwood, *Straight News: Gays, Lesbians and the News Media* (New York: Columbia University Press, 1996); and Larry Gross, *Up from Invisibility: Lesbians, Gay Men, and the Media in America* (New York: Columbia University Press, 2001).

9. See Pew Research Center, "5 Facts about Ethnic and Gender Diversity in U.S. Newsrooms," www.pewresearch.org/fact-tank/2013/07/18/5-facts-about-ethnic-and-gender-diversity-in-u-s-newsrooms/.

10. Don Hewitt, interview conducted by Richard Campbell on *60 Minutes*, CBS News, New York, February 21, 1989.

11. Alex T. Williams, "The Growing Pay Gap between Journalism and Public Relations," www.pewresearch.org/fact-tank/2014/08/11/the-growing-pay-gap-between-journalism-and-public-relations/.

12. Herbert Gans, *Deciding What's News* (New York: Pantheon, 1979), 42–48.

13. Ibid.

14. Ibid.

15. For reference and guidance on media ethics, see Clifford Christians, Mark Fackler, and Kim Rotzoll, *Media Ethics: Cases and Moral Reasoning*, 4th ed. (White Plains, N.Y.: Longman, 1995); and Thomas H. Bivins, "A Worksheet for Ethics Instruction and Exercises in Reason," *Journalism Educator* (Summer 1993): 4–16.

16. *SPJ Code of Ethics*, Society of Professional Journalists, 1996, www.spj.org/ethicscode.asp.

17. ASNE 2014 Census, Table A, http://asne.org/content.asp?pl=140&sl=129&contentid=129&utm_source=This+Week+%40+ASNE+7.31.2014&utm_campaign=This+Week+%40+ASNE&utm_medium=email.

18. For a summary and links to the 2012 study, go to www.poynter.org/mediawire/top-stories/174826/survey-nprs-listeners-best-informed-fox-news-viewers-worst-informed/.

19. For an overview of the PolitiFact network scorecard project and links to individual network scores, go to www.politifact.com/punditfact/article/2014/jul/01/introducing-scorecards-tv-networks/.

20. Michael O'Connell, "Fox News Nabs Historic Cable Ratings Victory," September 30, 2014, www.hollywoodreporter.com/live-feed/fox-news-nabs-historic-cable-736624.

21. David Broder, quoted in "Squaring with the Reader: A Seminar on Journalism," *Kettering Review* (Winter 1992): 48.

22. John Carroll, "News War, Part 3," *Frontline*, PBS, February 27, 2007, www.pbs.org/wgbh/pages/frontline /newswar/etc/script3.html.

MEDIA LITERACY CASE STUDY: From Uncovering Scandals to Being the Scandal, p. 82
1. Alan Rusbridger, "How We Broke the Murdoch Scandal," *Newsweek*, July 17, 2011, www.thedailybeast.com /newsweek/2011/07/17/how-the-guardian-broke-the-news -of-the-world-hacking-scandal.html.

CONVERGING MEDIA CASE STUDY: News Aggregation, p. 100
1. "What Is Newser?" *Newser*, accessed December 2011, www.newser.com/what-is-newser.aspx.
2. Ibid.
3. Mark Cuban, "My Advice to Fox & MySpace on Selling Content—Yes You Can," *Blog Maverick*, August 8, 2009, http://blogmaverick.com/2009/08/08/my-advice-to-fox -myspace-on-selling-content-yes-you-can/.
4. Michael Wolff, "Mark Cuban Is a Big Fat Idiot—News Will Stay Free," *Huffington Post*, August 12, 2009, www .huffingtonpost.com/michael-wolff/mark-cuban-is-a-big-fat -i_b_257483.html.
5. See "The New News," James Cameron Memorial Lecture, September 22, 2010, http://image.guardian.co.uk /sysfiles/Media/documents/2010/09/23/DownieCameron .pdf; and Jack Shaffer, "Len Downie Calls Arianna Huffington a Parasite," *Slate*, September 23, 2010, www .slate.com/articles/news_and_politics/press_box/2010/09 /len_downie_calls_arianna_huffington_a_parasite.html.
6. Arianna Huffington, "Leonard Downie's Downer," *Guardian*, September 23, 2009, www.guardian.co.uk/commentisfree /cifamerica/2010/sep/23/huffington-post-washington-post.

4 Magazines in the Age of Specialization

1. Sammye Johnson, "Promoting Easy Sex without the Intimacy: *Maxim* and *Cosmopolitan* Cover Lines and Cover Images," in Mary-Lou Galician and Debra L. Merskin, eds., *Critical Thinking about Sex, Love, and Romance in the Mass Media* (Mahwah, N.J.: Erlbaum, 2007), 55–74.
2. Jennifer Benjamin, "How *Cosmo* Changed the World," May 3, 2007, www.cosmopolitan.com/lifestyle/a1746 /about-us-how-cosmo-changed-the-world. See also Theodore Peterson, *Magazines in the Twentieth Century* (Urbana: University of Illinois Press, 1964), 5.
3. Pew Research Center's Project for Excellence in Journalism, "Magazines: By the Numbers," *State of the News Media 2011*, http://stateofthemedia.org/2011 /magazines-essay/data-page-4/.

4. See "Readex Research Survey Finds Professionals Not Replacing Print with Digital," October 2011, www.marketwired .com/press-release/readex-research-survey-finds -professionals-not-replacing-print-with-digital-1575198.htm.
5. Magazine Publishers of America, *Magazine Media Factbook 2012–13*, www.magazine.org/insights-resources /research-publications/magazine-factbook/2012-2013 -magazine-media-factbook, and Magazine Publishers of America, *2013/2014 Magazine Media Factbook*, www .magazine.org/node/26924.
6. See Gloria Steinem, "Sex, Lies and Advertising," *Ms.*, July–August 1990, 18–28.

MEDIA LITERACY CASE STUDY: The Evolution of Photojournalism, p. 124
1. Andrew Adam Newman, "3 Magazines Are Accused of Retouching Celebrity Photos to Excess," *New York Times*, May 28, 2007, http://www.nytimes.com/2007/05/28 /business/media/28fitness.html.

5 Sound Recording and Popular Music

1. Nolan Feeney, "Macklemore's 'Thrift Shop' Is First Indie Hit to Top Charts in Nearly Two Decades," *Time*, January 25,2013,http://newsfeed.time.com/2013/01/25/macklemores- thrift-shop-is-first-indie-hit-to-top-charts-in-nearly-two- decades; James C. McKinley Jr., "Stars Align for a Gay Marriage Anthem," *New York Times*, June 30, 2013, http:// www.nytimes.com/2013/07/01/arts/music/stars-align-for-a -gay-marriage-anthem.html.
2. Mark Coleman, *Playback: From the Victrola to MP3* (Cambridge, Mass.: Da Capo Press, 2003).
3. Mick Jagger, quoted in Jann S. Wenner, "Jagger Remembers," *Rolling Stone*, December 14, 1995, 66.
4. See Mac Rebennack (Dr. John) with Jack Rummel, *Under a Hoodoo Moon* (New York: St. Martin's Press, 1994), 58.
5. Ken Tucker, quoted in Ed Ward, Geoffrey Stokes, and Ken Tucker, *Rock of Ages: The Rolling Stone History of Rock & Roll* (New York: Rolling Stone Press, 1986), 521.
6. See "The 'Nashville Sound' Begins," *Living in Stereo*, September 19, 2006, http://livinginstereo.com/?p=252.
7. See Michael D'Arcy and Sherry Anderson, "What Is Countrypolitan Music?" January 2001, www.michaelfitz .net/blog/countrypolitan_101/.
8. RIAA, "2008 Year-End Shipment Statistics," http://riaa.com /media/D5664E44-B9F7-69E0-5ABD-B605F2EB6EF2.pdf.
9. "It Isn't Pretty: RIAA 2010 Sales Music Data," April 29, 2011, www.hypebot.com/hypebot/2011/04/it-isnt-pretty -riaa-2010-music-sales-data-chart.html.

10. Joshua P. Friedlander, "News and Notes on 2013 RIAA Music Industry Shipment and Revenue Statistics," http://riaa.com/media/2463566A-FF96-E0CA-2766-72779A364D01.pdf; and IFPI, "Digital Music Report 2014," www.ifpi.org/downloads/Digital-Music-Report-2014.pdf.

11. IFPI, "Digital Music Report 2014," www.ifpi.org/downloads/Digital-Music-Report-2014.pdf.

12. Spotify, "Some Fast Figures," accessed June 7, 2014, http://press.spotify.com/us/information.

13. Spotify, "Spotify Explained," accessed June 7, 2014, www.spotifyartists.com/spotify-explained.

CONVERGING MEDIA CASE STUDY: **360 Degrees of Music, p. 172**

1. See Sara Karubian, "360-Degree Deals: An Industry Reaction to the Devaluation of Recorded Music," *Southern California Interdisciplinary Law Journal* 18, no. 395 (2009): 395–462, www-bcf.usc.edu/~idjlaw/PDF/18-2/18-2%20Karubian.pdf.

6 Popular Radio and the Origins of Broadcasting

1. iHeartMedia, Inc., *Clear Channel Becomes iHeartMedia*, September 16, 2014, http://www.iheartmedia.com/Pages/Press.aspx.

2. Tom Lewis, *Empire of the Air: The Men Who Made Radio* (New York: HarperCollins, 1991), 181.

3. Michael Pupin, "Objections Entered to Court's Decision," *New York Times*, June 10, 1934, p. E5.

4. For a full discussion of early broadcast history and the formation of RCA, see Eric Barnouw, *Tube of Plenty* (New York: Oxford University Press, 1982); Susan Douglas, *Inventing American Broadcasting, 1899–1922* (Baltimore: Johns Hopkins University Press, 1987); and Christopher Sterling and John Kitross, *Stay Tuned: A Concise History of American Broadcasting* (Belmont, Calif.: Wadsworth, 1990).

5. Michele Hilmes, *Radio Voices: American Broadcasting, 1922–1952* (Minneapolis: University of Minnesota Press, 1997).

6. "Amos 'n' Andy Show," Museum of Broadcast Communications, www.museum.tv/archives/etv/A/htmlA/amosnandy/amosnandy.htm.

7. StreamingRadioGuide, "Radio Stations Streaming on the Internet," accessed April 14, 2015, http://streamingradioguide.com/internet-radio.php.

8. Arbitron, "The Infinite Dial 2013: Navigating Digital Platforms," www.edisonresearch.com/wp-content/uploads/2013/04/Edison_Research_Arbitron_Infinite_Dial_2013.pdf.

9. National Association of Broadcasters, "Equipping Mobile Phones with Broadcast Radio Capability for Emergency Preparedness: Additional Resources," accessed June 13, 2014, www.nab.org/advocacy/issueResources.asp?id=2354&issueID=1082.

10. Nielsen, "State of the Media: Audio Today 2014," February 6, 2014, www.nielsen.com/us/en/reports/2014/state-of-the-media-audio-today-2014.html.

11. Radio Advertising Bureau, "Network, Digital, Off-Air Shine as Radio Ends 2013 in the Black," March 14, 2014, www.rab.com/public/pr/revenue_detail.cfm?id=132.

12. Federal Communications Commission, "Broadcast Station Totals as of March 31, 2014," April 9, 2014, http://www.fcc.gov/document/broadcast-station-totals-march-31-2014.

13. Peter DiCola, "False Premises, False Promises: A Quantitative History of Ownership Consolidation in the Radio Industry," Future of Music Coalition, December 2006, www.futureofmusic.org/research/radiostudy06.cfm.

14. "Statement of FCC Chairman William E. Kennard on Low Power FM Radio Initiative," March 27, 2000, www.fcc.gov/Speeches/Kennard/Statements/2000/stwek024.html.

CONVERGING MEDIA CASE STUDY: **Streaming Music, p. 208**

1. Nielsen, "U.S. Music Year-End Review: 2013," January 17, 2014, http://www.nielsen.com/us/en/insights./reports/2014/u-s-music-industry-year-end-review-2013.html.

2. Nielsen, "Nielsen Entertainment and Billboards 2014 Mid-Year Music Industry Report," accessed May 8, 2015, http://www.nielsen.com/content/dam/corporate/us/en/public%20factsheets/Soundscan/nielsen-music-2014-mid-year-us-release.pdf?_ga=1.260224909.1211409962.1405087511.

3. Pandora, "Pandora Reports Q3 2014 Financial Results," accessed May 8, 2015, http://press.pandora.com/phoenix.zhtml?c=251764&p=irol-newsArticle&ID=1980997.

7 Movies and the Impact of Images

1. Box Office Mojo, *Gravity* box office totals, accessed September 15, 2014, http://boxofficemojo.com/movies/?page=intl&id=gravity.htm.

2. Douglas Gomery, *Shared Pleasures: A History of Movie Presentation in the United States* (Madison: University of Wisconsin Press, 1992), 18.

3. Douglas Gomery, *Movie History: A Survey* (Belmont, Calif.: Wadsworth, 1991), 167.

4. Based on MPAA reports over the past ten years.

5. Julianne Pepitone, "Americans Now Watch More Online Movies Than DVDs," CNN/Money, March 22, 2012, http://

money.cnn.com/2012/03/22/technology/streaming-movie
-sales/index.htm.

MEDIA LITERACY CASE STUDY: Breaking through
Hollywood's Race Barrier, p. 234

1. Douglas Gomery, *Shared Pleasures: A History of Movie
Presentation in the United States* (Madison: University of
Wisconsin Press, 1992), 155–170.
2. Scott Foundas, "Film Review: *Da Sweet Blood of
Jesus*," *Variety*, June 23, 2014. http://variety.com/2014
/film/reviews/film-review-spike-lees-da-sweet-blood
-of-jesus-1201242049/.

CONVERGING MEDIA CASE STUDY: Movie Theaters
and Live Exhibition, p. 244

1. "Comedy: Amos 'n' Andy," Radio Hall of Fame,
accessed February 10, 2012, www.radiohof.org/amos
_andy.htm.
2. "NCM Fathom Entertainment Events," National
CineMedia, updated March 30, 2011, www.ncm.com
/content/pdf/NCM_Fathom_Events_Chronology.pdf.
3. "Cinedigm's Live 3-D Broadcast of BCS Championship
Game Sees Huge Turnout," Cinedigm Digital Cinema
Corp., January 12, 2009, http://investor.cinedigm.com
/releasedetail.cfm?releaseid=358745.
4. Richard Verrier, "Movie Theaters Turn to Live Event
Screenings to Fill Seats," *Los Angeles Times*, April 20,
2010, http://articles.latimes.com/2010/apr/20/news
/la-ct-theater20-20100420.
5. Motion Picture Association of America, "Theatrical
Market Statistics 2012," accessed May 8, 2015, http://
www.mpaa.org/wp-content/uploads/2014/03/2012
-Theatrical-Market-Statistics-Report.pdf.

**8 Television, Cable, and Specialization in
Visual Culture**

1. Amanda Kondoloy, "'ABC World News with Diane
Sawyer' Closes Total Viewing Gap with 'NBC Nightly
News' by 3%," TV by the Numbers, June 5, 2012, http://
tvbythenumbers.zap2it.com/2012/06/05/abc-world-news
-with-diane-sawyer-closes-total-viewing-gap-with-nbc
-nightly-news-by-3/136864.
2. See Horace Newcomb, *TV: The Most Popular Art*
(Garden City, N.Y.: Anchor Books, 1974), 31, 39.
3. Michael Schneider, "America's Most Watched: The Top
50 Shows of the 2013–2014 TV Season," *TV Guide*, June
6, 2014, www.tvguide.com/news/most-watched-shows
-2013-2014-1082628.aspx.
4. "Just the Facts: Consumer Choice Explodes, 1992–2012,"
National Cable & Telecommunications Association, www
.ncta.com/statistic/statistic/Consumer-Choice-Explodes.aspx.
5. Schneider, "America's Most Watched."
6. *United States v. Midwest Video Corp.*, 440 U.S. 689 (1979).

MEDIA LITERACY CASE STUDY: The United Segments
of America, p. 270

1. Schneider, "America's Most Watched."

CONVERGING MEDIA: Shifting, Bingeing, and Saturday
Mornings, p. 278

1. Gail Sullivan, "Saturday Morning Cartoons Are No
More," *Washington Post*, September 30, 2014, www
.washingtonpost.com/news/morning-mix/wp/2014/09
/30/saturday-morning-cartoons-are-no-more.
2. PricewaterhouseCoopers, "Feeling the Effects of the
Videoquake: Changes in How We Consume Video Content,"
2014, https://consumermediallc.files.wordpress.com/2014/
12/pwc-videoquake-video-content-consumption-report.pdf.
3. "Netflix Declares Binge Watching Is the New Normal,"
PR Newswire, December 13, 2013, www.prnewswire
.com/news-releases/netflix-declares-binge-watching-is-the
-new-normal-235713431.html.

**9 The Internet and New Technologies:
The Media Converge**

1. Lori Grisham, "Timeline: North Korea and the Sony
Pictures Hack," *USA Today*, January 5, 2015, www.usatoday
.com/story/news/nation-now/2014/12/18/sony-hack
-timeline-interview-north-korea/20601645.
2. Dave McNary and Brent Lang, "'The Interview' Online,
VOD Sales Reach $31 Million," *Variety*, January 6, 2015,
http://variety.com/2015/film/news/the-interview-online
-sales-reach-31-million-1201394022.
3. NBC News, "Sony Hack Most Serious Cyberattack Yet
on U.S. Interests: Clapper," www.nbcnews.com/storyline
/sony-hack/sony-hack-most-serious-cyberattack-yet-u-s-interests
-clapper-n281456.
4. Andreas Kaplan and Michael Haenlein, "Users of the
World, Unite! The Challenges and Opportunities of Social
Media," *Business Horizons* 53, no. 1 (2010): 59–68.
5. Chris Anderson and Michael Wolff, "The Web Is Dead.
Long Live the Internet," *Wired*, August 17, 2010, www
.wired.com/magazine/2010/08/ff_webrip. See also
Charles Arthur, "Walled gardens look rosy for Facebook,
Apple—and Would-Be censors," *Guardian*, April 17, 2012,
www.guardian.co.uk/technology/2012/apr/17/walled
-gardens-facebook-apple-censors.

6. United States Securities and Exchange Commission, Form S-1 Registration Statement, Twitter, Inc., October 3, 2013, www.sec.gov/Archives/edgar/data/1418091 /000119312513390321/d564001ds1.htm; Twitter, "Twitter Reports Fourth Quarter and Fiscal Year 2013 Results," February 5, 2014, https://investor.twitterinc .com/releasedetail.cfm?ReleaseID=823321.

7. *Wikipedia*, s.v. "*Wikipedia* Seigenthaler Biography Incident," last modified March 24, 2015, http://en .wikipedia.org/wiki/Wikipedia_Seigenthaler_biography _incident.

8. Lucien Tessier, "Boy Scouts: Vote to End Your Anti-gay Policy So My Brother Can Earn His Eagle Award," Change .org, May 2013, www.change.org/petitions/boy-scouts -vote-to-end-your-anti-gay-policy-so-my-brother-can-earn -his-eagle-award.

9. Tim Berners-Lee, James Hendler, and Ora Lassila, "The Semantic Web," *Scientific American*, May 17, 2001, www .cs.umd.edu/~golbeck/LBSC690/SemanticWeb.html.

10. Liam F. McCabe, "Europe's Appliances Are Cooler, Prettier, and More Popular," September 5, 2013, Reviewed .com, http://refrigerators.reviewed.com/features/ifa-2013 -highlights-culture-gap-between-american-and-european -appliances.

11. Steven Musil, "Week in Review: Windows Woes," CNET, February 29, 2008, http://news.cnet.com/Week-in -review-Windows-woes/2100-1083_3-6232545.html.

12. Drew Fitzgerald, "Netflix's Share of Internet Traffic Grows," *Wall Street Journal*, May 14, 2014, http://www .wsj.com/articles/SB100014240527023049083045 79561802483718502.

13. Sucharita Mulpuru, "US eCommerce Grows, Reaching $414B by 2018, but Physical Stores Will Live On," *Forbes*, May 12, 2014, www.forbes.com/sites/forrester/2014/05/12 /us-ecommerce-grows-reaching-414b-by-2018-but-physical -stores-will-live-on.

14. Federal Trade Commission, *Privacy Online: Fair Information Practices in the Electronic Marketplace: A Report to Congress*, May 2000, www.ftc.gov/sites/default /files/documents/reports/privacy-online-fair-information -practices-electronic-marketplace-federal-trade-commission -report/privacy2000text.pdf.

15. Mark Zuckerberg, "Our Commitment to the Facebook Community," *Facebook Blog*, November 29, 2011, http:// blog.facebook.com/blog.php?post=10150378701937131.

16. "2013 Internet Ad Revenues Soar to $42.8 Billion," April 10, 2014, www.iab.net/about_the_iab/recent _press_releases/press_release_archive/press_release /pr-041014.

17. Federal Trade Commission, *Privacy Online*.

18. "Internet User Demographics," Pew Research Center, January 2014, www.pewinternet.org/data-trend/internet -use/latest-stats.

19. Kathryn Zickuhr and Aaron Smith, "Home Broadband 2013," Pew Research Center, August 26, 2013, www .pewinternet.org/2013/08/26/home-broadband-2013.

20. Pew Research Center, "Internet User Demographics," PewResearch Internet Project, accessed January 29, 2014, http://www.pewinternet.org/data-trend/internet-use/latest-stats. Also see Kathryn Zickuhr and Aaron Smith, "Home Broadband 2013," PewResearch Internet Project, August 26, 2013, http:/www.pewinternet.org/2013/08/26 /home-broadband-2013/.

MEDIA LITERACY CASE STUDY: Net Neutrality, p. 306

1. Federal Communications Commission, "In the Matter of Preserving the Open Internet Broadband Industry Practices," December 23, 2010, https://apps.fcc.gov /edocs_public/attachmatch/FCC-10-201A1_Rcd.pdf.

2. Rebecca R. Ruiz and Steve Lohr, "F.C.C. Approves Net Neutrality Rules, Classifying Broadband Internet Service as a Utility," *New York Times*, February 26, 2015, http://www .nytimes.com/2015/02/27/technology/net-neutrality -fcc-vote-internet-utility.html?_r=0.

3. Federal Communications Commision, "Fact Sheet: Chairman Wheeler Proposes New Rules for Protecting the Open Internet," accessed May 9, 2015, https://apps.fcc .gov/edocs_public/attachmatch/DOC-331869A1.pdf.

4. Brian Fung, "Here Are the First Lawsuits to Challenge the FCC's Net Neutrality Rules," *Washington Post* online, March 23, 2015, http://www.washingtonpost.com /blogs/the-switch/wp/2015/03/23/the-first-of-the-net -neutrality-lawsuits-has-now-been-filed/.

5. Open Technology Institute, "The Cost of Connectivity 2014: Data and Analysis on Broadband Offerings in 24 Cities around the World," www.newamerica.org/oti /the-cost-of-connectivity-2014.

6. James O'Toole, "Chatanooga's Super-Fast Publicly Owned Internet," CNN Money, May 20, 2014, http:// money.cnn.com/2014/05/20/technology/innovation /chattanooga-internet; Cedar Falls Utilities, accessed January 10, 2015, www.cfu.net/cybernet/default.aspx.

CONVERGING MEDIA CASE STUDY: Activism, Hacktivism, and Anonymous, p. 318

1. Chris Landers, "Serious Business: Anonymous Takes On Scientology (and Doesn't Afraid of Anything)," *Baltimore City Paper*, April 2, 2008.

2. David Kushner, "Anonymous vs. Steubenville," November 27, 2013, *Rolling Stone*, www.rollingstone .com/culture/news/anonymous-vs-steubenville-20131127.

10 Digital Gaming and the Media Playground

1. Entertainment Software Association, "Essential Facts about the Computer and Video Game Industry," 2014, www.theesa.com/wp-content/uploads/2014/10/ESA_EF _2014.pdf.

2. Roger Kay, "Facebook's $2 Billion Purchase of Oculus Is Just Crazy," *Forbes*, March 26, 2014, www.forbes.com /sites/rogerkay/2014/03/26/facebooks-2-billion-purchase -of-oculus-is-just-crazy; Jeff Reeves, "Why Facebook Was Smart to Buy Oculus," MarketWatch, March 31, 2014, www.marketwatch.com/story/why-facebook-was-smart-to -buy-oculus-2014-03-31.

3. Erkki Huhtamo, "Slots of Fun, Slots of Trouble: An Archaeology of Arcade Gaming," in *Handbook of Computer Game Studies*, ed. Joost Raessens and Jeffrey Goldstein (Cambridge, Mass.: MIT Press, 2005), 6–7.

4. Ibid., 9–10.

5. Seth Porges, "11 Things You Didn't Know about Pinball History," *Popular Mechanics*, accessed April 5, 2015, www .popularmechanics.com/technology/g284/4328211-new.

6. "Magnavox Odyssey," PONG-Story, accessed April 6, 2015, www.pong-story.com/odyssey.htm.

7. Fantasy Sports Trade Association, "Industry Demographics," accessed April 28, 2015, www.fsta.org/?page =Demographics.

8. "Number of World of Warcraft Subscribers from 1st Quarter 2005 to 4th Quarter 2014 (in Millions)," Statista, accessed April 28, 2015, http://www.statista.com/statistics /276601/number-of-world-of-warcraft-subscribers-by-quarter.

9. See Mark Rogowsky, "Without Much Fanfare, Apple Has Sold Its 500 Millionth iPhone," *Forbes*, March 25, 2014, www.forbes.com/sites/markrogowsky/2014/03/25/without -much-fanfare-apple-has-sold-its-500-millionth-iphone; Shara Tibken, "Six Takeaways from Apple CEO Cook's Earnings Call," CNET, April 24, 2014, www.cnet.com/news /six-takeaways-from-apple-ceo-cooks-earnings-call.

10. Henry Jenkins, "Interactive Audiences? The 'Collective Intelligence' of Media Fans," in *The New Media Book*, ed. Dan Harries (London: British Film Institute, 2002).

11. Douglas A. Gentile et al., "Pathological Video Game Use among Youths: A Two-Year Longitudinal Study," *Pediatrics* 127, no. 2 (2011), doi:10.1542/peds.2010-1353.

12. Florian Rehbein and Dirk Baier, "Family-, Media-, and School-Related Risk Factors of Video Game Addiction: A 5-Year Longitudinal Study," *Journal of Media Psychology: Theories, Methods and Application* 25, no. 3 (2013): 118–128.

13. "South Korean Couple Starved Child While Raising 'Virtual Baby,'" *CNN World*, March 5, 2010, http://articles. cnn.com/2010-03-05/world/korea.baby.starved_1_online -addiction-virtual-world-online-game?_s=PM:WORLD.

14. GamePolitics.com, "Newzoo Predicts Global Revenue from Gaming Will Hit $91.5 Billion in 2015," April 22, 2015, http://www.gamepolitics.com/2015/04/22/newzoo -predicts-global-revenue-gaming-will-hit-915-billion-2015#. VT_F1o2UCpp.

15. Ian Hamilton, "Blizzard's World of Warcraft Revenue Down," *Orange County Register*, November 8, 2010, www .ocregister.com/articles/blizzard-543767-world-warcraft .html.

16. "IGA Worldwide," YouTube video, posted April 8, 2009, www.youtube.com/watch?v=dGKum-lo9V8.

17. "Top 10 Most Expensive Video Game Budgets Ever," DigitalBattle.com, February 20, 2010, http://digitalbattle .com/2010/02/20/top-10-most-expensive-video-game -budgets-ever.

18. "John Madden Net Worth," CelebrityNetworth.com, accessed April 5, 2012, www.celebritynetworth.com /richest-athletes/nfl/john-madden-net-worth.

19. "ESRB Ratings Guide," Entertainment Software Rating Board, accessed April 8, 2015, www.esrb.org/ratings /ratings_guide.jsp.

20. Evan Narcisse, "Supreme Court: 'Video Games Qualify for First Amendment Protection,'" *Time*, June 27, 2011, http://techland.time.com/2011/06/27/supreme-court -video-games-qualify-for-first-amendment-protection.

21. Ibid.

22. Todd VanDerWerff, "#Gamergate: Here's Why Everybody in the Video Game World Is Fighting," *Vox*, October 13, 2014, www.vox.com/2014/9/6/6111065 /gamergate-explained-everybody-fighting.

23. Angela McRobbie, *The Uses of Cultural Studies* (Thousand Oaks: Sage, 2005).

CONVERGING MEDIA CASE STUDY: Anita Sarkeesian, #GamerGate, and Convergence, p. 342

1. Anita Sarkeesian, "It's Game Over for 'Gamers': Anita Sarkeesian on Video Games' Great Future," *New York Times*, October 28, 2014, www.nytimes.com/2014/10/29 /opinion/anita-sarkeesian-on-video-games-great-future .html?_r=0.

2. Todd VanDerWerff, "#Gamergate: Here's Why Everybody in the Video Game World Is Fighting," *Vox*,

October 13, 2014, www.vox.com/2014/9/6/6111065
/gamergate-explained-everybody-fighting.

3. Casey Parks, "Prank Call Sends Close to 20 Police
Officers to Southwest Portland Home," *Oregonian*, January
3, 2015, www.oregonlive.com/portland/index.ssf/2015/01
/prank_call_sends_several_polic.html.

4. Feminist Frequency 2014 Annual Report, www.dropbox
.com/s/q4z6qa561roidh5/femfreq_annualreport2014.pdf?dl=0.

**MEDIA LITERACY CASE STUDY: Writing about
Games, p. 352**

1. Todd VanDerWerff, "#Gamergate: Here's Why
Everybody in the Video Game World Is Fighting," *Vox*,
October 13, 2014, www.vox.com/2014/9/6/6111065
/gamergate-explained-everybody-fighting.

2. "Bow, Nigger," always_black.com, September 22, 2004,
www.alwaysblack.com/blackbox/bownigger.html.

3. Kieron Gillen, "The New Games Journalism," *Kieron
Gillen's Workblog*, March 23, 2004, http://gillen.cream.org
/wordpress_html/assorted-essays/the-new-games
-journalism.

11 Advertising and Commercial Culture

1. Archie Bland, "The Rise of GoPro: Why Wearable
Cameras Make Us Film Everything," *Guardian*, October 4,
2014, www.theguardian.com/technology/2014/oct/04
/rise-of-gopro-wearable-cameras.

2. *Advertising Age Marketing Fact Pack 2015.*

3. Randall Rothenberg, *Where the Suckers Moon: An
Advertising Story* (New York: Alfred A. Knopf, 1994), 20.

4. See Bettina Fabos, "The Commercialized Web:
Challenges for Libraries and Democracy," *Library Trends*
53, no. 4 (Spring 2005): 519–523.

5. Google, "Form 10-K for the Fiscal Year Ended December
31, 2012," www.sec.gov/Archives/edgar/data/1288776
/000119312513028362/d452134d10k.htm; eMarketer,
"Google Takes Home Half of Worldwide Mobile Internet Ad
Revenues," June 13, 2013, www.emarketer.com/Article
/Google-Takes-Home-Half-of-Worldwide-Mobile-Internet
-Ad-Revenues/1009966; Facebook, "Form 10-K for the
Fiscal Year Ended December 31, 2012," http://investor
.fb.com/secfiling.cfm?filingID=1326801-13-3.

6. See Michael Schudson, *Advertising: The Uneasy
Persuasion* (New York: Basic Books, 1984), 36–43; and
Andrew Robertson, *The Lessons of Failure* (London:
MacDonald, 1974).

7. Center for Responsive Politics, "The Money behind the
Elections," OpenSecrets.org, accessed September 2014,
www.opensecrets.org/bigpicture.

8. Nicholas Confessore, "Koch Brothers' Budget of $899
Million for 2016 Is on Par with Both Parties' Spending,"
New York Times, January 26, 2015, www.nytimes.com
/2015/01/27/us/politics/kochs-plan-to-spend-900-million
-on-2016-campaign.html?_r=0.

9. Editorial Board, NYT. "The Worst Voter Turnout in 72
Years," *New York Times*, November 11, 2014, http://www
.nytimes.com/2014/11/12/opinion/the-worst-voter-turnout
-in-72-years.html?_r=0.

**MEDIA LITERACY CASE STUDY: Idiots and Objects:
Stereotyping in Advertising, p. 382**

1. Gene Demby, "That Cute Cheerios Ad with the
Interracial Family Is Back," *National Public Radio*, January
30, 2014, www.npr.org/blogs/codeswitch/2014/01/30
/268930004/that-cute-cheerios-ad-with-the-interracial
-family-is-back.

12 Public Relations and Framing the Message

1. "Twitter Top 100 Most Followers," Twitter Counter,
accessed February 6, 2015, http://twittercounter.com
/pages/100.

2. Christie D'Zurilla, "Ashton Kutcher's Paterno Tweet
Sends Actor Running for PR Cover," *Ministry of Gossip, Los
Angeles Times*, November 10, 2011, http://latimesblogs
.latimes.com/gossip/2011/11/ashton-kutcher-paterno-tweet
-aplusk-ashton-kutcher.html.

3. Matthew J. Culligan and Dolph Greene, *Getting Back to
the Basics of Public Relations and Publicity* (New York:
Crown Publishers, 1982), 100.

4. Marvin N. Olasky, "The Development of Corporate
Public Relations, 1850–1930," *Journalism Monographs* 102
(April 1987): 15.

5. Michael Schudson, *Discovering the News: A Social History
of American Newspapers* (New York: Basic Books, 1978), 136.

6. "Lobbying: Overview," OpenSecrets.org, accessed
October 7, 2012, www.opensecrets.org/lobby/index.php.

7. Philip Shenon, "3 Partners Quit Firm Handling Saudis'
P.R.," *New York Times*, December 6, 2002, www.nytimes
.com/2002/12/06/international/middleeast/06SAUD.html
?ex=1040199544&ei=1&en=c061b2d98376e7ba.

8. Video of "Eisenhower Answers America" commercials
available online at www.c-span.org/video/?188176-1
/eisenhower-answers-america.

**CONVERGING MEDIA CASE STUDY: Military PR in the
Digital Age, p. 412**

1. Erik Ortiz, "String of Social Media Scandals Plagues
Military," *NBC News,* February 17, 2014, www.nbcnews

.com/news/military/string-social-media-scandals-plagues
-military-n40501.
2. Cori E. Dauber, *YouTube War: Fighting in a World of Cameras in Every Cell Phone and Photoshop on Every Computer*, Strategic Studies Institute, U.S. Army War College, November 2009, www.strategicstudiesinstitute .army.mil/pdffiles/pub951.pdf.

13 Legal Controls and Freedom of Expression

1. Allan J. Lichtman, "Who Rules America?" *Hill*, August 12, 2014, http://thehill.com/blogs/pundits-blog/civil-rights /214857-who-rules-america.
2. *Buckley v. Valeo*, 424 U.S. 1 (1976).
3. Lawrence Lessig, "An Open Letter to the Citizens against *Citizens United*," *Atlantic*, March 23, 2012, www .theatlantic.com/politics/archive/2013/03/an-open -letter-to-the-citizens-against-citizens-united/254902.
4. See Douglas M. Fraleigh and Joseph S. Tuman, *Freedom of Speech in the Marketplace of Ideas* (New York: St. Martin's Press, 1998), 77.
5. Fred Siebert, Theodore Peterson, and Wilbur Schramm, *Four Theories of the Press* (Urbana: University of Illinois Press, 1956).
6. Hugo Black, quoted in *New York Times Co. v. United States*, 403 U.S. 713 (1971), www.law.cornell.edu/supct /html/historics/USSC_CR_0403_0713_ZC.html.
7. Robert Warren, quoted in *United States v. Progressive, Inc.*, 467 F. Supp. 990 (W.D. Wis. 1979), www.bc.edu /bc_org/avp/cas/comm/free_speech/progressive.html.
8. Jenna Worthan, "Public Outcry over Antipiracy Bills Began as Grass-Roots Grumbling," *New York Times*, January 19, 2012, www.nytimes.com/2012/01/20/technology/public -outcry-over-antipiracy-bills-began-as-grass-roots-grumbling .html?_r=2&pagewanted=1&ref=technology.
9. "European Parliament Resolution on the EU-US Summit of 28 November 2011," European Parliament, www.europarl .europa.eu/sides/getDoc.do?type=MOTION&reference =P7-RC-2011-0577&language=EN.
10. See Edward W. Knappman, ed., *Great American Trials: From Salem Witchcraft to Rodney King* (Detroit, Mich.: Visible Ink Press, 1994), 517–519.
11. *Mutual Film Corp. v. Industrial Communication of Ohio*, 236 U.S. 230 (1915).
12. Human Rights Watch, "Become a Blogger for Human Rights," accessed June 17, 2008, http://hrw.org/blogs .htm.
13. "'First Wikileaks Revolution': Tunisia Descends into Anarchy as President Flees after Cables Reveal Country's Corruption," *Daily Mail*, January 15, 2011, www.dailymail

.co.uk/news/article-1347336/First-Wikileaks-Revolution -Tunisia-descends-anarchy-president-flees.html.
14. Bill Keller, "Dealing with Assange and the WikiLeaks Secrets," *New York Times Magazine*, January 26, 2011, www.nytimes.com/2011/01/30/magazine/30Wikileaks-t .html?pagewanted=1&_r=3&ref=magazine#.

CONVERGING MEDIA CASE STUDY: Bullying Converges Online, p. 453
1. "What Is Bullying," stopbullying.gov, accessed April 22, 2015, www.stopbullying.gov/what-is-bullying/index.html.
2. "What Is Cyberbullying," stopbullying.gov, accessed April 22, 2015, www.stopbullying.gov/cyberbullying /what-is-it/index.html.
3. CDC (2014). Youth Risk Behavior Survey (YRBS): Trends in the prevalence of behaviors that contribute to violence national YRBS 1991–2013, accessed May 5, 2015, http:// www.cdc.gov/healthyyouth/yrbs/pdf/trends/us_violence _trend_yrbs.pdf
4. "State Anti-Bullying Laws and Policies," stopbullying .gov, accessed April 22, 2015, www.stopbullying.gov/laws /index.html.

14 Media Economics and the Global Marketplace

1. "Our History in Depth," Google, accessed February 20, 2015, www.google.com/about/company/history.
2. Douglas Gomery, "The Centrality of Media Economics," in *Defining Media Studies*, ed. Mark R. Levy and Michael Gurevitch (New York: Oxford University Press, 1994), 202.
3. David Harvey, *The Condition of Postmodernity: An Enquiry into the Origins of Cultural Change* (Oxford: Basil Blackwell, 1989), 171.
4. Gomery, "Centrality of Media Economics," 203–204.
5. Nicholas Kristof, "The Cost of a Decline in Unions," *New York Times*, February 19, 2015, www.nytimes.com/2015/02 /19/opinion/nicholas-kristof-the-cost-of-a-decline-in-unions .html?&hp&action=click&pgtype=Homepage&module=c -column-top-span-region&region=c-column-top-span -region&WT.nav=c-column-top-span-region&_r=0.
6. Thomas Geoghegan, "How Pink Slips Hurt More Than Workers," *New York Times*, March 29, 2006, p. B8.
7. See James Stewart, *Disney War* (New York: Simon & Schuster, 2005).
8. Edward Herman, "Democratic Media," *Z Papers* (January–March 1992): 23.

15 Social Scientific and Cultural Approaches to Media Research

1. Sarah Anne Hughes, "Jamey Rodemeyer, Bullied Teen Who Made 'It Gets Better' Video, Commits Suicide," *blog-Post*, September 21, 2011, www.washingtonpost.com /blogs/blogpost/post/jamey-rodemeyer-bullied-teen-who -made-it-gets-better-video-commits-suicide/2011/09/21 /gIQAVVzxkK_blog.html.

2. Aylin Zafar, "Tumblr Bans Pro-Eating Disorder and Other Self-Harm Blogs," *Time NewsFeed*, February 24, 2012, newsfeed.time.com/2012/02/24/tumblr-bans-pro-eating -disorder-and-other-self-harm-blogs.

3. Steve Fore, "Lost in Translation: The Social Uses of Mass Communications Research," *Afterimage* 20 (April 1993): 10.

4. James Carey, *Communication as Culture: Essays on Media and Society* (Boston: Unwin Hyman, 1989), 75.

5. Daniel Czitrom, *Media and the American Mind: From Morse to McLuhan* (Chapel Hill: University of North Carolina Press, 1982), 122–125.

6. Ibid., 123.

7. Harold Lasswell, *Propaganda Technique in the World War* (New York: Alfred A. Knopf, 1927), 9.

8. See W. W. Charters, *Motion Pictures and Youth: A Summary* (New York: Macmillan, 1934); and Garth Jowett, *Film: The Democratic Art* (Boston: Little, Brown, 1976), 220–229.

9. Czitrom, *Media and the American Mind*, 132; see also Harold Lasswell, "The Structure and Function of Communication in Society," in *The Communication of Ideas*, ed. Lyman Bryson (New York: Harper and Brothers, 1948), 37–51.

10. See Joseph Klapper, *The Effects of Mass Communication* (New York: Free Press, 1960).

11. GLAAD. "GLAAD's Network Responsibility Index 2014," accessed May 12, 2015, http://www.glaad.org /nri2014.

12. See Nancy Signorielli and Michael Morgan, *Cultivation Analysis: New Directions in Media Effects Research* (Newbury Park, Calif.: Sage, 1990).

13. See Stuart Hall et al., *Policing the Crisis: Mugging, the State, and Law and Order* (London: Macmillan, 1978).

14. See Jack G. Shaheen, *Reel Bad Arabs: How Hollywood Vilifies a People* (Northampton, Mass.: Interlink Publishing Group, 2001).

15. See Janice Radway, *Reading the Romance: Women, Patriarchy, and Popular Literature* (Chapel Hill: University of North Carolina Press, 1984).

MEDIA LITERACY CASE STUDY: The Effects of Television in a Post-TV World, p. 504

1. Frank J. Prial, "Congressmen Hear Renewal of Debate over TV Violence," *New York Times*, April 16, 1983, www .nytimes.com/1983/04/16/arts/congressmen-hear-renewal -of-debate-over-tv-violence.html.

2. "What Is the PTC's Mission?" Parents Television Council, accessed April 24, 2015, http://w2.parentstv.org /main/About/FAQ.aspx.

3. INSP, "INSP Earns Coveted PTC Seal of Approval," May 17, 2012, www.insp.com/pressroom/insp-earns-coveted -ptc-seal-approval.

Glossary

A&R (artist & repertoire) agents talent scouts of the music business who discover, develop, and sometimes manage performers.

access channels in cable television, a tier of non-broadcast channels dedicated to local education, government, and the public.

account executives in advertising, client liaisons responsible for bringing in new business and managing the accounts of established clients.

account reviews in advertising, the process of evaluating or reinvigorating an ad campaign, which results in either renewing the contract with the original ad agency or hiring a new agency.

acquisitions editors in the book industry, editors who seek out and sign authors to contracts.

actual malice in libel law, a reckless disregard for the truth, such as when a reporter or an editor knows that a statement is false and prints or airs it anyway.

adult contemporary (AC) one of the oldest and most popular radio music formats, typically featuring a mix of news, talk, oldies, and soft rock.

affiliate stations radio or TV stations that, though independently owned, sign a contract to be part of a network and receive money to carry the network's programs; in exchange, the network reserves time slots, which it sells to national advertisers.

agenda-setting theory a media-research argument that says that when the mass media pay attention to particular events or issues, they determine—that is, set the agenda for—the major topics of discussion for individuals and society.

album-oriented rock (AOR) the radio music format that features album cuts from mainstream rock bands.

alternative rock nonmainstream rock music, which includes many types of experimental music.

AM (amplitude modulation) a type of radio and sound transmission that stresses the volume or height of radio waves.

analog recording a recording that is made by capturing the fluctuations of the original sound waves and storing those signals on record grooves or magnetic tape—analogous to the actual sound.

analysis the second step in the critical process, it involves discovering significant patterns that emerge from the description stage.

anthology drama a popular form of early TV programming that brought live dramatic theater to television; influenced by stage plays, anthologies offered new teleplays, casts, directors, writers, and sets from week to week.

arcade an establishment gathering multiple coin-operated games together in a single location.

ARPAnet the original Internet, designed by the U.S. Defense Department's Advanced Research Projects Agency (ARPA).

association principle in advertising, a persuasive technique that associates a product with some cultural value or image that has a positive connotation but may have little connection to the actual product.

astroturf lobbying phony grassroots public affairs campaigns engineered by public relations firms; coined by U.S. Senator Lloyd Bentsen of Texas (named after AstroTurf, the artificial grass athletic field surface).

Atari a video game development company that released Pong, the first big-hit arcade game, and established the home-video game market through a deal with Sears.

audience studies cultural studies research that focuses on how people use and interpret cultural content. Also known as *reader-response research*.

audiotape lightweight magnetized strands of ribbon that make possible sound editing and multiple-track mixing; instrumentals or vocals can be recorded at one studio and later mixed onto a master recording in another studio.

authoritarian model a model for journalism and speech that tolerates little criticism of government or public dissent; it holds that the general public needs guidance from an elite and educated ruling class.

avatar an identity created by an Internet user in order to participate in a form of online entertainment, such as *World of Warcraft* or *Second Life*.

bandwagon effect an advertising strategy that incorporates exaggerated claims that everyone is using a particular product, so you should, too.

barter in TV, giving a program to a local station in exchange for a split in the advertising revenue.

basic cable in cable programming, a tier of channels composed of local broadcast signals, nonbroadcast access channels (for local government, education, and general public use), a few regional PBS stations, and a variety of popular channels downlinked from communication satellites.

Big Six the six major Hollywood studios that currently rule the commercial film business: Warner Brothers, Paramount, Twentieth Century Fox, Universal, Columbia Pictures, and Disney.

block booking an early tactic of movie studios to control exhibition involving pressuring theater operators to accept marginal films with no stars in order to get access to films with the most popular stars.

block printing a printing technique developed by early Chinese printers, who hand-carved characters and illustrations into a block of wood, applied ink to the block, and then printed copies on multiple sheets of paper.

blogs sites that contain articles in chronological journal-like form, often with reader comments and links to other articles on the Web (from the term *Web log*).

blues originally a kind of black folk music, this music emerged as a distinct category in the early 1900s; it was influenced by African American spirituals, ballads, and work songs in the rural South, and by urban guitar and vocal solos from the 1930s and 1940s.

book challenge a formal complaint to have a book removed from a public or school library's collection.

boutique agencies in advertising, small regional ad agencies that offer personalized services.

broadband data transmission over a fiber-optic cable — a signaling method that handles a wide range of frequencies.

broadcasting the transmission of radio waves or TV signals to a broad public audience.

cathode-tube ray a key component of early television and computer screens that allowed the display of images.

CATV (community antenna television) early cable systems that originated where mountains or tall buildings blocked TV signals; because of early technical and regulatory limits, CATV contained only twelve channels.

celluloid a transparent and pliable film that can hold a coating of chemicals sensitive to light.

chapter shows in television production, situation comedies or dramatic programs whose narrative structure includes self-contained stories that feature a problem, a series of conflicts, and a resolution from week to week (for contrast, see **serial programs** and **episodic series**).

cinema verité French term for *truth film*, a documentary style that records fragments of everyday life unobtrusively; it often features a rough, grainy look and shaky, handheld camera work.

citizen journalism a grassroots movement wherein activist amateurs and concerned citizens, not professional journalists, use Internet tools like blogs to disseminate news and information.

codex an early type of book in which paperlike sheets were cut and sewed together along the edge, then bound with thin pieces of wood and covered with leather.

collective intelligence video game tips and cheats shared by players of the games, usually online.

commercial speech any print or broadcast expression for which a fee is charged to the organization or individual buying time or space in the mass media.

common carrier a communication or transportation business, such as a phone company or a taxi service, that is required by law to offer service on a first-come, first-served basis to whoever can pay the rate; such companies do not get involved in content.

compact discs (CDs) playback-only storage discs for music that incorporate pure and very precise digital techniques, thus eliminating noise during recording and playback.

conflict of interest considered unethical, a compromising situation in which a journalist stands to benefit personally from the news report he or she produces.

consensus narrative cultural products that become popular and command wide attention, providing shared cultural experiences.

console a device used specifically to play video games.

contemporary hit radio (CHR) originally called Top 40 radio, this radio format encompasses everything from hip-hop to children's songs; it remains the most popular format in radio for people ages eighteen to twenty-four.

content analysis in social science research, a method for systematically studying and coding media texts and programs.

cookies information profiles about a user that are usually automatically accepted by the Web browser and stored on the user's own computer hard drive.

copy editors the people in magazine, newspaper, and book publishing who attend to specific problems in writing such as style, content, and length.

copyright the legal right of authors and producers to own and control the use of their published or unpublished writing, music, and lyrics; TV programs and movies; or graphic art designs.

Corporation for Public Broadcasting (CPB) a private, nonprofit corporation created by Congress in 1967 to funnel federal funds to nonprofit radio and public television.

correlation an observed association between two variables.

country claiming the largest number of radio stations in the United States, this radio format includes such subdivisions as old-time, progressive, country-rock, western swing, and country-gospel.

cover music songs recorded or performed by musicians who did not originally write or perform the music; in the 1950s, cover music was an attempt by white producers and artists to capitalize on popular songs by blacks.

critical process the process whereby a media-literate person or student studying mass communication employs the techniques of description, analysis, interpretation, evaluation, and engagement.

cultivation effect theory in media research, the idea that heavy television viewing leads individuals to perceive reality in ways that are consistent with the portrayals they see on television.

cultural imperialism the phenomenon of American culture (e.g., media, fashion, and food) dominating the global market and shaping the cultures and identities of other nations.

cultural studies in media research, the approaches that try to understand how the media and culture are tied to the actual patterns of communication used in daily life; these studies focus on how people make meanings, apprehend reality, and order experience through the use of stories and symbols.

deadheading the practice in the early twentieth century of giving reporters free rail passes as bribes for favorable stories.

deficit financing in television, the process whereby a TV production company leases its programs to a network for a license fee that is actually less than the cost of production; the company hopes to recoup this loss later in rerun syndication.

demographic editions national magazines whose advertising is tailored to subscribers and readers according to occupation, class, and zip-code address.

demographics in market research, the gathering and analysis of audience members' age, gender, income, ethnicity, and education—characteristics to better target messages to particular audiences.

description the first step in the critical process, it involves paying close attention, taking notes, and researching the cultural product to be studied.

design managers publishing industry personnel who work on the look of a book, making decisions about type style, paper, cover design, and layout.

desktop publishing a computer technology that enables an aspiring publisher/editor to inexpensively write, design, lay out, and even print a small newsletter or magazine.

developmental editors in book publishing, the editors who provide authors with feedback, make suggestions for improvements, and obtain advice from knowledgeable members of the academic community.

development budget the money spent designing, coding, scoring, and testing a video game.

digital communication images, texts, and sounds that use pulses of electric current or flashes of laser lights and are converted (or encoded) into electronic signals represented as varied combinations of binary numbers, usually ones and zeros; these signals are then reassembled (decoded) as a precise reproduction of a TV picture, a magazine article, or a telephone voice.

digital divide the socioeconomic disparity between those who do and those who do not have access to digital technology and media, such as the Internet.

digital recording music recorded and played back by laser beam rather than by needle or magnetic tape.

digital video the production format that is replacing celluloid film and revolutionizing filmmaking because the cameras are more portable and production costs are much less expensive.

digital video recorder (DVR) a device that enables users to find and record specific television shows (and movies) and store them in a computer memory to be played back at a later time or recorded onto a DVD.

dime novels sometimes identified as pulp fiction, these cheaply produced and low-priced novels were popular in the United States beginning in the 1860s.

direct broadcast satellites (DBS) satellite-based services that for a monthly fee downlink hundreds of satellite channels and services; they began distributing video programming directly to households in 1994.

directories review and cataloguing services that group Web sites under particular categories (e.g., Arts & Humanities, News & Media, Entertainment).

direct payment in media economics, the payment of money, primarily by consumers, for a book, a music CD, a movie, an online computer service, or a cable TV subscription.

documentary a movie or TV news genre that documents reality by recording actual characters and settings.

e-book a digital book read on a computer or electronic reading device.

e-commerce electronic commerce, or commercial activity, on the Web.

economies of scale the economic process of increasing production levels so as to reduce the overall cost per unit.

electromagnetic waves invisible electronic impulses similar to visible light; electricity, magnetism, light, broadcast signals, and heat are part of such waves, which radiate in space at the speed of light, about 186,000 miles per second.

electronic publisher a communication business, such as a broadcaster or a cable TV company, that is entitled to choose what channels or content to carry.

e-mail electronic mail messages sent by the Internet; developed by computer engineer Ray Tomlinson in 1971.

engagement the fifth step in the critical process, it involves actively working to create a media world that best serves democracy.

Entertainment Software Rating Board the video game industry's self-regulating system, designed to inform parents of sexual and violent content that might not be suitable for younger players.

episodic series a narrative form well suited to television because main characters appear every week, sets and locales remain the same, and technical crews stay with the program; episodic series feature new adventures each week, but a handful of characters *emerge* with whom viewers can regularly identify (see also **chapter shows** and **serial programs**).

ethnocentrism an underlying value held by many U.S. journalists and citizens, it involves judging other countries and cultures according to how they live up to or imitate American practices and ideals.

evaluation the fourth step in the critical process, it involves arriving at a judgment about whether a cultural product is good, bad, or mediocre; this requires subordinating one's personal taste to the critical assessment resulting from the first three stages (description, analysis, and interpretation).

evergreens in TV syndication, popular, lucrative, and enduring network reruns, such as the *Andy Griffith Show* or *I Love Lucy*.

evergreen subscriptions magazine subscriptions that automatically renew on subscribers' credit cards.

experiments in regard to the mass media, research that isolates some aspect of content, suggests a hypothesis, and manipulates variables to discover a particular text's or medium's impact on attitudes, emotions, or behavior.

Fairness Doctrine repealed in 1987, this FCC rule required broadcast stations to both air and engage in controversial-issue programs that affected their communities and, when offering such programming, to provide competing points of view.

famous-person testimonial an advertising strategy that associates a product with the endorsement of a well-known person.

feature syndicates commercial outlets or brokers, such as United Features and King Features, that contract with newspapers to provide work from well-known political writers, editorial cartoonists, comic-strip artists, and self-help columnists.

Federal Communications Act of 1934 the far-reaching act that established the FCC and the federal regulatory structure for U.S. broadcasting.

Federal Communications Commission (FCC) an independent U.S. government agency charged with regulating interstate and international communications by radio, television, wire, satellite, and cable.

Federal Radio Commission (FRC) established in 1927 to oversee radio licenses and negotiate channel problems.

feedback responses from receivers to the senders of messages.

fiber-optic cable thin glass bundles of fiber capable of transmitting thousands of messages converted to shooting pulses of light along cable wires; these bundles of fiber can carry broadcast channels, telephone signals, and all sorts of digital codes.

fin-syn (Financial Interest and Syndication Rules) FCC rules that prohibited the major networks from running their own syndication companies or from charging production companies additional fees after shows had completed their prime-time runs; most fin-syn rules were rescinded in the mid-1990s.

first-run syndication in television, the process whereby new programs are specifically produced for sale in syndication markets rather than for network television.

flipper bumper an addition to the pinball machine that transformed the game from one of chance into a challenging game of skill, touch, and timing.

FM (frequency modulation) a type of radio and sound transmission that offers static-free reception and greater fidelity and clarity than AM radio by accentuating the pitch or distance between radio waves.

focus group a common research method in psychographic analysis in which a moderator leads a small-group discussion about a product or an issue, usually with six to twelve people.

folk music music performed by untrained musicians and passed down through oral traditions; it encompasses a wide range of music, from Appalachian fiddle tunes to the accordion-led zydeco of Louisiana.

format radio the concept of radio stations developing and playing specific styles (or formats) geared to listeners' age, race, or gender; in format radio, management, rather than deejays, controls programming choices.

Fourth Estate the notion that the press operates as an unofficial branch of government, monitoring the legislative, judicial, and executive branches for abuses of power.

fringe time in broadcast television, the time slot either immediately before the evening's prime-time schedule (called *early fringe*) or immediately following the local evening news or the network's late-night talk shows (called *late fringe*).

gag orders legal restrictions prohibiting the press from releasing preliminary information that might prejudice jury selection.

gangster rap a style of rap music that depicts the hardships of urban life and sometimes glorifies the violent style of street gangs.

gatekeepers editors, producers, and other media managers who function as message filters, making decisions about what types of messages actually get produced for particular audiences.

general-interest magazine a type of magazine that addresses a wide variety of topics and is aimed at a broad national audience.

genre a narrative category in which conventions regarding similar characters, scenes, structures, and themes recur in combination.

grunge rock music that takes the spirit of punk and infuses it with more attention to melody.

HD radio a digital technology that enables AM and FM radio broadcasters to multicast two to three additional compressed digital signals within their traditional analog frequency.

hegemony the acceptance of the dominant values in a culture by those who are subordinate to those who hold economic and political power.

hidden-fear appeal an advertising strategy that plays on a sense of insecurity, trying to persuade consumers that only a specific product can offer relief.

high culture a symbolic expression that has come to mean "good taste"; often supported by wealthy patrons and corporate donors, it is associated with fine art (such as ballet, the symphony, painting, and classical literature), which is available primarily in theaters or museums.

high-definition the digital standard for U.S. television sets that has more than twice the resolution of the system that served as the standard from the 1940s through the 1990s.

hip-hop music that combines spoken street dialect with cuts (or samples) from older records and bears the influences of social politics, male boasting, and comic lyrics carried forward from blues, R&B, soul, and rock and roll.

Hollywood Ten the nine screenwriters and one film director subpoenaed by the House Un-American Activities Committee (HUAC) who were sent to prison in the late 1940s for refusing to discuss their memberships or to identify communist sympathizers.

HTML (HyperText Markup Language) the written code that creates Web pages and links; a language all computers can read.

human-interest stories news accounts that focus on the trials and tribulations of the human condition, often featuring ordinary individuals facing extraordinary challenges.

hypodermic-needle model an early model in mass communication research that attempted to explain media effects by arguing that the media shoot their powerful effects directly into unsuspecting or weak audiences; sometimes called the *magic bullet theory*.

hypotheses in social science research, tentative general statements that predict a relationship between a dependent variable and an independent variable.

illuminated manuscripts books from the Middle Ages that featured decorative, colorful designs and illustrations on each page.

indecency the government may punish broadcasters for indecency or profanity after the fact; over the years, a handful of radio stations have had their licenses suspended or denied due to indecent programming.

indie rock independent-minded rock music, usually distributed by smaller labels.

indies independent music and film production houses that work outside industry oligopolies; they often produce less mainstream music and film.

indirect payment in media economics, the financial support of media products by advertisers, who pay for the quantity or quality of audience members that a particular medium attracts.

individualism an underlying value held by most U.S. journalists and citizens, it favors individual rights and responsibilities over group needs or institutional mandates.

infotainment a type of television program that packages human-interest and celebrity stories in TV news style.

instant book in the book industry, a marketing strategy that involves publishing a topical book quickly after a major event occurs.

instant messaging (IM) a Web feature that enables users to chat with buddies in real time via pop-up windows assigned to each conversation.

intellectual properties the material in video games—stories, characters, personalities, music, etc.—that requires licensing agreements.

Internet the vast central network of high-speed digital lines designed to link and carry computer information worldwide.

Internet radio online radio stations that either "stream" simulcast versions of on-air radio broadcasts over the Web or are created exclusively for the Internet.

Internet service provider (ISP) a company that provides Internet access to homes and businesses for a fee.

interpretation the third step in the critical process, it asks and answers the "What does that mean?" and "So what?" questions about one's findings.

interpretive journalism a type of journalism that involves analyzing and explaining key issues or events and placing them in a broader historical or social context.

inverted-pyramid style a style of journalism in which news reports begin with the most dramatic or newsworthy information—answering *who*, *what*, *where*, and *when* (and less frequently *why* or *how*) questions at the top of the story—and then tail off with less significant details.

irritation advertising an advertising strategy that tries to create product-name recognition by being annoying or obnoxious.

jazz an improvisational and mostly instrumental musical form that absorbs and integrates a diverse body of musical styles, including African rhythms, blues, big band, and gospel.

kinescope before the days of videotape, a 1950s technique for preserving television broadcasts by using a film camera to record a live TV show off a studio monitor.

kinetograph an early movie camera developed by Thomas Edison's assistant in the 1890s.

kinetoscope an early film projection system that served as a kind of peep show in which viewers looked through a hole and saw images moving on a tiny plate.

leased channels in cable television, channels that allow citizens to buy time for producing programs or presenting their own viewpoints.

libel in media law, the defamation of character in written or broadcast expression.

libertarian model a model for journalism and speech that encourages vigorous government criticism and supports the highest degree of freedom for individual speech and news operations.

limited competition in media economics, a market with many producers and sellers but only a few differentiable products within a particular category; sometimes called *monopolistic competition*.

linotype a technology introduced in the nineteenth century that enabled printers to set type mechanically using a typewriter-style keyboard.

lobbying in government public relations, the process of attempting to influence the voting of lawmakers to support a client's or an organization's best interests.

longitudinal studies a term used for research studies that are conducted over long periods of time and often rely on large government and academic survey databases.

low culture a symbolic expression allegedly aligned with the questionable tastes of the "masses," who enjoy the commercial "junk" circulated by the mass media, such as soap operas, rock music, talk radio, comic books, and monster truck pulls.

low-power FM (LPFM) a class of noncommercial radio stations approved by the FCC in 2000 to give voice to local groups lacking access to the public airwaves; the 10-watt and 100-watt stations broadcast to a small, community-based area.

magalogs a combination of a glossy magazine and retail catalogue that is often used to market goods or services to customers or employees.

magazine a nondaily periodical that comprises a collection of articles, stories, and ads.

manuscript culture a period during the Middle Ages when priests and monks advanced the art of bookmaking.

market research in advertising and public relations agencies, the department that uses social science techniques to assess the behaviors and attitudes of consumers toward particular products before any ads are created.

mass communication the process of designing and delivering cultural messages and stories to diverse audiences through media channels as old as the book and as new as the Internet.

mass customization the process whereby product companies and content providers customize a Web page, print ad, or other media form for an individual consumer.

massively multiplayer online role-playing game (MMORPG) an online fantasy game set in a virtual world in which users develop avatars of their own design and interact with other players.

mass market paperbacks low-priced paperback books sold mostly on racks in drugstores, supermarkets, and airports, as well as in bookstores.

mass media the cultural industries—the channels of communication—that produce songs, novels, news, movies, online services, and other cultural products and distribute them to a large number of people.

mass media channel newspapers, books, magazines, radio, television, and the Internet.

media buyers in advertising, the individuals who choose and purchase the types of media that are best suited to carry a client's ads and reach the targeted audience.

media convergence the process whereby old and new media are available via the integration of personal computers and high-speed digital distribution.

media effects (social scientific) research the mainstream tradition in mass communication research, it attempts to understand, explain, and predict the impact—or effects—of the mass media on individuals and society.

media literacy an understanding of the mass communication process through the development of critical-thinking tools—description, analysis, interpretation, evaluation, engagement—that enable a person to become more engaged as a citizen and more discerning as a consumer of mass media products.

mega-agencies in advertising, large firms or holding companies that are formed by merging several individual agencies and that maintain worldwide regional offices; they provide both advertising and public relations services and operate in-house radio and TV production studios.

megaplexes movie theater facilities with fourteen or more screens.

messages the texts, images, and sounds transmitted from senders to receivers.

microprocessors miniature circuits that process and store electronic signals, integrating thousands of electronic components into thin strands of silicon along which binary codes travel.

minimal-effects model a mass communication research model based on tightly controlled experiments and survey findings; it argues that the mass media have limited effects on audiences, reinforcing existing behaviors and attitudes rather than changing them. Also called the *limited effects* model.

modern era period from the Industrial Revolution to the twentieth century that was characterized by working efficiently, celebrating individuals, believing in a rational order, and reaching tradition and embracing progress.

monopoly in media economics, an organizational structure that occurs when a single firm dominates production and distribution in a particular industry, either nationally or locally.

Morse code a system of sending electrical impulses from a transmitter through a cable to a reception point; developed in the 1840s by the American inventor Samuel Morse.

movie palaces ornate, lavish single-screen movie theaters that emerged in the 1910s in the United States.

MP3 short for MPEG-1 Layer 3, an advanced type of audio compression that reduces file size, enabling audio to be easily distributed over the Internet.

muckraking a style of early-twentieth-century investigative journalism that referred to reporters' willingness to crawl around in society's muck to uncover a story.

multiple-system operators (MSOs) large corporations that own numerous cable television systems.

multiplexes contemporary movie theaters that exhibit many movies at the same time on multiple screens.

must-carry rules rules established by the FCC requiring all cable operators to assign channels to and carry all local TV broadcasts on their systems, thereby ensuring that local network affiliates, independent stations (those not carrying network programs), and public television channels would benefit from cable's clearer reception.

narrative films movies that tell a story, with dramatic action and conflict emerging mainly from individual characters.

narrowcasting any specialized electronic programming or media channel aimed at a target audience.

National Public Radio (NPR) noncommercial radio established in 1967 by the U.S. Congress to provide an alternative to commercial radio.

network a broadcast process that links, through special phone lines or satellite transmissions, groups of radio or TV stations that share programming produced at a central location.

network era the period in television history, roughly from the mid-1950s to the late 1970s, that refers to the dominance of the Big Three networks—ABC, CBS, and NBC—over programming and prime-time viewing habits; the era began eroding with a decline in viewing and with the development of VCRs, cable, and new TV networks.

news the process of gathering information and making narrative reports—edited by individuals in a news organization—that create selected frames of reference and help the public make sense of prominent people, important events, and unusual happenings in everyday life.

news and talk radio the fastest-growing radio format in the 1990s.

newshole the space left over in a newspaper for news content after all the ads are placed.

newspaper chain large companies that own several papers throughout the country.

newsreels weekly ten-minute magazine-style compilations of filmed news events from around the world organized in a sequence of short reports; prominent in movie theaters between the 1920s and the 1950s.

newsworthiness the often unstated criteria that journalists use to determine which events and issues should become news reports, including timeliness, proximity, conflict, prominence, human interest, consequence, usefulness, novelty, and deviance.

nickelodeons the first small makeshift movie theaters, which were often converted cigar stores, pawnshops, or restaurants redecorated to mimic vaudeville theaters.

objective journalism a modern style of journalism that distinguishes factual reports from opinion columns; reporters strive to remain neutral toward the issue or event they cover, searching out competing points of view among the sources for a story.

obscenity expression that is not protected as speech if these three legal tests are all met: (1) the average person, applying contemporary community standards, would find that the material as a whole appeals to prurient interest; (2) the material depicts or describes sexual conduct in a patently offensive way; (3) the material, as a whole, lacks serious literary, artistic, political, or scientific value.

off-network syndication in television, the process whereby older programs that no longer run during prime time are made available for reruns to local stations, cable operators, online services, and foreign markets.

offset lithography a technology that enabled books to be printed from photographic plates rather than metal casts, reducing the cost of color and illustrations and eventually permitting computers to perform typesetting.

oligopoly in media economics, an organizational structure in which a few firms control most of an industry's production and distribution resources.

online fantasy sports games where players assemble teams of real-life athletes and use actual sports results to determine scores.

open-source software noncommercial software shared freely and developed collectively on the Internet.

opinion and fair comment a defense against libel which states that libel applies only to intentional misstatements of factual information rather than opinion, and which therefore protects said opinion.

Pacifica Foundation a radio broadcasting foundation established in Berkeley, California, by journalist and World War II pacifist Lewis Hill; he established KPFA, the first nonprofit community radio station, in 1949.

pack journalism a situation in which reporters stake out a house or follow a story in such large groups that the entire profession comes under attack for invading people's privacy or exploiting their personal tragedies.

paperback books books made with less expensive paper covers, introduced in the United States in the mid-1800s.

papyrus one of the first substances to hold written language and symbols; obtained from plant reeds found along the Nile River.

Paramount decision the 1948 Supreme Court decision that ended vertical integration in the film industry by forcing the studios to divest themselves of their theaters.

parchment treated animal skin that replaced papyrus as an early pre-paper substance on which to document written language.

partisan press an early dominant style of American journalism distinguished by opinion newspapers, which generally argued one political point of view or pushed the plan of the particular party that subsidized the paper.

pass-along readership the total number of people who come into contact with a single copy of a magazine.

payola the unethical (and often illegal) practice of record promoters paying deejays or radio programmers to favor particular songs over others.

pay-per-view (PPV) a cable-television service that allows customers to select a particular movie for a fee, or to pay $25 to $40 for a special one-time event.

paywall an arrangement restricting Web site access to paid subscribers.

penny arcade an early version of the modern video arcade, with multiple coin-operated mechanical games gathered together in a single location.

penny papers (also *penny press*) refers to newspapers that, because of technological innovations in printing, were able to drop their price to one cent beginning in the 1830s, thereby making papers affordable to working and emerging middle classes and enabling newspapers to become a genuine mass medium.

phishing an Internet scam that begins with phony e-mail messages that pretend to be from an official site and request that customers send their credit card numbers, passwords, and other personal information to update the account.

photojournalism the use of photos to document events and people's lives.

pinball machine a mechanical game where players score points by manipulating the path of a metal ball on a playfield in a glass-covered case, and an early ancestor of today's electronic games.

plain-folks pitch an advertising strategy that associates a product with simplicity and the common person.

podcasting enables listeners to download audio program files from the Internet for playback on computers or digital music players.

political advertising the use of ad techniques to promote a candidate's image and persuade the public to adopt a particular viewpoint.

political economy studies an area of academic study that specifically examines interconnections among economic interests, political power, and how that power is used.

pop music popular music that appeals either to a wide cross section of the public or to sizable subdivisions within the larger public based on age, region, or ethnic background; the word *pop* has also been used as a label to distinguish popular music from classical music.

populism a political idea that attempts to appeal to ordinary people by setting up a conflict between "the people" and "the elite."

portal an entry point to the Internet, such as a search engine.

postmodern period a contemporary historical era spanning the 1960s to the present; its social values include opposing hierarchy, diversifying and recycling culture, questioning scientific reasoning, and embracing paradox.

premium channels in cable programming, a tier of channels that subscribers can order at an additional monthly fee over their basic cable service; these may include movie channels and interactive services.

press agents the earliest type of public relations practitioner, who sought to advance a client's image through media exposure.

press releases in public relations, announcements—written in the style of a news report—that give new information about an individual, a company, or an organization and pitch a story idea to the news media.

prime time in television programming, the hours between 7 and 11 P.M. (or 7 and 10 P.M. in the Midwest), when networks have traditionally drawn their largest audiences and charged their highest advertising rates.

printing press a fifteenth-century invention whose movable metallic type technology spawned modern mass communication by creating the first method for mass production; it reduced the size and cost of books, made them the first mass medium affordable to less-affluent people, and provided the impetus for the Industrial Revolution, assembly-line production, modern capitalism, and the rise of consumer culture.

prior restraint the legal definition of censorship in the United States, which prohibits courts and governments from blocking any publication or speech before it actually occurs.

product placement the advertising practice of strategically placing products in movies, TV shows, comic books, and video games so the products appear as part of a story's set environment.

professional books technical books that target various occupational groups and are not intended for the general consumer market.

Progressive Era the period of political and social reform lasting roughly from the 1890s to the 1920s that inspired many Americans—and mass media—to break with tradition and embrace change.

propaganda in advertising and public relations, a communication strategy that tries to manipulate public opinion to gain support for a special issue, program, or policy, such as a nation's war effort.

propaganda analysis the study of propaganda's effectiveness in influencing and mobilizing public opinion.

pseudo-events in public relations, any circumstance or event created solely for the purpose of obtaining coverage in the media.

pseudo-polls typically call-in, online, or person-in-the-street polls that don't use random samples and whose results thus don't represent the population as a whole.

psychographics in market research, the study of audience or consumer attitudes, beliefs, interests, and motivations.

Public Broadcasting Act of 1967 the act by the U.S. Congress that established the Corporation for Public Broadcasting, which oversees the Public Broadcasting Service (PBS) and National Public Radio (NPR).

Public Broadcasting Service (PBS) the noncommercial television network established in 1967 as an alternative to commercial television.

public domain the end of the copyright period for a cultural or scientific work, at which point the public may begin to access it for free.

publicity in public relations, the positive and negative messages that spread controlled and uncontrolled information about a person, a corporation, an issue, or a policy in various media.

public journalism a type of journalism, driven by citizen forums, that goes beyond telling the news to embrace a broader mission of improving the quality of public life; also called *citizen journalism.*

public relations the total communication strategy conducted by a person, a government, or an organization attempting to reach and persuade its audiences to adopt a point of view.

public service announcements (PSAs) reports or announcements, carried free by radio and TV stations, that promote government programs, educational projects, voluntary agencies, or social reform.

pulp fiction a term used to describe many late-nineteenth-century popular paperbacks and dime novels, which were constructed of cheap machine-made pulp material.

punk rock rock music that challenges the orthodoxy and commercialism of the recording business; it is characterized by loud, unpolished qualities, a jackhammer beat, primal vocal screams, crude aggression, and defiant or comic lyrics.

Radio Act of 1912 the first radio legislation passed by Congress, it addressed the problem of amateur radio operators increasingly cramming the airwaves.

Radio Act of 1927 the second radio legislation passed by Congress; in an attempt to restore order to the airwaves, it stated that licensees did not own their channels but could license them as long as they operated in order to serve the "public interest, convenience, or necessity."

Radio Corporation of America (RCA) a company developed during World War I that was designed, with government approval, to pool radio patents; the formation of RCA gave the United States almost total control over the emerging mass medium of broadcasting.

radio waves a portion of the electromagnetic wave spectrum that was harnessed so that signals could be sent from a transmission point and obtained at a reception point.

random assignment a social science research method for assigning research subjects; it ensures that every subject has an equal chance of being placed in either the experimental group or the control group.

rating in TV audience measurement, a statistical estimate expressed as a percentage of households tuned to a program in the local or national market being sampled.

receivers the target of messages crafted by a sender.

reference books dictionaries, encyclopedias, atlases, and other reference manuals related to particular professions or trades.

regional editions national magazines whose content is tailored to the interests of different geographic areas.

responsible capitalism an underlying value held by many U.S. journalists and citizens, it assumes that businesspeople compete with one another not primarily to maximize profits but to increase prosperity for all.

rhythm and blues (R&B) music that merged urban blues with big-band sounds.

right to privacy addresses a person's right to be left alone, without his or her name, image, or daily activities becoming public property.

rockabilly music that mixed bluegrass and country influences with those of black folk music and early amplified blues.

rock and roll music that mixed the vocal and instrumental traditions of popular music; it merged the black influences of urban blues, gospel, and R&B with the white influences of country, folk, and pop vocals.

rotation in format radio programming, the practice of playing the most popular or best-selling songs many times throughout the day.

satellite radio pay radio services that deliver various radio formats nationally via satellite.

saturation advertising the strategy of inundating a variety of print and visual media with ads aimed at target audiences.

scientific method a widely used research method that studies phenomena in systematic stages; it includes identifying the research problem, reviewing existing research, developing working hypotheses, determining appropriate research design, collecting information, analyzing results to see if the hypotheses have been verified, and interpreting the implications of the study.

search engines computer programs that allow users to enter key words or queries to find related sites on the Internet.

Section 315 part of the 1934 Communications Act; it mandates that during elections, broadcast stations must provide equal opportunities and response time for qualified political candidates.

selective exposure the phenomenon whereby audiences seek messages and meanings that correspond to their preexisting beliefs and values.

selective retention the phenomenon whereby audiences remember or retain messages and meanings that correspond to their preexisting beliefs and values.

senders the authors, producers, agencies, and organizations that transmit messages to receivers.

serial programs radio or TV programs, such as soap operas, that feature continuing story lines from day to day or week to week (see **chapter shows**).

share in TV audience measurement, a statistical estimate of the percentage of homes tuned to a certain program, compared with those simply using their sets at the time of a sample.

shield laws laws protecting the confidentiality of key interview subjects and reporters' rights not to reveal the sources of controversial information used in news stories.

situation comedy (sitcom) a type of comedy series that features a recurring cast and set as well as several narrative scenes; each episode establishes a situation, complicates it, develops increasing confusion among its characters, and then resolves the complications.

sketch comedy short television comedy skits that are usually segments of TV variety shows; sometimes known as *vaudeo*, the marriage of vaudeville and video.

slander in law, spoken language that defames a person's character.

small-town pastoralism an underlying value held by many U.S. journalists and citizens, it favors the small over the large and the rural over the urban.

snob-appeal approach an advertising strategy that attempts to convince consumers that using a product will enable them to maintain or elevate their social station.

social learning theory a theory within media effects research that suggests a link between the mass media and behavior.

social networking sites Internet Web sites that allow users to create personal profiles, upload photos, create lists of favorite things, and post messages to connect with old friends and to meet new ones.

social responsibility model a model for journalism and speech, influenced by the libertarian model, that encourages the free flow of information to citizens so they can make wise decisions regarding political and social issues.

social scientific research the mainstream tradition in mass communication research, it attempts to understand, explain, and predict the impact—or effects—of the mass media on individuals and society.

soul music that mixes gospel, blues, and urban and southern black styles with slower, more emotional, and melancholic lyrics.

sound bite in TV journalism, the equivalent of a quote in print; the part of a news report in which an expert, a celebrity, a victim, or a "person on the street" is interviewed about some aspect of an event or issue.

space brokers in the days before modern advertising, individuals who purchased space in newspapers and sold it to various merchants.

spam a computer term referring to unsolicited e-mail.

Spanish-language radio one of radio's fastest-growing formats, concentrated mostly in large Hispanic markets such as Miami, New York, Chicago, Las Vegas, California, Arizona, New Mexico, and Texas.

spiral of silence a theory that links the mass media, social psychology, and the formation of public opinion; it proposes that people who find their views on controversial issues in the minority tend to keep these views silent.

split-run editions editions of national magazines that tailor ads to different geographic areas.

spyware software with hidden codes that enable commercial firms to "spy" on users and gain access to their computers.

state model a model for journalism and speech that places control in the hands of an enlightened government, which speaks for ordinary citizens and workers in order to serve the common goals of the state.

stereo the recording of two separate channels or tracks of sound.

storyboard in advertising, a blueprint or roughly drawn comic-strip version of a proposed advertisement.

studio system an early film production system that constituted a sort of assembly-line process for moviemaking; major film studios controlled not only actors but also directors, editors, writers, and other employees, all of whom worked under exclusive contracts.

subliminal advertising a 1950s term that refers to hidden or disguised print and visual messages that allegedly register on the subconscious, creating false needs and seducing people into buying products.

subsidiary rights in the book industry, selling the rights to a book for use in other media forms, such as a mass market paperback, a CD-ROM, or the basis for a movie screenplay.

supermarket tabloids newspapers that feature bizarre human-interest stories, gruesome murder tales, violent accident accounts, unexplained phenomena stories, and malicious celebrity gossip.

superstations local independent TV stations, such as WTBS in Atlanta or WGN in Chicago, that have up-linked their signals onto a communication satellite to make themselves available nationwide.

survey research in social science research, a method of collecting and measuring data taken from a group of respondents.

syndication leasing TV stations the exclusive right to air older TV series.

synergy in media economics, the promotion and sale of a product (and all its versions) throughout the various subsidiaries of a media conglomerate.

Telecommunications Act of 1996 the sweeping update of telecommunications law that led to a wave of media consolidation.

telegraph invented in the 1840s, it sent electrical impulses through a cable from a transmitter to a reception point, transmitting Morse code.

textbooks books made for the el-hi (elementary and high school) and college markets.

textual analysis in media research, a method for closely and critically examining and interpreting the meanings of culture, including architecture, fashion, books, movies, and TV programs.

third-person effect theory theory suggesting that people believe others are more affected by media messages than they are themselves.

Top 40 format the first radio format, in which stations played the forty most popular hits in a given week as measured by record sales.

trade books the most visible book industry segment, featuring hardbound and paperback books aimed at general readers and sold at bookstores and other retail outlets.

transistor invented by Bell Laboratories in 1947, this tiny technology, which receives and amplifies radio signals, made portable radios possible.

TV newsmagazine a TV news program format, pioneered by CBS's *60 Minutes* in the late 1960s, that features multiple segments in an hour-long episode, usually ranging from a celebrity or political feature story to a hard-hitting investigative report.

underground press radical newspapers, run on shoestring budgets, that question mainstream political policies and conventional values; the term usually refers to a journalism movement of the 1960s.

university press the segment of the book industry that publishes scholarly books in specialized areas.

urban one of radio's more popular formats, primarily targeting African American listeners in urban areas with dance, R&B, and hip-hop music.

uses and gratifications model a mass communication research model, usually employing in-depth interviews and survey questionnaires, that argues that people use the media to satisfy various emotional desires or intellectual needs.

Values and Lifestyles (VALS) a market-research strategy that divides consumers into types and measures psychological factors, including how consumers think and feel about products and how they achieve (or do not achieve) the lifestyles to which they aspire.

vellum a handmade paper made from treated animal skin, used in the Gutenberg Bibles.

vertical integration in media economics, the phenomenon of controlling a mass media industry at its three essential levels: production, distribution, and exhibition; the term is most frequently used in reference to the film industry.

videocassette recorders (VCRs) recorders that use a half-inch video format known as VHS (video home system), which enables viewers to record and play back programs from television or to watch movies rented from video stores.

video news release (VNR) in public relations, the visual counterpart to a press release; it pitches a story idea to the TV news media by mimicking the style of a broadcast news report.

video-on-demand (VOD) cable television technology that enables viewers to instantly order programming, such as movies, to be digitally delivered to their sets.

viral marketing short videos or other content that marketers hope will quickly gain widespread attention as users share it with friends online, or by word of mouth.

vitascope a large-screen movie projection system developed by Thomas Edison.

Web browsers information-search services, such as Firefox and Microsoft's Internet Explorer, that offer detailed organizational maps to the Internet.

webzines magazines that publish on the Internet.

Wi-Fi a standard for short-distance wireless networking, enabling users of notebook computers and other devices to connect to the Internet in cafés, hotels, airports, and parks.

Wikis Internet Web sites that are capable of being edited by any user; the most famous of these sites is Wikipedia.

Wireless Ship Act the 1910 mandate that all major U.S. seagoing ships carrying more than fifty passengers and traveling more than two hundred miles off the coast be equipped with wireless equipment with a one-hundred-mile range.

wireless telegraphy the forerunner of radio, a form of voiceless point-to-point communication; it preceded the voice and sound transmissions of one-to-many mass communication that became known as *broadcasting*.

wireless telephony early experiments in wireless voice and music transmissions, which later developed into modern radio.

wire services commercial organizations, such as the Associated Press, that share news stories and information by relaying them around the country and the world, originally via telegraph and now via satellite transmission.

yellow journalism a newspaper style or era that peaked in the 1890s; it emphasized high-interest stories, sensational crime news, large headlines, and serious reports that exposed corruption, particularly in business and government.

Index

LaunchPad for *Media Essentials*

macmillanhighered.com/mediaessentials3e

Media Essentials doesn't just teach convergence—it also practices convergence, converging print and video with LaunchPad. LaunchPad for *Media Essentials* includes a full e-book as well as a library of video clips that complement the material in the text. These videos are called out in the margins of the book, as well as in the Converging Media and Media Literacy case study boxes and in the Chapter Essentials review section. Here is a quick list of all the videos featured in the book by chapter. For directions on how to access these videos online, please see the instructions to the right.